FORECLOSURE NATION

FORECLOSURE NATION

MORTGAGING

THE AMERICAN DREAM

SHARI B. OLEFSON, JD, LLM

Prometheus Books
59 John Glenn Drive
Amherst, New York 14228-2119

Published 2009 by Prometheus Books

Inquiries should be addressed to
Prometheus Books
59 John Glenn Drive
Amherst, New York 14228–2119
VOICE: 716–691–0133, ext. 210
FAX: 716–691–0137
WWW.PROMETHEUSBOOKS.COM

13 12 11 10 09   5 4 3 2 1

Library of Congress Cataloging-in-Publication Data

Olefson, Shari, 1963–
Foreclosure nation : mortgaging the American Dream / Shari Olefson.
p. cm.
Includes bibliographical references.
ISBN 978–1–59102–663–1 (pbk. : acid-free paper)
1. Real estate investment—United States. 2. Financial crises—United States. 3. Foreclosure—United States. 4. Mortgage loans—United States. I. Title.

HD255.O44 2008
332.7'20973—dc22   2008035687

Printed in the United States of America on acid-free paper

For my grandparents:
Lillian, Ben, Alma, and Dave

ACKNOWLEDGMENTS

Writing a book about an ongoing economic crisis is like herding cats. As you're proofreading one section, information critical to another section is changing. Thank you to the following cat herders without whom this book would not have been possible: Monique Ross, Wendy Lester, Sharon Podwol, Brad Hunter, Alan Hunter, Charlie Dowd, Amy McGrotty, Meghann French, Steven L. Mitchell, and to Devon, Brooke, and Pam for their patience. Thank you.

A special thanks to Metrostudy's chief economist and national director of consulting, Brad Hunter, and Senior Analyst Alan Hunter for graciously providing graphs, analysis, and statistical information.

CONTENTS

CHAPTER 2: THE MORTGAGE: AS AMERICAN AS APPLE PIE 31

CHAPTER 8: PREDICTIONS, RELIEF, AND REFORMS 225

INTRODUCTION

An introduction traditionally explains a book's subject matter and what led the author to write about it. At the very front of a book, the introduction is important real estate—too important, I think, to waste explaining to *you*, of all people, what the subprime real estate and mortgage crisis is. Chances are you have not just been rescued from a deserted island and opted to shop for a book before going home to reunite with your loved ones. I'm willing to bet you've heard about the crisis several times within the past twenty-four hours alone: on television before you went to bed last night, as you ate breakfast this morning, or maybe on the radio as you drove to work. You'll probably hear about it again on the news when you get home tonight, and again and again daily for months, maybe years to come. You know about the foreclosure mess our country is in—or perhaps you are one of the victims of subprime lending practices. Why else would you have picked up this book? Yet, even with everything you've heard on television, the radio, in the newspapers, at work, or from your friends—or perhaps because of it—you have unanswered questions.

When I began writing it in early 2007, this was going to be a book designed to help those who had lost or feared losing their homes or other real estate to foreclosure. At the time, the powers that be predicted 3 million of us would fall into this trap. But this book, like the subprime crisis, has evolved into something much bigger than what it first appeared to be. Subprime mortgages were only the first of even larger fault lines in our nation's financial foundation. Tremors continue reverberating, exposing layer after layer of devastating flaws; CDOs, auction-rate securities, and credit default swaps are crumbling. Perhaps even more significant to the fiber of our nation is the fact that the US economic landscape has become surreal. Only two of Wall Street's century-old investment firms remain: Goldman Sachs and J.P. Morgan, and even they have become a different breed of animal than they were just a few short months ago. Leading banks and mortgage lenders like Washington Mutual, Wachovia, and Countrywide no longer exist as they were. Our government is now part owner in AIG, the world's largest insurer, and some of our country's largest and oldest corporations—including General Motors, Ford, and American Express—are begging for public assistance. DHL has pulled out of the United States. Dozens of well-known retail companies, such as Circuit City, Sharper Image, Lillian Vernon, and the Bombay Company, have sought protection from bankruptcy. Virtually none of the major mortgage lenders from 2005–2006 even exist anymore. Discussion of money in figures as large as billions of dollars has become commonplace to us.

Foreclosure is replacing the American Dream of home ownership as a way of life. Foreclosure lawsuits were filed against 2,203,295 Americans in 2007, up 75 percent from 2006 and 148.83 percent from 2005. New foreclosures went up another 121 percent as of the second quarter of 2008. If this includes you, you know how utterly impossible it is to navigate the Kafkaesque automated bank voice-messaging systems. Even worse, when you finally do reach a real, live human being you can't understand a word of his offshore call-center accent. And he doesn't seem to have a clue—or give a damn—about helping to solve your problem. You simply want to know how to save your home and your credit without losing an arm and a leg in attorney fees and bank penalties. Maybe you want to make sure you are never put in this type of situation again. You may want to know how to get back at the mortgage broker or Realtor who got you into this mess in the first place. Or maybe you want to get a better handle on what the current Troubled Asset Relief Program (TARP) $700 billion bailout means to you—especially since the money is coming out of your pocket as a US taxpayer.

Enter *Foreclosure Nation*. As a real estate lawyer for almost twenty years,

I've enjoyed training hundreds of people from diverse backgrounds in real estate, mortgage, and law-related industries. Because we all have different levels of experience and attention spans, this book is organized into logical sections that will allow you to skim topics that are already familiar to you and refer back to subjects you are less comfortable with. Rest assured that the concepts are a lot less complicated once someone shows you what the legalese means and explains the dynamics motivating the people you must convince to help you. The goal of this book is to explain the pieces that together created our nation's subprime crisis in a user-friendly way so that average Americans can fully see and plan for the big picture. For those more inclined to enjoy the nitty-gritty details, references to resources are included so that you can conveniently access additional information about particular topics.

As the subprime crisis evolves, it's becoming increasingly clear that this is not your father's economic event. The savings and loan (S&L) crisis, the bursting of the dot-com bubble, and similar historical events exacted their heaviest toll on those people who chose to play. But the subprime crisis is not playing favorites. Because of the crisis, real estate and business credit is eluding *all* of us. Record-high fraud and the financial losses it is causing will cost all of us. Local governments are cutting services to everyone in their jurisdictions. We're watching helplessly as *all* of our real estate values melt away. Every corner of Wall Street and the global markets are feeling the impact—along with *each and every one of us* who has a horse in the race. Consumer spending, corporate growth, new jobs, and our country's gross domestic product are all stumbling as our collective American pride, pocketbook, and psyche—along with global confidence—continue to shrink. Still, no one knows where in the world all the bad debt will land or whose wallet it will drain the most. A lot of this debt is showing up as part of the investment holdings of companies that *our* pension and retirement funds bought stock in, which means we'll continue feeling the burn when we try to retire. Concerns about systemic discrimination, widening socioeconomic gaps, and even a lengthy recession are surfacing among the overall distrust of Wall Street risk assessment valuations and bank balance sheets, causing the stock and financial markets to have jitters that manifest themselves in wide daily up-and-down swings of stock prices. Now that the government has pulled up a seat at the table, it's anybody's game. Winners can become losers overnight—and vice versa—depending upon how Uncle Sam plays his cards.

The bottom line is that even if you considered the subprime crisis someone else's problem in early 2007, you've likely since discovered that if you have a home or any other real estate, a business, a dollar invested on Wall Street or anywhere in the American economy, or an interest in our country's moral fiber and its elected officials, you're at least curious, if not outright concerned, about what foreclosures in America will mean to *you*. This is precisely why this book will be of value for even those readers who managed to avoid the temptations of the real estate bubble, but who now see that there's no way on earth they can avoid the impact of the choices other people have made.

We've been hearing and reading news reports of first the subprime crisis and now the broader economic puzzle for months. Some cause us to have an "aha!" moment; others raise more questions than they answer. We all count on the mortgage loan application process to make sure we'll be able to repay the money a bank offers us. We place our good faith in the nation's mortgage industry without realizing that its infrastructure is contrary to our best interests. We trust bond-rating agencies implicitly, naively holding firm to the notion that "AAA" ratings are what Wall Street brokers buy all the time. We assume that regulators and government officials understand the idiosyncrasies of investment houses and brokerage firms and the impact their decisions will have on individual investors and on our country as a whole. In fact, we are little more than mere guinea pigs in trial-and-error legislative and regulatory experiments.

In bite-size, easy-to-follow sections, the book will connect the dots for you between what Realtors, banks, builders, rating agencies, Wall Street, and our government have really been up to and how they've affected us all, all the while providing solutions you can implement now. I'll also pose bigger ethical questions and conflicts of interest that could affect your pocketbook and the way you vote in the coming years.

You'll want or need to pay close attention to what follows if:

- You've lost or may lose your home or other property to foreclosure, or you're starting to think it may make financial sense for you to give your property back to the bank
- Your real estate investment is worth less now than in was in 2006 or your stocks or other investment values are down
- You want to understand what the subprime and broader economic crisis is all about or when the real estate market will turn around
- You're thinking about investing in real estate but want to know when

to buy, at what price to buy, and when you will be able to resell and make money; or you're wondering what types of opportunities the subprime crisis has created for making money
- You're having trouble trying to sell or refinance a home or other real estate
- You're having trouble getting credit for your business or your business sales are down
- You've lost your job or can't seem to find a job
- Your real estate taxes, insurance, and home owner or condominium association costs seem to be too high and you'd like to try to lower them
- You're thinking about suing a Realtor, lender, mortgage broker, developer, or Wall Street firm, or you're a Realtor, lender, mortgage broker, developer, or Wall Street firm at risk of being sued
- You want to know what your legislators and regulators have done and what they plan to do in response to the crisis
- You want to understand the terms running across news screens every day, what it all means to you, our country, and generations to come.

In short, if you want to make the best financial choices over the next few years or just want to be informed without spending weeks or months learning, I offer an easy, sometimes amusing read that fills you in on everything you need to know about the crisis as it relates to real estate, mortgages, Wall Street, and the economy. I'll share practical tools and resources designed to help you make educated choices, avoid loss, and even benefit from subprime-related economic shifts. I'll expose how we got here, how the systems really work, where we are headed, and how we can fix what's broken, while demystifying complicated, often intimidating financial and political processes that occur for the most part behind closed doors.

For those of you who always find the glass half full, not to worry: At the end of the day, banks, builders, Realtors, Wall Street, and our government all answer to you as consumers and voters. We'll see why "experts" are predicting that some of our nation's regional residential real estate markets will begin turning around in 2009, hopefully the beginning in a series of good news for Americans. In the meantime, I'll attempt to empower you with the knowledge to choose wisely.

1

CULTURAL ENTITLEMENT, CREDIT, AND THE AMERICAN DREAM

Welcome to our foreclosure nation. This may be the first time you've realized you're a resident of the nation, even if you never personallty bought into the current real estate, mortgage, and financial market mess, and that can be a bit of a shock. Understanding what a foreclosure nation is is easier when you have an understanding of the culture that created it, namely, our culture of credit.

REDEFINING THE AMERICAN DREAM

For most of us, the "dream" in American Dream is about money and the lifestyle it buys. Making the dream uniquely American is the promise that ours is a country in which anyone can achieve that dream. But what happens when we want the dream and don't have the money to afford it? Let's see how we've come to arrive at this dichotomy in the first place.

Our Grandparents' Definition of the Dream

The phrase "American Dream" was coined by and about turn-of-the-century European immigrants, an industrious group who arrived on our nation's shores with little more than the clothes on their backs. In this country, through hard work and perseverance, they had the opportunity to transcend financial and lifestyle barriers that were insurmountable in their respective homelands. Their core values, including financial values, are precisely what we'd expect from a generation struggling with two world wars, a Great Depression, a polio epidemic, and other woes. Their reward was not merely a new car, a house, jewelry, or the latest clothes. After living under monarchs and dictators, success in the land of plenty was more internal. Their desire to reap the benefits of their own efforts and control their own financial future was precious to them. They strove to create a better life for their children. Their firmly established work ethic, self-sufficiency, perseverance, practicality, and devotion to saving for a rainy day defined turn-of-the-century immigrants.

Baby Boomers' Interpretation of the Dream

The children of these immigrants are our baby boomers, optimistic kids who grew up on the crest of a postwar wave. Although their early years were marked by a predisposition toward cautious sprinklings of peace and love, boomers at once modeled the work ethic exemplified by their parents while relaxing the emphasis on saving. They chose instead to exchange some of their parents' seemingly endless sacrifice for the security and control of a big stash of cash in favor of life's little luxuries: a weekend cabin by the lake, a European vacation or maybe a cute convertible. As products of a newly emerged American world military power, boomers quickly rose as economic market leaders, their boundless optimism further empowering our country's collective relationship with money and, in turn, unwittingly initiating an important shift in Americans' core financial values. Boomers worked, in part, to get a piece of the pie, their "fair share" of material things. That they were entitled to benefit from their efforts to control their own financial future and to take their families to the next socioeconomic level (at least in the more external, material sense) was a given. True to the boomer version of the American Dream, the US government implemented a succession of programs that ensured future generations easier access to that signature dream lifestyle. Veterans Affairs (VA) and Federal Housing Authority (FHA) home loans were born, and we no longer had to work quite as hard or persevere quite as long to buy a house. Workforce protections, welfare benefits, and similar programs aimed at ensuring equal access to the dream for one and all rendered self-sufficiency a less critical factor in how we defined success.

The American Dream: Twenty-first Century Style

Fast forward fifty years to the boomers' children and grandchildren, post-postwar immigrants, and their progeny—a generation raised on home loans, car loans, and the litany of guaranteed government jump-start programs that followed: student loans, employment benefits, food stamps, and, perhaps most significantly, credit cards. We seem to have inherited the drive for the external rewards our parents and grandparents earned, but not the internal pride and motivation in earning them. Certain aspects of our modern economy actually make it more difficult for us to control our financial destinies, to get ahead the way former generations did. It used to be that we paid our dues and worked our way up the ladder, but today that's not necessarily the case. Young, newly minted MBAs trump years of work experience. Less expensive, fresh workforces replace existing workers who have become expensive and expendable. In response, some experts claim, we've acquired a form of learned helplessness that places material things we think we can control or we think make us appear rich, hip, and successful in a more important position. The psychology of material things and their priority for so many Americans makes for an interesting debate. Whether it's learned helplessness, instant gratification, or a feeling of entitlement, the outcome is the same: our grandparents' work ethic, self-sufficiency, perseverance, practicality, and penchant to save are viewed as quaint, comical, and even absurd to many modern-day Americans who have come to expect the dream lifestyle but reflect a growing lack of responsibility for personal financial well-being. Our primary career motivator is not building value, wealth, and security, but acquiring things—or, more aptly, covering the minimum monthly payments for things we've already acquired. Generations X and Y have replaced working hard with "working smart," which is often subjectively equated with working as little as possible.

The Dilemma

With help from Madison Avenue, positioning materialism as an entitlement and telling us we all deserve the best of everything, we've grown to believe our own rhetoric. We believe, for example, that because we're stressed out, or have been extra understanding or good about something, or maybe just because our neighbor has one, we've earned and can afford whatever it is we want at the moment as a "reward." For the majority of Americans, there is no reason to wait for anything. They view Benjamin Franklin's famous quote "A penny saved is a penny earned" as virtually meaningless, since a penny is worthless now anyway, right? Fast food, drive-thru banks and dry cleaners, instant download digital photos, text messaging, and the Internet reinforce the expectation that we can have everything *now*. Our worldwide reputation as Americans is for a love of flashy, material things. In short, the capitalism that defined our grandparents' generation—and indeed built our country's economy—has, over time, inadvertently bred a mentality of immediate material entitlement in which the end justifies the means. The view from the fast track to achieving the dream lifestyle is quite different from our grandparents' more traditional ride, when so much pride was experienced in the journey itself.

The Solution? Credit!

So we want lots of stuff, but we don't want to have to work and wait for it. It doesn't take a rocket scientist to see that the math just doesn't work. Unfortunately, for most of us, winning the lottery or having a rich uncle leave us millions is not likely. Enter the credit card: our fast-track ticket to the dream lifestyle. One often ignored reality is the fact that credit itself has become big business. Like most businesses, its goal is to sell, sell, sell, and make money, preferably as much money as possible. To do this, credit card companies have, over time, consciously aided in altering our society's core financial values.

There's nothing new about the concept of credit itself. It's a common thread throughout history. Some of our great-great-great-great-grandparents owed debt to lords and kings, and found themselves living as serfs in fiefdoms until the obligation was repaid. Seventeenth-century Americans regularly owed money to the blacksmith, the town doctor, or the banker. Why, then, is credit different for our generation?

For starters, look at who is granted credit today. Common sense tells us that credit card companies should lend money to those who can afford to repay it—and then, only as much money as they can comfortably repay. We tend to think that because a bank offers us credit, it must have verified in advance that we'll be able to pay back the debt. After all, banks are the experts at determining such complicated things. But that's not how modern credit works. The majority of credit cards today are sent unsolicited. In our grandparents' day it was the other way around: When Grandpa wanted credit, he went to the bank in his Sunday best, presented his case, and basically begged for a loan. Often the banker decided that Grandpa may not be able to repay the loan on time and turned him away empty-handed. Arguably, this system unfairly favored people of means. Theoretically, some folks who would have repaid their debts were denied the opportunity to better themselves. But lots of people who would have eventually found themselves in debtors' prison had they been granted the loan were spared the heartache of their own folly by prudent bankers.

OUTSMARTED BY CREDIT CARD COMPANIES

Today our senses are dulled by a constant barrage of mailings, televisions ads, and phone calls offering us credit. The average household currently has as many as thirteen credit cards, and most of these cards were issued without the cardholder having to prove even a modicum of personal worth or income. We don't need to have a job or demonstrate we're worthy of a loan to get a credit card. Only a fraction of credit card companies insist on any kind of background check, and a whopping two-thirds don't bother to see if we're employed. In fact, the credit card companies actually *prefer* when we don't pay our credit card balances in full. The industry's most profitable consumers are "revolvers," those people who carry a monthly balance. And credit card companies love late payments, since that translates to more profit in the form of substantial late fees.

Credit card companies are very much aware of human behaviors that influence us and generate more profits for them. Advertising is everywhere, suggesting that actual money is not really involved and equating spending with achieving favorable outcomes and emotions, like love and happiness. There is even an aura of respectability that comes with using credit cards and reaching the level of a "Gold" or "Platinum" card, even though we know in reality these cards are offered based on how much money we spend, not how much we earn or can afford to pay back. Who is not impressed when someone pulls out a "Black" card?

The credit card companies know that many of us associate "credit" with "free." They know we find "debt" distasteful, but "charging" is chic. Sadly, we aren't nearly as aware of our own behaviors as the credit card companies are. Some ads appeal to our desire for convenience: "Sign and drive. Leave your cash at home." Others appeal to a lack of accountability: "No Credit? Bad Credit? No problem!" What they don't say is that the reason it's no problem is that those cardholders with bad credit will pay the credit card company more by way of a much higher interest rate. A 2006 promotion for a credit line from the now-defunct Washington Mutual asked, "Just Can't Wait to Have It?"[1] But what is really so important to own that we can't wait for it, and is it really worth paying an extra 25 percent in interest to have it now? What would our grandparents have done? It's no wonder that the number of banks issuing credit cards increased by 68 percent in 2007. According to Federal Reserve statistics, of the total number of cards issued, more than 20 million in each system carry a balance forward each month, meaning we can't afford to repay what we've borrowed.[2]

LIFE, LIBERTY, AND THE PURSUIT OF GOOD CREDIT SCORES

Instead of approving or denying credit based on our true financial strength, today's borrowers' financial strength is evaluated in terms of a *credit rating* and our credit rating is used as a pricing mechanism.

Credit reporting originated more than a hundred years ago when small retail merchants started comparing financial information about their customers. This eventually evolved into localized credit associations that eventually consolidated into a few larger ones. Standardized credit-scoring systems were born in the 1960s. It was also during this time that controversy enveloped credit-rating associations, which were using credit information to deny services and opportunities to certain profiled populations. For example, credit reports tended to include only negative information and lifestyle factors such as sexual orientation. Credit reports weren't available to the public, so no one even knew what negative information their own credit report contained, nor could an individual contest and correct erroneous entries. In the early 1970s we gained the right to see, dispute, and correct our credit reports.

The advent of modern credit scoring propelled the credit industry forward by enabling companies to filter us into groups based on risk assessment, or the likelihood that we will pay our bills on time. This grouping provides the rationale credit card companies use to justify charging some of us more or less interest than others. Credit card companies believe those who are less likely to pay constitute more of a risk, and in return for taking this risk, the companies charge those individuals a higher interest rate. Today, creditors wanting access to the more than 1 billion US consumer credit reports issued annually must submit information about their own customers each month reflecting payment history and current unpaid balances to the Fair Issac Corporation (FICO). FICO uses this information in a formula that predicts the creditworthiness of each and every borrower, and awards each of us a corresponding score that ranges from a low of 300 to a high of 850. The median score is 725, and those who score above 770 usually get the best interest rates (meaning the lowest interest rates). A FICO score below 600 is subprime, meaning those borrowers will pay higher interest rates.

Amazingly, only 2 percent of us know our own credit scores, and even fewer of us take steps to improve our credit scores.[3] We'll drive miles out of our way to save money at a sale and spend hours clipping coupons, but only a very few hardy souls take the time to study and improve credit scores that may be costing tens of thousands of dollars in interest charges year after year. The same thing can be said of the manner in which we treat our credit card agreements and monthly statements. Surveys have shown that fewer than 10 percent of us review our credit card statements for accuracy. Errors have led to a plethora of other challenges, since such errors may lead to higher payments or denied credit. Among consumers with the lowest credit scores, almost 8 percent have credit reports containing errors. Twenty-five percent of these errors could result in credit denial. More than 50 percent contain outdated information or information belonging to someone else. Resources like FICO.com and annualcreditreport.com are important consumer protection tools available to all of us.[4] Credit scores will become increasingly important over the coming years as more and more companies make decisions about us—for example, our insurance rates, cell phone fees, rental car costs, and rental apartment lease approvals—based on this all-important number.

From time to time the US government has stepped in and forced the credit card companies to accept changes geared toward disclosing things more clearly to us or behaving in a manner that might be considered more fair. Judging by recent congressional hearings, we can expect to see a new series of credit card regulations soon. The challenge is balancing consumer protection with the fact that in our capitalist economy, credit card companies, like other businesses, are entitled to make money—theoretically as much as possible. In fact, they have an obligation to their investors to do so. So how can we logically expect a credit card company to earn less than top dollar? Certainly if we were the investors we wouldn't want to hear that our dividends had been cut so the company could give away credit! Some argue that credit card companies cross an ethical line with what they describe in the confusing fine print of the lending agreement, with misleading advertising, and with an overall lack of transparency. The credit card debt collection industry generates more complaints than any other business.[5] And industry insiders allege that some reporting agencies even deliberately include incorrect or incomplete information in our credit scoring so their competitors won't want to pursue us as customers.

Playing the Blame Game

The credit-debt blame game is a common waste of time some of us engage in with our credit card companies. It goes something like this: The credit companies tempt us with a variety of advertising and unsolicited offers into carrying more debt than our income justifies. When we drown in the debt, the house of cards crumbles. The credit card companies hit us with high penalties and collection fees. The companies claim they have to pressure us to collect the debt quickly, since once a debt is in default it becomes a riskier investment. With higher penalties and fees than we expected and the pressure to pay it all now, we cannot pay the companies back and place the blame on them. Clearly the game begins when we accept the credit card and begin to spend more than we can afford to repay. The credit industry is using every tool it can to tempt us into spending, but it's certainly not forcing us to buy things.

At the end of the day, America loves credit. Our economy has grown to need it, which is one reason the government is so hesitant to intervene. Credit keeps us all pumping money into the economy, even if we can't afford to pay it back. In our consumption-driven economy, all of us are pressed to spend if America's economy is to grow and flourish. On occasion it is almost presented as ones patriotic duty. We'll talk more about this later. For now, a timeline (pages 26–27) illustrating how the modern credit card industry evolved will give you a better idea of how our nation has progressed toward reliance upon the daily use of credit and show the common patterns in government intervention and deregulation, which, as you will see, also apply to how the subprime crisis was created and has been handled by our government.

Appropriate versus Inappropriate Use of Credit

No doubt life, including its financial components, is more complicated for us than it was for our grandparents. Let's face it: We have infinitely more spending opportunities and decisions than they did. Back then, someone could only use so many horseshoes, and I doubt any of them were Gucci. Which brings us to what is perhaps the most important controllable distinction between credit use then and now: necessity versus luxury.

Using credit cards is, hands down, far more convenient than using cash. (The same may be said of using debit cards, but at issue is our use of credit, not the fact that it can be accessed using a portable plastic card.) The magical convenience of plastic money is central to our famously compulsive consumer economy, an instrument of social as much as economic change. "Don't leave home without it" is not just a choice, it's a necessity. We can't rent a car or book a hotel room without a credit card. Our creditability has become our identity. Over time, this has led to an unrealistic comfort level with plastic that is not necessarily always in our best interest. We're comfortable using cards to finance unneeded luxuries or to buy daily necessities in between paychecks. In 2003 a residential developer named the Related Companies teamed with American Express to allow tenants to pay their rent using credit cards as landlords vied for ways to lure people away from home ownership and into rental properties. In 2007 American Express expanded the concept to allow the use of credit cards to pay mortgages. In some states we can now even use credit cards to pay our income taxes! It's easy, automatic, and convenient. Credit has become less a discretionary purchasing tool and more a financial management tool. In contrast to cars or real estate, most of our credit card purchases tend to be non-necessity depreciating assets, or things that lose their value over time, such as a television, in comparison to investing in an IRA, 401(k), or something intended to appreciate in value over time. There's no time frame for repayment and, in fact, at the time wc make our credit card expenditures, many of us have no idea how long it will take us to repay the debt.

Credit Industry Timeline

1958 Bank of America launches the first credit card, mailing sixty thousand to residents of Fresno, California.

1960 Lenders begin using a uniform credit-scoring system.

1966 A decade of trial and error in the credit card business, most notably a 1966 Chicago debacle when local banks mail 5 million unsolicited cards one week before Christmas. Among the recipients are children and convicted criminals.

1970 The interest rate banks can charge their customers is limited by law, while at the same time the rate these banks are charged for short-term borrowing from the Federal Reserve continues to increase, eating into their profits.

1971 Congress inquires into Credit Rating Association problems, including incorrect and misused information and secrecy, and initiates reforms.

1978 The US Supreme Court allows national banks to charge the maximum interest rate set by their home state in any state in which they offer credit cards, effectively lifting the cap on what credit card companies can charge. Citibank strikes a deal with South Dakota whereby South Dakota passes legislation removing its interest rate cap. Citibank moves operations, and hundreds of high-paying jobs, into the state. Other banks and states follow suit. Today's larger credit card companies are still based out of these states.

1980 The US government farms out student loan collections to debt collection companies. Backed by Wall Street and private equity firms recognizing the opportunity for investing in them, the debt collection industry booms.

1980–1990 Inflation propels the credit card industry to record profits, while the number of cards issued to Americans more than doubles.

1989 FICO develops a standard credit score measure in a joint project between Equifax (one of our nation's largest credit rating agencies) and the world's largest banks and companies, thereby widening credit card availability across the economic spectrum.

1996 The US Supreme Court lifts late payment fee restrictions, and credit card company profits double.

1997 Specialists develop a niche analyzing consumer data, more reliably predicting who will pay versus who will carry a balance, to more efficiently target newly developed market incentives such as higher credit lines, lower minimum payments, teaser rates, and rewards for using credit cards. Credit card companies realize another $12 billion in profit.

1997 Congress clamps down on credit repair schemes (such as companies charging a fee in return for their promise to repair a customer's credit rating and then doing nothing) targeting the customer.

2001 Consumers gain direct access to their credit scores.

2002 Bad debt (money owed to credit card companies by customers who are not paying it on time or at all) sold by credit companies increases from $910 million to $2.5 billion. Bad debt buyers pay far less than the face value of this debt. For example, $1,000 worth of debt might be purchased for $250. The buyers then put pressure on the credit card customers to pay the bad debt, often earning back close to the full $1,000 owed from the mere $250 investment.

2003 The credit industry charges off or sells a record $167 billion of bad debt (meaning more and more people are having a tough time paying their credit card bills on time).[6]

In a sense, a credit card is an instantaneous loan we issue to ourselves. The credit card companies don't ask what we will be buying. It's entirely up to us to use our credit cards in an appropriate manner. For the cash savvy, credit card incentives can be a windfall, allowing users to rack up reward points that translate to free trips and other perks. But for those less adept at financial restraint, it can spell disaster. With so many people living off credit, the growing question has been: What will happen when we finally have to pay the piper?

Credit on Steroids

With more than $1.5 trillion of total consumer spending each year, $800 billion more than what we earn, the US economy has clearly gone plastic. The only way we can collectively spend so much more than we earn is by using credit cards. Like everything else, we're super-sizing our credit card debt. Our household debt has grown from $680 billion in the mid-1970s to $14 trillion today, doubling since only 2001![7] The credit card industry is earning record profits, more than $30 billion a year. One-third of US families in bankruptcy in 2007 owed more than a year's salary on their credit cards! Seventy-eight percent of us roll over a balance each month, paying an average 1.5 percent service charge on top of other fees. According to the Federal Reserve, the total amount of outstanding revolving consumer credit exceeds $374 billion, nearly nine times the amount owed just twenty years ago.[8]

In the United States, annual outstanding credit card balances are now increasing at twice the rate of prior years. This indicates that people are either using their credit cards more often or using them for bigger expenses like mortgage and rent payments. Studies show that carrying so much debt is taking its toll on our lives. Seventy percent of us admit the debt we are carrying is making us unhappy, yet, as the Nike ad says, we "Just Do It." What most of us don't know is that our migration toward credit cards actually influences the way we spend money. That's right: Credit cards encourage spending. According to a research study conducted at MIT's Sloan School of Management, people who have more credit cards make larger purchases per store visit and are likely to underestimate or even entirely forget the amount spent on recent purchases. We overspend by an average of 20 percent when we use credit cards instead of cash.[9]

AMERICANS ARE IN DEBT DENIAL

Like many things in life, when it comes to credit card use there's a big gap between what we say and what we do. Seventy-five percent of us say we would not make a purchase we could not pay for, but the facts show more than 75 percent of us can't pay for what we buy each month. We are a nation in debt denial. Studies show that we prefer to talk about our age, weight, and even annual income than disclose the amount of credit card debt we owe. Our thought processes where credit is concerned defy common sense. Many of us put credit card debt on the psychological back burner because it can be paid back tomorrow. Some of us actually believe an incredible occurrence will happen—like winning the lottery or getting a huge bonus at work—that will make repaying the debt a cinch. Most of us don't even review our monthly statements.[10] Perhaps debt frustration and its related sense of hopelessness can keep us from connecting to our financial reality, while others cite a link between our country's overall aversion to numbers and mathematics, as reflected in student test scores. Or maybe online banking has removed us one step further from our money. How many of us still balance checkbooks or follow the regular monthly ritual of paying bills, as our grandparents once did?

Just when credit went from being a convenience to being a problem is hard to gauge, and debt denial compounds matters. Why we spend is a topic for another book. The 2007 Cadillac advertisement suggesting that after an exciting holiday season, as depression settles in, we should all buy new Cadillacs says it all. Automotive and other forms of "retail therapy" have become a normal way we all deal with life's daily challenges. Likewise, a trip to the mall has become a way we entertain ourselves and our kids.

Of course even when there's nothing we need, we seldom walk out empty-handed. Maybe just being aware of these behaviors is a first step in learning to keep them in check. Or maybe we'll decide that the time has come to really change our nation's cultural attitudes about credit, debt, and spending.

We often only truly address a problem when it's out of control. Most of us didn't give a second thought to global warming until Al Gore's *An Inconvenient Truth* hit movie theaters and captured audiences' attention. Terrorism officially became a problem only after 9/11. So it may be that only now, the buck will stop here with us, the consumers. Now that our debt denial has reached critical levels and America has become a full-fledged foreclosure nation, perhaps we can finally expect to see some changes. Experts at the not-for-profit Center for a New American Dream agree that changing our credit habits can make us a happier country. Current surveys show 90 percent of Americans want to take their financial power back. According to New American Dream executive director Lisa Wise, Americans are rethinking their priorities or what really matters to us. "Even before the crisis, it was obvious that the traditional American Dream had been displaced by a 'more is better' focus that promotes not quality of life, but rather the unbridled production and consumption of stuff. There was never any chance that could continue indefinitely."[11] A first step would be using cash more and our credit cards less, lending new meaning to the phrase "going green."

WHAT DOES ALL THIS MEAN TO YOU?

With the conclusion of this chapter, you have a bit more insight into how credit and debt have woven their way into our nation's fiber. If you're like most Americans, you have your own unique tales of the good, the bad, and the ugly that comes from having credit and debt in your life. But this is only the first chapter in the story of our foreclosure nation. In the next chapter, I will explain how credit and debt have infiltrated our homes.

NOTES

1. Washington Mutual branch promotion sign, February 2008.

2. Board of Governors of the Federal Reserve System, http://www.federalreserve.gov/releases/g19/20071207 (accessed January 1, 2008).

3. PBS, "Secret History of the Credit Card," *Frontline*, http://www.pbs.org/wgbh/pages/frontline/shows/credit (accessed February 3, 2008); "The Big Lie about Credit Card Debt," July 30, 2007, http://articles.moneycentral.msn.com/Banking/CreditCardSmarts/TheBigLieAboutCreditCardDebt.aspx.

4. Ibid.

5. Ibid.; Chris Arnold, "Credit Card Companies Abuse the Unwitting," *National Public Radio Morning Edition*, November 6, 2007.

6. "Discount Dining: How to Save Money When You Eat Out," *Today Show*, November 16, 2008; Liz Pulliam Weston, ""The Truth about Credit Card Debt," MSN Money, http://moneycentral.msn.com/content/Banking/creditcardsmarts/P74808.asp (accessed February 26, 2008).

7. Weston, "The Truth about Credit Card Debt."

8. Arnold, "Credit Card Companies Abuse the Unwitting."

9. "Discount Dining: How to Save When You Eat Out"; Weston, "The Truth about Credit Card Debt."

10. Weston, "The Truth about Credit Card Debt."

11. Center tor a New American Dream, http://newdream.org/about/pdfs/Economy-9-24.pdf.

2
THE MORTGAGE
AS AMERICAN AS APPLE PIE

For most of us, a home mortgage loan is the single biggest debt we'll ever incur. Like the credit cards we use to finance a variety of purchases, a mortgage loan is simply a credit vehicle used to finance a home purchase. In light of the progression over time in our society's comfort level with debt, our sense of entitlement to the American Dream, and lenders' aggressive tactics to engage us, it's easy to see how we've swallowed borrowing hundreds of billions of dollars in often overextended, costly mortgage loans. Our culture has further promoted the concept that home ownership is the ultimate symbol of achievement, responsibility, and maturity. We see this in our government's enthusiasm in allowing mortgage interest as a tax deduction and other benefits that encourage home ownership.

AMERICAN HOME = ATM

The problem, of course, lies not in simply owning our homes, but rather in our attitude about the credit used to acquire and maintain them. Until the early 1900s, mortgage loans were not commonly used to achieve home ownership. Instead, the majority of mortgage loans were used to finance farms.

It wasn't until around 1920 that home mortgages started to outnumber farm mortgages. Even then, people tended to buy more modest homes that they knew they could afford and pay off, the ultimate goal being to own one's home free and clear. When people became financially successful, they might trade up into a larger home, but seldom more than what they could comfortably afford and always with the goal of one day owning even the new home outright. True to our penchant for immediate gratification, the modern American view of home ownership has evolved. Today, very few of us are willing to wait and save for even a small down payment or spend years in a "starter home" before trading up into the bigger home we really want. We want our dream homes now, trading the comfort of building equity and an affordable payment for the prize of the biggest, fanciest home we can buy.

Because they are secured by our homes, mortgage loans are considered less risky for lenders than credit card, automobile, or other types of loans and thus are offered at lower interest rates. But once we're in the door, the modern tendency is to treat our homes as ATM machines, cashing out as much equity as possible as often as possible, most often to fund depreciating purchases by paying off credit card debt. Thanks in part to prime-time financial gurus encouraging us to refinance our homes to pay off higher-interest credit card debt, the home mortgage has evolved from an indispensable tool to help us achieve the American Dream of home ownership into a mechanism for easier access to cheaper credit. There are two fundamental problems with that approach, both of them even more serious than the issues of debt in general discussed in chapter 1. First, a mortgage loan puts our home in jeopardy if we don't pay the loan back on time. We are seeing this play out in foreclosures across America today, a process explained in more detail in chapter 6. Second, Americans have traditionally relied on this home equity as a nest egg for retirement. When we mortgage our homes and do not work hard to pay off our mortgages, rather than having money to live on when we retire and a home to live in with no monthly mortgage payment, we end up having to work long into our senior years just to pay our debts and eventually must rely more heavily on public assistance. Multiply that times millions of us hoping to retire in the coming years and you can see where we will run into problems we did not have when Americans believed in paying off their home mortgages. During the recent real estate bubble, the amount of home mortgage credit made available to higher-risk borrowers with higher-risk loan products on higher-risk properties, which we will discuss shortly, was prolific, tempting many with inappropriate loans. According to the US Federal Reserve, Americans took more than $700 billion in equity out of their homes in 2005 alone. Almost two-thirds of that money was used to pay down credit card debt.[1] The magnitude of these financing decisions on our lives and our nation is tremendous. As we are seeing, the difference between good and bad individual financial decisions can mean the difference between a healthy economy and a foreclosure nation.

WHAT THE MORTGAGE INDUSTRY DOESN'T WANT YOU TO KNOW

Today's mortgage business operates on several levels, from the frontline mortgage broker all the way to Wall Street. Each level has its own inherent loyalties and motivations, often running contrary to what is in the borrower's best interest. A bit of historical context, along with common industry terms and dynamics at work behind the scenes clarifying some of the things you've been reading and hearing about, will be helpful in better understanding how we have reached the huge number of foreclosures currently on the ledgers of banks and investment companies nationwide. Because it is written to accommodate a wide range of readers, this chapter is best used as a reference. Read those sections that interest you and refer to others that explain concepts you feel you need a refresher on in the context of the following chapters.

WHAT IS A MORTGAGE?

We use the term *mortgage* when referring to a loan or debt incurred to finance real estate. In some states, a mortgage is called a *mortgage deed* or a *deed of trust*. Each of these terms technically defines a legal device, a pledge, or a lien on property as security for the repayment of a debt. A more accurate use of the word would be phrased: "I am giving the bank a $100,000 mortgage lien against my home as collateral to ensure that I repay the bank the money that it loaned to me." All people on the title to a property will generally be required to sign a mortgage being filed against that property in order to indicate their consent to the creation of that encumbrance. The word "mortgage" originates in French law and literally translates to "dead pledge."

In fifteenth-century France, as is still the case in some jurisdictions which use a deed of trust rather than a mortgage, a lender actually owned a borrower's home until the loan was repaid. This concept, commonly referred to as title theory, is discussed more fully in chapter 6.

WHAT IS A PROMISSORY NOTE?

The debt itself is documented by a *promissory note* or *note*. Much like an IOU, a promissory note reflects the amount of money we've borrowed from the lender and the interest rate and time frame in which we've agreed to repay it. So a mortgage merely secures repayment of the debt documented by a promissory note. Borrowers often use the terms *mortgage* and *note* interchangably. It is possible for a person to sign or "be on" the note but not the mortgage if, for example, he is agreeing to be obligated to repay the loan to the bank but does not own the property (for example, a parent may "co-sign" a note for a grown child).

WHAT IS A LIEN?

A mortgage is *perfected* by recording it in the public records of the county in which the real estate is located. Recording the mortgage creates a *lien* or *encumbrance* on the real estate, putting future buyers and lenders on notice that the bank is owed money, which will need to be repaid when the home is sold or refinanced. A lien can be *consensual* or *nonconsensual*, *perfected* or *unperfected*. A mortgage lien is consensual, since we are in agreement with the lender placing it on our property. For purposes of example, a nonconsensual lien might arise when a person loses a lawsuit and the judge allows the winner of the lawsuit to place a lien on the loser's property in order to make sure the money owed from the lawsuit is paid. Another example of a nonconsensual lien arises when a person does not pay his income taxes. The IRS can place a nonconsensual lien on the property, again, to make sure the money owed is paid. Perfected liens are those for which a creditor has established a priority (which means a higher, senior, more important) right in the real estate with respect to other creditors, in comparison to an unperfected lien, over which even a lien recorded later might take priority or have higher rights. *Lien priority*, or which lien takes precedence or has higher rights over others, depends upon the legal priority theory employed by the particular state in which the lien is recorded. In some states, the lien recorded first in the local Office of Public Records takes priority over other liens recorded later, regardless of when the person owning the lien right acquired it; sometimes this is also referred to as a *superior lien*. For example, let's say you buy a $250,000 home with a $200,000 first mortgage loan from State Bank, but State Bank does not record its first mortgage document in the Office of Public Records right away. Two weeks later you decide to install a swimming pool. Pool Company arranges a $23,000 second mortgage loan to help you to cover the cost. If Pool Company records its $25,000 second mortgage in the Office of the Public Records before State Bank records its $200,000 first mortgage, Pool Company may have superior or higher rights than State Bank to foreclose on your home and sell it to pay off the debt. In fact, Pool Company could eliminate all rights State Bank has against the home. We'll explain these concepts in more detail in chapter 6. In other states, the lien that is signed, witnessed, and notarized first takes priority, regardless of which is actually recorded in the Office of Public Records first. Still other states take a hybrid approach, making the lien recorded first superior unless the party has actual notice of another lien that was signed first but not yet recorded.

WHAT IS THE CHAIN OF TITLE?

Buyers and lenders typically perform a title search before the purchase or refinance of a home. This search reveals any recorded mortgage and any other liens against the property securing repayment of outstanding debts. When a mortgage is paid off, the lien is released by recording a *satisfaction of mortgage* in the public records. This succession of recorded documents, which also includes documents called *deeds* that transfer ownership to and from various owners, is referred to as the *chain of title*.

WHAT IS A CONSTRUCTION LOAN?

Like we do with our homes, builders also obtain mortgage loans to buy real estate. In addition, they obtain *construction loans*, often secured by the real estate, to finance the building of homes, condominiums, and other structures on the real estate they eventually plan to sell to us. (Home owners can also use construction loans to finance building homes for themselves.) These loans are relevant to us because the builders' lenders often impose requirements on the builder that impact us. Many of these requirements eventually find their way into the purchase contracts that home builders require us to sign. For example, construction lender requirements may impact how much of a deposit the builder requires us to put down or how many units the builder must sell before he can begin construction, a practice commonly known as a *pre-sale requirement*.

HOW DO MORTGAGTE INTEREST AND AMORTIZATION WORK?

Principal versus Interest

Each payment we make under a mortgage loan has two parts, *principal* and *interest*. Principal is the actual amount of money we've borrowed. Paying principal is good. By paying principal we are actually relieving ourselves of debt by reducing the amount of the loan money we owe to the lender. Interest, on the other, hand is the fee we pay the bank or lender for loaning us the principal. Paying interest does nothing to reduce the amount of loan we still owe the bank.

What Is Default Interest?

Default interest is interest at a higher, more expensive rate that is normally charged if a loan is in default (i.e., when we fail to do something we are obligated to do under the terms of the loan documents we signed). There are two general types of default. A monetary default occurs when we don't pay all of the forms of payments we agreed to pay, for example, our monthly mortgage payment, real estate taxes, or home owner's insurance. A nonmonetary default occurs when we fail to do something else we agreed to do under the loan terms; for example, if we fail to maintain our home and a code enforcement violation is issued. Mortgage loan documents typically allow us a certain amount of time after we are notified of a default in which to cure, or fix, the default. If we don't do this within the cure period, the lender can exercise its default rights under the loan documents, including charging us the higher default interest rate and pursuing foreclosure. As we will see in chapter 6, foreclosure requires time. During the time that it takes for a lender to foreclose, the lender will usually charge us default interest.

What Exactly Is Loan Amortization?

The percentage of money from each month's mortgage payment that goes toward principal versus interest depends upon the interest rate and the *amortization period*, or the amount of time over which we've agreed to repay the loan. A fully amortized loan is one that is paid in full during its life. The amortization period for a home loan is typically fifteen, twenty, or thirty years. Because a picture is worth a thousand words, an amortization table for a thirty-year fixed-rate $100,000 mortgage loan is included as appendix A. You will note that as each payment is made, the amount of the payment going toward principal increases and the amount going toward interest decreases.

In general, the longer the loan amortization period, the lower the monthly payment but the more interest we end up paying over time. So those who have a thirty-year home loan will pay comparatively less money each month than someone with a fifteen- or twenty-year loan, but they will pay more interest because they are taking a longer time to pay back the loan and in the end will be making more payments. Since the actual dollar amount we pay each month in interest is based on how much principal we still owe and the interest rate we have agreed to pay, a larger portion of payments made at the beginning of the loan will be applied toward interest. Payments made at the end of the loan, when we owe less principal, consist of larger principal payments, since the amount of interest will be less because we will have already repaid most of the principal upon which the interest is calculated.

How Are Interest Rates Determined?

Like other types of credit companies, mortgage lenders provide mortgage loans to make a profit. They make a profit in the form of interest and the other fees we pay them at the time of closing or finalizing of the loan. The funds they lend us are typically borrowed from bank deposits, which are funded by bonds the lenders issue or money the lender has acquired by borrowing from other outside sources. The price lenders pay to borrow money impacts the interest rate they charge us, in turn, to borrow from them. Unlike our grandfathers' town bankers, who loaned their banks' own money and kept the mortgage loan in their own banks' portfolio until it was paid off, the modern mortgage industry involves multiple levels, as lenders now often sell the mortgage loans they make to third-party investors. Many home owners may notice this when their mortgage is sold to another bank or holding company and they are sent a letter instructing them to send their mortgage payment to a new bank or company. Sometimes this happens several times over the life of a mortgage. The price mortgage lenders can get and the type of mortgage loans they can most easily sell influence the amount and type of mortgage loans available to us. This will be explained in more detail when we discuss the sale of mortgage loans by lenders on the secondary market.

What Is a Negative Amortization Loan?

A negative amortization loan is one in which the principal loan amount is not only not paid in full during its life, but may actually increase in dollar amount over time. A negative amortization occurs in adjustable rate mortgages (explained more fully below). When the Federal Reserve interest rates go up, the amount of interest due with our mortgage payment each month likewise increases. In other words, a monthly adjustable rate mortgage payment increases if interest rates in general go up. With a negative amortization loan, rather than paying that additional increased amount of interest each month, the additional interest is tacked on to the principal amount of the loan (i.e., the overall amount we owe to the lender goes up). This allows a borrower's monthly payments under an adjustable rate mortgage to remain the same even after interest rates increases. However, it also creates a situation where the borrower could end up owing more on a mortgage loan than he originally borrowed or more than the property is worth when he tries to sell it. For example, if you borrowed $100,000 in an adjustable rate mortgage loan at an initial 7 percent interest rate, amortized over thirty years, your monthly mortgage payment would be $665.30. If the interest rate then increased to 10 percent, your monthly payment would increase to $877.57. Under a negative amortization loan, you could continue paying $665.30 each month and the additional $212.27 interest would be added to the $100,000 principal amount on your loan. So after one year, if the interest rate remained at 10 percent, you would need an additional $2,547.24 (12 months x $212.27 per month additional interest) to pay off the loan. In other words, you would owe the bank $102,547.24 instead of $100,000. For this reason, some people consider negative amortization loans more risky than fully amortized loans.

A MORTGAGE LOAN IS BORN

Originating the Mortgage Loan

The process of making a mortgage loan is referred to as *loan origination.* Loan origination begins by completing the loan application, referred to as a Form 1003, which contains information to help determine what type of loan is desired and can realistically be achieved. It includes blanks for borrower information, including monthly income and expenses, used to determine the maximum monthly mortgage loan payment a borrower should be able to afford. A sample 1003 is included as appendix B. The formula used by the industry to determine what loan a borrower qualifies for is explained later in this chapter. The various loan application tasks are performed by loan originators, discussed in more detail below.

Processing the Mortgage Loan

Once the loan application has been completed, the lender must obtain documentation to support or prove the information provided in the loan application. This typically includes conducting an appraisal to confirm that the price the buyer agreed to pay for the home is not more than the market value, verifying the buyer's employment and the buyer's income, the number of credit items (i.e., loans, other mortgages, etc.) outstanding, the number and frequency of late payments (on current or previous loans, utility bills, etc.), the buyer's credit score, any cash the buyer has on hand, and how much cash will be available after the purchase. Compiling all of this information, which is referred to as *processing*, is the reason it may take a few weeks for approval of a mortgage loan and is the job of the mortgage *processor*. The processor's job also entails packaging the application in a way that will be accepted by a mortgage lender. Processors are generally not licensed or regulated. Processors sometimes work directly for the same company as the loan originators but sometimes they are independent contractors hired on a per-loan basis at rates typically ranging from $250 to $650 per borrower loan. Processors who work directly for the same company as the loan originator are generally compensated by salary, but often receive bonuses based on the number of new loans they are able to process and that actually close each month. This motivates processors to make sure they present borrower information in a way that will be accepted by lenders and may be the reason for occasional allegations that processors have falsified mortgage loan application information.

Mortgage Loan Underwriting

Once the documents and information have been compiled, the next step is a detailed analysis of the borrower's employment history; verifying the borrower's salary; and reviewing financial statements, tax returns, and credit history to assess the borrower's ability to repay the loan. This is the job of the *underwriter*, to qualify borrowers through a procedure known as *underwriting.* Since most loans today are eventually sold to investors, many of the criteria used in underwriting mortgage loans today exist to please these investors. The underwriter is generally the only person in the loan process not being paid a commission when a loan closes, and these underwriters are typically the nemesis of most originators since underwriters are the folks who deny our loans. But underwriters are certainly not without blame in our current real estate fiasco. Since underwriters are salary based, the lender's goal is to get as much work out of each underwriter as possible. Underwriters are often evaluated on a basis of overhead cost per loan, in other words, the cost of their time to determine if a loan application should be approved. The more loans they approve, the less time it takes per loan, the lower their overhead cost per loan, and the more favorably they are evaluated by the lender. Perhaps the single factor that most influenced underwriters during the recent real estate bubble was their workload. The overwhelming workload created a tremendous incentive to get through each file as quickly as possible, thus creating a greater chance for carelessness, error, or oversight.

Here's one more twist: Unlike the good old days, in today's mortgage world the mortgage originator, processor, and underwriter sometimes work for different companies or are independent contractors who may not even know each other or their borrower. As is the case in many businesses, when employees don't know each other or workers don't know their customer, things like special attention to detail, going the extra mile, and picking up on nonverbal cues that might reveal helpful information in deciding if a borrower is telling the truth on his loan application may suffer. We will discuss in more depth later how this became a problem in the subprime mortgage crisis.

Closing the Mortgage Loan

Closing or *settlement* is the actual signing of the mortgage loan documents and the *funding* of the loan. Sometimes the mortgage loan is sold to another lender right at the closing table. Oftentimes the originator, the original lender, or another third party retains the right to *service* (i.e., collect payments, ensure taxes and insurance are paid, etc.) the mortgage loan even after it is sold. Out of this practice grew an entirely separate *mortgage servicing* industry. The separation of mortgage loan origination from servicing and ownership had many consequences for borrowers and lenders alike, some of which were pivotal in both our recent real estate bubble and the crisis that followed.

Who Was Your Mortgage Loan Originator?

Finding home buyers who need mortgages is typically the function of a *mortgage broker*, *mortgage banker*, or bank *loan officer*, often also referred to (along with the company he works for) as the *loan originator*. The primary difference between these various types of originators is that some work for the company lending the money, while others act as middlepersons, shopping the loan to several different lenders to find the best terms for the borrower. Obtaining a mortgage loan directly from the lender (say, your local bank) tends to be less expensive and, with no middleperson involved, it is often a simpler process. But the majority of us may not fit squarely into the loan programs offered by many direct lenders, and hence we need to use a mortgage broker to shop our loan to several different lenders. For example, before the real estate bubble, many local banks did not offer negative amortization loans or loans that allowed you to put down less than 10 percent for the purchase of a home. A borrower in need of a mortgage loan like that often had to work with a mortgage broker. Loan originators are the salespeople, the face of the mortgage industry. They are the salespeople we meet with when we go to the bank or the mortgage broker's office to talk about a mortgage.

Most states have several levels of mortgage licensing, each requiring a specific amount of experience, credentials, and business net worth, and each allowing for a corresponding amount of professional privilege. Mortgage brokers are at the bottom rung, with minimal education prerequisites. A mere two-day class and an hour-long state licensing exam is sufficient to earn a mortgage broker license in most states. The largest number of operators are mortgage brokers. Some may argue that because mortgage brokers are normally paid based on commission only, they tend to be more aggressive than salary-based bank loan officers in seeking customers. Accordingly, the majority of buyers tend to obtain home mortgages with the assistance of a mortgage broker.

Fortunately, many mortgage brokers are both knowledgeable and ethical. But because the home loan controversy is centered around those who are not—and in an effort to help us all identify the bad guys—we'll focus on the rotten apples for now. Likewise, for purposes of this discussion, we will focus on the home mortgage market for those buying their first home, but much of the same phenomenon applies to second home buyers and those purchasing income or investment properties. The amount of commission a mortgage originator earns depends on two things: the dollar amount of the mortgage loan and the interest rate involved. The more we borrow, the more the mortgage originator will make, and the higher the interest rate we pay, the greater the commission the mortgage originator will receive. Human nature tells us, then, that mortgage originators have tremendous incentive to encourage us to borrow as much as possible and to entice us into paying the highest possible interest rate. And those originators who are paid commission get paid only if we close. As is the case with processors, this may be the basis for allegations that some originators have falsified borrower loan applications and committed other variations of mortgage fraud, which we will discuss in chapter 3.

You can see now why it is important to know whether the originator you are working with is a mortgage broker or a loan officer and how they are being paid, as that fact may greatly influence the type of loan they suggest for you and how much you ultimately end up paying for it.

What Is a Broker of Record?

Unlike loan officers who work for a bank, complete with the infrastructure, protocols, and culture of larger more conservative institutions, mortgage brokers are hired, trained, and monitored by their company's *broker of record.*

Brokers of record are typically also licensed mortgage brokers and are legally responsible for the actions of those working under them. From a business standpoint, the broker of record is often a typical small businessperson, with rent, operating expenses, salaries, and income taxes to pay. Her income typically comes from commissions on loans she closes herself and a percentage of the commission on loans her mortgage brokers close—again a lot of incentive to make sure her mortgage brokers close loans.

Where Did the Money for Your Mortgage Loan Come From?

Mortgage loan money itself comes from lenders. The broker of record typically signs agreements with several different lenders, so that her mortgage brokers have several different loan products available, and if one lender turns down a borrower, there will be other potential lenders to accept that borrower's mortgage loan. Often, brokers of record are also required to sign *buy-back agreements* with lenders, whereby they promise to buy back loans that go into default in the event that originator fraud is involved. What exactly constitutes mortgage fraud and the different types of fraud we are seeing as a result of the subprime crisis is discussed in chapter 3.

What Is a Mortgage Wholesale Rep?

Lenders decide which mortgage originators they want to work with through an application process designed to investigate the originators in an effort to weed out the ones who try to sign high-risk mortgages and those originators with little or no experience, while retaining originators with a reputation or history of originating high-volume and high-profit loans. Each bank and lending institution typically has *wholesale representatives* who make daily sales calls on the various originators in their typically large territories, encouraging these originators to sell the lender's loan products. The wholesale representatives are also typically charged with ensuring that the originators they sign up are qualified (basically, that they know what they are doing) and with keeping an eye out for fraud. However, these wholesalers are too often compensated, at least in part, based on the profits generated by the mortgage originators in their territory. So, once again, the more you borrow and the higher the rate you pay, the more the wholesale representative will earn. If one of the mortgage originators happens to have an unhappy borrower or is accused of breaking the law, there are seldom actual consequences, other than a slap on the hand, to the wholesale representative. There has been little incentive for wholesale representatives to rein in originators whose practices might be considered overly risky.

How Do Lenders Decide How Much Money They Will Loan You?

In years past, the maximum amount someone seeking a home mortgage loan was allowed to borrow was determined by a combination of his credit score, the ratio between his gross income and his expenses, and the value of the property. Basically, lenders wanted to be sure that we would be able to pay the loan back, that our history indicated we would be willing to pay the loan back, and that if we didn't, the lender could gain enough money from the sale of the property to pay the loan. This is why the Form 1003 loan application requires borrowers to be so specific about listing all expenses and income.

What Are Front-End and Back-End Ratios?

Prior to our recent real estate bubble, the evaluation of how much money would be loaned to a particular borrower was accomplished by applying two different formulas. The first formula, called the front-end ratio, calculates the percentage of a borrower's total income that goes to pay his housing costs. This includes his mortgage principal, interest, real estate taxes, insurance, and, if he lives in a home where there is an association, the association fees. The second formula, called the back-end ratio, calculates all of the borrower's recurring debt payments, including those in the front-end ratio calculations. For conventional loans (which we will discuss shortly) the traditional front-end ratio cannot be higher than 28 percent of a borrower's income and the back-end ratio cannot exceed 36 percent. This is expressed as a 28:36 ratio requirement. During the real estate bubble these standards were lowered. For example, if prior to the real estate bubble, a borrower with a 700 FICO score and 26:38 ratios could borrow $300,000 at a 6 percent interest rate, during the bubble the same borrower may have been offered a $500,000 loan but with an interest rate of 7.5 percent. This provided the lender (and eventually, as we will discuss, the investor who bought the loan from the lender) an extra 1.5 percent interest for taking the higher risk by loaning the borrower more money than he might be able to comfortably repay. However, at the same time, this extra 1.5 percent and the extra $200,000 that was loaned translated to $1,627.34 more each month that the borrower had to pay for his mortgage, also actually increasing the risk that he would default on the loan. The FHA typically required 31:43 ratios, but back-end ratios up to 55 percent (meaning that the borrower's monthly debt payments eat up 55 percent of his gross income) became common during the bubble. Those who would have once been prevented from self-destructive financial behavior were, during the bubble, instead charged a higher interest rate, which further increased their risk of default.

What Does Loan-to-Value Ratio Mean?

The industry term for how much we can borrow based on the property value is the *loan-to-value ratio* (LTV). LTV is the percentage relationship the loan amount bears to the higher of the purchase price or appraised value of the property. (In the case of a refinance, only the appraised value is used.) So, for example, a 90 percent LTV means the individual is borrowing 90 percent of what the property is supposed to be worth. During the real estate bubble, however, as was the case with credit score and the credit card rates we discussed in chapter 1, a borrower's credit score, front- and back-end ratios and LTV evolved into mortgage loan pricing tools, influencing the interest rate but not necessarily limiting the amount of a loan.

During the bubble, mortgage loan products allowing home buyers to borrow 100 percent of the purchase price or appraised value of a home became commonplace. These loan products carried a higher risk for lenders since we, as borrowers, have no skin in the game. We are borrowing the entire value of the property. We have offered no down payment, or at best a very small one. In addition, mortgage originators and borrowers alike devised sometimes fraudulent ways to accomplish 100 percent mortgage financing without the lender actually knowing. These tactics are discussed in chapter 3. The important point here is that modern mortgage loan products and pricing have resulted in higher-risk investments for investors, higher interest rates and loan amounts and thus higher monthly payments for borrowers, and higher commissions for mortgage originators.

How Much Money Did Your Originator Make?

Each lender publishes a daily interest *rate sheet* that is provided to all originators selling its loans. An example of a rate sheet is provided for you here. The rate sheet reflects what is referred to in the industry as the *par pricing* for the day, or the interest rate at which the lender will lend money that day without the borrower having to pay *points* (also called discount points) to buy the interest rate down but also without the lender paying the mortgage originator any commission, referred to in the industry as back-end commission and explained in more detail below.

Was Your Interest Rate Below or Above Par?

When a borrower wants a loan with an interest rate below par, he can pay one point for every eighth of a percentage point he wishes to reduce the interest rate by. So to reduce the interest rate by a full 1 percent, the borrower would need to pay 8 points. Each point costs 1 percent of the loan amount (i.e., for a $200,000 loan, each point would cost $2,000). Buying 8 points to reduce the interest rate a full 1 percent would cost $16,000 ($2,000 x 8 points). Obviously, paying points in exchange for a lower interest rate can get expensive. If you planned to keep a loan long enough that the monthly savings in your mortgage payments would add up to more than the amount you paid in points for a reduction in the loan interest rate, it would be worthwhile.

Conversely, if you did not plan to keep the loan long enough, it might be worthwhile to agree to a higher interest rate, above par, in which case the lender pays the mortgage originator extra money, discussed shortly, and the mortgage originator may, in turn, agree to waive some of the fees she might otherwise charge you. The most significant other fee is normally a broker origination fee, referred to in the industry as front-end commission and explained in more detail below. This fee is also a percentage of the loan amount, although it is not tied to the interest rate and it is paid to the originator as part of her profit for coordinating your loan.

For example, if you are borrowing $200,000 for an interest-only loan and the par interest rate is 7 percent, you will be paying $14,000 during the first year in interest. If you could lower the interest rate to 6.5 percent, you would be paying only $13,000 in interest. If you only planned to keep the home for a year, it would not make sense to pay several thousand dollars in

CONVENTIONAL CONFORMING FIXED RATE LOANS — 3/7/08 10:28 AM

30-YEAR FIXED RATE

RATE	15 Days	30 Days	45 Days	60 Days
5.500	96.728	96.603	96.603	96.416
5.625	97.396	97.271	97.271	97.084
5.750	98.064	97.939	97.939	97.752
5.875	98.732	98.607	98.607	98.420
6.000	99.400	99.275	99.275	99.088
6.125	99.947	99.822	99.822	99.634
6.250	100.494	100.369	100.369	100.181
6.375	101.041	100.916	100.916	100.728
6.500	101.588	101.463	101.463	101.275
6.625	102.111	101.986	101.986	101.798
6.750	102.603	102.478	102.478	102.291
6.875	103.127	103.002	103.002	102.814
7.000	103.650	103.525	103.525	103.338
7.125	104.064	103.939	103.939	103.752
7.250	104.416	104.291	104.291	104.103
7.375	104.830	104.705	104.705	104.517
7.500	105.244	105.119	105.119	104.931
7.625	105.627	105.502	105.502	105.314
7.750	106.197	106.072	106.072	105.884
7.875	106.580	106.455	106.455	106.267
8.000	106.963	106.838	106.838	106.650

15-YEAR FIXED RATE

RATE	15 Days	30 Days	45 Days	60 Days
4.750	97.347	97.222	97.222	97.034
4.875	97.980	97.855	97.855	97.667
5.000	98.613	98.488	98.488	98.300
5.125	99.042	98.917	98.917	98.730
5.250	99.409	99.284	99.284	99.097
5.375	99.839	99.714	99.714	99.527
5.500	100.269	100.144	100.144	99.956
5.625	100.613	100.488	100.488	100.300
5.750	100.988	100.863	100.863	100.675
5.875	101.331	101.206	101.206	101.019
6.000	101.675	101.550	101.550	101.363
6.125	102.034	101.909	101.909	101.722
6.250	102.394	102.269	102.269	102.081
6.375	102.753	102.628	102.628	102.441
6.500	103.113	102.988	102.988	102.800
6.625	103.308	103.183	103.183	102.995
6.750	103.503	103.378	103.378	103.191
6.875	103.636	103.511	103.511	103.323
7.000	103.831	103.706	103.706	103.519
7.125	103.835	103.710	103.710	103.523
7.250	103.839	103.714	103.714	103.527

Price Adjustments

*** NC Predatory Lending Thresholds**
(If APR exceeds both thresholds, you may NOT offer a SIVA or SISA)

Treasury Yield Threshold	
10 yr Fixed (10 YR Treasury Yield + 3.00%)	6.780%
20 yr Fixed (20 YR Treasury Yield + 3.00%)	7.560%
30 yr Fixed (30 YR Treasury Yield + 3.00%)	7.590%
Conventional Mortgage Rate Threshold (Applies to All Stated Loans)	
H.15 Conventional Mortgage Rate + 1.75%	7.990%

Low Doc Adjustments * (See Above)	
SIVA (LTV <= 75%)	(0.750)
SIVA (LTV >75% <= 90%)	(1.625)
SISA (FICO >= 730)	(0.875)
SISA (FICO < 730)	(1.250)

Low Doc Adjustments (In Addition to Above)

LTV	2-4 Unit	Condo
<= 70%	(0.500)	-
70.01% - 75.00%	(1.750)	(0.250)
75.01% - 80.00%	(1.750)	(0.250)
80.01% - 95.00%	(1.750)	(0.250)

LTV > 70% (All Products w/ Amortization Period > 15 YR)
Except My Community, Home Possible, Expanded Approval, and A- Caution

Credit Score	Price Adjustment
<620	(2.000)
620-639	(1.750)
640-659	(1.250)
660-679	(0.750)

Additional Price Adjustments	
Cash Out 70.01%-80% LTV	(0.500)
Cash Out 80.01%-90% LTV	(0.750)
NOO <= 75% LTV	(1.500)
NOO 75.01%-80% LTV	(2.000)
NOO 80.01-90% LTV	(2.500)
NOO 3-4 Unit (Max CLTV = 75%)	(2.500)
2 Unit >75% LTV (Except My Community/HP)	(0.500)
3-4 Unit (80% LTV Max)	(1.000)
Sub. Financing CLTV > 75% <= 95% (Except MCM, HP, EA)	(0.250)
CLTV > 95% w/FICO = >700 (Includes 80/20 or 75/25)	(1.500)
CLTV >95% w/FICO <700 (Includes 80/20 or 75/25)	(2.000)
Escrow Waiver	(0.250)
Amount > $200,000	0.125
Manufactured Home	(1.000)
Streamlined Refi > Orig Bal	(0.250)
20-Year Mortgage	0.250

EXPIRATION DATES

60-Day	45-Day	30-Day	15-Day
05/06/08	04/21/08	04/07/08	03/24/08

Expanded Approval Price Adjustments
For LP A-Minus Pricing Please Contact Lock Desk

EA Level 1 w/ FICO = >620	(2.000)
EA Level 1 w/ FICO <620	(2.500)
EA Level 1 w/Sub. Fin LTV <=95% & CLTV 95.01-100%	(2.000)
EA Level 2 w/FICO = >620	(3.250)
EA Level 2 w/FICO <620	(4.250)
EA Level 3 w/FICO = >620	(4.500)
EA Level 3 w/FICO <620	(6.250)
EA Level II or Level III w/Condo/Coop and Cash Out	(0.500)
EA w/ Cash Out (In addition to other Cash Out Adjustments)	(0.500)

Flex Price Adjustments
For Flex Mortgages That Receive EA-I, EA-II, or EA-III Findings, Use EA Price Adjustments (See Above) In Lieu of Flex Adjustments.

Flex 90-95 w/ 35% MI	(0.500)
Flex 90-95 w/ 18% MI	(1.750)
Flex 90-95 w/ Subordinate Financing (In Addition to Above)	(1.500)
Flex 97 w/ 35% MI	(0.500)
Flex 97 w/ 18% MI	(1.750)
Flex 97 w/ Subordinate Financing (In Addition to Above)	(1.500)
Flex 100 w/ 35% MI	(1.000)
Flex 100 w/ 25% MI	(1.500)
Flex 100 w/ Subordinate Financing (In Addition to Above)	(1.500)

Interest Only Price Adjustments (10/20 Only)	
Interest Only	(1.250)
Interest Only with Subordinate Financing LTV >65% & <=90% AND CLTV >75% & <= 95%)	(1.750)

My Community/Home Possible Adjustments	
LTV > 97%	(2.625)
LTV <= 97%	(2.425)
2 Unit >95% & <=97% LTV	(0.500)
3-4 Unit (>90% & <= 95%, 95% Max)	(1.000)
Sub. Financing (In addition to LTV Adjustment) FICO >=720	(0.500)
Sub. Financing (In addition to LTV Adjustment) FICO < 720	(0.750)
Interest Only	(0.250)

Reductions to Standard MI Coverages	
MI 12%-17% & LTV 85.01% - 90%	(0.375)
MI 18%-25% & LTV 90.01%-95%	(0.750)
MI 18%-35% & LTV 95.01%-97%	(1.250)

40 YR Fixed Rate Adjustment
Add .50 % to RATE.

EXTENSION FEES	
7 Days:	(0.070)
15 Days:	(0.125)
30 Days:	(0.250)

points to buy the interest rate down from 7 percent to 6.5 percent to save only $1000 in interest. But if you planned to stay in the home longer, buying the interest rate down might make sense. This is the type of conversation and calculation your mortgage originator should help you with. At the same time, if you do elect to buy the interest rate down to below par, since your originator will not be making money from the lender for selling you a loan with an interest rate at or above par, your originator will probably charge you a higher broker origination fee instead. During the bubble, it was not unusual for mortgage brokers to make between 3 percent and 10 percent of the loan amount in commissions on some loans.

Back-End versus Front-End Commission

In addition to the par lender rate for the day, interest rate sheets also reflect the actual available interest rates in one-eighth of a percentage point increments above and below par. At each increment above par that a mortgage originator can convince a borrower to pay, the originator earns a higher commission. As we mentioned earlier, this commission is referred to in the industry as *back-end commission*, since it is paid by the lender to the mortgage originator and is usually paid without the borrower's knowledge. (Although back-end commission is legally required to be disclosed in writing, often borrowers still do not fully understand.) Also known as the *yield spread*, back-end commission is required by law to be reflected on the Housing and Urban Development Department's *HUD-1 Settlement Statement*, the document signed at the mortgage loan closing that reflects all costs the borrower is paying to have the loan processed and closed. Oftentimes if a borrower notices and inquiries about the yield spread on the *HUD-1*, the originator will simply dismiss it as "a fee the lender is paying me, and nothing that comes out of your pocket." In truth, of course, the back-end commission is indirectly paid by the borrower in the form of a higher interest rate. Those of us who call several different mortgage originators to shop and then negotiate our mortgage loan interest rate, and thus expect to receive the lowest interest rate we can find, may be able to obtain our mortgage at or under par, but only by paying the mortgage originator's commission directly, known as a *front-end commission*, and, as we said earlier, paying the lender points. Often mortgage originators earn commission on both the back end and the front end on a single mortgage loan. So, for example, a mortgage broker might give you three or four choices of interest rate and closing cost combinations, each designed to give him about the same profit. The sample rate sheet provided for you also reflects other factors that affect your loan interest rate and closing costs such as your FICO score, LTV, and how you want to lock in your interest rate for before you close.

Originator Profit on ARMs versus Fixed-Rate Loans

Originators typically make more money by selling adjustable-rate loans than fixed-rate loans, in part because lenders prefer the lower risk of an adjustable rate (we will discuss why shortly) and in part because the lower initial rate and payment on adjustable-rate loans enable borrowers to borrow more money than a fixed rate based on the front-end and back-end ratios we discussed above might allow, which increases the commissions of those who write the loans. The most profitable loans from an origination standpoint are often those loans we have come to refer to as *subprime mortgage loans*. In addition to generally caring more about making a profit than finding the loan best suited for borrowers and the fact that the most profitable loans for the originator tend to be riskier loans for the borrower, a further disincentive for mortgage originators to guide borrowers toward prudent mortgage loan decisions is the fact that if borrowers can't make their mortgage loan payments and unless actual fraud can be proven, the mortgage originator has zero responsibility. This means that mortgage originators have huge incentives to sell borrowers high-dollar, high-interest-rate loans and not much reason, absent their own conscience, to care whether or not the borrower will be able to make the payments. Common sense tells us the rotten-apple originators will soon earn themselves bad reputations and we, as consumers, will gravitate to ethical mortgage originators who help us choose the best mortgage loan, regardless of how much commission they will earn. But many of us never even know that a loan better suited for us exists or that our mortgage originators could be getting us a lower interest rate or charging us lower fees. In truth, the biggest pressure on mortgage originators to give us a good deal is the competition. Most mortgage originators sell, more or less, the same loan products. The best way to convince a mortgage originator to reduce his origination fee or absorb some of the discount points is to tell him that you've found another mortgage originator who will. (This is not to say that mortgage originators don't deserve to earn a living for what they do, but rather that you should be clear about how much money they will make from selling you your loan.) Unfortunately, perhaps because mortgage loans seem so complicated and we're just grateful to get approved or perhaps because we're just busy, we tend to take shortcuts in educating ourselves and rely heavily on the expertise of our mortgage originators. Seventy percent of us submit only one loan application. We don't shop around for competitive loan deals, like we would for a car or some other big purchase.

The Less You Know, the More You Pay

The bottom line is that it's a proven fact that when it comes to mortgage loans, the less we know, the more we'll pay. Lower-end borrowers (i.e., those with low FICO scores and whose expenses eat up more of their monthly income) statistically pay higher commissions and are sold higher-interest-rate loans because of their potentially higher risk of defaulting on loans. In some cases this may be due in part to the fact that some borrowers represent a higher credit risk for lenders. In many cases it is simply because they take less time to educate themselves and believe they have less negotiating leverage. It is precisely because they have not gone through the process before and tend to have the least knowledge of alternatives that first-time and minority borrowers are most intimidated and least likely to ask the right questions—and fall into this category of borrowers who pay more closing costs and get higher-interest-rate loans than they should in disproportionate numbers.[2]

You can see now why it is important to know what the par interest rate is and how much you are paying for an interest rate that is more or less than the par interest rate, as this is how your mortgage loan originator makes money—and if you don't ask there is little incentive for him to tell you.

WHAT IS THE SECONDARY MORTGAGE MARKET?

Secondary market is the catchall phrase used in reference to the various types of investors who purchase and then sell mortgage loans from loan originators, lenders, and others. We will discuss why they choose to sell the loans rather than keeping them and servicing them a bit later. The many types of mortgage loan purchasers and investors include banks and various funds assembled by, among others, Wall Street firms. Some hold the mortgage loans in their own portfolios, but recently, most have repackaged and sold the mortgage loans to end investors in the form of bonds or other *securities*. A security is simply ownership in a piece of something, secured or backed by some form of collateral or solid assurance, and intended to earn money in the form of interest or a dividend on the money invested. In the case of stock, for example, we are buying an ownership stake in a company. It is secured or backed by the company's assets and financial performance history and is intended to earn us money by way of profit generated by the company, which trickles down to shareholders in the form of dividends. Not unlike stock in a company, securities created by mortgage loan investors are backed by the mortgage loans themselves, and profits, based on the mortgage payments made by borrowers like us, trickle down to end investors in the form of distributions. Hence these are called *mortgage-backed securities* (MBS). A mortgage-backed security is simply an investment in which cash flows are backed by the payments anticipated to be received under a bundle of mortgage loans. This process of bundling, slicing up, and reselling is referred to as *securitization*. Again, like stock, the price end investors pay for mortgage-backed securities is based on the anticipated rate of return from the mortgage payments borrowers make, balanced by the risk of default and financial exposure to investors if those mortgages are not paid. And just as credit card companies like revolvers (borrowers who carry a balance) because they generate the highest profits, mortgage-backed securities investors like borrowers who don't prepay, or pay off their mortgage loans early. In fact, the likelihood of prepayment is factored into formulas investors use in valuing mortgage-backed securities as a negative event. The creation of the mortgaged-backed security allowed mortgage loan originators to turn once nonliquid mortgage loans (i.e., loans they had to keep their money tied up in) into a tradable commodity (i.e., loans they could sell to someone else and get their money out of), thereby allowing the mortgage loan originators to reuse that same money to generate more profit by replenishing their funds, making the monies available to make more mortgage loans to us. As we will discuss in the coming chapters, the Wall Street firms that handled the securitization of mortgages also had huge incentives to do so. A 2004 Securities and Exchange Commission (SEC) ruling essentially allowed US investment banks to take on more debt than was allowed before. They leveraged this debt to purchase, bundle, or sell mortgage-related securities. *Leverage* is borrowing by paying a lower interest rate to invest and earn or be paid a higher interest rate. The five largest investment banks on Wall Street increased their leverage, reporting more $4.1 trillion in debt during 2007—or 30 percent of the entire US economy! Three of the five, Lehman Brothers, Bear Stearns, and Merrill Lynch, eventually went bankrupt or were acquired in large part as a result of this extreme leveraging, creating global instability almost overnight. Critics say Wall Street decision makers take such huge leverage risks for the big year-end executive bonuses, not because they believe it is what's best for investors and their firm. According to the New York State Comptroller's Office, in 2006 alone, Wall Street executives were paid $23.9 billion in compensation.[3] We will discuss this in more detail in chapter 5.

At the end of the day, lenders are in the business of selling us the use of their money. The more times they can resell the same money, the more profit lenders can generate. The secondary mortgage market securitization process repeated itself over and over again, creating an endless proverbial circle of mortgage life.

WHAT DOES IT MEAN TO CASH OUT HOME EQUITY?

Mortgage loans are also important when we refinance our homes. *Refinancing* refers to the process of taking money out of home equity by replacing an existing loan with a larger new loan or replacing an existing loan with a new one that has better terms such as a lower interest rate. *Equity* is the difference between what a home is worth and what is owed to the bank—that is, how much of our home we truly own versus what belongs to the bank. If you bought your home for $100,000 and in a year you have paid $5,000 on the principal, then you have $5,000 of equity in the house. If during that year the value of housing in your area increased to such an extent that your house would now be worth $110,000 if you were to sell it, then you could say you have $15,000 of equity in the home. Thus, home equity is how much money we have saved up in our home—what our grandfathers worked so hard for, what they counted on for retirement, and what we seemingly couldn't care less about. Almost half of all home mortgage refinancing is intended to get cash out of home equity to pay off other debts and unexpected expenses, often to pay off or pay down credit cards. Credit card use and the debt that follows has been the single greatest drive behind the home mortgage refinancing business. Almost all other refinances are entered into in an effort to restructure overly burdensome mortgages and to make them more affordable at lower rates of interest.

As noted earlier, during the bubble many popular financial gurus advised home owners to use low-interest-rate home loans to pay off higher-interest-rate credit card debt. Certainly lowering overall monthly payments takes some of the pressure off, and if a refinance to pay off credit card debt is a one-time thing to fix a one-time mistake, the strategy might be a good one. But history has proven that is often not the case; many people have built a dream lifestyle entirely on an endless cycle of debt, refinance, and new debt at the cost of reducing the home equity that so many Americans have traditionally relied on for their retirement nest egg. The reality is that the refinance strategies of many Americans during the bubble show our complete lack of long-term wisdom.

WHAT DOES IT MEAN TO BE A SUBPRIME BORROWER?

We've established that those of us viewed by lenders as a higher risk pay more for our mortgage loans. This type of mortgage borrower is referred to as subprime. People may be *subprime borrowers* if their FICO scores are under 660, they've defaulted on credit payments in the past two years, had a foreclosure in the past two years (i.e., either not paid on time or not paid at all), or currently owe more than half of their annual income in debt. Like those of us who keep balances on our credit cards, the mortgage business has become most profitable by lending to subprime borrowers, and a wide range of mortgage loan products and slick advertising have evolved to attract this type of customer, the loans for whom are commonly referred to as subprime mortgages. Although they allow borrowers who would not qualify for other types of mortgage loans—and thus not be able to buy a home—access to the mortgage market, subprime mortgages are products designed, first and foremost, to be attractive to the investors to whom lenders look to sell the mortgages and to the end investors who will eventually buy them in the form of mortgage-backed securities. As such, subprime mortgages maximize profit for investors by providing for higher-than-average rates of return on their investment, which often adjust to ensure competitiveness in any market. In other words, the higher the risk of default on the mortgages, the higher the interest rate will be to attract investor money.

And like the credit card industry, most subprime mortgage loans are unsolicited, meaning the mortgage originators reach out to us, not the other way around. We've all seen them on television in advertisements for mortgage loans with no closing costs and low *teaser interest rates* designed to attract borrowers with bad credit or no credit. Lenders advertise whatever mortgage loan products they think will get us in the door. The problem, as is often the case with credit card solicitations, is that we frequently lack the necessary information and full disclosure needed to choose the right mortgage loan product for ourselves, and we lack awareness of our own behavior, thereby giving in to these attractive and tempting home loan deals. And mortgage brokers may not always have our best interests at heart. Often they do not understand the various mortgage loan products any more than we do. The past twenty years in particular have opened the mortgage market to an even more diverse group of borrowers whose personal financial situations are no longer barriers to loan approval. With a mortgage product to fit every shape and size now, we all theoretically have equal access to a home loan, though not equal types of loans. This is clearly a good thing, but it requires us to do more homework when choosing a home loan. We've already explained that those of us who take the time to understand the pros and cons of the various mortgage products and carefully consider our own needs, goals, and risk tolerance fare much better.

IS AMERICAN HOME OWNERSHIP A RIGHT OR A PRIVILEGE?

The history of the home mortgage industry in many ways parallels that of the credit industry in general, peppered with a series of government actions and unexpected market, industry, and government reactions.

The Great Depression

Perhaps most significant in the metamorphosis of home ownership from a privilege to a right was the Great Depression. Franklin D. Roosevelt's New Deal led to the Federal Home Loan Bank System (FHLBS), established in 1932 to, among other things, provide low-cost funds for home mortgages. The Federal Housing Administration (FHA) also emerged shortly after the

Depression, ensuring lenders that the home loans they made would be repaid—if necessary, by the federal government—thereby encouraging more lenders to make more home loans and enabling more of us to live the American Dream. Basically, for a fee borrowers pay at closing and monthly ongoing fees known as the *mortgage insurance premium* (MIP), the FHA promises the lender that if we default in paying the loan, it will step in and pay for us. Other mortgage insurance companies eventually emerged that encouraged lenders to lend us money with less and less money down, including *private mortgage insurance* (PMI) companies offering the same type of insurance provided by the FHA. Once we pay down the loan balance and our property appreciates, we can request that the mortgage insurance, and thus the monthly payment for mortgage insurance, be eliminated. The US Housing Act of 1937 created a public housing program that eventually led to the Department of Housing and Urban Development (HUD). Toward the end of World War II, in 1944, the Department of Veterans Affairs (VA) also got involved in the mortgage insurance game when Congress passed the Servicemen's Readjustment Act, enabling returning solders to live the dream by supplying GIs with thirty-year fixed-rate mortgages. Home prices appreciated, slowly but surely. This new, wider variety of home loan choices eventually created the "go-betweens" known as the mortgage banking and brokerage industries. Mortgage bankers and mortgage brokers played similar roles arranging loans for borrowers or properties that didn't quite qualify or didn't want conventional bank loans, and then sold these loans to investors. Home ownership rates climbed. Nine of the more significant US government and quasi-governmental agencies influencing our nation's mortgage and housing segments are briefly described in appendix C.

Inflation and the Savings and Loan Crisis

As more Americans achieved the American Dream, elevating our socioeconomic status, the savings and loan banking business grew. As the name suggests, these were local banks that held savings deposits for an expanding American middle class, paying customers a fixed rate of interest. Deposit monies were leveraged and loaned out as mortgage loans at a higher rate of interest, with the S&L banks earning as a profit the difference between the two interest rates. Savings and loan banks tended to handle highly regulated conventional loans on a local level. But in the 1970s, inflation wrecked

Some Common Interest Rate Indices

Cost of Funds Index (COFI): The average of interest costs, usually tracked by a regional regulatory body, incurred by banks in that particular region. Tends to fluctuate less than other indexes. Can change daily.

Prime Rate (Prime): The federal funds rate is the interest rate US banks charge each other for short-term loans designed to meet Federal Reserve requirements, a topic that in and of itself exceeds the scope of our discussion. The Federal Open Market Committee (FOMC) meets eight times a year to set the federal funds rate.

London Interbank Offered Rate (LIBOR): This index is calculated each day based upon rates banks charge to other banks in London's wholesale money markets.

havoc. Inflation is an increase in the prices of goods and services, or a corresponding decrease in currency value or what our money can buy. Economic theory is art, not science, but most economists agree that inflation is caused by excessive growth in the money supply. We will discuss shortly how lowering mortgage and other loan interest rates can help cause inflation. Almost overnight the savings and loan banks found themselves having to pay depositors higher interest rates to attract new money, but unable to increase the rates being paid to them on the mortgages they had already loaned out. Something had to give.

The ARM Is Born

The solution was the *adjustable-rate mortgage* (ARM), a mortgage loan with an interest rate that goes up and down depending on the interest rates lenders are charged to borrow money based on an *index* at any given time. As used in this context, an index is an agreed consistent reference benchmark. The index normally referred to by lenders to establish mortgage loan interest rates is the *Wall Street Journal* prime rate. The *Journal* surveys thirty of our nation's largest banks. When twenty-three of the thirty report a change in their prime rate, the *Journal* changes the prime rate it publishes accordingly. Therefore, the *Wall Street Journal* prime rate does not necessarily change daily. US prime rates generally end up being around three points above the

Federal funds rate at any given time. The banks report a change in their own rate when the Fed funds rate (the rate at which the Federal Reserve loans money to banks) changes. The Fed funds rate, in turn, is set by the Federal Open Market Committee (FOMC), which meets eight times a year to set the target rate for the Fed funds rate. The committee, of course, has to consider the rate at which our federal government itself is able to borrow funds from foreign nations as well as the state of our economy and the need, if any, to infuse liquidity, which we will discuss shortly. In addition to the prime rate, other well-known indices include the Cost of Funds Index (COFI) and the London Interbank Offered Rate (LIBOR). The sidebar on page 56 explains the differences between these various indices.

What Is a Hybrid ARM?

Hybrid and *option adjustable-rate mortgages* have evolved as variations of the ARM. Hybrid mortgages provide a fixed interest rate for an initial period (say, the first three years of the loan), after which time the interest rate adjusts daily, monthly, or annually depending upon the prime rate set by the Federal Reserve Bank. Hybrid ARMs are often referred to by their initial fixed-rate and subsequent adjustable-rate periods, for example 5/1 for an ARM with a five-year fixed rate of interest and then an interest rate that adjusts every year thereafter. Some option ARMs (called pick-a-pay loans) are thirty-year adjustable-rate mortgages that allow borrowers to choose from a limited number of monthly payment alternatives. For example, borrowers might be allowed to choose from a pre-set minimum payment, an interest-only payment, a payment amortized to pay off the loan in full over fifteen years, or a payment amortized to pay off the loan in full over thirty years. These newer loan products also incorporate a *prepayment penalty.* This is a fee charged by the lender to discourage repayment of the loan during the initial low-interest-rate period. Typically, this penalty is equal to the interest the lender would have earned had the borrower kept the mortgage loan for a longer time.

Early versions of adjustable-rate mortgages had dire consequences for borrowers as mortgage loan interest rates climbed to a record 17 percent in the 1970s. Consumers clamored again for the good old *fixed-rate mortgages*, home loans for which the interest rate remains unchanged during the entire life of the loan. Along with the adjustable-rate mortgage came serious, often confusing loan choices for borrowers. Rather than simply having to choose a loan amount, interest rate, and amortization period, as is the case when choosing a fixed rate mortgage, adjustable-rate mortgages have more moving parts borrowers must choose from and often do not realize the consequences of the choices they are making. For example, with adjustable-rate mortgages, borrowers must also consider the lender's initial interest rate, adjustment period, index, margin, adjustment caps, and lifetime caps. Each of these choices are highlighted and explained in the sidebar on page 59.

Regulators responded with the Truth in Lending Act (TILA) of 1968, contained in the Consumer Credit Protection Act, a law designed to protect consumers and to promote informed credit use by requiring disclosure of key lending terms and costs. The regulation implementing the Truth in Lending Act is commonly referred to as Reg. Z. This regulation also gave borrowers the right to cancel refinance transactions involving their primary residence within three days following the closing in case they did not get the loan terms originally promised or they were not happy with the loan.

WHAT ARE GOVERNMENT-SPONSORED ENTERPRISES?

The Federal Home Loan Mortgage Corporation (known as Freddie Mac or the FHLMC), created under the Emergency Home Finance Act in 1970; the Federal National Mortgage Association (Fannie Mae or FNMA), originally created as the National Mortgage Association of Washington in 1938; and the Government National Mortgage Association (Ginnie Mae or GNMA) are all quasi-governmental agencies designed to purchase mortgage loans from banks, bundle the loans, and sometimes sell the bundles to investors. Together they are commonly referred to as *government-sponsored enterprises* (GSEs). With the advent of government-sponsored enterprises, lenders were now able to make competitively priced fixed-rate mortgage loans with full knowledge that the risk of holding the loan would be transferred to one of the government-sponsored enterprises. In other words, banks now knew that if they made certain types of loans, they would be able to easily sell those loans, recovering their money to loan out again and again, each time making a profit. As with most businesses, having a guaranteed known buyer like that in advance helped make lending a very attractive business.

Choices Borrowers Must Make When Selecting an ARM

- Adjustable rate mortgages have an *initial interest rate*. This is the interest rate at the very beginning of the loan. During the real estate bubble, many lenders offered mortgage loans with a very low initial interest rate designed to lure borrowers to their loan products. These very low initial interest rates, referred to as *teaser rates*, ended up getting a lot of us into trouble. When the initial interest rate period ended, the interest rate and loan payment increased, sometimes drastically. This phenomenon has come to be referred to as *rate shock*. For example, the monthly payment for a $300,000 mortgage loan amortized over thirty years with an initial interest rate of 5 percent is $1,610.46. If, after the initial interest period, the interest rate jumps to 10 percent, the monthly mortgage payment jumps to $2,632.71.
- Adjustable-rate mortgage documents will state how frequently the interest rate on your loan can change. This is called the *adjustment period*.
- The amount of the initial interest-rate changes are tied to an *index*. Lenders add a percentage on top of the index to determine how much the interest rate on an adjustable-rate mortgage will be. This percentage is referred to within the industry as the *margin*.
- Some adjustable-rate mortgages include a maximum amount the interest rate can increase within a single adjustment period or over the entire life of the adjustable-rate mortgage. These are referred to as *adjustment caps* and *lifetime caps*, respectively. For example, an adjustable-rate mortgage may cap interest rate adjustments made to occur no more frequently than every year on the anniversary date of the loan closing, increase (or decrease) the interest rate by no more than 2 percent each time the interest rate adjusts, and not ever allow the interest rate to increase by more than 13 percent or less than 7 percent during the entire life of the mortgage loan. Interest rate caps are occasionally expressed as *initial adjustment cap/subsequent adjustment cap/life cap*, for example: a 3/4/6 for a loan with a 3 percent cap on the initial adjustment, a 4 percent cap on subsequent adjustments, and a 6 percent cap on total interest rate adjustments during the life of the mortgage loan.

The Difference between Conforming and Nonconforming Loans

Government-sponsored enterprises can only buy *conforming loans*. A conforming loan is a mortgage loan that does not exceed a specified dollar amount and meets other underwriting criteria. The maximum allowable dollar loan amount for conforming loans varies by geographical region (since the price of homes and therefore the size of the loans required to buy a home varies based on where the homes are located) and is set each year by the Office of Federal Housing Enterprise Oversight (OFHEO) based on the current price of homes in that particular region of the United States. Mortgage loans above this amount or those that do not meet the other underwriting criteria—as might be the case if a borrower has too much debt already or cannot or does not wish to document or prove her income—are considered nonconforming. Since government-sponsored enterprises will not buy these *nonconforming loans*, there is less competition for nonconforming loans among secondary market investors, making nonconforming loans harder for lenders to sell and thus less desirable for lenders to offer us. To make up for this, lenders charge us higher interest rates and more fees at closing for nonconforming loans.

Too Big to Fail

In response to recent problems and the mammoth size of government-sponsored enterprise holdings, many have called for greater regulation of government-sponsored enterprises. For example, in 2003 Freddie Mac understated its earnings by almost $5 billion. The ensuing investigation revealed that its records had been manipulated to conform to investor expectations. And in 2004 Fannie Mae was found to have shifted losses allegedly so that senior executives could receive bonuses. The mortgage industry has seen calls to limit the size of the government-sponsored enterprise loan portfolios. At the core of the issue is the fact that the government-sponsored enterprises are less regulated than private banks and they can sell mortgage-backed securities with half as much capital, or *reserves*, backing them as would be required in the private sector. Why does this matter to us? Because at the end of the day, government-sponsored enterprises are at least implicitly backed by our government's guarantee (which translates to our tax dollars). And as we will discuss in chapter 8, effective October 2008 this implicit guarantee became explicit when Fannie and Freddie, deemed "too big to fail," were effectively, at least temporarily, taken over by our government. At the end of the day, your tax dollars will go to cover their losses. We'll talk more about the problems Fannie and Freddie have forced and the role they may play moving forward in chapter 8.

WALL STREET DISCOVERS MORTGAGE LOANS

Until recently, real estate was thought of as being different from Wall Street investments. *Hedge funds* (relatively lightly regulated private investor money pooled together and managed by a paid leader) are somewhat similar to betting on both teams at a football game. These funds execute thousands of securities trades at the click of a computer key. But people buy homes one at a time, in a relatively illiquid and slow-moving manner. Unlike a savings or checking account that we can draw upon for ready cash, houses have to be sold before they can be turned into cash. Until Wall Street got involved, housing was not as liquid as securities and was harder to transform into usable cash. In 1970 the investment brokerage house Salomon Brothers' mortgage trading desk guru, Lewis Ranieri, recognized that mortgages could be traded like stocks and bonds. His story is told in *Liar's Poker*, the 1989 semiautobiographical book about Wall Street bond salesmen in the 1980s by Michael Lewis. Instead of keeping our mortgage loans locked away in a drawer, mortgage lenders began unloading their risk and freeing up funds by selling the mortgage paper to Salomon, which in turn took mortgages originated by lenders, stitched together bonds backed by payments on the mortgages, and sold them to investors as mortgage-backed securities. As we said before, mortgage-backed security investor cash flow comes from the mortgage payments. Recognizing an opportunity, the industry of private investors who purchased mortgage loans from lenders also grew. Thanks to the reasons we'll discuss later, as of 2006, US mortgage-backed securities exceeded \$6.1 trillion, up from only \$1 billion in 2001.[4]

What Is a Collateralized Debt Obligation?

The advent of collateralized debt obligations (CDOs) took mortgage-backed securities to a new level. Developed by 1980s junk-bond king Michael Milken, collateralized debt obligations are held by entities called special purpose vehicles (SPVs) created exclusively to bundle, slice up, and sell *pools* of securities. The SPVs holding CDOs are normally offshore entities, in part to avoid legal responsibilities and for tax purposes. The distinctions between mortgage-backed securities, collateralized debt obligations, and collateralized mortgage obligations mentioned below are not crucial to our discussion and understanding of the subprime crisis; in fact, for simplicity's sake, we will refer to all three types of investments as collateralized debt obligations, since they've each played more or less the same role in creating our foreclosure nation. Until the mid-1990s CDOs were little known in global markets. Since then, they have become popular investment vehicles and are credited with being the link between our nation's subprime crisis and eventually dragging down our broader economy and that of many other nations.

As we will discuss, CDOs were often underpinned with the riskier subprime mortgages but run according to a set of rules for ownership that makes investing in an SPV holding CDOs very different from investing in real estate. *Collateralized mortgage obligations* (CMOs) are a more complex type of mortgage-backed security, akin to CDOs. The mortgages behind CDOs are divided into *tranches*, with each tranche sold as a separate security. Tranches, or rankings, are classified based on cash flow and the risk assignment rules set by the particular collateralized debt obligation. The highest and least risky tranche is *senior*, or AAA. The next level is *mezzanine*, AA or BB. The lowest and the most risky level is referred to as *equity* or *unrated*, sometimes called the *toxic waste*.

In theory, the risk of owning individual mortgage loans is reduced by the process of bundling them together, again a process called securitization. Investors, including insurance companies, mutual funds, pension funds, and investment banks—in which many of us are often the ultimate end investors—buy CDO tranches and receive payments based on rules or structures set by the firm that creates the CDO. Cash flows are projected by mathematical models, also compiled by the CDO creator, which we'll discuss in more detail shortly. Over the past twenty-five years, Wall Street has helped turn real estate purchases into trading chips.

Wall Street Became Biggest Mortgage Loan Originator

Several Wall Street firms went so far as to buy mortgage loan origination companies to better guarantee a steady supply of new mortgage loans for their CDO pools. Wall Street's Lehman Brothers acquired BNC Mortgage in 2004, a decision that eventually contributed to Lehman's untimely demise. The British bank Barclays bought HomeEquity Servicing for $469 million in June 2006. In August 2006 Morgan Stanley bought Saxon Capital for more than $700 million, and a month later Merrill Lynch paid more than $1 billion for First Franklin Financial. In 2007 Bear Stearns bought Encore Credit for $26 million.[5]

Through these and other acquisitions, Wall Street became the biggest mortgage loan origination source. This development essentially converted the traditional lender from a long-term lender to a mere originator. The mortgage market thus obtained liquidity by quickly selling loans to investors. As a result, mortgages became cheaper, to the benefit of us all because there were more lenders competing against each other for our business and because once lenders sold the loans and recouped their money, they would loan the same money out all over again and again and again. As long as they could keep selling our loans, they could keep loaning us more money.

Wall Street's Flawed Assumptions

Grandpa always said, "When you assume, you make an ass of you and me." CDO investors are presumably buying a position in an entity that has a defined risk and reward. In truth, the investment merit of a CDO depends on the quality of the underlying mortgage loans (i.e., the likelihood that they will be paid by the borrower) and the accuracy of the assumptions (which unfortunately left little room for error) used to define the risk and reward of each tranche. For example, in assessing how safe or risky a pool of mortgage loans is, it seemed that Wall Street simply assumed that the mortgage loan originators (i.e., the mortgage loan processors and underwriters we discussed earlier) had thoroughly researched borrowers' ability to repay the loan, thereby rendering the risk that the borrowers would default minimal. We now know that the reality, on the other hand, is that subprime borrowers were qualified for their mortgage loans based primarily on their ability to repay only at the initial teaser interest rates (rather than the higher rates that would result when the ARM interest rate increase provision kicked in a few years later), and many mortgage loan originators are concerned only about closing loans and earning paychecks in the here and now, not what happens to the loan and to some anonymous investor months down the road.

Another flawed assumption was that even if a borrower defaulted, the value of the real estate collateral would remain solid. The originators were gambling that the housing price bubble wouldn't burst anytime soon. These factors were typically researched and determined by the investment bank that created the CDO. And the historical mortgage loan default rates, which Wall Street assumed were reflective of what future mortgage loan default rates would be in general, were based on traditional mortgage loans, not the newfangled, riskier hybrid and option ARMs. Some critics now claim that greed prompted many to ignore risks. The fact that virtually every expert on Wall Street was buying mortgage loans, pooling them and reselling them in the form of CDOs at gargantuan profits—seemingly as fast as they could—makes it look that way, since, at least in retrospect, even for a novice it is difficult not to spot serious flaws in the assumptions that allowed these securities to be labeled safe for investors.

Originating for Investors

US housing was turned from a market that responded to home owners to one that was driven by investors. As we've learned, historically the mortgage industry and government's intervention has been directed towards meeting borrower needs. For example, after the Depression, the goal was to make inexpensive mortgage money available to the masses. After the savings and loan crisis, the goal was again to make more affordable loans available for borrowers. But this does not appear to have been the case during our recent real estate bubble. Although other factors may be cited, in the big picture, the mortgage loans and homes that were sold during the bubble were not designed to be affordable for home owners. Instead, it seems they were designed to make the most profit possible for originators, lenders, and Wall Street. For example, many borrowers recount being told, flat out, when they applied for their mortgage loan that they would need to refinance in a few years when the interest rate on their mortgage loan increased, thereby garnering new fees for the mortgage loan originators when they closed the new loan and for lenders and Wall Street when they packaged and sold it.

Rules Remove CDOs Even Further from Real Estate Reality

Investment banks that create CDOs normally take a piece of the CDO and are paid a management fee to run it. The fact that the investment bank also plays the role of an intermediary, defining the risk and reward rules for the CDO, moves the end investor further from investing in a true real estate asset-backed security and closer to investing in little more than promises and mathematical models applied by the CDO creator, which, of course, is most motivated to generate profit for itself. For example, CDO rules establish, then select, which tranche absorbs losses from mortgage loan defaults first. The rules define certain occurrences that will require CDO managers to devalue the CDO assets. And the rules define how and when investors get paid. We will discuss in chapter 5 how CDO rules also govern how the actual mortgage loans held in the CDO can be handled. For example, many CDOs restrict the ability to modify a mortgage loan that is in default. Thus, investing in CDOs is very different from investing directly in mortgage loans. Critics have argued that their rules make CDOs an entirely different animal, even though CDO investors were encouraged to believe that they were investing in something as solid as real estate.

We've discussed that generating an attractive return for investors is a key consideration in structuring the CDO only inasmuch as that is what is required in order to sell tranches and generate profits for the CDO creater. In other words, the CDO creator's motive in crafting CDO risk and reward is not necessarily fully aligned with generating the best possible return for CDO investors. CDO creators have their own profit motive in the game as well. When investors win (i.e., earn a profit), CDO managers win. But CDO managers can also make money even when investors don't. Clearly, the most challenging aspect and thus a priority is finding investors for the riskiest toxic waste tranche. It is common for CDO managers to retain a piece of equity tranches at the behest of investors so they will have an economic incentive to ensure the CDO performs as promised. Because they are more similar to investing in a financial model than traditional investments, CDOs eventually became the link between the subprime mortgage crisis and the broader economic crisis in our country, unmasking just how convoluted and juxtaposed to real-life values and the best interest of investors Wall Street had become.

Until recently, CDOs were one of the fastest-growing sectors in the securities market. They overtook the market for US Treasury notes and bonds in 2000. The CDO market grew from $157 billion in 2004 to $503 billion in 2007. The global market was said to exceed $2 trillion in 2006. In fact, to buy our mortgage loans from originators, investment banks had to outbid each other. The risk exposure of mezzanine-level (medium-risk) CDOs to subprime mortgages was a whopping 70 percent. Nearly three-quarters of all CDOs were based on subprime mortgages.[6] Wall Street was essentially gambling on us little guys' ability to pay our mortgages. But, as we'll discuss later, as our ARMs reset, teaser rates were replaced with higher payments that we couldn't afford, and our property values went down, it has often become neither possible or nor worthwhile for us to pay our mortgages.

A FALLING KNIFE

A mortgage loan that is in default is worth less on paper to an investor than one that is not, since once in default there is a higher chance that the loan will not be repaid, thus making it riskier to invest in. As we default on our mortgages, the value of the CDOs built by pooling all of our mortgage loans together declines in value. Because no one knows how many of us will default and, if our homes have to be foreclosed and sold to pay off our mortgage loans, how much our homes can be sold for, lenders, funds, and investors holding the CDOs face difficulty in assigning an accurate price to these holdings. Because their values continue to fall with no known end point, the situation has aptly been compared to a "falling knife." Compounding the problem is the fact that mortgage defaults take time to appear as CDO losses. Some institutions buying these investments lack the infrastructure to track and respond to credit performance (they can't tell who will likely default and who will not) and properly reevaluate expected cash flows. Both are necessary pieces of information to value the investment, resulting in write-downs and loss of investor confidence in the AAA, AA, and BB ratings of the various levels of CDOs.

WHAT DOES "MARK TO MARKET" MEAN?

When a company writes down the value of the assets it holds, such as CDOs, the company reduces the value of that asset on the company's financial balance sheet. This has a negative impact on businesses such as lenders and investment firms, which are required by law to maintain a certain value or worth in reserves. The concept of reserve banking is discussed more fully in chapter 5. Most CDO holders who can afford to do so would elect to hold on to their investments until the values stabilize and presumably they can get more money for them than they can now. However, because of recently enacted accounting rules, when an asset cannot be valued, the institution is required to assign it the value at which similar assets are actually being sold in the open market. In a market where CDOs can be sold at only fire-sale prices, this creates quite a problem for those firms that do not wish to sell but are required to value the assets in this manner on their balance sheet. In fact, this can make an otherwise healthy company appear to be in dire financial straits literally overnight. Compounding the challenge is the fact that many of the companies governed by these *mark to market* accounting rules have created affiliated entities that are not subject to these rules in order to hold some of their assts, including CDOs, making it difficult to know the true financial strength of many companies.

How the Little Guys Defaulting on Mortgages Impacted CDOs and Eventually Brought Down Wall Street Firms

ONE: When word got out that borrowers were defaulting on their mortgages, investors stopped buying CDOs. The effect can be compared to the music being shut off during a game of musical chairs. Bear Stearns, for example, was left standing with $50 billion in CDOs no one wanted and the market did not know how to value. (Again, this is because they were originally valued using models and assumptions we've since learned were flawed.)

TWO: Firms holding the CDOs were required to write down the value of these assets, or mark to market, which resulted in reserve shortfalls for many.

THREE: In the case of Bear Stearns, the firm tried to raise capital to cover the shortfall but around the same time the ratings agencies (which we will discuss shortly) downgraded the firm's rating, meaning Bear Stearns and its securities were considered more risky for investors.

FOUR: In turn, many investors became skeptical about investing with Bear Stearns, and those who did invest demanded higher interest rates in return for the added risk (i.e., borrowing money became more expensive for Bear Stearns).

FIVE: As a result, investors started pulling their business and money from Bear causing an even larger resulting shortfall and eventually the demise of the company.

In June 2007 two hedge funds managed by Wall Street leader Bear Stearns crashed after unprecedented declines in the value the firm had placed on subprime mortgages underlying their CDOs. We'll discuss in more detail in chapter 5 how the plummet of these funds was precipitated by the bursting real estate bubble. Merrill Lynch (since acquired by Bank of America) and Citigroup, two other top players that created CDOs, faced similar challenges for similar reasons. In October 2007 Merrill Lynch reported almost $8 billion in losses on CDOs caused by mortgage loan defaults and subsequent CDO write-downs. Two days later, Merrill Lynch CEO Stan O'Neal resigned. One month later, Citigroup CEO Charles Prince resigned under similar pressure.[7] The sidebar on page 67 summarizes the five basic stages that pulled the rug out from underneath CDOs and the impact that had on one Wall Street firm.

A FALSE SENSE OF SECURITY

Investors will get little, if any, money back after these unprecedented declines in the value of the CDO they invested in. The paradox of secondary markets, in which mortgage loans are bundled and sold as high-return CDOs, is that their liquidity (the ease of turning them into cash), which investors perceived as their safeguard, created conditions for disaster. Each individual investor believes that his commitment is liquid—that *he* can cash out at any time—the belief that he can exit at will calms his nerves, in reality making him more willing to run a risk. The catch is that all investors, collectively, can *never* exit in unison. When they try, panic sets in, the value of the investments goes down as investors rush to sell their stake, and losses are the result. The true extent of many declines that occurred and are still occurring in the subprime lending area is being masked by the reluctance of investors to buy or sell what are essentially nonliquid securities.

IT'S ALL ABOUT THE RATING

In addition to brokerage house sales efforts, Wall Street is also driven by the credit rating agencies (CRAs). The top three agencies are Standard & Poor's, Fitch Group, and Moody's Investors Service. On their own Web sites, the top three describe themselves, respectively, as "the world's foremost provider of independent credit ratings, risk evaluation, investment research and data"; "a leading global rating agency committed to providing the world's credit markets with independent, timely and prospective credit opinions"; and "the world's most respected and widely utilized source, for credit ratings, research, and risk analysis." Assuming the descriptions are accurate, if the integrity of these ratings is compromised, serious consequences may follow.

The Creation of a Rating Agency Oligopoly

Until the 1970s the large rating agencies' business model was based on revenue from investors' subscriptions for ratings used to make their investing decisions. In the 1970s the Securities and Exchange Commission (SEC) established capital requirements for banks, insurance companies, and other financial institutions. These requirements governed the amount of money the institutions had to have on hand to respond to customers who sought to sell their securities. The specific requirements depended upon credit ratings from those ratings agencies designated by the SEC as *nationally recognized statistical ratings organizations* (NRSROs). The top three agencies were grandfathered in and codified as self-regulating entities.

New Model Allowed Wall Street to Shop for Ratings

Around the same time, the agencies modified their own business models to be based on revenue from the entities being rated. This meant that companies could essentially shop for a rating agency that would provide a positive rating, review their ratings before deciding to make them public, and fire a rating agency that did not provide a desirable rating. This raises serious questions about objectivity. In addition to setting capital requirements, only by receiving a favorable rating from one of these selected agencies can a security earn a place in a federally regulated bank's portfolio. In other words, a good rating from Standard & Poor's, Fitch, or Moody's can dramatically raise demand for a security in the market. For example, Credit Suisse Group was behind a CDO that Moody's, Standard & Poor's, and Fitch each rated a top-notch, or AAA, investment. Relying upon its high rating, clients invested more than $340 million. Unfortunately, the evaluation used to compute these high ratings was, as we've discussed, fundamentally flawed, and investors lost $125 million (losses may have since increased even more).[8]

Some say that this move toward a system that allowed shopping for the best rating was the beginning of the end for CDOs. We've already discussed how CDO creators may have motives other than generating the best profit for their investors (including generating profit for themselves). In some cases, the interests of those who issue securities are diametrically opposed to the interests of the investors who buy them. Accordingly, issuer-paid rating agencies should, in reality, have limited credibility. Rating agencies have acknowledged the potential for conflict of interest in this model. But, as we'll see, this change also catapulted the profit of the top three ratings agencies.

CDOs Became Huge Profit Center for the Ratings Agencies

After the dot-com meltdown of the 1990s, lawmakers became aware of this government-imposed oligopoly. In 2006 Congress passed the Credit Rating Agency Duopoly Relief Act, designed to increase the competition among nationally recognized statistical ratings organizations. Unfortunately, this may have been a case of too little, too late. Blessed by government regulators, with their unique and exclusive authority, the rating agencies institutionalized the notion that securities backed by subprime loans were essentially risk free by basically selling their seal of approval in the form of good ratings. In other words, rather than fulfilling their proper role in the market by warning investors about the now obvious risks involved in CDOs, the rating agencies instead helped to create a systemic problem. Some allege that there is no logical reason why securitized subprime mortgage obligations received high ratings, and that rating agencies have wrongly issued dubious, highly inflated ratings on hundreds of billions of dollars in securities backed by mortgages. Others add to the accusation that the reason the rating agencies turned a blind eye to CDO risks is that they were paid huge sums of money to stamp their approval on the companies who were packaging bad loans and selling them to investors everywhere.

CDOs quickly became cash cows for the rating agencies. Some rating agencies made upwards of fifteen times as much profit in connection with their ratings on CDOs in 2006 as they had ten years earlier. During the bubble, almost half of the ratings agencies' revenue came from rating CDOs. Often the agencies were paid to suggest the structure for the CDO and then paid again for blessing with a high rating the same structure they had helped design. Standard & Poor's, Fitch, and Moody's have been criticized for flaws in the analysis employed in rating CDOs, including allegations that their ratings of investments backed by subprime mortgages, failed to reflect quickly enough growing subprime mortgage default rates. Some securities lost more than 50 percent on the dollar before their ratings were downgraded.[9] The rating agencies claim that in many cases the fundamental flaw was mortgage fraud (explained in more detail in chapter 3) committed by borrowers and lenders. In defense of the rating agencies, it is true that late payments and defaults in the underlying mortgage loans, along with lender or servicer hesitancy or inability to report these defaults, when combined with the difficulty in determining the reduced value of the real estate that backed the loans, have made CDOs increasingly difficult to rate in any accurate way.

THE BEGINNING OF THE END

At the end of the day, investors dumped CDOs as they tried desperately to recover as much as they could of their original investments. This decreased the value, ratings, and demand for CDOs, which meant that fewer investors wanted to buy mortgage loans from lenders, which in turn limited lenders' ability to replenish the funds available to lend to us. The credit markets were tightening quickly as the desire to flee CDOs grew. Unfortunately, this came at a time when many adjustable-rate mortgages were adjusting upward to shockingly high levels, which should have generated higher profits, making them tremendously attractive to investors. Those home owners with adjusting mortgages were trying to refinance out of them but were faced with a serious credit crunch. With investors selling off their CDOs to recoup their money, few dollars were available for banks and others to lend to home owners and buyers seeking a mortgage.

WHAT'S NEXT

Whew! You have successfully made it over the subprime and financial crisis learning curve. Congratulations. You know all of the history, lingo, and dynamics indigenous to home ownership, the mortgage business, Wall Street securitization, and the government's intervention—so far. Together, these are the culprits that have led us to this unhappy economic situation. If you forget anything, the headings in this chapter and the glossary at the back of this book are designed to make topics easy to look up and refresh your memory. With this knowledge, we're fully equipped to tackle how on earth our country's real estate bubble happened.

NOTES

1. http://www.federalreserve.gov/pubs/oss/oss2/2004/bull0206.pdf.

2. "What Is a Subprime Mortgage Lender?" mtgprofessor.com/A%20-%20Shopping%20for%20a%20Mortgage/how_to_avoid_mortgage_overcharges.htm; Roger Lowenstein, "Subprime Times," *New York Times Magazine*, September 2, 2007, p. 11; David Lereah, "The Subprime Reckoning," *Realtor's Magazine* (May 2007): 8; Paul Owens, "Facing the Pain of Foreclosure," *South Florida Sun-Sentinel*, February 24, 2008, pp. 1A, 8F; Marshall Brian, "Subprime Mess: Still Don't Get It? Here's the Scoop," *Keys Sunday*, December 23, 2007, p. 14; Bob Tedeschi, "How to Get a Cheaper Loan," *New York Times*, January 20, 2008, p. 6; Jack Rosenthal, "A Subprime Glossary for the Mortgage Scandal," *International Herald Tribune*, August 18, 2008, p. 7.

3. Gregory Zuckerman, "Hedge Funds Feels New Heat," *Wall Street Journal*, February 23, 2008, pp. A1, 7; Gretchen Morgenson, "In the Fed's Cross Hairs: Exotic Game," *New York Times*, March 23, 2008, pp. 1, 8; Nelson D. Schwartz, "What Created This Monster?" *New York Times*, March 23, 2008, pp. 1, 7; Michael S. Grynbaum, "Wall Street's Wild Ride Believed to Be Far from Over," *New York Times*, January 19, 2008, p. C4; Martin Arnold, "Questions over Sectors and Debt Purchases" *Financial Times*, August 18, 2008, p. 16; James Grant, "Why No Outrage?" *Wall Street Journal*, July 19, 2008, p. W6; Greg Hitt, "Economic Woes Get a Fix: Witch Hunt," *Wall Street Journal*, July 19, 2008, p. A3; Henry Sander, "Hedge Fund's Risky Bets Come to Roost," New York State Comptroller's Office, *Wall Street Journal*, March 8, 2007, p. C1, http://online.wsj.com/article/ SB117331538462530298.html?mod=home_whats_news_us; Carick Mollenkamp and Ian McDonald, "Behind Subprime Woes, a Cascade of Bad Bets," *Wall Street Journal*, October 27, 2007, p. B1.

4. Rosenthal, "A Subprime Glossary for the Mortgage Scandal"; Schwartz, "What Created this Monster?"; Gregory Zuckerman, "The More Hedges the Better," *Wall Street Journal*, October 17, 2007, p. C1; Sender, "Hedge Funds Risky Bets Come to Roost."

5. Bert Ely, "Let's Try Market-Oriented Reform" *Wall Street Journal*, May 31, 2008, p. A11; Gretchen Morgenson, "What Created This Monster," *New York Times*, March 23, 2008, pp. 1, 7; Kate Kelly, "The Fall of Bear Stearns," *Wall Street*

Journal, May 28, 2008, p. A13; Jeffrey M. Levine, "The Verticals of Integration Strategy," *Mortgage Banking* (February 2008): 58–65; Jenny Anderson and Vikas Bajaj, "Lehman Plans to Close a Lending Unit and Layoff 1,200," *New York Times*, August 22, 2007, p. 4B.

6. Saha- Bubna Aparjat and Carrick Moltenkamp, "CDO Ratings Are Whacked by Moody's," *Wall Street Journal*, October 27, 2007, p. B1; Peter S. Goodman, "This Is the Sound of a Bubble Bursting," *New York Times*, December 23, 2007, p. 7; James B. Stewart, "Risks of a 'Safe' Investment Are Found Out the Hard Way," *Wall Street Journal*, February 27, 2008, p. D4; Schwartz, "What Created This Monster?"; Grynbaum, "Wall Street's Wild Ride Believed to Be Far from Over"; Rosenthal, "A Subprime Glossary for the Mortgage Scandal"; Andrea Tryphondes, "More Pain Seems Likely for Firms' Earnings," *Wall Street Journal*, August 11, 2008, p. 20; Tyler Cowen, "So We Thought. But Then Again . . . ," *New York Times*, January 13, 2008, p. 6.

7. Grant, "Why No Outrage?"; Hitt, "Economic Woes Get a Fix"; Robin Sidel, "Citigroup CEO Plans to Resign as Losses Grow," *Wall Street Journal*, November 3, 2007, p. A4; Jed Horowitz, "Merrill Defends Its Transactions," *New York Times*, August 28, 2008, p. 1B.

8. Schwartz, "What Created This Monster?"; Judith Burns, "Unclear Review for Revamp," *Wall Street Journal*, March 22, 2008, p. A11; Nat Worden, "Why the Ratings Agencies Flunked," TheStreet.com, January 3, 2008, http://www.thestreet.com/story/10396742/1/why-the-ratings-agencies-flunked.html; Martin D. Weiss, "Next Phase of the Crisis: The Great Ratings Debate," *Money and Markets*, November 12, 2007, http://www.moneyandmarkets.com/next-phase-of-the-crisis-the-great-ratings-debacle-9241.

9. Schwartz, "Who Created This Monster?"; Burns, "Unclear Review for Revamp."

3

BUILDING A REAL ESTATE BUBBLE

Between the years 2003 and 2006, US home ownership hit an all-time high. More than 69 percent of American citizens had realized the American Dream (about 5 percent more people than before).[1] A sampling of specific ownership rates in seven different states is reflected in the sidebar (see p. 76) to illustrate the variance by region. Even today, America still offers unique access to that dream. In addition to advancing individual pride, this level of nationwide home ownership is good for our country. Whether it be a humble abode, a family estate, or a new "McMansion," the family residence remains the backbone of the American economy. Once we get through our current crisis, the home will reemerge as something we appreciate in a manner more like our grandparents did. If there's one point I'd like to make in this book, it is that the family residence be revered as the most valuable and enduring asset for those who have achieved a financial foothold and not leveraged for lesser reasons. One need only look at the following facts to be convinced. The average net worth of a US renter is only $4,000, while the average American home owner's net worth (at least before the current real estate crash) was a whopping $184,000. A recent MSNBC interview of millionaires offering advice for the rest of us collectively supported this view: "Our entire panel agreed, real estate ownership is key."[2] Popular financial

Home Ownership Rates in Key US States

West Virginia	78.4%	California	60.2%
Michigan	77.4%	Hawaii	59.9%
Delaware	76.8%	New York	55.7%
Mississippi	76.2%	Washington, DC	45.9%

guru Suze Orman preaches that home ownership can help Americans achieve solid financial goals and wealth. Another national benefit is that home owners contribute more to our overall economy in several ways. Home owners tend to spend more than renters, helping to support important business sectors such as construction, home improvement, maintenance, services and repairs, furniture, and decor. When it is time to retire, most of us count on our home equity as a nest egg to draw upon, augmenting our Social Security benefits and lessening Medicaid and other public eldercare burdens. Added to that is the sense of community, security, and pride that solid shelter and owning the roof over your own head can bring.

THE McMANSION PHENOMENON

All other things being equal, it would be ideal if all American citizens could own their home. However, between 2003 and 2006, thanks to easier access to more mortgage money for more and more of us, the homes we chose to buy morphed to a level some say far exceeded the basic necessity of solid shelter. Average home size increased. What were once considered luxury amenities, such as expensive Italian tile, stainless steel appliances, and granite countertops, have come to be expected standard features as builders competed for our money. Dollarwise, we can compare it to a nation driving Toyotas one year and Mercedes Benzes the next—all thanks to credit. The same public and private industries that were built to help us achieve the American Dream of home ownership are, at once, our best friend and our worst foe. The biggest impact of easier access to home loan credit was not merely enabling more of us to buy homes, since even though (as a percentage of total population) US home ownership rates today are higher than before, they were almost this high in the 1960s. Instead, the biggest impact was that easier access to home loans enabled a larger percentage of us to buy bigger, more expensive homes and even investment properties. In fact, the record-breaking number of properties listed for sale today throughout the country is a testament to just how much of the housing bubble was speculative. The graph in the sidebar reflects this peak spending phenomenon. Real estate investing grew predominantly in the area of new construction as more and more of us learned that for a mere 10 or 20 percent deposit, we could reserve and then flip (quickly sell) a unit (a house, townhouse, or condominium), more than doubling our initial investment. Little did we know that so many of us would eventually have to actually close on those units, tie up our capital, and be burdened with unaffordable payments.

As much as our country values equality, the fact is that not all of us are equally adept when it comes to assessing our own abilities and being disciplined enough to manage the financial responsibilities of home ownership without at least some education on the skill sets involved. Without further professional guidance, some of us should not be home owners. Others do have the basic skills to successfully own homes, but ended up buying houses that soon became unaffordable. We should have bought that Toyota, but with

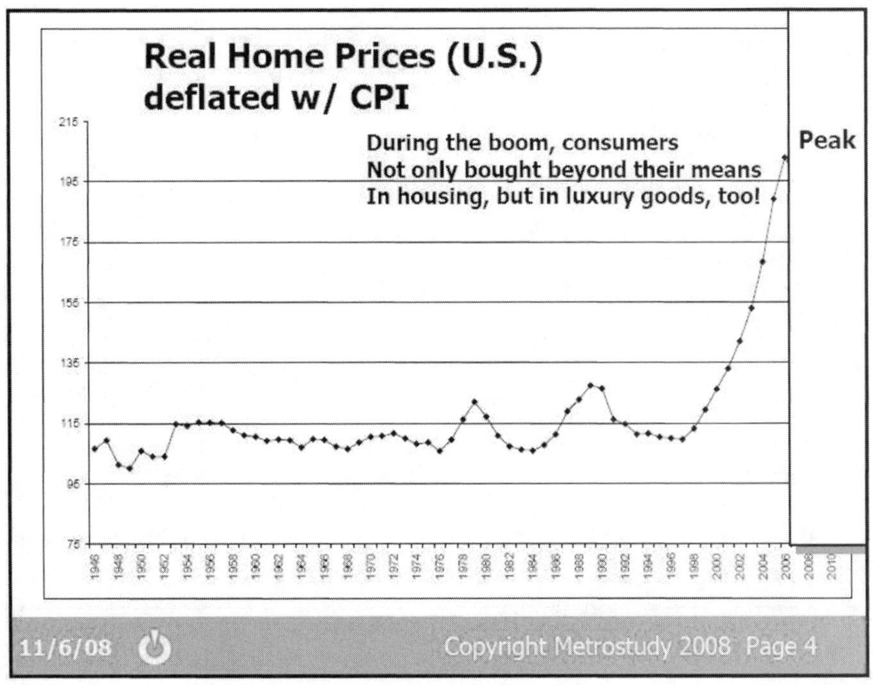

Wall Street hungry to buy our mortgage loans, originators convinced us—although with precious little resistance from our end—that we could afford the Mercedes. Most of us succumbed to the temptation, thanks to our blossoming comfort level with credit and debt in general, and found this concept easy to swallow.

THE PERFECT REAL ESTATE STORM

Armed with an appreciation for US societal attitudes, the historical context, and the mortgage industry infrastructure, understanding how we came to this steep precipice is simple. The perfect real estate storm began heating up in 2003 (as we'll discuss later, the problems that subsequently emerged on Wall Street can be traced even further back to the 1970s), when several factors collided. When you are done reading this chapter, you will understand the factors—summarized in the sidebar below—that together created a perfect real estate storm.

It should be noted that the propensity to succumb to these various temptations is not uniquely American. We now know that other countries, including the United Kingdom, experienced real estate bubbles during approximately the same period as we did. We will explore these influential international factors in more detail later in this chapter.

Summary of Factors Contributing to Perfect Storm

- Delocalization
- The role of the Internet
- Mortgage lead aggregation
- Wall Street's insatiable appetite for mortgage-backed securities
- Emerging mortgage loan markets
- Speculative real estate investors
- ARMs, subprime, and Alt A loan products
- The FHA and the Federal Reserve's reaction
- An influx of inexperienced mortgage and real estate professionals
- Increasingly relaxed loan-underwriting practices
- Tempting predatory lending
- Record levels of mortgage fraud

What Is Delocalization?

Delocalization is simply the opposite of local businesses, localization. Our nation was built on local businesses. They become closer or nearer, and consequently more familiar with their customers. Customers likewise were familiar with the companies and the people behind them. With delocalization, businesses grow more distant from their customers both geographically and in familiarity. The mortgage industry has become increasingly delocalized in four key ways.

Community-Based Origination No More

First, as banks consolidated and grew into national institutions, mortgage loan origination was no longer a community-based business, as it had been in our grandparents' era, driven by local bankers who knew the local market and their potential borrowers. In fact in 2007, 40 percent of all subprime loans were originated by automated underwriting.[3]

Securitization Adds More Distance

Second, as the secondary market grew, home loans quickly left their local arenas to be sold off to larger firms or bundled into pools and sold as securities. The percentage of subprime mortgages securitized after origination increased from 54 percent in 2001 to 75 percent in 2006.[4] Rather than work with their local bankers to solve problems after closing, a handful of national mortgage loan-servicing companies handled the bulk of post-closing customer relationship management. This often decreased their ability to respond to borrower needs. The post-origination lives of mortgage loans became further and further removed from their original sources.

Ratings Replaced Prudent Underwriting

Third, distancing borrowers from lenders has contributed to the development of lax underwriting standards. Investors in CDOs, being far removed from the actual real estate, can hardly be expected to scrutinize the underlying mortgages, loan by loan. Many instead delegated this task to the rating agencies that evaluated the quality of loans being made and supposedly rate the securities that rest on them. As we discussed in chapter 2, over time, the rating agencies, also grew lax.

Distance Increases Communication Issues

Fourth, while layers of players we discussed in chapter 2 were added, systems to get critical information from one level to the next had not yet been perfected. The mortgage industry is still inefficient in sharing information. Each time a mortgage loan changes hands the chances that information will be misplaced or misinterpreted increase much like a childhood game of telephone. The way the modern-day mortgage industry is structured, mortgage loans often change hands in terms of ownership several times after being originated as they are securitized and sold. The loans also change hands in terms of rights and responsibilities (as opposed to ownership) when intermediary companies are brought in to service the loans. As we explained earlier, these folks, appropriately referred to as *mortgage loan servicers*, are often the ones who send you your statements, take your calls when you have a question, and call you when you're late on a payment. Even within a mortgage servicing company we find different layers of players who may not be compiling and maintaining critical information efficiently and accurately. For example, at many mortgage servicing companies your statements are handled by one department, your payments by another, and your phone calls by yet another. Mortgage loan customer Pamela Axelrod (some names have been changed at the request of interviewees) recounts her firsthand experience with a mortgage loan servicing department for us in the sidebar.

As a result of these factors, mortgage loan delocalization increased both borrower and investor risk.

Mortgage Loan Lead Aggregation

The Internet is credited with vastly improving mortgage loan marketing and the efficiency of making loans. It is the most common source of information for mortgage loans and, as such, perhaps the single largest contributor to delocalization. Almost half of us shop online for mortgage loans, which further lessens the originator's ability to accurately assess our comprehension of the obligation we are taking on and our loan risk. The anonymity of the Internet arguably increases the likelihood that borrowers will be tempted to misrepresent impor-

Caught in a Mortgage Servicing Department Nightmare

"About a year ago we received a letter from our bank saying we had not paid our home owner's insurance. I was pretty sure I'd paid it. I checked our records, and sure enough, there was the cancelled check. So I called the local branch for the mortgage company, spoke with my loan officer, and then e-mailed him the cancelled check. He assured me it had been handled.

A few weeks later I got another letter from the bank, again saying we had not paid the insurance. So I called our local banker, again e-mailed him the cancelled check, and again he said not to worry.

A few weeks later another letter arrived. This one threatened if we didn't pay our insurance the bank would buy us insurance and charge us for it [sometimes called "forced place insurance"]. This time I called an 800 number at the bottom of the letter. That put me into an automated phone system with 4 or 5 levels until you get to a live person. The first time I called I must have pressed a wrong option because the person said I needed to speak with a different department. When she transferred me the call was disconnected, so I started over again. Eventually I spoke with someone, a very nice guy, who told me to mail him the cancelled check and it would be handled. So I did that.

Three weeks later I noticed a $4,500 charge on my mortgage statement. I freaked out. I'd heard stories about banks making mistakes that even lead to foreclosure. So I called our local banker again. This time he said there was nothing he could do and gave me another 800 number to call. I called there and navigated the usual automated system. Eventually I found out that I could either send a check for $4,500 or the bank would add 1/12 of the insurance premium into my mortgage payments. Mind you, I'd already paid a premium to my insurance company. We'd been saving for hurricane shutters, so luckily we had some money set aside. I overnighted a check for $4,500 to the bank and was assured that if I got a letter from my insurance company, the bank would refund this money to me.

Literally, the next day I got our monthly mortgage statement and the bank had added 1/12 of the insurance into our payment. This time I went ballistic.

Eventually, I spoke with my local banking supervisor and she helped us straighten the whole thing out. She said the problem is there are so many departments that these things sometimes happen."

tant loan application information. Even though mortgage underwriters do the best they can to verify the information on borrowers' loans applications, as we'll discuss in a bit and as often is the case in other businesses, we all know that people who want to get away with lying will always find a way to do so.

But perhaps even more significant is the explosion of the online mortgage lead aggregation business. Lead aggregation companies capture potential borrower information from public records, Web sites, and other sources, selling these "leads" to mortgage loan originators, who contact potential borrowers by standard mail, e-mail, and telephone in an attempt to sell them mortgage loans. Sometimes would-be borrowers are aware that their information is being sold and sometimes they are not. One well-known example of mortgage lead aggregation is Lending Tree. During the bubble, Lending Tree television advertisements appeared regularly: "With Lending Tree, lenders compete for your business." When we knowingly submit our information to a lead aggregation company such as Lending Tree, the company can sell leads for a higher price because this type of lead represents potential borrowers who are actively shopping for a mortgage loan. Lead aggregation companies that extract our information without our knowledge from other sources, such as public records, generally sell leads at a lower price. Some aggregation companies offer further lead-filtering services, allowing home loan originators to identify those of us with pending interest rate adjustments we may wish to avoid by refinancing or those with equity in our homes we may wish to cash out. Some companies charge a flat monthly fee; others charge based on the number of searches an originator conducts when utilizing their database. Still others charge on a per lead basis. Mortgage lead aggregation further increases a loan mortgage originator's motivation to sell us a mortgage loan, since buying the leads involves cash out of the originator's pocket he will no doubt want to recoup. Unfortunately, it also reduces the trusted relationship or personal referral component that had been a key factor in our country's home loan industry.

The Emerging Markets Influence

According to "The State of the Nation's Housing in 2008," produced by Harvard University's Joint Center for Housing Studies with support from some fifteen government entities and other groups, home ownership has expanded to a statistical high in every racial, income, and geographical category, although equality issues remain. A 2007 First American Title Insurance Company survey showed 72 percent of whites nationwide owned their own home, versus 50 percent of Hispanics and African Americans. But a wider choice than ever before in loan types has helped open the door to what is known in the industry as "emerging markets" or first-time, minority, immigrant, and low-income home buyers. This group contributed to almost half of recent new home ownership. Over the next fifteen years, this group is projected to account for two-thirds of total household growth. Yet experts at the Federal Reserve; the Center for Responsible Lending in Durham, North Carolina; the National Community Reinvestment Coalition in Washington, DC; and Greenlining Institute in Berkeley, California, report two disturbing trends: First, the historical gap, which in some areas is as big as 50 percent between white and black home ownership continues.[5] Second, studies suggest African Americans and Latinos pay disproportionately more than whites for mortgages, even after legitimate pricing factors such as income, credit, and debt have been taken into account. There is growing evidence that loan originators often place borrowers who qualify for conventional loans into subprime mortgages, not because the subprime loans better suit the borrowers, but because subprime loans generate more profit for the loan originators. Latino borrowers accounted for 40 percent of the newly emerged category of subprime borrowers. More than half of the subprime mortgages are originated in predominantly African American census tracts.[6]

Facilitating this trend is the fact that conventional banks tend to locate branches in neighborhoods that will generate savings deposits. Emerging market, minority, and first-time home buyers typically have less money to save and deposit. As a result, banks are less likely to locate branches in the neighborhoods in which these individuals live. Enter the aggressive mortgage brokers who target these vulnerable neighborhoods with mailings, phone calls, even door-to-door solicitations. The result is that most emerging market, minority, and first-time home buyer loans are originated by mortgage brokers rather than banks. Our government has tried to prevent discrimination in the mortgage business with the Fair Housing Act, the Equal Credit Opportunity Act, the Home Mortgage Disclosure Act, the Truth in Lending Act, the Real Estate Settlement Procedures Act, and the Community Reinvestment Act. Each of these acts is explained in more detail in appendix D. Some of these attempts work; others do not. Lenders are held accountable, in particular via "redlining" prohibitions (i.e., rules that prevent lenders from refusing to make mortgage loans on property that is located in certain "bad" neighborhoods). Underwriters are under more pressure to review and approve or deny loan applications without regard to race, color, religion, marital status, age, disability, or national origin. While that may influence loan approvals versus denials, it does not impact the *type* of loans emerging market borrowers are getting and how much it costs them. This time the buck stops with mortgage loan originators, who have the greatest impact on the mortgage loan product we're put into and how much we're charged for home loans.

Illegal Kickbacks

Many mortgage originators have found other "creative" ways to increase revenue, as well. As the competition increased among title search companies for mortgage loan closing referrals from originators, some companies engaged in *kickbacks.* Even though the Real Estate Settlement Procedure Act (RESPA), passed in the 1970s, prohibits the payment of fees or kickbacks by title companies to mortgage originators or real estate professionals for the referral of closing business, rumors of title companies paying hundreds of dollars per loan became commonplace. Theoretically, these costs incurred were eventually passed on to borrowers like us in the form of higher closing costs.

Now Infamous "Predatory Lending"

In some cases, the practices of loan originators have sunk to the level of predatory lending. A 2002 joint report by the US Department of Housing and Urban Development and the Department of Treasury defines predatory lending as lending that strips home equity and places borrowers at increased risk of foreclosure. It can be more broadly explained as deliberately leading borrowers who are unlikely to be able to meet the terms of their loans into a financial obligation for the originators' own profit. Many of the loans made between 2003 and 2006 fall under this definition.

Prepayment Penalties

The Center for Responsible Lending believes that prepayment penalties (fees charged by a lender for paying off a home loan early) are, by definition, predatory because they may operate to prevent borrowers from refinancing at lower interest rates. According to the Mortgage Bankers Association (MBA),

80 percent of the adjustable-rate mortgages originated between 2003 and 2006 have prepayment penalties. During 2007 and 2008, Fannie Mae and Freddie Mac changed their standards to prohibit prepayment penalties, or no longer purchased subprime loans with prepayment penalties.[7] Obviously with legislation placing these government-sponsored enterprises into a receivership-type situation in the fall of 2008, we can expect more changes in how they do business. Some of these changes are discussed in chapter 8.

Counseling

It has been argued that emerging market borrowers require more education and thus more time, entitling mortgage loan originators to more profit. Mortgage loan originators tend not to refer borrowers to housing counselors for this education for fear that housing counselors are already overburdened and may delay the loan process. They also fear that a counselor may refer a borrower to another mortgage loan originator. A brief description of some of the relevant organizations conducting research and providing information available to assist home buyers is included as appendix E.

Tips to avoid predatory lending are also included in the sidebar (see p. 86) for you. Record growth in emerging market borrowers, in combination with an educational void, contributed significantly to our foreclosure nation. Many of these borrowers are the folks who unknowingly took on too much mortgage, could not afford their rate adjustments, and are now losing their homes.

Enter the Real Estate Speculator

Between 2003 and 2006, second-home and speculative-investor purchases hit 7.5 and 10 percent of all transactions, respectively. That's three and a half times more home loans made to buyers of second homes and speculative investors than in prior years. By 2006 nearly 40 percent or 3 million US units were purchased as second homes or for investment.[8] By some estimates nearly 85 percent of condominium purchases in some of the harder-hit areas such as Miami, Florida, were for investment and resale. Many investors assumed highly leveraged positions on several units at once. The demand for new construction became so compelling that builders utilized lotteries, awarding winners the "right" to buy a home. In some highly sought-after areas such as Florida, Nevada, and California, it became commonplace to see people lining up days

Tips to Help You Avoid Predatory Lending

- Beware of no-money-down offers.
- Check professional licenses and credentials for all Realtors, mortgage loan originators, and appraisers.
- Don't be convinced to borrow more than what you really need. Remember, the more mortgage loan money you borrow, the more commission your mortgage loan originator will earn.
- Don't pay costs you did not agree to or that were not fully disclosed.
- Read and understand everything you sign.
- Don't sign any form if all of the blanks are not completely filled in.
- Choose a reputable, experienced mortgage lender.
- Consider your lifestyle priorities and spending patterns. Make sure the loan you get won't require you to change your patterns or compromise your priorities.
- Find a lender with strong in-house processing, underwriting, and funding departments to control these processes locally and quickly.
- Don't blindly follow advice you don't understand.
- Don't automatically expect the right advice from all experts.
- Structure purchase contracts so that time pressures will not force you to go along or accept things you are not comfortable with. For example, make sure there is plenty of time for you to find and get approved for the right mortgage loan before you have to close.
- Get at least three quotes from different mortgage loan originators.
- Make sure you get answers to the questions you ask, and not just what they want to tell you.
- Don't expect everyone involved, including mortgage loan originators, processors, and underwriters, to do their job correctly.
- Take responsibility for your own decisions.
- Do not keep asking the same question over and over again until you hear the answer you want.

in advance of the opening of a new project sales office. As a result, builders were easily able to sell new homes, despite an apparent shortfall in the creation of new households.

In 2005, some appraisers were factoring double-digit annual appreciation into their valuations. The excitement was palatable. These new investors were never planning to take occupancy. Profits on the sale of one unit went to new purchases and the resulting mortgage payments until another resale occurred. The *flip* became commonplace. Some investors were even selling or *flipping* their contracts, never closing on the units before cashing out. Realizing that many of their customers were buying on speculation, builders began-at the urging of their construction lenders—adding resale restriction clauses to their purchase contracts, requiring buyers to hold their units for at least one year before reselling, thus prohibiting investors from competing with the home builder for the new buyers.

THE FHA ASLEEP AT THE WHEEL

Until recently, Federal Housing Authority (FHA)–insured loan products were the most common loan utilized by what might now be considered subprime borrowers, potential home buyers who were less likely to secure a conventional loan because they lacked a large enough down payment. So not only did the FHA's borrowers tend to be higher risk, but so did the loan products. But bigger lender discounts for introductory adjustable-rate mortgages, mentioned earlier, commonly known as "teaser rates," lower down payment requirements (by 2005 median down payments for first-time home buyers were only 2 percent, with 43 percent of these buyers making no down payment at all!), and the increasing popularity of hybrid adjustable rate mortgages, resulted in a decline in the number of FHA loans. Compared to the wide variety of creative new loans that emerged during the bubble, FHA loans were viewed by many borrowers as costly, burdensome, and old-fashioned. The agency's red tape was legendary, and its mandatory mortgage insurance fees weren't competitive with the private market. Perhaps even more significantly, homes in high-demand states such as California became so expensive they didn't even qualify for FHA loans. The National Housing Act of 1934, passed as a result of the Great Depression to make home mortgage loans and housing more affordable, provides that the mortgage limit for any given area be set at 95 percent of the median house price in that area, except that the FHA mortgage limit cannot exceed 87 percent of the Freddie Mac loan limit or be lower than 48 percent of the Freddie Mac loan limit. So if the median home price in your area is, for example, $150,000, the mortgage loan limit would be $142,500. In simple terms, this means that FHA loan limits were out of step with rising home prices. Accordingly, in many markets, people wanting to buy a house could not borrow enough money from the FHA to purchase a property, and were consequently driven into the arms (and ARMs) of subprime lenders, who happily filled the void.

Because of these factors and the attractive, higher commission subprime loan alternatives were paying, many mortgage loan originators dropped the FHA programs altogether, and the number of FHA home loans decreased dramatically. Historically, the point of FHA loan approval requirements was protecting borrowers against risky home loan decisions. The FHA requires the borrower to provide a down payment so she has some equity, a stake in the home from the beginning and therefore a reason to try hard to pay off the loan. The home must be inspected by an FHA inspector to avoid unexpected repair costs. And, of course, the lender is assured of being repaid by the FHA if the borrower defaults.

But even the FHA was not immune to the 2003 to 2006 mind-set that all of us deserve to own a home and we'd better hurry and buy one now before prices go even higher! Despite its decreasing market share, the FHA may have also played a role in the mortgage meltdown. In its quest to compete with the private sector for its share of the home loan market, the agency decided, over time, to lower its own lending standards. For example, in 1934 the FHA required borrowers to first save a 20 percent down payment. That requirement was gradually whittled down to only 3 percent. Also at issue is where the FHA has begun to allow down payments to come from. According to the FHA Mortgage Whistleblowers, in 2000, 76 percent of FHA borrowers came up with their own down payment. About 20 percent came from nonprofit agencies and the rest from the borrower's family members. The delinquency rate for these borrowers was under 10 percent.[9] The challenge clearly lies in offering government-backed mortgage loans that allow access to the housing market and at the same time follow prudent lending practices. This is no easy task. And, in fact, some critics say it is literally impossible because that 30 percent to 40 percent of Americans who have historically never seemed able to own their own home (remember we discussed that US home ownership rates have historically hovered at around 65 percent) in truth, for financial reasons, should be renters not owners.[10] FHA delinquency rates have been even higher than those for subprime mortgages. Almost 20 percent of FHA single-family borrowers are currently delinquent or in foreclosure on their mortgage loan payment. But under 50 percent of down payments are now coming from the borrowers themselves. Thirty-seven percent of FHA down payments are now coming from nonprofits.[11] Agency-insured loans have been at the heart of some of the worst excesses, including false income verifications and inflated appraisals.

We have also learned that some of the so-called not-for-profit FHA down payment assistance agencies were often nothing more than a scam at taxpayer expense (although some of these agencies are completely legitimate and provide a valuable service). These bad guys merely collected the down payment from the seller and then charged a fee to act as the middleman in crediting it to the buyer/FHA borrower. The result was a higher-priced transaction for everyone, which the sales price paid by the buyer was typically increased to absorb. Both HUD and the IRS attempted to address this problem in 2005 and 2006 but the problem persists. In fact, a Senate subcommittee has determined that the federal government has essentially subsidized much of this fraud. The reality is that when a federal agency steps in to help people finance a home, it's not surprising that some lenders and borrowers would seek to take advantage and cheat the system. This is an important fact to keep in mind as we explore the government's involvement in solving the subprime crisis.

A DOT-COM HANGOVER?

The Federal Reserve sets the interest rate at which banks can borrow money. If the Fed wants to increase our borrowing and spending as consumers, one tool it has is to decrease the interest rate at which banks can borrow. The theory is that this will cause banks to decrease the interest rate they can offer to us, thereby encouraging us to borrow and spend more. This tool has been utilized, some would say overutilized, to boost us out of the post-dot-com slump and the economic slowdown that it caused. With lower interest rates, consumers borrowed more to buy homes, borrowed against their home's equity to buy more consumer goods, and increased their credit card debt. When the Fed decided to increase short-term interest rates to reduce inflation pressures and slow down the economy, it caused the most notable impact on adjustable-rate mortgage interest rates. As the difference in the interest rates charged for thirty-year fixed mortgages (which are typically higher because they remain constant over a long period of time) and adjustable-rate mortgages becomes smaller, the adjustable mortgages look less attractive, so lenders generally offer borrowers larger initial interest rate discounts, or teaser rates, on these adjustable mortgages to attract them.

In part because of potentially frequent fluctuations in Federal Reserve rates, mortgage interest that adjusts annually made potential home buyers leery of committing to a loan. Who knew the Fed could raise its rate any time and a borrower could find himself paying more interest than necessary on his home loan? For this reason, the adjustable-rate mortgages with an initial fixed-rate period of more than one year, commonly known as hybrid adjustable-rate mortgages, which were discussed earlier in chapter 2, grew to become among the most popular mortgage loan products available. Adjustable-rate mortgages with an initial fixed rate period of five years, known as 5/1 ARMs, became the dominant consumer choice.

The average initial interest rate on 5/1 ARMs has normally been priced slightly above the traditional one-year adjustable rate but slightly below the thirty-year fixed rate in order to lure borrowers away from a solid fixed-rate home loan, which, as we have learned, many lenders prefer to avoid because they are less profitable. Most borrowers went along with it because that's what the mortgage loan originator offered and made so easy for us and because we believed our homes would continue to appreciate, mortgage money would continue to flow, and refinancing when our interest rate went up would not be a problem (or, if the home was an investment, we would have sold it before the interest rate went up). According to the Mortgage Bankers Association, between 2003 and 2006, the 5/1 ARM was offered by almost 90 percent of all mortgage loan lenders. In comparison, during this same period, the more traditional one-year adjustable rate mortgage was offered by only half of all mortgage loan lenders, the lowest in its twenty-three-year history.[12] As we discussed in chapter 2, a 5/1 ARM provides borrowers the comfort of knowing that the interest rate will be fixed over the first five years of the loan. However, the interest rate may jump as much as 5 points on the fifth anniversary. In comparison, mortgages that adjust more frequently have less severe interest rate changes.

In the recent past, we safely relied on increasing property values and continued low interest rates to assure ourselves that we would have sufficient home equity to refinance again before our home loan interest rate adjusted, causing our mortgage payment to increase. Hundreds of thousands of borrowers, and their lenders, made increasingly optimistic assumptions about our ability to handle subprime debt. We ignored the fact that our monthly payments would someday reset. Our universal hope was that housing prices would continue rising and we would be able to refinance before our mortgage loan interest rate increase hit. In 2006, this safety net disappeared as the downward cycle of interest rate increases, mortgage defaults, home price decreases and mortgage loan credit scarcity began, leaving many borrowers with higher monthly mortgage payments that they could not afford as our ARMs adjusted upward—and unfortunately most borrowers had no Plan B.

Commercial Banks v. Investment Banks

Following the Great Depression, Congress decided that banks that engage in traditional banking activities, such as holding customers' deposits, should not also be involved in capital markets activities, such as creating and selling securities. The Glass-Steagall Act was passed in 1933. But the Gramm-Leach-Bailey Act in 1999 effectively repealed the application of Glass-Steagall for many of our nation's large financial institutions.

Commercial Banks: Commercial banks are what most of use mean when we speak about banks. But the term is actually used in two contexts. First, it refers to a bank that deals primarily with deposits and loans from corporations or large businesses. Second, the term is used to distinguish a bank from retail banks, or those banks providing services directly to consumers. Many banks offer both commercial and retail services.

Investment Banks: Investment banks issue and sell securities in the equity and bond capital markets and provide advice on transactions including mergers and acquisitions. They are subject to SEC oversight. This involves helping clients raise funds for acquisitions and corporate finance. During the bubble, global investment banking increased, reaching $84.7 billion in 2007, more than double the 2003 revenue. Fifty-three percent of the 2007 global investment banking revenue can be attributed to the United States. The industry hubs are New York City, London, Tokyo, and Manila. The industry is highly competitive, attracting high performers with sky-high compensation, and is thus prone to extreme pressure toward innovation. New products with ever increasing higher profit margins are continuously devised to attract and keep clients.

DID THE GOVERNMENT HAVE ITS HEAD IN THE SAND?

The most cynical among us may have a creepy sense of something even more diabolical than anything else we've discussed so far. Could Washington have possible been deliberately turning its head to the subprime warning signs? Many of our nation's wealthiest citizens, most of whom presumably make it a point to support their friendly politicians of choice, were making bundles of money during the bubble. And what appeared to be a boom economy was making our nation's leaders look like economic rocket scientists. It certainly wouldn't be the first time regulatory or legislative sway was effectively bought. Some historians believe that the legislation behind the separation of investment banks from commercial banks, a decision eventually, some say, leading to leaner oversight of investment banks than commercial banks (which has been blamed for allowing the unmonitored creation and growth of risky CDOs), was nothing more than an exercise of rich businessmen power (in this case the Rockefeller and Morgan families) over Washington. Although the legislation itself, the Banking Act of 1933 also referred to as the Glass-Steagall Act, is not crucial to our discussion, the distinction between commercial banks and investment banks explained for you in the sidebar on the previous page is. It's true that we had expensive wars in Afghanistan and Iraq to pay for. Certainly when money seems to be flowing freely at home, Americans are less apt to object to spending it on wars abroad. While there is plenty of fodder for theories, in light of the abundance of now obvious overt causes leading to the crises, we're likely to see the politically correct pursuit of reforms in the areas we've discussed in this chapter so far and will discuss in the coming chapters, as opposed to support for exploring darker possibilities.

THE SUM OF THE PARTS

As we discussed in chapter 2, in the world of home loan borrowers, the term "subprime" refers to those buyers who do not qualify for the best market interest rates because lenders believe they are less likely than other borrowers to make their mortgage payments. About 25 percent of us fall into this category. The term *Alt A* refers to loans on property types that lenders consider to be at higher risk, such as investment properties and second homes. From the lender's standpoint, borrowers are more apt to default on these loans and walk away from these types of properties than borrowers with loans on their primary residence. Subprime loans originated in the 1990s, but, as we discussed earlier, between 2003 and 2006 their popularity grew to record levels as demand from borrowers eager to get into the booming housing market and end investors anxious to make quick profits rose astronomically: according to the Mortgage Bankers Association, from $35 billion in 1994, to $65 billion in 1995, to $332 billion in 2003, and to $600 billion, or 20 percent of all mortgages, in 2006, a record number. By March of 2007, US subprime mortgages were estimated to have a total value of $1.3 trillion out of the total $12 trillion US mortgage market. A graph reflecting the growth of subprime mortgages according to the Mortgage Bankers Association is included for you below. Likewise, the rate at which subprime loans were transformed into securities grew from less than 30 percent in 1995 to over 58 percent in 2003, with mortgage loan originators bringing risky borrowers in the front door and selling their loans to investors out the back. Then came the day of reckoning. In early 2008, the Mortgage Bankers Association reported that the subprime mortgage loan delinquency rate was already almost six times that of the number of conforming loans and the foreclosure rate ten times higher.[13]

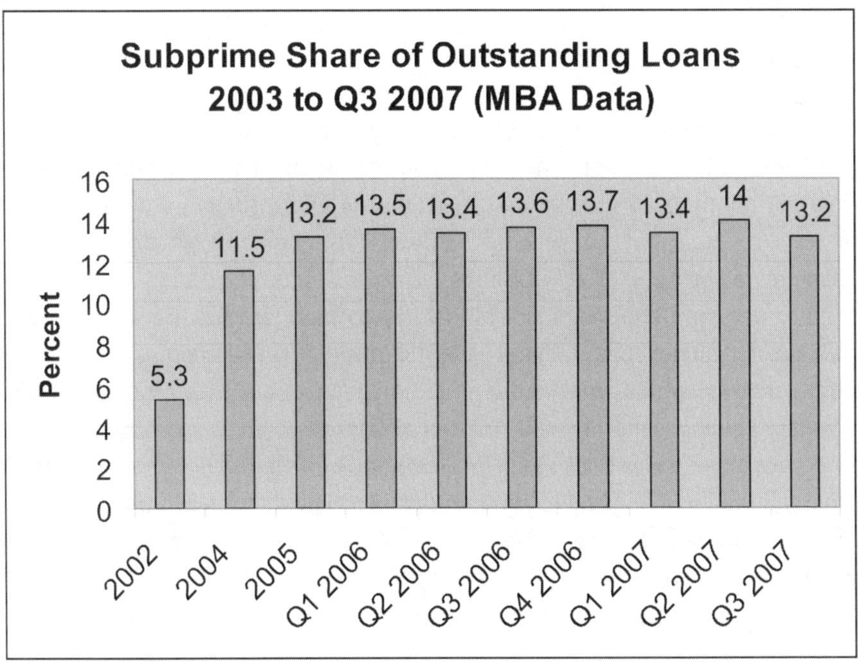

Did You Rely on an Inexperienced Mortgage or Real Estate Professional?

Attracted by big dollars and a housing market that seemed to always increase in value, according to the Mortgage Banking Association and National Association of Realtors, the number of US mortgage originators and Realtors tripled between 2003 and 2006. Many of these folks were inexperienced newcomers with little time to learn the best business practices and the many complicated loan products, given the rate at which we were buying, borrowing, selling, and refinancing. With the wide array of complex and constantly evolving new mortgage loan products available, including subprime and Alt A products, and few barriers to entering the professions, it is a safe bet to say that many of these new brokers and Realtors did not fully understand what they were selling. Many had never known anything but an extremely bullish real estate market and they assumed that it would go on indefinitely, unwisely advising their customers accordingly. Relying on inexperienced professionals to advise us in choosing the home and loan product best suited for us—the single biggest investment most of us will ever make—has proved not to be a good idea. Many home owners are now in dire situations that may well have been avoided with better counseling.

Did You One-Stop Shop?

One-stop shopping, the practice of locating a real estate, title, and mortgage company under one roof, often with common ownership, injected additional risk that conflicts of interest and higher costs to consumers would arise. To increase revenue and compete for Realtors, mortgage brokers, and customers alike, many brokers of record engaged in this business model. Oftentimes smaller one-stop shops are not able to beat larger lenders on interest rates because the bigger lenders have more loan options available and can usually offer better loan rates. Instead, the smaller lenders compete on timing and convenience, enabling us to apply for our mortgage loan at the same time and place we make the real estate offer. Brokers, knowing that we as consumers aren't all that knowledgeable about home loans and so we will rarely decide to look outside their company for competitive quotes from unrelated and often unknown mortgage loan originators, expect to sign or "capture" an average 40 percent of the loan seekers who come to them. This model creates a huge secondary source of income for home loan brokerage firms and helps drive interest in the company among real estate agents, who are often compensated for bringing these likely customers in the door. On the negative side, it's a challenge keeping real estate associates up to date on the latest loan products and the many companies that underwrite them. Many will agree that it is just too complex for real estate agents to be good at both sides of the deal. And certainly, a Realtor, for example, who will be paid commission on a sale only if our mortgage loan is approved and we can close the sale, has an added incentive to do whatever it takes to make sure our mortgage loan is approved.

To complicate the matter even more, during the housing bubble many builders opened their own one-stop shops, offering buyers incentives and more or less aggressively encouraging buyers to use these in-house services. While it is illegal to literally require buyers to use the builder's title or mortgage company, many builders offered to pay for the mortgage fees or title insurance, which often costs several thousand dollars, only if a buyer used the builder's in-house companies. In reality, this cost the builder nothing since he was basically paying himself. Most buyers, not realizing that that this would leave them with no one truly representing their interests, happily went along to save the money.

MORE ABOUT MORTGAGE FRAUD

Some of the key factors we've discussed and will discuss now that together are credited with having contributed to what appear to be historically high levels of mortgage fraud are recapped in the sidebar on page 96.

Mortgage fraud can be defined as any misrepresentation in the loan process made with the intention of influencing the lender's decision regarding the loan. The motive is to generate a profit by causing lenders to extend mortgage loan credit beyond that which they would otherwise have done, either in the form of a larger mortgage loan or different (better) mortgage loan terms, most typically a lower interest rate. There are two basics types of fraud, fraud for property or housing and fraud for profit.

Fraud for Housing

Fraud for housing, which according to the FBI accounts for 20 percent of all mortgage fraud, usually involves a single borrower attempting to purchase property for himself and, accordingly, involves smaller lender losses.[14] Perhaps the most common versions of fraud for housing we've all heard about involve misrepresentations about income, debt, down payment, or the property value made by borrowers on their loan applications. Terms like *liar loans* or *Ninja loans* have emerged to describe this type of industry-created fraud. Liar loan refers to low-documentation or no-documentation mortgages that we now know encouraged borrowers to lie about income, debt, assets, and other things on their mortgage loan applications because they knew they would not have to produce the documentation such as tax returns and pay stubs to prove that what was on their loan application was true. Ninja loans are loans that required no income, no job, and no asset verification. These are said to have self-induced fraud in the mortgage industry because

Some Key Factors That Contributed to Fraud

- Relaxed mortgage loan underwriting guidelines including stated income, and no documentation mortgage loan products based on lower-quality borrower credit.
- Little or no oversight of mortgage originators and appraisers.
- Borrower willingness to pay higher than usual mortgage origination fees since they were under the impression that they would be making plenty of money themselves on the real estate investment.
- The massive influx of new inexperienced mortgage brokers into the industry.
- Once mortgage loan originators became a supplier to Wall Street, new, often unregulated nonbanking companies jumped into the game of brokering and issuing mortgage loans, over time further weakening lending standards.
- The absence of scrutiny and an insatiable appetite for buying mortgage loans on Wall Street had a profound effect on mortgage loan originations. As originators discovered that investors would buy anything and they could literally flip a loan in a day, they naturally lowered standards.
- The shared perception among mortgage and real estate industry insiders that "everyone does it (fraud)," often encouraging borrowers by suggesting a fraudulent method to apply for a loan assuring borrowers and then looking the other way or even participating themselves in mortgage fraud.

again it now seems obvious that the industry knew it was encouraging borrowers to lie. In most cases of fraud for property, borrowers fully intend to pay their mortgages. Assuming they are able to do so, their fraud is seldom, if ever, discovered.

In fact, it is questionable whether the number of fraud-for-property cases are higher now than ever before or perhaps we are simply uncovering more of it as a result of higher delinquency and foreclosure rates. In the past, our strong real estate market hid a number of frauds that occur at the time a loan or mortgage is originated, including appraisal fraud or valuing a property for more than its actually worth. However, as the housing market changed and property values fell dramatically, borrowers who intended to pay their mortgages have become unable to do so. This has led various agencies to investigate and their investigations uncovered more fraud than had initially been estimated. A 2007 Litton Loan Servicing study showed that 18 percent of loans currently in default were on properties that were, much to the lender's surprise, entirely uninhabitable, vacant, or occupied by tenants when the loan application said the property was to be owner-occupied.[15] Among the most common forms of mortgage fraud for housing involve loan originators falsifying W-2s, tax returns, and other proof of borrower income along with borrowers who claimed that they will occupy homes that they actually plan to rent or immediately resell. Again, banks give more favorable mortgage loan terms to borrowers who will be occupying the property—less down payment, lower interest rate, and so on—because lenders believe a borrower is less likely to walk away from the property if it is where he lives. But as we have learned, borrowers wanting the benefit of these better loan terms, even if they do not plan to live in the property, simply lie. Among borrowers in foreclosure or faced with fraud-for-property allegations, many claim to have been counseled by their mortgage loan originator to make false statements or provide false income figures because "everyone does it." People who would never steal cash or property seem hardly to hesitate in committing mortgage fraud, instead justifying it as an anonymous act against a rich lender. The prevalence of mortgage fraud has bred a generation of mortgage loan originators who believe that these schemes were the industry norm and therefore acceptable. The sidebar on page 100 explains some of the ways you can spot mortgage fraud.

Some Common Fraud-for-Profit Schemes

The Flip

In the popular deception known as the flip, a buyer contracts to purchase a property for its actual market value. A second buyer contracts with the first buyer to repurchase the property from the first buyer for more than what it is actually worth. Loan originators and property appraisers often work together to document the inflated property values and dupe the lenders into making mortgage loans based on the unreal second purchase value and concealing the real first purchase value from the lender. When the new loan is approved, the buyer and seller split the difference between the inflated value and what the property is actually worth.

The Straw Buyer

In straw buyer loans, the borrower may be completely fabricated. For example, one scam involved second mortgage and real estate professionals working together. The gang would hire a homeless person, and create a false name, driver's license, social security card, and identity for him. A bank account would be set up in the "straw" borrower's name. One member of the gang would then contract to purchase a home for market value (for example, for $100,000) with the real seller. That buyer would then contract to resell the same home to the straw buyer for a much higher price (say, $175,000). Another gang member, often a licensed appraiser, would then falsify an appraisal to provide to the lender. Another gang member, this one a mortgage loan originator, would submit the straw borrower's loan application to the lender. When the loan closed, the gang would pocket the additional $75,000. The straw borrower would of course never move into the property or make any mortgage payments. Lenders would not discover the fraud until they noticed that even the very first mortgage loan payment was never made, collection notices were being returned indicating that the home was unoccupied, and collection telephone calls to the number provided on the straw buyer's loan application revealed that the number was not in service.

Silent Second

With the *silent second,* the buyer borrows down payment funds from the seller or someone else but the bank believes the borrower is using his own money for the down payment. Remember, banks approve loans based on the risk. If a borrower has his own money invested in the property, there is less risk that he will walk away from the loan than if the seller has provided the down payment vis-à-vis a second mortgage the lender has not been informed of.

Fraud for Profit

Fraud for profit is usually a larger scheme involving multiple mortgage loans, bigger losses, and mortgage or real estate industry insiders; sometimes several work together as co-conspirators, and therefore it traditionally draws more attention from regulators. Some prevalent variations of fraud for profit include *flipping*, *straw buyers*, and *air loans*. Appraisal or valuation fraud is almost always an element when large mortgage losses occur.

Professional involvement in mortgage fraud is not limited to mortgage brokers and appraisers; real estate brokers and title companies are also being accused of participating in or at least blindly ignoring mortgage fraud. Entire businesses have emerged based on these sketchy practices. For example, The Formula, a Florida-based organization, allegedly enabled home builders to meet construction loan presale requirements (in other words, as we said before, a certain number of homes had to be committed to buyers before initial construction could begin), by signing up large pools of investor-buyers who were willing to enter sale contracts. Seldom did the lenders know that the builders had agreed to enable The Formula to flip all the contracts. In other words, the "buyers" represented to the lender to be people who would buy the homes once they were built, but in truth, they were not real buyers at all. As long as the new construction condo market stayed strong, The Formula investors were able to flip (resell) their contracts, actual condo buyers could then close on their units before their construction loans came due, and the lack of full disclosure to the lender was inconsequential. When the real estate market unraveled, so did The Formula.

Mortgage Fraud "Red Flags"

- The buyer wants to re-sign the purchase contract with higher prices after the parties have already agreed to terms (but you don't get to keep the additional money).
- The deal is structured in a way that there will be money going back to the buyer, often without the lender's knowledge.
- You are being asked to do something that is outside of the closing or not in the paper work.
- The sellers show payoffs for unrecorded or undocumented debts on the settlement statement.
- The sellers agree to pay amounts to the buyers or other third parties.
- Contractors who help home owners find loans for home improvements they can't comfortably afford to pay for.
- Something just doesn't "feel right."
- If someone tells you "we do this all the time," remember that doesn't mean it's legal to do.
- Buyer, Realtor, or mortgage loan originator insistence on using a specific appraiser.
- Commission is based on something other than the contract purchase price.
- The Realtor, mortgage loan originator, or other party (buyer or seller) asks you to sign a separate addendum that the lender cannot be shown.
- Anything that seems important but someone tells you the lender cannot know about may indicate fraud.
- If a deal seems too good to be true, it probably is.

Just a Cost of Doing Business?

For a long time, lenders have viewed mortgage fraud as an unfortunate cost of doing business. But as fraud continues to impact lenders in increasingly higher dollar amounts and involves actual damage to consumers in the form of increased servicing costs and delinquencies, this view is changing. According to the FBI's 2005 Financial Crisis Report to the Public and subsequent updates, approximately $1 billion worth of mortgage fraud was perpetuated in 2005, but industry experts later estimated actual losses at closer to $3 billion

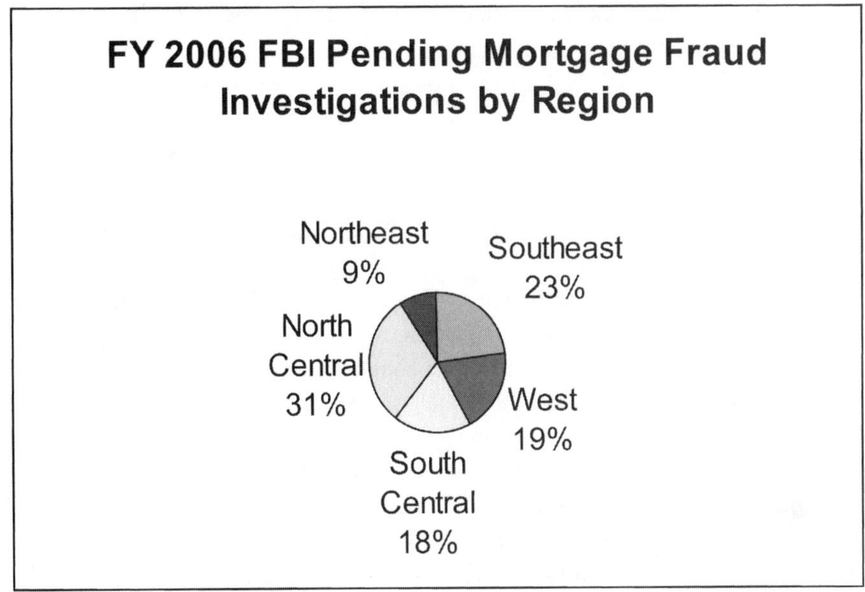

and it is likely that the number is even higher. Forty percent of subprime mortgages and 20 percent of less risky Alt A mortgages are estimated to have involved mortgage fraud. An estimated 60 percent of these fraudulent loans were broker originated. Top fraud hot spots have been identified as Arizona, New Jersey, Maryland, Florida, Illinois, Michigan, New York, Connecticut, and South Carolina. The pie chart above reflects FBI fraud investigations in each US region for 2006. Not surprisingly, these are also some of the states with the highest foreclosure rates. Adding to the problem of fraud is a lack of adequate coordination and communication between states. A large percentage of mortgage fraud is perpetrated by repeat offenders who are caught in one state and simply move to another.[16] The mortgage industry is just not efficient in sharing fraud information and hesitates to do so because of potential liability such as defamation and slander lawsuits by parties if for some reason allegations are not correct or cannot be proven.

THE BIGGER PICTURE

Comprehending the forces we've explored in chapter 3 is an important step toward clearly seeing the bigger picture crisis. From this new perspective we will now see how, in early 2005, our glorious real estate bubble sprung a leak, eventually bursting into a metaphorical geyser. The next chapter titled, "Pop," explains exactly what happened.

NOTES

1. US Census Bureau, "Census Bureau Reports on Residential Vacancies and Homeownership," October 6, 2007.

2. "HUD Gives Up on Zero Down," *National Mortgage News*, March 5, 2007, p. 20; Anna Bahney, "Most Americans Strain to Meet Housing Costs," *USA Today*, September 23, 2008, p. 3A; www.habitatla.com/habitatla/news/thrivent.pdf.

3. Lynnley Browning and Arthur Ochs Sulzberger Jr., "The Subprime Loan Machine," *NYTimes.com*, http://www.nytimes.com/2007/03/23/business/23speed.html?_r=1&scp=1&sq=The%20Subprime%20loan%20machine&st=cse (retrieved September 1, 2008); Arshad Masood, "The Limits of Offshore Outsourcing," *Mortgage Banking (News)*, March 7, 2007, pp. 70–79; Brenda B. White and Andy Woodward, "A Meeting of the Minds: The Council to Shape Change," *Mortgage Banking (News)*, February 7, 2007, pp. 19–20

4. Yuliya Demyonyk and Otto Van Hemert, "Understanding the Subprime Mortgage Crisis," *Working Paper Series*, Social Science Electronic Publishing, http://papers.ssrn.com/sol3/papers.cfm?abstract_id=1020396 (retrieved on October 5, 2008); S. A. Ibraham, "Managing Risk to Find Profit," *Mortgage Banking (News)*, February 7, 2007, pp. 22–24; David Henry, "How the Bad News Could Get Worse," *Business Week*, May 7, 2007, p. 35; John Mauldin, "$250 Billion in Subprime Losses?" *Weekly Newsletter*, June 29, 2007; David Lerech, "The Subprime Reckoning," *Realtor Magazine*, May 2007, p. 18; Carrick Mollenkamp and Ian McDonald, "Behind Subprime Woes, a Cascade of Bad Bets," *Wall Street Journal*, October 27, 2007, p. A14; Roger Lowenstein, "Subprime Times," *New York Times Magazine*, September 2, 2007, p. 11.

5. Edmund L. Andrews, "Blacks Hit Hardest by Costlier Mortgages," *New York Times*, September 14, 2005, p. 69.

6. Erik Eckholm, "Hispanic Homebuyers Pay Higher Interest a Mortgage Banking Study Finds," *New York Times*, June 1, 2006, p. 7C, "In Economic Slump, Hispanics Are Losing Tenuous Prosperity," *New York Times*, May 13, 2008, p. C4; Vivian Vasallo, "From Smith to Sanchez," *Florida Report 2007*; Jackson Clarion Ledger, "Minorities Pay More for Loans in 6 Cities," *New York Times*, March 9, 2007, p. C7; Neil J. Morse, "Getting Educated on the Ethnic Homeownership and Pricing Gaps," *Mortgage Banking (News)*, February 2007, pp. 133–41.

7. HUD, Center for Responsible Lending, Mortgage Banking Association, FNMA Freddie Mac.

8. "New Home Sales Fell by Record Amount in 2007," *Real Estate, MSNBC .com*, http://www.msn.com/id/22880294/ (retrieved June 1, 2008).

9. "FHA Mortgage Whistleblowers," http://whistleblower.ml-implode.com/.

10. www.frbsf.org/community/resources/wacraroundtable/hispanicpurchasing power.ppt.

11. www.fha.com/fha-programs.cfm.

12. Banking City Business Series, www.ifsl.org.uk/upload/CBS_Banking _2008.pdg (retrieved September 2, 2008).

13. Mortgage Bankers Association; National Public Radio, "Economists Brace for Worsening Subprime Crisis" (2008), http://www.npr.org/templates/story/story .php?storyId=12561184 (retrieved July 12, 2008). "How Severe Is Subprime Mess?" MSNBC.com, Associated Press, March 13, 2007, http://www.msnbc.msn .com/?id=11881780&q=How%20severe%20is%20subprime%20mess&p=1&st=1 (retrieved July 19, 2008).

14. FBI; "How to Spot Mortgage Fraud," *Florida Realtor*, January 2007, p. 12; "Loan Fraud Alert," *Realtor*, December 2006, p. 24; Anthony Carr, "Cash Back," *Agent Direct News*, February 2007, p. 5.

15. Litton Loan Servicing Study 2007, http://www.intervopice.com/downloads/ CS.LITTON811.12.13.07.pdf.

16. FBI, Jonathan Goodman, "Loan Fraud Alert," *Realtor Magazine*, December 2006, p. 24; Carr, "Cash Back" *Agent Direct News*, p. 5.

4

"POP"

We need to reset the clock back to the year 2004, when real estate sales were hitting record volumes. Prices were at an all-time high and the sexy investment condominium market was making headlines daily.

It was a surreal real estate market, especially in places like Miami and Las Vegas. These units were the perfect example of how much money could be quickly made in the market. Even folks who had never considered speculating on real estate investments were jumping into the game. First-time speculator Sandy Clark recounts her personal experience for you in the sidebar (see p. 106).

To some degree, the surge experienced in other market segments, first-time single-family homes, attractive Midwest locations, and the like can be traced to a highly contagious copycat mentality. In many places throughout the country, new construction developments sold out the first day, with units often put back on the market right away, at much higher prices because the demand for real estate was soaring. Contracts changed hands two or three times, each party taking a profit off the top, before a buyer who intended to keep the property stepped in. It was real estate gone wild. In the next sidebar (see p. 106), Carol Boyd tells us how her own family relied on bad advice and got caught up in the bubble.

Sandy Clark Remembers Her Experience as a Novice Bubble Speculator

"I'd just ended a relationship and moved to Las Vegas from Indiana. I had bought and sold a few homes in Indiana so I knew a little about real estate. The Nevada market seemed pretty hot so I decided to try my hand as a Realtor and maybe make some investments myself. I was only there a few months before things really started picking up. You could put a $10,000 deposit down on a condo and then sell the contract for $40,000 or $50,000 more in a matter of days. I realized I could make much more money doing that than selling real estate to other people.

After the first year I decided to invest a little more conservatively and actually buy a few condos to use as rentals. I was able to finance them without much money down so rather than just buy one or two I eventually bought seven. I was making a TON of money because the initial interest rates on my loans were so low. I grew up in a small town and am not a big spender. So rather than drive a fancy car or something, I just kept putting the profit into more real estate. I remember going home one Christmas and being introduced by my best friend from high school as a real estate millionaire. And on paper I was.

I don't know when everything first started to change but the last 2 years have been the most stressful time of my life. In the end I had $475,000 in total deposits on 4 condos. I'd planned to sell the contracts but couldn't find any buyers. I gave the developers 3 of the deposits to get out of the contracts. The fourth one said if I didn't close he would sue me. The price is $675,000. I can't get a loan and even if I could, the unit is worth maybe $450,000 now. The tenants in all but one of the condos I own have moved out. I'm trying to evict the last one because he's not paying rent. I paid a lawyer to negotiate with the banks to take the condos back and two of them will. But I have no money left to pay the lawyer anymore, so I'm not sure what I'll do."

Carol Boyd's Real Estate Frenzy

In the beginning of 2005 we were a family of three (my husband, my son, and myself.) I was expecting my second child. We were a normal working-class family. We owned a condo that we bought in 2002 and our loan was under $100,000. As a result, by 2005 we had a lot of equity. We started to think about buying a bigger house (our condo was a very small three bedroom) to accommodate our new family, which also included my mom, who was going to take care of our children. In my research I found a local mortgage company. I made an appointment and met with them in early 2005. Our plan was to sell our condo and buy a new house, and I wanted to find out about what kind of loans were out there. This mortgage company owned an impressive three-story beautiful building and apparently had been in business for a very long time; they also had a radio show about finances, mortgages, and investments, which I listened to.

After meeting with the broker our plans changed. The broker explained that we had a great opportunity. I had great credit so our current mortgage could be refinanced to a lower interest rate, I could also pull equity from my condo and receive cash which would allow me to buy an investment property that could be rented out. We were also introduced to the negative amortization loan; they called it "the investor loan." The way the loan worked was explained to us; we could refinance our current condo and put our loan in a negative amortization loan, cash out and put a down payment on an investment home, which would also be financed by a negative amortization loan. This way I could pay the minimum monthly payments (which is what investors do I was told) on both properties while I collected rent on both of the properties and basically the rent would pay the mortgages. I was told that real estate would go up for at least ten more years and that I should just rent my properties and not sell them. I was told that by 2010 I could retire!!!! It was difficult at that time not to believe all this, when everyone around us was making money in real estate. My neighbors were selling their home for $150,000 more than what they'd bought it for.

So toward the end of 2005 we bought our first investment home and rented it out. In the beginning of 2006, against what we were advised, we decided to put our condo up for sale; at this time we saw a downward shift in the real estate market but we were optimistic. In April of 2006, we received a written offer for our condo that we accepted. We had been looking for a house to buy and live in for almost a year. In May of 2006 we found the house. We decided to move forward with financing (our current condo was under contract), the bank approved us, and the closing date was scheduled. I closed on my new home in July and not long after that the offer on my condo fell through. By the end of July we received a second offer on our condo, which we accepted. This offer fell through in August. Property values were going down and banks were not financing as easily anymore. Now we've got three properties. Our interest rates have gone up to the point where we can'teven afford one of the mortgage payments, no less three. We have no idea what we're going to do.

Q: HOW DO YOU SPOT A BUBBLE? A: WITH 20/20 HINDSIGHT

Even in the middle of it all, some of us wondered where it would end. It doesn't take a genius to see that prices cannot appreciate that quickly indefinitely, especially when salaries and qualified buyers don't increase proportionately. US home prices increased by 124 percent from 1997 to 2006. Prior to that the national median home price had gone up and down but remained at 2.9 to 3.1 times median household income. By 2006, the income to home cost ratio was a whopping 4.6.[1] Eventually buyers would have to just say no because the sales price would be too high. No one will ever know for sure exactly when we reached the tipping point at which the housing market fell to somewhere below the previously justifiable peak. But there came a time when prices grew so high and both real estate and the quality of CDOs fell so low that the wide disparity between the cost being paid and the value of the real estate being sold could no longer be denied. That's when buyers and investors flushed the proverbial toilet, the cycle reversed, and home prices started spiraling downward. Rather than enjoying a healthy real estate market that generated a constant stream of new mortgage loan originations, that in turn fed Wall Street's desire to turn these mortgage loans into tradable securities that promised to pay dividends to those who invested in them, thereby allowing mortgage loan originators to replenish the amount of mortgage loan money available to make more mortgage loans to prospective new home owners, the exact opposite began happening.

REAL ESTATE'S "HIDDEN" COSTS

Unlike other types of investments, real estate requires an eventual user. At some point, someone has to want to take occupancy and live in the unit, at least for a little while. To do so, that someone has to be able to afford it. Whereas stock valuations are based on objective components of a company's financial statements such as revenues, assets, and inventory, home values are determined at least in part by what buyers are willing to pay, which makes real estate more susceptible to the irrational exuberance witnessed between 2003 and 2006 when housing prices seemed to be escalating to heights unknown. But unlike stock, owning real estate entails *carrying costs*, those unavoidable repeat expenses incurred in connection with owning the property. And unlike stock and other investment vehicles that increase in value without triggering corresponding increases in other costs to the owner, growth in real estate values triggers increases in its carrying costs. As demand-driven real estate values go up, so do the property taxes, insurance costs, and, in the case of condominiums or association-governed properties, fees that are linked to the valuation of the property.

Real Estate Tax Costs

Local county taxing authorities calculate property real estate taxes in order to raise funds sufficient to cover the annual county budget. The tax rates for specific properties are expressed as *annual millage rates* (aka mill levy or permille meaning amount of tax per thousand currency units of property value). The property's assessed value multiplied by the property millage rate, then divided by 1,000 equals the real estate tax for that property. For example: If your property is assessed by the county to be worth $150,000 and the county millage rate has been set at .15, your real estate tax bill would be $150,000.00 × .15 ÷ 1,000 or $2,250.00. The county property appraiser's office periodically values, or reassesses, each property within the county based on that property's fair market value. However, properties are also reassessed each time they are sold since the sale price indicates a property's then-current market value. Therefore, as a property's sales price increases, so does the property's real estate tax. Across the nation, the rise in home values during the bubble has sharply boosted property tax bills. According to the US Department of Commerce, the average annual property tax burden in the United States stood at $1,132.00 per home in 2005, up 10 percent from 2000.[2] In some regions, housing prices rose too quickly for local property assessors to keep pace. Ironically, real estate reassessments and corresponding tax increases are only now catching up, at a time when home owners, already in dire financial straits, can least afford it and as the properties themselves are now decreasing in value. Because decreases in property values are not reported as transactions, as property sales are, they do not automatically trigger a reassessment downward, meaning the tax rate may remain the same, based on the higher value when the property was last sold, unless the owner petitions the county and contests the higher taxes.

Insurance Costs

Insurance premiums, too, are based in part on purchase price and loan amount. Higher real estate purchase prices translate to higher insurance premiums. Many owners of condominium units that were built between 2003 and 2006 are shocked to learn that their assessments, which often include insurance pass-throughs (i.e., insurance costs the developer or association has to pay but has legally arranged to require the home owner to reimburse or has "passed it through" to the home owner), are higher than anticipated, creating a further burden for owners and a deterrent for possible buyers.

As properties were repeatedly sold and resold at higher and higher prices, carrying costs also climbed, eliminating more and more potential home buyers who could afford to purchase and own those properties. Even without other contributing factors, high real estate taxes coupled with scarce and costly insurance and other carrying costs would have been sufficient to start a slowdown in the housing markets. Over time, real estate once attractive to possible end users became increasingly less so as housing prices continued to rise and the carrying costs of ownership increased to the point of becoming prohibitive. In some cases, existing residents relocated out of increasingly expensive areas for the same reason, adding unanticipated supply to the market. Around the same time real estate carrying costs were inching their way upward, other notable occurrences happened. The Federal Reserve, fearing that housing costs could cause inflation, began increasing its interest rates. In the old Rust Belt of Ohio, Michigan, Illinois, and Indiana, job losses in the automotive and related industries were having a flattening effect on area economies. Once oil prices soared, gasoline prices started to spike, and increased energy prices had Americans tightening their belts. In the Southeast, hurricanes and tropical storms intimidated some would-be buyers. The Northwest dealt with unusual floods, California suffered an early and severe wild fire season, and Tornado Alley through the nation's midsection was particularly active and destructive. Beginning in 2005, the more obvious succession of human-made simultaneous events we've been discussing in the real estate and lending markets and on Wall Street began to feed and exacerbated each other.

THE LAW OF SUPPLY AND DEMAND

As real estate demand began to slow, builders were still flooding the market with new units they had just completed. Fundamental principles of supply and demand soon took over. Investors were unwilling to put money into new home construction until the market sold its existing inventory of housing. Increasingly fewer end-user home buyers stepped in. Unprepared speculative buyers who had planned on flipping their contracts began having to actually make good on what they thought were merely going to be paper purchases. Some elected to walk away instead, leaving hefty deposits on the table and creating issues for builders and lenders, who saw construction stop because they no longer had enough units purchased in advance to satisfy the lender's presales requirement under the terms of their construction loans. Homebuilder D. R. Horton initially reported a 48 percent cancellation rate, while Beazer Homes posted a 68 percent rate. Earnings were suddenly down 84 percent at Toll Brothers, the nation's largest luxury home builder.[3] This dramatic decrease in new home construction was caused by both fearful buyers and those who could not sell their existing homes or who were unable to find suitable financing to close. Builders cut prices to move unsold units, leaving those investors who had previously closed on units unable to compete for buyers against prices lower than what they'd paid. Some builders conducted well-publicized auctions, dumping inventory at fifty cents on the dollar, explaining that they simply had to make payroll. Housing projects that prohibited short-term rentals required investors to choose between continuing to try to sell their units and committing to long-term rentals. Because many of these units were sold decorator ready, without floor coverings and other finishing touches, those investors who elected to rent out their empty units to help cover carrying costs were faced with additional expenses. Many blame the media for worsening the panic. Certainly banner headlines deepened buyer apprehension, increased investor fallout, gave people reasons to hold off on buying a house in the hope of further price reductions, and helped jump start the overall domino effect.

MAIN STREET PROBLEMS REACH WALL STREET

As the housing market cooled, we began seeing an ever-increasing number of financially strapped investors and borrowers who had bought more real estate than they could afford, and may have taken on even more credit card debt to finish and furnish their properties. They were caught in the middle, having left themselves little room for error, unable to sell or refinance and make their debt load more manageable. The mortgage loan defaults that followed were the beginning of the end, as CDOs began unraveling, Wall Street's demand for CDOs withered, and loan originators found it increasingly more difficult to sell mortgage loans in the secondary market to replenish funds available for loans to new borrowers and the mortgage credit available to potential borrowers tightened. Adjustable rate mortgages began adjusting. Falling prices, difficulty obtaining financing, and the growing challenge of selling their own homes further spooked potential buyers. The sentiment, in general, was one of wait and see. Why buy now when the home will cost less tomorrow? As prices continued to fall, the equity we had in our homes shrank, leaving many of us *upside down*, or owing more in mortgage principal than our property was actually worth. This further diminished our chance of refinancing when our ARMs adjusted to the higher interest rate we'd planned to avoid.

LOAN SERVICERS ARE SIMPLY NOT PREPARED

Financial innovation, marketing and sales, often get ahead of the operations and delivery mechanisms necessary to regulate, monitor, and service the market. Lenders and mortgage loan servicers continue finding themselves underequipped to handle the increasing number of mortgage loan defaults as the surge in foreclosures continues adding to the glut of homes already for sale, further depressing already declining property values and escalating the overall doom and gloom. According to the Mortgage Banking Association, in the past those who serviced mortgage loans began by taking slow action at around 45 days after a delinquent payment is noticed. Today that happens at a maximum of 30 days, with some reaching out to borrowers as early as 15 days. Some creditors are even calling borrowers considered high risk days before their payments are due just to remind them to make the payment on time. How this will be impacted by promises by lenders to prioritize modifications and stop foreclosures has yet to be seen. When a borrower misses three payments, the gloves generally come off and they're notified that the bank intends to foreclose. Mortgage loan servicing is no longer a collection tool, but rather a real effort to get everything lined up for foreclosure and to prepare home owners for moving out quickly. Servicers are on an aggressive campaign to cut their losses, expanding from an average 7 calls per month for past due accounts to 30 or more. This, in turn, drives up loan-servicing costs. Today, subprime loan servicing costs have more than doubled.[4]

Mere Capacity Is Also an Issue

Current risk management practices (i.e., the procedures lenders and mortgage loan services have in place to make sure we pay our mortgage loans and minimize their losses) may not fully address the entire set of risks inherent in nontraditional and subprime mortgages. In other words, the risks that we will not pay our mortgage loan are different for nontraditional mortgages like subprime and Alt A loans, than they are for more traditional mortgage loans, such as 30-year fixed rate loans, and lenders and mortgage loan services may not have the procedures in place to address this. Mere capacity is also a key issue. Many who service mortgages have failed to update their methods to keep up with this different loan origination environment. Overburdened, insufficiently trained staff members frustrate parties on both sides of the collection telephone call. The debtor is nagged and embarrassed by frequent calls, and creditors are frustrated by debtors dodging their telephone calls and responding defensively to aggressive efforts to obtain payment. The various levels of services have not heretofore had to work together as quickly, as often, and as efficiently as the volume of delinquent mortgage loan debtors now demands. Costs are being further driven up in the face of an apparent inability to look beyond the outdated business model to find new ways to save people's homes. Some of the rigid procedures are unproductive and waste precious time, while regulators impose unrealistic deadlines often prohibiting finding solutions that could have otherwise saved people's homes. Differences in procedures, relationships, and infrastructure from one organization, vendor, state, and regulatory body to the next, as well as state-to-state bureaucracy, discourages efforts to pool resources and craft universal solutions.

Default Servicing

Traditionally, once it is clear that a borrower will not be able to pay a mortgage loan, lenders have put a great deal of pressure on their mortgage loan servicers (and yet another layer of professionals brought in when a mortgage loan goes into default, the mortgage default servicers) as well as the attorneys to get the property through the foreclosure process and resold to pay off the mortgage loan as quickly as possible. There are two primary reasons for this. First, some borrowers are notorious for trashing the homes their lenders are going to take back from them. They remove everything of value including appliances, air conditioning units, and light fixtures, often taking their anger and frustration out on what's left by breaking windows and damaging walls and flooring. Abandoned vacant properties then naturally attract more attention from vandals. Second, loans listed as in default or in foreclosure require lenders to increase their reserves for regulators (a topic we will explain in more detail in chapter 5). Some lenders have gone so far as to penalize their foreclosure attorneys with reduced pay if the foreclosure process extends beyond a certain amount of time. Government-sponsored enterprises will require that their foreclosures be completed within a certain amount of time and for a certain set fee, meaning that if the foreclosure takes longer, the attorney is not paid for the additional time. The bottom line is that this puts a great deal of pressure on anyone involved on the lender's side in the foreclosure process. We'll discuss in chapter 8 how this dynamic is changing as some lenders realize they may not be able to resell the foreclosed real estate due to an illiquid market.

Compromised Safeguards

Pressure on mortgage loan servicers to speed up the foreclosure process together with the dizzying number of new foreclosure cases may be the cause for the number of alleged inappropriate shortcuts in proper procedures. One circuit court judge who asked to remain anonymous shares her frustration in the sidebar on page 115.

Questions surrounding data accuracy and inquiry process diligence have arisen. Left unchecked, with seemingly insurmountable workloads and insufficient resources, there is a tendency for mortgage loan default servicers to circumvent important safeguards. For example, toward the end of a foreclosure case, the lender needs to provide the court with an accurate accounting of the total amount of all principal, interest, default interest, advances, fees and other costs due from the borrower. This is important because it will be the total amount for which the borrower is liable. When the

Foreclosure Judge's Insights

"The number of foreclosure cases we all have now is beyond absurd. Everyone's doing the best we can but no one feels they can be as thorough as they'd like. The entire foreclosure process is taking two or three times as long as it used to because there's only so much time in a day for hearings and sales and only so many rooms to hold them in. All in all, everyone's being pretty patient and understanding. Everyone is doing the best they can to chip in, like they would in a natural disaster or something. I had a case here yesterday where the borrower, who spoke very little English, showed up with his Realtor who showed me a contract offer for a short sale, the borrower owed the bank $375,000. The offer was for $175,000, based on what I've seen, the bank will probably take it. The problem was this Realtor showed me calls and letters he'd been sending to the bank for seven months with no response. The lawyer for the bank was there. He said he never heard a word from his bank client about the short sale offer. His marching orders were to foreclose on the property. So I told the bank's lawyer he needed to talk to his client and see if they can work out a deal. I can't force the bank to take less than what they're owed but I can help bridge this communication gap and ask them to resolve it without the court before they come in here. Unfortunately, it doesn't seem those systems are in place. The left hand is not talking to the right and the home owners are stuck in the middle. Hopefully, this guy claiming to be the Realtor is not a scam artist."

property is sold at the foreclosure sale, if the property does not sell for that amount (and nowadays it seldom does), the lender may be able to sue the borrower for the difference. Obviously, these "total debt certifications" must be prepared immediately before they are due to the judge in order to be as current and accurate as possible. But examiners have reported repeated abuses. For example, incidents of presigned total debt certifications, meaning they are being prepared in advance, probably to save time and ease workload, but therefore may not be current and/or accurate.

With the entire foreclosure process, explained in more detail in chapter 6, stretched by sheer volume, from default notifications to real estate owned (REO) property valuation and preservation through resale, efficiencies are lost, resulting in higher losses to us and our lenders and lower foreclosure sale prices, driving the real estate market even further down. Unfortunately, many borrowers in default certainly cannot afford an attorney and have no other advocate.

THE MODIFICATION CATCH-22

Those struggling home owners who seek mortgage relief may hear a tough message from their mortgage loan servicers, who remain justifiably wary of cutting interest rates, extending amortization periods, or forgiving debt as long as borrowers are still current with their payments. Help may not be an option unless a borrower first falls behind on his payments, which creates a dilemma given that mortgage loan default immediately triggers all kinds of other problems such as kinks in the borrower's future FICO score (making us less credit-worthy and subject to higher interest rates on future loans), increases in credit card interest, and other charges. Some mortgage companies won't even consider a mortgage modification until a customer defaults on three separate occasions. For those who are in desperate need of financial counseling to salvage their debt situation, such a policy almost encourages them to fall behind. Changing the interest rate on a home loan is time consuming and costly. Lesser changes may not be considered loan modifications under the servicing and pooling agreements. For example, getting a borrower current by adding past due payments that are owed in to future mortgage payments over time is technically considered a forbearance as opposed to a modification. In other words, if you are behind by $10,000 and do not have $10,000 to pay all at once, your lender might allow you to add $208.33, assuming you can afford that, to your mortgage payment each month for four years. This foreclosure alternative will be discussed in more detail in chapter 6. Many borrowers would benefit exponentially from the relatively small amount of education required to know where these lines are drawn and what to ask for.

Securitization Makes Modification Difficult

Those who service loans point to delocalization and the way home loans are packaged and sold on the secondary market as the problem. Fifty-six percent of all outstanding loans today have been pooled into CDOs, versus only 12 percent in 1980. What was once a simple relationship is now a complex structure involving many parties. Because many loans are held not by federally insured banks or thrifts, but by aggressive hedge funds and investors pushing hard to stop their financial bleeding, the industry has tied its hands by packaging loans and selling them in pools. Only an estimated 5 percent of loans can be easily modified.[5]

Since the loans are no longer owned by their originators but are sold worldwide as securities, the servicers who collect payments for a fee often define their service as maximizing return for the loan owners. As such, these servicers have to make sure that they can defend their actions, including any loan modifications they might attempt to make. Servicers fear that their decision to enter into modification agreements will be challenged by investors asking if the borrowers were truly not able to pay. Investors are naturally concerned about frivolous, dishonest claims. Until now modified loans averaged around 2 percent, but these altered loans may prove to be the only viable strategy, since as many as 50 percent of all home loans are in or at risk of default.[6] Adding to the confusion is the fact that the steep rise in second mortgages (loans taken against equity in a home) has lenders fighting with each other over which creditor has the right to modify a loan and who has the right to equity in cases of foreclosure. At the same time, other lenders are reaching out to some borrowers in the hope of fending off foreclosures. Included as appendix F is an example of the loan modification offers some lenders are making. Shortly before it was acquired, the lender Countrywide had announced that it was prepared to actively refinance or restructure $16 billion in loans with rates adjusting by the end of 2009. Since then, not all borrowers who have tried to modify their Countrywide loans have had success, or even a pleasant customer service experience.

BUY-BACK DEMANDS

Often mortgage loan defaults or foreclosures trigger buy-back demands in the pooling and servicing agreements between mortgage originators, servicers, and investors, particularly if fraud at the origination stage is discovered. A buy-back, again, may be compared to returning a faulty product to the store where you bought it. The store will, if you follow their return policies, refund your money. Lenders more or less guarantee investors that the mortgage loans they sell are in compliance with applicable regulations and will be repaid. Essentially, the guarantee is that there is no fraud, an accurate appraisal, appropriate underwriting standards, and the loan documents are complete and accurate. Like a store's return policy, most buy-back agreements have requirements that must be met. Specifically, the loan must go into default within a certain time after it is closed (normally 3 to 6 months) or otherwise violate the guarantee.

As borrowers, our ability to obtain a modification to our mortgage loan may be tied to something as irrelevant to us as the date the lender transferred our loan to the mortgage servicing company or pooled and sold it to an investor or how many other borrowers might have requested a modification before we did. Borrowers who obtained loans from lenders willing to modify may remain in their homes while borrowers with loans from banks not equipped or willing to modify may lose theirs, serious consequences that are nothing more than the luck of the draw. Between 2003 and 2006, many of these buy-back agreements were revised to place more risk for mortgage loan problems on the lenders selling them and thus be more appealing to secondary market investors for the purpose of generating quicker sales and higher prices for the CDOs based on the mortgage loans. Some of these buy-back relationships lacked transparency and created additional layers of conflict. One example of this potential conflict is that not everyone who could potentially be impacted knew that a buy-back agreement existed, what it said, or how it could potentially play out. For example, most of Countrywide's loans are serviced by its own home loan servicing unit. Because of this relationship and the underlying buy-back agreements, the home loan servicing and default servicing unit have less incentive to help troubled borrowers, because doing so would likely trigger a quality control review of the loan documents. If the review reveals a breach of one of the buy-back guarantees, this could put its parent company, Countrywide, on the hook to buy back the loans. Compare this to what is the wrong way to handle the situation but the way Countrywide may have a financial incentive to see it play out, namely, by just letting the borrower default, foreclosing on his home, and keeping the loan off their investor's quality compliance review radar screen. It is likely that Countrywide put this language in its agreements as an incentive to make its mortgage pools more attractive to investors and generate more money for Countrywide when they were sold. Market research says banks received roughly $35 billion in subprime revenue during the bubble.[7] Agreements for pools backed by mortgages issued by Fannie Mae and other government-sponsored enterprises also now typically include such buy-back language. Likewise, under some agreements the amount of loans that can be modified in any pool is limited to 5 percent unless the mortgage borrowers are in default or about to default.[8]

Repurchase Demands Can Be Devastating

Buy-back provisions have had dire consequences on mortgage originators already strapped with reduced funds available to loan. Repurchase demands from Morgan Stanley, Citigroup, Goldman Sachs, Bank of America, and others hastened the decline of a subprime market that was unprepared for the hit. By March 2008, buy-back demands were five times as prevalent as they were a mere six months earlier. Risky loans today are already estimated at $600 billion, more than six times that of the last subprime cycle in 1998. Analysts originally estimated that it would cost more than $1 billion if lenders were forced to buy-back only 1 percent of these loans. Five percent would cost more than $6 billions. In 2007, twenty-five of the most active subprime originators closed shop or filed for bankruptcy protection.[9] Companies that had been the biggest source for mortgage loan originations, companies that had been acquired by Wall Street firms only a few years earlier, began shrinking. Lehman Brothers, which is no longer with us as it was then, but which acquired BNC Mortgage in 2004, let twelve thousand employees go. Accredited Home Lenders stopped taking US home loan applications and cut its staff in half to cope with the credit market turmoil. Substantially all of its retail lending closed and the company elected to trade $1 billion in home loans to an investor in exchange for the right to buy them back later at a premium.[10] This complex deal essentially protected the lender from loans that were losing their value while offering the chance to turn a profit if the market improved. The overall effect on consumers was to reduce even further the mortgage loan options available, thereby driving real estate sales and prices down even more, forcing foreclosures and eventually tightening credit another notch on Wall Street.

FACING THE MUSIC

In chapter 1 we discussed how, as borrowers we are our own worst enemies. In chapter 2 we talked about how many of us just don't take the time to become educated about our mortgage loans and often trust the wrong folks. We tend to do the same thing when we run into trouble paying our mortgage loan, we stick our head in the sand. This lack of understanding and awareness of better possible mortgage loan alternatives and foreclosure avoidance, and, when we do have a problem paying, deliberate delay of inevitably having to deal with it, often facilitates our own financial demise, driving costs up even further.

Unlike a stock market crash that happens relatively quickly, forcing us to reckon with it, the real estate downturn has been a slow and painful financial death. Many borrowers cashed out their real estate equity with expensive home equity loans in order cover mortgage payments and avoid default, only to find that had they sought bankruptcy protection they may have preserved these valuable assets. We naturally tend to avoid bad news, confrontation, and unpleasantness. Creditors certainly fall into this category. Collection personnel historically have lacked compassion and the personal touch normally deemed appropriate in stressful, emotionally charged circumstances. Banks, in particular, are associated with age-old inflexible attitudes. They make us feel embarrassed, angry, defensive, and helpless. In their defense, many banks will agree that next to meter maids, collections employees are top on the public's list of people to despise, but someone has to do it.

Since 2006, an entire industry has blossomed around helping us further delay the inevitable. The number of Web sites appearing in response to a simple Google search of the word "foreclosure" has grown exponentially. Some offer valid assistance, solutions that can help us save our credit scores and our homes; others merely aim to generate a profit at our expense, suggesting they can arrange the impossible—a low-cost refinance, a quick sale, settlement with our lender, or merely buy us more time-to delay the agony. In reactionary mode and desperate to believe, some of us are at a loss when it comes to spotting the difference between a legitimate offer and a scam. Filing bankruptcy can also delay foreclosure by imposing an automatic "stay." When there is a bankruptcy, everything, even a foreclosure case, stops until the bankruptcy judge decides how it should be handled. Lenders, eager to recoup money tied up in bad loans, find that today's foreclosure environment is a fight all the way.

AMERICANS LEARN ABOUT FORECLOSURES

The Center for Responsible Lending (for a detailed explanation of who they are and what they do, see appendix E) has conducted studies showing that for every home lost to foreclosure, the values of surrounding homes within a mile decrease by 1 percent. Nationally, foreclosures were initially predicted to cause US property values to sink by a total of $223 billion, with the most severe impact being felt in minority communities. The historic average for foreclosure is only 1 percent of all mortgages.[11] By December 2006, Treasury Secretary Henry M. Paulson Jr. publicly announced at an Office of Thrift Supervision meeting that mortgage delinquency and foreclosure rates were on the rise and worried that "the impact could be greatest on low-income families" that took out higher-interest and more risky loans. This prediction is proving to be correct. Increases in delinquency rates have been noticeably larger for subprime loans, particularly subprime ARMs that have adjusted. By January 2007, America's foreclosure rate was one filing for every ninety households, driven primarily by slow housing sales and mortgage payment increases on riskier loans. In chapter 8 we discuss more specifically how high this is likely to grow. In an economically challenged areas like Detroit the rate was one in every twenty-one households, four and a half times the national average. During 2007, nearly 1.3 million properties were in the process of foreclosure, up 70 percent from 2006.[12]

Experts originally predicted that more than 2 million Americans would lose their homes and as much as $164 billion of wealth in the process, estimating that 20 percent of all subprime mortgages would end in foreclosure.[13]

The surge in late payments and defaults on subprime and slightly less risky Alt A mortgages quickly reverberated up the chain to Wall Street. As early as November 2006, an article in *Asset Securitization Report*, advised that subprime pools for that year were the poorest-performing loans in history. Issuance of securities backed by subprime mortgages fell by more than half in 2007, as originators ran into trouble placing new securities with investors. Analysts warned that subprime and Alt A mortgages accounted for 25 percent of all mortgage-backed securities.[14] The danger for Wall Street was obvious: Would lenders be left holding billions of dollars in subprime mortgage loans that they had hoped to sell to investors while at the same time other lenders that were trying to return poorly underwritten loans to the mortgage originators were having difficulty doing so? Even if some of the loans were protected with buy-back agreements, experts were beginning to worry that their former owners would not be around to buy them back.

THE RATINGS AGENCIES FINALLY REACT

The ratings agencies that helped catapult the CDOs industry suddenly downgraded the ratings for major originators like New Century Financial resulting in a 69 percent decrease in the value of its assets and eventually led to that company's demise. Accredited Home Lenders and NovaStar faced a similar fate, being downgraded to "sell" and seeing values immediately drop 27 and 41 percent, respectively, before eventually being forced out of business. Lehman Brothers, once a leader in packaging subprime mortgages into securities, shut down its home-lending unit, taking a $52 million charge against earnings. Fremont, barred by regulators from offering mortgages to borrowers with poor credit, agreed to sell its subprime holdings for an expected $100 million pretax loss. Hard hit by mortgage market turmoil, the now defunct brokerage firm Bear Stearn's hedge fund fell 23 percent between January and April 2007. Concerned that an internal hedge fund at Bear Stearns wouldn't be able to meet obligations, Merrill Lynch, one of the fund's biggest investors, seized $400 million worth of assets in preparation to auction them off, a move that threatened to trigger dissolutions of other funds that had made questionable bets on the subprime market. At the same time, Bear Stearns scrambled to sell hundreds of millions of dollars in bonds to satisfy demands for cash and assets from its creditors to stave off liquidation. In total, between the third quarter of 2007 and the second quarter of 2008 the agencies lowered ratings on $1.9 trillion in mortgage-backed securities.[15] Having to sell higher-quality mortgage bonds to cover lower-quality losses eventually had dire consequences on the company. Some feared the move could spur other lenders to seize hedge fund assets of other firms. Especially concerned were the other funds that were eventually forced to "mark to market" or lower the value of their own assets when the Bear Stearns sale fetched bids below what the funds said their Bear holdings were worth. Who suspected that in a matter of months, Bear Stearn and other Wall Street giants would change forever?

Some of the Major Headliners . . . So Far

The second quarter of 2008 brought with it a succession of rapid-fire impacts that, despite the warning signs, somehow seemed unreal. Lenders, ratings agencies, investors, and consumers alike responded by hunkering down. Government, big banks, and even investment icon Warren Buffett stepped up. Some of the leading stories are recapped for you here.

Countrywide. Are Our Nation's Big Banks Becoming "Too Big to Fail"?

The breaking news headliners began with Countrywide's estimated liability for mortgage loan repurchase claims resulting from alleged fraud and early defaults climbing from $365 million a year earlier to $935 million. Experts estimate Countrywide buy-backs tripled in one year. With $133 million already paid out, it was determined that a sale of Countrywide to Bank of America, worth approximately $4 billion, was the best alternative. While these numbers sounded big, they paled in comparison to some of the headliners that followed. Bank of America will benefit from Countrywide's extensive retail, wholesale, and distribution networks, with more than 1,000 field offices to add to Bank of America's 6,100 banking centers, a leading mortgage technology platform, and a well-known brand in home lending. Countrywide also serviced about $1.5 trillion with 9 million loans in its portfolio. The transaction price presumably reflected the challenges Countrywide had faced within the housing and mortgage industry and was the beginning of what has since become a pattern of consolidation of midmarket banks into a handful of our nation's largest banking institutions. Some fear a second wave of ever larger failures if these mammoth acquirers cave under the burden of the bad assets acquired with the good. Others say our country's largest banks are now becoming too big to ever be allowed to fail.[16]

Indy Mac. Are the FDIC Pockets as Deep as You May Think?

The Federal Deposit Insurance Corporation (FDIC) was established in 1933. In 1937 it served as user interface between 77 insured banks that failed and the American public. In 1969, the insured account limit was raised to $20,000 in order to keep up with the times, and in 1980 it was raised to

$100,000 for the same reason. The FDIC intervened in 1982 and 1984 when more banks failed and again in 1988 when the S&L crisis brought down 423 banks and thrifts. In 1991 another 121 banks failed. In July 2008, the FDIC became conservator for Indy Mac Bank, the fifth but most publicized bank to fail in 2008 as a direct result of the subprime crisis. As conservator, the FDIC will operate Indy Mac to maximize value for an eventual future sale. Few will deny that the initial news stories, complete with images of folks standing outside locked Indy Mac bank branches wondering how they would get their money, were eerily reminiscent of Depression era photographs. The FDIC initially estimated, the cost to stabilize and dispose of Indy Mac would be between $4 and $8 billion. But losses so far are closer to $9 billion and that does not take into account Indy Mac's estimated $500 million in uninsured deposits. As of this writing, 14 other US banks have failed. With over 8,000 banks remaining and 150-plus deemed "troubled" by the FDIC, that number will, no doubt, grow. The $100,000 deposit cap the FDIC insures was recently temporarily raised to $250,000. Of concern is the little known fact that the FDIC only has about $1 for every $100 of deposits it insures. No one has lost money on an FDIC insured deposit in seventy-five years. But, in real numbers, this translates to $4.5 trillion in our deposits insured by the FDIC with only $45 to 50 billion in actual funds available to it at the moment to make good on that insurance should things ever get that bad.[17]

Bear Sterns. What Happens When the Government Steps into Uncharted Territory?

The March 2008 financial headlines were all about Bear Sterns. More accurately, the buzz was over how the federal govenment responded to the Bear Sterns drama. During the weeks that followed, the rest of us learned how Bear Stern's demise unfolded. This series of events was to be repeated in the lives of other firms to follow.

Apparently rumors that Bear was strapped for cash had been proliferating Wall Street. Bear Sterns was sitting on almost $50 billion in mortgages and mortgage-backed assets. But no one knew their true worth. Twenty-nine billion dollars were valued using computer models derived from some kind of observable market data. The other $17 billion were based on internally developed models. No doubt the new "mark to market" accounting rules are to blame for much of the continued problems. Again, these rules require firms to value holdings with no current buyers, such as subprime mortgage related holdings, at fire sale prices, even though they may be worth more in the not to far off future. Things began to unravel when Moody's downgraded mortgage backed securities issued by a Bear affiliate in response to concerns that the underlying home loans were at greater risk of borrower default than originally estimated. The market value for Bear Sterns' shares plummeted. What began with one European lender telling the company that it would not be renewing a $500 million loan due later that week, snowballed into other nonrenewal notifications on loans that the company needed to fund it's daily operations. It wasn't long before the cost of five-year contracts to protect against default on Bear Sterns' debt rose to a point notably higher than what investors were paying to insure against Bear Sterns' competitors, a clear sign that the market had decided things were heading south for the firm. Institutions that had bought *credit default swaps*, insurance policies designed to protect against corporate bond defaults, were scrambling to undo those trades as the firm's ability to pay claims grew increasingly more doubtful. Eventually Bear experienced a full-fledged "run on the bank."

Up until this point, average folks like us had no idea how leveraged institutions like Bear had been allowed to reach such a perilous point, but the market insiders understood. Bear Sterns had borrowed more than thirty times the value of its actual equity base. Despite the lack of transparency to which much of our current problems are attributed, we know that for the insiders, Wall Street is built on trust. Billions of dollars in securities are traded each day in reliance upon a mere implied understanding that trading partners will pay up. Bear Sterns' experience highlights the fact that, when Wall Street investors become concerned that a partner won't honor this understanding, the investors simply take their money and go home.

In no time at all, Bear Sterns called in the Federal Reserve in the hope that the Fed would accelerate a special program for lending to investment banks set to begin shortly. With lenders refusing to replenish necessary financing, it did not take Bear Sterns long to blow through its cash reserves. At that point, then Federal Reserve chairman Benjamin Bernanke initiated a conference call with top officials, including Timothy Geithner, then president of the Federal Reserve Bank of New York, and then treasury secretary Henry Paulson, to discuss what would happen if Bear Sterns were simply allowed to collapse, a move that seems to have since become standard operating procedure. Word has it that the phone call focused on concern that this one failure could spread. Wall Street firms like Bear Sterns conduct business with many individual, corporations, financial companies, pension funds, hedge funds and the like, exchanging billions of dollars with each other daily. Normally when a Wall Street firm fails, the Securities Investor Protection Corporation (SIPC) steps in to take over customer accounts. But this time regulators feared they were facing further potential widespread deterioration in multiple markets that they would not be able to predict, no less control. As we've all heard, some experts feel many of our financial institutions have, arguably, become too big to allow to fail.

The decision was made that government needed to step in. Only a week before the end, Bear Sterns put out press releases assuring the world that "There is absolutely no truth to the rumors of liquidity problems." At the end of the day, a deal was crafted whereby J.P. Morgan agreed to take over Bear Sterns with money backed by the US government. Because J.P. Morgan settled transactions for Bear Sterns as a main clearing bank, it was in a better than average position to assess the collateral Bear Sterns could provide against a loan. Most significant is the fact that this was the first time since the Great Depression that our government made a commitment of this nature to an entity other than a federally regulated bank, "back stopping" or guaranteeing to limit losses on $29 billion worth of troubled assets. The authority to do this was extrapolated (some say by too much of a stretch) under the Federal Reserve Act, which allows government to lend to nonbanks under "unusual and exigent" circumstances. Investors who had purchased credit insurance on the Bear Sterns deals were happy to get new, more solid, debt obligations from the acquirers. The story further fueled the constantly growing distrust and animosity toward those Wall Streeters who have walked about with millions, sometimes billions even after what most of us would consider big-time screw-ups on their part. The immediate losers were those who had speculated against Bear Sterns, and Bear employees who never saw it coming.

The fear was that this decision by the Fed would open the floodgate for federal loans due to the countless "unusual and exigent" circumstances we may potentially encounter over the coming months and years as a result of the crisis, backed by our taxpayer money, to nonregulated, for-profit institutions. Compounding that is the long-term possibility of added risk from "moral hazard" or the appearance that rewarding reckless behavior may have on our nation's financial well-being.[18]

UBS. Insider Bidding, How Much Will What We Don't Know Hurt Us on Wall Street?

Auction-rate securities, a popular derivative strategy among tax-exempt borrowers like our nation's cities and counties, are designed to help local governments, schools, museums, and hospitals lower their borrowing costs by borrowing for the long term at lower short-term interest rates. The interest rates reset at weekly or monthly auctions. The money comes from investors who buy bonds backed by payments from the public entities at designated interest rates determined by investor bidding at auctions.

More than $500 billion has been loaned to public entities using this strategy. Normally, the interest rate paid by the public entity and the interest rate paid to the investors move in sync. However, during the summer of 2008, investors became nervous and demanded a higher interest rate in return for the added risk they were taking by investing their funds, given the subprime crisis and problems on Wall Street, causing these two interest rates to diverge and the bond issuers to pay much higher rates to investors than they were getting. Some public entities were forced to pay the higher interest rates to borrow, and some may be forced into bankruptcy. Others will cut back on the services they provide to us. One example is highway safety rangers, the guys who drive tow trucks on our nation's highways and come to our rescue when we break down or have an accident. Some counties have now cut back the hours that this assistance will be available and are charging drivers who we need to use them.

But the immediate story was more about the fact that insiders at UBS were accused of, unbeknownst to investors, bidding at their own auctions in order to prop up and maintain the market impression that the auction-rate securities were desirable and, therefore, keep demand and prices stable and so mislead investors about the safety of these investments. At Merrill Lynch, since acquired by Bank of America, client monthly statements reflected these securities as "other cash." The majority of marketing materials reflected the securities as AAA rated. UBS is accused of having bid at its own auctions in 69 percent of almost 60,000 auctions between 2006 and 2008. UBS, like others, paid brokers an unusually high 0.25 percent for selling these securities in comparison to 0.05 percent for selling Treasury securities and 0 percent for selling its clients traditional money market funds. In a settlement with regulators, UBS agreed to buy back $19 billion of auction-rate securities from investors who claim to have been misled. Other firms, including Citigroup who will be paying $100 million in fines, reached similar settlements as we learned that the practice had become a widespread, even standard, operating procedure for doing auction-rate security business, which begs the question, what else happens on Wall Street without our knowledge?[19]

The good news is that the negative press and fines may cause some of these firms to make some internal changes to avoid this type of occurrence in the future. Selling off or separating some of their riskier divisions, organizational management revisions designed to improve communication, and revising bonus structures to be more consistent with accountability and client outcomes could all be moves in the right direction. Bank of America, for example, now reflects the value of auction-rate securities on client statements as "not available," meaning they are not valued but not worthless.

Lehman Brothers. Government "Just Says No."

Described as a "controlled demise," mid-September 2008 saw 158-year-old Lehman Brothers file bankruptcy. As has come to be the pattern, overt events began with a series of emergency meetings at the Federal Reserve building in lower Manhattan, this time called by Fed officials with then treasury secretary Henry Paulson in attendance along with top bankers. Faced, after Bear Sterns, with the question of where to draw the line on government intervention into Wall Street's affairs with our money, this time the bankers were told the government would not bail out Lehman. It was up to Wall Street to solve the Lehman problem itself. Without the government to count on, Lehman scrambled for a buyer as its stock tumbled and funds headed for the door. Barclays and Bank of America considered a transaction but eventually declined. Bank of America pulled out when the government refused to take any responsibility for losses on some of Lehman's most troubled assets as it had done when J.P. Morgan Chase bought Bear Sterns. Barclays' proposal involved separating out Lehman's bad divisions, which would be absorbed by a group of Wall Street banks, with Barclays buying the parts that performed well so that taxpayer money would not play a role. Eventually Lehman was forced into a bankruptcy it will not likely survive. Ten banks agreed to create an emergency fund of $70 billion to $100 billion that financial institutions can use to protect themselves from the Lehman fallout.[20]

Merrill Lynch. When Volunteering to Be Acquired Beats the Alternatives

Lehman's troubles forced ninety-four-year-old Merrill Lynch's leadership to take a hard look at its own situation. A look that, in not much time, resulted in the decision to offer itself up for sale. The buyer was Bank of America. The price tag was $50 billion, a big drop from the $100 billion offer Merrill had turned down less than a year earlier. With 17,000 brokers, 60,000 employees in total, Merrill had the largest brokerage force in the country. Together with the Countrywide deal, this acquisition made Bank of America the biggest brokerage house and consumer banking franchise in the nation.

AIG. Should Our Government Own an Insurance Company?

In mid-September 2008, ratings agencies threatened to downgrade American International Group's (AIG) rating if it did not immediately raise $40 billion to offset losses caused in large part by mark to market accounting requirements. Within a few days, the number had climbed to $75 billion. The company's stock was already down 94 percent for the year. The firm had hoped to raise funds by selling off certain of its businesses but suitors had backed out. The troubles traced back to AIG Financial Products (AIGFP), a relatively small division of AIG that had allegedly found a way to make a quick buck on the back of AIG's solid credit rating and strong balance sheet as a seller of credit default swaps. There was fear that AIG's weakness could force losses on US, European, and Asian financial institutions that had bought the credit default swaps. Banks and mutual funds, major holders of AIG debt, would also take the hit if AIG failed. Goldman Sachs was AIG's largest trading partner. An AIG collapse could have cost Goldman $20 billion. The government tried to get private sector money, but when that failed it decided that AIG's failure would be "catastrophic" and stepped in, seizing control of one of the world's biggest insurers in an $85 billion deal. But this time the Fed drove a hard bargain, getting a 79.9 percent equity stake in the form of "warrants." Warrants are the right to buy a company's stock in the future, usually at a price higher than it's value today. The purchase of warrants is to allow the warrant holder an opportunity to benefit from the company's growth and profitability. The two-year loan will pay a solid interest rate to the government and is secured by AIG's assets, meaning that if AIG rebounds, taxpayers could earn a big profit.

AIG will sell certain assets in a orderly fashion. But most significant is the fact that the AIG deal put the federal government in control of the insurer, a historic move in that AIG isn't directly regulated by the government. Once again, the Fed got authority under the Federal Reserve Act, which allows it to lend to nonbanks under "unusual and exigent" circumstances.[21]

Money Market Funds. To Insure or Not to Insure, That Is the Question

During the last week of September, the $62 billion Primary Fund, a New York money market firm, "Broke the buck." This term means that it's net asset value fell below the minimum $1 per share most money market funds maintain. This well-established and expected minimum is what has historically given money market funds their reputation as conservative, safe, reliable places to keep money. In fact, money market funds are restricted by federal regulations and can only invest in vehicles deemed conservative. The decline in value at Primary Fund was attributed to soured investments in Lehman Brothers' debt. The Primary Fund had $785 million in unsecured debt issued by Lehman, which mark to market accounting forced it to write down to $0. At the time, the Primary Fund had been left with $23 billion in assets, down from $65 billion in August, reducing its holdings to .97 for each $1 of investors funds. At the same time, the Reserve Yield Plus Fund and the Reserve International Liquidity Fund, two other well-established money market funds, also broke the buck. Together, these funds hold $3.5 trillion.[22]

Unlike savings deposits, money market funds are not insured by the FDIC. Because our nation's ten biggest money market funds hold 75 percent of all money market money, there is concern that breaking the buck by these three funds would cause a run on money market funds.[23] As a result, the government moved to provide $50 billion to insure money market funds. Unlike FDIC deposit insurance, which comes with a $100,000.00 cap since raised to $250,000.00, there is no cap on the dollar amount a depositor may have in a money market fund that is now government insured. However, the commitment to insure money market funds, as currently written, only applies to purchases made prior to September 19, 2009, and is a temporary fix that the government can elect to extend only up until September 2010.

Washington Mutual (WaMu). A Failure of Historic Proportions

Washington Mutual, the nation's largest savings and loan association, was founded in 1989 and tended, more than others, to cater to our country's middle class. More recently, one of the bank's top products was home mortgages, eventually leading the bank to become the nation's leader in servicing mortgages. The same strategy that allowed for the company's rapid growth, focusing on lower income borrowers, eventually caused losses that brought it down. On September 25 federal regulators seized Washington Mutual after a series of deposit withdrawals, and helped negotiate a deal to sell most of its operations to J.P. Morgan Chase, making this the largest bank failure in US history.[24] Some of the stories that have since emerged about just how lax WaMu's loan approval process had become would make any mortgage loan underwriter's hair stand on end. For example, borrower income verification, a crucial part of prudent loan underwriting that normally requires legitimate documentation, was allegedly reduced at WaMu to including a photograph of a pickup truck with the borrower's company name on it in the loan application file.

The Fight Over Wachovia, a Good Sign

Less than a month before the Wachovia Corporation's problems with mortgage-related loans became public, the biggest problem was finding anyone willing to step in and buy a firm in its dying hour. The fact that Citicorp and Wells Fargo both wanted Wachovia, our nation's fourth-largest bank, just days after WaMu's demise, was good news. And the fact that Citicorp was willing to pay $2 billion in a crunch, but Wells Fargo offered eight times that price, or $16 billion, when given a few more days to consider the asset, highlights the heavy toll urgent "fire sales" are taking on asset values. Under certain circumstances, merely buying a few days time can be significant. Wachovia's stock had been down almost 80 percent from a year earlier, but plunged 27 percent after the WaMu takeover. Wachovia's failure has been attributed in large part to its ill-timed 2006 acquisition of Golden West Financial Corp. Golden West was parent company to World Savings Bank, a lender know for creative home loan products such as the "pick a pay" and negative amortization loans, which provide terrific financial planning tools in the hands of borrowers who understood them but proved fatal to those who did not.[25]

WHAT IT MEANS TO BE "TOO BIG TO FAIL"

Perhaps the most common phrase on in Washington during the summer of 2008 was "Too big to fail." The phrase became the government's litmus test for when it would involve itself and taxpayer dollars in the business of business. But no one was clear where the feds were drawing the lifesaving line that would render a business too big to fail.

Until now, saving business was something other countries did (for example, Japan in the 1990s) and Americans shunned as contrary to the capitalism that is at the foundation of our country's economy. Letting weak companies fail is rule number one. But then Fannie Mae and Freddie Mac were saved because, you guessed it, they were too big to fail. Critics argued that, to the contrary, these entities were too big to save since doing so would either require the government to get more money from taxpayers or print more itself (which may debase the value of the dollar and encourage inflation, ultimately costing taxpayers more anyway). Apparently holding or insuring nearly half of the country's $12 trillion in home mortgages put Fannie Mae and Freddie Mac on the right side of the line.

Or is the real meaning of the phrase "too big to fail" more global? China, Japan, the Persian Gulf nations, and dozens of other foreign central bank and soverign wealth funds have hundred of billions invested in Fannie Mae and Freddie Mac bonds. The last thing the US Treasury wanted to do was to see our foreign allies sweat. We count on their investment funds to run our country; that's the now almost $10 trillion national deficit you hear about every so often. It's basically loans these foreign nations have made to us. Just as banks charge higher interest rates for higher-risk borrowers with low FICO scores and investors demand higher returns for high-risk securities, if the financial risk foreign countries take by investing in the United States increases, as would have been deemed the case if Fannie Mae and Freddie Mac failed, foreign investors may force the treasury to pay them higher interest rates on the next tranche of US Treasury bonds. This would, in turn, increase the cost of credit all Americans pay on homes, business credit, cars, student loans, everything. You and I, the average American consumers, as well as US industry are at the heart of America's global spending capacity. As long as we're spending money in their countries for the goods and services they import to us, presumably all will be well since they are essentially lending us back our own money. If American consumers stopped shopping, the world would feel it. But perhaps the bigger concern, certainly beyond the scope of this book, is that as our nation's deficit grows and foreign governments hold increasingly more of our debt, we should all be aware of the potential that someday they may decide to pull out. At least for the moment, where global economies are concerned, the United States itself is too big to fail.

It's a Small World after All

They say when America sneezes the world catches a cold. Four of the world's five largest economies—the United States, the Euro zone, the UK, and Japan—are now officially in a recession and markets are loudly pointing to a worsening forecast as a result of the US subprime crisis and its underlying causes. Britain, like the United States, is experiencing a housing downturn, tightening credit, and high commodity prices. More than 3,560 companies were forced out of business in England and Wales during the second quarter of 2008, a 15 percent increase over last year. Commercial property values abroad are falling to values lower than the loans on the property. With values falling and credit tight, transactions have all but stopped. Analysts predict that the UK real estate market will decline another 10 percent and remain under this cloud through 2010. Every region, with the exception of some of the oil-rich Middle Eastern and North African nations, is in a similar situation. Even Dubai's gold standard real estate market does not seem to be immune. That country's Real Estate Regulatory Authority (RERA) is cracking down on real estate flipping. Dubai real estate prices, up 79 percent since 2007, are also being driven to a great extent by speculation rather than market fundamentals. Some Dubai developers are likewise imposing resale rules requiring buyers to wait a year or until the purchase price has been paid down by at least 30 percent before reselling. The securities firm Morgan Stanley predicts that Dubai's real estate prices will fall as much as 10 percent within the coming year. The Fitch rating service says Dubai's commercial markets are likely to see corrections over next two years.[26]

OFF-BALANCE-SHEET TRANSATIONS IMPACT INVESTOR CONFIDENCE

It's not just talk of further write downs that's fueling the fear and caution in the markets. The real driver is uncertainty. A lack of transparency such as not making clear the types of assets a company holds and their likely market value in the mortgage securities industry has become apparent, but it's far from being resolved. Financial institutions, in particular, have been wary of disclosing much about their exposure to subprime-backed securities. No doubt they fear that investors will attempt to sell their shares to cut their losses and further devalue the remaining stock. It's a fragile, even dangerous situation. Some, like Merrill Lynch, may have tried to delay taking losses by using off-balance-sheet transactions with hedge funds, which the Securities and Exchange Commission is likely to examine. Off-balance-sheet transactions are permitted in some transactions in order to control liability risk that could hurt earnings or to take advantage of tax incentives. (But they can be abused as in the Enron case when they are used to make a company seem more solid than it is.) Merrill initially wrote down almost $8 billion in mortgage-backed securities in the third quarter of 2007 alone. Because home values had plummeted, the securities were no longer worth as much and investors bid the price lower. Merrill Lynch showed a $2.2 billion quarterly loss that resulted in the resignation of the company's CEO.[27] Initial losses were much bigger than even the firm's own experts originally expected but less than were expected to see before this is all over. The discrepancy probably stemmed from the use of computer models, the only way to price securities if there's no open market trading. We've discussed how computer models are used on Wall Street sometimes to replace human instinct, using mathematical formulas to transform historical trends into predictions upon which financial products are designed, rated, bought and sold. During the bubble, most lenders and firms instinctively used brighter assumptions than we would now deem prudent, making the model spit out higher values than today's gloomier scenarios would. Again, this inability or unwillingness to value existing and potential new-issue CDOs is causing illiquidity, an inability to sell assets in order to raise money and diminished credit availability for average people.

It has become clear that while bankers were adept at constructing and selling these CDOs, they weren't very good at valuing them. We explained in chapter 3 that ratings agencies grade the financial products produced by Wall Street. As of the first quarter of 2008, ratings agencies that evaluate the quality of securities had already downgraded more than $50 billion worth of mortgage-backed securities.[28] Even today the agencies are still saying they can't rerate some funds until they know for sure what the losses are. When funds lose their ratings, many institutions are forced to put themselves up for sale because their charters only allow them to invest in rated securities. This is the type of uncontrolled unwinding that Washington wants to protect us all from.

As we've said, as a result of higher risks in CDOs, investors are demanding higher returns, reducing CDO prices and making them harder to sell. Previously issued CDOs are almost impossible to sell, at least at prices their creators thought they would be worth. The quick action on Wall Street to stop backing subprime mortgages is blamed for freezing credit lines, and so the now reverse cycle of credit tightening repeats itself. As we will see in chapter 7, the fallout has since spread to other financing tools also tied to these investments. Unlike in the 1980s, when banks failed because of bad loans, there is a much larger pool of investors in all sorts of instruments (many of which few people realized were even tied to subprime mortgages in any way) holding the bag now.

Thanks to the especially heavy attention the media paid to the happenings we've discussed here in chapter 4, by the end of 2006 Americans knew there would be trouble. But we still had no idea how much trouble. And a lot of us still thought we'd be off the radar screen since we hadn't bought or refinanced any real estate in years. How did the factors we've discussed in chapters 3 and 4 end up playing out? Enter chapter 5 in our story "The Great American Awakening," or how we all came to realize that no one's coming out of this mess unscathed.

NOTES

1. Terry Sheridan, "Cash Strapped," *Daily Business Review*, May 1, 2008, p. 5; Paola Lupsi-Abbott, "Delinquency Deluge," *Daily Business Review*, May 2, 2008, pp. 1, 13; Jeannine Aversa, "Look for Signals of a Turnaround," *South Florida Sun Sentinel*, May 23, 2008, p. 3; Tom Lauricella, "Signs Say US Recovery Isn't Here," *Wall Street Journal*, August 11, 2008, p. 19; Peter Goodman and Amanda Cox, "A Slowdown with Trouble at Every Turn," *New York Times*, July 19, 2008, p. A10; Noelle Knox, "Foreclosure Proceedings Set Record," *USA Today*, September 7, 2007, p. A1; David Jaberi, "Helping Struggling Homeowners," *Mortgage Banking*, February 2007, pp. 42–47; Christopher Rubaber, "Cases of Mortgage Fraud Up, FBI Says," *Washington Post*, March 8, 2007, p. D4; June Fletcher, "The Custom McMansion," *Wall Street Journal*, July 24, 2008, p. D1, D3; "Mortgage Fraud," sherlterrock.com, FBI.com; Rachel Beck, "Homeowners Bail Loans Due to More Than Just

Mortgage Rate," *South Florida Sun Sentinel*, December 18, 2007; Anna Bahney, "More Americans Straining to Meet Housing Costs," *USA Today*, September 23, 2008, p. 3A; ATIF 2008 Real Estate Forecast, *National Economic Forecast*, January 2008; Lisa Prevost, "Confronting the House Loan Dilemna," *New York Times*, February 24, 2008, p. 19; John Leland, "Facing Default, Some Walk Out on New Homes," *New York Times*, February 29, 2008, p. 7; Michelle Archer, "Slump Hasn't Caused House Cost," *USA Today*, January 21, 2008, p. 6B.

2. US Department of Commerce Web site. Connor Dougherty, "States Slammed by the Shortfalls," *Wall Street Journal*, July 29, 2008, p. 1; Anna Bahney, "More Americans Strain to Meet Housing Costs," *USA Today*, September 23, 2008, p. 3A.

3. Michael Contery, "Hortons Cancellation Woes Construction Chill," *Wall Street Journal*, October 17, 2007, p. B9; Justin Lahort, "Why Investors May Want to Shun Builders," *Wall Street Journal*, September 27, 2007, p. C1; Jim Freer, "Levit Eliminates Jobs, May Sell Some Commercial Property," *South Florida Business Journal*, September 21, 2007, p. 4; Kelly Evans, "Decline in Home Prices Accelerates," *Wall Street Journal*, February 17, 2008, pp. A1, A14; Jonathan Clements, "Price Fixing: In This Market, Selling Requires Savvy," *MSN.com*, February 27, 2008, http://cc.msncache/cache.aspx?q=price+fixing+in+this+market+selling+requires+savvy&d=75332678272007&mkt=en-US&setlang=en-US&w=3953d662,88eaae5; Michael Corkery, "Beazer Restates Results for 9 Years," *Wall Street Journal*, May 13, 2008 ; Amy Merrick, "Drop in Home Prices Accelerates to 14.1%" *Wall Street Journal*, May 30, 2008, p. A3.

4. Mortgage Banking Association; Neil J. Morse, "Servicing's Tough New Challenges," *Mortgage Banking (News)*, February 2007, pp. 33–40; S. A. Ibraham, "Managing Risk to Fund Profit," *Mortgage Banking (News)*, February 2007, pp. 22–24; Gretchen Morgenson, "Foreclosure Hits, a Snag for Lenders," *New York Times*, November 15, 2007, pp.1–3; James Donnell, "Small Services Can Stay in the Game," *Mortgage Banking (News)*, March 2007, pp. 133–34; Brenda B. White and Andy Woodward, "A Meeting of the Minds: The Council to Shape Change," *Mortgage Banking (News)*, February 2007, pp. 19–20.

5. Ibraham, "Managing Risk to Fund Profit," pp. 22–24; Morse, "Servicing's Tough New Challenges, " pp. 33–40; Vikas Bajaj, "Assurance of Buybacks a Burden for Countrywide," *New York Times*, August 23, 2007, p. C2; "Investors Press Lenders on Bad Loans," *Wall Street Journal*, May 28, 2008, pp.C1, C4.

6. Ibraham, "Managing Risk to Fund Profit," pp. 22–24; Morse, "Servicing's Tough New Challenges," pp. 33–40; Bajaj, "Assurance of Buybacks a Burden for Countrywide," p. C2.

7. Bajaj, "Assurance of Buybacks a Burden for Countrywide," p. C2; Simon, "Investors Press Lenders on Bad Loans," pp. C1, C4; Gretchen Morgenson, "Borrowers and Bankers: A Great Divide," *New York Times*, August 2, 2008, pp.1, 2; David Whitford, "A Bank Built on a Bubble," *Fortune*, August 18, 2008, pp. 83, 84;

James R. Hargerty, "Countrywide Reaches Eye of Storm," *Wall Street Journal*, October 27, 2007, p. A3.

8. Bajaj, "Assurance of Buybacks a Burden for Countrywide," p. C2; Simon, "Investors Press Lenders on Bad Loans," pp. C1, C4; Morgenson, "Borrowers and Bankers: A Great Divide," pp. 1, 2; Morse, "Servicing's Tough New Challenges," pp. 33–40; Bob Brooks, "The Right Compliance Tools," *Mortgage Banking (News)*, February 2007, pp. 72–79; Jeff D. Opdyke, "Figuring Out Big-Mortgage Helper Plan," *Wall Street Journal*, March 22, 2008, p. A9.

9. Bajaj, "Assurance of Buybacks a Burden for Countrywide," p. C2; James R. Hagerty and Serena Ng, "Mortgage Giants Take Hit on Fears Over Capital," *Wall Street Journal*, July 8, 2008, p. A15; Conrad de Aenlle, "Good Banks Are Punished with the Bad," *New York Times*, March 15, 2008; p. B6; Jenny Anderson and Vikas Bajaj, "Behind Rescue Effort: Wall Street Domino Theory," *New York Times*, March 15, 2008, p. A12; Opdyke, "Figuring Out Big-Mortgage Helper Plan," p. A9; Morgenson, "Borrowers and Bankers: A Great Divide," pp. 1, 2.

10. Jenny Anderson, "Lehman Is Shutting Down Loan Unit," *Wall Street Journal*, August 23, 2007, p. 10; Kevin Kingsbury, "Accredited to Halt Home Loans, Cut More Than Half of Staff," *Wall Street Journal*, August 23, 2007, http://online.wsj.com/article/SB118778585156105263.html?mod=hpp_us_whats_news; Suzanne Craig, "In Subprime Retreat, Layoffs," *Wall Street Journal*, August 23, 2007, pp. C1, C4; Morse, "Servicing's Tough New Challenges," pp. 33–40; Morgenson, "Foreclosure Hits a Snag for Lenders," pp. 1–3; Simon, "Investors Press Lenders on Bad Loans," pp. C1, C4; Mark Fleming, "The New Risk Revolution," *Mortgage Banking (News)*, March 2007, pp. 87–93.

11. "The Biggest Housing Losers," *New York Times*, May 12, 2008, p. A14; Neil J. Morse, "Afraid to Call," *Mortgage Banking (News)*, February 2007, pp. 133–41; Vikas Bajaj and Ford Fessenden, "What Is Behind the Race Gap?" *New York Times*, November 4, 2007, p. 16.

12. John Mauldin, "$250 Billion in Subprime Losses?" *Weekly Newsletter*, June 29, 2007, p. 1; Alex Verza, "Foreclosure Filings Nearly Double," *Weekly Newsletter*, October 11, 2007; Paul Owens, "Facing the Pain of Foreclosure," *South Florida Sun Sentinel*, February 24, 2008, pp. 1A, 8A; David Jaberi, "Helping Struggling Homeowners," *Mortgage Banker*, February 2007, pp. 42–47; David Lereah, "The Subprime Reckoning," *Realtor's Magazine*, May 2007, p. 8; Carrick Mollenkamp and Ian McDonald, "Behind Subprime Woes, a Cascade of Bad Bets," *Wall Street Journal*, October 17, 2007, p. A14; Ruth Simon, "Mortgage Defaults Start to Spread," *Wall Street Journal*, March 1, 2007, p. D1; Marc Hochstein, "Foreclosures Overstated by Some American Banks," *Wall Street Journal*, March 9, 2007, p. 17; Noelle Knox, "Foreclosure Proceedings Set Record," *USA Today*, September 7, 2007, p. A1.

13. Henry Sender, "Hedge Fund Risky Bets Come to Roost," *Wall Street*

Journal, March 8, 2007, p. C1; James J. Cramer, "The Bear Stearns Bull," *New York Times Magazine*, March 31, 2008, p. 16; Gabriel Sherman, "Angry Bear," *New York Times Magazine*, March 31, 2008, p. 28; Al Shinklekirk, "Subprime Firms Five as Problems Rise, Mortgage Investors Flee," *Investors Business Daily*, March 6, 2007, p. 3; Vikas Bajaj, "Lender Stops Accepting Mortgage Applications," *New York Times*, March 9, 2007, p. C3; Kate Kelly, "A Subprime Fund Is on the Brink" *Wall Street Journal*, June 16, 2007, p. B1.

14. James Grant, "Why No Outrage," *Wall Street Journal*, July 19, 2008, p. 6; Judith Burns, "Unclear Review for Revamp: The Credit Ratings Firms," *Wall Street Journal*, March 22, 2008, p. A11; Nelson D. Schwartz, "Wait, Weren't These the Safer Bets?" *New York Times*, March 16, 2008, p. 2; Carrick Mollenkamp and Ian MacDonald, "Behind Subprime Woes, a Cascade of Bad Bets," *Wall Street Journal*, October 17, 2007, p. A14; Yalman Onaran, "Subprime Losses Top $379 Billion of Balance Sheet Marks: Table," *Bloomberg.com*, May 19, 2008, http://www.bloomberg.com/apps/news?pid=20601087&sid=aK4Z6C2kXs3A&refer=home (retrieved on September 1, 2008); "Investors Now Shrug at Debt Downgrades," *Wall Street Journal*, May 31, 2008, http://cc.msnscahce.com/cache.aspx?q=investors+now+shrug+at+debt+downgrades&d=775332920353456&mkt=en=US&setlang=en-US&w=d3018db2,5c269d80.

15. "Wait, Weren't These the Safer Bets?" p. 2; Omran "Subprime Losses Top $379 Billion of Balance Sheet Marks Table"; Nelson D. Schwartz, "What Created This Monster?" *New York Times*, March 23, 2008, pp. 1, 7; Jed Horowitz, "S&P Flags Goldman, Lehman," *Wall Street Journal*, March 23, 2008, p. A15; Conrad DeAenlle, "Thrown by Housing's Shaky Foundation," *New York Times*, January 13, 2008, p. 28; Michael S. Grynbaum, "Wall Street Wild Ride Believed to Be Far from Over," *New York Times*, January 19, 2008, p. C4; Floyd Navrs, "For Some Lenders the Risk Is Too Great," *New York Times*, March 15, 2008, p. 4; John Mauldin, "$250 Billion in Subprime Losses?" *Weekly Newsletter*, June 29, 2007, p. 1; Mollenkamp and McDonald, "Behind Subprime Woes, a Cascade of Bad Bets," p. A14; Noelle Knox, "Foreclosure Proceedings Set Record," *USA Today*, September 7, 2007, p. A1; Kate Kelly and Serena Ng, "Bear Stearns Fund Hurt by Subprime Loans," *Wall Street Journal*, June 13, 2007, p. 3B; Kingsbury, "Accredited to Halt Home Loans, Cut More Than Half of Staff"; Jenny Anderson, "Lehman Is Shutting Loan Unit," *Wall Street Journal*, August 23, 2007, p. 10; Jed Horowitz, "Merrill Defends Transactions," *New York Times*, August 28, 2008, p. 7C; Aparajati Saha-Bubna and Carrick Mollenkamp, "CDO Ratings Are Whacked by Moody's," *Wall Street Journal*, October 27, 2008, p. B1; Kelly, "The Fall of Bear Stearns," p. A13; Floyd Norris, "In Lehmans Fallout, Two Stars Are Given Lesser Roles," *New York Times*, June 13, 2008, pp. C1, C5; David Henry, "How the Bad News Could Get Worse," *Business Week*, May 7, 2007, p. 35; Ben Stein, "Tattered Standard of Rating on Wall Street," *New York Times*, September 20, 2008, p. 1C; "Bank Earnings, Housing Fears Take a

Toll," *USA Today*, November 17, 2007, p. 6B; Ian McDonald and Carrick Mollenkamp, "Banks Look to Salvage Profitable Funds," *Wall Street Journal*, October 26, 2007, p. C2; Peter S. Goodman, "This Is the Sound of a Bubble Bursting," *New York Times*, December 23, 2007, p. 7; Tim Paradis, "Slump Pushes Subprime Lenders to Precipice," *South Florida Sun Sentinel*, March 10, 2007; John Poirier, "FDIC Sanctions Fremont Over Subprime Loans," Reuters, March 8, 2007; Bruce Elder, "Property Drags Stocks Down," *Financial Times*, August 14, 2008, p. 28; Martin Arnold, "Questions Over Sectors Own Debt Purchase," *Financial Times*, August 18, 2008, p. 16; Andrea Tryphondes, "More Pain Seems Likely for Firms' Earnings," *Wall Street Journal*, August 11, 2008, p. 20; James Hagerty and Serena Ng, "Mortgage Giants Take Hit on Fears Over Capital," *Wall Street Journal*, July 8, 2008, p. A15.

16. "Bank of America Agrees to Purchase Countrywide Financial Corp.," *Newsroom*, January 11, 2008; Ruth Simon, "Bank of America Buys Stake in Countrywide," *New York Times*, January 11, 2008, p. 7C; "Assurance of Buybacks a Burden for Countrywide," *New York Times*, August 23, 2007, p. 4B; Robin Sidel, "Countrywide Reaches Eye of the Storm," *Wall Street Journal*, November 3, 2007, p. A4.

17. Kathy M. Kristof and Andrea Chang, "IndyMac Bank Seized by Federal Regulators," *Wall Street Journal*, July 12, 2008, p. 7C.

18. Kate Kelly, "Fear, Rumors Touched Fatal Run on Bear Stearns," *Wall Street Journal*, May 28, 2008; James J. Cramer, "The Bear Stearns Bull," *New York Magazine*, March 31, 2008, p. 16; Gabriel Sherman, "Angry Bear," *New York Times Magazine*, March 31, 2008, p. 4B; Kate Kelly and Serena Ng, "Bear Stearns Fund Hurt by Subprime Loans," *Wall Street Journal*, June 13, 2007, p. 3B; Kate Kelly, "The Fall of Bear Stearns," *Wall Street Journal*, May 28, 2008, p. A13.

19. Dakin Campbell, "Broker Dealers Face Auction Rate Failures," *Bond Buyer*, February 14, 2008, p. 10; Carrick Mollenkamp, "UBS Revises Its Practices to Reduce Risks," *Wall Street Journal*, August 13, 2008, p. 1; Jeffrey Goldfarb, "UBS Races to a New Future; It Is Dogged by Mistakes of Past," *Wall Street Journal*, August 13, 2008, p. 17; Liz Rappaport and Randall Smith, "UBS Takes $19 Billion Hit in Widening Auction Rate Scandal," *Wall Street Journal*, August 11, 2008, p. 17; Liz Rappaport and Randall Smith, "UBS to Pay $19 Billion as Auction Mess Hits Wall Street," *Wall Street Journal*, August 9, 2008, p. A8; Jack Rosenthal, "A Subprime Glossary for the Mortgage Scandal," *International Herald Tribune*, August 18, 2008, p. 7; Gretchen Morgenson, "Addressing Disclosure Backwater," *International Herald Tribune*, August 18, 2008, p. 11; Carrick Mollenkamp, "Pressure Grows for Big Changes Over UBS Woes," *Wall Street Journal*, August 11, 2008, pp.1–2.

20. Anderson, "Lehman Is Shutting Loan Unit," p. 10; Jed Horowitz, "Merrill Defends Transactions," *New York Times*, August 28, 2008, p. 1B; Norris, "In Lehmans Fallout, Two Stars Are Given Lesser Roles," pp. C1, C5; Horowitz, "S&P Flags Goldman, Lehman," p. A15.

21. www.reuters.com/article.wtmostread/idustre.

22. John Waggoner, "Reserve Primary Money Market Fund Breaks a Back," *USA Today*, September 17, 2008, p. 7.

23. Tara Siegel Bernard, "Money Market Funds Enter a World of Risk," *New York Times*, September 17, 2008, p. C1.

24. Sandra Block, "What's Next for Bank Customers at Failed Washington Mutual?" *USA Today*, September 30, 2008, p. 1.

25. Michael Corkery, "Wachovia Unloads Troubled Loans," *Wall Street Journal*, August 20, 2008, p. C12.

26. Peter S. Goodman, "Too Big to Fail," p. 4; Bruce Elder, "Euro Zone Ensnared in Global Slowdown," *International Herald Tribune*, August 15, 2008, p. 12; Chris Flood, "More Gloom to Increase Fears of Global Recession," *Financial Times*, August 1, 2008; Justin Lahart, "Global Economy Slows," *Wall Street Journal*, August 15, 2008, p. 1; Marcus Walker, "Éuro Zone GDP Shrinks in New Signs of Global Downturn," *Wall Street Journal*, August 15, 2008, p. 28; Lawrence Norman, "UK Divided on Mortgage Reforms," *Wall Street Journal*, August 11, 2008, p. 21; William Boston, "More Trouble Looms for UK Property Firms," *Wall Street Journal*, August 13, 2008, p. 28; Stefania Bianchi, "Dubai Property Sector Loses Luster," *Wall Street Journal*, August 13, 2008, p. 17.

27. Conrad DeAelle, "Thrown by Housing's Shaky Foundation," *New York Times*, January 13, 2008, p. 28; Grynbaum, "Wall Street Wild Ride Believed to Be Far from Over," p .C4; "Merrill Defends Transactions," *New York Times*, August 28, 2008, p. 1B; Saha-Bubna and Mollenkamp, "CDO Ratings Are Whacked by Moody's," p. B1; Nelson Schwartz and Julie Creswell, "What Created This Monster?" *New York Times*, March 23, 2008, http://iepecdg.com/DISK%201/Arquivos/Leiturassugeridas/080323_What%20Created%20This%20Monster_%20NYT.pdf.

28. Horowitz, "S&P Flags Goldman, Lehman," p. A15; Jenny Anderson and Vikas Bajaj, "Behind Rescue Effort: Wall Street Domino Theory," *New York Times*, March 15, 2008, p. A12; DeAelle, "Thrown by Housing's Shaky Foundation," p. 28; Grynbaum, "Wall Street Wild Ride Believed to Be Far from Over," p. C4; Saha-Bubna and Mollenkamp, "CDO Ratings Are Whacked by Moody's," p. B1; Bruce Elder, "Property Drags Stocks Down," *Financial Times*, August 14, 2008, p. 28; Judith Burns, "Unclear Review for Revamp; the Credit Ratings Firms," *Wall Street Journal*, March 22, 2008, p. A11; "The Biggest Housing Losers," *New York Times*, May 12, 2008, p. A14; "Investors Now Shrug at Debt Downgrades"; Henry Snyder, "Hedge Fund Risky Bets Come to Roost," *Wall Street Journal*, March 8, 2007, p. C1; Al Shinklekirk, "Subprime Firms Dive as Problems Rise, Mortgage Investors Flee," *Investors Business Daily*, March 6, 2007, p. 3.

5

THE GREAT AMERICAN AWAKENING

Because it reflects the biggest picture, we'll begin our discussion of America's awakening with the impact that being a foreclosure nation has on our general economy. Mortgage default rates have clearly shaken our nation's financial institutions. The fallout continues to spread beyond lenders and borrowers and CDO investors. It's influencing how much we spend and where we spend it in the general economy. Collateralized debt obligations can be compared to a cancerous mole that appears months, sometimes years, after the cancer has taken hold and spread, in this case to credit default swaps, auction-rate securities and into an entire financial system we will discuss shortly.

EMPLOYMENT

One traditional economic indicator, a type of market MRI that helps identify the cancer, if you will, is employment statistics. We discussed visible employment reductions in construction businesses in chapter 4. Levitt and Sons, and Toll Brothers—two of this country's largest builders—initially cut their workforces in half. Six out of every ten new American jobs created during the real estate bubble were real estate or mortgage-related. Hundreds of thousands of financial service jobs have been lost. Residential Capital, the home lending arm of GMAC Financial Services and its former crown jewel, for example, reduced its work force by 25 percent not long after, and over and above the thousand jobs it had already cut due to reduction in available mortgage funds to loan and thus less need for staff to do so. The next major job fallout was on Wall Street with more than 2 million jobs cut as of November 2008. The graph below illustrates job loss in Florida (one of the hardest hit states) and the nation as a whole. The next graph illustrates the reverberations that construction losses are generating in the economy in one state. Levitt, of course, subsequently filed bankruptcy notwithstanding the job cuts. In the third quarter of 2008, US job losses averaged 199,000 a month. During the fourth quarter that number had increased to an average of 510,000 jobs lost each month.[1] According to sources at economy.com, our nation's unemployment rate is expected to rise to 7.3 percent by the end of 2009. Still not even close to the 25 percent unemployment during the Depression, but some fear if the situation is not well managed, we may be headed in that direction.

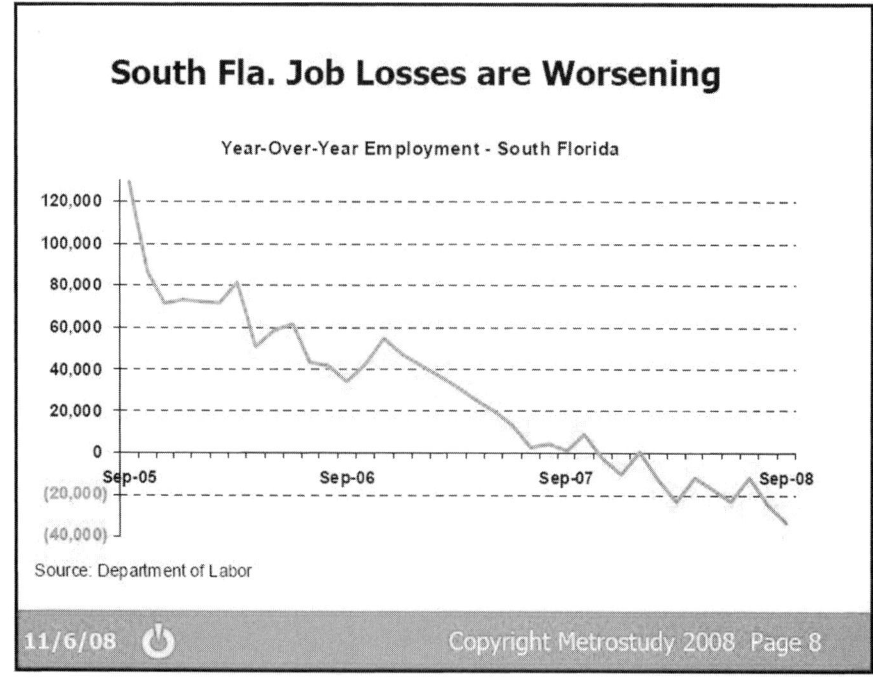

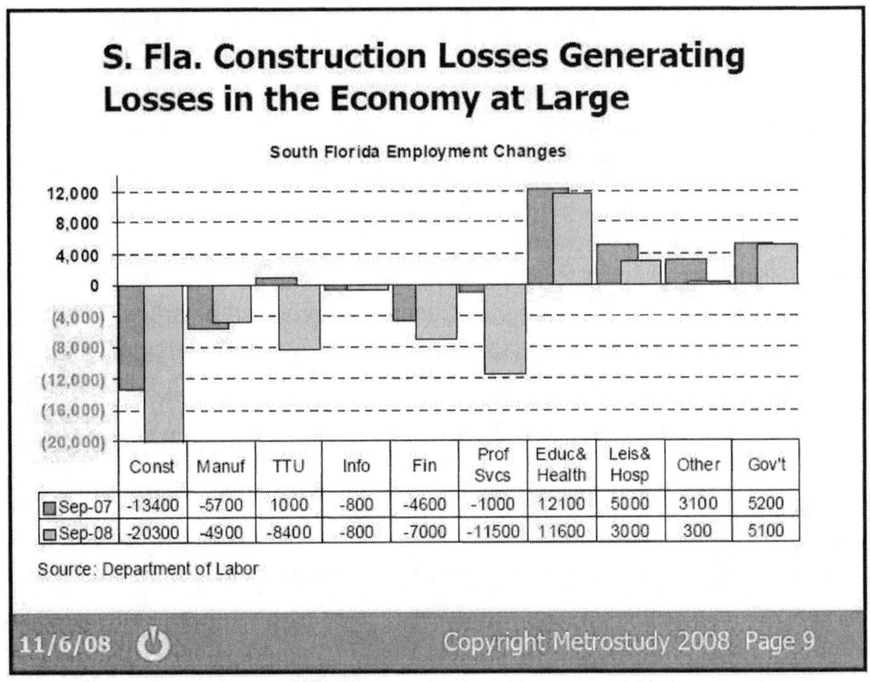

	Const	Manuf	TTU	Info	Fin	Prof Svcs	Educ& Health	Leis& Hosp	Other	Gov't
Sep-07	-13400	-5700	1000	-800	-4600	-1000	12100	5000	3100	5200
Sep-08	-20300	-4900	-8400	-800	-7000	-11500	11600	3000	300	5100

THE CYCLE: UNEMPLOYMENT BEGETS LESS CONSUMER SPENDING, AND LESS CONSUMER SPENDING BEGETS MORE UNEMPLOYMENT

The unavoidable impact on consumer spending, reduced GDP (explained below) and corporate profits, which, in turn results in even more jobs lost, is a logical consequence. But there have also been less obvious impacts. For example, within weeks of the crisis spreading to Wall Street, computer giant IBM saw sales to its biggest consumer segment, the financial industry, fall dramatically as lenders battled their subprime problems, As we mentioned earlier, major retailers like Sharper Image, Linens n Things, Lillian Vernon, and Circuit City, and more recently the travel and automotive industries, are publically feeling the pain. When we stop spending money with companies like this, some will file bankruptcy and vacate retail spaces, eventually taking a toll on commercial real estate as well. The companies that supply businesses with goods and services will, of course, be impacted, meaning more job losses. The process is not merely trickling down; it is gushing. Job loss begets curtailed spending in every area that relies, directly or indirectly, in whole or in part, on consumers receiving their paychecks, which in turn begets further job loss. These businesses must also reduce their spending, which in turn spreads the impact further, to other businesses and their spending and employment rosters in an endless cycle. Not to mention the losses incurred by those of us with stock in these companies. Since January of 2008, investors in US corporations have lost $8 trillion on paper.[2] The largest declines came near the end of 2008, as investors decided that our government's efforts to fix the problems weren't exactly working as they'd planned. The good news is that the cycle of US borrower confidence can, theoretically, reverse itself in virtually the same manner, though typically not as quickly. Consumers normally lose confidence and panic easier than they regain it. Hence all the talk we've been hearing about the importance of consumer confidence in our economic recovery.

As of the beginning of 2008, the combined effect on overall consumption and future lending attitudes by financial institutions had reduced manufacturing business activity by about 5 percent and is expected to have a negative effect on US gross domestic product (GDP)—the sum of all goods and services bought and sold in this country—and our economic growth generally.[3] This is the reason the United States is now officially in a recession until

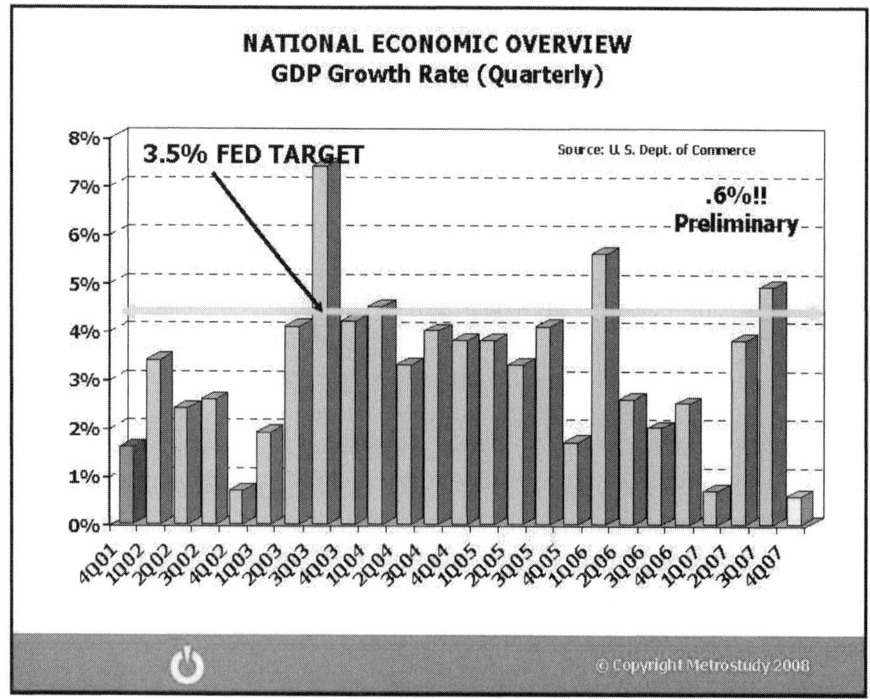

consumer confidence is restored. A *recession* means our GDP reflects a loss for two consecutive fiscal quarters. The Fed's target GDP rate for 2008 was 3.5 percent, but our economy is clearly contracting. A graph reflecting GDP trends is included for you here.

THE CREDIT CRUNCH BROADENS

Like mortgage credit, business credit, even for bigger companies, is now markedly more difficult to obtain and just at a time when it is most needed. When sales are temporarily down, smaller businesses in particular rely more heavily than usual on credit. Thirty percent of small entrepreneurial business owners tap into their home equity for capital to start up businesses, cover temporary shortfalls, buy equipment, expand, or hire more staff. When the subprime markets imploded and home prices slipped, lenders made it far more difficult for entrepreneurs to borrow against their homes to feed their businesses. Three years ago, Bank of America had a program that allowed business to borrow up to $100,000 in an unsecured line of credit, even if the borrower had been in business for just one day. The bank's portfolio of small business loans increased by 30 percent in one year to $14 billion.[4] Even banks that managed to avoid making risky residential mortgages could not resist the urge of riskier than usual small business loans, oftentimes approved without prudently assessing a borrower's business strategy and finances. Bank of America discontinued its business "Credit Express Program" several months ago and is now focusing instead on mature businesses with a good credit history. The difficulty businesses, large and small, are having getting credit today receives even more attention than our nation's residential foreclosure crisis. And not without reason, major business are cutting back employment, expenditures, and expansion plans and, on occasion, even folding for lack of ongoing capital. Now that another $700 billion in federal bailout money is on the table, some of the companies that helped define our nation are asking for help, including major "big three" players in the auto and credit industries. We'll discuss this shortly.

What began as a small business credit crunch arguably hit young minority females hardest, because they often lack the means to qualify for the best terms on other types of financing. More than 60 percent of woman-owned businesses are service firms, compared to about 50 percent of the overall small business population. Service firms lack the hard assets—like inventory, a building, or delivery trucks—to use as collateral for loans. Without collateral, these loans are riskier for the banks and other lending institutions, and thus costlier and harder for business owners to obtain. For many of the same reasons, African Americans are twice as likely to use credit cards to fund start-ups.

During the second half of 2008, the business credit crunch spread to bigger businesses we would otherwise have expected to have more alternatives to get through rough times like these. Topping the headlines during November 2008 was the credit crunch impact on car dealerships and individual car loans.

THE BAD NEWS SPREADS INTO OUR RETIREMENT YEARS

There is another potential impact that could destroy what many Americans have been looking forward to their entire lives: those much-anticipated retirement years. Experts initially estimated $500 billion of potentially worthless paper was on the balance sheets of the biggest global banks. These and other losses have spilled into the huge pension and mutual funds that average American workers and investors depend on for retirement savings not to mention the hit to retirement savings for those of us with more direct investments in real estate. Twenty years ago, the average American had 70 percent equity in his home at retirement age. Ten years ago, the number was about 50 percent.[5] If we look at all of the people who refinanced their mortgages in recent years and all of the folks who are upside down (owe more than the present value of their home), how many will have home equity for retirement now? As of March 2008, an estimated 8.8 million Americans, or almost 10.8 percent of us, had zero or negative equity in our homes.[6] It's no wonder that the experts are worried about the baby boomers, most of whom have little or negligible savings, whose biggest assets are the houses they occupy. The crisis coincides exactly with the 2008 timeframe these folks have always been expected to begin retiring in. Coupled with a negative savings rate, if continued weakness in the housing sector reduces equity even further for this group, it will be difficult for them to save enough in their potential remaining working years to offset the loss. Fast-forward another ten years and we may be faced with supporting, in a much more literal sense, a much larger retirement population than ever before. And this support is in addition to the costs our government has already expressed serious concern about, such as Medicaid and Medicare, costs that this population is likely to incur.

THE CRISIS GOES GLOBAL

All of this bad debt seems to have scattered in the wind. Exactly where in the world all the bad debt ended up still remains a mystery. It has been and likely will continue to pop up where and when we least expect it. The *New York Times*,[7] for example, recently reported that the Norwegian town of Narvik lost about $64 million so far in complex securities investments backed in part by subprime mortgages that turned bad. The investments represent 20 percent of Narvik's annual budget. Covering the loss will require a long-term loan that can be paid only by cutting town services. Narvik's story is a common one. The financial giant Citigroup created investments bought by the town through Terra Securities, a trusted Norwegian broker with which the town had been doing business for years. As a result of the losses, Narvik has cut local services like free kindergarten, nursing homes, and cultural institutions. The town itself has already missed payroll for its employees and is considering legal action against Citigroup. Terra Securities took a financial hit, too. The company's license was revoked and it has filed for bankruptcy. Narvik's leaders allege that they were duped by brokers and weren't warned that the securities were risky and subject to being cashed out at a loss if their market price fell below a certain level. Town opposition leaders are calling for an investigation to determine exactly how the investment decisions were made and by whom.

As of early 2008, it was estimated that Chinese banks had invested $9 billion in subprime-backed securities. Bank of China alone, the second biggest bank in that country, as of early 2008 had set aside more than $150 million to secure itself against possible losses. The Industrial and Commercial Bank of China had another $1.2 billion potentially at risk. And Mitsubishi, the Japanese automaker, had a whopping $2.6 billion tied up in the US subprime and related markets. Estimates are that Taiwanese banks had about $1.2 billion on the line. The United Kingdom's Barclays Bank, France's BNP Paribas, and Germany's Deutsche Bank all had big dollar amounts at risk.

Banks worldwide were estimated to have almost $900 billion at risk because of credit agreements based on asset-backed paper programs. Although these numbers seemed astronomical they have actually grown over 2008, but as we've said, the bigger concern, in terms of our nation's global standing, is that extreme volatility can increase general global anxiety and harm America's reputation as a safe place to invest.[8] This would discourage economic commitments from other countries in the United States and could rock our economy to the core. Where the US will end up, in terms of world economic powers, after this crisis is yet to be seen. Anti-American sentiment should not be overlooked as a possible impact of our mess having infected foreign shores. We'll discuss in chapter 9 how the crisis itself (as opposed to just US investments made in the US by other countries) spread during late 2008.

EXPOSED FLAWS IN OTHER WALL STREET CREATIONS

As the subprime crisis began impacting employment, consumer spending, and business credit, fatal flaws in other Wall Street creations and our nation's financial infrastructure were exposed. The next few pages provide specific examples of other routes the crisis has taken in its spread from our nation's mortgage and real estate market into broader financial markets.

Credit Default Swaps, the Trojan Horse of Wall Street

Credit default swaps were crafted by Wall Street as a type of insurance to cover bank and bondholder losses when companies default on their debts. Briefly, those who buy this insurance agree to pay the seller (the insurer) a premium. The seller agrees to pay the buyer if a particular event, like a default, occurs.

Credit default swaps may be sold and resold several times. And, more recently, about a third have been written against groupings of debt from multiple insurers, the values of which were calculated using computer models. Because credit default swap sales are not highly regulated, the parties may not tell each other when they sell or may wind up sold to a third party who is not able to honor the credit default swap obligation to pay up if a default takes place. The buyer, who is relying on the credit default swap, may not know that a new, potentially weaker insurer has assumed the obligation to pay. When markets were growing at a steady pace, defaults were minimal, which led several commercial banks to consider credit default swaps a low-risk income generator of premiums and so they issued increasingly more of them. Experts worried that the total credit default swap market far exceeded the face value of underlying company bonds.

Like mortgage-backed securities, the credit default swap market was founded to diversify the risk among many investors. The credit default swap market boomed, doubling each year during the past five or so years from $9 billion to more than $45 billion. As of January 2008, the top twenty-five US banks accounted for $14 trillion of credit default swaps, with J.P. Morgan, Citibank, and Bank of America heading the list. Speculators, including hedge funds, eager to make quick profits, were in this market, too. In light of the subprime crisis, increased defaults that would trigger demands for payment under credit default swaps by investors who have purchased them were inevitable. Initial estimates were that 16 percent of credit default swap contracts insured mortgage-backed securities.[9] The inability to determine an insurer's financial stability rendered banks' valuation of the contracts on their books questionable. In other words, banks may believe they are leveraged (i.e., insured) against exposure when, in reality, they could never collect on the coverage they had purchased.

Auction-Rate Securities

We explained auction-rate securities in the context of the UBS scandal in chapter 4 in which that firm was accused of misleading its investors by covertly bidding in the auctions to keep interest in the investments and prices up. The particular type of auction process used to sell auction-rate securities is called a "Dutch" auction. In a Dutch auction, buyers determine the number of shares they want to buy and the lowest interest rate they will accept. The bids are then ranked, from lowest to highest. The lowest bid rate for which all shares can be sold at par is called the "clearing rate" This will be the interest rate paid. Buyers who bid above the clearing rate get no bonds. Buyers who bid below clearing rate get paid the clearing rate of interest. If there aren't enough orders for shares offered at an auction, the auction is said to have "failed." When an auction fails, the interest rate will be set at a predefined maximum rate in order to compensate shareholders who could not sell their shares due to the failure.

During 2008, firms that had been bidding at their own auctions were forced to stop doing so in part as a result of a shortage of funds with which to bid because of subprime crisis–related impacts. Auctions began to fail at rates never seen before. This was yet another faulty market crafted by Wall Street whose flaws were exposed when the subprime mortgage market came unglued.

Conflicts of Interest

Many people are wondering just what those on Wall Street knew and when they knew it. And if there are things they should have known but didn't, then why not? It was recently reported that, despite the tremendous financial losses suffered by so many of its clients, the investment firm of Goldman Sachs generated for itself one of the biggest windfalls the securities industry has seen in years. Like other Wall Street firms, Goldman weighs its financial risk by calculating its average daily *value at risk* (VaR), in other words, how much money the firm could lose under adverse market conditions. Firms try to leverage VaR by betting both sides of the coin. In this case, for example, Goldman's mortgage department continued selling CDOs to its clients while its own structured products trading group, located within the firm's same mortgage department, was betting big that the same CDO values would fall.

Public Financial Writedowns as of Early September 2008

Firm	Writedowns	Capital Raised
Citigroup	55.1	49.1
Merrill Lynch	51.8	29.9
UBS	44.2	28.3
HSBC	27.4	3.9
Wachovia	22.5	11.0
Bank of America	21.2	20.7
IKB Deutshce	15.3	12.6
Royal Bank of Scotland	14.9	24.3
Washington Mutual	14.8	12.1
Morgan Stanley	14.4	5.6
J.P. MorganChase	14.3	7.9
Deutsche Bank	10.8	3.2
Credit Suisse	10.5	2.7
Wells Fargo	10.0	4.1
Barclays	9.1	18.6
Lehman Brothers	8.2	13.9
Credit Agricole	8.0	8.9

Foris	7.4	7.2
HBOS	7.1	7.6
Societe General	6.8	9.8
Bayerische Landesbank	6.4	0.0
Canadian Imperial	6.3	2.8
Mizuho Financial Group	5.9	0.0
ING Group	5.8	4.8
National City	5.4	8.9
Lloyds TSB	5.0	4.9
IndyMac	4.9	0.0
WestLB	4.7	7.5
Dresdner	4.1	0.0
BNP Paribas	4.0	0.0
LB Baden-Wuerttemberg	3.8	0.0
Goldman Sachs	3.8	0.6
E*Trade	3.6	2.4
Nomura Holdings	3.3	1.1
Natixis	3.3	6.7
Bear Stearns	3.2	0.0
HSH Nordbank	2.8	1.9
Landesbank Sachsen	2.6	0.0
UniCredit	2.6	0.0
Commerzbank	2.4	0.0
ABN Amro	2.3	0.0
DZ Bank	2.0	0.0
Bank of China	2.0	0.0
Fifth Third	1.9	2.6
Rabobank	1.7	0.0
Bank Hapoalim	1.7	2.4
Mitsubishi UFJ	1.6	1.5
Royal Bank of Canada	1.5	0.0
Marchsall & Ilsley	1.4	0.0
Alliane & Leicester	1.4	0.0
U.S. Bancorp	1.3	0.0
Dexia	1.2	0.0
Caisse d'Epargne	1.2	0.0
Keycorp	1.2	1.7
Soverign Bancorp	1.0	1.9
Hypo Real Estate	1.0	0.0
Gulf International	1.0	1.0
Sumitomo Mitsui	0.9	4.9
Sumitomo Trust	0.7	1.0
DBS Group	0.2	1.1
Other European Banks	7.2	2.3
Other Asian Banks	4.6	7.8
Other US Banks	2.9	1.9
Other Canadian Banks	1.8	0.0
Total	***501.4***	***351.2***

The bet against CDOs generated nearly $4 billion in profits for Goldman in 2007, erasing other firm losses but raising questions about how the firm, and others on Wall Street like it, balance their responsibilities to shareholders and clients with its own drive for profits.[10] Another area of conflict garnering plenty of media attention is the gargantuan bonuses paid on Wall Street and the fact that those incentives due are not always structured consistently with producing the best outcomes for the firm's clients.

Risky CDOs were once big business for the firms, bringing in hundreds of millions of dollars in profits from CDO trading and not requiring much overhead. Citigroup's Centauri Fund, for example, paid core investors almost $63 million in 2006.[11] That business is now gone. The strategies and products Wall Street will devise to replace lost market share and revenues with entirely new sources and how executives will be compensated remain to be seen. We can only speculate about the likely long-term effects of the financial reverberations we've discussed. One result will no doubt be lawsuits aplenty (to be discussed in more detail below). Another will be a changing of the leadership at many levels. We now know it will likely be influenced by our government's bailout plan discussed in more detail in chapter 8.

Early estimates indicated that the new owners of Merrill Lynch could face as much as $10 billion in additional writedowns on CDOs and subprime mortgage bonds, in addition to the $8.5 billion that forced the company's CEO to resign.[12] Some of the write-downs taken thus far are reflected in the sidebar on pages 150–51. We can expect the list of corporate casualties to grow as causes and effects become increasingly transparent and publicly known.

Commercial Paper Troubles

In the midst of the credit crunch, banks still need to do business, as they borrow money from depositors and others to relend it to us. With consumer debt high, oil prices still stretched, and confidence in the economy at a low ebb, the commercial paper market shrank the most it has this decade. Companies saw sales dip and couldn't justify incurring debt to expand or develop new products. Those who wanted to take out loans to expand found money scarce. Banks faced a scarcity of short-term loans to provide to companies facing the credit squeeze. After the market hesitated, the Federal Reserve began to lower the interest rate it charges member banks to lend them the funds needed and encourage the purchase of commercial paper. Although in prior years subprime mortgages accounted for only around 20 percent of the mortgage market, during the bubble subprime mortgages accounted for almost half of all loans.[13] Home loan woes are likely to continue squeezing regional lender profits over the next several years, as greater loan charge-offs are expected. These lenders can't sell their home loans to investors as easily as they once did, so they have to service them and take any losses that defaults bring. Whether their money is tied up in active home loans or stuck in defaulted loans leading to foreclosure, these lenders have less money to lend to even the more creditworthy home buyers. Analysts expect the pace of bank mergers and consolidations to accelerate. As concern over the quality of bank assets continues, we can expect the value and sale prices for many of these banks to decrease.

Balance Sheet Bingo

One challenge to recovery is that banks don't trust each other's balance sheets. This makes loans from one bank to another, even short-term ones, less likely. Investors don't trust banks either, so bank stock prices have tumbled. Only the banks know where their bad debts lie. Some have adopted the practice of granting extensions on the loan repayment dates for entire higher-risk loan types, such as vacant land loans. Rather than call these loans into default now and having to deal with the high cost of foreclosure, lenders are choosing to grant automatic two- or three-year extensions to borrowers in the hope that this will enable the borrowers to repay their loans. Some say banks merely delaying the inevitable. On the other hand, there is something to be said for controlling the timing of the financial hits. The point is, only the banks know what they are doing behind closed doors.

Obsolete Methods for Controlling the Money Supply

Regulators used to determine how much debt banks could create by simply limiting the amount of money regulators supplied, which formed the base of all loans, and by requiring banks to hold sufficient reserves for every loan on their books. This made mortgage lending somewhat finite. Once banks developed the practice of shifting loans off their books (literally selling the loans to holding companies and others), this form of regulatory control became obsolete. Regulators could no longer determine how much debt was being created. The lending capacity of US banks became infinite. Most experts agree that until the banks reckon with the bad mortgage loans both on and off their books, the problems will fester. We'll discuss some of the alternatives banks may have, along with the bailout plan in chapter 8.

LENDERS RECOGNIZE THE NEED TO MAKE CHANGES

We are already seeing changes in the way banks conduct business. We've discussed some of the industry infrastructure flaws in chapter 2. Although mortgage brokers were a low-cost sales force, making it easier for lenders to ramp up production, utilizing delocalized loan originators removes control over loan quality. Some lenders are indicating that they will stop using mortgage brokers, who used to provide access to new markets for loans, in an effort to regain control over the assessment of borrowers. Brokers are arguably a leading cause behind much of the mortgage fraud now being blamed for high defaults and losses. We've discussed how the massive influx of inexperienced brokers into the industry over the past five years resulted in lower than usual quality control. The stated-income and no-document mortgage loan products based on lower-credit-quality applicants, discussed in chapter 2, resulted in more loan products for borrowers with FICO scores of 550 and below. Relaxed loan underwriting guidelines, with an emphasis on producing more mortgages, though not necessarily quality mortgages, led to many of the problems we see today. Bank of America is among those leading the way in focusing on high-quality, direct-to-consumer lending, a practice that could pressure other banks to follow. Mortgage brokers had been involved in 25 percent of Bank of America's loans. The move to more direct lending lowered that number and eliminated 5 percent of the bank's workforce.[14]

On the back end, banks are grappling with the logistics of servicing an unprecedented number of foreclosures for which they weren't prepared. No doubt changes will emerge on this front as well. With fewer takers on Wall Street, the exotic loan products like the interest-only ARMs and teaser rates that got so many into trouble are moving toward extinction. Banks are finally meeting increased investor scrutiny by requiring more detailed documentation and larger down payments in addition to tightening their requirements for appraiser approval. Basically, there is a gradual return to old-fashioned tried-and-true lending, which is increasing both the cost of creating and servicing loans for everyone.

COURTS RESPOND

Other businesses and regulatory organizations are likewise questioning their operating and other systems as a result of failures apparent under the current strains. Courts across the country, for example, are experiencing longer than usual foreclosure time lines. Some have created *complex business litigation divisions* to handle cases that might otherwise delay the progression of other more clear-cut ones. Other jurisdictions, like the Circuit Court of the Fifteenth Judicial Circuit in Palm Beach County, Florida, are requiring institutional lenders foreclosing on a borrower's homestead property to provide proof that the lender has tried to reach a short sale or mortgage modification with the borrower before proceeding with the foreclosure in court. A copy of Administrative Order No. 3.305–10/08 is included for your reference at Appendix G as an example of what these new protections for home owners and our nation will resemble.

COMMERCIAL REAL ESTATE MARKETS WAKE UP AND SMELL THE COFFEE

The subprime mortgage weakness and the ensuing consolidations and closures have hurt the office, retail, resort, industrial, and other commercial real estate market segments as first lenders and other real estate and finance businesses and later businesses in general laid off workers and closed operations. During economic downturns, small and mid-level companies take the first hit. Class "A" space, the most expensive, prestigious space for the highest quality tenants initially remained solid, but Class "B" tenants were moving down to Class "C" space meant for lower quality tenants. And big-league tenants are waiting to see how their business would be impacted before making new commitments for space. The condominium office market is on hold, with many units intended for sale being utilized as rentals instead. "Condo" has become a dirty word across all markets. For the most part, slowdowns in the commercial real estate markets, like the residential market, are attributable to the credit crunch, and overall apprehension about the markets in general.

Unlike our homes, decisions to buy or sell commercial real estate are typically made strictly based on the numbers. The *capitalization* or *cap rate* of a building, a rule of thumb used to value commercial real estate, is its cost divided by the rental profit it generates. Commercial real estate developers and buyers look for certain minimum cap rates. As costs such as real estate taxes and insurance increase, cap rates decrease, as does the price buyers are willing to pay for a particular property and, therefore, its market value. This can be counterbalanced by increasing rental profit, but only when tenants are willing to pay more. At least for now, that does not seem likely. At a "State of the Market" meeting sponsored by Gibraltar Bank in early 2008, speaker Dennis O'Shea, president of Stiles Corporation, a large commercial real estate development and management firm, observed: "Some folks just want out of the commercial properties. Many who can't repay their construction loans are being pushed to get out by their lenders. The rest of us are more or less sitting tight and watching for opportunities."

As our economic slow down and consumer confidence and spending slumps continue making their way onto business balance sheets, business spending and expansion, including expansion into new real estate space, is put on hold. National smoothie retailer Jamba Juice's real estate manager Becky Smith explained to a group of commercial Realtors in Boca Raton, Florida, in 2008: "Our company's plans for new location openings have been slashed to a fraction of what was anticipated in 2006. Our cutbacks will probably run through 2010, especially in locations planned to accommodate nearby new residential developments, since that new space was planned in anticipation of the new residents who never materialized into the market."

GETTING A HANDLE ON MORTGAGE FRAUD

As the market evaluates its recent indiscretions and mortgage fraud continues to take an even wider and more obvious toll we still have no better handle on the actual number of fraud cases. From 2000 to 2006, the number of *suspicious activity reports* (SARs), discussed in more detailed in chapter 8, rose from about thirty-five hundred to more than twenty-eight thousand, with estimated losses of a billion dollars. A reported 55 percent of fraud

One Realtor's Insight into New Types of Mortgage Fraud

"Like other people who are still selling real estate today, most of the transactions end up being short sales. We're all sort of learning by doing. And from my experience, that goes for the people we negotiate with who work for the bank as well. The banks each have their own procedures and forms. As far as I know there are no laws telling them how they have to handle a short sale so each bank has more or less made up its own forms and procedures but there are some things that they all seem to be doing and asking for. For example, when a home owner wants to negotiate a short sale with their bank, the bank will usually require a broker price opinion (BPO) from a local Realtor like me, someone who knows the market and can attest to a property's probable value. They really don't seem to have any other process in place to value the properties other than that. I think this type of procedure can expose the banks to people wanting to take advantage of the situation. In fact, I know it can. I've received calls from people I sold houses to during the boom offering to pay me what sounds like a lot of money to provide them with a BPO for their bank. Once you start asking about the transaction you find out that their "buyer" is really a friend and they're planning to buy the house back from the friend right after the lender approves the short sale. In other words, they're telling the lender they can't afford the mortgage payment and have to sell the house but can only get, say, $100,000 for a house they owe $250,000 on. At the end of the day they're hoping the lender will eat the $150,000 difference and they'll end up owning the same house with only a $100,000 mortgage. I say no, but I'm certain there are Realtors out there providing BPOs on fraudulent short sales like this and the lenders have no idea. I'd report this if I knew where to go because it's so unfair to other home owners in the neighbor and to Realtors like me whose pay depends on the value of the homes we sell. Once these fraudulent, under-market-value transactions are recorded in the public record, anyone looking to buy a home in that neighborhood or appraisers trying to value other homes in the area will see it, probably not know the price is entirely fabricated, and undervalue other homes in the neighborhood, too. This pushes down home values for everyone."

cases occurred at the loan application stage, and 65 percent occurred in subprime mortgages. Reported incidents have typically involved more than one type of fraud. Easy-to-use Web sites that enable borrower and loan originators to create false documentation and even false identities have no doubt compounded the problem. A 2006 study released by the Mortgage Asset Research Institute (MARI), an agency explained in more detail in appendix E, indicated that borrower income may have been exaggerated in as much as 60 percent of stated-income loans. The following year, a survey by Litton Loan Servicing, a leading US mortgage loan servicing company, estimated the number of incidents of fraud to be between 30 and 35 percent of subprime loans. As of January 2007, nationwide incidence of mortgage fraud during the boom was estimated by the Mortgage Brokers Association to be 35 percent.[15]

As of March 2008, Florida led the nation in reported incidents of fraud.[16] The chart below reflects other high-fraud locations. This information is important in deciding where industry reform is needed and focus should be directed. It is also helpful in predicting which markets will recover quicker and whether or not fraud may be impacting values in a geographic area.

One thing is for sure, cheating on mortgage applications was so wide-

Suggestions for Handling Suspected Mortgage Fraud

- Dig deeper. Ask questions.
- Don't stop until you're sure you've figured out what's really going on.
- Ask the other party (buyer or seller), Realtor, mortgage loan originator, or appraiser questions privately. Compare the answers you get from each person.
- Get written explanations for things that seem unusual or you don't understand.
- Read the documents you are given carefully. If you don't understand them, things don't match up or something just doesn't seem right, get a second opinion.
- Follow your instincts.
- Don't rush. And don't trust anyone who tells you that you have to rush. Take all the time you need to get comfortable.
- Don't respond to unsolicited mailings, phone calls, or e-mails from mortgage loan originators.
- Report any suspicious activity to local law enforcement authorities. If the transaction involves over $1 million, report it to the FBI.

spread and, before now, so seldom punished that the Office of Thrift Supervision (a government agency whose purpose, history, and authority is explained for you in more detail in appendix C) speculates that mortgage fraud is fueling an increase in foreclosures that will prolong the housing slump. For example, hidden fraud can delay determination of the market value of a property. If a lender has loaned $250,000 based on a false appraisal, inflating the value of a property that is actually only worth, say, $150,000, it may take longer to sell that property as a short sale or after foreclosure until the lender understands and can justify selling it for such a loss. Since only federally regulated financial institutions have to file suspicious activity reports, current data on mortgage fraud is likely to be only the tip of the iceberg. Experts say it will take an estimated three to five years to get a more accurate handle on the actual numbers of mortgage fraud cases.

New Varieties of the Same Old Fraud

We know that very active, high-loan-volume markets will attract fraud because that type of environment makes it easier to conceal the fraud. But we're learning that downturn markets can encourage fraud as well. Slow markets frustrate sellers, encouraging them to turn a blind eye to some of the telltale signs of mortgage fraud such as buyers asking to raise the price of the

Mortgage Asset Research Institute's (MARI) Top 10 States for 2007 Reported Fraud in Single-Family Loan Types[17]

State	*MFI Rank 2007*	*MFI Rank 2006*
Florida	1	1
Nevada	2	6
Michigan	3	3
California	4	2
Utah	5	11
Georgia	6	4
Virginia	7	14
Illinois	8	8
New York	9	9
Minnesota	10	5

property, buyers who insist on using certain appraisers, basing the Realtor commission on something other than the purchase price in the contract, attempting to get cash back at the closing, agreeing to terms they will not put in the contract, or asking for separate addendums they do not intend to show the lender.

A new variation of the flip scenario explained in chapter 2 has emerged with borrowers in default now making misrepresentations to lenders, such as false contracts for short sales to a buyer (who is actually the borrower's friend) with the plan to buy the property back from this buyer-friend at a lower price after the lender agrees to take the loss. Residential Realtor Karon Carpenter explains her own exposure to this trend for you in the sidebar on page 163.

According to initial estimates from the Mortgage Bankers Association, as many as twenty-two thousand new incidents of fraud occurred after the market started going down in 2007.[18] The FBI says mortgage fraud is still one of the fastest-growing white-collar crimes in the United States.[19] It costs borrowers and lenders alike, and both are responsible for combating the problem. Fortunately, there are things you can do when you suspect mortgage fraud. They are summarized for you in the sidebar on page 158.

While the presence of one or more of these conditions does not definitely mean fraud is involved, it does mean that you should ask more questions.

Predators Find New Ways to Make (or Take) a Buck

Predators, too, have adjusted to the market shift. New predatory lending schemes are emerging, particularly of the "foreclosure prevention" or "rescue" type, to be discussed in chapter 7. Home owners claim they are being misled into believing that predatory opportunists can help them save their homes from being foreclosed upon. Some accomplish this by convincing home owners that they will pay the home owner's mortgage for a year to give the home owner time to catch up with financial obligations. In reality, these home owners unknowingly deed their property over to the bad guy. The bad guy then technically "leases" the home owner his own property back. At the end of the year the predator kicks the home owner out and keeps the home. In another variation, predators convince distressed home owners to send their monthly payment to the predator because they believe the predator has paid off or bought their mortgage loan, the predator then keeps the money. Their approaches vary, but in the end their efforts are aimed at convincing home owners to give up control, transfer money, and often to give up actual ownership of their homes. Thriving on home owner despair, these companies solicit their victims by phone, door-to-door canvassing, and through direct mail. Sadly, foreclosure rescue firms are not required to be licensed, leaving them open to do or say almost anything.

THE VIEW FROM A BUILDER'S WORLD

We've talked about another frontier where our nation has been forced to wake up and deal with the crisis, namely, residential development. Even when the signs told builders to stop building, many could not. Once construction began, many builders determined that their losses would be bigger if the projects were not completed. That's why many builders completed the projects, even if it meant being stuck holding units for longer than they had originally planned.

We will discuss in chapter 8 how in some areas excess inventory is estimated to last years. Builders have to generate cash to make payroll. In most cases, the only way for builders to expedite the sale of this inventory has been to lower prices. Clearly reducing housing production until more existing houses are absorbed is a necessary evil and key to bringing the market back to equilibrium. This normal market correction in available housing is prolonged due to an anticipated flood of foreclosed homes on the market, which naturally makes selling new units more competitive for builders, and home owners alike. As publicly traded companies, some of our nation's largest home builders, mentioned earlier in this chapter, filed for bankruptcy protection as their stock prices plummeted. We'll discuss how what is now an observable decrease in new unit construction real estate market is one indicator used to predict recovery (see chapter 8).

Other developers had no choice but to cease construction, or sales and marketing, in projects already underway as lenders declared them in default under their construction loans. Halted construction has left some residents staring at unfinished homes next door. Owners of new units in some condominiums are discovering that only a few people are sharing the expenses that were meant to be shared by an entire building full of new owners. Lenders faced with taking back these properties have to grapple with completing the projects, finding buyers willing to complete them, or trying to secure the sites against vandals, trespass, deterioration of exposed partially completed construction, and permit expiration, and then just sit tight in hopes that the market will turn around. One real estate turn-around specialist explains some of the challenges she faces foreclosing on commercial projects for you in the sidebar on page 163.

Some developments designed between 2003 and 2006 are no longer state of the art. At the height of this earlier period of demand, design, construction, and even location quality slipped a notch or two. Pressed by permit and entitlement deadlines, many lenders who now have control of these developments find themselves between a rock and a hard place. The market is already glutted with very desirable housing that competes with these less attractive units for a scarce number of available buyers. Faced with having to close and then carry empty units, many speculators and developers have taken to luring residential renters with attractive deals to help defray the carrying costs, which risks flooding the rental market and negatively impacting residential rental properties and landlords who had considered themselves removed from the affects of the subprime crisis.

Once it became apparent that the housing bubble was bursting, values were dropping, and speculative development was no longer a good idea, virtually all developers nationwide withdrew offers on land intended for new projects, at least where it was possible for them to do so according to the terms of existing contracts. Developers have walked away from multimillion-dollar deposits in cases where losses due to longer than originally estimated carrying times and costs and purchase prices negotiated during better times would have resulted in even bigger losses had they closed. In some cases residents, relying on contracts from developers, had already bought new homes in anticipation of the big payday. For example, the town of Briny Breezes, a small enclave of mobile homes situated for more than fifty years directly overlooking the Atlantic Ocean, was approached a few years back by a developer who eventually convinced every owner to sell. Some owners, in anticipation of walking away with a million dollars in their pocket, went ahead and bought new boats, cars, or other homes. In light of the subprime crisis, the developer canceled the contract.[20] Adam Reiss, general counsel for Ross Realty Investments, Inc. (RRI), another development, acquisition, leasing, and management company for upscale commercial retail and office projects, notes that even before specifically spreading to commercial real

A Real Estate Development Project in Limbo

"I've been involved in real estate development, management, marketing and finance for a long, long time but I've never seen anything like what we're seeing today. I think the main difference between this and prior real estate busts, including the RTC (Resolution Trust Corporation, an entity established after the S&L crash to sell real estate assets held by those banks after borrower defaulted on their loans), is that the market is almost completely illiquid. You just can't sell these assets right now. There's so much risk involved for potential buyers because no one knows how long it will take the market to recover, meaning no one knows how long they will have to carry these assets. And that's where the real added costs come in, the difference in cost between buying a condo project today and being able to sell the units for $100,000 each in six months verses having to carry the project and sell the same units for the same price in two years can make or break a real estate investor. So in the mean time, the banks are just fighting with developers for title to the projects and hoping to find a way to sell them once they get title.

Most of my time now is spent playing negotiator between the developer —a guy who may be losing everything he has and dealing with a wife who's divorcing him because of all the stress but still swears his project is worth every penny he and the bank have in it—and the bank. One project like this is a $37 million luxury residential development. The concrete walls and floors are in but that's about it. Our building permits expire in 7 days. The bank's going to have to lay out a few thousand dollars to get those extend since the borrower has no money. If we allow the permits to expire it could take another two years to get them back and we may not ever be able to get approval for the number of units we're building now. Without the permits, all we have to sell is a useless vacant lot, and the bank would have to take a huge loss on the loan. On top of that, if the permits expire, we'll have to tear down the construction that's been done so far. I just finished working with a contractor we brought in to coat the exposed rebar and make sure what's been done there so far doesn't deteriorate or blow away in a storm. Speaking of which, the bank just laid out another $37 thousand yesterday for insurance since the developer hadn't paid that either. And that's just the tip of the iceberg. I'm seeing a lot of lawyers and Realtors trying to jump into the business of preserving these projects like I do. I hope they get themselves up to speed quickly, but there are so many aspects of this business and so many people you really need to know to get things done. There's no easy answer but at least I feel as if I'm doing the best I can to help solve our country's bigger problem by stopping the bleeding one project at a time from my end. The more the banks, developers, and investors I work for can salvage from the projects, the less will have to be written off or maybe even paid for by taxpayers and the better off we all will be."

estate, the subprime mortgage problem had affected commercial real estate finance opportunities for even financially sound developers like RRI who would be willing to do deals even in this market, as the lender pools had a increasingly limited interest in providing desirable financing. Says Reiss, "Although loans are still available for upscale projects, interest rates on new loans have jumped to prohibitive rates. Until the credit markets stabilize, even financially sound developer interest in the loans Wall Street is willing to offer will be limited." Virtually all builders are being forced to write down the value of the properties they still own.

OTHER IMPACTS AMERICA'S WAKING UP TO

Oddly enough, the stagnant housing market has inadvertently trapped seniors. Many who want to move into assisted living facilities, retirement complexes, or move in with their children are unable to sell their homes. As a result, some families are tapping into savings to bring in home healthcare aides. In some locations, condominiums sit empty after seniors pass away and heirs are unable to sell the property. Many home owners in this situation or even those just financially strapped for any number of reasons may vote to turn down needed improvements suggested by the building's home owner association in which their elder was a member. This creates an unexpected obstacle for associations and boards as well as the other unit owners in the building trying to pass votes through for maintenance and improvements or manage excessively late maintenance fee payments.

No One Is Immune

How many of us steered well clear of buying real estate or refinancing our real estate during the bubble? Another *New York Times* article titled "Can the Mortgage Crisis Swallow a Town?"[21] said it all. The article highlighted one Ohio family who never took out a risky loan, never borrowed more than they could afford, and never missed a loan payment. But because others on their street did take these risks, and eventually couldn't pay their mortgages, one house after another went into foreclosure and now many stand vacant. When home owners can't pay their mortgages they certainly are not going to spend money taking care of their property. Lenders, already taking a loss by having to foreclose, likewise do not spend money maintaining a real estate owned (REO) property unless it is absolutely necessary. Their town has already had to shut down its two community pools, cut back its police force and fire department, and eliminate free snow plowing for its senior citizens. The family in Ohio, no longer feeling safe in their own neighborhood, put their home on the market. But because they were competing for buyers with bank-owned properties and the neighborhood had fallen on rough times, there were no buyers. The family kept lowering the asking price for their home but the competition to sell was prohibitive.

The fallout from nationwide foreclosures has engulfed middle-class communities across the country. People living next door to foreclosed properties are getting discouraged and middle-class families are leaving. As they depart, they leave behind fewer and fewer people to share the costs of maintaining their towns. The cost per home for routine services like trash collection as well as water and sewer levies increases. The number of transient students in local school districts increases. Crime increases. Virtually every aspect of community life is impacted in a foreclosure nation.

The View from Home Owner Associations

We mentioned earlier in this chapter how the challenges facing our country's 300,000 home owners and condominium associations are worsening as these associations grapple with shrinking budgets. Many banks are systematically refusing to pay association dues on properties they take back by foreclosure and, in fact, many of the mortgage and association documents explicitly limit bank liability for these fees. Developers long ago stopped building promised improvements. Delinquent home owner association payments, which historically run around 2 percent, are now reaching as high as 25 percent.[22] As a result, clubhouse repairs and essential services, such as trash removal and lawn cutting, continue to be compromised.

In new developments, owners continue to see their own pocket books hit as they cover the share of expenses intended to be covered by owners of units still sitting vacant. Those remaining owners who are honoring their obligation to pay assessments and covering for owners who are not are not getting anything extra for the added expense they're paying. Aside from reading association bylaws to determine what services are guaranteed and if there is a cap on how much money the association can demand from unit owners, individual unit owners are finding they have limited power as association boards generally make the decisions. As long as a board follows the association rules, they can't be questioned. There is, likewise, little recourse against delinquent unit owners other than lawsuits. It makes little sense to sue a unit owner who simply has no money to pay as, even if the suit is won, the unit owner still has no money to pay. Surprisingly few association bylaws address foreclosure contingencies.

With $41 billion in association operating revenue and 1.7 million people serving on association boards throughout the United States, this is not a small matter.[23] Most states still have no agencies to oversee association reserves and budgets, meaning, at least in the short term, there will be no relief.

Local Government's Perspective

We mentioned in chapter 4 how the dramatic increase and subsequent decrease in real estate values, together with various lag times involved for local government tax bases to catch up with these value shifts is creating a significant challenge. Some locales have increased taxable values and based budgets on the anticipated higher revenue. Others are only now seeing the increase hit their record books. In both cases, home owners across the nation are looking to their local governments to reassess the values of their homes significantly downward in the face of falling prices. The need for downward reassessments is anticipated to be skewed in favor of lower- and middle-class areas. In some locations almost ten times the usual number of home owners are asking for reduced real estate tax assessments.[24] We can't sell our homes. We can't afford our mortgage payments. We can't understand why our local governments are now raising our real estate taxes and demanding more money from us at the worst time ever.

On the other hand, as we've discussed, local governments rely heavily on real estate tax revenue and will have to find ways to either replace the money or cut local services. Government has clearly been a beneficiary of increased home values. Public education in particular is often a beneficiary of real estate tax dollars. Some geographic areas require that the government make up any tax loss. Many local governments are already cutting back on building department staff and resources they no longer need due to decreased new construction in their areas. The value of taxable land in California, for example, declined almost $3 billion between 2005 and 2008. The state of

Florida could lose more than $23 billion from its tax base. Nationally, the loss in the real estate tax base is anticipated to reach $223 billion, with the most severe impact in minority communities.

Exacerbating the problem is the fact that many local governments are now spending new unbudgeted money, for example, cutting lawns on abandoned properties in foreclosure since people under water on their homes often just leave. Shelved projects, in turn, mean expected jobs that don't materialize. Some local governments report that residential burglaries are up by more than 30 percent.[25] Abandoned or foreclosed houses prove to be irresistible targets.

As business revenues shrink and, in particular, as Wall Street buckles down under repeat punches with the possibility of paying huge settlements, those on the receiving end of their dollars are feeling the pinch. Among the beneficiaries of Wall Street business, in the form of taxes, is New York City. Banks provide 20 percent of New York's tax revenue, which is similar to other international financial hub cities. With numbers like this, it is making sense for some to follow the lead of companies like Merrill Lynch and book deals in London, where the 28 percent UK corporate tax rate applies, rather than New York, where the federal tax rate is 35 percent and states taxes add even more.

Counties and states throughout the United States continue to cut spending, including jobs, in response to what some estimate will be a $40 billion shortfall in annual tax revenues.[26] The total gap between budgeted and actual municipal revenue, attributed predominately to plummeting real estate taxes due to foreclosures and property value decreases, sales tax loss due to less consumer spending and corporate tax revenue reductions due, also, to losses resulting from less consumer spending, has grown to more than three times what it was in prior years and is expected to continue through 2010, as personal income tax reductions also become a factor. Unlike the federal government, most states are required to balance their budgets. Many have resisted passing tax increases on to us, but that does not mean we're not paying the price. We've already begun paying in the form of increased prices for tolls, college tuition, and reduced public services.

Home Values

As we discussed earlier, because we borrowed so much and our property has decreased in value, more and more of us are upside-down in our homes: We owe far more principal on our mortgage loans than our homes are now worth. One in every three households will see their property value drop, in some cases wiping out wealth that took a lifetime to build. According to the Office of Federal Housing Enterprise Oversight, between 1980 and 2000, average nationwide annual home appreciation was about 5 percent. Between 2000 and 2006 some markets saw appreciation skyrocket to as high as 200 percent! But since 2006, nationwide, the same real estate has already experienced an average 12.5 percent decline in value. In some markets the decrease has or is expected to be as much as 30 percent.[27] While this is wreaking havoc on some home owners, as we'll discuss in chapter 7, for others it is an opportunity for wealth creation, theoretically redistributing money and widening the gap between the haves and the have-nots.

Bankruptcies

Further losses will result in the current market from an ongoing decrease in normal appreciation as excess inventory is slowly absorbed and the housing industry returns to equilibrium. US personal bankruptcies are up 40 percent for 2007,[28] a shift universally attributed to the mortgage crisis and credit card debt. As we lose control of our finances, the tendency is to lose hope and eventually financial accountability, which often leads to defaulting on obligations we might otherwise have been able to manage. In our new foreclosure nation, 60 percent of us are behind on our car loans.[29] Experts anticipate a steady flow of increasing defaults on car loans, student loans, credit cards, and other debts. Those of us who have lost our homes face the prospect of rebuilding our financial lives. Many of us will never achieve home ownership again. And 2 million Americans are collectively carrying another $600 billion in subprime loans with ARMs due to reset in the near future[30] of whom 75 percent say an interest rate increase will hurt their finances, and many bank accounts will not survive the strain.[31] Some of us will eventually make it back into the real estate market. For those who are fortunate enough to make it into the group that will fully recover, and for future generations of new home owners, saving to buy a home will just take longer. We'll have to save for a down payment, build income, and show we can manage mortgage payments just like in the good old days.

THE LAWSUITS ARE ONLY JUST GETTING STARTED

Borrowers v. Originators

True to the American way, the lawsuits have begun. Some buyers are going to great lengths to paint someone other than themselves as the bad guy, claiming to have been duped by Realtors or loan originators into purchasing houses they couldn't afford or victimized through fraudulent investment schemes. With the understanding acquired in chapter 2, we can now predict that the lawsuits against loan originators are based upon allegations that they knew buyers would not be able to afford payments on loans they were placed in, encouraged buyers with no down payment to rely on overly optimistic future property appreciation, facilitated liar loans, did not adequately explain interest rate adjustments, and generally acted with disregard for their professional responsibilities as a result of the fact that they would not be retaining the loans and the risk of default but would instead be paid an immediate commission and be off the hook.

One somewhat amusing short-lived trend of lawsuits emerged in mid-2008. Some buyers were claiming that their Realtors misled them into purchasing or paying more for houses than they should have by guaranteeing unrealistic continued appreciation rates or failing to disclose lower comparable sales in the neighborhoods where these homes were purchased. These lawsuits did not seem to take hold or become widespread. Instead, courts tended to agree that buyers, whether it be buyers of shoes, cars or homes, should be aware of the fact that a salesperson's job to sell will entice them to make the product as desirable as possible. The responsibility is on us, at least to some extent, to do our homework (literally and figuratively), know the neighborhood, and comparison shop. At least to some extent we should know to not simply believe everything we hear, especially when we're placing hundreds of thousands of dollars at risk.

Investors v. Originators and Lenders

Lawsuits by Wall Street firms against mortgage loan originators and lenders center around allegations that the originator and lender knew, or should have known, that the loans being sold on the secondary market involved fraud or were more likely to default than they actually disclosed. Many are simply suing under buy-back agreements that require loans to be repurchased if fraud is found or default occurs within a certain amount of time following origination, regardless of knowledge or culpability. In many cases they are winning only to find out that the originators obligated to buy back the loans do not have the money to do so.

Investors v. Wall Street

On Wall Street the allegations of wrongdoing against investment firms, bond insurers, lenders, and rating agencies are mounting. We've already discussed some of these and will address more in a few moments. Most are based on accusations that Wall Street brokers knew, or should have known, that the loans backing the CDOs or other financial instruments they were crafting were junk. Wall Street firms are alleged to have wrongly assumed and assured investors that pooling, slicing, and insuring this junk reduced the risk, since only some would not be repaid and housing would continue to appreciate, rendering the risk minimal. For example, dividing CDOs into tranches or quality levels, as discussed in chapter 2, falsely allowed the creation of a relatively higher-level investment bond that insurance companies would cover and rating agencies would inappropriately label as AAA grade. By retaining much of the toxic waste themselves, Wall Street firms also paid themselves the highest interest rates. And utilizing shell special purpose vehicles (SPVs), companies located in places like the Cayman Islands allowed the firms to avoid having to show junk subprime mortgage collateral on their balance sheets. For example, Bear Stearns managed to sidestep scrutiny, accountability, and taxes in this way by registering subprime-related vehicles in the Cayman Islands. Courts in these foreign places may be less friendly to complaints by fund investors when fund managers support the local economy by parking billions of dollars there. Prior to now, funds such as these were open to investment only to very wealthy, sophisticated investors. As recently as 2003, a Securities and Exchange Commission study found that hedge fund investors were mostly institutions. During the bubble, however, investments in increments as low as $250,000 by less sophisticated investors less able to absorb huge hits were allowed. Many of the investors are now alleging that they did not understand the risk of these investments, often marketed to sound like high-grade securities. Allegations include that firms misrepresented the risk to investors, the risk controls in place to cut losses (for example, that markets were not being accurately monitored on an ongoing basis to know when defaults were going up or borrower quality and property values down), and the funds' performance were misinterpreted on a series of conference calls scheduled to avoid investors seeking to take their money out of these funds. The bottom line is that Bear funds have plummeted as much as 91 percent.[32] We have also seen claims against organizers or administrators of mortgage pools for losses resulting from misrepresentation at sale, misclassification of loans in the pool, mismanagement, and bad reporting of impending borrower defaults. As we discussed in detail in chapter 4, when home owners couldn't pay the subprime mortgages that were backing the CDOs, and housing prices stopped appreciating as promised, everything fell apart. It became obvious that the rating agencies had been wrong, the insurers did not have the resources to honor their obligations, investors were stuck, and the flow of money back into the market just froze. Some of these cases were highlighted for you earlier in chapter 4.

We've discussed settlements in auction-rate securities cases against UBS and others. Recently publicized cases include criminal charges against Bernard Madoff and attorney Marc Drier. Similar lawsuits have arisen between credit default swap and auction-rate securities buyers and sellers as well as various levels of lenders, their investors, and guaranty insurers, and possibly against the receivers of these entities as they fall.

Buyers v. Builders

Many residential projects that sold out quickly during the boom days became and still continue to become ready for closing and occupancy now. As the market cooled, buyers started seeking ways to get out of their contracts. Builders faced a rash of unforeseen cancellations and lawsuits. The majority simply involve people who don't want to close because they can no longer flip the unit and make a quick bundle of money or because they agreed to pay more than the units are now worth. This type of buyer is faced with a tough decision. If he closes, even a few months carrying the unit could well deplete his saving accounts. For many, it's worth the fight. Some are scrutinizing their contracts looking for loopholes or searching for tiny flaws in finished homes that might allow them to back out without losing their deposits. A newly formed brigade of lawyers is eager to help. A recent lawyer ad reads: "Do you want your money back? Your contract for purchase of a new house or condominium may be illegal. To see if you are entitled to a refund, call us for a free consultation." This type of crisis impact has become an opportunity for some and is discussed in more detail in chapter 7. The remedy provisions in mid-bubble builder contracts tended to be one-sided because they could be. At that time, buyers were willing to sign anything. Many contracts allow the builder to keep deposits and sue buyers for damages on top of that if they don't close. On the other hand, if the builder defaults, the contract only allows buyers to get their deposit back. Some builders may have violated the Interstate Land Sales Full Disclosure Act, enacted by Congress in 1968 to help protect buyers against abuses including fraud when buying land, which requires builders to provide buyers with certain disclosures and rights, and that the contract include certain provisions and registration of certain projects. For example, in some cases, if the project is not completed within a certain amount of time after the contract is signed, there have been changes to the project or documents, or a full set of association-related documents was not provided, buyers can cancel the contracts and get their deposits back. Other builders have wrongly utilized our deposits and the money is just gone. Suing an illiquid builder makes no sense; even if the buyer wins, the builders don't have the money to give back anyway.

Realtors v. Builders and Builders v. Realtors

We're also seeing Realtors suing builders for commissions deemed earned when they sold the units and now payable at closing or from the deposit if buyers wrongly cancel the contracts and are deemed in default. Builders are also suing Realtors in an attempt to force them to return commissions paid on contracts that are now being legally cancelled. Again, the likelihood is small that these Realtors have the resources to repay the commissions, even if the builders prevail.

Title Insurance Underwriters, the Deep Pocket

One group of players being dragged into lawsuits precisely because they *do* have the financial resources and are perceived as having deep pockets are the title insurance agents and their underwriters. In mortgage lending there are two types of title insurance policies. The first is a *lender* or *mortgagee policy*. All lenders require a buyer to have a mortgagee policy when closing on a mortgage to purchase or refinance property. A lender policy ensures the bank that its mortgage is a valid first lien on the property. In other words, there are no other debts owed by the current property owner for which he has put his property up as collateral to secure those debts. The amount of lender title insurance coverage is usually equal to the dollar amount of the mortgage. If it turns out that there is another lien that is superior to the lender's, the lender's title insurance policy will pay off the other lien or take whatever steps are necessary to make sure the lender's mortgage is a valid first lien or pay the lender for any loss up to the amount of the title insurance coverage. The second type of title insurance policy is an *owner's title insurance policy*. Buyers typically purchase an owner's title insurance policy when buying property. An owner's policy ensures that the buyer acquired good title to the property unencumbered by prior liens. The coverage amount is the purchase price. If it turns out that someone else has an interest in the property, the owner's title insurance policy will pay whatever is necessary to eliminate the other interest or pay the buyer for any loss up to the insured amount.

Much like other types of insurance, such as hazard insurance, title insurance is often sold by local agents. Some states require that attorneys close real estate transactions and issue title insurance at that time. Other states allow non-attorneys to become licensed by the state as title insurance agents in order to conduct real estate closings and issue title insurance. Becoming a title insurance agent also requires being approved as an agent by one of several title insurance underwriters, who actually assume legal responsibility for the policy. Such approval, in turn, requires that the agent carry adequate professional liability, malpractice, or errors and omission (EIO) insurance and is bonded to protect any monies that are changing hands. Title insurance underwriters include smaller regional companies as well as larger national companies some of which are also diversified in other information-related business sectors such as mortgage loan servicing, credit reporting, and aircraft or marine vessel insurance. One of the country's largest title insurance underwriters, for example, is First American Title Insurance Company (FATIC), a publicly traded Fortune 300 company. First American has over thirty subsidiary and affiliated companies.

When a title insurance agent is alleged to have made an error or, even worse, to have knowingly participated in wrongdoing, such as collusion with a loan originator to perpetuate mortgage fraud, which results in a threat to the first priority status of a lender's mortgage or a threat to an owner's valid ownership, a claim is filed with the title insurance underwriter against the policy issued by the agent and the agent notifies the professional liability insurance carrier. In today's shaky housing and lending market, title insurance underwriters and agent professional liability insurance carriers are often the only companies still standing after the mortgage loan closing that can be relatively easily located and have a modicum of financial stability, especially given the crisis which has caused so many lenders, originators, and Realtors to have left the business. Suing title insurance underwriters and agents by naming them as additional defendants in lawsuits against loan originators, builders, Realtors, and others simply to take a shot at getting some money from them, is becoming commonplace. The majority of current cases are based upon the highly speculative allegation that the underwriter's agent was involved in the fraud. Home buyers have little to lose by simply adding the title insurance underwriter's name to the lawsuit. Although many such suits will be dismissed, all nonetheless require underwriters to defend themselves, the cost of which may eventually be passed on to new buyers in the form of higher-priced title insurance. In the meantime, those who hold stock in the title insurance underwriters are sure to see a decline in stock values. One of the nation's top three title insurance underwriters has already been forced to place itself on the auctionblock, in part because of the costs associated with defending claims such as these. We may see consolidation among some of the smaller title insurance underwriters or even closures if efforts to defend the volume of claims become too burdensome for smaller firms.

Class Action Suits

We can expect to see class action suits of the widest variety, many of which will result in positive long-term change. One example filed in 2008 involved allegations made by a group of borrowers of illegal kickbacks and price-fixing between mortgage loan servicers and the law firms they hire to handle foreclosure on behalf of the lender. Another such suit alleges illegal practices were being employed by lenders, who supposedly sought to ease the burden on their overworked staff in the midst of heavy foreclosure filings, by pre-signing affidavits before the facts stated in these documents had been proved to be true. Still another alleges underhanded practices between lenders and their foreclosure attorneys to collect fees not approved by the court.

Municipalities v. Originators

Perhaps one of the most interesting legal arguments is that made by some local governments, which are buckling under the strain of decreasing tax bases and increasing demand for services resulting from foreclosed vacant homes. Some of these governments have sued mortgage originators. The allegation is that the local governments have been damaged as a direct result of loan originators who sold their residents loans without full and adequate disclosure and based on the false pretenses. It is not likely these local governments will prevail given the legal distance between their budget expenses, the real estate tax income, the price of homes, and the impact loan originators had on the price of homes in enabling buyers to pay that much money by approving their allegedly unlawful mortgage loans.

Other Lawsuits

The allegations against Wall Street and government leaders, oftentimes based on conflict of interest, have only just begun. In June 2008, for example, allegations that Washington insiders received special loan terms from Countrywide Financial Corp. emerged.[33] We'll discuss other situations where folks are being rightly or wrongly dragged into court in the coming chapters.

LEADING THE WAY OUT OF A FORECLOSURE NATION

The signs of America awakening extend beyond local government all the way up to the US presidency. The election of 2008 was an important one, and the subprime and broader financial crisis was a central election topic. The "R" word—recession—was shot around by candidates like a poison arrow. The fact that the incumbent historically owns the economy, housing, and economic turmoil no doubt hurt the Republican Party. As president, Barack Obama will influence our country, from legislation to life-tenured judicial appointments. The 2008 presidential election drew one of the highest number of voters ever, in part because of concern over our nation's economic situation. The fact that so many Americans are taking ownership and engaging in our nation's future is one of the crisis' many silver linings that we will discuss in chapter 7.

Our nation's awakening to the crisis has not been a quick one. We've discussed how it first began as a few of us started running into problems selling or refinancing our homes and paying our mortgage loans. The great awakening continues as we watch, sometimes in amazement, and learn more each day about how much our lifestyles and finances have become interconnected and out of control. There is only one more subject we need to discuss before we're fully equipped to talk about where our nation can and should go from here and the best choices each of us can make for ourselves. That subject is the foreclosure process itself so that those of you facing foreclosure will be better equipped and the rest of you will have a better sense of what is going on in our nation's courtrooms, defining American culture today.

NOTES

1. Editorial, "The Stimulus Debate," *New York Times*, January 11, 2009.

2. Peter S. Goodman, "Foreigners Buy Stakes in US at Record Price," *New York Times*, January 20, 2008, p. 18; Fred A. Bernstein, "For Foreign Investors, Profit Isn't Only Goal," *New York Times*, March 16, 2008, p. 20; Tal Abbady, "Venezuelan, Guatamalan and Brazilian Immigrants Have Made South Florida Their Home," *South Florida Sun Sentinel*, January 14, 2008, p. 6; "Global Trends in Real Estate," p. 9G.

3. Peter S. Goodman and Amanda Cox, "A Slowdown with Trouble at Every Turn," *New York Times*, July 19, 2008, p. A10; Paul J. Lim, "A Recession's Impact Is All in the Timing," *New York Times*, January 20, 2008, p. 6; Frank Rick, "It's the Economic Stupidity, Stupid," *New York Times*, July 20, 2008, p. 11; Justin Lahart, "Businesses Feel Pinch as Credit Grows Tight," *Wall Street Journal*, p. A1; Michael S. Grynbaum, "Businesses Worried about Economy Invest Less," *New York Times*, February 28, 2008, p. C8; Edmund L. Andrews, "Growth Is Top Concern, Bernanke Tells Congress," *New York Times*, February 28, 2008, p. C3; Edmond L. Andrews, "Inflation Rise and Drop of Dollar Complicate Fed's Calculations," *New York Times*, February 28, 2008, p. A16; David Ranson, "Inflation May Be Worse Than We Think," *Wall Street Journal*, February 27, 2008, p. A17; Vikas Bajaj, "New Worries on Inflation and the Home," *Wall Street Journal*, February 27, 2007, p. 4; Gregory Mankin, "How to Avoid a Recession? Let the Fed Work," *New York Times*, December 23, 2007; Sue Kirchoff, "Housing Turmoil a Risk to Economy," *USA Today*, July 2, 2008; Kelly Evans, "Economy's Weak Signals Persist," *Wall Street Journal*, October 26, 2007, p. 8; Scott Peterson, "Treasury Shows a Disconnect with Inflation," *Wall Street Journal*, December 4, 2007, p. C1; Tony Jackson, "All Quiet

as Front Switches from Inflation to Recession," *Financial Times*, August 18, 2008, p. 17; Tony Lauricella, "Signs Say Recovery Isn't Here," *Wall Street Journal*, August 11, 2008, p. 19; "Contraction" *Wall Street Journal*, August 15, 2008, p. 12.

4. "Bank of America Agrees to Purchase Countrywide Financial Corp.," *Newsroom*, January 11, 2008.

5. "Delinquencies and Foreclosure Increase in Latest MBA National Delinquency Survey," *Mortgage Bankers Association* press release, December 6, 2007.

6. J. Alex Tarquinio, "This Type of Rate Cuts May Not Be a Panacea," *New York Times*, January 20, 2006, p. 6; John Leland, "Facing Default, Some Walk Out on New Homes," *New York Times*, February 29, 2008, p. 1; Michael Corkey and Ruth Simon, "As Market Cools Home Buyers Seek a Way Out," *Wall Street Journal*, May 4, 2007, p. A11; Rachel Beck, "Homeowners Bail Loans Due to More Than Just Mortgage Rate," *South Florida Sun Sentinel*, December 14, 2007, p. 15.

7. Mark Landler, "US Crisis Adds to Gloom of Long Nights in Arctic Norway," *New York Times*, December 2, 2007, pp. 1, 17.

8. "Trouble in Banking Sector Hurts Europe, Asia Markets," *Wall Street Journal*, November 3, 2007, p. B3; "Global Trends in Real Estate," *Key*, September 2007, p. 9; "British Mortgage System Is Challenged," *New York Times*, August 24, 2007, p. C5; Aaron Kirchfeld and Hellmunt Tromm, "WestLB Post EU 11 Billion Loss, Will Raise Capital," *Bloomberg.com*, February 12, 2008; Aaron Kirchfeld and Oliver Suess, "WestLB to Cut 25% of Staff, Get EU15 Billion Bailout," *Bloomberg.com*, February 12, 2008, pp. 1–3; "WestLB Expects Billion Euro Loss," *BBC News*, January 21, 2008; Lionel Laurent, "Germany Steps in to Save WestLB," *Forbes*, February 8, 2008, pp. 1–5; Joe Bel Bruno, "Mortgage Meltdown a Global Nightmare," *South Florida Sun Sentinel*, January 24, 2007, p. 7; Chris Giles, "UK Forecast Punishes Sterling," *Financial Times*, August 14, 2008, p. 10; Carter Dougherty, "Euro Zone Ensnared in Global Slowdown," *International Herald Tribune*, August 15, 2008, p. 12; Chris Flood, "More Gloom to Increase Fears of Global Recession," *Financial Times*, August 18, 2008; Justin Lahart, "Global Economy Slows," *Wall Street Journal*, August 15, 2008, p. 1; Marcus Walker, "Euro Zone GDP Shrinks in New Signs of Global Downturn," *Wall Street Journal*, August 15, 2008, p. 28; Nina Koepper, "Euro Banks Lending," *Wall Street Journal*, August 11, 2008, p. 20; Laura Santini, "Debts the Way China Likes It," *Wall Street Journal*, August 28, 2008, p. 18; Polyana da Costa, "Global Connections," *Daily Business Review*, December 14. 2007, p. A6; David Roche, "The Global Money Machine," *Wall Street Journal*, December 14, 2007, p. A21.

9. Martin Arnold, "Questions Over Sectors Own Debt Purchases," *Financial Times*, August 18, 2008, p. 16; Gretchen Morgenson, "Addressing a Disclosure Backwater," *International Herald Tribune*, August 18, 2008, p. 11; Serena Ng, "Liffe Joins Credit Default Arena," *Wall Street Journal*, July 8, 2008, p. C2; Craig

Karmin, "Swap Backfire as Cost Saver on Public Debt," *Wall Street Journal*, March 22, 2008, pp. 9, 15; Kate Kelly, "How Goldman Won Big on Mortgage Meltdown," *Wall Street Journal*, December 14, 2007, pp. A1, 17; Ben Stein, "The Long and the Short of It at Goldman Sachs," *New York Times*, December 2, 2007, p. 9.

10. Kate Kelly, "How Goldman Won Big on Mortgage Meltdown," *Wall Street Journal*, December 14, 2007, pp. A1, 7; Ben Stein, "The Long and Short of It at Goldman," *New York Times*, December 2, 2007, p. 9.

11. Robin Sidel, "Citigroup CEO Plans to Resign as Losses Grow," *Wall Street Journal*, November 3, 2007, p. A4.

12. Jed Horowitz, "Merrill Defends Its Transactions," *New York Times*, August 28, 2008, p. 1B; Robin Sidel, "Citigroup CEO Plans to Resign as Losses Grow," *Wall Street Journal*, November 3, 2007, p. A4.

13. Conrad de Aenlle, "Good Banks Are Punished with the Bad," *New York Times,* May 15, 2008, p. B6.

14. Associated Press, "Bank of America Buys Stake in Countrywide," *New York Times*, January 11, 2008, p. C7.

15. Charles Wisniowski, "Mortgage Fraud Expert Rachel Dollar—The Mortgage Fraud Blog," *Mortgage Banking (News)*, February 2007, pp. 26–30; Jonathan Goodman, "Loan Fraud Alert," *Realtor Magazine*, December 2006, p. 24; John Mechem, "FBI Sign Memo of Understanding on Mortgage Fraud Warning," *Mortgage Bankers Association*, March 9, 2007.

16. www.marisolutions.com.

17. Ibid.

18. David Subar, "The New Battle against Fraud," *Mortgage Banking (News),* March 2007, pp. 109–13; Mortgage Bankers Association Web site.

19. Subar, "The New Battle against Fraud," pp. 109–13; Mechem, "FBI Sign Memo of Understanding on Mortgage Fraud Warning"; Michael Murray, "Fraud against Lenders Not Going Away," *Mortgage Bankers Association*, March 9, 2007; Christopher Rubaber, "Case of Mortgage Fraud Up, FBI Says," *Washington Post*, March 8, 2007, p. D4.

20. Paul Davidson, "Millionaire Hopefuls Cash Gone with Breeze," *USA Today*, August 14, 2007, p. 3B.

21. Nelson P. Schwartz, "Can the Mortgage Crisis Swallow a Town?" *New York Times*, September 2, 2007, p. 9.

22. "Slump Pinches Association Fees," *New York Times*, May 13, 2008, p. D3; Stephanie Chen, "As Dues Dry Up the Neighbors Pay," *Wall Street Journal*, May 13, 2008, p. D3.

23. Chen, "As Dues Dry Up the Neighbors Pay," p. D3.

24. Mark Whitehouse, "Florida Homes Plan Overhaul Property Taxes," *Wall Street Journal*, May 29, 2007, p. C7; Jennifer Steinhauer, "Taxes Reassessed in Housing Slump as Prices Decline," *New York Times*, December 23, 2007, p. 30.

25. Ibid.

26. Steinhauer, "Taxes Reassessed in Housing Slump as Prices Decline," p. 30.

27. Associated Press, "Key Home Price Index Shows Record Decline," February 26, 2008.

28. www.bankruptcyaction.com/usbankstats.htm.

29. www.marketwatch.com/news/story/transunion.com-national-auto-loan; www.marketwatch.com/news/story/transunion.com-delinquency/story.

30. Metro Study Rate Resets.

31. Terry Sheridan, "Cash Strapped," *Daily Business Review,* May 1, 2008, p. 5.

32. Kate Kelly, "The Fall of Bear Stearns," *Wall Street Journal*, May 28, 2008, p. A13; Kate Kelly and Serena Ng, "Bear Stearns Funds Hurt by Subprime Losses," *Wall Street Journal*, June 13, 2007, p. 3B.

33. Kathy M. Kristof and Tom Hamburger, "Lender a Major Beltway Operator," *Los Angeles Times*, June 14, 2008, p. C1.

6

FORECLOSURE 101

Foreclosure is a legal procedure with roots going back to English common law by which a lender takes title to a parcel of real estate following a borrower's failure to comply with the mortgage loan agreement entered into with the lender. The most frequent failure is a default in payment under the promissory note, but in some cases, particularly construction loans, defaults under other agreement terms are common. For example, a developer default may be triggered if multiple buyers of the homes the developer planned to build cancel their purchase contracts or if the construction involves too many changes, runs over budget, or takes longer than the agreed time frame for completion. Many commercial loans provide that if the borrower's sales, collateral property value, income, or occupancy rates falls below a certain level or even if the bank is simply feeling that the borrower's business has been negatively impacted, the bank can call the loan. These provisions are causing many commercial loans to go into default even though the borrower is still paying on time and from a business standpoint might still be considered a safe loan risk. Because many borrowers do not realize the variety of events that can cause a default or the remedies available to lenders when we default, examples of typical mortgage loan default and remedy provisions are included in appendix G. This chapter provides you with an overview of foreclosure processes and terms, incorporating many frequently asked questions. Like chapter 2, this chapter is written to be used as a reference, allowing you to read those sections that interest you and refer to others as needed.

WHAT IS ACCELERATION?

The legal concept of *acceleration* allows a lender to declare the entire mortgage loan amount due in full if an event of default occurs. Once a lender accelerates a loan, the borrower must repay the higher default interest rate we discussed in chapter 2 along with late penalties, attorney fees, and other costs incurred by the lender in foreclosing, in addition to the mortgage loan principal, if he wants to keep the property. Often, borrowers who have reached the foreclosure stage also owe real estate taxes, association assessments, and even insurance advanced by the lender when they fail to pay for those items themselves.

WHICH FORECLOSURE THEORY DOES YOUR STATE FOLLOW?

There are two different types of foreclosure processes employed by states, depending upon the underlying legal theory each adopts. In the United States we have *judicial* or *lien* foreclosure theory states and *trustee* or *title* theory foreclosure states. We reviewed in chapter 2 that a mortgage creates a lien against the property that is normally recorded in public records. The titleholder during the loan period can be either the borrower or lender depending on which foreclosure theory is practiced in the state where the property is located, "lien theory" or "title theory." In a title theory state, the borrower conveys title to the lender during the loan term.

In a lien theory state, a *deed of trust* essentially serves the same purpose as a mortgage; however, there are important differences with respect to parties involved, the titleholder, and foreclosure process. Unlike a mortgage, a deed of trust involves three parties—the borrower, the lender, and the trustee. The trustee is a neutral third party that holds title to the property to secure repayment of the loan until the loan is paid. In some states, attorneys can act as trustees; and in others, title companies normally provide trustee services.

Another significant difference is in the foreclosure process. When a deed of trust is involved, foreclosure can be quicker, less expensive, and less complicated than when a mortgage is the security instrument. If the loan becomes delinquent, the trustee has the power to sell the home. Of course, the lender must provide the trustee with proof of delinquency and request that foreclosure proceedings be initiated. And the foreclosure must progress according to law and as dictated by the deed of trust. However, the foreclosure does not have to go through the court system in the same time-consuming manner that applies in lien theory states. In lien theory states, the borrower retains title to his property during the loan period and instead gives the lender a mortgage, discussed more fully in chapter 2, to secure repayment of the loan. If the borrower defaults, the lender can foreclose on the mortgage in a process commonly referred to as judicial foreclosure. Most states are lien theory and use judicial foreclosure procedures, so we will explain that process in more detail below. A list of which US states follow which theory is included as appendix H so you can check which theory your own state follows. Appendix H also explains the process used in title theory states in more detail for those of you with properties or loans in those jurisdictions.

WHAT IS A FORECLOSURE COMPLAINT?

Each party reflected in the chain of title or foreclosure title report needs to be named in the *foreclosure complaint*, the legal document filed with the court that officially begins the judicial foreclosure process. An example of a mortgage foreclosure complaint is included as appendix I so that readers at risk of foreclosure can see exactly what to expect and other readers will have a better understanding as well. We discussed mortgage insurance in chapter 2. Those home owners with mortgage insurance will hear from their mortgage insurance carrier when they default on payments under the mortgage since the mortgage insurance company will be required, under the terms of the mortgage insurance policy, to step in and pay the lender any outstanding principal and interest. Once the mortgage insurance company has paid the lender, it will pursue the home owner for payment. The Fair Debt Collection Practices Act (FDCPA) also requires that under some circumstances a specific notice be served upon the borrower with the complaint lodged against him. The notice explains the borrowers options in more layman terms.

It is important that all parties with an interest in the property be notified of the foreclosure action. Every interest or lien that is recorded after the lender's mortgage is *inferior* to the lender's and will be eliminated, or wiped out, when the lender takes back the property. When the property is sold at the foreclosure sale, these parties will be paid the money that is due to them in accordance with their lien priority, as discussed in chapter 2, but only after the first lender gets paid. Every interest of lien superior must be paid by the foreclosing lender, who will acquire title "subject to" these interests. For this reason, a foreclosure complaint literally lists or names every interest holder as a *defendant*, or party being sued. If the property happens to be a rental home, condominium, or building that is occupied by tenants, these tenants and associations will also be named in the complaint and an eviction action may be necessary.

The foreclosure complaint is formally delivered or *served* on each of these parties by a certified process server in the same manner as it is delivered to the borrower in default. The residential borrower has a specified amount of time to contact the lender for validation of the debt. In validating the debt, the lender provides a copy of the promissory note, the mortgage, the loan payment history, and any escrow account statement, as well as other relevant documents that show what is owed and that payment is in arrears. If the borrower does not request validation of the debt within the time allotted, the debt is presumed to be valid under the FDCPA.

WHAT IS A LIS PENDENS?

A *Lis Pendens* (pronounced Liz-Pen-danz) is recorded in the public records office to put other third parties on notice that the property is now subject to foreclosure litigation. The Lis Pendens puts any potential buyers or lenders for the property on notice that a legal action which might affect that property is pending. A sample Lis Pendens is included as appendix J to give you more complete understanding of what this document says.

WHAT IS AN ANSWER?

Likewise, each defendant has an opportunity to respond to the complaint within a certain period of time. This also means that each of these parties will or should hire an attorney to handle that response and represent their interests in the foreclosure action.

Defendants wishing to do so may file a response, or *answer*, to the foreclosure complaint. Often residential borrower-defendants cannot afford to hire an attorney and thus do not file a proper answer or sometimes file no answer at all. A sample answer is included as appendix K.

WHAT IS A MOTION FOR SUMMARY JUDGMENT?

The lender's course of action at this point often depends upon the content of the various defendants' answers. If no answers are filed or the answers filed contain no legitimate responses—*defenses* or *counterclaims*, also known as the defendant's own allegations of wrongdoing against the lender—to the defaults cited or *counts* in the foreclosure complaint, the lender may file a *motion for summary judgment* (MSJ) asking the judge to simply rule in the lender's favor and authorize, or *order*, a foreclosure sale for the property. In many states, the borrower is required to file an affidavit in opposition to the MSJ at least forty-eight hours prior to the MSJ hearing if he intends to oppose the MSJ. However, again since many residential borrowers cannot afford to hire an attorney they are therefore not aware of this and other important rules. Instead, many borrowers simply show up in the courtroom on the day of the hearing and tell the judge what circumstances have befallen them and how they hope to resolve their situation. If an actual contract for a short sale or concrete solution is presented at the time of the hearing, judges are more apt to allow time. If the borrower and other defendants have no credible defense or solution, the court will enter the order granting the MSJ at the time of the hearing and the clerk of court will set the foreclosure sale date. This is generally the last chance for the borrower, unless he retains an attorney who discovers some irregularity in the judgment that is sufficient to set it aside.

WHAT ARE DEFENSES AND COUNTERCLAIMS?

Again, if legitimate affirmative defenses are raised or if the borrower or other defendants files any counterclaims, the case is moved to contested status, and the lender must reply to any affirmative defense or counterclaim raised by the borrower or other defendants. Some examples of defenses or counterclaims are, if the borrower claims that the mortgage loan originator committed predatory lending (as discussed in chapter 5), the mortgage loan servicer modified the terms of the mortgage, the lender cannot produce proof that it actually owns the mortgage loan, or the amount the lender claims is due is incorrect. This will lead to a more protracted foreclosure suit, with the judge setting the date for trial, which permits all sides an opportunity to present their respective cases.

WHAT IS DISCOVERY?

Discovery is the legal process by which each side in the foreclosure lawsuit is allowed an opportunity to gather information about the facts surrounding the case from the other side and third parties (such as witnesses) before starting a trial. Oftentimes, one of the parties learns about something during discovery that they did not know before, which gives them incentive to try to resolve the matter. For example, a lender may learn that a borrower made the mortgage payments that the lender claims were never made at the bank's branch office and the lender's employee did not enter the payments properly into the computer system. There are several different types of discovery. *Interrogatories* are written questions one side gives to the other to respond to, also in writing. *Requests for production* are written requests one side gives the other to produce various documents and information. And *depositions* are questions one side asks the other (or third parties such as witnesses) in person, which are documented word-for-word by the court reporter. One or more of the parties may *subpoena* an individual to appear and testify. Contested cases are often referred to *mediation* before a trial is set. Mediation is a process outside the court where a third party, called a mediator, who the parties all agree to, meets with the parties to help them try to negotiate a mutually agreeable solution. Often the case settles in mediation by executing a loan modification agreement or by granting a forbearance or repayment plan allowing the borrower to refinance or sell the property to satisfy the loan. Mediation is quickly emerging as a top alternative to foreclosure for lenders and borrowers alike. For more information about mediation, go to www.foreclosurenationthebook.com.

HOW DOES BANKRUPTCY FIT IN?

One common last resort for borrowers trying to delay foreclosure and buy time to find another solution such as a refinance or a sale of the property is to file for bankruptcy since this automatically stops, or *stays*, the foreclosure process. Depending on the creditor(s) and type of bankruptcy (chapter 7, 11, or 13) sought, the borrower's creditors are prevented from collecting on the debts owed until the bankruptcy is decided upon. On the other hand, residential borrowers who elect to file personal bankruptcy are faced with the prospect of having to rebuild their credit, which may lead to difficulty buying another home or even renting an apartment. Conversely, in commercial settings lenders may force a borrower into involuntary bankruptcy and request the appointment of a receiver or chief restructuring officer (CRO) to oversee or run the property as a strategy to pressure the borrower or to protect or get control over the property sooner. In the sidebar below, bankruptcy attorney Brad Shraiberg shares his expertise about bankruptcy as an option if your home is being foreclosed upon.

If you elect to file bankruptcy, it is very important to choose an experi-

Insight from a Foreclosure Attorney

"If all else fails, a debtor's last option to preserve his, her, or its equity in real estate is to seek protection under one of the various chapters of the bankruptcy code. The filing of a bankruptcy delays, if not outright stops, a foreclosure proceeding as it automatically freezes the lender's lawsuit in its tracks including the cancellation of a foreclosure sale if one is scheduled. Once in bankruptcy, the debtor may set forth a plan of reorganization which pays back its past due obligations (including mortgage payments) over a period of up to five years. When used properly, due to this ability to automatically stay (or freeze) a foreclosure proceeding, the filing of a bankruptcy can be a powerful tool to help a debtor (borrower) reorganize. With this said, the filing of a bankruptcy may only be utilized in certain circumstances. If there is no equity in the property the debtor seeks to save or it is not feasible for the debtor (borrower) to repay the past due obligations, including mortgage payments, over time, then the filing of a bankruptcy could be deemed a bad faith filing which could subject the debtor (borrower) to sanctions (punishment by the court such as having to pay the lender's attorneys fees)."

enced, qualified bankruptcy attorney. Likewise, it is important that lenders are represented by a qualified bankruptcy attorney when a borrower files bankruptcy in order to design the best possible strategy to get the stay lifted, or removed, so the lender can proceed with the foreclosure or negotiate the best possible plan with borrower's counsel so as to avoid added costs and delays. It is also important that borrowers understand which of their debts their bankruptcy attorney will help to alleviate. If a debt is overlooked or not properly addressed by your bankruptcy attorney, you may go through the bankruptcy process only to find that you are still on the hook for an obligation that could have been dealt with in bankruptcy court.

WHAT IS A FINAL JUDGMENT AND NOTICE OF SALE?

If the judge determines that the defendant's case outweighs the lender's or that proper procedure has not been followed, the judge may dismiss the case, in which event the lender may need to amend the complaint and start over again and refile for foreclosure. On the other hand, if the judge agrees with the lender, he will issue a *final judgment* in favor of the lender and order the foreclosure sale. Notice of the foreclosure must be published in a designated area newspaper, and, again, a certain period of time must pass. This allows as many people interested in buying the property as possible to know about it so that the highest price can be achieved. While the notice is running, the lender or servicer of the mortgage is computing the bidding instructions for the lender's attorney, who will represent and bid for the lender at the foreclosure sale. Sometimes the bid will be whatever the judgment provides; other times the highest bid will be lower than the judgment amount. This generally occurs when the property has decreased in value. If no one else is bidding, the lender's attorney will try to keep the bid as low as possible since the transfer tax, taxes paid to the state or county every time a property changes hands, often including by foreclosure, is based on the price and may have to be paid by the winning bidder. A higher price means higher taxes. In the past, all the lender wanted was a return of the principal, accrued interest, and any outstanding fees and costs. However, as the market has changed, lenders now consider more in determining how much to bid at their own foreclosure sales. Lenders or servicers sometimes but rarely now consider only how much they have loaned and what they have spent in collection and base the bid on those figures alone. Most lenders or servicers now also consider what the property will cost them if they get it back, such as costs to secure the property against vandalism, costs to maintain the property, costs associated with any outstanding building code violations, and costs associated with marketing and selling the property, in deciding whether or not they want to own the property. If the property is a construction project, commercial real estate lenders also need to consider the possibility of exposing themselves to something called *successor developer liability* if they elect to take back the project and finish construction. Under certain circumstances and in some jurisdictions such "successor developers" can be held liable by unit buyers for construction defects. If a lender is held liable as a successor developer, its exposure could be much more than the original loan amount. In other words, lenders and servicers are now looking at the big picture. If they keep their blinders on, they will have too many real-estate-owned (REO) properties in their inventory. Sometimes it makes more sense to instead keep the highest bid at a level that will encourage purchasers at the foreclosure sale to take the property off their hands, get the cash now, and avoid further costs and potential liability.

Professional Foreclosure Investors

Often the other bidders at foreclosure sales are what we might call professionals, experienced folks who have made full or part time careers of buying foreclosed properties. They, like the lender, know ahead of time what their highest bid for a particular property will be. An example of the type of information used by some investors available by subscription from foreclosure data providers is included as appendix L for those readers considering taking advantage of the market by investing in foreclosures. The lender's attorney and other bidders may know each other and even discuss in advance how high they each intend to bid. The important point is that the relationships between the lender's attorney and the professional bidders may influence how much the property sells for at a foreclosure sale and, ultimately, how much money the borrower may get back or may still owe the lender after the sale. Foreclosure attorney Amy McGrotty, remembers the first foreclosure sale she attended as young counsel for a national lender and shares these memories with us in the sidebar on page 190.

Insight from a Bank's Foreclosure Attorney

"The professional foreclosure bidders in some regions are a pretty tight group. They tend to be street-smart kind of guys. It's still very much a boy's club. These guys saw a young girl and figured they'd give me a hard time. But my dad was a foreclosure attorney for thirty years. He'd warned me about them. Even a few specifically by name. The clerk started the bids on my lender's property. No one else wanted the property. But rather than let me just finish the bidding for a minimum hundred-dollar bid and be done with it, these guys figured they'd mess with me by bidding the price up. Everyone knows that's not great for my lender, since it also drives up the price we have to pay in transfer tax. We're talking about a difference of hundreds, maybe thousands of dollars. There was nothing I could do about it during the bidding. But I also happen to have a black belt in marital arts. After the sale I cornered one of the guys. I gave him my card and told him I'd appreciate if he made sure that didn't happen again. He looked at my card and said "Oh. You're McGrotty's kid. Sorry about that." And that was that. It never happened again, at least not to me, and the guy ended up becoming a personal friend. I see them do it to younger attorneys all the time still. It's kind of a foreclosure attorney's right of passage. Having a good relationship with the other regular bidders can be important for your lender client."

In cases where the investors outbid the attorney, the attorney will confirm that the deposit has been paid by the investor bidder to the clerk and follows up again later for the disbursement of funds to the lender to pay off the mortgage loan. In most jurisdictions if the highest bidder doesn't deliver the full purchase funds on time, the property will go to the next highest bidder. Likewise, if proper procedures are not followed at the foreclosure sale, the sale may be set aside and have to be rescheduled for another day. Some foreclosure rescue firms have become quite adept at using this type of technicality to delay foreclosures and buy home owners more time.

WHAT HAPPENS AFTER THE FORECLOSURE SALE?

As we've said, state statutes specify exactly what needs to be included in the foreclosure complaint and other documents, or *pleadings*, which together comprise the foreclosure process, as well as the time frames lenders must adhere to. These documents and time frames vary from state to state.

Certificate of Title and Right of Redemption

Although procedures vary from state to state, in general on the day of the foreclosure sale, anyone interested may bid at the sale. This requires first posting a deposit with the clerk of the court. Successful bidders must pay in full by the end of the day. (Bidding at foreclosure sales, including associated risks, is discussed in more detail in chapter 7.) Included as appendix L is an administrative order explaining foreclosure proceedings in one jurisdiction as an example for those readers interested in pursuing this opportunity.

After the sale, a *certificate of title* is issued to the successful bidder. This process normally takes a few days to several months, depending upon the state, during which time the borrower may still have the opportunity, called the right of redemption, to pay off the mortgage loan and *redeem* the title to the property or get it back. We briefly discussed the right of redemption in chapter 2. This right varies by state from under a day to up to a year, which is relevant to our discussion now as this variance makes managing huge volumes of mortgage loan foreclosures that much more challenging for lenders and servicers. For example, Texas has a shorter foreclosure time than Pennsylvania, and courts in some states disallow various lender fees allowed in others. More recently, some courts began disallowing lender broker price opinion and inspection charges.

What Is a Deficiency Judgment?

As we've said, the proceeds from the foreclosure sale go first to pay off the lender and the lender's lawyers and then to pay off remaining debts against the property. Once the lender gets title to the property it has to pay any outstanding county real estate taxes, Internal Revenue Service liens, and state taxes. Any money left after everyone is paid and the second mortgage or other liens, if any, are paid, goes to the borrower as his equity in the property. As you can imagine, in today's market it is rare that there is any money left over to go back to the borrower. If the amount generated from the foreclosure sale is less than what is owed to the lender, the lender may continue suing the borrower for a *deficiency judgment,* requiring the borrower to repay the shortfall from other assets he may have. With real estate prices dropping, the foreclosure sale is likely to yield far less than what is owed and deficiency judgments have become commonplace. When a deficiency judgment applies, the lender may pursue forcing the sale of these other assets owned by the borrower. The *statute of limitations,* or time during which a lender is entitled to pursue and enforce a deficiency judgment, varies from state to state, sometimes extending for several years after the foreclosure is done.

The primary purpose for foreclosure statutes is to ensure that *due process*, or the legal rights of all interested parties are assured. If the statutes are not properly followed, the lender or, a third party if someone else buys the property as the eventual successful bidder foreclosure at a sale, may not acquire good title and the foreclosure process may have to be repeated. For example, if there was a second mortgage on the property but the second lender was not named as a defendant in the complaint and included in the foreclosure suit, the second lender's mortgage lien will not be eliminated or wiped out by the foreclosure suit. The process to reforeclose on property in order to cure a defect like that in the original foreclosure process is shorter, but it's a step that shouldn't have to be taken if all procedures are properly followed the first time.

HOW IS FORECLOSING ON A SECOND MORTGAGE DIFFERENT?

In cases where borrowers have more than one mortgage on their home, circumstances may arise where the borrower stops paying on a home equity loan or otherwise defaults on the second mortgage, but not the first. If a second mortgage holder, or the holder of any encumbrance inferior to the first mortgage, decides to foreclose, that lender or the buyer at the foreclosure sale takes title to the property "subject to" the superior first mortgage. This means the buyer will need to pay off the first mortgage holder.

REOs

Once the property is owned by the lender, it becomes part of the lender's *real estate owned* (REO) portfolio. The lender's job of securing, maintaining, and marketing the property begins at this time. Most lenders will obtain a current *broker price opinion* (BPO) to determine the current property value and list the property for sale with a local Realtor with whom they typically have a preexisting relationship. An example of a BPO is included for you as appendix N. Most lenders also have designated REO repair and maintenance companies who care for the properties they own or prepare them for sale. Generally lenders spend as little as possible on the property. They don't want to have a lot of expenses to deduct from the sale price when one of their properties is sold. The procedures, opportunities, and challenges involved for lenders trying to sell REOs are discussed in more detail in chapter 7. Over the years, the politics involved in securing contracts to act as a lender servicer, foreclosure attorney, closing company and title insurer, BPO provider, Realtor, and repair and maintenance resource have become increasingly heated. Larger national businesses, including the country's largest title insurance underwriters, now vie for the business once handled by local firms. These contenders are financially positioned to provide other services to the lender at discounted prices, or even free of charge, in return for winning the lender's servicing or foreclosure-related business. Some of these relationships result in conflicts of interest and arrangements that do not necessarily create the best resources and support for us as borrowers. For example, because of the other benefits a lender may get from the relationship, the lender may not shop for the absolute best price for the services. Since the cost of these services is normally passed on to the borrower, the bottom line is borrowers may sometimes pay more than they might otherwise have to.

WHAT ARE FORECLOSURE "MILLS?"

Because the competition for contracts to do business with lenders has become so intense, lender's service providers often must compete on price, and therefore need to reduce their own costs of providing the service in order to maintain a profit. This intense competition for foreclosure-related business, together with the increase in sheer volume and time required for the industry to gear up to handle it, has contributed to the lack of adequate staff and training we've mentioned we encounter when attempting to work with lenders' servicing, default, and foreclosure departments. The larger residential foreclosure attorney offices have for some time been referred to in the industry as "factories" or "mills." This is because, while there are smaller attorney offices that handle residential foreclosures for (usually the smaller) lenders, most often foreclosures for larger residential mortgage lenders are handled by a handful of large firms that do very little work for any other type of client.

These firms have established a factorylike infrastructure where large numbers of employees are trained to each handle only a specific small piece of the overall foreclosure case in the most cost effective manner possible. Because each person is only responsible for one part of the process, each person is expected to handle a very large volume of cases. This type of cost efficiency is necessitated in part by the fact that part of the agreement government-sponsored enterprises (GSEs), like Fannie Mae, CDO investors, and others have with mortgage lenders to purchase or insure mortgage loans from those lenders is that, if the loans go into default, the GSEs only have to pay a specified amount for the servicers to foreclose on the mortgage loans, often as little as $1200 per loan foreclosure file, and the foreclosure has to be completed within an often impossibly short amount of time. The sidebar on page 195 reflects an example of these timeframes, which some now say, due to court backlogs, are impossible to comply with. Most require the foreclosure attorney to lay out costs up front (such as foreclosure complaint filing fees and title searches, often totaling hundreds of dollars per foreclosure case) a burden many smaller legal practices simply cannot afford. Only being able to charge a particular small amount of money per case, of course, also ties the lawyer's hands in terms of the number and quality of people and amount of time he can afford to have working

Foreclosure Time Frames (Fannie Mae—150 Days)

Task	*Day*
File Received	3
First Legal Action	30
Service Completed	55
Judgment Entered	100
Scheduled Sale Date	150
Foreclosure Sale Held	150
Foreclosure Sale Confirmed/Ratified	165
Foreclosure Deed Recorded	180

on a foreclosure file and may account for why so little time can be invested in trying to resolve a borrower's defaults and prevent foreclosure altogether. These attorneys basically have to get each foreclosure off their desk as quickly and inexpensively as possible. This explains why so many borrowers complain that their bank's foreclosure attorney won't return their calls or respond to short sale offers. The other reason for this apparent lack of service is that many lenders have their foreclosure attorneys work on the foreclosure case but want any calls or questions regarding a workout, modification, or short sale to still go the the internal default servicing department, meaning that a borrower in foreclosure who wants to work it out has to do so with several people from the lending side at the same time.

COMMERCIAL REAL ESTATE FORECLOSURES

Because commercial real estate foreclosures and workouts tend to be for higher dollar amounts and more complicated, often involving relationships and projects that need to be managed and preserved, most commercial real estate lenders will hire lawyers better equipped to address the wider variety of legal issues that tend to emerge, in addition to simply litigating a foreclosure case, such as construction litigation, land use, successor developer liability, permits and entitlements, contract law, and bankruptcy. In larger commercial real estate foreclosure cases, especially in today's environment, business acumen, negotiating skills and an understanding of human psychology are as critical as top-notch legal skills for a lender's counsel. One such case that I am currently handling illustrates the needs for these various skills and is described for you in the sidebar on page 196.

WHAT ARE THE ALTERNATIVES TO FORECLOSURE?

Foreclosure is usually a last resort for borrower and lender alike. The process is time consuming and costly, and while it is pending, a foreclosure prohibits everyone from putting the default behind them and moving on. Lenders are not in the business of owning, maintaining, and marketing properties and generally try to avoid it. In today's market, lenders know that until excess inventory is absorbed in the areas where they do business, new homes will

An Example of Some of the Issues Complicating Commercial Real Estate Foreclosure Cases Today

The foreclosure involves eighty-seven oceanfront condominiums originally designed in 2005 to be sold for between $3 and $7 million each. Thirty-one were presold to buyers who still have active contracts but who are all either actually in litigation or threatening litigation to cancel their contracts and get their deposits back. Unfortunately, the developer-borrower has already spent the deposit money. (Whether this was legal or not for him to have done is also in dispute but may be moot since the fact is he now has no money whatsoever to pay back the deposits.) The buildings are approximately 30 percent complete. The construction site is fenced off but that is clearly not stopping vandals and homeless people from entering the property. And, in the event of a hurricane the fence will not stop the loose construction materials from becoming projectiles, possibly harming people and damaging surrounding properties. The county has cited the borrower for a variety of building code violations and placed liens on the property with thousands of dollars in fines accruing daily. The borrower has filed for bankruptcy and has been named, along with the lender (my client), as a defendant in lawsuits filed by the general contractor and several Realtors. The insurance protecting both the developer-borrower and the lender recently expired. Again, the developer-borrower has completely run out of money. So if any of these items are going to be addressed, the money will have to come from the lender, who is already owed $37 million from the loan, which is now over a year in arrears. As of this writing, the building permits will expire in fourteen days. If the permits expire, all construction done so far on the property will have to be torn down and the permits will need to be re-applied for, a process that could take several years. There is no guarantee that new permits for 87 units will be issued. If that is allowed to happen and only 70 units, for example, are later permitted, the profit lost on the seventeen additional units would be over $60 million!

delay the resale of foreclosed ones, especially if an area has depreciated or the foreclosure property is in poor condition.

Fortunately there are often other options that could be taken before the more drastic foreclosure route is explored. In recent years, one of the newer buzzwords among lenders is *loss mitigation*, or the attempt to employ foreclosure alternatives in order to cut losses incurred by lenders and borrowers alike. Regrettably, borrowers are often not aware of the options available to them and mortgage loan servicers are too overburdened to invest the resources to explore alternative possibilities.

Forbearance Agreements

Often the first alternative is a *forbearance*, or repayment agreement either formal or informal, under which lenders refrain from immediately exercising their default rights and give borrowers more time to cure (resolve) the default. A forbearance agreement is basically a "timeout" to allow the borrower a chance to solve the defaults. Forbearance agreements have become extremely effective tools in dealing with foreclosures on commercial projects in our current environment simply because they allow both borrower and lender to get a better idea of what the property is now worth. A forbearance period may also behoove both sides to work together to make sure the property is protected; for example, that permits will not expire, as we discussed earlier. This is in comparison to the typical lender foreclosure strategy pre-2006, which was to foreclose as quickly as possible, get the property sold, and pay off the loan. We'll discuss in chapter 8 how forbearance agreements have become extremely popular for large commercial real estate projects as lenders and borrowers decide that it is also in their mutual best interest to sit tight and see if either side will be eligible for relief from the government's bailout.

Mortgage Modifications

A similar alternative is a *mortgage loan modification*, in which the lender agrees to formally change the terms of the mortgage loan in an effort to facilitate the borrower's ability to get caught up and repay the debt. Most modifications involve drafting an agreement that alters the terms of the loan on a permanent basis and may involve paying documentary stamp taxes, recording fees, and sometimes even title insurance premiums, depending on how significant the changes to the loan are. A sample mortgage modification agreement is included as appendix O to give you a better understanding of this option.

Short Sales

We've discussed how recent declines in property values are leaving some of us upside down in our homes. Often we are not fully aware of the disparity until after meeting with a Realtor to list our home, at which point we discover that what the home needs to sell for in order to pay off the mortgage and cover the selling costs, including a commission to the Realtor, is much more than what the market is likely to pay. In other words, we owe more than our house is actually worth. One solution may be to ask the lender or servicer to allow a *short sale* of our home for less than what will be needed to cover these costs. To work, the sale requires a corresponding reduction in the amount the lender expects from us to pay off the mortgage loan. Because a short sale involves the lender or servicer, more work is involved. As we discussed earlier, the lender or servicer may need to justify the decision to accept a short sale to its investors. Typically this involves presenting the servicer with reasons for and evidence of our financial hardship as well as a current market value estimate for the property. More information about short sale basics is included as appendix P for readers considering that option. Realtors can be key in the short-sale process. Many real estate agents have undergone new training and are becoming more and more experienced in navigating the short-sale process for their seller-customers. Short sales are equally applicable in the commercial real estate context where many investors actually buy the defaulted note and foreclosure rights from the lender at a discount rather than wait until the lender forecloses and acquire the propertly itself.

Refinancing or Renting

In prior housing markets, refinancing a mortgage before or during foreclosure was an option, as was renting out the property (if the rent would cover the owner's costs), and temporarily moving in with friends or family, or into a less expensive home. We've discussed that refinancing has become an increasingly less viable alternative as credit tightens and the credit rating of a borrower in default falls. However, as we'll discuss in more detail in chapter 8, we can expect to see refinance and modification money free up as a result of the government bailout. Likewise, with the excess new housing yet unsold and investor inventory flooding the rental market, further driving down rent rates, the prospect of renting out an existing home to avoid foreclosure and being able to cover costs has become slim.

Deed-in-Lieu of Foreclosure

Another foreclosure alternative is the *deed-in-lieu of foreclosure*, in which the borrower voluntarily gives the lender ownership of the property (he hands over the deed) in return for release from the promissory note and mortgage obligations. Because a deed-in-lieu does not involve legally foreclosing on the property and wiping out inferior encumbrances (liens and debts against the property that are inferior to the lender's mortgage), other arrangements must be made to address those parties and their interests. Typically this involves time-consuming negotiations that may ultimately prove to be unsuccessful. In other words, the other creditors may expect to be paid before the owner turns over the deed to the mortgage lender but the home owner is unable to pay these debts. For this reason, when inferior encumbrances are involved, a deed-in-lieu may not be an option. Likewise, if a borrower files bankruptcy, the deed-in-lieu may be set aside by the bankruptcy court, further increasing lender's hesitancy to accept this alternative. Borrowers considering giving their lender a deed-in-lieu of foreclosure should be sure that in return, their lender gives them a release from all liability under the mortgage loan. Do not assume that just because you give the bank the property, you are automatically released from the obligations agreed to in the original mortgage loan documents. This is a common mistake being made by borrowers every day when they elect to literally mail the lender the keys to the property, commonly referred to as "jingle mail." These lenders still have the legal right to sue the borrower for deficiency judgment payment under the loan documents if, after selling the property, they do not get enough money to pay off the entire loan amount. A sample of a deed-in-lieu of foreclosure is included as appendix Q so that readers considering that option will have a better understanding of what they will be expected to sign.

DOES FORECLOSURE ACTUALLY BEGIN WITH THE MORTGAGE LOAN CLOSING PROCESS?

People are the heart of our foreclosure nation. We've discussed the visible impact of foreclosure, but what of the more elusive emotional destruction?

With so many problems in our economy, we tend to forget that each foreclosure complaint filed in US courts has one of our country's citizens behind it, each with his or her own story.

The Application

In some ways, the foreclosure process actually begins when a borrower first applies for a mortgage loan and willingly moves forward without understanding the loan terms. Within three days after making an application for a home loan, federal law, specifically, the Truth in Lending Act of 1968, requires that the borrower be provided certain written disclosures, commonly referred to in the industry as the *three-day notices*. This includes four documents; first, a good faith estimate reflecting what the closing costs will be. If actual costs at closing consistently vary from good faith estimates given by more than 10 percent, a mortgage loan originator may be subject to discipline or fines; second, a Truth in Lending disclosure showing borrowers, among other things, how much the credit or mortgage loan will actually cost them over time; third, a servicing notice advising the borrower that the lender may sell the loan or assign servicing rights for the loan; and fourth, an interest rate lock-in agreement which allows the borrower to either lock in their interest rate or wait and hope rates will go down before they close by letting the rate "float." Each time a borrower executes a document, including the three-day notices, or provides information in connection with their mortgage loan application, as usually occurs between the time of application and the time of closing, the borrowers are making representations and acknowledging awareness of facts that, in the event that we fail to pay off the mortgage, may come back to haunt us.

Closing

At the closing table, borrowers sign and execute dozens of lengthy documents, often in small type. This is often done in front of other people, normally the Realtors, seller, and title or closing settlement agent, all of whom somehow always seem to be rushed. Borrowers may be embarrassed to ask questions. Certainly no one else at the table wants the borrower to make the closing take any longer than it has to. On the other hand, of all people, the mortgage loan originator who sold the borrower the loan is often not present to answer questions at closing. When a borrower does ask questions, the title agent, often the only representative for the lender at closing, is hesitant to get involved with anything that has to do with the loan terms, and with good reason: Closing agents have been held legally liable for statements made about mortgage loans at closing and are not generally knowledgeable enough about the mortgage loan products to adequately answer questions. Further, if the mortgage loan officer is the person who referred the borrower to the title agent (i.e., the title agent counts on the mortgage originator to refer her business), she certainly would not want to answer a borrower's question in any way that might make the mortgage originator look bad. For example, the title agent would not want to tell the borrower that the loan is not well suited for him or that the mortgage costs are too high. It is not uncommon now to hear title agents say how ridiculous the terms of loans they closed during the bubble were but extremely rare to hear any say that they shared these thoughts with the borrowers. Conversely, it is not the job or responsibility of a title agent to educate borrowers about their mortgage loans. Oftentimes, title agents are undercompensated as it is for the work they do and the risks involved if they make a mistake. In fact, sharing their own opinions about loan products with borrowers could result in legal liability to the seller, Realtor, and mortgage originator if, as a result of a title agent's input concerning the mortgage loan terms or costs, a borrower refused to close.

A typical mortgage loan closing lasts less than an hour. If a borrower is buying a home, he is also under pressure from the Realtor and seller to close, even if he doesn't understand or agree with something in the loan documents. Failure to close at that point may put the borrower's deposit and the purchase of the home at risk. Again, a borrower's lack of understanding of the details in these documents will resurface in the event he defaults. Some borrowers ask to see their mortgage loan documents before closing, but, since the emailing of loan packages has become common, and as busy as the housing market has been in recent years, even the title company doesn't get the mortgage loan documents and fees from the lender until as late as an hour before we are to close on the sale.

Closing Instructions

When they do arrive, the loan package is accompanied by lengthy lender *closing instructions* (directions from the lender explaining how the documents are to be signed, whom they must be signed by, what the lender intends to hold the closing agent responsible for, what the closing agent must fax to the lender before they will be authorized to disburse the mortgage loan funds, how many copies of each loan document the lender wants the closing agent to send back and specifics of that nature) resulting in a last-minute crunch for everyone involved. It is not unusual for the title company to have no choice but to wait until minutes before closing to tell us how much money we will need to bring for down payment, closing costs, mortgage insurance, etc. Often the title agent has been selected by the bank, and like the mortgage loan originator (perhaps based on an affiliated arrangement replete with potential for added conflict of interest), is a complete stranger to the borrower with little incentive to ensure that the borrower understands what is being signed. As we've noted, if the title company counts on the mortgage loan originator or our Realtor for business referrals, the title company may actually have an incentive to make sure the borrower closes, regardless of what's best for them, since the loan originator and the Realtor get paid their commission only if the borrower closes.

Closing or Title Insurance Agents

The title agent has no responsibility to make sure our good faith estimate matches the actual fees (such as the title insurance premium, survey, appraisal, credit report, broker fees, and mortgage loan origination fees described in chapter 2) that appear on our final HUD-1 Settlement Statement (the document listing all of the closing costs for institutional lender residential mortgage closings on primary residences at closing). During the real estate bubble it was not uncommon for the mortgage loan terms a borrower saw at closing to differ from what the borrower recalled being promised by his mortgage loan originator at application. Because things were moving so quickly and borrowers figured they'd be making a lot of money on the real estate deal anyway, they often did not object too loudly. There are no laws with teeth that ensure that borrowers get the mortgage loan terms they are promised and-in fact, there are many reasons why they may not. Interest rates may have changed, or perhaps the borrower did not qualify for the loan program he initially wanted. On the other hand, a better loan program or rate may have been used by the mortgage loan originator as a bait-and-switch plan, or as we discussed in chapter 2, the loan originator may simply put a borrower in a program that earns the originator more money.

Collection Calls

In the past, real problems paying the mortgage arose when some major life event occurred that affected our ability to pay basic bills. It could be a divorce, a family member gets sick or injured or you lose your job. We miss a mortgage payment, and soon we get a call from our lender, a complete stranger, typically five to ten days after the payment was due. This is a call we'll lie awake in bed worrying about at night, but never return. We assure ourselves that we'll catch up with our next paycheck and never hear from the lender again, but it turns out that we never seem to have enough money to catch up. Nowadays the first calls aren't even from the loan servicer but are from a call center, often based offshore in India or some similar place to reduce costs. The caller leaves a voice mail with a toll-free number for us to call back. Most do not use their real names and, in fact, many companies employ high security at their facilities, largely in unpublished locations, because of the often emotional, irrational nature of borrowers in the process of having their homes foreclosed upon. Servicers report making an average of four calls before a borrower calls back.

If the mortgage included a provision allowing the lender to confiscate money from savings, checking, or other accounts the borrower may have with them (often home owners take mortgages with their own bank, where they have checking and savings accounts), the lender may do that, a move that often catches us entirely by surprise.

When we return the lender's call, it is often the beginning of a Kafkaesque process seemingly designed to reject all common sense and humanity. We'll first hear an automated message known in the industry as the *mini-Miranda warning* (see appendix R). After that, as in most situations when we call a large organization, we wait on hold and are asked to select among several computerized options. When we reach an actual human, the person's demeanor is typically impersonal. If we do not know our loan number, we are asked to provide sufficient personal information for the customer service person to pull up our loan in the computer system. The servicer then normally tries to gather information from us to understand why we are not paying our mortgage. Depending on the reason, most servicers are trained to make the conversation more personal, often asking if a family member might be able to help us pay or determining if we have any other assets (CDs, retirement accounts, etc.) with which the loan may be repaid. The servicer's goal at this stage is to get our money in their hands quickly.

Insight between Loss Mitigation Departments for Two Different Lenders (with the Same Borrower)

Countrywide

"I first contacted Countrywide on September 10, 2008. It took approximately 10 minutes to get to an individual in the Loss Mitigation Department. When someone was finally willing to speak to me, the representative would not give me their direct dial, their extension, or their last name. I confirmed that Countrywide would require an Authorization Letter executed by the borrowers in order to discuss the file with me.

I drafted the Authorization Letter and faxed it to the fax number provided by Countrywide's representative on September 11, 2008. When I called back on September 12, 2008, to confirm that Countrywide received the fax, I was told to call back in 3 days, because it takes Countrywide 5 to 7 days to process Authorization Letters into its system. I also confirmed the fax number previously given, which was confirmed, and I was given an additional fax number to fax the Authorization Letter. I re-faxed the Authorization Letter to both fax numbers, to ensure that there was no error on our part. I called Countrywide again on September 15, 2008, and was placed on hold while two different representatives looked for the Authorization Letter. I was on hold and spoke to the two representatives for approximately 40 minutes. Again, I was asked to call back the following week.

"On September 18, 2008, Countrywide sent a letter which alleged that the borrower's signature on the Authorization Letter did not match the signature in Countrywide's file or on the loan documents. I re-faxed the Authorization Letter previously signed by the borrower along with a copy of the signature page from the Mortgage. I called Countrywide again on September 23, 2008, to confirm receipt of the Authorization Letter and verification of signature. I was then told that the documents had not been processed and were not in its system and that I would have to wait another 5 to 7 days. On September 30, 2008, I spoke to "Leon" regarding the Authorization Letter. He confirmed that it had been received and processed. He also informed me that Countrywide would not accept any financial statements via fax or e-mail and that I would have to provide all of the client's financial information over the phone. He asked that I call back the following day and provide that information.

On October 1, 2008, I spoke to "Janet" from Countrywide because Leon wasn't available. I provided all of the client's financial information over the phone, including his list of assets and liabilities. This process took approximately 1½ hours. Once Janet inputted all of the information into her database she told me that the loan modification request was instantly rejected and that she would have to take the information to her supervisor to request an override, but that she didn't think it would make a difference since my client's monthly expenses exceeded his monthly income.

"I explained that if the client's monthly payments were reduced, by either reducing his interest rate or allowing him to pay interest only for a year, he could afford his monthly payments and take the properties out of foreclosure. I also requested a forbearance for at least 3 to 6 months to allow the client to catch up. Finally, I requested that the term be extended so that the payments would be reduced. Janet told me to call back when the client's financial status had changed and then I would have to go through the entire process over the telephone again. Under normal circumstances the client's bill for my legal services would be around $3,500 and we accomplished nothing. At this point the property will go into foreclosure."

Washington Mutual (WaMu)

"My experiences with Washington Mutual was entirely different. I originally contacted WaMu on September 10, 2008, and again on September 11, 2008, since I was immediately assigned to a representative, Stephen, who unlike the Countrywide representatives, had no problem telling me his last name. I faxed the Authorization Letter to WaMu and confirmed receipt of the letter on September 12, 2008. Stephen requested certain financial information which I faxed to him and discussed over a conference call on September 16, 2008. Stephen requested additional financial information, which I obtained from the client and forwarded to him on September 19, 2008. On September 23, 2008, I contacted Stephen to check on the status of the loan modification. Stephen asked that I contact him on October 1, 2008. During that call Stephen told me that the loan modification package we requested had already been mailed to the client. On October 17, 2008, the client forwarded the loan modification package to me and on October 23, 2008, we discussed the terms of the modification and the proposed restructuring for the loan.

The client's mortgage payment was reduced from approximately $1,500 per month to $406.51 per month (1% interest only for the first year and 2% interest only for the second year), which will hopefully be sufficient to help him get his finances back on track and avoid foreclosure."

WHAT IS LOSS MITIGATION?

The various foreclosure alternatives we've discussed in this chapter, along with everything else lenders do to reduce their losses, is commonly referred to as *loss mitigation*. A work sheet designed to help evaluate which loss mitigation option might work for you is included as appendix S. One foreclosure attorney who represents borrowers but wished to remain anonymous shares his thoughts about the current state of foreclosure loss mitigation in the sidebar below. But as we noted in chapter 5, courts in some jurisdictions are stepping in to effectively ensure that lenders do a better job with loss mitigation before clogging the courts with foreclosures that can be resolved in another way. And, as we'll discuss in chapter 8, government rescue is slowly but surely on its way.

There is such a tremendous difference among banks in terms of how they are handling requests for assistance from borrowers in default and foreclosure. The customer service is different and so is the help they're willing to offer. Sometimes the difference between a borrower being able to modify his loan and losing it to foreclosure depends on nothing more than what lender has his loan now. The sidebar on pages 204–205 illustrates the difference in response and outcome between two recent cases handled for a developer client first with Countrywide and then Washington Mutual (WaMu), both recently acquired financial institutions.

Insight about Loss Mitibation from a Borrower's Foreclosure Defense Lawyer

"I have found that most attempts at loss mitigation are still usually a waste of time. And it's labor intensive-letters, e-mails, phone calls. Clients don't want to pay for that time if it doesn't yield results, so I usually try to persuade them away from that. It avoids having to argue with them about the bill for my time later on. Servicer staff are still only giving lip service to loss mitigation. I am not impressed with their ability to handle it. It's really a result of poor training and GSE or CDO investor requirements and the requirements in the pooling and servicing agreements that prohibit many loss mitigation options. Right now mortgage loan default servicers and lenders don't know what they want or how to go about mitigating their losses. It's like they're immobilized between a rock and a hard place."

Insight about Life Events That Resulted in Mortgage Foreclosure

Trina, a single mother, and a now grandmother, providing for both her daughter and her five-year-old grandson, purchased a single-family home in May 2000 with the help of two mortgages. The first mortgage loan was from a conventional bank and had a five-year balloon provision. The second was held by the seller. By 2002, Trina had built enough equity in her home to consolidate the two loans and refinance at a lower interest rate. By coincidence, she received an unsolicited sales call from a mortgage loan originator from the now defunct Ameriquest Mortgage Company. Trina recalls how "easy" the originator made refinancing sound and how fast he was able to get the refinance loan approved. Based on that alone, Trina decided to accept the loan he offered her. She says: "I did not have a lot of experience with mortgages at that time, so I believed everything he said or led me to believe. I did ask how the adjustable rate worked, as he insisted I was better with that than the fixed rate. It was one of those loans with a really low rate, something like 3 percent, that they call a teaser rate now. He assured me the adjustable rate would never be a problem and, if anything, after the first increase, he said the interest rate would more likely adjust down rather than up. If I took the fixed rate, he said, I would be stuck with that higher rate when everybody else's rate went down. With home prices rising, interest rates staying so low, and mortgage money and refinances so easy to come by, it seemed like a really great deal. The first year went by with no adjustments, but after that the interest rate just started going up and up and up. I didn't understand why. That certainly was not what he'd told me was going to happen. Along with the insurance rates going up [because the value of the house was increasing], I was starting to feel trapped. I would have sold my house to get out of that situation, but around the same time my boyfriend moved out and started claiming he had a legal right to my house. He found a lawyer who would take his case and filed liens, making it impossible for me to sell or refinance. The judge eventually told him to go take a hike but by late 2006 I was going into foreclosure.

Karen and Tom Found That after Their Foreclosure, Rebuilding Their Credit Was Even More Challenging Than Losing Their House

"Our foreclosure experience began in early 2005 when we decided to refinance our house so that we would be able to put a pool in the backyard. We figured a pool would be beneficial for the family and also be a bonus when it came time to sell the house. At that time everyone we knew was either buying property or refinancing it. Interest rates were low and property values were going up. We refinanced our $149,000 mortgage with a new mortgage of $242,000 that even covered the closing costs, so we figured it cost us nothing at all. And even then, our new payment was only $1,600 a month!

A year after the refinance, my husband took a new job a few hours away. That was when the real problems began. My husband rented an apartment and started his new job. The children and I would visit him every other weekend. In November of 2006 we decided to put the old house on the market and began looking for a house closer to where my husband was working, planning to move at the end of the school year. We bought the new house with a $242,000 ARM we were approved for right away.

The old house had been appraised at $339,000. We listed it for $310,000 so it would be the lowest priced pool home in the neighborhood, figuring it would sell quickly. But overnight everything stopped selling. In March we reduced the price to $299,000. We'd left it vacant, trying to make things easier for the agent to sell. In July we decided to put a renter in the house to help with the mortgage payment, since we had now eaten up much of our savings making two mortgage payments and home insurance payments for five months. When my husband was laid off from his job we just didn't have any money to give the bank and finally started falling behind. At first we thought something would come through and we'd be able to get caught up. But after we missed two payments I tried to contact the mortgage company. I was hoping to talk to someone about payment options so we could get caught up again—maybe spreading the payments out or something along those lines. I explained the whole situation to them. It was a no-go. Plain and simple. The bank's telephone representative said I had three options. Pay the bank back in full now. Sell the house. Or lose the house in foreclosure. I tried to explain that we had been trying to sell the house for over a year. The only "advice" the bank offered was that maybe we should lower the price, since the market had dropped.

After that conversion we started to wonder if the property was even worth what we'd have to pay the bank back. I called the bank again a few weeks later, this time to inquire about short sales. We'd heard of them but didn't really understand them. The representative told me if we could get an offer that is less then the mortgage amount, we could fill out a bunch of paperwork and hope that the bank would accept it.

We've reduced the price to exactly what we owed the bank but the house is still on the market and we have not even had a showing. The foreclosure paperwork was filed on January 11, 2008, and we had twenty days to pay all monies due or lose the house. The way I see it, there were a lot of factors involved. When we refinanced the old house, prices of the homes were at an all-time high. We did not take the full amount that the house was appraised at, but we took out more then we needed for the pool because we were able to. When my husband suggested we buy a house near his new job, I figured we would never get financed for a second loan when we already had one mortgage, since we are not rich by any means. I was very surprised when we received approval and since we had already dealt with an ARM, I figured that in two years we would be able to refinance the new house. I also figured that the old house would sell. Now it looks like we may not be able to refinance the mortgage on the new house as planned when the rate goes up because the foreclosure on the old house will destroy our credit. Was I ever wrong. Now we are paying the price for making some bad decisions.

Unfortunately, even in many cases where a modification or foreclosure payment plan or some other foreclosure alternative is reached there soon comes a point (especially if the borrower's life situation doesn't change) at which even these lower payments can't be met. Eventually another default occurs and foreclosure takes place.

Distressed home owner Trina Beasley's story is not uncommon. Financially stressed as the head of household for her grown daughter and five-year-old grandson, a break up with her boyfriend threw her life into a whirlwind. Trina recounts her story in the sidebar on page 207.

Thankfully, with the help of good friends and an attorney who helped her for free, Trina was able to save her home, but because of her bad credit rating now (resulting from not being able to pay her prior mortgage on time), she is now considered a higher-risk borrower by lenders who are therefore charging her a higher interest rate and her mortgage payments have almost doubled since

2000. Trina says, "I have learned a lot, but it was an expensive lesson. I am still struggling to survive in this down market but things can only get better."

For Karen and Tom Jones, the life event was the loss of Tom's job and the ending was not quite as happy. You can read their story on pages 208–209.

GETTING HELP

For most of us, the *writ of possession*, often nailed to our front door, issued after the foreclosure sale in order to physically force a borrower out of his home, is the beginning of a most embarrassing public spectacle. A foreclosure complaint may be the first legal document we've ever seen. It's wordy and intimidating. Some home owners ask around for advice at work or from friends. Maybe someone knows a lawyer who can give a few minutes worth of free advice. Others are just too embarrassed to let anyone know. At this point we'll take one of three paths, normally dictated simply by what we can or cannot afford. We either hire a lawyer, decide to try to handle the foreclosure ourselves, or just pretend it's not happening. Those who hire a lawyer to defend a basic residential foreclosure in today's market will spend an average of $2,500 and typically need to pay at least half up front. In many cases, the best approach even a borrower's foreclosure defense attorney can offer will only delay the foreclosure for about another six months. Because they are accepting so many cases at such a relatively small fee, it is not realistic to expect a lot of attention or a custom-crafted approach from a foreclosure defense lawyer hired on these terms. A lawyer may be effective in negotiating a loan modification, a short sale, or even a forbearance or deed-in-lieu, but she cannot make our mortgage go away. We'll discuss in chapter 8 that consumer advocacy organizations and court assistance programs are increasingly available to assist those of us who cannot afford to hire an attorney.

EVICTION

Ignoring a foreclosure complaint creates a no-win situation. Eventually, the notices will stop when the sheriff or other official knocks on the door. The swiftness of the foreclosure process catches most people by surprise. Friends or family may help with the all-night move when word comes that law enforcement will be there the next day. Some handle the move out in the middle of the night alone, to avoid further embarrassment. When a property is occupied by renters, even though they may be named in the foreclosure complaint in order to wipe out their rights as tenants, it is seldom worthwhile for renters who can afford to do so to try to fight the bank. Owners who are in denial often don't even tell family members or make arrangements. Eviction crew members tend to be respectful and somber. They'll leave what remains of a borrower's belongings on the front lawn or near the curb. If the borrower leaves his possessions unattended, scavengers may quickly take what they want. Neighbors might complain. After the foreclosure sale, it's up to the lender or the new owner to cart away what remains.

WHO IS TO BLAME FOR AMERICA'S FORECLOSURES?

It is impossible to take sides with borrowers or lenders in all cases. In addition to the challenges lenders must overcome, often lenders are faced with questionable practices from the borrower. They are accustomed to being treated badly and often lied to by borrowers who blame all their financial troubles on the big, bad bank. Even experienced developers, especially in this market downturn, tend to behave as if their lender *has* to work with them.

The reality is that borrowers tend to ignore written default notifications and requests for payment. Telephone calls generally generate a higher contact and response rate. However, under the Fair Debt Collection Practices Act, as debt collectors, lenders may not communicate with any person other than the consumer and are prohibited from using any false, deceptive, or misleading representation or engaging in any conduct to harass, oppress, or abuse the consumer. While these sound like reasonable restrictions, in the hands of borrowers grasping at any defense to save their homes, these rules and a servicer's actions are often twisted to imply fraud, harrassment, or some illegal action where none exists. Many servicers, in fear of running afoul, don't leave voicemail messages or leave only minimal information. At the same time, they are required to make a meaningful disclosure. Some experiment with prerecorded voice messages, but these unfortunately tend to increase the impersonality of the relationship and lead borrowers to become even more distrustful. The point is that many lenders and the people who work for them are in a difficult position, too.

When the proverbial subprime and economic dust settles it will be up to each of us individually to decide whether we want to view our glass as half-full or half-empty. No doubt there will be more surprises that result from the interconnectedness and lack of transparency in our markets as well as from the way we react each time a new surprise emerges. Our nation's economic situation will likely get worse before it gets better. But eventually it will get better and each of us already has the opportunity to seek a silver lining if we so choose. Armed now with everything you've ever wanted to know about the facts and dynamics that have brought our nation's real estate and mortgage market and the American Dream to this precipice, let's look at what we can do to help ourselves and each other move forward by focusing on the silver-lining and where we want our nation to go from here.

7

THE SILVER LINING

As the old adage goes, when one door closes, another one opens. So it will be with our nation's subprime crisis and the housing and financial shifts that have followed.

REAL ESTATE PROFESSIONALS

Tens of thousands Realtors and mortgage brokers (among others) are out of business, but for those still standing, competition is already less of an issue. From our perspective as consumers, the crisis is eliminating many real estate professionals who jumped into the market looking for a fast buck and who may have helped lead us astray.

Realtors and mortgage loan originators who choose to tough it out are finding new niches that may help them weather the storm. Before they were placed in a conservator ship, government-sponsored enterprises Fannie Mae and Freddie Mac were reworking their criteria for approving loans to be more prudent, but also to be more current and attractive in today's market. Together with the government bailout plan, this creates opportunity for loan originators. Chances are these entities will be used to help return liquidity to our nation's mortgage loan and real estate markets, meaning opportunities. In the meantime, many of the folks who originated mortgage loans during the bubble are now busy modifying them for a fee. Realtor Sharon Podwol of Preferred Property Finders has found a silver lining. She shares her enthusiasm with you in the following.

One Realtor's Enthusiasm about Emerging Post-bubble Opportunities

"Everyone knows the number of transactions Realtors can be involved in has gone down. But what a lot of people don't realize is the huge opportunities that present themselves for those of us who remain when so many people exit the market. As a smaller company, we had a tough time competing for big developer business during the bubble. Now they're looking for Realtors just like us who know how to move product [real estate] on a smaller budget. A few months ago we made a deal with one of the biggest developers in the country to sell their remaining units. They would not have even returned our calls in 2005. That's a relationship that will last long after the crisis is over. But for the crisis we probably would never have had the chance to get a foot in the developer's door.

For top-quality real estate and mortgage professionals, a business downturn provides the opportunity to demonstrate superior skills at a time when customers need them most. These are the folks who are using this time to intensify business relationships, re-educate, cross-market, selectively focus on market niches, and reinvent themselves. Like the mortgage originators, Realtors are adapting to the environment, educating themselves in short sales, selling REOs, providing BFOs and the other tools needed to get their job done.

Many title companies that were doing massive numbers of closings in 2004 have now closed up shop. Lawyers who were doing real estate title closings have shifted their practice and many are now busier than ever supplementing their reduced workload of closings with loan modifications, forbearances, foreclosure defenses, and helping buyers get out of purchase contracts. Litigation associated with predatory lending and mortgage fraud is boosting law firm revenues as are lender foreclosure work, developer representation in contract and deposit disputes, and correcting sloppy title work often executed by inexperienced, overstretched workers during the height of the housing bubble. Some law firms have set up special distressed or special asset practice groups in the hope of eventually handling the resale of larger commercial projects on behalf of lender, investor, or developer clients.

HOME IMPROVEMENTS

For home buyers and sellers the numerous advantages of owning a home still far outweigh the risks. Eventually our homes will begin appreciating again, albeit at more reasonable rates similar to those before the bubble, meaning that investing in the home we own is still a good idea for some of us. For now, dramatic decreases in new home construction have left countless subcontractors searching for work. This translates to notably better labor pricing than before for those of us inclined to have home improvements done. In some regions and job types, prices are down by as much as 20 percent. Some material prices are down too (although others are up, largely due to fuel

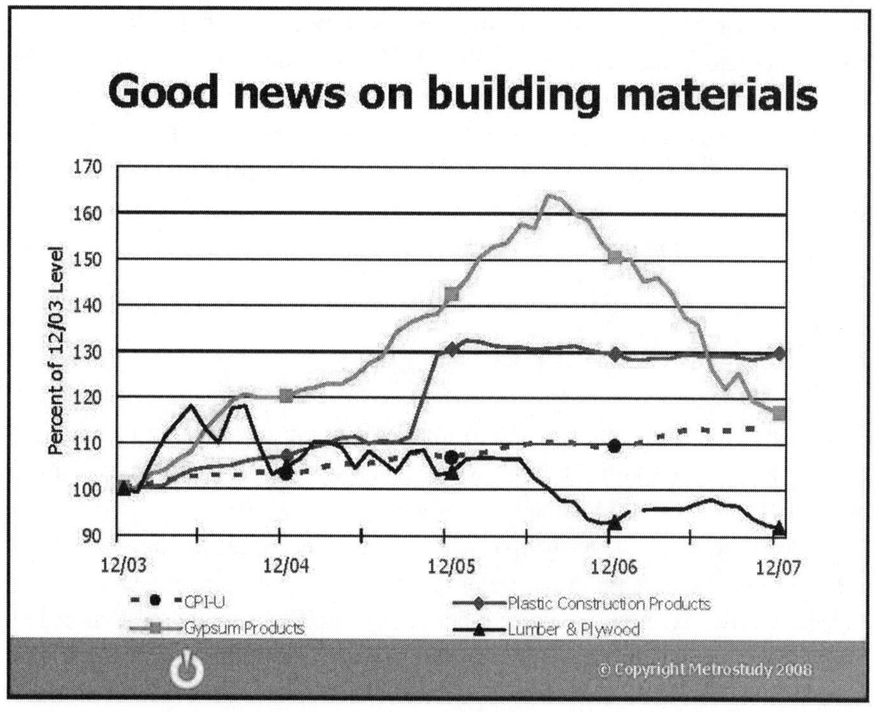

prices). For example, by the peak of the bubble in 2005–2006, the cost of the building material sheetrock had risen to 165 percent of its 2003 cost. The price of sheetrock has since decreased 15 to 30 percent depending on location. The graph provided on the previous page reflects the decrease in building material costs.

With the major automakers predicting as much as a 50 percent decrease in auto sales for 2009, now is a great time to buy a car. And since virtually all sectors of the retail markets are down, the same presumably holds true for other purchases and expenditures, assuming, of course, that one has disposable income to spend.

AFFORDABLE HOUSING

As buyers, the price reversion opens up home ownership possibilities that, not long ago, were rising beyond the grasp of the mere working mortal. Many of our country's future home owners will be minorities. By 2010, an estimated 60 percent of first-time home buyers will be found in emerging markets, 44 million Hispanics and 39 million African Americans. By 2050, new home ownership among Hispanics is estimated to be 102 million and among African Americans, 61 million.[1] The big questions of when will be the right time to buy and at what price point will the housing market bottom out are discussed in more detail below but the point is that affordable housing, both for average Americans and in the context of government-subsidized programs for lower-income folks, is no longer the oxymoron it was during the bubble.

BUYING FORECLOSED HOMES

The first opportunity that comes to mind for many of us when considering the subprime crisis is the possibility of generating a profit by buying short-sale, distressed, or REO foreclosed properties.

No doubt, some clever people who are adept at capturing these and other related opportunities will emerge in the next few years much wealthier than before. Ironically, now is a much better time to buy real estate than a few years ago when everyone and his brother was buying it and helping to create our bubble. Amazon.com, Barnes and Noble, and other book sellers stock several excellent titles specifically written to teach would-be investors how to go about buying distressed or foreclosed properties. The Internet is also a good resource for information, as long as we keep in mind that many Web sites tempt us with offers of free information, and may even give away tid-bits, but eventually they require us to pull out a credit card to access the content we really need.

For the purposes of this discussion, it suffices to say that buying foreclosures for profit has become a fairly specialized field with a learning curve that not everyone will choose to invest in. It requires knowledge of the geographic areas in which properties are located, knowing at what price we should buy and at what price we can sell, and possibly the price we could get if we needed to rent the property until it sold. It requires knowing what repairs and improvements we will need to make to the property, how long they will take and what they will cost. It requires knowing how to research the title to the distressed property or pending foreclosure to be sure there are no interested parties or encumbrances, that the legal processes have been properly followed, and for how long the redumption period will run. Any of these could create expensive problems for us once we take ownership. Most important, buying distressed and foreclosed properties requires money. In this market, who is likely to have it? The people prudent enough *not* to have gotten into the real estate bubble using risky loans and paying too much for properties (or those who got out when they saw the downturn coming). They are probably also the same people and companies who aren't drowning in other debt.

Those buyers who have attempted to purchase REO properties can attest to the fact that, as property owners, lenders are nowhere near as responsive during the negotiating process as the typical individual seller would be. Most lenders require the use of their own purchase contract form, which typically provides that both the property's physical condition and the title are being sold "as is." This applies to both lenders holding residential REOs and those holding larger commercial projects. While individual sellers typically respond to offers within hours or days, it is not unusual to wait weeks or even months for a lender's response to a purchase offer. And while individual sellers will often propose a counteroffer to an offer that is in their eyes not acceptable on its face, many lenders will merely reject the offer, leaving it up to the buyer to choose whether or not to continue making offers. The reasons for this often relate to the fact that the lender's staff has grown accustomed to receiving unreasonable, lowball offers, have heavy workloads, and need to be able to justify their decisions to investors. In fact, fear of making decisions, often the result of the unclear direction the government bailout and regulatory requirements will take, is one of the largest causes of delay. But each of these factors has been magnified by the subprime crisis. As we've said, banks aren't in the business of property management. Every day the bank owns a property, it loses money. Banks seek quick sales of REO property, as this enables them to avoid paying real estate taxes and maintenance. From a safety and soundness perspective, the Federal Deposit Insurance Corporation (FDIC) wants banks it insures to dispose of REOs as quickly as possible, since they are nonearning assets—but the permitted time frame is up to ten years.

FORECLOSURE-RELATED LENDER SERVICE PROVIDERS

A similar, albeit less risky, learning curve is faced by Realtors seeking to capitalize on distressed and foreclosed properties. For them, it's not merely a matter of knowing the neighborhood and how to market and sell an REO property for an owner or bank, but also an understanding of how to capture the bank's business in the first place and, once that is accomplished, how the banks want to work.

Capturing the larger bank's REO and other business has become increasingly competitive and political. Often it's a matter of who you know: some banks prefer to enter into large territory contracts with one or two approved real estate firms. This system may minimize the time and thus the cost involved in getting an REO property to market. Whether it maximizes the attention given by the Realtor to marketing the listing and the price the lender will eventually get for the property is questionable. Less well-connected Realtors may have a shot at getting an REO contract from smaller banks on a case-by-case, property-by-property basis.

The increased frequency at which the foreclosure process is repeating itself has created increased opportunity for other service providers who play a role in that process. From broker price opinion providers—the folks who drive by the property and provide the lender a price analysis in light of current surrounding resale values—to auction firms that help lenders sell their special assets, to construction consultants who help lenders complete development projects (a role taken by many of the folks who were building the developments during the bubble), to firms that specialize in cleaning and maintaining REO properties, many have doubled their workforces. We know that properties are taking longer to sell. The longer a property sits vacant on the market, the more the biggest maintenance issues—trash, algae-infested swimming pools, leaky roofs, and mold-grow. We discussed in chapter 6 that home owners in foreclosure often simply leave their junk behind for the new lender-owner to haul away. Like hiring Realtors to market REOs, larger banks often enter into contracts for these services with national firms.

Most banks want frequent periodic inspections and status reports from their service providers. Many expect their service providers to lay out the costs they incur servicing the REO properties (for example, as we mentioned earlier, the foreclosure mills lay out the cost for title searches and filing fees). Realtors are expected to pay vendors for maintenance and repairs, then file for reimbursement. It is easy to see how this would create a cash-flow challenge for smaller real estate companies. But for those who can handle it, the opportunity to make a lot of money selling a wide variety of foreclosure-related services to lenders has never been better.

DISTRESSED HOME OWNER ASSISTANCE

A vast number of non-attorney companies have emerged offering to assist distressed home owners in negotiating a modification or short sale, sometimes for a flat fee typically ranging from $250 to upwards of $900. Some provide valuable assistance. Others negotiate terms that are no better than those home owners would have fairly easily obtained on their own or do nothing. But for those qualified consultants and counselors inclined to do so, many of whom, as we said earlier, were originating mortgage loans during the bubble, the subprime crisis has created unprecedented opportunity for generating revenue in this type of business. Who among us would not be thrilled to pay an expert a few hundred dollars to help get us avoid paying tens of thousands out of pocket of dollars to pay off a mortgage that the sale price of our home will not cover, or to simply be able to walk away from a home we're upside down in?

On the other hand, we discussed in chapter 4 that some shady companies are actually taking the home owner's mortgage payment and allegedly forwarding it to the lender, or taking title to the property, often without the home owner's knowledge, and "leasing" it back to the home owner. Sometimes these predatory schemes are designed to allow the company to tie up the property, allowing time to try to sell it themselves for a profit. When that effort fails, home owners end up losing their money and their home. Questionable practices are on the rise, with the Internet making it increasingly easy for con artists to find home owners in trouble. Fortunately, there are precautions we can all take to protect ourselves from the bad guys. These include carefully screening any offers, not signing anything without obtaining a professional review, seeking out only financial counselors endorsed by legitimate professional associations or personal reference, and not agreeing to any upfront fees, all of which are discussed in greater detail in chapter 8. But for those interested in helping people and making a good living over the next few years, assisting distressed home owners may be your silver lining. Precautions you can take to protect yourself from these predators are reflected in a sidebar in chapter 3 (p. 86).

FRACTURED CONDO PROJECTS

A *fractured condominium* project is one that was built during the bubble and in which some, but not all, of the building's units were sold and closed. Investors are learning that some of these projects can be bought for 40 to 50 percent discounts. Some are apartments purchased at top dollar during the bubble to be converted to condominiums which can now easily be converted back into rental apartments. This requires relatively nominal time and funding to generate quick cash flow and cover carrying costs. An interesting side note is that since, by definition, these projects contain at least some units that were sold to individual buyers, those owners will be living among a building of renters, probably not what they expected. Further, if fewer than 50 percent of the units have been sold, the developer normally retains control of the association, meaning that the new investor will now control the association and may be able to take actions that require association approval such as changing the budget or eliminating services and features, even over the objections of the remaining unit owners.

WALL STREET FIRE SALES

The same holds true for Wall Street and other types of investments that are currently suffering from deflated values. Many believe the value of stocks, securities, and other more traditional investments have been pushed down too far by the panic. Even blue chip business stocks now trade at a fraction of their realistic market value. It is in times like these that fortunes are made. Now may be the time to buy!

BANKS BUYING BANKS

Lenders who can accurately navigate the storm and safely but smartly acquire other banks and customer market share may not ever see an opportunity like this again. The trick, as discussed in chapter 5, is that many banks that are or will become available for acquisition are not accurately reflecting their exposure to the subprime crisis on their balance sheets, rendering their actual market value questionable. The ultimate role of government bailout money in funding these acquisitions and back-stopping, or generating against unforeseen loss, remains to be seen. The same opportunity exists for businesses in all market spaces. Experts predict we will see notable consolidation and fewer small banks.

BUYING DEFAULTED MORTGAGE LOAN PAPER AND JUDGMENTS

Like the securitization process itself, the foreclosure process is being divvied up into pieces. Investors of all genres continue to explore other niches of opportunity, from buying loans in default to buying mortgage loan servicing contracts to buying deficiency judgments. Distressed debt and other paper, often discounted significantly off the face value of the loan amount, is emerging as a hot investment opportunity.

LOOKING FOR THE UPSIDE

Other businesses seeing the silver lining of opportunity in the midst of the subprime storm cloud include those that provide fraud protection for banks, foreclosure-related education for professionals as well as the general population, Web sites and seminars, REO and other foreclosure and regulatory compliance–related software, and even home-staging companies offering us a competitive edge in selling our house by giving it that all-important curb appeal. But far more significant than any of these opportunities is the fact that our nation's situation itself is, at once, a crisis that has a silver lining.

Perhaps the brightest silver lining relates to the opportunity we all have now to take a step back and consider where our country has come from and where we want to go. We discussed the metamorphous of our collective core financial values in chapter 1. Now that we are all in the midst of an economic time-out, we have a unique, perhaps once in a lifetime opportunity to reconsider our individual and our nation's attitudes about credit and the American Dream. The good part about the fact that consumer spending is down is that we're all spending less money and most of us are cutting back on luxury consumption, not necessity. Maybe some of us are being a little less wasteful or flashy. Maybe instead we're appreciating those other things we refer to as the "things that really matter." Certainly less credit card debt will make us all less stressed. Even situations that at first appear dire, generations of family having to move in together under the same roof, for example, have some upside. Maybe we're returning to some of the core financial values our grandparents had. Maybe our grandparents would be proud.

The reality is that average Americans have already shown the ability to effect a major change of that nature. Beginning in 2006, millions could no longer afford to pay their mortgage loans. At first it seemed the problems were mostly concerned with people normally considered to be at the bottom of our nation's socio-economic totem pole, subprime borrowers. As more and more of us eventually defaulted, the pole began shaking until eventually the guys we've always considered to be at the top, maybe even godlike and untouchable, felt the tremors. If that doesn't speak to the power of the average American's ability to influence our nation, what does?

Even if we did miss the red flag of a plunging economy, including ridiculous subprime mortgage loan terms, overly complicated securitized financial instruments based on flawed assumptions, relaxed regulation of the mortgage and investment banking industries, supersonic real estate prices, homes sizes on steroids, a long list of conflicts of interest, and the various other signs we've discussed together, we all know that what goes up must come down. That appears to be the case with the house of cards that much of our economy and financial markets have become.

Did anyone really think that real estate and our general economy would continue moving in the direction and at the rate it was going indefinitely? That we would simply continue borrowing increasingly more in loans we could never possibly repay? And that home prices would just continue to increase forever? Some people wonder how the subprime and broader economic crises could have happened. Having read the first six chapters of this book you of course know that the better question is how could this crisis not have happened! The good news is that the sooner our worst economic fears from this latest bubble and crash are being realized, the sooner we'll have nothing left to fear.

NOTE

1. Steven Holland, "Getting Educated on the Ethnic Homeownership and Pricing Gaps," *Mortgage Banking (News)*, February 2007, pp. 123–24; Vikas Bajaj and Ford Fessenden, "What Is behind the Race Gap?" *New York Times*, November 4, 2007, p. 16.

8

PREDICTIONS, RELIEF, AND REFORMS

THE NATURE OF ECONOMIES

We've discussed some of the many interconnected causes of our subprime and broader financial crises as well as the countless continually emerging impacts. Crafting relief for distressed home owners, and now for commercial property and other individuals and businesses, and reforming the various dynamics that got us here in the first place is a slippery slope of gargantuan proportion. For the purposes of our discussion, our primary focus will remain on the subprime real estate crisis. But first a little background on economies and economic crises in general, our banking system's structural safeguards to combat such crises, what's been done so far, and some of the reasons it has not worked.

We've discussed how some of the solutions to past challenges, such as government-sponsored enterprises, adjustable-rate mortgages, lower interest rates, looser credit standards, and Wall Street deregulation, actually contributed to today's problems. Sometimes relief and reform works as intended. Other times it does not. But oftentimes even those ideas that appear to be working have unanticipated, even initially unobservable, undesired side effects. To illustrate this point, the next sidebar contains some of the rela-

Some of the US Government Intervention Blamed for Causing the Current Crisis

- The conversion of Fannie Mae and Freddie Mac from Federal government entities into GSEs in 1968
- The Community Reinvestment Act of 1977, requiring lenders to provide loans for lower income borrowers
- The 1980 Depository Institutions Deregulation and Monetary Control Act, which neglected to regulate certain types of lenders
- The Federal Housing Enterprises Financial Safety and Soundness Act of 1992, which required Fannie Mae and Freddie Mac to dedicate a certain amount of funds to affordable housing
- The Riegle-Neal Interstate Banking and Branching Efficiency Act in 1994, which reduced regulation of bank holding companies
- Former president Clinton's enhancement of the Community Reinvestment Act in 1995 by requiring lenders to loan to Fannie Mae and Freddie Mac and Fannie Mae and Freddie Mac to buy less qualified loans
- Further easing of requirements by Fannie Mae in 1999 intended to increase affordable home ownership
- 1999 Gramm Leach Bliley Act further deregulating banking and securities
- The Commodity Futures Modernization Act of 2000 effectively preventing regulation of credit default swaps
- The 2001 lowering of the Fed interest rate eleven times to stimulate recovery from the dot-com crises, together with further lowering in 2003.
- The 2006 mark to market accounting rules, intended to protect investors

tively recent instances of US government intervention that have allegedly contributed to the current crisis.

Constantly Moving Parts

Economies are like living creatures. They have many parts constantly in motion, ebbing and flowing, growing, contracting and evolving in a survival of the fittest. Evolving economies are not exempt from the occasional growth spurt that arguably ends up taking them in a wrong direction. When nonnative species are introduced (such as artificially setting prices or regulating industry), indigenous species may be inadvertantly compromised. The possibilities are endless. Every relief and reform proposed has several sides and personal agendas to weave through. Every yin has its yang.

So it has been with our nation's real estate, mortgage, banking and securities markets, and the many economies that have been impacted as the subprime crisis sheds it skin. Having read chapter 2, we now know that this is not the first time our nation has faced economic crisis. History teaches us that Americans have survived economic adversity and emerged from it for the better. In fact, keeping this in mind is crucial to maintaining an accurate perspective and short circuiting counterproductive, irrational panic.

Trial-and-Error

Although few of us were old enough at the time to remember (in fact most of us had not even been born yet), there are good reasons that our nation's central banking system, the Federal Reserve, was created and charged with, among other things, addressing banking crises like this in the first place.

The First Bank of the United States was chartered in 1791 by Alexander Hamilton. By 1816, our founding fathers had scrapped the first bank for the Second Bank of the United States. Even the second bank did not cut it and, between 1837 and 1862, America had no formal central bank at all. From 1862 to 1913, a system of banks, operating under the National Banking Act of 1862, seemed to be the answer. But after nationwide banking panics in 1873, 1893 and, in particular, 1907, our Congress switched banking theory gears again, enacting the Aldrich-Vreeland Act and establishing the National Monetary Commission to study and advise Congress on national central banking reform. Then commission chair and Republican leader Nelson Aldrich appointed two investigative boards, one to study America's monetary system and the other to study Europe's systems. The combined result of each commission's observations and recommendations was the Federal Reserve Act of 1913.

Since that time our nation's banking system has been revisited time and again including by the Banking Act of 1935, the Employment Act of 1946, the Federal Reserve-Treasury Department Accord of 1951, the Bank Holding Company Act of 1956, as amended in 1970, the Federal Reserve Reform Act

Basic Functions of the Department of the Treasury

- Managing federal finances
- Collecting taxes, duties, and monies paid to and due to the United States and paying all the bills of the federal government
- Producing all postage stamps, currency, and coinage
- Managing government accounts and the US public debt
- Supervising national banks and thrift institutions
- Advising on domestic and international financial, monetary, economic, trade, and tax policy—fiscal policy being the sum of these, and the ultimate responsibility of Congress
- Enforcing federal finance and tax laws
- Investigating and prosecuting tax evaders, counterfeiters, forgers, smugglers, illicit spirits distillers, and gun law violators

Basic Functions of the Federal Reserve

- Addressing the problem of bank panics
- Elastic currency
- Check clearing system
- Lender of last resort
- Central bank
- Federal funds
- Balance between private banks and responsibility of government
- Government regulation and supervision
- Preventing asset bubbles
- National payments system

of 1977, the International Banking Act of 1978, the Full Employment and Balanced Growth Act of 1978, the Depository Institutions Reform, Recovery and Enforcement Act of 1989, the Federal Deposit Insurance Corporation Improvement Act of 1991, and the Gramm-Leach-Bailey Act of 1999. You get the picture. This litany of banking regulatory trial and error does not even take into account the multitude of ideas and explorations at all levels of government that never made it into law, hopefully because the investigation and debate processes yielded more appropriate alternatives. But likely, at least in part, because of political pressures and agendas.

In addition to the Federal Reserve, the other major player in our nation's financial health is the United States Department of the Treasury, part of the president's cabinet established by Congress in 1789. The department is run by the United States secretary of the treasury. Among other things, the treasury recommends and implements the president's economic policy, regulates US chartered financial institutions, and enforces US financial laws. A more detailed description of what the Federal Reserve and the US Department of Treasury do is included for you on page 228.

Yet, in spite of all this effort, we still had the Great Depression in the 1930s, inflation in the 1970s, the savings and loan crisis in the 1980s, the dot-com era of the 1990s, and a fair share of tough economic times in between, each necessary by-products of a constantly evolving economy and a trial-and-error approach to reigning it in. In the late 1980s and early 1990s, the Resolution Trust Corporation (RTC) sold $304 billion in assets from 747 failed savings and loan associations at a cost of $76 billion to US taxpayers. And our nation survived. The point is, we've never employed anything other than a trial, error, and improve approach to economics, banking, and finance. Government and reform have always gone hand-in-hand. Our national approach to regulation of the real estate market, mortgage market, banking, and Wall Street has been no exception. Economic policy making is an art, not a science. Among other challenges, policy makers rely on estimates of economic variables. The exact impact that relying on mere estimates of important economic variables will have on policies is unknown and will be further influenced by other future conditions, both known and unknown. The methods available for measuring economic policy effectiveness are equally speculative. In fact, as we said, a series of government initiatives, founded on honorable intentions, have actually been cited for having *caused* America's most recent crises.

WHAT IS A "RUN ON THE BANK"?

Likewise, the concept of a *run on the bank* is nothing new. A run on the bank occurs when bank depositors get nervous that their bank or investment firm is becoming illiquid and, all at once, demand their deposits or investments back, ironically actually causing their bank or investment firm to become illiquid. Bank runs occur because, in addition to holding deposits, banks also lend money. US banking is based upon a theory (which is itself beyond the scope of our discussion) that allows banks to loan out more money than what they are holding in deposits. In other words, banks only have to hold a certain percentage of the amount they loan out in reserves. Accordingly, a bank will simply never have enough cash in reserves to give all of its depositors all of their money back at the exact same time.

WHAT IS ELASTIC CURRENCY?

Knowing that bank runs may happen, the Federal Reserve was designed to minimize these occurrences and to forestall runs on US banks. The primary way the Federal Reserve accomplishes this is by having its own supply of money to inject into the banking systems when needed or remove when it is not. This is known as *elastic currency*. The Federal Reserve also serves as a central check clearing system because we've learned from trial and error that banks tend to not trust each other during financial crises. And, as we learned in chapter 5, the Fed plays the role of lender of last resort by funding lenders in certain cases of need.

WHAT EXACTLY IS THE FEDERAL RESERVE SYSTEM?

The Federal Reserve is a hybrid of private banking business and government regulation. There are twelve regional Federal Reserve banks in the United States. Private US banks elect their regional Federal Reserve Bank's board of directors. Seven members of the Federal Reserve's Board of Governors in Washington, DC, are appointed by the president of the United States and confirmed by the Senate. This system is designed with the idea that the private banks will provide input about the current economics in their regions, which the government appointees in DC will then use in crafting and adjusting federal banking policy. Federal banking regulations come out of these policies. Some recent examples have been the Truth in Lending Act, the Equal Credit Opportunity Act, and the Home Mortgage Disclosure Act, all discussed earlier. As the bubble burst, the current chairman of the board of governors was, of course, Benjamin Bernanke. As such, he frequently met with other government divisions and with the president and then treasury secretary Henry Paulson, on banking and economic issues.

At the heart of much of the recent criticism of the Federal Reserve is what is alleged to be it's outdated box of tools to ward off, and when necessary respond to, financial crises. As we've discussed, the Fed utilizes open market operations, or the purchase and sale of US treasury and federal agency securities to regulate the supply of bank reserves, the discount rate or the interest rate charged to lenders for loans from the Federal Reserve discount window, and reserve requirements (the amount a lender must retain in its reserve account). Criticism of the Federal Reserve is nothing new. Some claim the Fed actually worsened the Great Depression of the 1930s and the hyperinflation of the 1970s and has been used for political gain in favor of some business or economic sectors over others. Others have criticized its secretiveness.

Artificial Manipulation

No doubt, the Fed does artificially manipulate our nation's monetary system, an invasion of nonnative species into natural economic ecosystems, subject to human error. The question is: Can the US banking system, created and re-created over the past two centuries and the humans operating it do a better job than our economic systems would do naturally, without intervention from the Fed? Given its deep entrenchment in American government and politics, the question is moot but for the direction we, as a nation, wish to see the Fed take in response to our current crisis and over coming generations. History suggests that the Fed is more susceptible to overhaul following shaky economic times like this. President Barack Obama will fill three vacant seats currently on the seven-member board of governors of the Federal Reserve, each of which will have to be approved by the Senate. If you're not happy about Federal Reserve policies, now is the time to speak out.

WHAT DID WE DO THE LAST TIME THIS HAPPENED?

Faced with a similar foreclosure challenge during the Great Depression, in 1933 Franklin D. Roosevelt and Congress crafted the Home Owners Loan Corporation (HOLC) and the Reconstruction Finance Corporation (RFC) to inject large amounts of federal cash into institutions. We've mentioned the HOLC before. The HOLC replaced mortgages near or in default with new ones that home owners could presumably afford. About half of the mortgage loan applications received by the HOLC were granted, in total a million mortgages adding up to $3.5 billion in loans. To put this in better perspective, one in every five mortgages in the United States was owned by the HOLC. In the end, 20 percent of the HOLC borrowers defaulted anyway, leaving the HOLC with two hundred thousand REOs.[1] As we've discussed, many things have changed over the past seventy-five years. A detailed comparison of our current crisis and prior crises our country has weathered would probably make for an interesting discussion but is beyond the scope of this book. For purposes of our discussion though, one important distinction between then and now is personal accountability. Roosevelt's distressed home owners were caught between a rock and the Depression. Today's distressed home owners were directly involved in making their own bad choices. Bernanke, a well-known student of the Depression, once wrote that the RFC and the HOLC were "the only major New Deal programs which successfully promoted economic recovery." A similar solution today would render our government the sixth-biggest bank in the country overnight and require hundreds of billions of dollars.[2] Although some of our nation's larger banks and Wall Street firms are stepping up with dollars to strategically acquire weaker companies (sometimes with urging and assistance from Treasury Department and Federal Reserve leaders), we now know for sure that most of the relief dollars for distressed home owners (as well as for businesses, investors, and individuals impacted by the broader economic crisis) will be coming from taxpayers by way of our government's first $700 billion Troubled Asset Relief Program bailout passed in October 2008 and subsequent provisions that have and will continue to follow, which we will discuss shortly. The question has now become who will get those dollars, how will those decisions be made and will that be enough to solve our nation's economic problems? These decisions are likely to be works in progress, changing many times as the crisis evolves. One component that we can be certain the solution will involve is good, old, tried-and-true trial-and-error.

Recent Economic Crisis in Other Countries

1977	Spain
1987	Norway
1990	Singapore
1991	Finland
1991	Sweden
1994	Mexico
1997	Japan
1997	South Korea
1998	Russia

ECONOMIC CRISIS IS NOT UNIQUELY AMERICAN

As we've said before, America has not cornered the market on real estate crises. Singapore's prices fell 80 percent in eighteen months in 1990. The world has seen eighteen other major banking crises in industrial countries since World War II, the most serious of which have resulted directly from real estate bubbles and lending changes. Some of these are illustrated for your reference in the sidebar on page 232. Much can be learned from this more recent trial-and-error of others. Between 1998 and 2003, Japan's bailout cost that country $440 billion, mostly to protect bank depositors, nationalize the weakest banks, and provide capital for the others. Much of that expense was attributed to the fact that the Japanese government waited several years, until the nation's banks began to fail, before stepping in.[3] Japan's bank failures began in 1991. The government takeovers were not put in motion until 1998. In fact, prior bailout costs incurred by other nations reflect the success of the strategies utilized in each case. A recap of these costs as a percentage of GDP is included for your insight in the following chart. One reason bailouts are so expensive is that it is extremely difficult to prevent abuse.[4]

Bailout Costs Incurred by Other Nations

Country	*Crisis Year*	*Bailout Cost as % of GDP*
Finland	1991	12.8%
Sweden	1991	3.6%
Mexico	1994	19.3%
Japan	1997	24.0%
South Korea	1997	31.2%
Average cost to resolve economic crisis	(past 30 years)	16.0%

The stock market crashed in 1929, but it was not until 1932 that many of the more effective responses were implemented. In the interim, unemployment reached 25 percent.[5] Even though our S&Ls began to fail in the early 1980s, the Resolution Trust Corporation (RTC) was not formed to dispose of their assets until 1989. This has been cited as one of the reasons our leaders felt it was imperative to move ahead with the $700 billion October 2008 bailout right away, even as critics argued that more time was needed to craft a better approach. The biggest potential risk of responding so quickly is that the government may pay too much for the distressed assets, which could result in an unnecessarily larger US budget deficit. We have since learned that safeguards written into the plan, dictating, among other things, how the money was to be spent and requiring periodic detailed public accountings, may have also been compromised in haste. As is the case in the United States, the people of Japan resented using public funds to assist big banks that had made big profits on risky real estate speculation. The notion some of you may have is that, while other people were mortgaging big homes and doing cash out refinances to buy new cars and going on lovely vacations, you were busy working hard so why should your tax dollars go to help them. This view is not uncommon. But the government is telling us that our dollars are going to save *us*, not *them*. The Japanese government provided much of the funding in the form of loans and stock purchases, some of which eventually generated healthy returns for the country and its citizens. In fact, much of the investment was recovered after just five years.[6] Industry experts say the two primary lessons to be learned from the experience of our friends in Japan is that, first quicker government intervention is important and, second, government must be selective in determining which banks to save, since not every bank can survive.

WHAT'S NEXT?

Although it took nearly two years for the subprime crisis to begin getting the attention it deserved, it eventually moved to the forefront of our government, corporate, and private individuals' agendas. Unfortunately, what began as a problem for US home owners has become a series of much bigger problems for much bigger groups. And much of our government's attention seems to have shifted away from home owners and onto these other concerns. That given, the real challenge for us as individuals and as a nation lies in determining how to best utilize the next few years to our best advantage for both short- and long-term well-being. It may be another eighty-plus years before we have this unanimous opportunity to focus on and potentially improve our collective core financial values, practices, and policies again, especially as they relate to our individual and national use of credit and the American Dream of home ownership.

SOME OF THE REASONS WHY OUR GOVERNMENT'S TOOLS MAY NOT BE WORKING

Some historians say the US Congress made its most important contribution to taming business cycles when it created the Federal Reserve System in 1913 and equipped it to respond to banking crises. After that, whenever banks needed cash and couldn't sell their assets or borrow against them because markets were panicked, the Fed could lend to banks that had solid collateral. The Fed's control over the money supply in this manner is a powerful lever and is still our government's first line of defense. When its trading desk buys bonds and expands the money supply, the Fed operates to lower interest rates, encouraging the private sector to borrow and spend more. Influence over interest rates on the economy is strongest in housing where buyers are more rate sensitive. Investors, on the other hand, turn to the equity market and bid up stock prices, making consumers richer (because their stock is now worth more). Richer consumers are willing to take a chance that the stock will stay high or go even higher. In turn they spend more, making it easier for businesses to expand with equity financing. As a result, regulators' knee-jerk reaction to decreased consumer spending is to make money easier for us to get our hands on so we'll spend it more freely. We've seen this so far since the real estate bubble burst in a series of Federal Reserve rate cuts aimed at increasing the flow of credit. When the rates are cut the cost of credit is lowered on all types of loans and on credit costs, in theory making people more interested in borrowing money.

Off-Balance-Sheet Leveraging

Unfortunately, this particular Federal Reserve tool was not honed with twenty-first century banking dynamics in mind. In fact, our entire banking regulation system is based on more traditional banking and liquidity concepts. For example, government deposit insurance (the FDIC) protects depositors' money. Government supervision makes sure the banks behave prudently and the government insists that banks have a set amount of currency in reserve to respond to those who wish to take their money out of the bank. But, as we discussed in chapter 2, this is not necessarily how banking and liquidity work today. Traditional liquidity depends upon real world money or value. Over time, our tougher regulatory capital requirements encouraged banks to keep fewer loans on their books and instead financially engineer ways to spread the risk around since only loans actually on the bank's balance sheet get counted as real money at risk for which reserves were required. A bank or company balance sheet is also used by other banks and companies to assess its value for acquisition or merger and its strength for borrowing money to and otherwise doing business. With no governmental capital requirements in place to limit this type of off balance sheet leveraging, as we discussed in chapter 2, lenders have increasingly devised creative ways to borrow and loan more and more money. Because available cheap credit is simply not counted in traditional banking definitions of liquidity, this newer model had remained off the radar screen for regulators and had never been fully tested for flaws until now.

Irrational Exuberance

The simple fact that Americans chose to buy real estate because they could get the cheap credit we've been discussing from banks and not because what they were using that credit to buy (in this case, real estate) was a good value changed everything. The real estate bubble lead to little correlation between

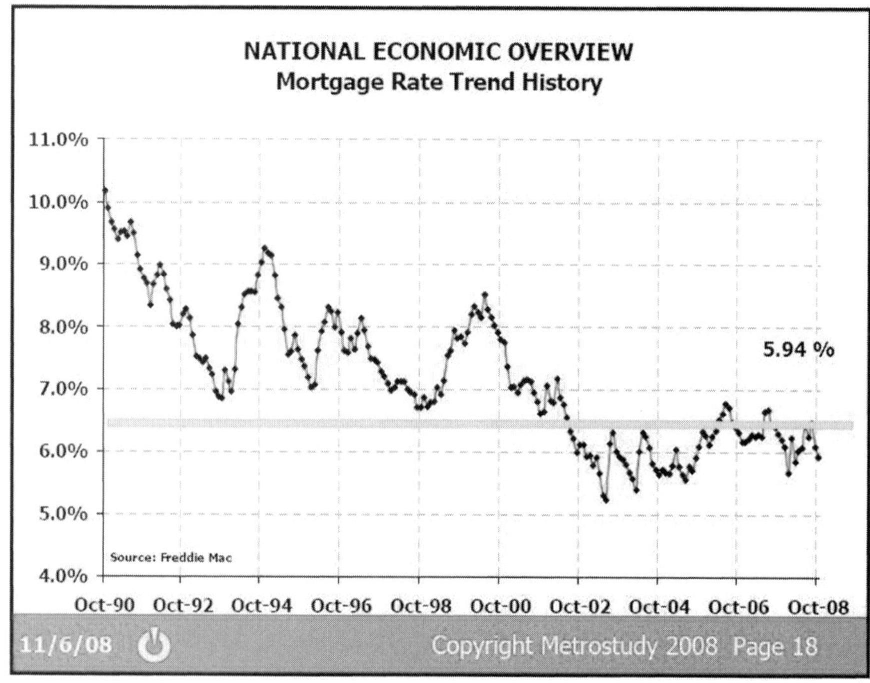

real-world money or value and purchase prices paid for real estate. In other words, real estate prices were driven up based on the seemingly endless supply of cheap credit and irrational investor and buyer exuberance, not because the true asset value of the real estate. The graph on the previous page reflects just how cheap mortgage credit had become from a high of 10 percent in October 1990 to the 6 percent range during the bubble. We discussed in chapter 5 that this is contrary to healthy real estate appreciation, in which real estate values have and in most cases always and logically should be tied to traditional tested methods for real estate valuation such as borrower income for residential properties and income potential or cap rates for commercial properties. The process of negotiating who is going to absorb the different between big loans made on real estate during the bubbles and the smaller values the same real estate now has has been a long one, at first between borrowers and lenders but now also involving our government.

Banks Hoarding Money

Some banks and investors today are flush with funds but reluctant to lend and buy because they no longer trust the market values (of real estate, CDOs, etc.) or each other's balance sheets (since they now know that everyone is playing balance sheet bingo with bad loans and investments that may not be on balance sheets). This is the reason banks don't want to lend to us or other borrowers, including other banks, and are said to be hoarding money. One emerging result, which we discussed earlier alone with commercial paper, is a serious lack of solvency for once healthy borrowers as sources relied on by other banks and companies for new capital dry up.

Some say the distrust is merely a temporary lack of confidence. But most agree that at least for now we can probably expect still more losses in the housing and mortgage sectors and beyond as the crisis continues its spread into even more industries and markets. For example, we mentioned earlier one bank's strategy of issuing automatic, unsolicited, two-year extensions on all vacant lot loans maturing this year, a move that quietly keeps defaults and refinances off that bank's books but supports the suspicion that there is still a lot we don't know about as from the outside these loans still appear to be perfectly fine. The nonbank-affiliated financial intermediaries, to whom some banks transfer their riskier assets in order to avoid regulatory hassles, are not eligible for central bank loans. Much of this debt may eventually have to be moved back onto the banks' balance sheets and written off as bad (unpaid) debt. Clearly this will impact many banks' lending capacity as well as their reserve requirements. In other words, they will have to carry more money on hand to offset the bad debt and so they won't be able to lend that money, potentially making it harder for us to get loans. Perhaps the knowledge that this "other shoe" is bound to drop soon is another reason some banks are holding on to what loanable funds they have. Some are suggesting that more lending needs to be kept on the banks' own balance sheets in order for banks to remain responsible for quality when loans are securitized and prudent reserves retained. At the end of the day, this could all lead to slower future liquidity expansion. How can the Federal Reserve be expected to fix all of this by using its circa 1930s tool of simply pumping more money into the system?

Intertwined Markets

While it is the responsibility of the world's central banks to insure proper functioning of our financial markets by providing temporary liquidity (increasing the money supply), they are not intended to be a bailout for banks' bad assets. By comparison, the saving and loan problems of the 1980s were largely contained, allowing relatively simple government intervention and rescue through a $125 billion bailout.[7] Today's financial systems, however, are not self-contained but instead are more interconnected, both domestically and globally, than ever before. In our new global banking markets, a simple, self-contained government intervention and rescue is no longer an option.

MORE TRIAL-AND-ERROR, SUBPRIME CRISIS STYLE

True to form, Washington has taken a series of stabs at trying to contain and subsequently solve our nation's current economic crisis. The irony that one of the earliest proposals actually considered $2 billion sufficient is now laudible and puts the speed at which and the size to which the problem has grown into perspective. The following recaps some of the more memorable proposals.

Fed Discount Window

While Federal Reserve chairman Bernanke's initial response to banks' hoarding money and calls for crisis assistance was to pump money into short-term money markets, when that didn't work, he and others began a series of other recovery attempts. In August 2007 the Fed sweetened the terms of lending and loosened collateral standards at the *federal discount window* (again, the term used when referring to federal credit available for banks to borrow when they're short on cash themselves). However, long viewed as a last resort for banks because of possible investor alarm at a bank seeking capital, there were no takers. So the powers that be turned to the powers of persuasion, calling on our country's four biggest banks together to borrow a collective $2 billion from the federal discount window; the goal was to lift the perceived stigma of borrowing from the discount window and boost market confidence. Citigroup, Bank of America, J.P. Morgan, and Wachovia (since sold) each borrowed $500 million. The move was largely symbolic but it set a precedent for government big bank solidarity, working together to improve investor confidence.[8]

Super Conduit

Not long after that came the super conduit, a proposal designed to enhance special purpose vehicle (SPV) liquidity. The super conduit was a government-created entity intended to issue short-term notes to investors who would invest in it and use the proceeds to buy the securities from the SPVs that appeared to have frozen due to market conditions. In reality the super conduit was nothing more than a middleman between SPVs and the potential end investors, put in place to make the potential investors more comfortable in order to jump start their demand again for the commercial paper sold by the SPVs, which the investors had stopped buying. But again the efforts did not succeed as intended. It seems investors realized the super conduit did nothing more than effectively offer to resell them the same SPV paper they didn't want in the first place. In short, investors didn't trust the super conduit either.[9]

Interest Rate Freeze

Then president George W. Bush and Treasury Secretary Paulson initially proposed an interest rate freeze for home borrowers who closed on loans between January 1, 2005, and July 31, 2007; still lived in the home; had a low credit score; were still current on their mortgage payments; and were able to prove they would not be able to afford an upward adjustment in their mortgage interest rate. This proposal was rejected, in part because the group it proposed to help was too narrowly defined, effectively eliminating a great many who needed it.

Economic Stimulus Act

The government made another stab at the problems with the 2008 Economic Stimulus Act designed to put more cash in our pockets so we, in turn, would spend it and boost the economy. The act also increased the amount of expenses small businesses could write off in an effort to encourage them to spend more on equipment and expansion.[10]

Tax Relief for Forgiven Mortgage Debt

In further attempts, the House Ways and Means Committee, where tax bills start, proposed a bill to allow home owners in foreclosure to forego paying tax on any debt that is forgiven by their lenders. Prior to that, forgiven debt of this

Some of the Initial Government Steps Taken in Response to the Subprime Crisis

- October 2007, the Hope Now Alliance was created by government and private lenders to help subprime borrowers.
- October 2007, a consortium of US banks, backed by the government, created the $100 billion Master Liquidity Enhancement Conduit (MLEC) or Super Conduit to buy mortgage backed securities.
- The Term Auction Facility was created by the Fed in December 2007 to inject cash into the system.
- Around the same time, then president Bush announced plans for an Economic Stimulus Act, giving many Americans $600 to spend.
- December 2008, President Bush announced FHA Secure, a voluntary plan to freeze interest rate adjustments; asked Congress to pass legislation modernizing FHA and the tax code so people could refinance their mortgages; and requested funding for mortgage counseling and legislation to reform Fannie Mae and Freddie Mac.
- The Term Securities Lending Facility was created in March 2008 to inject treasury securities into the system.

- March 2008, then Fed chairman Bernanke openly advocated the voluntary reduction by lenders of loan principal on mortgages where the loan amount exceeds the property value in order to avoid home owners walking away from their homes.
- March 2008, the Primary Dealer Credit Facility was implemented.
- March 2008, the Fed increased funds available through the Term Auction Facility from $60 billion to $100 billion.
- Between September 2007 and April 2008, the Fed took action to lower lending rates six times. The stated goal was to provide funds to entities with illiquid mortgage-backed securities so that they can avoid selling those securities at a loss, potentially triggering other impacts, and stimulate the economy in general.
- In April 2008, the US House passed a bill offering government insurance on $300 billion in new refinance mortgages for 500,000 borrowers and $15 billion to affected states.
- The SEC began a series of crackdowns on short selling in July 2008 but has met criticism surrounding the companies not included and failure to regulate more heavily before.
- The Housing and Economic Recovery Act of 2008 was passed by Congress on July 24, 2008, and signed into law by the President Bush six days later. The act enabled expanded regulatory authority of Fannie Mae and Freddie Mac by the newly established Federal Housing Finance Authority (FHFA) and gave the US Treasury authority to advance funds to stabilize both companies, effectively raising the treasury debt ceiling by $800 billion to a total of $10.7 trillion. The legislation was landmark in that it also allowed government to take equity positions in Fannie Mae and Freddie Mac.
- Shortly thereafter Fannie Mae and Freddie Mac are placed into conservatorship.
- In July 2008, the Fed finalized new mortgage lender rules designed to prevent future mortgage crises. In particular, the new rules require lenders to verify income, assets, and ability to make payments as well as establish real estate tax and insurance escrow accounts on certain loans.
- In September 2008, the SEC temporarily banned short selling of stock.
- After what appeared from outside the beltway to be a lot of drama and name-calling, in October 2008, Congress fine-tuned and passed the so-called $700 billion Housing and Economic Recovery Act.
- An $800 billion increase in the national debt ceiling enabling the treasury to further support secondary housing market and GSEs.
- Ease of mark to market accounting rules.

nature was treated as income and taxed accordingly. To pay for the tax revenue shortage this would produce, the bill proposed to eliminate the right of those with second homes to reduce or avoid the taxes they pay when they sell those second homes. In short, second home owners would pick up the tab.

A summary of crisis-related relief initiatives through October 2008 is included for your quick reference in the sidebar on the previous two pages. At the time supporters said this series of recovery stimulators would eventually turn the markets around, but the downward trend persisted.

We discussed earlier that the timing of relief and reform can have as big of an impact as the type of intervention itself. Trigger-happy intervention has risks and drawbacks, too. But most agree that our government's moves have not come too early. In fact, the criticism is more along the lines that government reaction has been piecemeal and too slow. Many say we could have skipped right past the initial voluntary initiatives. Bernanke had initially been focusing on trying to make our toxic debt liquid as opposed to focusing on the burdens of losses caused by the toxic debt that has since trickled downward and left institutions and individuals short of capital. After Lehman Brothers went bankrupt and AIG ran into trouble in October 2008, the even bigger problem emerged and the market seemingly lost faith in Bernanke's strategy of saving one financial institution at a time.

As is always the case with economic policy trial and error, we have seen side effects from some of the measures taken thus far. For example, FHA loans (with their very specific requirements for lending and the need for down payment), which had fallen from 1.3 million in 2002 to only 300,000 in 2006, have already, together with Fannie Mae and Freddie Mac, accounted for 90 percent of all loans originated in 2008, the highest rate in fifty years.[11] Of course much of this may be due to lack of availability of other funding. On the other hand, safe treasury securities were 92 percent of the Fed's assets in June 2007; now they are under 50 percent.[12] Overall, most agree that the Fed has earned some credibility on Wall Street and on Main Street as a result of unrelenting initiatives, flexibility in changing its approach, and successfully managing the media.

Political Party Lines

Although at the height of a national crisis we can anticipate both Democrats and Republicans to be on board with the need for immediate action, division along political party lines, with Democrats tending to favor immediate and more extreme government intervention and Republicans favoring a more laissez-faire approach, allowing the problems to play themselves out, was observable prior to the fall of 2008 and should be expected again as we move forward.[13] Since the Democrats now control the White House, the House of Representatives, and the Senate, we can expect relief and reform leaning more toward the former. On the other hand, many agree that Paulson and Bernanke have been doing a good job; their work should not be interrupted by the transition to a new Obama team just now. Private sector suggestions often carry thinly veiled windfalls for their advocates and even government initiatives are not without favoritism. Treasury Secretary Paulson, a former Goldman Sachs chairman, has been accused of favoring Goldman and other Wall Street firms in some of the more significant actions he has proposed, supported, and actually taken to date. And even as we try to determine how to correct the markets, they continue to move and grow in directions we've yet to imagine.

Our goal in this final chapter is not to conquer the world's subprime-related problems, but to clarify the areas in which relief and reform are likely, provoke thought about what we feel that relief and reform should look like, prepare for the possibilities and learn how we can protect ourselves as changes are effected. Again, as the title of this book suggests, ours is a discussion first and foremost about the American Dream of home ownership and our nation's culturalization of mortgage and mortgage foreclosure. Our discussion of relief and reforms will focus on distressed home owners and our nation's mortgage systems, including suggestions for the broader economic sectors as they relate to the subprime crisis.

STOP THE BLEEDING

On the road to relief and reform, our first stop is to clot the proverbial bleeding as soon as possible. For both ethical and financial reasons, halting foreclosures and keeping people in their homes must top the list of priorities. Few will disagree that the idea of more families being thrown out of their homes and onto the street is downright un-American. Some also believe that if we can stop the foreclosures, we will stop the series of other financial reverberations that have entered into our broader economy. Others of course believe we have exceeded the point where that will solve the problem.

How Do We Decide Who to Help?

Among the various relief proposals, the most hotly debated aspect involves the need to distinguish between those who will and those who will not be considered for relief assistance. This applies at the distressed home owner level as well as the illiquid, potentially insolvent institutional level. There is much challenge involved in simply building consensus in terms of which home owners and institutions deserve relief. For some of us, sending the right value message with our taxpayer money is just as important as saving homes and thwarting further economic disintegration. Some have likened the outcomes thus far to a game of Russian roulette. Once the trigger has been pulled on banks and distressed Wall Street firms (usually, by a ratings downgrade due to write downs or losses, and regulators requiring additional capital or reserves), it remains to be seen whether the Fed has loaded the pistol chamber with a deadly bullet, as we saw in the case of Lehman Brothers, or with a lifesaving bailout, as was the case for AIG. At least at the time there appeared to be little rhyme or reason for who was saved and who was not, other than the Fed's position, we discussed earlier, that some firms are simply too big too allow to fail. Toward that end, the criteria used to determine which home owners and institutions will qualify are just as important as the relief proposal itself. Also to be considered is the practicality of making those determinations. In other words, do we have the time and resources to make precise case-by-case decisions regarding who should be helped, or are we better off making broader decisions? Perhaps the best approach to answering that question is to first discuss how we would craft solutions in a perfect world and then apply real-life constraints to achieve the best balance between what we wish we could do and what we need to do. If, for example, we are to separate out from the millions of distressed home owners those we feel should not receive government assistance, what should this separating process look like?

Should Ignorance of the Law Be an Excuse?

Let's start with the easiest criteria, namely, those borrowers who committed mortgage fraud. Does anyone disagree that folks who knowingly lied to lenders and broke the law should not be bailed out with taxpayer money? Unfortunately, this piece of our analysis may not be quite so clear. If some home owners were encouraged or even duped into committing fraud by the mortgage and real estate professionals they relied upon, the lines become fuzzy. The challenge in crafting relief based on that distinction of course lies in knowing who is telling the truth. After all, given the choice between claiming they were duped and receiving relief or accepting responsibility with no relief, can we realistically expect people to come clean and opt for the later?

The Hazard of Moral Hazard

We discussed in chapter 5 the fear that rewarding people and companies for making bad financial choices will only encourage more bad choices in the future, even among folks who otherwise would have acted with prudence. Why not take a risk if you know that if you fail the government will bail you out? For this reason, critics argue that not all foreclosures *should* be stopped. When we consider the large number of people who bought or refinanced during the bubble and now face foreclosure, it is clear that this list includes borrowers who knowingly extended themselves far beyond their means, gambling on what, with the benefit of 20/20 hindsight, seemed to be the absurd assumption that home prices would increase at record rates indefinitely and that approval for a refinance loan down the road was guaranteed. The idea of rewarding people for poor judgment by allowing them to stay in homes they could never have afforded and therefore should never have purchased in the first place seems counterintuitive and unfair to those who chose more modestly, wisely, or consistently with their capabilities, not to mention those of us who will be forced to subsidize these poor choices. Lest we forget the context, in some of the cases we are talking about subsidizing borrowers so they can stay in spacious homes with granite countertops, stainless steel appliances and Italian marble floors. Making national compromises so that those of us who can barely afford Toyotas are now able to drive Mercedes Benzes instead may indeed perpetuate poor financial decision making or moral hazard. Exactly how realistic was it for a borrower who knew he could only afford an $85,000 ten-year-old two-bedroom, two-bath town home in 2003, to believe someone who told him he could afford a brand new $300,000 five-bedroom, four-bath home in 2005 on the same income? The same has been said of securities investors who elected not to read the fine print and blindly believed they could earn a 20 percent annual return on the same money that had been earning, on historial average, only 8 percent annually without added risk. Given our cultural relationship with credit (discussed in chapter 1), which itself could use some evolutionary correcting, one might argue that the subprime crisis is merely natural correction of the marketplace and we should not meddle with these naturally occurring corrective measures that have worked since the dawn of capitalism.

Determining exactly where personal accountability for our own choices lies is a topic beyond the scope of this chapter, but it should certainly be a consideration in deciding who gets help. Even in cases where borrowers were legitimately and justifiably mislead into making bad choices, as in situations involving predatory lending (discussed in chapter 5), a consequence of some sort, perhaps financial education, seems appropriate as a prerequisite for public money receiving.

Delaying the Inevitable

In cases where bad financial choices were made by borrowers, overlooking the threat of moral hazard and providing assistance may merely be delaying the inevitable for many. As we discussed in chapters 3 and 4, today's foreclosures are a symptom of larger problems that were allowed to grow in the years leading up to the bubble. The true maladies behind the foreclosures are threefold: first, monthly mortgage payments are unmanageable after interest rates reset on adjustable rate mortgages; second, even for borrowers who can afford to pay their mortgage, other carrying costs, such as real estate taxes, insurance, condominium or home owners' association assessments, utilities, and maintenance are increasingly unaffordable; and third, the true value of the underlying home is oftentimes less than what is owed to the bank, leading some home owners to want the bank to take back their home and their mortgage loan along with it. Whether or not we can realistically help this category of distressed home owners who inappropriately stretched to get into their bubble homes will depend, in part, upon which bracket a particular borrower falls into and the type of relief we propose to provide.

SO SHOULD WE FREEZE OR REDUCE INTEREST RATES?

One logical way to address the primary cause behind our nation's mounting foreclosures, namely, freezing or reducing interest rate resets, seems simple.

Since initially the leading cause of foreclosure is interest rate adjustments that cause mortgage payments to increase to unaffordable levels, just freeze or even reduce the interest rate resets. As of November 2008 that seemed to be something we could expect will happen. The latest buzz is that lenders are encouraging borrowers to call them for modifications and carte blanche ninety-day moratoriums on new foreclosure filings.

A Leading Proposal

Freezing or limiting interest rate adjustments and providing new sources of less expensive mortgage loans for home owners experiencing distress as a result of interest rate adjustment has been an area of relief that the government has been attempting to utilize for several months now, first with the FHA Secure program and with the Hope for Homeowners program, both mentioned earlier. Critics say that both programs are not broad enough to make a noticeable dent in the subprime problem. A graph depicting the limited impact these initial proposals would have is provided below.

Initially the Treasury Department, and more recently others, were leaning on mortgage loan lenders and servicers to voluntarily freeze rates.

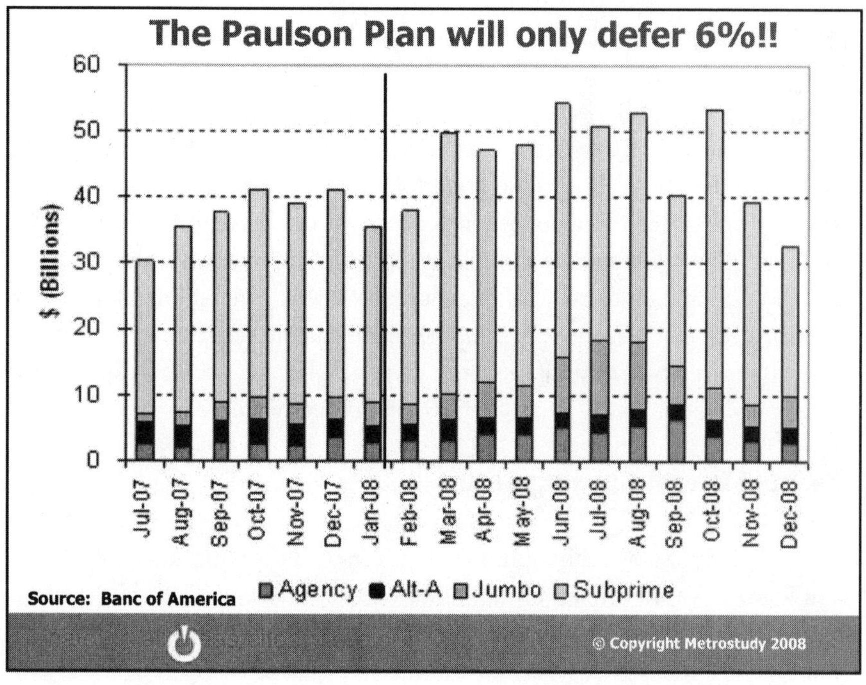

Then senator Hillary Clinton was among the first outspoken proponents of a five-year freeze, while industry executives suggested that one year would be sufficient. Barney Frank, chair of the House Financial Services Committee, supported a voluntary lender-subsidized reprieve. FDIC chairman Sheila Bair took the proposal a step further, urging lenders to make those low mortgage loan teaser rates permanent. Democrats went even further, suggesting a bill that would allow bankruptcy judges to modify loan terms to help people keep their homes, a notion that opponents argued would dry up mortgage loan financing altogether by removing the security that investors would be repaid. The concept of providing new affordable home loans to replace those with interest rates adjusting to unaffordable levels solves this dilemma by taking the original lenders and investors who anticipated higher returns out of the picture by paying them off with loans, most likely from or subsidized by our government, from lenders who agree to the lower, presumably fixed, interest rate and return. Even so, as we mentioned earlier, investors factor mortgage loan prepayment (which will be essentially what happens if the bailout facilitates new loans to replace the unaffordable ones home owners now have) in as something that negatively impacts the return on their investment, which means we simply may not be able to avoid a chilling effect.

A Rate Freeze or Reduction May Not Solve the Problem

Unfortunately, in addition to the chilling effect it could have on mortgage loan investors, an across-the-board interest rate reset freeze or reduction may cause a series of other yet-to-be-realized problems and, because such a solution only addresses one of the three underlying causes for our current foreclosures, it is not likely to have the results sought for all distressed home owners. In particular, those home owners who purchased McMansion bubble homes well beyond their means may lose their homes even with an interest rate freeze. And we'll discuss below why those home owners who are upside down in their homes may elect to walk away even in spite of a rate freeze or reduction.

The Trouble with Carrying Costs

Why will a freeze or reduction on rate resets or providing affordable mortgage loans have no impact on the other carrying costs we've discussed that are making homes unaffordable? Because buying a home is not like the other purchases we make. For example, a pair of black leather Payless pumps may cost $9.99 while a pair of black leather Manolo Blahnik pumps may cost $999.00. Once you buy the pumps, the cost difference stops there. When either pair needs new heels, the shoemaker charges us the same price for his handy work, regardless of the name on the label. With a house, however, the difference between affordable and unaffordable does not stop with the purchase price and mortgage payment (the only issue that would be addressed by a rate freeze). For those of us who choose to purchase a home which is above our means, even if the government were to freeze our interest rate or give us a more affordable loan, we will still be saddled with ongoing real estate taxes, insurance, repairs, maintenance and even monthly utilities that cost more than the same items would cost in a smaller, less expensive home. For example, the cost to heat or cool a 5,000 square foot home is about twice as much as the cost to heat or cool a 2,500 square foot home. And since the larger size home will have twice as many air conditioning units as the smaller home, it will cost the home owner two times as much money to maintain them in terms of service calls and the filters, condensers, and coils, which require continual cleaning and replacement. Likewise, the roof on a 5,000 square foot home is typically larger and more expensive to maintain than the roof on a 2,500 square foot home. There are more windows, doors, even more paint required to keep the larger home in good repair in comparison to the smaller home. In the sidebar one home owner shares her story about buying a super-sized bubble home only to find that the bucks she needed didn't stop there. An interest rate freeze will have no impact whatsoever on these hidden costs of ownership which, together, often exceed our mortgage payment and, unlike our mortgage payment, usually get more expensive over time and can never be permanently paid off. Absent another solution, eventually home owners who purchased a bubble home they cannot realistically ever afford may succumb to these other financial burdens and lose their homes regardless.

One solution that at once reduces the hazard of moral hazard and carves out those home owners for whom an interest rate freeze or reduction would not likely work in the long run is requalifying interest rate freeze or reduction applicants based on traditional mortgage loan underwriting criteria. The requalification process fleshes out those borrowers who will still not be able to afford the home even with a rate freeze or reduction so that they can be offered a short-term solution designed to help them hold on until they can eventually

Insight from a Home Owner Struggling with Hidden Home Ownership Costs

Elisa Patchage bought her 5,000 square foot home in a gated community in 2006. She shares with us, "In my neighborhood everyone is a young professional with young kids. We all stretched to buy new homes during the bubble. My husband and I spent $650,000 for our 4,500 square foot, 5 bedroom, 4 bath home. And now me and all my neighbors are living in these beautiful homes which none of us can afford to furnish or decorate. It's ridiculous. I don't know what we were thinking. Now we're much more careful than we were in our old condo about turning off the lights when we leave a room or turning the air-conditioning down if we'll be gone for the day. And my husband goes out of his way to save on other expenses we didn't even think about before we bought this house. He cuts the lawn and cleans the pool. We had a lady clean the condo for us every week. But for the house she charges six times as much so I do it myself. We never go out to dinner anymore. It's like we're slaves to our house. We can afford to pay our mortgage. But honestly if I had it to do over again, I'd buy a smaller house so we could still afford to do all of the other things we used to enjoy."

trade down into a more affordable home. For example, there's the temporary mortgage payment reduction or loan. We're seeing some lenders such as Citibank and Bank of America doing this already with offers to modify loans by reducing interest and increasing amortization (i.e., the life of the loan) for people who are qualified to make the payments. Exactly how short term such a solution can be depends of course upon how long it takes for the real estate market to recover and the difference between how much money will be required to pay off the borrower's mortgage and how much the borrower can eventually sell his home for. We will discuss both of these important variables shortly. In the meantime, the sidebar on page 251 illustrates this dilemma by reflecting on the difference between estimated carrying costs on a property a borrower can afford and one he cannot afford utilizing the traditional loan qualification front-end and back-end ratios we discussed earlier. Herein lies one of the reasons absorption, which we will discuss shortly, may take longer than it should. Namely, much of the bubble inventory of housing is larger, fancier, and more expensive than what many of us should have ever been able to afford to begin with.

AFFORDABLE v. NOT AFFORDABLE

Traditional Loan		**Bubble Loan**	
Borrower Monthly Income Based on $65,000 = $5,416		Borrower Monthly Income Based on $65,000 = $5,416	

28% Traditional Front-End Qualifying Ratio	=	$1,520
36% Back-End Ratio	=	$1,950
55% Bubble Qualifying Ratio	=	$2,978

Max Price of Home with 10% Down $132,000.00		Max Price of Home with 3% Down $360,500.00	
Maximum Traditional Loan Qualified for $120,000		Maximum Bubble Loan Qualified for $350,000	
Loan Terms: 30-Year, 6.5% Fixed Rate Interest		ARM, 3% Teaser Rate	
		Monthly Payment before rate resets	$2,950
Monthly Payment	$1,446	(Rate adjusts to 7%)	
Hidden Carrying Costs for $120,000 Home:		**Hidden Carrying Costs for $350,000 Home:**	
Real Estate Taxes	$215	Real Estate Taxes	$620
Insurance	$105	Insurance	$325
Association Fees	$ 85	Association Fees	$265
Utilities based on 2,400 SF	$130	Utilities based on 4,500 SF	$275
Total	**$535**	**Total**	**$1,485**
Total Monthly Expense	**$1,981**	**Total Monthly Expense**	**$4,435**

When the rate on the bubble loan resets to 7%, the mortgage payment will increase to $4,650 and total monthly expenses to $6,135. Granted, freezing the rate at 3% will keep the total monthly expenses down for this borrower, but, in truth, he should be living in a home that costs, in total, $1,981 a month, not $4,435 a month.

What If the Borrower Wants to Walk?

Although interest rate resets were initially the leading cause for foreclosures, as we discussed in chapter 5, more and more borrowers are electing foreclosure regardless of whether or not they can afford to pay their mortgage. With purchase prices having fallen so much that these home owners have no hope of reselling their homes at or above the mortgage loan amount they must now repay. In effect, they would lose money by paying off their mortgage loan principal even if we made their interest and monthly payment more affordable. Those home owners who are upside down may elect to walk away from their homes even in spite of an interest rate freeze or availability of affordable home mortgages. One of the more unfortunate impacts of the crisis is what appears to be an emerging cultural acceptance of borrowers shirking their financial responsibility in this way. In fact, my guess is that some readers would consider an upsidedown home owner who has the opportunity but does not walk away from excess debt to be naive, maybe even foolish. If we are not going to hold these borrowers liable to repay their full mortgage loan, regardless of the value of their property, *someone* else will need to either repay this valueless debt or write it off as a loss. This is precisely what borrowers, banks, investors and regulators keep tossing around in what has become a game of financial hot potato.

Can We Reconcile This with Core Financial Values?

We've discussed how, as time passes, we acquire an increasingly clearer image of just how unrealistic everyone at every level had become during the bubble in terms of their assumptions, and choices, including borrowers, mortgage loan originators, and investors. One of the things that still seems to be stumping us is to what extent should these various participants be held responsible for the losses resulting from their own decisions? At the heart of the answer to that question is how much of what we now know can we reasonably have expected these participants to have known, or at least, have suspected, at the time their decisions were being made? If they relied upon others in making their decisions as we know was the case, for example, with many borrowers who relied upon guidance from mortgage loan originators or investors who relied upon guidance from brokers and ratings agencies, how reasonable was it for the participants to have so relied without indepen-

For Example, What If Homes Were Pencils?

Let's say the price of pencils had held steady at $1.00 for the past ten years but recently, for no apparent reason, the price shot up to $50.00. If a borrower with only a little money needed a pencil and an originator, knowing this, offered him a pencil for free today provided he pay $50.00 for it tomorrow, this may seem to be a risky proposition. First, we all know the borrower has very little money to begin with. How will he come up with $50.00 tomorrow? Historically, the price of pencils is $1.00, not $50.00, and the value of a piece of wood with lead in the middle and some rubber at the end logically makes sense at $1.00, maybe even a little more, but certainly not $50.00. Given these facts, most would agree that an originator who gives a pencil on these terms and a borrower who accepts the pencil on these terms are both, at best, pretty big risks takers. Enter the investor who, on the advice of Mr. Rating, tells him that to buy the $50.00 receivable from the originator is a great deal. The next day, the price of pencils returns to $1.00. The borrower calls the originator to say, first, that he does not have the $50.00 to pay him and, second, even if he did he would never pay $50.00 for a pencil he can buy anywhere for only $1.00. The originator says too bad, either pay me or be sued and then calls the investor to tell him the bad news. Should the borrower have known better? Should the originator have known better? What about the investor? Should any of these folks be bailed out with your taxpayer dollars?

dently verifying what they were being told? And even if their reliance was reasonable, should they have still been conscious of the risks inherent in blind reliance? Should they have reasonably known that the profits investors were promised and the absurdly low teaser rates on McMansions were too good to be true? In part because of the complicated nature of mortgages and securities themselves, which we explained in chapter 2, it may be difficult for us to say whether or not we ourselves would have made the same choices or whether we would have known to ask more questions or at least expected (and prepared for) the other shoe to drop. Can the same level of prudence realistically be expected from everyone? For example, do we believe that not all borrowers and investors are equal? Not all are as experienced or even as intelligent, and some, therefore, need more protection against their own poor decision making than others. Should they therefore not be expected to have exercised the same standard of care? Or are there minimum prudence, experience, and intelligence requirements that we should impose regardless before enabling a person to buy a home. Some requirements designed to qualify investors for the purchase of complicated securities already do exist but apparently did not prevent losses.

Perhaps in a simplified context the answers to some of these questions may be easier to reach: for example, if we were talking about making good old-fashioned common pencils and not complicated, seemingly foreign mortgage loans or securities. The sidebar on the previous page contains such an example for your consideration.

Clearly homes are not pencils and $50.00 receivables are not complex CDOs. Then again, it is hard to explain why folks with little money (relative to the purchase) paid $700 a square foot for condominiums in 2005 that were selling for $300 a foot just three years earlier and had never sold for a price anywhere close to $700 per square foot. And then there's the case of home owners who refinanced with subprime mortgages. As we discussed in chapter 2, most of the time the money from these refinances went to buy flat-screen televisions, new cars, or other nonessentials (or to pay off the credit card debt from having already purchased these items). How can we justify forgiving any of this debt and essentially forcing taxpayers to foot the bill for these luxury-type expenditures? Given these facts, some of us may be able to justify holding borrowers, lenders, and investors alike responsible for bad decisions made during the bubble. Some people feel that our response with respect to accountability should be just this simple. Others agree but believe that the scope of relief action needed now far exceeds what would be accomplished by merely allowing natural consequences to take their course. One thing is for sure, the $700 billion bailout of October 2008 and any other economic incentive efforts that may be contemplated by the government will set the tone of our nation's core financial values for years to come. It is up to each of us to decide whether we want to live in a nation that encourages and rewards core financial values consistent with those of our grandparent's—hard work, perseverance, and self-sufficiency—or a nation that has decided it stands for something else.

Is This Reverse Discrimination?

Yet another distinction keeps popping up along socioeconomic lines in what some might argue is a reverse discriminatory manner. Many of the interest rate freeze and affordable mortgage loan proposals exclude borrowers who are in distress now as a result of having purchased or refinanced a second home, an income property (or even a high-end primary residence valued at more than a certain price point), as opposed to those who are suffering from having purchased a less expensive primary residence. Another question to consider is whether or not this amounts to discrimination against wealthier borrowers who have just as much to lose in terms of dollars, even though it may be in the form of loss on a second home or investment property as opposed to a primary residence.

What Is the Investor Perspective?

On the other side of the coin are the investors who were promised higher interest rates in return for the investments they made in subprime mortgage backed securities and related instruments. Some initially proposed that the money to cover the rate reset freeze should come at the expense of these, presumably big and wealthy investors, a concept not far off from socialist ideals of the 1960s. The logic was that these were the same investors who had made large sums of money during the subprime bubble, so they could afford to pay some of it back. Of course, without further examination, no one actually knew for sure how much money investors made or whether the investors who would have been paying after the bubble burst were the same ones who made fortunes, in the same percentages, during the bubble. Even in the unlikely event that the overlap was exact, the argument that investors should forgo their profits to bail us all out is contrary to the fundamentals of capitalism and is clearly not without flaws. And besides, many of the so-called big and wealthy investors include our own pensions and retirement funds! There was a real fear that if a rate reset freeze requiring investors to absorb the costs were approved, investors would start selling their estimated hundreds of billions of dollars worth of financially secured debt, thereby causing our problems to spiral even further out of control.

The investors and securities experts themselves, like mortgage lenders and servicers, were forced to weigh substantially lower returns against the probability that mortgage loan defaults would skyrocket if interest rates are allowed to reset. Investor losses that may follow if such an event were allowed to occur could be enormous. Following the passage of the initial $700 billion TARP bailout, we now know that the government will be leading the rescue of distressed home owners, CDO investors, and mortgage lenders. But until all of the relief details are solidified, we cannot eliminate the possibility that investors and lenders will be asked to absorb some of the losses. Fannie Mae and Freddie Mac stand to gain or lose the most. These government-sponsored enterprises have hundred of billions at stake. Now that the federal government has taken control of both Fannie Mae and Freddie Mac, the burden of an investor absorbed interest rate freeze, should it come to fruition, will fall on the US taxpayers.

Even if we could get ourselves intellectually comfortable with the idea of a partial lender- or investor-subsidized interest bailout freeze, pragmatists point out that it will be impossible to secure all of the necessary and appropriate approvals from lenders and investors and subsequent assignees in each collateralized debt obligation tranch and, because of the number of parties and contracts involved, many of which may be unknown, the likelihood of success is operationally impossible. As we discussed in chapters 3 and 4, unlike years past, when only a bank and a borrower were involved in a mortgage loan, today's loans have been sliced into pieces and sold to countless investors worldwide. This is, in fact, one of the reasons solutions that worked in prior years, such as mortgage loan modifications and loan forbearance, are also no longer an option. No doubt we can expect any move forward with a rate reset freeze or other investor subsidized bailout, absent appropriate investor approvals to spark a hailstorm of investor lawsuits. For purposes of example, in a most extreme case, now that the loans have been securitized, in some cases, the shareholders (or others entitled to vote on decisions) of the companies holding these investments might actually have to vote on whether or not to approve any a modification of the terms of any of the loans in those pools.

IS INCREASING CONSUMER SPENDING THE ANSWER?

We've talked about how economics evolve. Damaged economic markets are supposed to heal themselves. That's how our nation's capitalist system was designed to work. Demand decreases, supply increases, and bargain hunters rush in and absorb excess supply; supply declines and the price increases as the market returns to normal. But, as we discussed in chapter 5, that's not happening now, or at least not quickly enough to avoid collateral damage. Instead, you'll also remember from chapter 5, consumer spending is down, and with it so is business growth, job growth, and the gross domestic product (GDP). Some economists tell us that consumer spending is the chemotherapy to our subprime and economic crisis cancer. Once people start buying up the home supply again and investing and spending money in general, we'll be back on track. Until then, our leaders are hoping that consumers won't stop buying a whole lot of other things, too.[14] But there's an even bigger picture here: during this decade, 5 million Americans effectively earned less than before as increases in the cost of living outpaced increases in their income. As a result, many people are losing their financial foothold and moving from America's middle socioeconomic class down to a lower class.[15] Where consumer spending is concerned, many Americans may just have less money to spend than they did before. Theoretically, this may be one of the reasons Americans have been spending so much using credit card debt and chose to take equity out of their homes. We've discussed in chapter 1 some of the negative impacts that our use of credit has had on our core financial values. There may be an inherent conflict between the trouble overuse of credit causes us and the trouble not using it may cause our nation's economy (once again a topic for another book). In any event, it is unlikely that Americans will start spending again until our home mortgage woes are resolved. Which again begs the question, if we can stabilize our nation's real estate market will broader economic stabilization follow?

THE CASE FOR STABILIZING REAL ESTATE

The idea that real estate or land is at the heart of a society's economy is nothing new. Land has been the foundation of wealth and power since the beginning of humankind. Since our woes began with real estate and then transitioned into the broader economy, should our solution also begin with real estate and will it likewise then transition into the broader economy? Ensuring that Americans can afford their homes will improve consumer spending. Reestablishing home values and affordable home loans will resolve real estate supply and demand issues, restoring health in construction and the various real estate related industries. Restoring investor confidence in the value of mortgages underlying securities will help return liquidity to CDOs and could potentially reverse at least some of the domino effects we've discussed that were caused when that market froze.

Emergency Economic Stabilization Act of 2008

- Treasury purchase up to $700 billion in mortgage-backed securities and other troubled assets from US financial institutions to help restore liquidity
- $250 billion immediately
- $100 billion available upon report to Congress by the president
- $350 billion if the president provides Congress with a written report detailing secretary's plan and Congress doesn't jointly disapprove
- Insurance program to guarantee troubled assets and encourage private sector to participate in purchase of troubled assets and invest in financial institutions.
- Increased FDIC insurance to $250,000 until December 31, 2009
- SEC ability to soften market to market accounting rules
- Several revenue ringers
- Establishes a five-member oversight panel (Financial Stability Oversight Board) for comprehensive reform of US financial system—study due January 20, 2009
- Troubled Asset Relief Program (TARP) creates new Treasury Offices of Financial Stability under a Treasury Assistant Secretary
- Participating lenders issue warrants on senior debt designated to cover losses and administrative costs and allow taxpayers to share in equity appreciation
- Asset price set by reverse auction—can hold asset until maturity or resell; secretary established vehicles to purchase, manage, price, sell—criteria to identify assets for purchase, guidelines prohibiting conflicts of interest
- Procedures to value; select asset margins
- Requires treasury to modify troubled loans it controls and direct other federal agencies to modify loans they own or control to minimize foreclosures
- Relief for banks that hold Fannie Mae and Freddie Mac stock
- Revised to include foreign bank relief.[16]

But, as we have learned, in addition to being an event in its own right, the real estate crisis exposed a plethora of other flaws within the mortgage industry, banking, government, Wall Street, and in our nation's underlying values, including questions as big as America's role in the global economy, most of which will require more than a real estate market recovery to fix.

WHAT IS THE $700 BILLION BAILOUT?

For now, all eyes are on the $700 billion and subsequent bailouts, and further money bound to be pledged, formally know as the Emergency Economic Stabilization Act of 2008. The original aspects of this act, which have already evolved, are summarized in the sidebar on page 258.

Investment versus Expense

It was initially anticipated that because participating institutions would have to issue warrants or preferred stock in exchange for bailout funds, the plan would be more along the lines of a series of investments than a straight bailout. Furthermore, Americans would also theoretically benefit as employees and consumers of many of the companies whose hands would no longer be tied as tightly as a result of the crisis. If taxpayers were completely insulated from bailout losses, the bailout itself most agreed would probably not succeed since, by definition, a bailout socializes losses. To this Treasury Secretary Paulson said, "The ultimate taxpayer protection (gained from the bailout) will be the market stability provided."[17]

Ironically, at the end of the day the return on the bailout investment as originally proposed would have depended upon whether or not Americans pay their mortgages. If we did pay our mortgages, then the toxic mortgage-backed securities purchased as part of the bailout would prove to have been a decent investment. However, also figured into the equation was how much the government would pay for these assets. For example, a mortgage-backed security that may be worth $2.00 if it is held until it matures might only fetch $1.00 if it were sold in today's market. The valuation detail of the original $700 billion bailout plan would presumably be ironed out when the investigative commission reported its suggestions to Congress, originally slated for January 2008. A leading proposal was to be the utilization of reverse auctions at which the Fed and others could bid on the assets, starting at the highest price and bidding down. The theory was that a huge buyer like the Fed would wind up paying more than today's value but still get a price that reflected the chance of defaults. If in practice this theory operated to establish fair market valuations for the toxic assets, it could have broken the cycle of panic and pessimism that had been keeping asset buyers on the sidelines. Or it could have had the reverse effect and scared off some private investors.

In addition to its potential for deciding whether or not taxpayers are able to recoup the investments, asset valuation would have also been crucial to the success of the plan for the banks selling the assets since, if the sale prices were too low, banks would not receive the capital needed and the plan might ultimately not succeed. One important detail was to have been asset purchase oversight since, as we've seen in the auction-rate securities market discussed earlier, it is not unheard of for sellers and other interested parties to rig auctions. Also important was the anticipated timing and terms for the resale of these assets.

Is $700 Billion Enough?

The $700 billion price tag may have seemed more appropriate to those who were aware of the $53 trillion we were already on the hook for. At the time American taxpayers were already on the hook for $34 trillion for Medicare obligations, $7 trillion for Social Security liabilities, and $12 trillion for the balance of our national debt. The bailout amount exceeded the $500 billion the FDIC estimated was at risk vis-à-vis delinquent residential mortgages as of June 2008 out of the total $10.6 trillion residential mortgage market. Under the bailout plan the treasury had the authority to buy anything related to mortgage-backed securities, including credit derivatives and equity in companies weakened by their bad loans. Before the bailout was proposed, our nation's 2009 federal budget deficit was projected by the Congressional Budget Office to be more than $400 billion (3% of GDP). With the $700 billion bailout and other crisis expenditures, our 2009 deficit was projected to reach 10 percent of the GDP. Given the average costs of previous bailouts in other countries discussed earlier, it will come as no surprise if actual costs exceed these numbers.[18]

As you can guess, there was no shortage of criticism of the bailout plan or so much of it as had been spent. Most obvious was the fact that the bailout and TARP for the most part addressed the initial symptom of the crisis—mortgage defaults and mortgage-backed securities—but the crisis had since spread into many other areas, including car loans, credit cards, and student loans. Another criticism was that the bailout might delay crisis resolution by interfering with natural home price adjustments, encouraging more home owners to default in the hope that the government would bail them out, too, and dissuading potential buyers from stepping into the market until the glut of government-owned homes was absorbed. Other experts believed that only

Some Alternatives Suggested at the Time the $700 Billion Bailout Was Approved

- Former Freddie Mac senior economist Arnold Kling suggested replacing loans for certain low down payment home buyers with home renting programs. Kling referred to buyers who put too little money down on their home purchases as nominal owners or "Home borrowers."
- Investor Warren Buffett said government should pay the current distressed market price for toxic assets rather than an artificially high hold-to-maturity price (market price would be determined by selling a portion of the assets to private investors).
- Economist Paul Krugman recommended equity investments in banks, like government did for the recent GSE bailout, since this approach avoids valuation questions involved in purchasing toxic assets.[19]

market-based solutions would resolve the crisis, alleging that a non-market-based solution such as the bailout only created artificial pricing floors. Some of the alternatives to the bailout suggested by experts at the time are summarized for you in the sidebar above.

TIME WILL TELL

It will take time for the actual impact of the initial $700 billion and subsequent bailout funds on our nation to become apparent. And as we now know, the bailout that we thought was approved has proven to be much different in terms of the manner in which the money has ultimately been disbursed. And as of January 2009 we've learned that the number we'll likely be on the hook for after implementation of only initial Obama stimulus proposals is closer to $1.9 trillion. The Congressional Budget Office projections reflect a 2009 deficit of $1.2 trillion, three times 2008's budget deficit. Effectively implementing this and the further funding we can expect to see will require trained staff and an organizational structure. The market was down the week after the first bailout passed. The Dow Jones Index declined 22 percent, the worst week in the index's 118-year history.[20] Lender-borrower mortgage loan completions as well as real estate investor's acquisitions virtually froze. Now that Uncle Sam has taken a seat at the metaphorical real estate poker table, the rest of the players want to see how he is going to play his hand before they play their own. After all, he is holding cards that will turn some of them into lucky winners.

JUST THE TIP OF THE REFORM ICEBERG

We've said that the lion's share of initial government intervention was aimed at reducing the real estate and financial markets' downward spiral. The government's theory, at the epicenter of both of these strategies, was the need to restore market confidence and liquidity. The initial bailout proposed attempted to address both strategies. But the relief and reform "to do" list does not stop there.

Regulating Wall Street's Instruments

For example, we still have not heard how credit default swaps and other derivatives will be better regulated. Even former Treasury Secretary Alan Greenspan, who at one time said that derivatives "enhance the ability to differentiate risk and allocate it to those investors most able and willing to take it" has since warned "in reality it spread a virus through the economy because these products are so opaque and hard to value. . . . I don't believe anybody understood the significance of this."[21] Investment icon Warren Buffett has referred to derivatives as "weapons of mass destruction."[22] One criticism is that the industry has no central clearing system. The Federal Reserve began cracking down on credit default swap traders for their alleged sloppiness in 2005. In July of 2008 the feds again demanded cleaner practices from some of the larger traders. The backlog of trade confirmations has already reportedly been reduced by 50 percent. But still only 50 percent of the over-the-counter interest trades are reportedly automated. The technology is available but appears to not be implemented.[23]

Executive Compensation and Ratings

More may remain to be done in the realm of executive compensation. Some say tying it more closely to longer-term, consumer-focused outcomes will result in less risk taking. Also needed are transparency, particularly in regard to what is now off-balance-sheet, limits on permitted leverage, limits on the size certain firms and divisions are allowed to become, review and approval processes for new exotic financial instruments, and enhanced consumer protections and disclosures on ratings agencies. At a minimum, these firms need to examine what appears to be a tendency toward underestimating the risk of default, overestimating liquidity, and relying on inappropriate historical data when rating mortgage-backed securities. Rules need to force ratings agencies to distance themselves from the firms and institutions they rate. At a minimum, we should prevent executive compensation from being tied to the rating of the company's securities. And the rest of us need to remember that ratings agencies are not always accurate.

Consumer Protection

We can expect consumer protection to be a top priority for Congress in the form of anti-predatory-lending legislation and uniform national mortgage licensing standards. Paulson has voiced concern over home owners being harmed by the complexity of our mortgage system. He and others have called for nationwide rules for mortgage lenders, changes in credit rating agency practices, and tougher scrutiny by federal banking regulators. The Federal Reserve likewise urged lenders to toughen subprime loan standards. Guidelines already in effect cover several areas related to interest-only and adjustable rate mortgages, including underwriting standards, risk layering, third-party originators, consumer disclosures, and portfolio risk management as well as management reporting and monitoring. More than twenty states have published similar guidelines. Paulson and Bernanke have both expressed frustration with complex mortgage securities that are inscrutable to many investors and probably to some Wall Street insiders. Until investors are confident in mortgage loan valuations and the securities they back, the lack of liquidity (money available for loans) will persist

WILL GOVERNMENT-SPONSORED ENTERPRISES PLAY A ROLE IN RELIEF?

If they can be fixed Fannie Mae, Freddie Mac, and the FHA may provide an excellent user interface between government plans and getting that relief to

Americans. Even before the bubble burst, Federal Reserve Chairman Bernanke and others had urged Congress to bolster the regulation of Fannie Mae and Freddie Mac, suggesting that their massive holdings be limited to guard against the danger that their debt posed to the overall economy. Both entities were effectively put into receivership in the fall of 2008, but some of the ideas produced by and around them before that are worth considering as we search for solutions. Shortly after the subprime crisis began, Freddie Mac announced it would be buying subprime adjustable rate mortgages only if the borrower qualified based on the maximum rate that the interest could reset to, not just the teaser rate. The goal of course was to ensure that the same mistake would not be made moving forward and future borrowers would be able to afford their homes even after interest rate resets. Recommendations were being made by banks issuing Fannie Mae and Freddie Mac loans regarding money from borrowers held in escrow to pay taxes and insurance. Freddie Mac unveiled a $20 billion proposal to help make sure lenders could offer fair and affordable financing to home owners seeking to refinance problem loans and the cap on loans Fannie Mae and Freddie Mac could buy was raised in order to encourage lenders to make more large home mortgage loans in housing markets in which the prices exceeded the maximum amounts that both Freddie Mac and Fannie Mae would consider eligible for loans. High default rates on loans to borrowers who received down payment assistance prompted initiation of a rule-making process for assistance programs run by nonprofit housing groups.

The Untouchables?

We've talked about the origins of Fannie Mae and Freddie Mac. They, like many of our government housing programs, are eventual byproducts of the New Deal, which created their predecessor, the Federal Home Loan Mortgage Association when private lending dried up in the 1930s. Though publically traded for years, Fannie Mae and Freddie Mac had been exempt from SEC registration and filing requirements. Over the years, with government backing, the companies' financial positions have been complicated by a series of the same derivatives, insurance contracts and guarantees that plague many of our country's financial entities now. The primary difference is that Fannie Mae and Freddie Mac are enabled by special treatment from our government and backed by our taxpayer dollars.

Wall Street loved the profits, selling Fannie Mae and Freddie Mac mortgaged-backed securities as being as safe as treasury notes but with much higher yields. Capital Hill was all for the idea of supporting affordable housing. Some say it is this combination of liberal ideology and private profit that made Fannie Mae and Freddie Mac untouchable. Most private companies would not have survived the storm Fannie Mae and Freddie Mac have recently weathered. But government has put taxpayers in a difficult situation by allowing Fannie Mae and Freddie Mac to become too big to let fail at the risk of our social security and Medicare money.

Attempts to Reform

In 2002 both companies agreed to register with the SEC and in 2004 Fannie Mae actually did. Freddie Mac ran into some accounting and business challenges that prevented it from registering at that time. In 2005, Senator John McCain encouraged passage of the Federal Housing Enterprise Regulatory Reform Act. The act, which never passed in the House or the Senate, was intended to have increased oversight of Fannie Mae and Freddie Mac. Instead, concerns over the companies caused Paulson to request temporary authority from Congress allowing the government to buy shares of both companies and increasing the amount of money it could lend them. The Housing and Economic Recovery Act of 2008 was passed by Congress on July 24, 2008, and signed into law by the President Bush six days later. The act enabled expanded regulatory authority of Fannie Mae and Freddie Mac by the newly established Federal Housing Finance Authority (FHFA) and gave the US Treasury authority to advance funds to stabilize both companies, effectively raising the treasury debt ceiling by $800 billion to a total of $10.7 trillion. The legislation was landmark in that it also allowed government to take equity (ownership) positions in Fannie Mae and Freddie Mac. The stated intent was that this new government authority would be at no expense to the taxpayers and, in fact, was not likely to be exercised. One interesting side note, following the passage of the Housing and Economic Recovery Act of 2008, the fact that twenty eight members of Congress owned shares in Fannie Mae or Freddie Mac and would be impacted by the legislation, and the fact that both Fannie Mae and Freddie Mac had contributed to members of both the House and the Senate, caused some to question the motives of some in Congress.

Around the same time, Fannie Mae and Freddie Mac made internal changes to help keep Americans in their homes and help the companies preserve cash by delaying some of the subprime fallout. They increased the time allowed and fees paid to mortgage loan servicers for arranging a workout with the home owner to avoid foreclosure. The fee for arranging a mortgage modification was increased from $400 to $800 and the fee for arranging a short sale rose from $1,100 to $2,200. The time period went up to as many as 300 days. In addition, Fannie Mae has been offering a $15,000 unsecured loan to borrowers who are behind in their mortgage payments as the result of a temporary setback. It remains to be seen whether these moves merely delay the inevitable for the companies and borrowers alike. The companies also announced a refocusing of business moving forward on less purchasing of mortgaged-backed securities and more focus on more secure, larger loans to borrowers with better credit, highlighting the need to better balance their stated purposes of providing liquidity in the mortgage markets and access to affordable housing with the need to generate a profit. However, at first blush, this appears to be inconsistent with part of the mission of Fannie Mae and Freddie Mac, which again is to enhance affordable housing.

Fannie Mae and Freddie Mac Take a "Time Out"

But less than two months later, the government expressed further concern over perceived illiquidity of Fannie Mae and Freddie Mac, fearing the companies lacked sufficient funds in reserve to handle growing mortgage delinquency rates. Both continued taking hits to the value of their assets and to suffer from apparent distrust of accounting and management decisions. Fear of their future failure could induce an actual lack of money and failure now if investors shied away from buying their debt. Only a few short weeks after Congress passed the legislation most thought would not be exercised, Treasury Secretary Henry Paulson used the power to effectively place Fannie Mae and Freddie Mac into a government conservatorship, a "time out" that permitted him to extend up to $200 billion to the companies. The stated goal was to protect the mortgage market until the government could decide what to do with Fannie Mae and Freddie Mac long term. Pundits told us we shouldn't be surprised—in government blank checks almost always get filled in and cashed.

GSE Leverage and Losses

Although some were surprised to see the new authority exercised so quickly after being told it would probably not be used, most agreed with the need to have better control over and a clearer idea of what Fannie Mae and Freddie Mac portfolios should look like. Fannie Mae had been leveraged 20:1 and Freddie Mac a whopping 70:1 or more if calculations include the mortgage-backed assets they guarantee. Together, whether viewed as on or off their respective balance sheets, obligations for the two companies totaled $5.2 trillion, about half of all outstanding US mortgage loans. FHFA director James B. Lockhart III blamed "inherent conflict and a flawed business model embedded in the GSE structure and the ongoing housing correction" for the combined reported Fannie Mae–Freddie Mac losses thus far in excess of $15 billion and concern about their ability to raise new capital that led to the conservatorship. As of summer 2008, Fannie Mae stock was down 76 percent for the year, Freddie Mac 80 percent.[24]

What Is the Future of Fannie Mae and Freddie Mac?

The deal Fannie Mae and Freddie Mac got requires them to insure that their retained mortgage and mortgage-backed securities portfolio will be reduced to under $850 billion by the end of 2009 and further reduce the balance by ten percent each year until it reaches $250 billion, leaving the future of Fannie Mae and Freddie Mac in question.[25] One would hope the companies will be pushed to raise capital privately. The question in the long run is, should the companies be fully nationalized, privatized, or divided and specialized? Former Federal Reserved chair Alan Greenspan has called the companies fundamentally flawed institutions that privatize profits and socialize losses. As such, he believes they should be nationalized; divided into smaller, viable private entities; and auctioned off.[26] The common denominator seems to be that both companies need to somehow muddle through the next few years but that, ultimately, we need to avoid creating similar giants again in the future. Fannie Mae and Freddie Mac's net losses will depend on our nation's housing price declines and the companies' future losses on their mortgage assets. In the meantime, it was hoped that the government's actions would reassure lenders that Fannie Mae and Freddie Mac have funds to free lenders of their mortgages, encouraging lenders to loan more and increasing overall market liquidity.

Outcomes So Far

While no one is certain that Fannie Mae and Freddie Mac have actually been saved, there have been certain instantaneous outcomes. When the government steps in, rules change, turning would-be winners into losers and visa versa, overnight. It might be compared to betting on a high school basketball game only to have Shaquille O'Neal make a surprise appearance and join the other team after bets have been placed and the game starts. For example, for commercial banks that own Fannie Mae or Freddie Mac preferred shares, dividends were suspended and their investment subordinated to the senior preferred stock issued to the Treasury as part of the deal. The market value of their shares plunged, leaving many with no choice but to write down the value of their investments. In the case of smaller banks that owned an interest in Fannie Mae or Freddie Mac, this type of result can be fatal. Likewise, for investors in credit default swap contracts, the government's placing Fannie Mae and Freddie Mac into a conservatorship triggered an event of default under those contracts, leaving investors holding the bag.[27] We are learning again by trial and error how many obvious and not so obvious, long-term and shorter-term, direct and less direct, impacts resulted when decisions were enacted to reign in our economy.

What Role Might the FHA Play?

Given that it was at the heart of one of the first attempts for relief, the Federal Housing Administration (FHA) Secure and other programs may also play a role in recovery. In chapter 3 we discussed how the agency's failure to keep up with market changes created a void that subprime mortgages happily filled. As we discussed before, the FHA allows down payment assistance from family, employers, other government entities and even charities. Proposed FHA refinance loan programs allowed families with strong credit histories who were making timely payments to qualify for refinances allowing distressed home owners to hold on longer while their homes rebuild the equity needed to sell. Both the House and the Senate proposed bills that would raise the permissible maximum dollar size of FHA loans, especially in higher-cost regions of the country. Also, proposed were reforms enabling FHA to create a risk-based premium structure for mortgage insurance so that borrowers do not all have to pay the same premium. Lower-risk borrowers and those who put more money down would pay less for mortgage insurance. A similar reform had passed in the House a year earlier but was stalled in the Senate because it allowed for 100 percent financing instead of the then current minimum 3 percent required down payment. In light of the mortgage meltdown, this failure to pass turned out to be a good thing. As we'll see shortly, the brightest signs of real estate recovery are in the price ranges and buyer types most often traditionally associated with FHA, meaning that there is potential for FHA to help lead the residential real estate market recovery.

Has Government Gotten Too Complicated to Be Effective?

We've discussed how effectively implementing the bailout will require infrastructure. Before starting from scratch it makes sense to inventory the infrastructure already in place, including Fannie Mae, Freddie Mac and the FHA. This leads us to consideration of the appropriateness of government infrastructure as it relates to our mortgage and broader investment and financial industries. One thing to be wary of is the fact that economic crises tend to result in the creation of more government, which tends to not go away when the crises subside.

No doubt one of the reasons relief, recovery, and reform has been slow and challenging is the fact that we have so many levels of government with so many agencies, groups, and individuals at each level. Achieving the most efficient and best outcomes requires coordination between each of these sectors, which is no easy task. Not long ago, five federal regulatory agencies—the Office of the Comptroller of the Currency (OCC), the board of governors of the Federal Reserve System, the Federal Deposit Insurance Corporation, the Office of Thrift Supervision, and the National Credit Union Administration—issued a single policy document called Interagency Guidance on Nontraditional Mortgage Product Risks, primarily concerned with the negative-amortization mortgages that allow borrowers to defer principal and/or interest. The guidance established safety measures for lenders designed to lessen the risks of nontraditional loans such as recommendations on underwriting standards, collectability of the portfolio, sufficient consumer information, and servicing. But this type of collaboration is the exception, not the rule. We've discussed the many government agencies relevant to our foreclosure nation and even included a list and description of each in appendix C. And we've discussed how many of these agencies have come into being and evolved by trial and error. Like a home built in 1776, after two hundred forty-two years of additions, renovations and remodeling, there exists the possibility that tearing the home down to its foundation and rebuilding it from scratch with new technologies might theoretically be more efficient and effective than yet another addition or renovation. For many reasons (including folks in Washington who naturally would prefer to keep their jobs and power), we all know this is not going to happen with our many government agencies making up the infrastructure. And even if it could, it might amount to throwing the baby out with the bathwater since some agencies are working just fine. The point is that again, infrastructure reform should begin with a comprehensive look at the entire "big" picture and a plan for what our modern day home would look like if built from the foundation up. With that ideal in mind, we can create more practical renovations and additions that get us as close as possible to a best-case scenario.

WHAT ARE THE STATES DOING TO HELP?

We've seen more and more states taking action to help distressed home owners, punish deceptive lending practices, and license and regulate originators, in part because the federal government did not appear to be doing it quickly or effectively enough. Some states lead the way with creative approaches to relieve distressed home owners. Illinois, New York, and Massachusetts, for example, each formed task forces to identify and explore ways to rework troubled home owner loans. In some states, housing finance agencies helped tap low-cost funds for distressed home owner relief by selling bonds. Maryland, Massachusetts, New Jersey, New York, Ohio, and Pennsylvania were among the first to introduce programs to refinance at-risk loans by using state bonds and federal lending agency money. Other states found ways to keep more money in home owners' pockets. New Jersey, New York, Indiana, and Montana, for example, proposed tax breaks aimed at helping distressed home owners. Many states and even local municipalities have devised methods for purchasing foreclosed property to use as low-income housing.[28]

States Focus on Fraud

In other states, the focus has been on mortgage fraud prevention and punishment. Massachusetts and Florida were among the first to initiate plans aimed at ending home rescue fraud schemes like equity stripping discussed earlier. Florida's mortgage fraud task force apprehended whole groups of people involved in fraud in various aspects of the real estate business, including mortgage loan originators, Realtors, title agents, and appraisers. In one such bust, participants were alleged to have taken bribes to help borrowers conceal from lenders the fact that the borrowers were defrauding lenders into awarding loans for more than the amounts actually needed to buy the property. In this scheme, one person would recruit home sellers willing to overstate the price of their property and people willing to pose as home buyers. Another person would prepare the mortgage loan application in the false buyer's name, including fraudulent employment verification, pay stubs, and IRS forms. A different person would prepare fraudulent appraisals. Together they collected the difference between the loan amount and the actual sales price for each home. Ohio's mortgage fraud task force broke up similar schemes.[29]

Collectively, hundreds of millions of dollars are being spent at the federal, state, and local levels to track down professionals who have committed mortgage fraud during the bubble. Efficiency in these stings may be improved by implementing a borrower-driven reporting mechanism. But critics argue that such a system would be rampant with deliberate or mistaken false accusations. Another idea worthy of consideration is a temporary amnesty period, during which time mortgage and real estate professionals who know they are at risk of being discovered and prosecuted for having committed fraud would be encouraged to surrender and be given amnesty or immunity from prosecution.

The FBI has increased the attention it is paying to mortgage fraud. Initial estimated losses due to mortgage fraud were in the billions. The number of agents assigned to mortgage-related cases increased by 50 percent between 2007 and 2008. Its mortgage fraud caseload has doubled. The FBI is working with the United States Treasury Department's Financial Crimes Enforcement Network (FinCEN), the agency that collects suspicious activity reports (SAR), reports submitted by lenders who suspect fraud. There are currently twenty-six cases of potential subprime-related fraud being investigated. Institutions under investigation are said to include Lehman Brothers, AIG, Fannie Mae, and Freddie Mac.[30] Because in the past there was no "safe harbor" for reporting mortgage fraud, there has been a lot of hesitancy on the part of industry insiders to do so. Mechanisms are being devised to correct this as well.[31]

One of the biggest challenges in prosecuting mortgage fraud is the fact that, until now, the act of mortgage fraud had not been specifically defined as a crime in most state laws. Instead, lawmakers prosecuted mortgage fraud offenders under mail fraud, wire transfer fraud, and other similar laws. Unfortunately, in many states mortgage fraud still didn't fit squarely into any of those boxes, so those states couldn't indict under their own statutes and accordingly had to rely on federal prosecutors. But new state laws specifically spelling out mortgage fraud as a crime and stiffening the penalties for mortgage fraud have been enacted across the country. For example, the Georgia Residential Mortgage Fraud Act was signed into law to assist local authorities in prosecuting these cases. Well over a hundred state bills have been introduced to stem deceptive mortgage lending practices and those related to foreclosure.[32]

States Address Mortgage Licensing Laws

According to the National Association of Mortgage Brokers (NAMB), the number of licensed mortgage professionals in some of the busiest states is estimated to have grown threefold during the bubble.[33] Perhaps the best strategy for correcting internal mortgage industry flaws is to make the business less attractive to the bad guys in the first place. North Carolina legislators have limited the mortgage broker's ability to charge above-par rates and prepayment penalties and have taken steps to protect subprime borrowers from risky adjustable rate mortgage loans. Minnesota implemented tighter restrictions on subprime lending. Pennsylvania's Department of Banking issued new guidelines to advise thousands of mortgage licensees in the state on what the state considers "dishonest, fraudulent, illegal, unfair, unethical, negligent, or incompetent" practices under the Pennsylvania Mortgage Bankers and Brokers Consumer Equity Protection Act. Massachusetts targeted subprime lenders with a new bill that requires loan officers making subprime loans to first obtain a special license and pay a $250 special licensing fee. The move is projected to raise millions of dollars for the state to use in hiring loan co-examiners and funding for distressed home owner foreclosure relief.[34]

States and Fed Need to Coordinate

Of equal significance was the variance from state to state and from our federal government to the state level, along with a lack of unification that made effective governing difficult, allegedly creating law avoidance opportunities within the mortgage industry. For example, although some states have tried to control the use of prepayment penalties, a 1996 decision by the US Office of Thrift Supervision exempted certain finance companies from state restrictions against prepayment penalties, resulting in an increase in loans that exacted a fee if borrowers paid their mortgage off early. The decision was later repealed. There were cases in which originators were prosecuted in one state only to move to another and commit the same crimes all over again. It was a common practice. The Conference of State Bank Supervisors and the American Association of Residential Mortgage Regulators are striving to create a standardized licensing system that regulates requirements and procedures in states. The State Foreclosure Prevention Working Group is a coalition of eleven state attorneys general and bank regulators. In April of 2008 the group reported that loan services could simply not keep up with the pace of foreclosures. As a result, 70 percent of distressed home owners were not getting helped. The group has recommended a broad sweeping systematic workout method since the case-by-case procedures do not work quickly enough.[35]

States Coordinating with Each Other

The National Conference of State Legislatures has loosely divided state legislative responses to the subprime crises into two categories; foreclosure-related laws and predator lending-related laws. The former generally encompasses emergency mortgage assistance funds, foreclosure consultants, and the foreclosure process. The latter encompasses loan flipping or repeatedly refinancing loans, excessive fees, lending based on a borrower's assets rather than his ability to repay the loan and on outright fraud and abuse. Most states are also revisiting their mortgage and appraiser licensing laws and penalties, bearing in mind the more uniform Secure and Fair Enforcement (S.A.F.E.) Mortgage Licensing Act of 2008 at the federal level.[36] Specific state laws and legislation can be found at the NCSL Web site, www.ncst.org.

RELIEF AND REFORM AT THE COUNTY LEVEL

More localized cities and counties have organized their own efforts. One example is the task force appointed by county commissioners in Broward County, Florida. In June 2008, the seventeen-member task force made twenty-three recommendations for local foreclosure prevention and assistance including establishing a specialized foreclosure court, quicker and improved foreclosure education, volunteer foreclosure cleanup crews, mandatory pre-foreclosure mediation, and donating foreclosed properties to cities and non-profit agencies for affordable housing.[37]

WHAT IS THE MORTGAGE INDUSTRY DOING TO IMPROVE SELF-REGULATION?

When the subprime crisis began to unfold, among the first calls for reform came from within the mortgage industry itself. As early as the first quarter of 2007, the Mortgage Bankers Association entered a Memo of Understanding with the FBI addressing mortgage fraud. MBA members were warned to expect consumer protection to be a top priority for Congress in the form of anti-predatory-lending legislation and a uniform national standard. Among the problems cited was the fact that lenders have lacked a safe way to share information. As a result, we can expect increased utilization and popularity of cooperative databases like that of the Mortgage Asset Research Institute (MARI) and the Mortgage Industry Data Exchange, which allow lenders, insurers, and agencies to exchange information about individuals and companies that have originated loans known to be fraudulent. Former MBA chair Regina Lowrie was active in creating the "Council to Shape Change." Participants represented a broad spectrum of residential and commercial, small and large, prime and nonprime real estate finance companies. Among other things, the council identified trends it believed have and will continue to impact the mortgage industry. Identifying such trends may be helpful to lawmakers in anticipating necessary and appropriate regulatory changes.[38] Included in the sidebar on page 275 are some of the trends observed by the council.

The MBA has promoted the use of voluntary fraud disclosures by its members and initially asked the House and Senate appropriations committees for more than $30 million over the next five years to be used by an FBI and

Council to Shape Change Observations

- Changing borrower demographics. Emerging markets include more first-time home buyers as well as home buyers who do not speak English as their first language. Accommodating this market with appropriate educational prerequisites to home ownership, especially those using government-purchased or insured home mortgage loans, may be appropriate.
- Consolidation of mortgage business ownership by larger financial institutions. Anticipating the impact this may have on borrowers and on investors, as well on avoiding future institutions that become to big to fail may be appropriate.
- Increasing integration of mortgages with other financial products and business lines for the purpose of increasing product sales to an existing customer base and achieving a greater share of the consumer wallet. This trend may necessitate further consumer protection including disclosure and competitive pricing and alternatives.
- Increasing regulatory demand. Known side effects of increased regulatory requirements are increased cost of doing business and, sometimes, unanticipated chilling effects on those doing business. As we've said, new regulations can result in unanticipated side effects.
- Technology as, at once, an enabler and inhibitor. As in other applications of technology, efficiency may be improved, but human elements, such as common sense and the various benefits of personal relations, are lost.
- Disintegration of the real estate finance process itself into smaller components that can be optimized, automated, outsourced, and offshored. The pros and cons of this trend were discussed in chapter 2.

Department of Justice interagency task force. The MBA is seeking over $6 million in dedicated funding for new FBI field investigators, new dedicated prosecutors at the Justice Department to coordinate prosecutions with the US attorneys' offices, and $750,000 to support the operations of FBI interagency task force in areas with the highest concentrations of mortgage fraud. In a "State of the Real Estate Industry" press briefing that took place as the subprime mortgage crisis was first unfolding, MBA chairman John M. Robbins reaffirmed a genuine need and business benefit for customers to be better educated about the mortgage lending process, acknowledging that financial education should be a "shared responsibility" between borrower and lender.[39] But critics say much of the MBA's interest in combating fraud stems from its own agenda to control any reforms to which the industry may be subject.

Appraiser groups are likewise seeking solutions. Title XI of the Financial Institutions Reform Recovery and Enforcement Act of 1989 (FIRREA), was designed, in part, to prevent appraisal-associated mortgage fraud by unethical or unqualified professionals. But industry experts feel it has proven ineffective due to lack of enforcement and lack of resources. The legislature has taken stabs at resolving the deficiencies, including the 2005 Responsible Lending Act (intended, among other things, to protect consumers against unfair and deceptive practices in connection with higher-cost mortgage transactions; strengthen remedies available; provide more uniform lending standards; improve housing counseling, mortgage servicing, appraisal standards, and oversight; and establish licensing and minimum standards for mortgage brokers) and the 2006 Stop Fraud Act (intended primarily to stop fraud). Appraiser regulatory reform includes tougher prohibitions against and clearer penalties for appraiser coercion, bribery, and collusion. Educating borrowers to be on the lookout for appraiser wrongdoing is also cited as key. Numerous states enacted legislation and revised mandatory appraiser licensing, noting that nondesignated appraisers are sanctioned six times as often as appraisers who elect to register as "designated" under applicable guidelines.[40]

BUSINESS INCENTIVES TO CLEAN UP

As we've said, in a cooling housing market, with fewer purchases and fewer requests to refinance, lenders who survive the downturn will eventually experience greater stability and, presumably, an enhanced ability to better focus on and improve customer needs as well as streamlining their own operations. Increased legal exposure, more loan servicing and default costs, and secondary market and REO resale risks are pressuring lenders to realize the benefits of growing a stable customer pool and cleaning up their operations to make sure they keep customers and gain referrals. Quality control is receiving increased attention as a profit center as opposed to merely something lenders were forced to do by regulators or investors simply because originating bad loans is not profitable. As in other businesses, the cost to acquire new customers is significantly higher than the cost of retaining current ones. From a practical standpoint, only by qualifying the expected value of long-term customer cross-sell relations (i.e., identifying how much additional money lenders can make and losses they can avoid by providing better service to keep existing customers happy and sell them other products) will lenders be able to justify the additional money they will have to invest to improve customer service and retention. We can expect lifetime customer value and loyalty measurements to become increasingly important as the value of educating, better servicing, and cross-selling synergies.

Customer Retention

Understanding a customer's product and service needs is critical to acquiring, retaining, and cross-selling profitable relationships. In a survey of refinancing borrowers, when asked why they did not contact their current lender, the majority indicated they did not think they could modify their loan or refinance with their current lender. Thirty-seven percent of those borrowers who switch lenders indicate they would have preferred to stay if they had known that was an option. The service-related attributes important to the borrowers surveyed when they speak with their bank representative are reflected in the sidebar.

The subprime crisis has made abundantly clear that it is imperative that what is in most businesses considered the sales aspects (i.e., relationship building and education) of the mortgage industry needs to continue beyond the loan originator and closing and not just in a thinly veiled effort to sell the borrower more products. Mortgage servicers must also know their customers. Even at the loss mitigation level, a deeper relationship with the borrower will benefit both sides since professionals need to know who they are dealing with in order to identify the most effective and efficient method for even things as basic as borrower contact. Most banks are still using traditional methods like voicemail, associate interaction contact and snail mail. But the

Top Service-Related Mortgage Lender or Servicer Attributes Sited as Being Important to Borrowers

- Explaining things clearly
- Providing information needed about the borrower's current mortgage
- Treating the borrower with courtesy
- Providing consistently high service quality
- Resolving complaints (as is the case when a borrower believes a late fee has been wrongly charged to his account) quickly
- Reacting to requests quickly and knowing products and services thoroughly[41]

new generation borrower often prefers face-to-face communication. Others, especially those of the younger generations, prefer electronic communications like e-mail or text-messaging. The poor customer communication experienced by borrowers like Trina and Michelle recounted for us earlier, including forty-minute telephone on-hold times, can be dramatically reduced by simply taking advantage of modern-day technology with borrowers who prefer to communicate that way. We can expect progressive banks to emphasize viewing the financing process, from application through nonpayment or payoff, as an entire process, devising ways to work with borrowers in a similar manner during nonpayment as they do during the loan application. Despite the distrust and legal constraints we've discussed throughout this book, innovative lenders are already developing their own foreclosure preventive loan products to offer current borrowers who clearly cannot afford to make their current payments.

Contrary to other industries, where smaller firms tend to score better in terms of consumer satisfaction, the larger players in the mortgage business often deliver better service. According to the survey company J. D. Power and Associates, the three primary factors that drive overall customer satisfaction with mortgage lenders are the application/approval process, the loan officer/representative or mortgage broker, and the closing process.[42] With an overall index score of 782 on a 1,000-point scale, SunTrust Mortgage performed particularly well in the three factor areas. Bank of America followed, with a score of 781. Twenty-eight percent of those responding to the survey reported experiencing some type of problem during the mortgage origination process, such as miscommunication of loan terms and unresponsive or unavailable mortgage brokers. One of the biggest sources of dissatisfaction is not keeping commitments. In particular, surprises at the closing table such as getting an interest rate of 7 percent, when the originator promised a rate of 6.5 percent at the time of application, have been a big customer service issue. Some of the reasons a borrower may get a different interest rate than first promised were discussed in chapter 2 but we may be seeing banks implementing better ways to avoid interest rate and other important loan term changes during last few days before closing.

Customers of the five highest-ranking lenders made 20 percent more recommendations to friends and were significantly more likely to turn to their existing provider for new purchase mortgages, refinances, and home equity loans. Turnaround time for loan approval and not being asked for the same information twice were other indicators demonstrating satisfaction and are indicative of industry issues.[43] Other top improvements borrowers feel lenders need to make are reflected in the sidebar below.

What Is Regulation AB?

As we discussed in chapter 2, during the bubble many changes were made in the way the mortgage industry works in order to improve ratings awarded to

Borrower Perception of Improvements Their Lenders Need to Make

- 77 percent of borrowers feel their lender should do a better job to guarantee rates and fees. Despite the federal disclosure requirements we discussed in chapter 2, borrowers are still finding that their closing costs are higher than what they were told they would be by the originator. This is most likely because originators have an incentive to underestimate what the cost of the loan will be in order to secure the borrower as a customer and prevent him from shopping for a better price. In particular, the fees of third party service providers (such as survey, home owner's insurance, and title insurance) are often underestimated since if the borrower is upset the originator can easily blame the third party vendor for charging higher than expected fees and if need be pressure the vendor (who often depends upon business referrals from the originator) to lower his charges at the last minute (after the vendor has already performed the work) without impacting the originators own profit.
- 75 percent of borrowers feel their lender should do a better job to communicate benefits and risks of loan products. As we've discussed, many distressed borrowers now claim they did not understand their loan. Originators have personal incentives to sell loans that generate the most profit for them, which may impact how well they explain the various alternatives to borrowers.
- 64 percent of borrowers feel that their lender should do a better job to provide incentives for existing customers. Surveys show that many borrowers are not even aware of the fact that they may be able to refinance their mortgage loan with their current lender.
- 63 percent of borrowers feel their lender should do a better job to keep the customer apprised of the loan status. Anyone who has ever bought a home understands the importance of this.
- 53 percent of borrowers feel that their lender should do a better job to provide more education. This appears to be the common denominator in all areas cited for reform.[44]

mortgage-backed securities by the ratings agencies. These moves to please investors, such as outsourcing mortgage loan servicing departments, implementing quicker mortgage loan default response and foreclosure timelines, and imposing penalties against mortgage loan servicers who do not meet them, often turned out to be the opposite of what would help borrowers. For those on the backend of the mortgage business, servicing loans, attempting to mitigate default losses, prosecuting foreclosures, and marketing REOs, the need for reform is abundantly clear. Staff and systems are above maximum capacity since no one was prepared for the crisis. Many in this sector of the business are anxious for an interest rate reset freeze simply so they will have time to get caught up with their workloads. In fact, just as the bubble was bursting, the Securities and Exchange Commission beefed up its Regulation AB designed to protect securities investors, by clarifying and formalizing investor disclosure requirements, broadening the definition of "servicer," and creating minimum servicing criteria intended to be applied to a broad range of asset-backed securities (ABS) including mortgage-backed securities. The new regulation took effect January 1, 2006, and servicers had until March 2007 to produce compliance assertions and accounting firm attestations. Servicers who failed to do so risked having their servicer rating downgraded. A reduced rating for the servicer impacts the rating of the securities based upon the mortgage loans of that servicer, and we've discussed how crucial a top rating is to getting top dollar for mortgage-backed securities.

Regulation AB separates minimum servicing criteria into four categories: general serving considerations, cash collection and administration, investor remittances and reporting, and pool asset administration. The new reporting requirements significantly expand on the earlier Uniform Single Attestation Program for Mortgage Bankers (USAP) certification, accepted until now as the industry standard. Many complained that achieving Regulation AB compliance in a timely manner was a challenge.[45] With servicing being such a price-sensitive business, no one was happy with the expense that Regulation AB compliance added. One can only imagine how staying above water was achieved given the sheer caseload. Successful servicers will need to maximize value and manage cost, and capacity while complying with the regulation. They will need to manage defaults and repurchases, understand customer value, and retain customers. RBC vice president Charles Dowd shares his insights on some of the reforms needed in the sidebar. Certainly a return to pre-bubble mortgage loan qualifying standards is a good first step.

A Banker's Insights on Needed Reform

RBC Bank vice president Charles Dowd cites several areas for banking reform. From a banking perspective there were a few things during the bubble that clearly did not make sense. "First and foremost is the fact that loan originators had no incentive to secure the best loan terms for their customers. Instead, originators were paid more if they could sell customers larger loans at higher interest rates. Many even scheduled closings to maximize their compensation based on their companies' monthly bonus structure. Another problem area was banking regulations and guidelines. In many instances, mortgage loan originators and their customers are given twenty or more pages of complicated rules they're supposed to follow. Common sense tells us these are often not read, even more often not understood. On top of this, the guidelines change all the time. There have been times originators tell a customer something only to find the guidelines just changed and what they told the customer was wrong. Compliance definitely needs to be less complicated. Probably the biggest single contributor to the subprime crisis though, was the fact that everything just grew too big too fast. In a normal market; lenders, investors, and borrowers are all confident [that] the principal sum on [the] mortgage loans being made can be repaid. But this past market grew too quickly to be properly managed. Everyone was focusing on the initial teaser interest rates and monthly payments, overlooking the borrower's ability to actually repay the loan. The rating agencies could not possibly properly and accurately rate the loans securities were being built on. If we had based decisions on the worst-case scenarios, instead of the best cases, none of this would have happened. We really need to change the way loan officers are compensated by limiting front-end and back-end commissions, simplifying and unifying regulations, underwriting loans based on the worst case instead of underwriting to please investors, and providing borrowers with a clear worst-case amortization schedule up front."

ARE WE MAKING NEW MISTAKES WHILE CLEANING UP THE OLD ONES?

Finally, while everyone is focusing on relieving distressed home owners and crafting reforms to fix the problems, attention should be paid to not repeat the same types of mistakes. With subprime pools performing at an all-time low and the mortgage-backed securities market in turmoil, many lenders are not willing or able to continue originating the types of loans that until recently had filled their pipelines. The pressure is on originators to keep writing a high number of loans but in a slower market. The only avenue available to them is attracting more borrowers with other types of mortgage loan products. Because of this pressure on originators to produce, there seems to be a reinvention of old loan products, including the Home Equity Conversion Mortgage (HECM) commonly known as the reverse mortgage. A reverse mortgage is a loan available to borrowers sixty-two and older. It is intended to allow borrowers access to convert their home equity into cash either as a lump sum or in monthly payments borrowers receive from their lender. The borrower is not obligated to repay the loan until he dies, the home is sold, or the borrower moves out of the home.

Because it is a more complicated loan than others and the borrower by definition must be elderly (and thus may require more careful explanations), and originator's compensation for this product is higher than other loan types, care should be taken to ensure that borrowers understand the consequences of a reverse mortgage loan. For example, the maximum allowed principal amount advanced with a reverse mortgage increases with the age of the borrower. If the borrower is a married couple, the amount allowed will be the larger dollar amount based on the older of the two. However, if the older spouse dies, the younger spouse will be required to pay the loan amount down to the lower allowable amount that corresponds with her age. If she does not have funds available to do this, it may be necessary to refinance with a conventional loan or sell the home. And if both elderly borrowers die or leave the home, for example to move into an assisted living facility, their heirs will have to refinance and pay off the reverse mortgage or sell the home. What's more, the closing fees for reverse mortgages are relatively high, since all fees projected to accrue over the life of the loan are paid up front. However, if one of the foregoing scenarios plays out and the loan is repaid earlier than projected, none of the fees are refunded. Because most lenders play up the fact that reverse mortgages are government insured, the fear is that some elderly borrowers may misunderstand that to mean that the government is somehow protecting *them*, when in truth the government is protecting the lender. Perhaps most significant is the fact that the eligibility age of sixty-two was established when life expectancy was much lower. If the intent of a reverse mortgage is still to assist home owners in their retirement years we may want to increase the eligibility age to be more consistent with the age at which folks actually retire now. Allowing borrowers to cash out sooner may leave them no money when they actually do retire and need it.

A bipartisan bill to temporarily increase the allowable loan amounts of the reverse mortgage overwhelmingly passed in the House of Representatives. The FHA's HECM program accounts for 90 percent of all reverse mortgages.[46] While increasing the caps will make more cash available to widows and widowers, it will also place additional burden on those who must eventually pay back these funds. And again we are faced with the question: How prudent is it to project future valuations on the current real estate price that is still expected to decline?

ELIMINATING WALL STREET AND RATING AGENCY CONFLICTS OF INTEREST

For free-market capitalism to work, we need to know we can trust in the understood standards of care that require those who are handling our money to behave honestly. There can be no conflict of interest, and there must be full disclosure, much like the concepts that were codified on state and federal levels after the stock market crash of 1929. But during the 1980s, we started seeing a breakdown. Investment firms began effectively placing their own values on the investments they sold, the same hocus-pocus we've recently seen in valuing mortgage-backed securities. Well-established underwriter names turned out to be worthless. We discussed in chapter 5 how, unbeknownst to the rest of us, Wall Street players hedged their bets, some say breaching their fiduciary obligations, and getting away with it. We can anticipate these practices and others like them, to be scrutinized. But if the insinuations that Wall Street and Washington have an unspoken pact to take care of each other are true (or even if they are not, simply because of human nature and greed) this will not be the last time we uncover questionable practices on Wall Street. The concept of vertical integration within Wall Street operations, including all facets of mortgage loan origination and servicing, along with securitization are also being reexamined for potential conflicts and consumer disclosure needs. And billions in bonuses being paid to Wall Street executives despite the financial crises the rest of us are enduring are making headlines difficult for Washington to ignore.

We discussed in chapter 5 the fact that the rating agencies also have possible conflicts of interest, since they are often paid to rate the creditworthiness of firms and governments and are eager for clients. Posting disclaimers advising investors that: "You should not make an investment based on our ratings," will likely no longer cut it. This tattered standard of duty on Wall Street is playing a big part in current investor hesitancy. Critics have argued that the rating agencies need to provide more detail about the exposures they struggle to value such as the risk that subprime borrowers would default on their mortgage loans. Investors deserve to at least know which firms are using more or less conservative valuation assumptions. Certainly if investors had known and understood, for example, that borrower payment history for traditional mortgage loans were being used to predict subprime borrower default rates, many investors would have better understood the risk they were taking by investing in securities backed by the payment of these riskier mortgage loans. Market consensus on valuation might help a measure of price stability return and improve liquidity. One suggestion is "stress tests" to value mortgage loans under a number of future market assumptions. For example, models using the highest possible interest rate adjustment may have yielded predictions closer to what actually happened (and rating agencies may have therefore given these securities a lower rating so that investors would be aware of the risk) than models making mortgage loan payment and default predictions based on low teaser rates.

WHAT ROLE ARE CONSUMER ADVOCACY GROUPS PLAYING?

In the shadows of the subprime crisis, consumer advocacy groups are expanding or forming. Among them is the Association of Community Organizations for Reform Now (ACORN), which tripled its size last year now that this type of community outreach is quickly becoming imperative in areas where borrowers are increasingly likely to feel totally disempowered. ACORN workers assist borrowers in communicating with their lenders to reach reasonable workout plans to forestall foreclosure, take action against servicer wrongdoing, apply for home preservation programs, engage in financial counseling, restructure debts, and work with loan servicers by going into neighborhoods and knocking on the doors of those borrowers who are proving the toughest to reach. Historically this includes the most disenfranchised groups, such, as non-English-speaking, low-income, or elderly borrowers. Another group, the Homeownership Preservation Foundation (HPF), a private Minneapolis charitable foundation, was also established to help reduce foreclosures and preserve home ownership. Borrowers across the country can call the toll-free HPF national hotline at (888) 995-HOPE for free, expert foreclosure prevention counseling. Consumer Credit Counseling Service (CCCS) advises that credit counseling can help get people back on track, but only if they seek help before it's too late because far too many distressed borrowers instead elect to go into hibernation. As of 2008, CCCS was reporting a 60 percent success rate in helping distressed home owners and consumers. And Homecoming Financial's Home Ownership Preservation Enterprise (HOPE), a joint effort among lenders to reach borrowers face-to-face, is working with high-risk customers through its relationships with organizations such as HUD and the FDIC. The original program consists of three primary components: education, counseling, and on-site assistance. It is aimed at borrowers who are at least sixty days delinquent and those who have had no contact with their mortgage company. HOPE representatives note that many borrower-callers facing foreclosure are living through a "perfect storm" of several unforeseen crises hitting them within a short period of time. Leading factors include layoffs, poor budget management, death, divorce, and medical crisis. Some of these groups are also beginning to partner with local nonprofit housing organizations, city governments, and faith-based leadership to sponsor workshops, seminars, and counseling events. One such local group is the Eastside Organization Project Advocacy Group, affectionately nicknamed the "Mod Squad." The team, whose members renegotiate loans for distressed borrowers, compared recent increases in requests to a "cattle call."[47]

Nonetheless, according to a poll by Freddie Mac and New York–based Roper Public Affairs and Media, more than six out of every ten home owners delinquent in their mortgage payments are still not aware of loss mitigation services their mortgage lender offers.[48] As we discussed in chapter 6, these home owners fail to contact their lenders because they're embarrassed, they don't believe their lender can help, or they believe it will cause them to lose their home more quickly.

Critics say advocacy groups need to be careful not to be too optimistic. As we've seen, some borrowers are only qualified to have smaller loans and smaller, less elaborate homes than the ones they bought and financed during the bubble. Others, based on their income, debt, financial discipline, and other factors, should probably not be home owners at all. Americans for Fairness in Lending, a national consumer and civil rights organization coalition, rolled out a national campaign against predatory lending promoting enhanced disclosure and stricter regulation. Participants include the Consumer Federation of America, Consumers Union, The NAACP, and the National Council of La Raza.[49] Information about some of the relevant consumer advocate groups are included for reference as appendix E.

In the bigger picture, two of the factors we've discussed that will probably never go away are originators' motivation to close as many loans and make them as large as possible and our government's motivation to keep consumers spending. If the disentanglement of the subprime crisis amounts to the massive redistribution of US wealth some are predicting, the average American consumer will need advocates more than ever before. You are encouraged to e-mail information or links to other groups you may become aware of to www.foreclosurenationthebook.com for sharing with other readers.

Even the best possible protection and assistance from Washington, the separate states, and the various consumer advocacy groups will never be enough to permanently stop the bad guys (who will always find ways to get around the rules) or even to ensure that we always understand the possible ramifications of our important financial choices. Consumer education is important but taking ownership for the responsibility to become better educated is crucial. It is potentially the difference between a nation that strives to be the best that it can be and one in which making the best choices really doesn't matter. The financial choices we made as individuals and as a country are precisely what have brought us to today. Home ownership is a privilege, not a right. Armed with education, awareness, and core financial values, aggressive and even unethical credit card companies and mortgage originators face a formidable foe. The beautiful thing about a foreclosure nation is that it gets our attention long enough for each of us to decide whether we want to live with that label or not.

THE BUZZ WORD IS CHANGE

Change most logically begins where it all started with the American Dream. We (as both mortgage loan borrowers and as consumers) will have to seriously reconsider the importance of self-sufficiency and savings in our culture. If we agree with our grandparents that these are important core financial values then we also need to take steps to reincorporate them into

Prudent Refinance Considerations

- What are your current mortgage(s) details?
  - Interest rate
  - Remaining amortization term
  - Principal balance
- What is the current market interest rate you can get if you refinance?
- What is the cost of refinancing (i.e., closing costs)?
- What are your current income and expenses?
- Will your current income and expenses continue at the same rates?
- Are there any events that may be coming up that could influence your income or expenses?
- Are you using conservative estimates of what you think your home is currently worth?
- Are you borrowing more money than you need?
- Are you cashing out equity for anything other than absolute necessities?
- Are you essentially cashing out equity for basic living expenses?
- What is your target date to have your mortgage paid off in full and own your home free and clear?
- How will a refinance impact your target "nest egg" date?
- Are you willing to make that sacrifice?

our daily lives. Already industry leaders like Bank of America are promoting products that allow us to round up the dollar amount of our credit card purchases and have the overage direct-deposited into our savings accounts. Responsible businesses, politicians, and decision makers will continue reinforcing this new trend, reminding us all on a daily basis of the importance of savings and financial accountability. Not treating our homes like ATM machines with repeated periodic cash-out refinances, is key to this strategy. In fact, a life-long restriction prohibiting cash-out refinancing for any home owner using government funds or insurance to purchase a home would be consistent with these values. For the rest of us, the right time and reasons to refinance are case specific, but the sidebar on the left reflects the considerations suggested for rendering smart refinance decisions.

Ideally, our nation's public school systems will expand on the independent living skills currently being taught that espouse these values. Parents will set good examples for their children. Politicians will initiate and support bipartisan legislation to reward financially responsible lifestyle decisions. Public sports and entertainment figures will become involved in reemphasizing financial responsibility and self-sufficiency as politically correct values. In the alternative, if America is shifting in the direction of being a domestic consumer-driven economy in which imports exceed exports with increasingly larger annual trade deficits, alternative spending resources that will not drive our nations' consumers into a life of overwhelming debt will be necessary (yet another discussion that far exceeds the scope of this book). In many cases folks do not earn enough income to live without incurring debt and simply have no other choice, a trend which, as we've discussed, appears to be growing. Some of the things experts are telling us to do to protect ourselves from a full-scale crisis are to purchase long-term healthcare insurance and invest in tax-free instruments such as IRAs and 401(k)s. But, before we can expect Americans to save money we need to ensure that all Americans who try to do so have enough income on which to live. Herman Melville once wrote, "Of all the preposterous assumptions of humanity over humanity, nothing exceeds most of the criticism made on habits of the poor by the well-housed, well-warmed and well-fed." The richest 1 percent of Americans earned 22 percent of our nation's total adjusted gross income in 2006, the highest in 19 years.[50] Many are concerned by what appears to be a long-term trend toward economic inequality and that the gap may find its deepest points along racial lines. Construction during the housing boom was responsible for the 46 percent employment growth among foreign-born Hispanics from 2004 to 2006.[51]

But for the housing boom, American's financial condition has generally worsened. Compared to even a generation ago, we no longer have the same corporate and social safety nets our parents had. During the years following World War II, America was the poster child of corporate responsibility. But with the resurgence of Japanese and European competition during the 1960s and 1970s, along with Wall Street's demand for visible steady growth, the squeeze on profit margins took its biggest toll on employee security. It is predicted that the current recession will devastate 10 percent of our nation and have a noticeable impact on the average American's standard of living, at least into the near future. A chief contributor will be reduced credit card spending simply due to less amounts of such credit being made available.[52] This, in combination with the disappearance of home equity and, thus, home equity lines of credit, will force many Americans to live within what their paychecks and other actual income will allow.

We discussed in chapter 1 how our nation's reliance upon debt has grown.

As we've discussed, consumer debt is up 22 percent since 2000, often at the cost of savings, which is down 50 percent since 1968. Interestingly, the rate of credit card debt increase slowed because of a shift from the use of credit cards to the use of home equity debt. Between 2000 to 2006, Americans borrowed $1.3 trillion from their homes. Household debt was 120 percent of annual income, up from 60 percent in 1984. As the real estate market slowed, credit card debt began climbing again, growing as much as $20 billion per quarter in 2007, clear evidence that many of us have become accustomed to living beyond our means.[53] We have become a culture built around spending. Even our government's favorite tools are tax measures and spending initiatives. This begs the question, is the average American earning enough money to live a reasonable lifestyle in the first place? If not, chalk another one up for government's "to do" list. If so, then it is up to each us of to make long-term changes in our spending. Unfortunately, so many of us are buried so deep in debt at the moment, that it may seem impossible to get ourselves back on track without some help. It is hoped that those who can manage a workout plan to pay off their debt will do so now, while creditors are open to that idea and of the mind-set that it is better to work with us. Those who cannot will be among the millions of Americans making foreclosure and bankruptcy a household word and a more socially acceptable alternative. In the meantime, some tips to help you weather the credit crunch are included in the sidebar. As we demand government action in solving a crisis with so many contributing causes, perhaps it would be wise if we also follow the now famous advice of President John F. Kennedy, and ask not what our country can do for us, but what we can do for our country and ourselves. Some of the suggestions from the FDIC in the sidebar on page 291 may be a good place to start.

THE BIG QUESTION ON EVERYONE'S MIND

At the end of the day, the big question on everyone's mind is when and at what price will the real estate market bottom out? Armed with this information, we'll know when to buy, when to sell, and for how long those in distress will need to hold on. This information will help lenders price REOs (and get bad debt off their balance sheets), developers decide when to start building again, Wall Street to know when to expect a decrease in mortgage loan defaults (and restoration in CDO value and liquidity and the broader

Credit Crunch Home Buying Suggestions

- At any point during your pending purchase, your lender can back out or go out of business. For this reason, it's important to consider a lender's stability and credentials. Look for a large, nationally recognized lender with a presence in your area. And make sure you have a Plan B.
- If loan approval is not an option (perhaps because the home costs too much or you have poor credit), consider a lease purchase. Most lenders allow sellers to contribute to the transaction on the buyer's behalf by buying down the interest rate on the buyer's new loan. Also, explore seller-held loan options.
- Prepare in advance: review your credit report for accuracy, if possible improve your FICO score, and have income and expense verification information handy.
- Determine if you would qualify for an FHA loan.

financial markets), and along with the rest of the world, when we can regain confidence in the US economy.

Ironically, while we wait and wonder, in truth, we ourselves will be the ones to determine when the real estate market bottoms out and recovery begins. Consumers have historically led economic recovery. Recovery or equilibrium in our nation's real estate market needs to involve five basic steps. First, we have to get comfortable buying again. Second, we need to work off excess builder inventory. Third, we must absorb excess resale supply. Fourth, we have to absorb foreclosure units. And fifth, we need to buy up the inventory deferred for resale and disguised as rental properties to defray the carrying costs until the crisis subsides. It is logical to think that, at that point, housing market equilibrium will normalize. Each of these five steps is explored below.

Getting Comfortable

Underlying the necessary equilibrium is, of course, the law of supply and demand. As supply increases, demand and prices decrease. Conversely, as supply decreases, demand and prices increase. Which begs the question: what's it going to take to get us comfortable buying real estate so that demand and price do stabilize? We've discussed the most significant causes behind our hesitancy for jumping back into the housing market: high real estate taxes and other carrying costs, affordability or purchase prices, trouble selling our existing homes, and difficulty getting home mortgage loans. But perhaps the biggest single deterrent holding us back from real estate purchases now is an overall discomfort with real estate valuations and the economy in general. To some extent, our discomfort with the overall economy is a catch 22: once we get comfortable we'll start buying and seeing some signs of recovery, but we all want to see some signs of recovery to help us get comfortable before we'll start buying. Some of the things in play now we have very little control over. But real estate valuation is not one of them. In fact, we've already talked about the power we've always had to value real estate. So the real question is how do we get comfortable again with our ability to value real estate? The answer is simple: We value it the same way we always did before the bubble: we use comparable sales, replacement cost, and income potential for investment property or capitalization rate and looking to various statistical indicators to confirm our valu-

FDIC Borrower Tips

- Pay bills on time to maintain good credit and qualify for low rates.
- Don't have too many credit cards (there is a cost higher interest).
- Check your credit report for accuracy.
- Periodically review your existing loans and credit cards.
- Compare your loans and credit with what a few of your lender's competitors offer.
- Focus on the long term, not just monthly payments.
- Use the Internet for research.
- Read the fine print.
- Don't buy the extra insurance (originators sometimes try to sell life insurance, etc.)
- Limit interest charges by making payments on time.
- Avoid late payments by making payments on time.
- Read all statements and other mail from your lenders (creditors are often allowed to change the terms of your loan and will notify you by letters many people never read).
- Don't be afraid to ask questions of your originator of by calling the toll-free numbers.
- Make sure you use only reputable companies (if you can't verify a company by speaking with people who have used them or information on the Internet that reflects a good reputation, don't use them).

Traditional Real Estate Valuation Methods

The Replacement Cost Approach

The replacement cost approach analyzes land, construction, and all other costs to replicate the home at current market rates. Existing improvements are normally depreciated to account for their current, less than brand-new condition.

The Comparative Sales Approach

This is the most often used valuation method for homes. But as we've learned in markets like our recent bubble, we can't rely solely on this method to determine value. Had we also been factoring in area income, rental prices, and the like, home prices may not have gone quite so high. This approach involves locating recent sales of similar properties in the same neighborhood and making adjustments by adding to the estimated value of the home you are considering buying if it has features the comparative property does not have or deducting from the estimated value of the property you are trying to value if it does not have features that the comparative property has. For example, if you are buying a 2,500 square foot home with a swimming pool and you are trying to determine its value based on the recent sale of a 3,500 square foot home in more or less the same condition and similarly desirable but without a swimming pool (for purposes of our example we will assume a pool adds $25,000 to a home's value) that sold for $350,000, the analysis would be as follows:

$350,000 divided by 3,500 square feet = $100 per foot
$100 per foot times 2,500 square feet = $250,000
Plus $ 25,000 for swimming pool
Equals $275,000 estimated value for home

Appraisers typically use three comparative sales to complete the analysis.

The Income Capitalization Approach

This method uses the estimated income that can be generated from a property to determine its value. For purposes of our discussion we will use an example of a residential quadplex.

First decide what rate of return is desired for the investment. This is referred to as the cap rate, which we discussed earlier. Second, calculate the property's gross income by adding together all rental income and subtracting the mortgage loan payment. Let's say this result is $20,000 and the desired cap rate is .08. To value the property based on the income approach, you would simply divide $20,000 by .08 and the property value would be $250,000.

ation opinions (which we'll discuss shortly). Each of the valuation methods is explained in the sidebar on the following page. Further, residential sales have always borne a fairly stable relationship to rental prices and household income. Our discussion will focus on valuing residential real estate.

Clearly the bubble has made utilizing comparable sales to value real estate a bit more challenging. In a perfect world we would be able to eliminate all bubble sales (since those purchase prices were irrationally high). We would likewise eliminate all crisis-related sales (in particular those involving a lender that tend to be artificially low, such as foreclosures, REOs, and short sales). Unfortunately, it would be impossible to isolate these two artificially influenced extreme segments of home sales. But fear not, the market is clearly creating its own solution thanks to four reasons. First, we all need a place to live. Second, even though historical rent versus ownership cost ratios are way out of whack in some regions (because of vacant units flooding the market and competing for renters juxtaposed to the heights that home ownership costs reached during the bubble), and the national median mortgage payment is $1,687 a month, nearly twice the median rent payment of $868 a month,[54] as long as you buy on the right terms, for most of us it still makes more sense to own than to rent. As our grandparents believed, paying rent is like flushing money down the toilet. Third, most of us view our homes as relatively long-term investments. While we want to buy for the best price we can, it is more important to know that when we eventually sell, the home will be worth more than what we paid for it. Fourth, we choose our homes based on several factors, not just the cheapest price. For example, even if less expensive comparable homes are available, we may choose another home because of the school district or room layout. For these reasons, despite gloomy overall economic predictions Americans are already getting off the fence when it comes to buying homes.

How are these buyers deciding what price they will pay? At least for now they appear to be going back to prices they were comfortable with, namely, prebubble prices. More specifically, circa 2002–2003 prices. Bubble price increases varied by region. Out of the twenty largest metropolitan areas tracked by S&P/Case-Shiller house price index, six regions; Dallas, Cleveland, Detroit, Denver, Atlanta, and Charlotte, saw less than 10 percent real estate price growth during the bubble.[55] On the other hand, seven; Tampa, Miami, San Diego, Los Angeles, Las Vegas, Phoenix, and DC, appreciated by more than 80 percent. Price reversions now will likewise vary by region. Based on historic trends, prices are predicted to decrease from a few percentage points to over 50 percent off peak bubble values with a median 30 percent reduction. From 2006 to 2007 median national existing home prices had dropped 6 percent.[56]

While some investors are looking to 2002–2003 prices as home buyers are doing, for the reasons discussed before, most are using the income approach or replacement cost to value property and determine offer prices. Large-scale investment funds are using broad stroke valuations to buy REOs and mortgage loans from lenders seeking to "dump" them. Formulas of 20 percent to 50 percent of face value are common as both parties are factoring in high levels of anticipated continued default and depreciation. It remains to be seen whether these valuations will prove to be profitable for large-scale investors or not.

Whether prices will fluctuate between now and the end of the crisis remains to be seen, but once we are through this, we can be certain that real estate prices will land in accordance with the solid valuation methods we have always used.

IT'S ALL ABOUT INDICATORS

As we've discussed, appropriate statistical compilation and analysis is critical in predicting when real estate markets will recover and at what price points they will begin to turn around. Information accuracy is key. Although there are several sources for information and analysis, finding the most credible is not always easy. Most rely on extensive databases. Some, like Metrostudy (referenced below), also have researchers literally drive the streets of new home subdivisions, inspecting every home site and recording primary data every ninety days to provide the most complete and current information on undeveloped and vacant building lots, housing starts and real estate closings, products, and pricing. This primary research information is then combined with secondary information and data obtained from other sources on future developments, demographics, job growth, and the economy.

Supply Indicators

When the landing will occur, again, depends in great part on basic laws of supply and demand. On the supply side, the number of available *finished vacant units* in a particular geographical real estate market at any given time tells us how much excess supply needs to be absorbed in order for demand and price to increase and that market to stabilize. Likewise, the number of *multiple listing service (MLS) listings* is another indicator of available supply. The number of *units under construction* tells us how much additional supply will be hitting the market and, likewise, need to be absorbed in the near future. The number of *new construction starts* tells us what supply will look like a bit further in the future. And the number of *finished vacant lots* gives us a glimpse of supply we can expect even farther down the road.

Thanks to the subprime crisis, *mortgage foreclosure filings* are now also reaching numbers significant enough to impact supply and absorption, and therefore, will have to be factored into the recovery equation. However, as to foreclosures, a six- to nine-month gap normally exists between filing a foreclosure, prosecuting the action to completion, and the date the property can be expected to actually hit the market as an REO. The number of certificates of title will be less than the number of foreclosures filed as a result of short sales during the foreclosure process. About a third of foreclosure filings end in REO. Some overlap is also noted between foreclosure filing statistics and MLS listings due to short sales. The primary impact of these units on statistics, already reflected in our market supply as MLS listings before they are foreclosed, is normally price since price typically drops after the property becomes a bank REO. Initially we were able to predict the number of REOs that would be added to the supply inventory. The primary indicator used to predict future foreclosure levels was interest rate resets. This is because when interest goes up, borrower's ARM mortgage payments go up and, if they cannot afford to make the new mortgage payment amount, foreclosures will go up, too. So there is a direct correlation between increases in interest rates and increases in foreclosure rates. Early 2008 rate resets resulted in an average 26 percent increase in monthly payments for many home owners.[57] Since resets surged again in June, July, August, and October 2008, analysts predicted even larger foreclosure numbers than before, between $40 and $55 billion in mortgages, during each of these months,[58] with the heaviest impact being in subpar locations.[59] But actual foreclosure numbers have been higher than predicted since, as we've discussed, as prices continue to fall, many home owners will voluntarily elect to allow their properties to be foreclosed, regardless of whether their rate is resetting or they can afford their mortgage payments. Consequently, it has become increasingly difficult to predict the number of future foreclosures. Certainly if all home owners who are upside down in their properties elected to walk away from those properties, the impact on foreclosure rates, REO supply inventory, and prices would be devastating.

Predicting Miami Supply Using Statistical Indicators

Since supply and demand indicator numbers vary by state and county, in addition to national statistics, for purposes of our discussion, we'll look at Miami, Florida, one of the hardest-hit housing markets in the United States, as well as South Florida and nationwide indicators. As a provider of market information to the housing and related industries nationwide, Metrostudy is recognized for its consulting expertise on development, marketing, and economic issues, and is a key source of research studies evaluating the marketability of residential and commercial real estate projects. Metrostudy has generously provided some basic numbers and insight for our consideration. Statistical indicators are likewise broken down into property type, for example, new construction and existing single-family homes and condominiums. For the purposes of our discussion, we will examine a sampling of property type indicators as well.

As we can see from graph A, as of the third quarter of 2008, Miami had almost a seven-month supply of finished vacant single-family properties, up from almost four months about a year earlier and prior years before that of only one or two months' worth of real estate supply.

Graph B illustrates the tremendous influx of new condominium projects in Miami over the past few years, from 3,205 large new projects started in the first quarter of 2006 to 886 in the fourth quarter of 2007, meaning Miami's condo supply will certainly taper off over time and prices will stabilize.

The same region has another eleven and a half months' supply of attached residences, townhomes, and condominiums, as reflected in graph C, up from only a four months' supply a year earlier and as little as one to two months' supply in prior years. Also helpful in determining Miami-Dade housing supply is an analysis of properties available on the realtor MLS. As you can see from graph D, this region has over twenty-four thousand condominiums and over fifteen thousand single-family homes listed as available for sale as of November 2008. But also visible is what appears to be a slowly emerging downward curve in numbers, meaning that Miami-Dade's MLS listing supply is perhaps slowly being absorbed. Nonetheless, with a pre-bubble average of 8,500 MLS listings, Miami is now home to almost 40,000 MLS listings! The dramatic surge in MLS listings over the past twenty-four

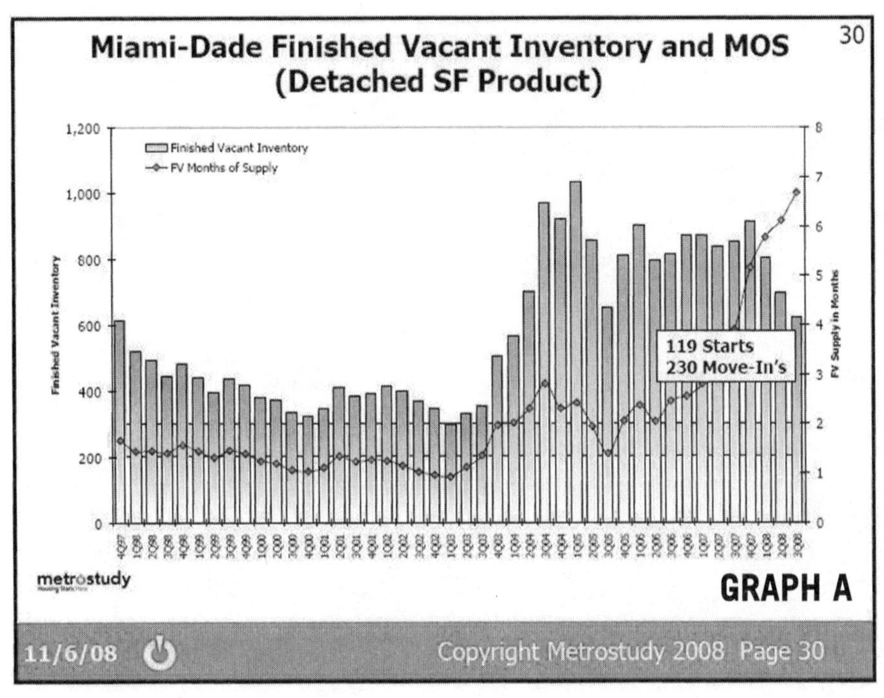
30
Miami-Dade Finished Vacant Inventory and MOS
(Detached SF Product)
Finished Vacant Inventory
FV Months of Supply
Finished Vacant Inventory
FV Supply in Months
119 Starts
230 Move-In's
metrostudy
GRAPH A
11/6/08
Copyright Metrostudy 2008 Page 30

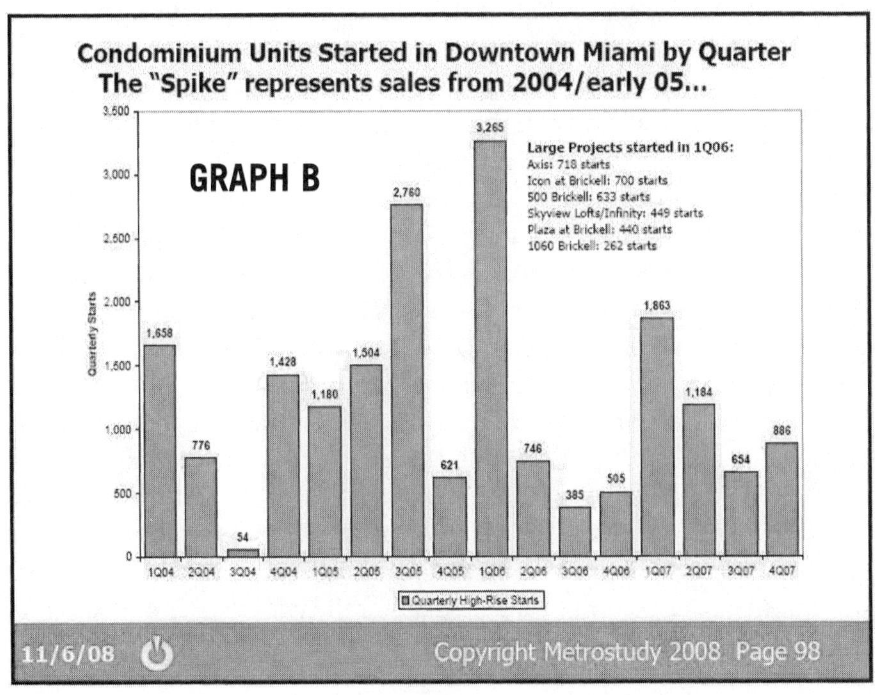
Condominium Units Started in Downtown Miami by Quarter
The "Spike" represents sales from 2004/early 05...
GRAPH B
Large Projects started in 1Q06:
Axis: 718 starts
Icon at Brickell: 700 starts
500 Brickell: 633 starts
Skyview Lofts/Infinity: 449 starts
Plaza at Brickell: 440 starts
1060 Brickell: 262 starts
Quarterly Starts
1,658
776
54
1,428
1,180
1,504
2,760
621
3,265
746
385
505
1,863
1,184
654
886
1Q04 2Q04 3Q04 4Q04 1Q05 2Q05 3Q05 4Q05 1Q06 2Q06 3Q06 4Q06 1Q07 2Q07 3Q07 4Q07
Quarterly High-Rise Starts
11/6/08
Copyright Metrostudy 2008 Page 98

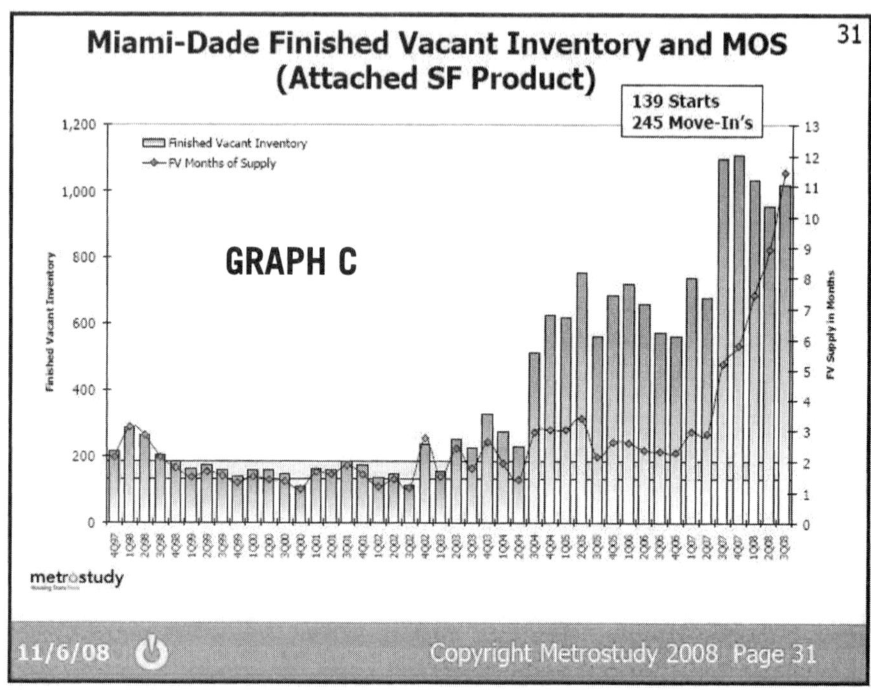

months tells us that much of the bubble buying was speculative, and is one reason properties have been taking more than twice as long to sell (a conclusion that can be drawn by examining time on market statistical indicators). Add to these supply numbers the thousands of new foreclosure filing REOs expected to hit the Miami real estate market and a growing number of predicted new foreclosure filings, based on interest rate resets and loss of equity, as reflected in graph E, up to 6,000 for the month of September 2008 from 2,500 in September 2007 and about 4,500 only a month earlier in August 2008! No doubt Miami's inflated supply level will further increase price pressure on builders, lender REOs, and MLS sellers alike.

Let's take it up a notch and look at similar supply indicators for all of South Florida. As we can see from graph F, unit completions (or raw supply) are down to under 2,000 for the third quarter of 2008, from a high of over 7,000 in the third quarter of 2004 and almost 4,000 in the third quarter of 2007. This same graph also reflects the demand side of our equation. We can see that move-ins, discussed in more detail shortly as a statistical indicator of demand, are also down to about 2,000 for the third quarter of 2008 from almost 7,000 at the third quarter of 2004 peak and 3,000 one year ago.

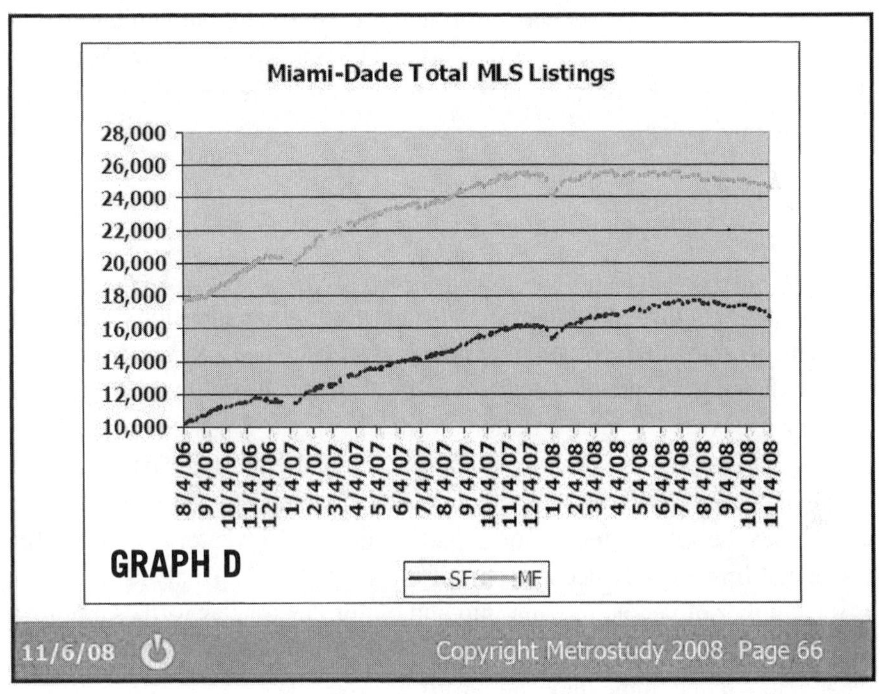

GRAPH D

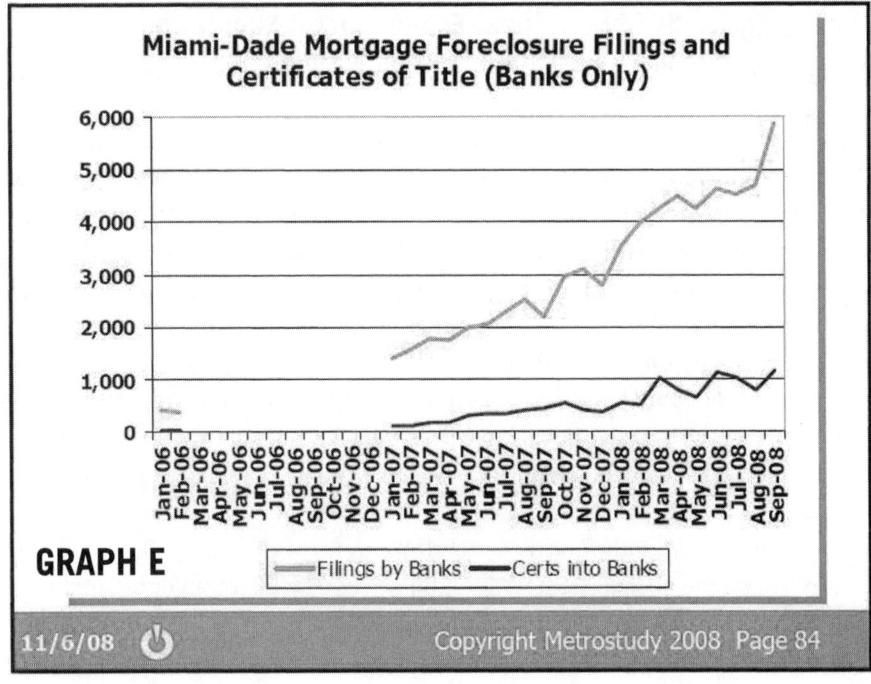

GRAPH E

The next graph (G) reflects information in a broader but similar annual picture as well as new construction starts that help us predict new supply for the near future. Obviously, many of these units were under construction when the bubble burst.

Demand Indicators

For how much longer and how much farther down will prices be forced to fall compared to the excess supply? The answer to these questions will lie in the demand side of the equation. On the demand side, *closings* and *move-ins* indicate the current rate of absorption, allowing us to predict how long it will take for excess real estate inventory to decrease and for prices to begin to recover. Closings alone are not a sufficient demand indicator, since a closing does not necessarily mean that the new owners are moving in. After closing, a unit may be rented and become part of deferred inventory or listed for resale and immediately become part of the supply again. Analysts also look at the number of people moving into and out of the area, as well as employment and other economic factors that influence how many buyers there will be and how much home they can afford.

Predicting South Florida's Real Estate Market Supply and Recovery Timeline Using Statistical Indicators

Let's look at closings or move-ins in Miami-Dade. During the last quarter of 2007, about fifteen thousand units were absorbed via closings, half the number of closings at the peak of the bubble. Based on this rate of absorption, analysts predict that Miami's supply will begin to stabilize with demand after 2009, at which point prices will begin stabilizing. Graph H illustrates the demand side of Miami's real estate market equation, move-ins and closings (in comparison to completions).

The impact this tug-of-war between supply and demand (as well as builders' response to the need for less expensive housing that we can actually afford to pay for) has had on real estate prices is reflected in statistical indicators tracking the prices of units listed and sold. As you can see from graph I, prices in South Florida are shifting in favor of units in the $200,000 range. This trend is consistent with rental prices as well as buyer income and, therefore, supports the notion that we can still rely on tried-and-true traditional real estate valuation matrixes and theories.

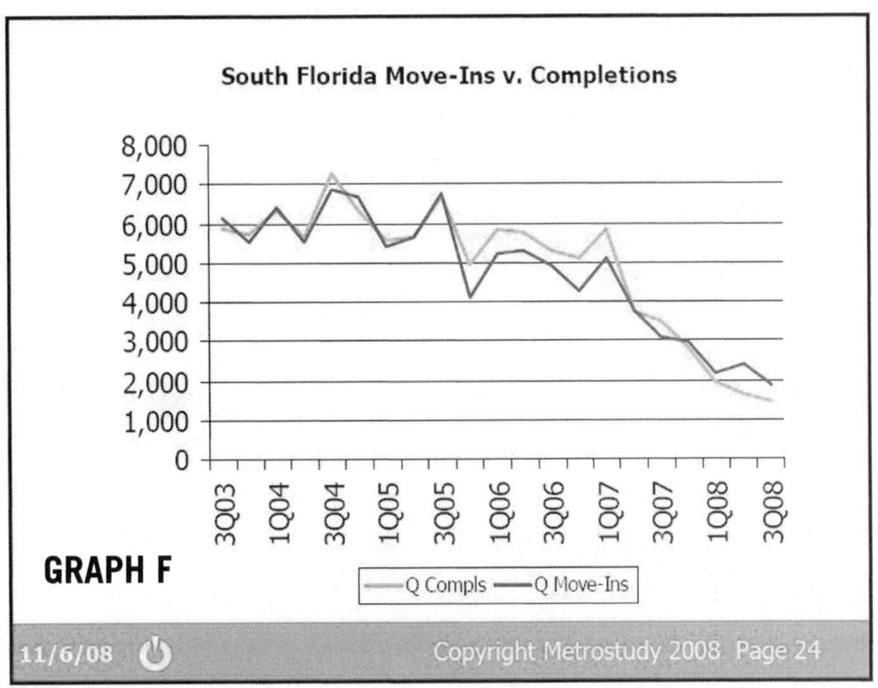
South Florida Move-Ins v. Completions
8,000
7,000
6,000
5,000
4,000
3,000
2,000
1,000
0
3Q03
1Q04
3Q04
1Q05
3Q05
1Q06
3Q06
1Q07
3Q07
1Q08
3Q08
GRAPH F
Q Compls
Q Move-Ins
11/6/08
Copyright Metrostudy 2008 Page 24

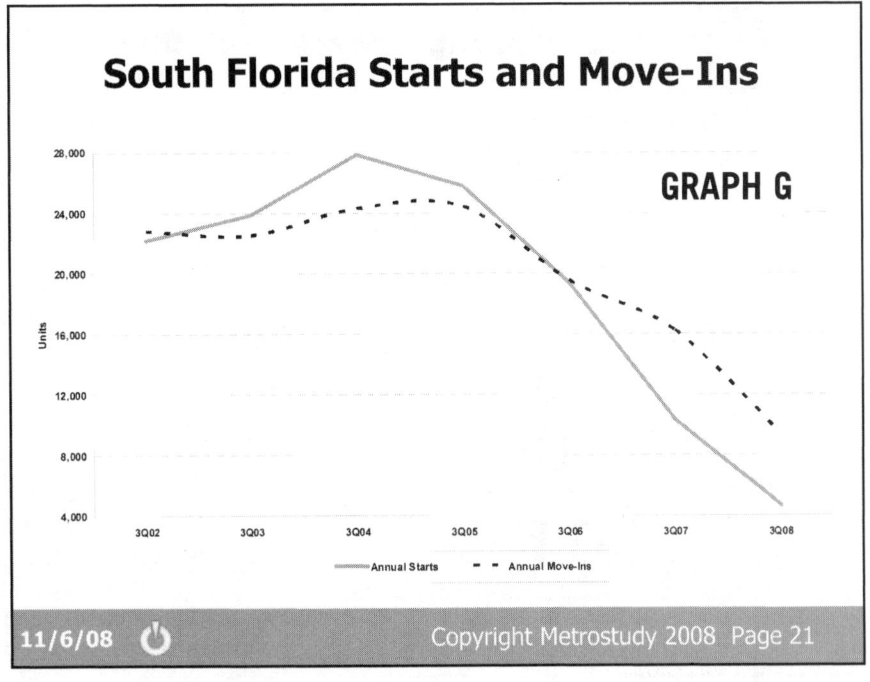
South Florida Starts and Move-Ins
GRAPH G
28,000
24,000
20,000
16,000
12,000
8,000
4,000
Units
3Q02
3Q03
3Q04
3Q05
3Q06
3Q07
3Q08
Annual Starts
Annual Move-Ins
11/6/08
Copyright Metrostudy 2008 Page 21

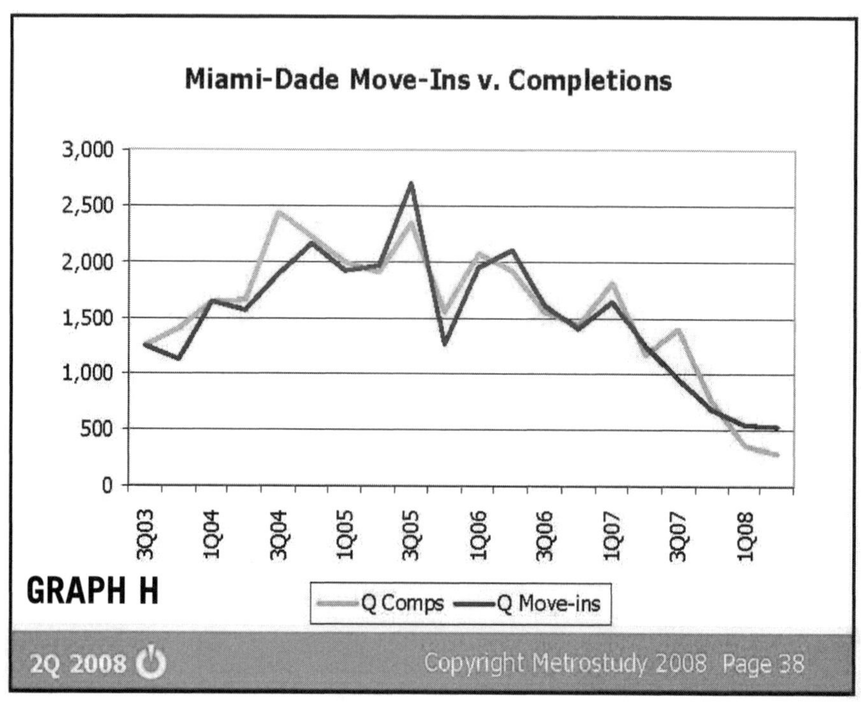

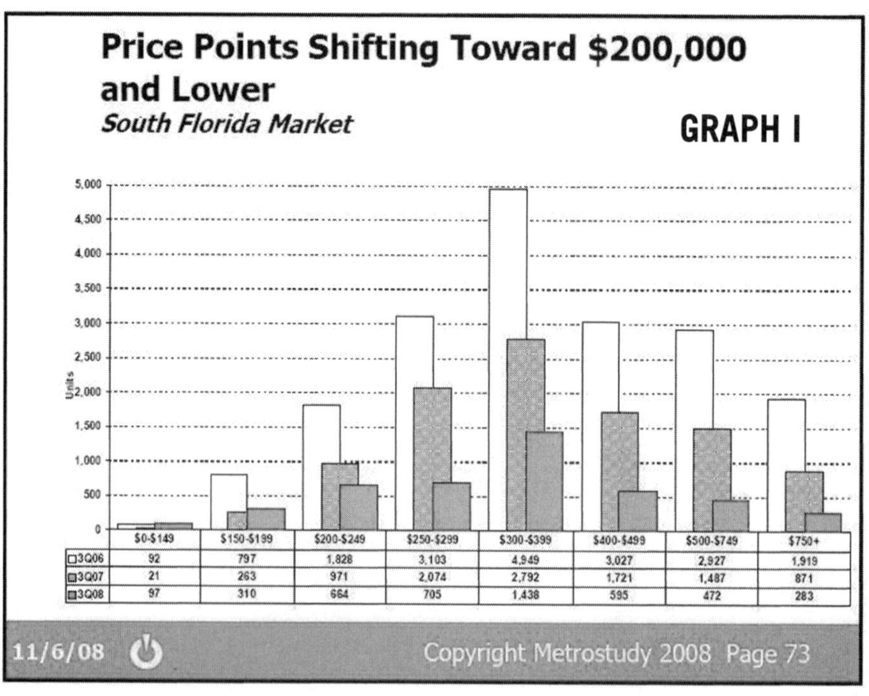

	$0-$149	$150-$199	$200-$249	$250-$299	$300-$399	$400-$499	$500-$749	$750+
3Q06	92	797	1,828	3,103	4,949	3,027	2,927	1,919
3Q07	21	263	971	2,074	2,792	1,721	1,487	871
3Q08	97	310	664	705	1,438	595	472	283

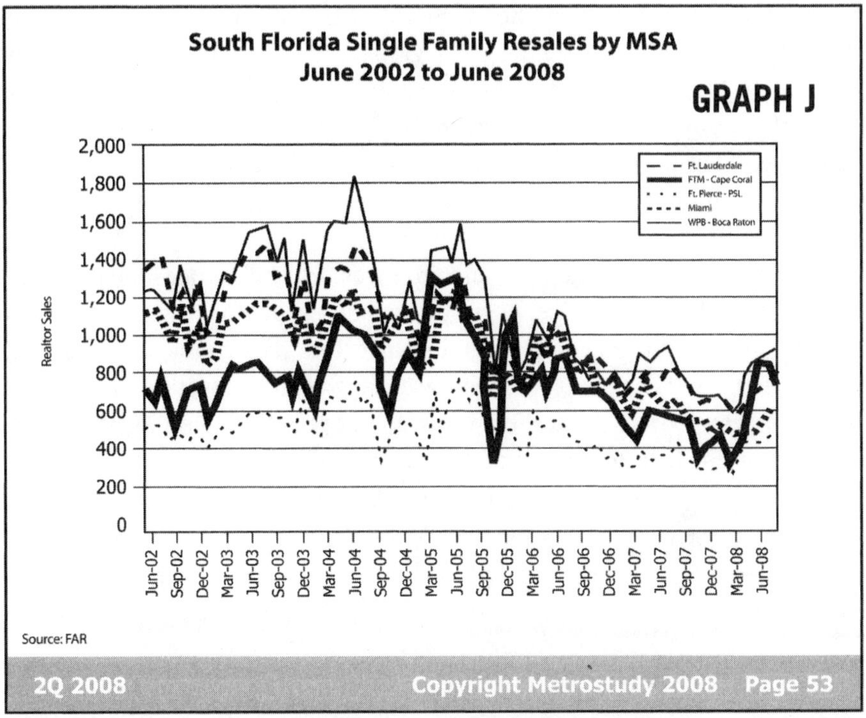

South Florida Single Family Resales by MSA
June 2002 to June 2008
GRAPH J
Ft. Lauderdale
FTM - Cape Coral
Ft. Pierce - PSL
Miami
WPB - Boca Raton
Realtor Sales
2,000
1,800
1,600
1,400
1,200
1,000
800
600
400
200
0
Jun-02
Sep-02
Dec-02
Mar-03
Jun-03
Sep-03
Dec-03
Mar-04
Jun-04
Sep-04
Dec-04
Mar-05
Jun-05
Sep-05
Dec-05
Mar-06
Jun-06
Sep-06
Dec-06
Mar-07
Jun-07
Sep-07
Dec-07
Mar-08
Jun-08
Source: FAR
2Q 2008
Copyright Metrostudy 2008 Page 53

NATIONAL HOUSING MARKET
Finished Vacant Inventory & Months of Supply
by Market
Finished Vacant Inventory
Finished Vacant Inv. Mos
20,000
18,000
16,000
14,000
12,000
10,000
8,000
6,000
4,000
2,000
-
10.0
9.0
8.0
7.0
6.0
5.0
4.0
3.0
2.0
1.0
0.0
SOUTHEAST - Central Florida
SOUTHEAST - South Florida
SOUTH-ATLANTIC - Atlanta
CALIFORNIA - LA Coastal
SOUTHEAST - Naples-Ft. Myers
DESERT-MOUNTAIN - Reno
DESERT-MOUNTAIN - Las Vegas
SOUTHEAST - Sarasota-Bradenton
CALIFORNIA - San Diego
CALIFORNIA - San Francisco Bay Area
MIDWEST - Twin Cities
DESERT-MOUNTAIN - Boise
MIDWEST - Chicago
DESERT-MOUNTAIN - St. George-Mesquite
SOUTHEAST - Tampa
SOUTHEAST - North Florida
DESERT-MOUNTAIN - Denver
DESERT-MOUNTAIN - Phoenix-Tucson
CALIFORNIA - Inland Empire
SOUTH-ATLANTIC - Raleigh - Durham
DESERT-MOUNTAIN - Salt Lake City
MID-ATLANTIC - Suburban Maryland
CALIFORNIA - Sacramento
MID-ATLANTIC - Northern Virginia
CALIFORNIA - Central Valley
SOUTHWEST - Dallas/Ft. Worth
SOUTH-ATLANTIC - Charlotte
SOUTHWEST - Houston SF & Condo
SOUTHWEST - Austin
MIDWEST - Indianapolis
SOUTHWEST - San Antonio
MID-ATLANTIC - Baltimore
GRAPH K
11/6/08
Copyright Metrostudy 2008 Page 10

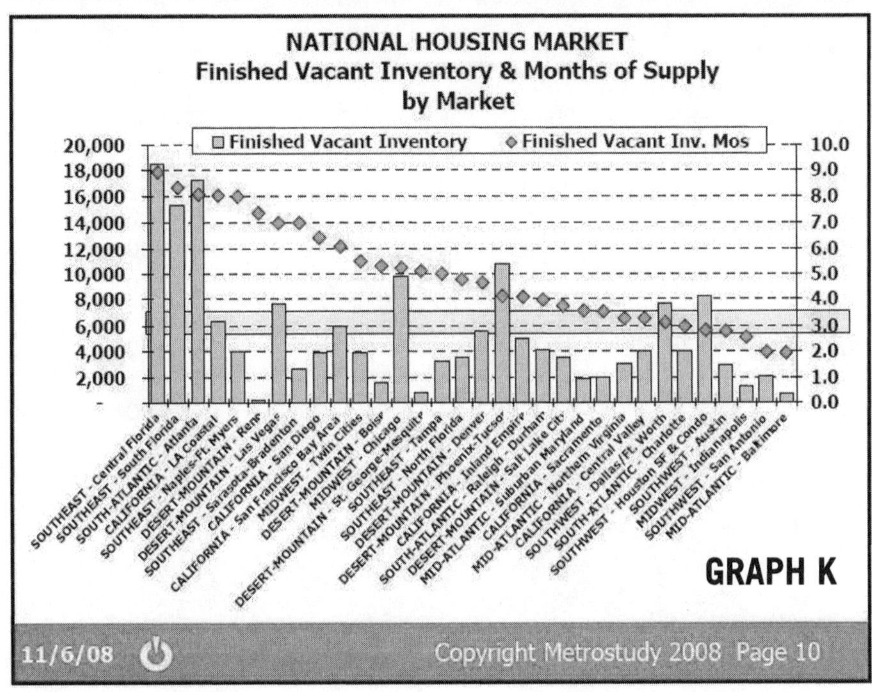

Look at the graph titled "South Florida Median Single-Family Housing Prices from June 2002 to June 2008," graph J. As you can see in the graph, prices hit a high toward the end of the bubble in 2005 and as of June 2008 had declined by more than 20 percent in some areas. In between you will note several abrupt jolts up and down. These may be attributed to things like temporary builder discounts or events in the broader economy, which we discussed earlier.

Because so many Miami buyers are investors and second-home buyers, one factor that will influence where prices bottom out that region especially heavily is unit rental income potential. Investors factor unit carrying costs into their buy/sell decisions. In most cases they want to cover most, if not all, of the carrying costs so that these costs do not present a burden and cut into their net profit. Investors use rental income to cover carrying costs. In other words, if an investor can get more rental income from a unit, she can pay a higher purchase price to buy the unit, and vice versa.

Average National Sales Price of Existing Homes

Year	*Month*	*Existing Home Price*	*Single Family*	*Condo/Co-op Price*
2005		$266,600	$267,400	$260,800
2006		268,200	269,500	259,300
2007		266,000	266,200	264,300
2007	Sept.	257,300	256,300	262,100
2007	Oct.	255,100	253,600	260,300
2007	Nov.	255,700	255,500	257,000
2007	Dec.	254,000	253,000	262,200
2008	Jan.	245,500	243,900	258,700
2008	Feb.	242,000	240,700	252,100
2008	Mar.	247,100	245,400	259,600
2008	Apr.	247,200	246,200	255,000
2008	May	252,600	251,200	263,400
2008	Jun.	257,900	256,800	265,500
2008	Jul.	253,300	252,400	259,700
2008	Aug.	245,400	244,700	251,200
2008	Sept.	234,700	233,900	241,500
vs. last year:		*–8.8%*	*–8.7%*	*–7.9%*

National Supply Indicators

A similar set of supply and demand indicators apply on the national level. Graph K, provided for you on page 303, illustrates our national housing market inventory (finished vacant units) in terms of months of supply by region. Available supply varies greatly by region, with a low of two months' supply in San Antonio and Baltimore and a high of nine months' supply in Central Florida. As we said before and will discuss again, this combined with the variation in bubble price increases (and other factors such as higher unemployment in some areas) is what will lead some real estate markets in certain regions to recover before others.

A chart reflecting home inventory by month over the past two years is included on page 306 to illustrate the variation among providers of indicators and the need to seek more than one source for an accurate assessment. As we can see, these numbers indicate a current national supply of just under ten months' worth of housing units (fourteen months for condominiums) as of September 2008. Supply has peaked during the past few months but may be beginning to be absorbed.

GRAPH L

To help us forecast future supply on a national level, the next graph, L, reflects new housing starts in the United States. We are down to about a third of the level of new construction for 2009 as seen in 2005 (and the lowest level in twenty years). The positive impact this will eventually have on demand and price is good. The negative impact it is already having in construction jobs and manufacturing and related GDP is not good.

National Demand Indicators

On the demand side, graph M reflects national housing market annual closings (in comparison to starts). As you can see, the number of move-ins began dropping off during 2005–2006 and has continued to decline from a high of almost twenty-five thousand units in the third quarter of 2005 to less than ten thousand in the third quarter of 2008. The downward trend in move-ins nationwide has yet to turn around.

Home Inventory by Month

Year	Month	*National Mos. Supply*	*Single Family Mos. Supply*	*Condo/Co-op Mos. Supply*
2005		4.5	4.4	4.7
2006		6.5	6.4	7.8
2007		8.9	8.7	10.7
2007	Sept.	10.3	10.0	12.1
2007	Oct.	10.5	10.2	12.5
2007	Nov.	10.1	9.8	12.3
2007	Dec.	9.7	9.4	11.9
2008	Jan.	10.2	10.0	11.8
2008	Feb.	9.6	9.2	12.6
2008	Mar.	10.0	9.6	12.8
2008	Apr.	11.2	10.7	14.2
2008	May	10.8	10.5	14.1
2008	Jun.	11.1	11.0	12.1
2008	Jul.	10.9	10.4	15.3
2008	Aug.	10.6	10.0	15.7
2008	Sept.	9.9	9.4	14.3
vs. last month:		**–6.6%**	**–6.0%**	**–8.9%**
vs. last year:		**–3.9%**	**–6.0%**	**18.2%**

National Price Indicators

A table illustrating the changes in existing home sale prices nationwide is included on page 304. As demand increases, supply decreases and therefore price increases. The bubble price points for new construction (as opposed to existing homes) was signficantly higher. Hence we can expect to see a comparatively bigger decrease now in the resale prices of those new units. The average national home price for existing homes during the 2006 bubble was $268,200, compared to an average national price of $234,700 as of September 2008.

A Warning about Statistical Indicators

As the chart below illustrates, it is worth noting, however, that from time to time statistical indicators sometimes prove to be misleading. For example, as we've discussed, one traditional indicator is new home sales, which began decreasing in early 2006. But about a year later, indicators told us the market was turning around and we began seeing a healthy increase in the sales of

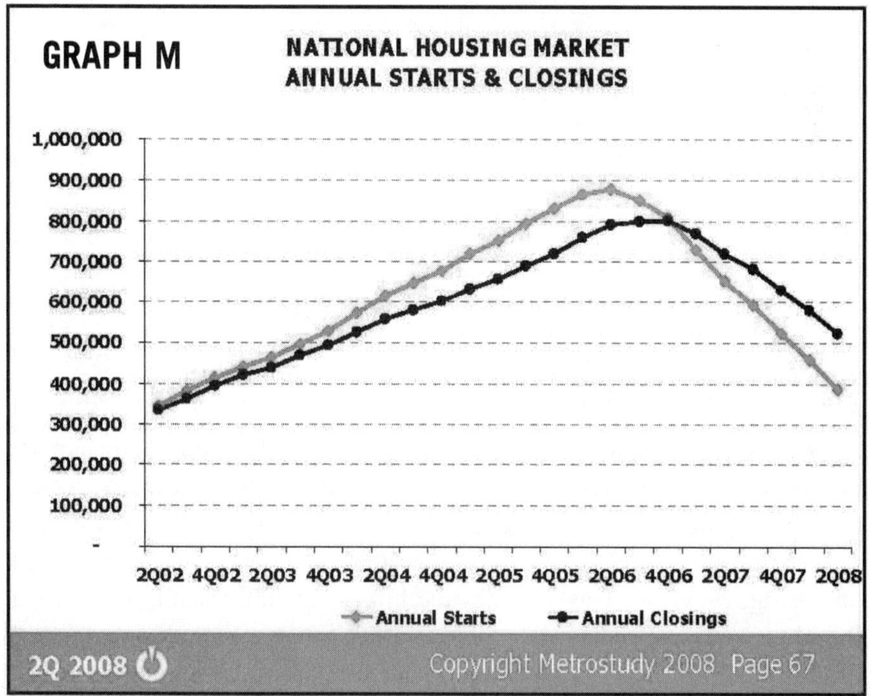

Some of the Up-to-the-Date Statistical Indicators Available to You Online

- New and Existing Home Sales
- New and Existing Single-Family Home Prices
- New Existing Homes Sold by Region
- New and Existing Single Family Home Prices, US
- Housing Economics, Builders' Forecast
- Long-Term Forecast
- Price per Square Foot by Location
- Single-Family Square Footage by Location
- State Starts Forecasts
- Top 100 Metro Forecasts
- Executive-Level Forecast
- Housing Market Statistics
- Long-Term Forecast
- Multifamily Forecast Report
- Remodeling Forecast
- Building Permits
- Employment
- Existing Home Sales and Prices Overview
- Breakouts of Single-family, Condo and Co-op
- Single-Family Existing-Home Sales and Prices
- Condo and Co-op Sales and Prices

new homes. We later learned, however, that this apparent increase in new home sales was a false indicator, because it was fueled not by renewed sustainable market confidence but by deep builder price cuts on new homes. It turned out that roughly half of these new sales were not real, but instead were buyers lured by sales incentives who eventually didn't close because they were unable to obtain financing, or to sell their prior home, or they became once again uncomfortable with the market.

And again it should also be noted that real estate market indicators do not reflect the many subprime crisis reverberations that previous chapters have shown infiltrated other markets. Many of these could, potentially, have further impacts that ricochet back to the real estate and mortgage markets, hampering recovery. This includes the broader credit crunch, job loss, reduced consumer spending, and the overall cloud of gloom that is no doubt holding many of us back from buying our first home, trading up, or investing. Likewise, the fact that there are multiple companies around the country compiling and/or providing market information, some more reputable and precise than others, also influences statistical predictions. As with any endeavor of that nature, undisclosed assumptions and imperfect techniques are often a factor. Given this, in attempting to pinpoint the time frame for the beginning of the end of the subprime crisis and where prices will wind up, it is prudent to look at multiple indicators from different sources. Making the most accurate predictions possible requires looking at a specific market scientifically, regarding price range, competition, builders, foreclosure rates, and other variables. As we've seen, some areas in the United States did not experience extreme bubble prices. Therefore, price reductions, if any, in these areas may be attributed to the overall economic conditions, not to a retraction to 2003 prices. For example, when national unemployment reached 6.1 percent in August 2008, it was 8.9 percent in Michigan. As the automotive industry worsens, so may Michigan's real estate prices and absorption rates. We've also discussed an apparent widening of the socioeconomic wealth gap. With the exception of higher-paid executives in financial and related markets, for the most part our nation's wealthier citizens, while feeling temporary pain in their investment accounts, are far better equipped to weather our financial storm than our already financially stretched middle and lower socioeconomic class citizens (many of whom can be completely wiped out by a job loss, illness, divorce, lawsuit, or foreclosure). Home prices by socioeconomic class reflect this, with prices on the middle and lower end of the range reflecting the more severe challenges their owners are facing, and prices at the higher end of the scale holding more steady.[60] Even for those who are financially sound, however, the mere appearance of economic trouble around us has a noticeable impact on their consumption behavior. Graphs N and O on page 310 reflect market sentiment in terms of new home buyer traffic and contract cancellations as of September 2008. Similar behaviors were observed during the fall of 2008 in the retail sector with retail returns at an all time high.

Analysts predict that supply and demand imbalance is also impacting our commercial real estate market absorption and prices as a result of the credit crunch and reduced consumer spending. For example, further perpetuating the crisis may be almost $18 billion in option ARM mortgage loans set to recast through 2011 as reflected in graph P on page 311.

Together with Prometheus Books I have gone to great lengths to ensure

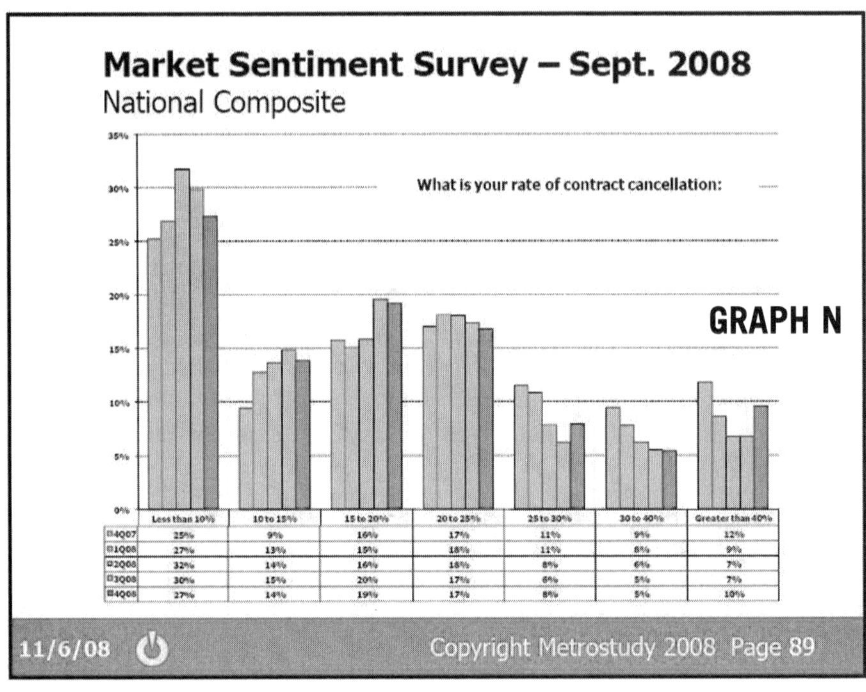

	Less than 10%	10 to 15%	15 to 20%	20 to 25%	25 to 30%	30 to 40%	Greater than 40%
4Q07	25%	9%	16%	17%	11%	9%	12%
1Q08	27%	13%	15%	18%	11%	8%	9%
2Q08	32%	14%	16%	18%	8%	6%	7%
3Q08	30%	15%	20%	17%	6%	5%	7%
4Q08	27%	14%	19%	17%	8%	5%	10%

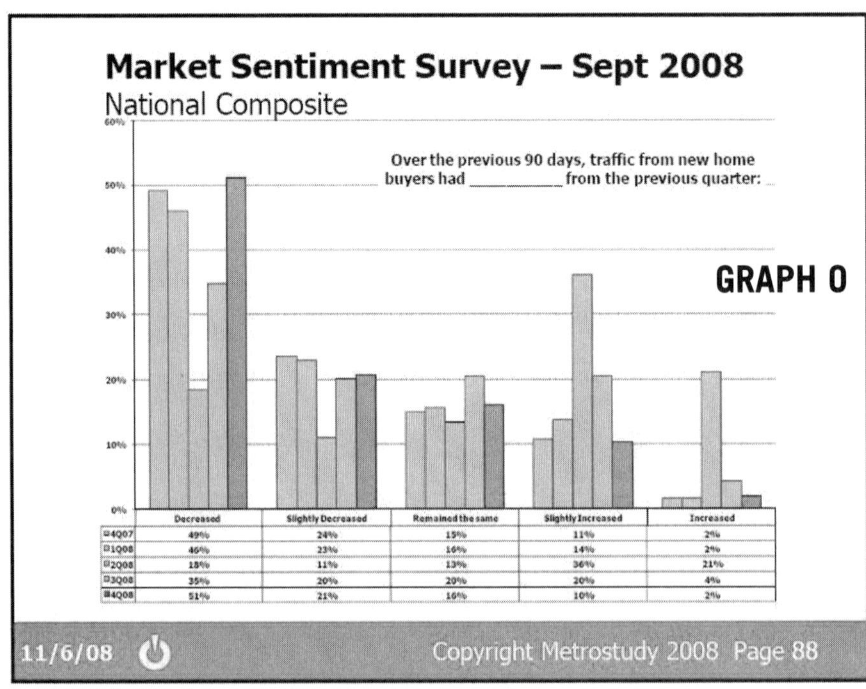

	Decreased	Slightly Decreased	Remained the same	Slightly Increased	Increased
4Q07	49%	24%	15%	11%	2%
1Q08	46%	23%	16%	14%	2%
2Q08	18%	11%	13%	36%	21%
3Q08	35%	20%	20%	20%	4%
4Q08	51%	21%	16%	10%	2%

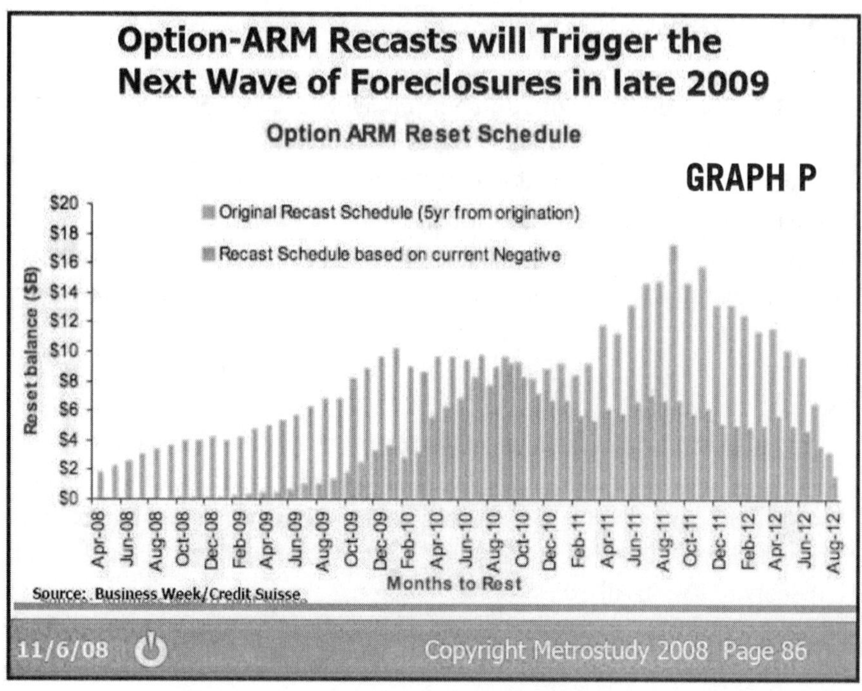

that the information, including statistical indicators, provided for you in this book was as current as possible as of the date it was printed. To accommodate the fact that our economy will continue to evolve daily, a postscript and links are delivered to you online at www.foreclosurenationthebook.com, rather than in traditional fixed print. In addition, statistical indicators online are available, often times for free, to the general public and is an excellent resource for up-to-the-minute information about where our nations' real estate is headed. For example, both the National Association of Home Builders and the National Association of Realtors provide statistical indicators on their Web sites (www.nahb.org and www.realtor.org, respecitively). A list of some of the types of charts and graphs generally available to you is included in the sidebar. As we move forward toward recovery, it is precisely this type of factual information, as opposed to media buzz or irrational panic, upon which prudent real estate purchase decisions will be made. Armed with these powerful tools, there is nothing the experts have that you cannot also have.

CONCLUSION

What else can we say about a foreclosure nation? It is replete with illiquid, distrustful, often insolvent lenders; distressed companies; industry leaders who stand accused of wrongdoing at the expense of an entire country; and innocent (and not so innocent) citizens who are losing their homes. It is a nation with a lot of questions and very few definitive answers. When the foreclosure nation is America, it is a one-time world leader potentially redefining its place in the global community and at risk of becoming something much different from what it's founding fathers, and most of our grandfathers, intended.

Even before it is over, financial losses from the US-originated subprime crisis are already astronomical: $200 billion to save Fannie Mae and Freddie Mac, $85 billion for AIG, $1.2 trillion in loans to financial institutions, millions in federal loans to mitigate states' deficits, investor losses on collateralized debt obligations in excess of $150 billion, subprime mortgage defaults in the $200 to $300 billion range with estimated eventual impacts between $350 and $600 billion. US corporations have suffered about $8 trillion in losses as their holdings declined in value from $20 trillion to only $12 trillion. Losses in other countries have averaged 40 percent of those investment values. Financial institutions in other countries have written down a total of $501 billion in US investments. The International Monetary Fund (IMF) predicts worldwide losses of $945 billion. Profits from the 8,533 US banks insured by the FDIC are down 89 percent, from $35.2 billion to $646 million between 2007 and 2008 and another 46 percent as of the first quarter of 2008. An estimated $1.2 trillion reduction in housing prices and slowing of the economy are expected to further reduce state and local property tax revenues significantly and recently another $700 billion burned a hole in Washington's pocket.[61]

While many are already losing the financial foothold home ownership provided, the rest of us are anxiously awaiting what may still be yet to come. Together we have now explored the various dynamics that are said to have resulted in the subprime and broader economic crises. We have discussed the crises' many impacts thus far and considered its probable outcomes both in our own lives and in the larger context of US economic history. But most important, we have begun a dialogue about the roles each of us play in this historic drama. America has been a world leader, not because we have a cool flag, but because of the position we have carved for ourselves in the world.

We are second, third, and fourth generations of immigrant parents, grandparents, and great-grandparents who lived their lives in accordance with certain core values that helped them to help their country become an example for the rest of the world of how great a capitalist economy governed by democracy can be, a leader among nations.

We've discussed how, together, we spent $800 billion more than we earned last year. Our household debt has grown to $14 trillion, doubling over the past six years alone![62] Some will say we have grown fat and complacent on borrowed money. In that sense the subprime crisis can be viewed as a resounding wake-up call we simply cannot afford to ignore.

Former chairman of the Federal Reserve Alan Greenspan has said that "the current credit crisis will come to an end when the overhang of inventories of newly built homes is largely liquidated, and home price deflation comes to an end. That will stabilize the now-uncertain value of the home equity that acts as a buffer for all home mortgages, but most importantly for those held as collateral for residential mortgage-backed securities. Very large losses will, no doubt, be taken as a consequence of the crisis. But after a period of protracted adjustment, the US economy, and the world economy more generally, will be able to get back to business."[63]

That's great news. But even better is the hope that Americans and the nation will not be going back to business as usual. Perhaps the fact that an overwhelming majority of us voted for change in our nation's recent presidential election is a sign that we will recognize and act on the need for economic change, beginning in our own homes. And perhaps now that our new administration is in place, we'll listen to their advice, starting with White House Chief of Staff Rohm Emmanuel's suggestion that we "Never let a serious crisis go to waste." The news about US home ownership is more positive. The media knows we're tired of hearing how bad things are. Viewers like something fresh and different. The media seems to be done reporting about half-empty glasses and to have moved on to bringing us information about the half-full ones. In August of 2007 the morning news interviewed foreclosed home owners in Santa Barbara, California, who had taken to sleeping in their cars. In an effort to improve safety, the city had begun chaining parking lots at night so these newly homeless could sleep soundly, bringing new meaning to the term "gated community" in a foreclosure nation.[64] Fast-forward a year to August 2008 and the *Today* show feature segment titled "The New Mortgage Rules; Recession Proofing Your Life, " during which first-time home buyers were urged to save

3 percent to 5 percent for a down payment (the rest of us were urged to save 20 percent), think twice before applying for a home equity loan (the reporter noted that a home is not a piggy bank), not buy a home that is too big for their budget, and never borrow more than 30 percent of take home pay for a home mortgage.[65]

But we already know that. We've taken a long objective look at the America our grandparents gave us and what we've done with it so far. We've seen what happens when an entire nation takes its home equity for granted. We've stared credit in the eyes and glimpsed a foreclosure nation. This crisis is a once in a century opportunity for Americans to decide whether or not the nation we want to leave for our next generation is a foreclosure nation.

NOTES

1. Mark Gongloff, "Like S&L? Paying the Tab for a Cleanup," *Wall Street Journal*, July 21, 2008, p. C1.

2. Emily Kaiser, "A Long Year of Lessons for the Fed," *International Herald Tribune*, August 18, 2008, p. 13.

3. Yuka Hayashi, "Japan's Bailout Lessons," *Wall Street Journal*, August 13, 2008, p. 31.

4. James Surowiecki, "Too Dumb to Fail," *New Yorker*, February 2008; Carter Dougherty, "Mason–Lessons from Bailouts, Part 2," http://www.rgemonitor.com/financemarkets-monitor/253015/lessons_from_bailout_history_ii; Carter Dougherty, "Stopping a Financial Crisis, the Swedish Way," *New York Times*, September 22, 2008.

5. Alan S. Blinder, "From the New Deal, A Way Out of a Mess?" *New York Times*, February 24, 2008, p. 6.

6. Hayshi, "Japan's Bailout Lessons," p. 31.

7. Gongloff, "Like S&Ls? Paying the Tab for a Cleanup," p. C1.

8. Eric Dash, "Four Major Banks Seek Federal Reserve for Money," *New York Times*, August 23, 2007, p. C7; Robin Sidel and Greg Ip, "Banks Step Up to Fed's Window," *Wall Street Journal*, August 23, 2008, p. A3.

9. Randalle Smith, "Behind Banks Credit Rescue Fund," *Wall Street Journal*, October 17, 2008, p. C1; Carrick Mollenkamp, "Rescue Readied by Banks Is Bet to Spur Market," *Wall Street Journal*, October 15, 2007, p. 16.

10. Dwight Cass and Robert Cyran, "Freeze May Generate Heat," *Wall Street Journal*, December 1, 2007, p. B16; Edmund L Andrews, "US Urges Freezing Some Rates on Loans," *Wall Street Journal*, December 1, 2007, p. B1.

11. James R. Hagerty and Aparajita Saha-Bubna, "Fannie Loss of $2.3 Billion Exceeds Forecast," *Wall Street Journal*, August 9, 2008, p. A3; James A. Hagerty and Serena Ng, "Mortgage Giants Take Hits on Fears Over Capital," *Wall Street Journal*, August 8, 2008, p. A15.

12. Nicole Gelinas, "Uncle Sam Can Bail Out Fannie, but Who Will Bail Out Uncle Sam?" *Wall Street Journal*, July 21, 2008, p. A17.

13. "I Want Your Money: The Left Accuses the Bailout of Ripping Off Taxpayers While the Right Damns It as Socialism," *Economist*, September 27, 2008, p. 17.

14. "Once in a century rip-off . . ."

15. Gregory Mankin, "The Wealth Trajectory: Reward for the Few," *New York Times*, April 20, 2008 p. 9; Jesse Drucker, "Richest Americans See Their Income Share Grow," *Wall Street Journal*, July 23, 2008 p. A3; Naomi Scheiber, "What Safety Net?" *New York Times*, July 6, 2008, p. 14.

16. Christie, Les, "Housing Relief," *CNN Money.com*, April 8, 2008.

17. "Briefing America's Bailout Plan," *Economist*, September 27, 2006, p. 83.

18. Lori Montgomery and David Cho, "Rescue Plan Grows to $700 Billion," *Washington Post*, September 21, 2008, p. A13.

19. http://www.AmericanBanker.com/article.html/whats_new.html.

20. Tom Paradis, "Stocks End Worst Week Ever," *Huffington Post*, October 10, 2008, p. 1.

21. Nelson Schwartz, "What Created This Monster?" *New York Times*, March 23, 2008, p. A13.

22. Ibid.

23. Serena Ng, "Liffe Joins Credit Default Arena," *Wall Street Journal*, July 8, 2008, p. C2.

24. Hagerty and Saha-Bubna, "Fannie Loss of $2.3 Billion Exceeds Forecasts," p. A3.

25. Phil Izzo, "Fannie, Freddie, Bailout?" *Wall Street Journal*, August 15, 2008, p. 9.

26. Ibid.

27. Hagerty and Ng, "Mortgage Giants Take Hit on Fears Over capital," p. A15.

28. Clifford Krauss, "Belatedly, Some States Move to Limit Damage from Subprime Lending," *New York Times*, August 24, 2007, p. 5; Reginald Fields, "State Agency to Help Strapped Homeowners," *Wall Street Journal*," March 8, 2007, p. A4.

29. John Mechem, "FBI Signs Memo of Understanding on Mortgage Fraud Warning," *Mortgage Bankers Association News*, March 9, 2007, p. 17; John Mecham, "Fraud against Lenders Not Going Away," *Mortgage Bankers Association News*, March 9, 2007, p. 13; Christopher Robacher, "Cases of Mortgage Fraud Up, FBI Says," *Washington Post*, March 8, 2007, p. D4.

30. Ibid.

31. Ibid.

32. www.legis.state.ga.us/legis/2005_06/sum/sb100.htm.

33. www.namb.org.

34. www.mortgagenewsdaily.com.

35. www.csbs.org/Content/NavigationMenu/Home/StateForeclosurePrevention WorkGroupDataReport.

36. www.washingtonwatch.com/bills/show/110_SN_2595.html.

37. Terry Sheridan, "Task Force Gives Recommendation to Broward," *Daily Business Journal*, June 24, 2008, p. A3.

38. Brenda B. White and Andy Woodward, "A Meeting of the Minds: The Council to Shape Change," *Mortgage Bankers Association News*, February 13, 2007, p. 19.

39. John Mecham, "Anti-Predatory-Lending Standard, Mortgage Fraud Top MBA Agenda," *Mortgage Banking Association News*, February 13, 2007, p. 7.

40. www.appraisalfraud.com; money.cnn.com/2008/01/17/real_estate/wamu_law suit.moneymag/index.htm; money.cnn.com/2005/05/23/real_estate/financing/ appraisalfraud/index.htm; www.mortgagenewsdaily.com/522005_Appraisal_Fraud _Suggestions .asp.

41. www.jdpower.com/corporate/news/releases/pressrelease.aspx?ID=2008217.

42. www.nationalnotary.org/news/index.cfm?Text=newsNotary&newsID=1565.

43. www.jdpower.com/corporate/news/releases/pressrelease.aspx?ID=2008217.

44. www.jdpower.com/corporate/news/releases/pressrelease.aspx?ID=2008217.

45. www.mbaa.org/IndustryResources/ResourceCenters/RegAB.

46. Christine Dugas, "Reverse Mortgage Aren't for Everyone," *USA Today*, January 18, 2008, p. 4B.

47. Eduardo Gomez, "Coalition to Fight Predatory Lending," *Los Angeles Times*, March 6, 2007, p. 11.

48. www.freddiemac.com/news/archives/corporate/2008/20080131_07roper survey.html.

49. Jim Frer, "Changes to Mortgage Law Expected to Combat Fraud," *Real Estate Journal*, September 2008, p. 10.

50. Gregory Mankin, "The Wealth Trajectory: Reward for the Few," *New York Times*, April 20, 2008, p. 9; Drucker, "Richest Americans See Their Income Share Grow," p. A3.

51. Nelson Schwartz, "In Economic Slump, Hispanics Are Losing a Tenuous Prosperity," *New York Times*, May 13, 2008.

52. Naomi Scheiber, "What Safety Net?" *New York Times*, July 6, 2008, p. 14.

53. Andrew Ross Sorkin, "The Ranks of the Comfortable Are Still Thinning," *New York Times*, September 2, 2007, p. 11; Roger Lowenstein, "Subprime Times,"

New York Times, July 14, 2008; Anna Bahney, "More Americans Strain to Meet Housing Costs," *USA Today*, September 23, 2008, p. 3A.

54. Courtney Albers, "The High Price of Ownership," *USA Today*, August 10, 2006, p. B4; www.catalystexhibit.com/catalyst_speaks.html.

55. www.marketwatch.com/news/story/continued-record-home-price-declines/story; www.standardandpoors.com/portal/site/sp/en/us/page.topic/indices_csmahp/.

56. www.marketwatch.com/news/story/continued-record-home-price-declines/story; www.standardandpoors.com/portal/site/sp/en/us/page.topic/indices.

57. Noelle Kno, "Foreclosure Proceedings Set Record," *USA Today*, September 7, 2007, p. A1; Paola Lupsa-Abbot, "Delinquency Deluge," *Daily Business Review*, May 2, 2008, p. 1.

58. MetroStudy Mortgage Interest Rate Resets.

59. money.cnn.com/2007/02/12/news/economy/subprime_realestate/index.htm.

60. S. Giles, "The Center of the Storm," *Economist*, September 27, 2008, p. 44.

61. Justin Lahart, "Egg Cracks Differ in Housing, Finance Shells," *Wall Street Journal*, December 24, 2007; http://dallasmorningviewsblog.dallasnew.com/archives/2008/09/the-root-of-all.html.

62. http://dallasmorningviewsblog.dallasnew.com/archives/2008/09/the-root-of-all.html.

63. www.huffingtonpost.com/2008/03/16/greenspan-financial-cris_n_91786.html.

64. "Santa Barbara Steps Up," CNN, August 13, 2007.

65. "Recession Proof Your Mortgage," *Today*, August 28, 2008.

GLOSSARY

Acceleration: The right of the lender to demand payment on the outstanding balance of a loan.

Adjustable-Rate Mortgage (ARM): A loan with an interest rate that changes periodically in keeping with a current index, such as one-year treasury bills.

Air Loans: A type of mortgage fraud where there is no collateral because the loan is on a nonexistent property.

Alt-A Mortgage: A classification of mortgages where the risk profile is between prime and subprime. The borrowers behind these mortgages will typically have clean credit histories, but the mortgage itself will generally have some issues, such as higher loan-to-value and debt-to-income ratios or inadequate documentation of the borrower's income, that increase its risk profile. Lenders find these loans attractive because the rates are higher than rates on prime classified mortgages, but they are still backed by borrowers with stronger credit ratings than subprime borrowers. However, there is additional risk for lenders because of a lack of documentation—including limited proof of the borrower's income.

Amortization: A plan of monthly payments of principal and interest that enables a borrower to reduce his debt gradually over a period of time.

Answer: The legal document filed by a party in response to a lawsuit that has been filed. It admits or denies facts alleged in the complaint and sets forth legal defenses to the complaint.

Broker Price Opinion (BPO): An estimated value of a property based on the characteristics of the property. It is determined by a real estate broker or other qualified individual.

Buyback Agreement: An agreement by a seller to buy back an asset at a specific price for specific conditions, normally used as a sales incentive.

Capitalization Rate (Cap Rate): A ratio used to compare properties based on the income they generate. The Cap Rate is computed by taking the rental net operating income (NOI) and dividing it by the property's fair market value (FMV). A higher capitalization rate makes a property more attractive to a prospective purchaser.

Carrying Costs: Loan costs imposed by a lender, including interest, negotiation fee, processing fee, and penalties.

Center for a New American Dream: A nonprofit organization based in Maryland, on the border of Washington, DC, that promotes sustainable consumption. The organization works with individuals, institutions, communities, and businesses to conserve natural resources, counter the commercialization of the culture, and change the way goods are produced and consumed.

Center for Responsible Living (CRL): A nonprofit, nonpartisan research and policy organization working to eliminate abusive financial practices and to protect home ownership and family wealth.

Certificate of Title: A written opinion, executed by the examining attorney, stating that a title is vested as stated in the abstract.

Closing: The process of executing legally binding documents, such as deeds and mortgages, commonly associated with the purchase of real estate and borrowing money to assist in the purchase. Also known as "escrow" or "settlement."

Collateralized Debt Obligation (CDO): A debt security collateralized by a variety of debt obligations including bonds and loans with different maturities and credit quality.

Collateralized Mortgage Obligation (CMO): A type of mortgage-backed security that creates separate pools of pass-through rates for different classes of bondholders with varying maturities, called tranches. The investors in the CMO are divided up into three classes called Class A, B and C. The order in which they receive principal payments differs by class, but all classes receive interest payments as long as the mortgage is not completely paid off. Class A investors are paid out first with prepayments and repayments until they are paid off. Then Class B investors are paid off, followed by Class C investors. In this example, Class A investors bear most of the prepayment risk, while Class C investors bear the least.

Combined (Hybrid) Loans: A combination of fixed and adjustable rate loans, combined (hybrid) loans come in different varieties: a fixed-period ARM will remain at a fixed rate of interest from three to ten years before the initial interest rate changes. At the end of the fixed period, the interest rate will adjust annually. A two-step mortgage has a fixed rate for a certain time, usually five or seven years, after which the interest rate changes to a current market rate and then remains at the new fixed rate for the remaining twenty-three or twenty-five years. Convertible ARMs have an option to convert them to a fixed-rate mortgage, usually on the adjustment date during the first five years. The new rate is the current market rate for fixed-rate mortgages.

Commerce Department: A cabinet department of the United States that promotes and administers domestic and foreign trade, including management of the census and the patent office, created in 1913.

Commission (Front-End, Back-End): A commission or sales fee charged at the time of the initial purchase (front-end) or at the time of the sale (back-end) for an investment. These fees are usually in connection with mutual funds and insurance policies.

Common Area Maintenance (CAM): Amounts charged to tenants for expenses to maintain the common areas such as hallways, restrooms, and parking lots.

Common Law: A system of laws that was originated and developed in England based on court decisions, the doctrines implicit in those decisions, and customs and usages rather than on codified written laws.

Community Reinvestment Act (CRA): Enacted by Congress in 1977, the CRA encourages banks to help meet the credit needs of their communities for housing and other purposes, particularly in neighborhoods with low or moderate incomes, while maintaining safe and sound operations.

Complaint: The legal document filed to commence a lawsuit.

Conference of State Bank Supervisors: Founded in 1902 as a clearinghouse for ideas to solve common problems of state bank regulators, it has evolved into a force that strengthens state banking departments. It is the only national organization dedicated to protecting and advancing our nation's dual banking system by continuing to champion a system that offers competitive chartering options, efficient and effective supervision, and a lower cost of regulation for all banks.

Conforming Mortgage Loan: A conventional home loan that equals or is less than the government limits established by Fannie Mae and Freddie Mac or a residential mortgage loan that is of sufficiently high quality to be bought and packaged as a collateralized mortgage obligation.

Consensual: Existing or entered into by mutual consent without formalization by document or ceremony.

Construction Loan: Short-term loan (usually for three years) to cover the cost of land development and building construction secured by a mortgage on the property being financed. The loan is disbursed (1) as needed, (2) as each stage is completed, (3) according to a prearranged schedule, or (4) when some condition is met. Construction loans are paid off from the proceeds of permanent financing (usually for 20 to 30 years), which in turn is repaid from the cash flow generated by the completed building, and is arranged before the construction loan is disbursed. Also called building loan, construction mortgage, or development loan.

Counterclaim: A claim by a defendant opposing the claim of the plaintiff and seeking some relief from the plaintiff for the defendant.

Counts: Each separate statement in a complaint that states a cause of action that, alone, would give rise to a lawsuit, or each separate charge in a criminal action.

Credit Default Swap: A contract in which a buyer pays a series of payments to a seller in exchange for the right to a payoff if a credit instrument goes into default or on the occurrence of a specified event such as a bankruptcy or restructuring—originally used as a form of insurance against bad debts.

Credit Rating Agency Duopoly Relief Act: Legislation recommended by the House Financial Services Committee in order to improve ratings quality by fostering competition, transparency, and accountability in the credit rating agency industry.

Decorator Ready: Condo units (usually luxury high-rises) sold as basic shells or blank slates without flooring, cabinetry, or appliances so owners can completely customize the unit to their personal style by contracting an interior designer or construction firm to complete the unit. There are two types of "decorator ready" units, white box and grey box. White box units typically have drywall and some moldings and doors. A grey box unit is "bare bones" with no drywall or fixtures. Both require a licensed general contractor and some local permits.

Deed-in-Lieu of Foreclosure: A deed given by a borrower/owner to a lender to satisfy a mortgage debt and avoid foreclosure.

Default Interest: A higher interest rate payable after a borrower defaults on a loan.

Defendant: The person defending or denying; the party against whom the complaint is filed in an action or suit, or the accused in a criminal case.

Defense: The totality of the facts, law, and contentions presented by the defendant against whom a civil action or criminal prosecution is instituted in order to defeat or diminish the plaintiff's cause of action or the prosecutor's case.

Deficiency Judgment: A judgment for an amount exceeding the value of security put up for a loan or installment payments. These judgments are often sought to obtain the difference between the loan amount and what a property sold for at auction after a foreclosure.

Department of Housing and Urban Development (HUD): The federal department of the United States that administers federal programs dealing with better housing and urban renewal; created in 1965.

Department of Treasury: A cabinet department and the treasury of the United States government established by an Act of Congress in 1789 to manage government revenue.

Department of Veterans Affairs: A federal agency that guarantees loans made to veterans.

Deposition: The testimony of a party or witness in a civil or criminal proceeding taken before trial, usually in an attorney's office.

Derivative: A contract between two or more parties where the security is dependent on the price of another investment.

Dismiss: The ruling by a judge that all or a portion of the plaintiff's lawsuit is terminated or thrown out at that point without further evidence or testimony.

Encumbrance: Any item that hinders someone from holding clear title to a property, such as a loan, lease, easement, or restriction.

Equal Credit Opportunity Act (ECOA): A federal law requiring lenders to make credit available equally without discrimination based on race, color, religion, national origin, age, sex, marital status, or receipt of income from public assistance programs.

Equity: The amount of financial interest an owner has in a property after subtracting the amount still owed on the mortgage loan(s) from the fair market value of the property.

Equity Skimming: A form of predatory lending aimed at vulnerable, often low-income, uninformed home owners that began in the early 2000s in which investors or small companies take properties from foreclosed home owners in exchange for allowing the home owner to stay in the property as a tenant. Victims are often unaware that they are giving away their property and equity because of the complexity of the transaction and the false assurances given by rescue artists.

Event of Default: A term used in commercial loan documentation that refers to the occurrence of an event (e.g., late payments) that allows the lender to demand repayment of the loan in advance of its normal due date. When revolving credit is involved, an event of default usually also allows the lender to cancel any obligations for additional loan advances.

Fair Debt Collection Practices Act (FDCPA): A federal law passed in 1977 outlawing debtor harassment and other types of collection practices and regulating collection agencies, original creditors who set up a separate office to collect debts, and lawyers hired by the creditor to help collect overdue bills.

Fair Housing Act: Legislation requiring all covered multifamily dwellings built for first occupancy after March 13, 1991, to be designed and constructed in a manner that incorporates certain basic features of both accessibility and adaptable design, including usable doors, kitchens and bathrooms, reinforced walls for grab bars, and accessible and usable public and common-use areas.

Fair Issac Corporation (FICO): A person's credit score based on credit history and information from the three major credit bureaus; usually between a range of 300 and 850 points. The credit score is used by lenders and credit card companies to decide whether or not to grant a person credit and the interest rate that person will pay.

Fannie Mae (FNMA): The Federal National Mortgage Association—a quasi-governmental corporation authorized to sell bonds in order to supplement private mortgage funds by buying and selling FHA (Federal

Housing Administration) and VA (Veterans Affairs) loans at market prices.

Federal Deposit Insurance Corporation (FDIC): Provides deposit insurance that currently guarantees checking and savings deposits in member banks up to $100,000 per depositor. The insured amount was temporarily increased to $250,000 until 2010.

Federal Discount Window: An instrument of monetary policy (usually controlled by central banks) that allows eligible institutions to borrow money from the central bank, usually on a short-term basis, to meet temporary shortages of liquidity caused by internal or external disruptions.

Federal Home Loan Banking System (FHLBS): A government-sponsored enterprise established in 1932 to improve the supply of funds to lenders, including credit unions, thrifts, banks, and insurance companies that finance loans for home mortgages. With an AAA credit rating the system is able to borrow money at relatively low cost and pass the savings through to borrowers in the housing market.

Federal Housing Administration (FHA): A federal agency that insures first mortgages, enabling lenders to lend a very high percentage of the sale price.

Federal Reserve: The Fed, as it is commonly called, is the central bank of the United States and it regulates the US monetary and financial system. The Federal Reserve System is composed of the board of governors, a central governmental agency in Washington, DC, and twelve regional Federal Reserve Banks in major cities throughout the United States.

Final Judgment: The written determination (final decree or final decision) of a lawsuit by the judge who presided at trial that makes rulings on all issues and completes the case unless it is appealed to a higher court.

Financial Crimes Enforcement Network (FinCEN): A network administered by the United States Department of the Treasury whose goal it is to prevent and punish criminals and criminal networks that participate in money laundering. FinCEN operates domestically and internationally, and it consists of three major players: law enforcement agencies, the regulatory community, and the financial-services community.

5-1 Hybrid Adjustable-Rate Mortgage—5-1 Hybrid ARM: An adjustable-rate mortgage with an initial five-year fixed-interest rate, after which the interest rate adjusts on an annual basis according to an index plus a margin. The speed and the extent to which the interest rate can adjust are usually limited by an interest rate cap structure.

Fixed-Rate Mortgage: A mortgage loan where the interest rate on the note remains the same through the term of the loan.

Flipping: A term, most often applied to real estate and initial public offerings, which refers to the practice of buying an asset and quickly reselling ("flipping") it for profit.

Forbearance: A lender may decide not to take legal action when a borrower is late in making a payment. Usually this occurs when a borrower sets up a plan that both sides agree will bring overdue mortgage payments up to date.

Foreign Investment in Real Property Tax Act (FIRPTA): A US law that applies to the sale of interests held by nonresident aliens and foreign corporations in real property located within the United States. FIRPTA authorized the Internal Revenue Service (IRS) to apply a withholding income tax on nonresident aliens and foreign corporations with sales of US real property as well as sales of shares in certain US corporations that primarily hold and sell real property in the United States. When a person or corporation purchases a US real property interest from nonresident aliens or a foreign corporation, he is required to withhold 10 percent of the amount realized in order to ensure that the United States is able to tax the gains realized on the sale of such interests. A common exception to FIRPTA withholding is when a person purchases real estate to build or extend his or her own home and the purchase price is $300,000 or less.

Fraud for Profit: This type of fraud involves industry professionals and multiple loan transactions with several financial institutions involved. These frauds include numerous gross misrepresentations, including overstated income, assets, and collateral. Length of employment is overstated or fictitious employment is reported, and employment is backstopped by conspirators. The borrower's debts are not fully disclosed, nor is the borrower's credit history, which is often altered. Often, the borrower assumes the identity of another person (straw buyer). The borrower states he intends to use the property for occupancy when he/she intends to use the property for rental income, or is purchasing the property for another party (nominee). Appraisals almost always list the property as owner-occupied. Down payments do not exist or are borrowed and disguised with a fraudulent gift letter. The property value is inflated (through a faulty appraisal) to increase the sales value to make up for no down payment and to generate cash proceeds in fraud for profit.

Freddie Mac (FHLMC): Federal Home Loan Mortgage Corporation; a federally chartered corporation that purchases residential mortgages, securitizes them, and sells them to investors; this provides lenders with funds for new homebuyers. Also known as a Government-Sponsored Enterprise (GSE).

Ginnie Mae: Government National Mortgage Association (GNMA); a government-owned corporation overseen by the US Department of Housing and Urban Development that pools FHA-insured and VA-guaranteed loans to back securities for private investment.

Good Faith Estimate: An estimate of all closing fees, including prepaid and escrow items as well as lender charges, that must be given to the borrower within three days after submission of a loan application.

Government-Sponsored Enterprise (GSE): A collection of financial services corporations formed by the United States Congress to reduce interest rates for farmers and home owners, including, for example, Fannie Mae and Freddie Mac.

Greenlining Institute: A public policy, research, and advocacy nonprofit organization based in Berkeley, California. According to its mission statement, it "works to improve the quality of life for low-income and minority communities." It emphasizes encouraging and assisting the providing of business opportunities in the communities it serves. The institute takes its name from the practice of redlining, by which various services are denied or restricted in particular areas. "Greenlining" is a neologism for the opposite of redlining.

Gross Domestic Product (GDP): The total market value of all final goods and services produced within a country in a given period of time (usually a calendar year).

Hard-Money Loan: A specific type of asset-based loan financing in which a borrower receives funds based on the value of a parcel of real estate. Hard-money loans are typically issued at much higher interest rates than conventional commercial or residential property loans and are almost never issued by a commercial bank or other deposit institution. A hard-money loan is a species of real estate loan collateralized against the quick-sale value of the property for which the loan is made. Most lenders fund in the first lien position, meaning that in the event of a default, they are the first creditor to receive remuneration. Occasionally, a lender will subordinate to another first lien position loan; this loan is known as a mezzanine loan or second lien.

Harvard University's Joint Center for Housing Studies: The Joint Center for Housing Studies is Harvard University's center for information and research on housing in the United States.

Hearing: A legal proceeding where an issue of law or fact is tried and evidence is presented to help determine the issue.

Home Mortgage Disclosure Act HMDA (pronounced HUM-duh): An act passed in 1975 that requires financial institutions to maintain and annually disclose data about home purchases, home purchase pre-approvals, home improvement, and refinance applications involving one-to-four-unit and multifamily dwellings and also requires bank branches and loan centers to display a HMDA poster. HMDA was designed to help public officials to distribute public-sector investments, discover if financial institutions are serving the housing needs of communities, and identify where there are discriminatory lending practices.

Home Owners Loan Corporation (HOLC): A former US government agency established in 1933 to help stabilize real estate that had depreciated during the Depression and to refinance the urban mortgage debt. It granted long-term mortgage loans to some one million home owners facing the loss of their property. The HOLC ceased its lending activities in June 1936, by the terms of the Home Owners Loan Act.

HUD1 Statement: A "settlement sheet," or "closing statement," itemizing all closing costs, which must be given to the borrower at or before closing. Items that appear on the statement include real estate commissions, loan fees, points, and escrow amounts.

Inflation: The number of dollars in circulation exceeding the amount of goods and services available for purchase resulting in a decrease in the dollar's value. The annual rate at which consumer prices increase.

Interest: A fee charged for the use of borrowing money. The price paid for the use of capital.

Interrogatories: Written questions submitted to a party from his or her adversary to ascertain answers prepared in writing, which are signed under oath and have relevance to the issues in a lawsuit.

Interstate Land Sale Full Disclosure Act (ILSA): A federal law administered by HUD to control the sale of large, unimproved residential subdivisions and that requires certain disclosures and advertising procedures when selling land to purchasers in other states.

Judicial Foreclosure State: Any state in the nation in which foreclosed property is exposed to auction by a county sheriff or some other officer of the court in order to protect any equity a debtor may have in that property, in case the value of the debt being foreclosed on is substantially less than the market value of the immovable property.

Kickback: A clandestine payment in return for a favor, usually an illegal one.

Liar Loans: A mortgage loan in which the lender does not verify the borrower's stated income by looking at his or her pay stubs, W-2 forms, income tax returns, or other records; instead, the borrower is simply asked to state his or her income, and is taken at his or her word. These loans are intended for self-employed borrowers, or other borrowers who might have difficulty documenting their income but have been extended to customers with a wide range of credit histories, including subprime borrowers. The lack of verification makes these loans particularly easy targets for fraud.

Lien: A legal claim against property that must be satisfied when the property is sold. A claim of money against a property, wherein the value of the property is used as security in repayment of a debt. Examples include a mechanic's lien, which might be for the unpaid cost of building supplies, or a tax lien for unpaid property taxes. A lien is a defect on the title and needs to be settled before any transfer of ownership can take place. This is done through recording of a lien release (a written report of the settlement of a lien) in the public record as evidence of payment.

Lis Pendens: Latin for "suit pending." Any pending lawsuit or a specific situation with a public notice of litigation that has been recorded where the title of real property secures a plaintiff's claim on the property so that the sale, mortgage, or encumbrance of the property will not diminish the plaintiff's rights to the property, should the plaintiff prevail in its case. A foreclosure will wipe out a lis pendens.

Loan-to-Value (LTV) Ratio: A percentage calculated by dividing the amount borrowed by the price or appraised value of the home to be purchased; the higher the LTV, the less cash a borrower is required to pay as a down payment.

Loss Mitigation: A process to avoid foreclosure in which the lender tries to help a borrower who has been unable to make loan payments and is in danger of defaulting on his or her loan.

Mediation: A settlement of a dispute or controversy by setting up an independent person between two contending parties in order to aid them in the settlement of their disagreement.

Mezzanine Lender: Lenders that look for a certain minimum internal rate of return which can come from four sources: arrangement fee, cash interest, payment in kind, and warrants. The arrangement fee, usually payable upfront, contributes the least return and is more aimed to cover administrative costs. Cash interest is the same as interest, usually payable on the principal in equal periods until maturity. Payment in kind (PIK) is in addition to cash interest and accrues period after period, thus increasing the underlying principal (i.e., compound interest). The PIK part is due on maturity of the principal. The achieved selling price of the shares acquired under the warrant are also part of the total return of the lender. (See Mezzanine Loan.)

Mezzanine Loan: A relatively large loan, typically unsecured (i.e., not backed by a pledging of assets) or with a deeply subordinated security structure (e.g., third lien on the property but non-recourse vis-à-vis the borrower). Maturities usually exceed five years, with the principal payable at the end of the loan term. In a standard offer, the loan carries a detachable warrant (the option to purchase a certain number of shares of stock or bonds at a given price for a certain period of time) or a similar mechanism to allow the lender to share in the future success of the business. Mezzanine loans can be used in financing a start-up company or leveraged buyouts, usually as part of a larger financing package. Mezzanine loans are often used by developers to secure supplementary financing for development projects (typically in cases where the primary mortgage or construction loan equity requirements are larger than 10%). These types of mezzanine loans are often collateralized by the stock of the development company rather than the property itself, which allows the lender to seize underlying collateral in the event of default and foreclosure more rapidly.

Millage Rate: A permille or per mille (Latin "for (every) thousand") is a tenth of a percent or one part per thousand and when used to describe property taxation in the United States, it is called the millage rate.

Mini-Miranda Warning: A required disclosure in all communications made to collect a debt that the debt collector is attempting to collect a debt and that any information obtained will be used for that purpose.

Modification: A change or alteration in existing materials. The parties to a completed and binding contract are free to change the terms of the contract. Changes to a preexisting contract are called contract modifications.

If the parties agree to modify the contract, the modification will be enforceable in a court of law.

Mortgage: A lien on any property that secures the promise to repay a loan. A security agreement between the lender and the buyer in which the property is collateral for the loan. The mortgage gives the lender the right to collect payment on the loan and to foreclose if the loan obligations are not met.

Mortgage Asset Research Institute (MARI): A risk management service for the mortgage and banking industries and a leading provider of information services to the financial services industry, to provide innovative solutions and expand upon fraud-fighting services. MARI developed MIDEX to defend its subscribers against mortgage fraud and the perpetrators of fraudulent schemes.

Mortgage-Backed Security (MBS): A Fannie Mae security that represents an undivided interest in a group of mortgages. Holders of a security interest receive payments of principal and interest from the group of individual mortgage loans.

Mortgage Bankers Association (MBA): The national association, headquartered in Washington, that represents the real estate finance industry. The MBA works to help its members conduct the business of single and multifamily mortgage finance by promoting fair and ethical lending practices, fostering professional excellence through educational programs and publications, providing news and information, and holding conferences.

Mortgage Broker: An intermediary who locates mortgage loans from qualified lenders on behalf of individuals or businesses.

Mortgage Insurance Premium (MIP): A monthly payment usually included in the mortgage payment that is paid by a borrower for mortgage insurance that will pay the mortgage off if the insured dies or is incapacitated and unable to pay the loan.

Mortgage Servicing Rights (MSR): The right to collect monthly payments and penalties, record keeping, payment of insurance and taxes, and possible settlement of default involved with a mortgage loan.

Motion for Summary Judgment: A written request for a judgment in favor of one party before a lawsuit goes to trial and based on recorded (testimony outside court) affidavits (or declarations under penalty of perjury), depositions, admissions of fact, and answers to written interrogatories (written questions), claiming that all factual and legal issues can be decided in the requester's favor. These alleged facts are accompanied by a written legal brief (points and authorities) in support of the motion. The opposing party needs to show by affidavits or written declarations, or by points and authorities (written legal argument in support of the motion), that there are "triable issues of fact" and/or of law. If there are any triable issues, the motion must be denied and the case can go to trial. Sometimes, if there are several claims (causes of action), such a motion may cause the judge to find (decide) that some causes of action can be decided under the motion, leaving fewer matters actually to be tried. The paper work on both sides is complex, burdensome, and in many states, based on strict procedures.

National Community Reinvestment Coalition (NCRC): The NCRC was formed in 1990 by national, regional, and local organizations to develop and harness the collective energies of community reinvestment organizations from across the country so as to increase the flow of private capital into traditionally underserved communities. The NCRC has grown to an association of more than six hundred community-based organizations that promote access to basic banking services, including credit and savings, to create and sustain affordable housing, job development, and vibrant communities for America's working families. Members include community reinvestment organizations, community development corporations, local and state government agencies, faith-based institutions, community organizing and civil rights groups, and minority- and women-owned business associations, as well as local and social service providers from across the nation. The NCRC acts as the collective voice for its member organizations to Congress, bank regulatory agencies, the executive branches of the federal government, and the national press.

National Credit Union Administration (NCUA): The US federal agency that supervises and charters federal credit unions and insures savings in federal and most state-chartered credit unions across the country through the National Credit Union Share Insurance Fund (NCUSIF), a federal fund backed by the full faith and credit of the United States government.

National Housing Act: Passed in 1934 during the Great Depression, the act was to make housing and home mortgages more affordable. It created the Federal Housing Administration (FHA) and the Federal Savings and Loan Insurance Corporation. It was designed to stop the tide of bank foreclosures on family homes.

Nationally Recognized Statistical Ratings Organizations (NRSRO): A credit rating agency that issues credit ratings that the US Securities and Exchange Commission (SEC) permits other financial firms to use for certain regulatory purposes.

Negative Equity: See Upside-Down Mortgage Loan.

Nonconforming loan: A loan that exceeds Fannie Mae's and Freddie Mac's loan limits. Freddie Mac and Fannie Mae loans are referred to as conforming loans.

Nonconsensual: Existing or entered into without mutual consent or formalization by document or ceremony.

Office of Federal Housing Enterprise Oversight (OFHEO): An agency within the Department of Housing and Urban Development charged with ensuring the capital adequacy, financial safety, and soundness of two government-sponsored enterprises—the Federal National Mortgage Association (Fannie Mae) and the Federal Home Loan Mortgage Corporation (Freddie Mac).

Office of the Comptroller of Currency (OCC): A government office with an official, appointed by the president of the United States, who controls all national banks and receives reports from the banks at least quarterly, to be published in newspapers.

Office of Thrift Supervision (OTS): An agency of the US Treasury Department responsible for the US savings and loan industry.

Order: A direction of a court or judge normally made in writing, and not included in a judgment, which determines some point or directs some step in a legal proceeding.

Origination: The process through which a mortgage lender creates a mortgage secured by some amount of the mortgagor's real property, also known as loan origination, the terms of the mortgage agreement (amount of loan, interest rate, compounding frequency, etc) are established, and the involved parties legally bind themselves to the transaction.

Perfected: Having completed all necessary legal steps to achieve a result, such as perfected title to property.

Pleadings: The formal presentation of claims and defenses by parties to a lawsuit. The specific papers by which the allegations of parties to a lawsuit are presented in proper form; specifically the complaint of a plaintiff and the answer of a defendant plus any additional responses to those papers that are authorized by law.

Points: A point is equal to one percent of the principal amount of a mortgage.

Pool: A combination of similar mortgages used as collateral for loans or for participation certificates sold to investors. Also called mortgage pool.

Prepayment Penalty: A provision contained in some loans that charges a fee to a borrower who pays off a loan before it is due.

Principal: The amount borrowed or the amount still owed on a loan, separate from interest.

Processor: A person who prepares a loan for underwriting by making certain the borrower's income is properly documented and verified, the appraisal is being performed, and title and escrow are opened.

Promissory Note: A written, dated, and signed two-party instrument containing an unconditional promise by the maker to pay a definite sum of money to a payee on demand or at a specified future date.

Rate Adjustment Cap: A limit on an adjustable-rate mortgage on how much the interest rate or mortgage payment may rise or fall on the adjustment dates and over the life of the loan.

Rate Cap: An upper limit on the interesst rates charged for a loan.

Rate Sheet: A term used to describe how lenders communicate via computer or fax, the interest rates, terms, and costs of loan products available to mortgage brokers. Interest rates can change several times a day. Each lender provides its approved mortgage brokers with the current rate sheet for its loan products.

Ratings Agency: A company that assigns credit ratings for issuers of certain types of debt obligations as well as the debt instruments themselves. In some cases, the servicers of the underlying debt are also given ratings. In most cases, the issuers of securities are companies, special purpose entities, state and local governments, nonprofit organizations, or national governments issuing debtlike securities (i.e., bonds) that can be traded on a secondary market. A credit rating for an issuer takes into consideration the issuer's credit worthiness (i.e., its ability to pay back a loan) and affects the interest rate applied to the particular security being issued. (In contrast to credit reporting agencies, companies that issue credit scores for individual credit worthiness are generally called credit bureaus or consumer credit reporting agencies.)

Real Estate Owned (REO): A term used for property acquired through lender foreclosure that is currently held in inventory by a bank.

Real Estate Settlement Procedures Act (RESPA): A law requiring lenders to disclose all settlement costs, practices, and relationships in order to protect consumers from abuses during the residential real estate purchase and loan process.

Reassess: The process of revising or updating the estimate of value of property for taxation purposes.

Recession: A general economic slowdown in the general business economy and/or a condition officially declared by the government after two consecutive quarters of reduced gross domestic product.

Refinance: The paying off of an existing mortgage loan obligation by extending or renewing existing financing or taking on a new loan obligation in its place.

Regulation Z (Reg Z): The regulations issued by the board of governors of the Federal Reserve system to aid in the implementation of the Truth-in-Lending Act that require lending institutions to disclosure to and inform borrowers of the true cost of obtaining credit.

Reverse Mortgage (Home Equity Conversion Mortgage [HECM]): A loan used by senior home owners age sixty-two and older to convert the equity in their home into monthly streams of income and/or a line of credit to be repaid when they no longer occupy the home. A lending institution such as a mortgage lender, bank, credit union, or savings and loan association funds the FHA-insured loan.

Satisfaction of Mortgage: The document issued by the mortgagee when the mortgage loan is paid in full. Also called a "release of mortgage."

Secondary Mortgage Market: The place where primary mortgage lenders sell the mortgages they make to obtain more funds to originate more new loans. It provides liquidity for the lenders.

Securities and Exchange Commission (SEC): A government commission created by Congress to regulate the securities markets and protect investors. In addition to regulation and protection, it also monitors corporate takeovers in the United States. The SEC is composed of five commissioners appointed by the US president and approved by the Senate. The statutes administered by the SEC are designed to promote full public disclosure and to protect the investing public against fraudulent and manipulative practices in the securities markets. Generally, most issues of securities offered in interstate commerce, through the mail or on the Internet, must be registered with the SEC.

Securitization: The process through which an issuer creates a financial instrument by combining other financial assets and then marketing different tiers of the repackaged instruments to investors. The process can encompass any type of financial asset and promotes liquidity in the marketplace. Mortgage-backed securities are an example of securitization. By combining mortgages into one large pool, the issuer can divide the large pool into smaller pieces based on each individual mortgage's inherent risk of default and then sell those smaller pieces to investors. The process creates liquidity by enabling smaller investors to purchase shares in a larger asset pool. Using the mortgage-backed security example, individual retail investors are able to purchase portions of a mortgage as a type of bond. Without the securitization of mortgages, retail investors may not be able to afford to buy into a large pool of mortgages.

Security: The property that will be pledged as collateral for a loan.

Servicing: The supervising and administering of a loan after it has been made that involves such things as collecting the payments, keeping accounting records, computing the principal and interest, delinquent loan follow-up, and foreclosing on defaulted loans.

Short Sale: The sale of a property by a financially distressed borrower for less than the outstanding mortgage balance due where the sale proceeds will be used to repay the lender and the borrower will be released from the mortgage obligation. The lender then accepts the less-than-full repayment of the mortgage in order to avoid what would amount to larger losses if it were to foreclose on the mortgage.

Stagflation: A condition of relatively high unemployment and slow economic growth accompanied by a rise in prices, or inflation.

Stare decisis (Latin for Let the decision stand): The policy of courts to abide by or adhere to principles established by decisions in earlier cases.

Stay: A provision under the US Bankruptcy Code prohibiting creditors from beginning or continuing proceedings for collecting owed amounts from a firm who files for bankruptcy under Chapter 11.

Straw Buyers: A form of fraud in which an investor may use a third person, false income documents, and false credit reports to obtain a mortgage loan in the third person's name. Subsequent to closing, the straw buyer signs the property over to the investor in a quit claim deed that relinquishes all rights to the property and provides no guarantee to title. The investor does not make any mortgage payments and rents the property until foreclosure takes place several months later. The identity of the borrower is concealed through the use of a nominee who allows the borrower to use the nominee's name and credit history to apply for a loan.

Structured Investment Vehicle (SIV): A pool of investment assets that attempts to profit from credit spreads between short-term debt and long-term structured finance products such as asset-backed securities (ABS). Funding for SIVs comes from the issuance of commercial paper that is continuously renewed or rolled over; the proceeds are then invested in longer maturity assets that have less liquidity but pay higher yields. The SIV earns profits on the spread between incoming cash flows (principal and interest payments on ABS) and the high-rated commercial paper that it issues. SIVs often employ great amounts of leverage to generate returns. SIVs are less regulated than other investment pools and are typically held off the balance sheet by large financial institutions such as commercial banks and investment houses. They gained much attention during the housing and subprime fallout of 2007; tens of billions in the value of off–balance sheet SIVs was written down as investors fled from subprime mortgage–related assets.

Many investors were caught off-guard by the losses because little is publicly known about the specifics of SIVs, including such basics as what assets are held and what regulations determine their actions. SIVs essentially allow their managing financial institutions to employ leverage in a way that the parent company would be unable to due to capital requirement regulations.

Subpoena: A legal document requiring a person to appear before a court of law at a specified time to give testimony.

Subprime Mortgage: A type of mortgage that is normally given to borrowers with lower credit ratings. Due to the borrower's lowered credit rating, a conventional mortgage is not offered because the lender views the borrower as having a larger-than-average risk of defaulting on the loan. Lending institutions often charge higher interest rates on subprime mortgages than on conventional mortgages in order to compensate themselves for carrying more risk.

Summons: An official order requiring a person to attend court, either to answer a charge or to give evidence.

Suspicious Activity Report (SAR): One of the tools provided under the Bank Secrecy Act (BSA) as a way of monitoring suspicious activities that seem out of the ordinary, if they give rise to a suspicion that the account holder is attempting to hide something or avoid reporting under the BSA that would not ordinarily be flagged under other reports (such as the currency transaction report).

Teaser Interest Rate: An initial rate on an adjustable-rate mortgage (ARM) that is typically below the going market rate and is used by lenders to entice borrowers to choose ARMs over traditional mortgages. The teaser rate will be in effect for only a few months, at which point the rate will gradually climb until it reaches the full indexed rate, which will be a static margin rate plus the floating rate index to which the mortgage is tied (usually the LIBOR index).

Title Insurance: Insurance that protects the lender against any claims that arise from arguments about ownership of the property; also available for homebuyers. An insurance policy guaranteeing the accuracy of a title search that protects against errors. Most lenders require the buyer to purchase title insurance protecting the lender against loss in the event of a title defect. This charge is included in the closing costs. A policy that protects the buyer from title defects is known as an owner's policy and requires an additional charge.

Toxic Waste: A slang term referring to securities that are unattractive due to certain underlying provisions or risks making them generally illiquid (unable to sell for cash) with poor pricing schemes and transparency.

Tranche: A group of related securities offered as part of the same transaction, the word *tranche* is French for slice, section, series, or portion. In the financial sense of the word, each bond is a different slice of the deal's risk. Transaction documentation usually defines the tranches as different "classes" of notes, each identified by letter (e.g., the Class A, Class B, Class C securities).

Truth-in-Lending: A federal law obligating a lender to give full written disclosure of all fees, terms, and conditions associated with a loan.

Underwriter: A company or other entity that administers the public issuance and distribution of securities from a corporation or other issuing body by working closely with the issuing body to determine the offering price of the securities, buying them from the issuer and selling them to investors via the underwriter's distribution network.

Upside-Down Mortgage Loan: Refers to owing more on a loan than the value of the asset for which the loan was used to purchase and occurs when the asset depreciates in value or was overvalued when the buyer purchased the asset. Also known as Negative Equity

Value at Risk (VaR): A technique used to estimate the probability of portfolio losses based on the statistical analysis of historical price trends and volatilities.

Workout: A variety of negotiated agreements one might arrange with creditors to address a debt that one is having trouble paying. Most commonly, a workout is devised between a mortgagee and mortgagor to restructure or modify a loan to avoid foreclosure.

Writ of Possession: An order directing a sheriff to put a person in peaceable possession of property recovered after ejection.

Yield Spread: The difference between yields on differing debt instruments that is calculated by deducting the yield of one instrument from another. The higher the yield spread, the greater the difference between the yields offered by each instrument. The spread can be measured between debt instruments of differing maturities, credit ratings, and risk.

APPENDIX A

SAMPLE AMORTIZATION TABLE

Amortization Schedule

Month	**Interest**	**Principal**	**Balance**
First Two Years			
Nov, 2008	$812.50	$135.60	$149,864.40
Dec, 2008	$811.77	$136.34	$149,728.06
Jan, 2009	$811.03	$137.08	$149,590.99
Feb, 2009	$810.28	$137.82	$149,453.17
Mar, 2009	$809.54	$138.56	$149,314.60
Apr, 2009	$808.79	$139.31	$149,175.29
May, 2009	$808.03	$140.07	$149,035.22
Jun, 2009	$807.27	$140.83	$148,894.39
Jul, 2009	$806.51	$141.59	$148,752.80
Aug, 2009	$805.74	$142.36	$148,610.44
Sep, 2009	$804.97	$143.13	$148,467.32
Oct, 2009	$804.20	$143.90	$148,323.41
Nov, 2009	$803.42	$144.68	$148,178.73
Dec, 2009	$802.63	$145.47	$148,033.26
Jan, 2010	$801.85	$146.26	$147,887.01
Feb, 2010	$801.05	$147.05	$147,739.96
Mar, 2010	$800.26	$147.84	$147,592.11
Apr, 2010	$799.46	$148.64	$147,443.47
May, 2010	$798.65	$149.45	$147,294.02
Jun, 2010	$797.84	$150.26	$147,143.76
Jul, 2010	$797.03	$151.07	$146,992.69

Aug, 2010	$796.21	$151.89	$146,840.80
Sep, 2010	$795.39	$152.71	$146,688.08
Oct, 2010	$794.56	$153.54	$146,534.54

Middle Two Years

Nov, 2023	$589.54	$358.56	$108,480.15
Dec, 2023	$587.60	$360.50	$108,119.65
Jan, 2024	$585.65	$362.45	$107,757.20
Feb, 2024	$583.68	$364.42	$107,392.78
Mar, 2024	$581.71	$366.39	$107,026.39
Apr, 2024	$579.73	$368.38	$106,658.01
May, 2024	$577.73	$370.37	$106,287.64
Jun, 2024	$575.72	$372.38	$105,915.27
Jul, 2024	$573.71	$374.39	$105,540.87
Aug, 2024	$571.68	$376.42	$105,164.45
Sep, 2024	$569.64	$378.46	$104,785.99
Oct, 2024	$567.59	$380.51	$104,405.48
Nov, 2024	$565.53	$382.57	$104,022.90
Dec, 2024	$563.46	$384.64	$103,638.26
Jan, 2025	$561.37	$386.73	$103,251.53
Feb, 2025	$559.28	$388.82	$102,862.71
Mar, 2025	$557.17	$390.93	$102,471.78
Apr, 2025	$555.06	$393.05	$102,078.73
May, 2025	$552.93	$395.18	$101,683.56
Jun, 2025	$550.79	$397.32	$101,286.24
Jul, 2025	$548.63	$399.47	$100,886.77
Aug, 2025	$546.47	$401.63	$100,485.14
Sep, 2025	$544.29	$403.81	$100,081.33
Oct, 2025	$542.11	$405.99	$99,675.34

Last Two Years

Nov, 2036	$115.29	$832.82	$20,450.73
Dec, 2036	$110.77	$837.33	$19,613.40
Jan, 2037	$106.24	$841.86	$18,771.54
Feb, 2037	$101.68	$846.42	$17,925.11

Mar, 2037	$97.09	$851.01	$17,074.11
Apr, 2037	$92.48	$855.62	$16,218.49
May, 2037	$87.85	$860.25	$15,358.24
Jun, 2037	$83.19	$864.91	$14,493.32
Jul, 2037	$78.51	$869.60	$13,623.73
Aug, 2037	$73.80	$874.31	$12,749.42
Sep, 2037	$69.06	$879.04	$11,870.38
Oct, 2037	$64.30	$883.80	$10,986.57
Nov, 2037	$59.51	$888.59	$10,097.98
Dec, 2037	$54.70	$893.40	$9,204.58
Jan, 2038	$49.86	$898.24	$8,306.33
Feb, 2038	$44.99	$903.11	$7,403.23
Mar, 2038	$40.10	$908.00	$6,495.22
Apr, 2038	$35.18	$912.92	$5,582.30
May, 2038	$30.24	$917.86	$4,664.44
Jun, 2038	$25.27	$922.84	$3,741.60
Jul, 2038	$20.27	$927.84	$2,813.77
Aug, 2038	$15.24	$932.86	$1,880.91
Sep, 2038	$10.19	$937.91	$942.99
Oct, 2038	$5.11	$942.99	$0.00

APPENDIX B

MORTGAGE LOAN APPLICATION (1003)

Uniform Residential Loan Application

This application is designed to be completed by the applicant(s) with the Lender's assistance. Applicants should complete this form as "Borrower" or "Co-Borrower," as applicable. Co-Borrower information must also be provided (and the appropriate box checked) when ☐ the income or assets of a person other than the Borrower (including the Borrower's spouse) will be used as a basis for loan qualification or ☐ the income or assets of the Borrower's spouse or other person who has community property rights pursuant to state law will not be used as a basis for loan qualification, but his or her liabilities must be considered because the spouse or other person has community property rights pursuant to applicable law and Borrower resides in a community property state, the security property is located in a community property state, or the Borrower is relying on other property located in a community property state as a basis for repayment of the loan.

If this is an application for joint credit, Borrower and Co-Borrower each agree that we intend to apply for joint credit (sign below):

Borrower

Co-Borrower

I. TYPE OF MORTGAGE AND TERMS OF LOAN

Mortgage Applied for: ☐ VA ☐ Conventional ☐ Other (explain): ☐ FHA ☐ USDA/Rural Housing Service | Agency Case Number | Lender Case Number

Amount $ | Interest Rate % | No. of Months | **Amortization Type:** ☐ Fixed Rate ☐ Other (explain): ☐ GPM ☐ ARM (type):

II. PROPERTY INFORMATION AND PURPOSE OF LOAN

Subject Property Address (street, city, state & ZIP) | No. of Units

Legal Description of Subject Property (attach description if necessary) | Year Built

Purpose of Loan ☐ Purchase ☐ Construction ☐ Other (explain): ☐ Refinance ☐ Construction-Permanent | Property will be: ☐ Primary Residence ☐ Secondary Residence ☐ Investment

Complete this line if construction or construction-permanent loan.

Year Lot Acquired	Original Cost	Amount Existing Liens	(a) Present Value of Lot	(b) Cost of Improvements	Total (a + b)
	$	$	$	$	$

Complete this line if this is a refinance loan.

Year Acquired	Original Cost	Amount Existing Liens	Purpose of Refinance	Describe Improvements ☐ made ☐ to be made
	$	$		Cost: $

Title will be held in what Name(s) | Manner in which Title will be held | Estate will be held in: ☐ Fee Simple ☐ Leasehold (show expiration date)

Source of Down Payment, Settlement Charges, and/or Subordinate Financing (explain)

Borrower — III. BORROWER INFORMATION — Co-Borrower

Borrower	Co-Borrower
Borrower's Name (include Jr. or Sr. if applicable)	Co-Borrower's Name (include Jr. or Sr. if applicable)
Social Security Number / Home Phone (incl. area code) / DOB (mm/dd/yyyy) / Yrs. School	Social Security Number / Home Phone (incl. area code) / DOB (mm/dd/yyyy) / Yrs. School
☐ Married ☐ Unmarried (include single, divorced, widowed) ☐ Separated / Dependents (not listed by Co-Borrower) no. ages	☐ Married ☐ Unmarried (include single, divorced, widowed) ☐ Separated / Dependents (not listed by Borrower) no. ages
Present Address (street, city, state, ZIP) ☐ Own ☐ Rent ____ No. Yrs.	Present Address (street, city, state, ZIP) ☐ Own ☐ Rent ____ No. Yrs.
Mailing Address, if different from Present Address	Mailing Address, if different from Present Address

If residing at present address for less than two years, complete the following:

Borrower	Co-Borrower
Former Address (street, city, state, ZIP) ☐ Own ☐ Rent ____ No. Yrs.	Former Address (street, city, state, ZIP) ☐ Own ☐ Rent ____ No. Yrs.

Borrower — IV. EMPLOYMENT INFORMATION — Co-Borrower

Borrower	Co-Borrower
Name & Address of Employer ☐ Self Employed / Yrs. on this job / Yrs. employed in this line of work/profession	Name & Address of Employer ☐ Self Employed / Yrs. on this job / Yrs. employed in this line of work/profession
Position/Title/Type of Business / Business Phone (incl. area code)	Position/Title/Type of Business / Business Phone (incl. area code)

If employed in current position for less than two years or if currently employed in more than one position, complete the following:

Borrower	Co-Borrower
Name & Address of Employer ☐ Self Employed / Dates (from - to) / Monthly Income $	Name & Address of Employer ☐ Self Employed / Dates (from - to) / Monthly Income $
Position/Title/Type of Business / Business Phone (incl. area code)	Position/Title/Type of Business / Business Phone (incl. area code)
Name & Address of Employer ☐ Self Employed / Dates (from - to) / Monthly Income $	Name & Address of Employer ☐ Self Employed / Dates (from - to) / Monthly Income $
Position/Title/Type of Business / Business Phone (incl. area code)	Position/Title/Type of Business / Business Phone (incl. area code)

V. MONTHLY INCOME AND COMBINED HOUSING EXPENSE INFORMATION

Gross Monthly Income	Borrower	Co-Borrower	Total	Combined Monthly Housing Expense	Present	Proposed
Base Empl. Income*	$	$	$	Rent	$	
Overtime				First Mortgage (P&I)		$
Bonuses				Other Financing (P&I)		
Commissions				Hazard Insurance		
Dividends/Interest				Real Estate Taxes		
Net Rental Income				Mortgage Insurance		
Other (before completing, see the notice in "describe other income," below)				Homeowner Assn. Dues		
				Other:		
Total	$	$	$	**Total**	$	$

* Self Employed Borrower(s) may be required to provide additional documentation such as tax returns and financial statements.

B/C	Describe Other Income Notice: Alimony, child support, or separate maintenance income need not be revealed if the Borrower (B) or Co-Borrower (C) does not choose to have it considered for repaying this loan.	Monthly Amount
		$

VI. ASSETS AND LIABILITIES

This Statement and any applicable supporting schedules may be completed jointly by both married and unmarried Co-Borrowers if their assets and liabilities are sufficiently joined so that the Statement can be meaningfully and fairly presented on a combined basis; otherwise, separate Statements and Schedules are required. If the Co-Borrower section was completed about a non-applicant spouse or other person, this Statement and supporting schedules must be completed about that spouse or other person also.

Completed ☐ Jointly ☐ Not Jointly

ASSETS Description	Cash or Market Value
Cash deposit toward purchase held by:	$
List checking and savings accounts below	
Name and address of Bank, S&L, or Credit Union	
Acct. no.	$
Name and address of Bank, S&L, or Credit Union	
Acct. no.	$
Name and address of Bank, S&L, or Credit Union	
Acct. no.	$
Name and address of Bank, S&L, or Credit Union	
Acct. no.	$
Stocks & Bonds (Company name/number & description)	$
Life insurance net cash value Face amount: $	$
Subtotal Liquid Assets	$
Real estate owned (enter market value from schedule of real estate owned)	$
Vested interest in retirement fund	$
Net worth of business(es) owned (attach financial statement)	$
Automobiles owned (make and year)	$
Other Assets (itemize)	$
Total Assets a.	$

Liabilities and Pledged Assets. List the creditor's name, address, and account number for all outstanding debts, including automobile loans, revolving charge accounts, real estate loans, alimony, child support, stock pledges, etc. Use continuation sheet, if necessary. Indicate by (*) those liabilities, which will be satisfied upon sale of real estate owned or upon refinancing of the subject property.

LIABILITIES	Monthly Payment & Months Left to Pay	Unpaid Balance
Name and address of Company Acct. no.	$ Payment/Months	$
Name and address of Company Acct. no.	$ Payment/Months	$
Name and address of Company Acct. no.	$ Payment/Months	$
Name and address of Company Acct. no.	$ Payment/Months	$
Name and address of Company Acct. no.	$ Payment/Months	$
Name and address of Company Acct. no.	$ Payment/Months	$
Name and address of Company Acct. no.	$ Payment/Months	$
Alimony/Child Support/Separate Maintenance Payments Owed to:	$	
Job-Related Expense (child care, union dues, etc.)	$	
Total Monthly Payments	$	
Net Worth (a minus b) ► $	**Total Liabilities b.**	$

Freddie Mac Form 65 7/05
Fannie Mae Form 1003 7/05
VMP-21N (0507)

Page 2 of 4

Initials: ________

VI. ASSETS AND LIABILITIES (cont'd)

Schedule of Real Estate Owned (If additional properties are owned, use continuation sheet.)

Property Address (enter S if sold, PS if pending sale or R if rental being held for income)	▼	Type of Property	Present Market Value	Amount of Mortgages & Liens	Gross Rental Income	Mortgage Payments	Insurance, Maintenance, Taxes & Misc.	Net Rental Income
			$	$	$	$	$	$
		Totals	$	$	$	$	$	$

List any additional names under which credit has previously been received and indicate appropriate creditor name(s) and account number(s):

Alternate Name	Creditor Name	Account Number

VII. DETAILS OF TRANSACTION

a. Purchase price	$
b. Alterations, improvements, repairs	
c. Land (if acquired separately)	
d. Refinance (incl. debts to be paid off)	
e. Estimated prepaid items	
f. Estimated closing costs	
g. PMI, MIP, Funding Fee	
h. Discount (if Borrower will pay)	
i. Total costs (add items a through h)	
j. Subordinate financing	
k. Borrower's closing costs paid by Seller	
l. Other Credits (explain)	
m. Loan amount (exclude PMI, MIP, Funding Fee financed)	
n. PMI, MIP, Funding Fee financed	
o. Loan amount (add m & n)	
p. Cash from/to Borrower (subtract j, k, l & o from i)	

VIII. DECLARATIONS

If you answer "Yes" to any questions a through i, please use continuation sheet for explanation.	Borrower Yes	Borrower No	Co-Borrower Yes	Co-Borrower No
a. Are there any outstanding judgments against you?	☐	☐	☐	☐
b. Have you been declared bankrupt within the past 7 years?	☐	☐	☐	☐
c. Have you had property foreclosed upon or given title or deed in lieu thereof in the last 7 years?	☐	☐	☐	☐
d. Are you a party to a lawsuit?	☐	☐	☐	☐
e. Have you directly or indirectly been obligated on any loan which resulted in foreclosure, transfer of title in lieu of foreclosure, or judgment? (This would include such loans as home mortgage loans, SBA loans, home improvement loans, educational loans, manufactured (mobile) home loans, any mortgage, financial obligation, bond, or loan guarantee. If "Yes," provide details, including date, name, and address of Lender, FHA or VA case number, if any, and reasons for the action.)	☐	☐	☐	☐
f. Are you presently delinquent or in default on any Federal debt or any other loan, mortgage, financial obligation, bond, or loan guarantee? If "Yes," give details as described in the preceding question.	☐	☐	☐	☐
g. Are you obligated to pay alimony, child support, or separate maintenance?	☐	☐	☐	☐
h. Is any part of the down payment borrowed?	☐	☐	☐	☐
i. Are you a co-maker or endorser on a note?	☐	☐	☐	☐
j. Are you a U.S. citizen?	☐	☐	☐	☐
k. Are you a permanent resident alien?	☐	☐	☐	☐
l. Do you intend to occupy the property as your primary residence? If "Yes," complete question m below.	☐	☐	☐	☐
m. Have you had an ownership interest in a property in the last three years?	☐	☐	☐	☐
(1) What type of property did you own - - principal residence (PR), second home (SH), or investment property (IP)?	____		____	
(2) How did you hold title to the home - - solely by yourself (S), jointly with your spouse (SP), or jointly with another person (O)?	____		____	

IX. ACKNOWLEDGEMENT AND AGREEMENT

Each of the undersigned specifically represents to Lender and to Lender's actual or potential agents, brokers, processors, attorneys, insurers, servicers, successors and assigns and agrees and acknowledges that: (1) the information provided in this application is true and correct as of the date set forth opposite my signature and that any intentional or negligent misrepresentation of this information contained in this application may result in civil liability, including monetary damages, to any person who may suffer any loss due to reliance upon any misrepresentation that I have made on this application, and/or in criminal penalties including, but not limited to, fine or imprisonment or both under the provisions of Title 18, United States Code, Sec. 1001, et seq.; (2) the loan requested pursuant to this application (the "Loan") will be secured by a mortgage or deed of trust on the property described in this application; (3) the property will not be used for any illegal or prohibited purpose or use; (4) all statements made in this application are made for the purpose of obtaining a residential mortgage loan; (5) the property will be occupied as indicated in this application; (6) the Lender, its servicers, successors or assigns may retain the original and/or an electronic record of this application, whether or not the Loan is approved; (7) the Lender and its agents, brokers, insurers, servicers, successors, and assigns may continuously rely on the information contained in the application, and I am obligated to amend and/or supplement the information provided in this application if any of the material facts that I have represented herein should change prior to closing of the Loan; (8) in the event that my payments on the Loan become delinquent, the Lender, its servicers, successors or assigns may, in addition to any other rights and remedies that it may have relating to such delinquency, report my name and account information to one or more consumer reporting agencies; (9) ownership of the Loan and/or administration of the Loan account may be transferred with such notice as may be required by law; (10) neither Lender nor its agents, brokers, insurers, servicers, successors or assigns has made any representation or warranty, express or implied, to me regarding the property or the condition or value of the property; and (11) my transmission of this application as an "electronic record" containing my "electronic signature," as those terms are defined in applicable federal and/or state laws (excluding audio and video recordings), or my facsimile transmission of this application containing a facsimile of my signature, shall be as effective, enforceable and valid as if a paper version of this application were delivered containing my original written signature.

Acknowledgement. Each of the undersigned hereby acknowledges that any owner of the Loan, its servicers, successors and assigns, may verify or reverify any information contained in this application or obtain any information or data relating to the Loan, for any legitimate business purpose through any source, including a source named in this application or a consumer reporting agency.

Borrower's Signature	Date	Co-Borrower's Signature	Date
X		X	

X. INFORMATION FOR GOVERNMENT MONITORING PURPOSES

The following information is requested by the Federal Government for certain types of loans related to a dwelling in order to monitor the lender's compliance with equal credit opportunity, fair housing and home mortgage disclosure laws. You are not required to furnish this information, but are encouraged to do so. The law provides that a lender may not discriminate either on the basis of this information, or on whether you choose to furnish it. If you furnish the information, please provide both ethnicity and race. For race, you may check more than one designation. If you do not furnish ethnicity, race, or sex, under Federal regulations, this lender is required to note the information on the basis of visual observation and surname if you have made this application in person. If you do not wish to furnish the information, please check the box below. (Lender must review the above material to assure that the disclosures satisfy all requirements to which the lender is subject under applicable state law for the particular type of loan applied for.)

BORROWER	☐ I do not wish to furnish this information.			**CO-BORROWER**	☐ I do not wish to furnish this information.		
Ethnicity:	☐ Hispanic or Latino	☐ Not Hispanic or Latino		**Ethnicity:**	☐ Hispanic or Latino	☐ Not Hispanic or Latino	
Race:	☐ American Indian or Alaska Native	☐ Asian	☐ Black or African American	**Race:**	☐ American Indian or Alaska Native	☐ Asian	☐ Black or African American
	☐ Native Hawaiian or Other Pacific Islander	☐ White			☐ Native Hawaiian or Other Pacific Islander	☐ White	
Sex:	☐ Female	☐ Male		**Sex:**	☐ Female	☐ Male	

To be Completed by Interviewer	Interviewer's Name (print or type)		Name and Address of Interviewer's Employer
This application was taken by:			
☐ Face-to-face interview	Interviewer's Signature	Date	
☐ Mail			
☐ Telephone	Interviewer's Phone Number (incl. area code)		
☐ Internet			

CONTINUATION SHEET/RESIDENTIAL LOAN APPLICATION		
Use this continuation sheet if you need more space to complete the Residential Loan Application. Mark **B** for Borrower or **C** for Co-Borrower.	Borrower:	Agency Case Number:
	Co-Borrower:	Lender Case Number:

I/We fully understand that it is a Federal crime punishable by fine or imprisonment, or both, to knowingly make any false statements concerning any of the above facts as applicable under the provisions of Title 18, United States Code, Section 1001, et seq.

Borrower's Signature:	Date	Co-Borrower's Signature:	Date
X		**X**	

Freddie Mac Form 65 7/05
Fannie Mae Form 1003 7/05
VMP®-21N (0507)

APPENDIX C

RELEVANT GOVERNMENT AGENCIES

CONFERENCE OF STATE BANK SUPERVISORS (CSBS)

http://www.csbs.org/

Founded in 1902 as a clearinghouse for ideas to solve common problems of state bank regulators, the Conference of State Bank Supervisors (CSBS) has evolved into a vital force that strengthens state banking departments. For one hundred years, CSBS has been uniquely positioned as the only national organization dedicated to protecting and advancing our nation's dual banking system. Through CSBS, state bank regulatory agencies and state-chartered banks continue to champion a system that offers competitive chartering options, efficient and effective supervision, and a lower cost of regulation for all banks. CSBS works to: optimize the authority of individual states to determine the activities of their financial institutions, enhance the professionalism of state banking departments and their personnel, represent the interests of the state banking system to federal and state legislative and regulatory agencies, and ensure that all banks continue to have the choice and flexibility of the state charter in the new era of financial modernization.

FEDERAL FINANCIAL INSTITUTIONS EXAMINATION COUNCIL (FFIEC)

http://www.ffiec.gov/default.htm

The council is a formal interagency body empowered to prescribe uniform principles, standards, and report forms for the federal examination of financial institutions by the board of governors of the Federal Reserve System, the Federal Deposit Insurance Corporation, the National Credit Union Administration, the Office of the Comptroller of the Currency, and the Office of Thrift Supervision, and to make recommendations to promote uniformity in the supervision of financial institutions. In 2006, the State Liaison Committee (SLC) was added to the council as a voting member. The SLC includes representatives from the Conference of State Bank Supervisors, the American Council of State Savings Supervisors, and the National Association of State Credit Union Supervisors.

FEDERAL DEPOSIT INSURANCE CORPORATION (FDIC)

http://www.fdic.gov

The FDIC was created in 1933 in response to the thousands of bank failures that occurred in the 1920s and early 1930s. America's Great Depression of the late 1920s and early 1930s caused many financial problems. Thousands of banks failed between the stock market crash of October 1929 and March of 1933. Many people who had money in banks lost some or all of it when their banks failed. President Franklin D. Roosevelt and Congress made several changes. In June of 1933, the FDIC was created to provide a federal government guarantee of deposits. The guarantee says a person's money, within certain limits, would be safe. Since the start of FDIC insurance, no one has lost a cent of insured money because of a bank failure. The FDIC's biggest job is insuring the savings of millions of Americans in all the FDIC insured banks across the country. The FDIC also visits banks on a regular basis to make sure they are following the rules they need to follow. These rules, called regulations, make sure the bank operates profitably and fairly. For example, one rule banks have to follow is called the Equal Credit Opportunity Act. It says that a bank can't refuse to loan money to someone just because of his or her color, religion, national origin or for a number of other reasons. When a bank has a sign on it that says "Insured by FDIC" it means that if the bank doesn't have enough money to pay back the people it owes money to, including the bank's depositors, and is closed, the FDIC will make sure all of the depositors get their money, up to the FDIC insurance limit. To be insured by the FDIC, a bank must prove it is being run profitably and fairly.

There is more to the FDIC's mission, however, than standing ready to protect depositors when a financial institution fails. The FDIC also is the federal bank regulator responsible for supervising certain savings banks and state-chartered banks that are not members of the Federal Reserve System. As a regulator, the FDIC strives to prevent bank failures by monitoring the industry's performance and enforcing regulations intended to make sure financial institutions operate in a safe and sound manner. Banking, however, is a competitive business. The FDIC's oversight of the industry is not designed to stifle competition or to prevent the failure of banking businesses that cannot compete effectively. Banks fail, and when they do the FDIC is working for you. The FDIC staff is on location at the failed institution, using money from the FDIC insurance fund to promptly reimburse insured depositors. Later, the FDIC staff will recover a portion of this money by selling the failed financial institution's loans and other assets. Approximately 4,500 people working within seven specialized operating divisions now work in FDIC offices throughout the country. The FDIC's main office is in Washington, DC. Six cities host major regional offices. They are: Atlanta, Georgia; Chicago, Illinois; Dallas, Texas; Kansas City, Missouri; New York, New York and San Francisco, California. There are two area offices located in Memphis, Tennessee, and Boston, Massachusetts. There also are more than 80 small field offices throughout the country.

The FDIC preserves and promotes public confidence in the US financial system by insuring deposits in banks and thrift institutions by identifying, monitoring, and addressing risks to the deposit insurance funds; and by limiting the effect on the economy and the financial system when a bank or thrift institution fails.

The FDIC receives no Congressional appropriations—it is funded by premiums that banks and thrift institutions pay for deposit insurance coverage and from earnings on investments in US Treasury securities. With an insurance fund totaling more than $49 billion, the FDIC insures more than $3 trillion of deposits in US banks and thrifts—deposits in virtually every bank and thrift in the country.

Deposits held in different categories of ownership—such as single or joint accounts—may be separately insured. Also, the FDIC generally provides separate coverage for retirement accounts, such as individual retirement accounts (IRAs) and Keoghs, insured up to $250,000. The FDIC does not insure securities or similar types of investments that banks and thrift institutions may offer. (*Insured and Uninsured Investments* distinguishes between what is and is not protected by FDIC insurance.)

The FDIC directly examines and supervises about 5,250 banks and savings banks, more than half of the institutions in the banking system. Banks can be chartered by the states or by the federal government. Banks chartered by states also have the choice of whether to join the Federal Reserve System. The FDIC is the primary federal regulator of banks that are chartered by the states that do not join the Federal Reserve System. In addition, the FDIC is the backup supervisor for the remaining insured banks and thrift institutions.

To protect insured depositors, the FDIC responds immediately when a bank or thrift institution fails. Institutions generally are closed by their chartering authority—the state regulator, the Office of the Comptroller of the Currency, or the Office of Thrift Supervision. The FDIC has several options for resolving institution failures, but the one most used is to sell deposits and loans of the failed institution to another institution. Customers of the failed institution automatically become customers of the assuming institution. Most of the time, the transition is seamless from the customer's point of view.

The FDIC is managed by a five-person board of directors, all of whom are appointed by the president and confirmed by the Senate, with no more than three being from the same political party.

FEDERAL RESERVE BOARD (FED)

http://www.federalreserve.gov

Congress created the Federal Reserve System on December 23, 1913, with the signing of the Federal Reserve Act by President Woodrow Wilson. The Federal Reserve System includes the board of governors and the twelve regional reserve banks. It took nearly a year from the time President Wilson signed the act to determine the boundaries of the twelve Federal Reserve Districts and to establish the twelve regional reserve banks. The board of governors oversees the Federal Reserve System. It is made up of seven members who are appointed by the President and confirmed by the Senate. The full term of a board member is 14 years, and the appointments are staggered so that one term expires on each even-numbered year. After serving a full term, a board member may not be reappointed. If a member leaves the board before his or her term expires, however, the person appointed and confirmed to serve the remainder of the term may be later reappointed to a full term.

The chairman and vice chairman lead the board. They are also appointed by the president and confirmed by the Senate. The nominees to these posts must already be members of the board or must be simultaneously appointed to the Board. The terms for these positions are four years, but the chairman and vice chairman may be reappointed for additional four-year terms, as long as their term as board member is active. Under the Federal Reserve System, the United States is divided into twelve regions, or districts. Each district has a reserve bank serving it. The twelve reserve banks are named after the city in which they are located: Boston | New York | Philadelphia | Cleveland | Richmond | Atlanta | Chicago | St. Louis | Minneapolis | Kansas City | Dallas | San Francisco. The Federal Reserve's responsibilities include:

- Conducting the nation's monetary policy to help maintain employment, keep prices stable, and keep interest rates relatively low.
- Supervising and regulating banking institutions to make sure they are safe places for people to keep their money and to protect consumers' credit rights.
- Providing financial services to depository institutions, the US government, and foreign central banks, including playing a major role in clearing checks, processing electronic payments, and distributing coin and paper money to the nation's banks, credit unions, savings and loan associations, and savings banks.

The Federal Reserve System also

- Conducts research on the US and regional economies.
- Distributes information about the economy through publications, speeches, educational seminars, and web sites.

Interest rates, like other prices, are determined by the forces of supply and demand. Higher interest rates provide incentives for people to save more and borrow less. Likewise, lower interest rates provide incentives for people to borrow more and save less. When interest rates rise, businesses are likely to invest less in capital and households are likely to spend less on housing, cars, and other major purchases. Lower interest rates are likely to cause businesses to invest more in capital and households to buy more big ticket items. In this way, interest rates affect the level of economic activity in the economy. The

Federal Reserve System is able to affect the level of interest rates through its monetary policy. Inflation means that the general level of prices of goods and services is increasing. When inflation is rapid, the prices of goods and services can increase faster than consumers' income, and that means the amount of goods and services consumers are able to purchase goes down. In other words, the purchasing power of money has declined. With inflation, a dollar buys less and less over time. The Federal Open Market Committee (FOMC) tries to keep inflation low and stable in the long run because that helps the economy to keep growing over long periods of time. When inflation is low and stable, businesses and households can make better spending and investment plans because they do not have to worry about high inflation decreasing the purchasing power of their money. The FOMC consists of twelve members—the seven members of the board of governors, the president of the Federal Reserve Bank of New York, and four of the other eleven reserve bank presidents. The four reserve bank presidents serve one-year terms on a rotating basis. Nonvoting reserve bank presidents attend the meetings of the committee, participate in discussions, and contribute information about economic conditions in their district. The purpose of the FOMC is to determine the nation's monetary policy. The FOMC holds eight regularly scheduled meetings each year in Washington, D.C. At these meetings, the FOMC reviews economic and financial conditions and sets monetary policy. The term "monetary policy" refers to the actions taken by a central bank, such as the Federal Reserve, to help encourage a healthy economy. The actions taken influence the availability and cost of money and credit, which affect a range of economic variables, including output, employment, and prices of goods and services. At each of its meetings, the FOMC decides whether or not to change its target for the federal funds rate, and if so, by how much. The FOMC also issues a statement after each meeting explaining its decision, and these statements contain some important information about the FOMC's evaluation of the economy.

FEDERAL HOME LOANS BANK SYSTEM (FHLB)

http://www.fhlbanks.com

Federal Home Loan Banks and their members are the largest source of residential mortgage and community development credit in the United States.

There are twelve FHLBanks, each with its own president and board of directors, located in different regions of the country, with twelve distinct sets of customers, all with differing kinds of demand for their products, services and expertise. The FHLBanks' cooperative structure is ideal for serving the system's 8,100 member lenders. Each regional FHLBank manages and is responsive to its customer relationships, while the twelve FHLBanks use their combined size and strength to obtain the necessary funding at the lowest possible cost. The FHLBanks provide billions of dollars of primary liquidity to approximately 80 percent of the nation's financial institutions. By providing this assured liquidity to its members, the FHLBank system allows member institutions to remain active lenders, in all economic cycles, to help their local economies grow.

"The mission of the Federal Home Loan Banks is to provide cost-effective funding to members for use in housing, community, and economic development; to provide regional affordable housing programs, which create housing opportunities for low- and moderate-income families; to support housing finance through advances and mortgage programs; and to serve as a reliable source of liquidity for its membership."

Advance lending is the FHLBanks' main business line. It currently represents about two-thirds of all the FHLBanks' assets. These loans, known as advances, are well-collateralized loans used by members to support mortgage lending, community investment and other credit needs of their customers." Another innovative component of the FHLBanks member services is their acquired mortgage assets (AMA) or mortgage programs. These FHLBank mortgage programs serve as an alternative to the secondary mortgage market. The programs split the associated risks according to expertise of the member lenders and home loan banks. Member lenders keep the credit risk and maintain the customer relationship, while the FHLBanks manage the interest rate risk. Unbundling these risks allows the member and the FHLBanks to manage what each knows best. The FHLBanks deliver on their commitment to promote community development through two of the nation's most successful housing programs: the Affordable Housing Program (AHP) and the Community Investment Program (CIP). Since its inception in 1989, AHP has provided over $2.9 billion dollars in grants to help create 575,000 housing units. Forty-seven billion dollars in CIP-funded loans, also since 1989, have financed nearly 600,000 housing units and thousands of economic development projects.

FHLBanks issue debt to institutional investors through the Office of Finance. FHLBank debt is the joint and several liability of all the FHLBanks. Each year, 30 percent of FHLBank net earnings are paid into two separate programs. Ten percent of gross earnings go to the Affordable Housing Program (AHP) and 20 percent of the net income is paid into REFCORP. These statutory obligations are tantamount to a 30 percent federal levy on FHLBank income.

FEDERAL HOUSING ADMINISTRATION (FHA)

http://www.hud.gov
http://www.fha.com

During the Great Depression, the US banking system failed, causing a drastic decrease in home loans and ownership. At this time, most home mortgages were short term (three to five years), no amortization, balloon instruments at loan-to-value (LTV) ratios below 50 to 60 percent. The banking crisis of the 1930s forced all lenders to retrieve due mortgages. Refinancing was not available, and many borrowers, now unemployed, were unable to make mortgage payments. Consequently, many homes were foreclosed, causing the housing market to plummet. Banks collected the loan collateral (foreclosed homes) but the low property values resulted in a relative lack of assets. Because there was little faith in the backing of the US government, few loans were issued and few new homes were purchased.

In 1934, the federal banking system was restructured. The National Housing Act of 1934 was passed and the Federal Housing Administration was created. Its intent was to regulate the rate of interest and the terms of mortgages that it insured. These new lending practices increased the number of people who could afford a down payment on a house and monthly debt service payments on a mortgage, thereby also increasing the size of the market for single-family homes. The FHA calculated appraisal value based on eight criteria and directed its agents to lend more for higher appraised projects, up to a maximum cap. The two most important were "Relative Economic Stability," which constituted 40 percent of appraisal value, and "Protection from adverse influences," which made up another 20 percent. A community with even one African American family was deemed economically unstable because the prevailing theory of housing markets was that racial integration greatly lowered home values and lead to the decline of neighborhoods. This racist point of view was ubiquitous among white Americans and explains why the FHA refused to grant mortgage loans to innumerable African American households, as well as home owners, who were mostly from non Anglo-Saxon backgrounds, who lived in or near African American neighborhoods, or wanted to do so. Data on the geography of actual FHA loans was mostly kept secret, but when data was released, scholars have found that FHA's generous programs were targeted disproportionately and almost exclusively to white Americans building homes in suburbs. Between 1935 and 1939, 220 out of 241 loans in St. Louis (91 percent) were located in the suburbs. From 1934 to 1960, the county of St. Louis received five times more FHA loans than the city of St. Louis, despite greater economic need in the city. Similarly, the average resident of Bronx County New York received just $10 in home mortgage loans from the FHA during its first 25 years, while the average resident in the wealthy Nassau County received $601. Overall, the FHA has been accused of an anti-urban bias, and its practices precipitated the decline of many important American cities, by subsidizing the departure of white middle-class Americans and refusing to give nearly as many loans for rental units, which would have been necessary to house low-income workers. In 1968, Senator Paul Douglas of Illinois summed up the federal role in home finance: "The poor and those on the fringes of poverty have been almost completely excluded."

In 1965, the Federal Housing Administration became part of the Department of Housing and Urban Development (HUD). Since 1934, the FHA and HUD have insured over 34 million home mortgages and 47,205 multifamily project mortgages. Currently, the FHA has 4.8 million insured single-family mortgages and 13,000 insured multifamily projects in its portfolio. The Federal Housing Administration is the only government agency that is completely self-funded. It operates solely from its own income and comes at no cost to taxpayers. This department spurs economic growth in the form of home and community development.

During budget planning for 2008 HUD had been projecting a $143 million budget shortfall stemming from the FHA program. This is the first time in three decades that HUD had made a request to Congress for a taxpayer subsidy. Currently new budget numbers are projecting "windfall revenues" for FHA due to the collapse of the subprime market and a flood of new loans being originated with FHA.

FHA loans are insured through a combination of a small upfront mortgage insurance premium (UFMIP), as well as a small monthly mortgage insurance premium. The UFMIP is often financed into the loan. Unlike other forms of conventional financed mortgage insurance, the UFMIP on an FHA loan is prorated over a five-year period, meaning that should the home owner refinance or sell during the first five years of his loan, he is entitled to a partial refund of the UFMIP paid at loan inception. The monthly mortgage insurance premium paid is less than that of what a borrower with a conventional mortgage and excellent credit pays per month providing the LTV is 85% or greater (in other words, providing the borrower has less than 15% equity in her home). In instances where the home owner has a poor-to-moderate credit history, his monthly mortgage insurance premium will be substantially less expensive with an FHA loan than with a conventional loan regardless of LTV—sometimes as little as one-ninth as much per month depending on the borrower's exact credit score, LTV, loan size, and approval status. The monthly mortgage insurance premium on an FHA loan has the ability to save a credit-challenged home owner thousands of dollars per year depending on the size of his home loan, his credit score, and his LTV. Currently, a borrower with an FHA loan always pays the same mortgage insurance rate regardless of her credit score. This is especially of benefit to borrowers who have less than 22% equity in their homes and credit scores under 620. Conventional mortgage insurance premium rates factor in credit scores, whereas FHA mortgage insurance premiums do not. When a borrower has a credit score under 620, conventional mortgae premiums spike dramatically. If a borrower has a credit score under 575, he may find it impossible to purchase a home for less than 20% down with a conventional loan, as the majority of mortgage insurance companies no longer write mortgage insurance policies on borrowers with credit scores under 575 due to a sharply increased risk. When they do write mortgage insurance policies for borrowers with lower credit scores, the annual premiums are sometimes as high as 4% to 5% of the loan amount. Based on this, if a consumer is considering purchasing a new home or refinancing her existing home, she would often be well-advised to look into the FHA loan program. When a home owner purchases a home utilizing an FHA loan, he will pay monthly mortgage insurance for a period of five years or until the loan is paid down to 78% of the appraised value—whichever comes first. Mortgage insurance is available for housing loan lenders, protecting against home owner mortgage default. For a small fee, lenders can obtain insurance for a value of 97% of the appraised value of the home or building. In the event of a mortgage default, this value is transferred to the FHA and the lenders receive a large percentage of their investment. The other 3% is received from the original down payment for the home.

A borrowers downpayment may come from a number of sources. The 3 percent requirement can be satisfied with the borrower using their own cash or receiving a gift from a family member, their employer, labor union, non-profit or government entity. Since 1998, nonprofits have been providing downpayment gifts to borrowers who purchase homes where the seller has agreed to reimburse the nonprofit and pay an additional processing fee. In May 2006, the IRS determined that this is not "charitible activity" and has moved to revoke the nonprofit status of groups providing downpayment assistance in this manner. This has led to a new downpayment program conducted by a Native American government. This program is exempt from IRS regulations and essentially works similarly to the nonprofit programs.

The FHA offers various types of housing loans. These include:

- Adjustable Rate Mortgages
- Fixed Rate Mortgages
- Energy Efficient Mortgages
- Graduated Payment Mortgages
- Mortgages for Condominium Units
- Growing Equity Mortgages

In order to qualify for an FHA housing loan, applicants must meet certain criteria, including employment, credit ratings, and income levels. The specific requirements are:

- Steady employment history, at least two years with the same employer.
- Consistent or increasing income over the past two years.
- Credit report should be in good standing with less than two thirty-day late payments in the past two years.
- Any bankruptcy on record must be at least two years old with good credit for the two consecutive years.
- Any foreclosure must be at least three years old.
- Mortgage payment qualified for must be approximately 30 percent of a person's total monthly gross income.

The creation of the FHA successfully increased the size of the housing market. By convincing banks to lend again, as well as changing and standardizing mortgage instruments and procedures, home ownership has increased from 40% in the 1930s to nearly 70% today. By 1938, only four years after the beginning of the FHA, a house could be purchased for a down payment of only 10 percent of the purchase price. The remaining 90 percent was financed by a twenty-five year, self amortizing, FHA-insured mortgage loan. After World War II, the FHA helped finance homes for returning veterans and families of soldiers. It has helped with purchases of both single-family and multi-family homes. In the 1950s, 1960s and 1970s, the FHA helped to spark the production of millions of units of privately owned apartments for elderly, handicapped and lower-income Americans. When the soaring inflation and energy costs threatened the survival of thousands of private apartment buildings in the 1970s, FHA's emergency financing kept cash-strapped properties afloat. In the 1980s, when the economy didn't support an increase in home owners, the FHA helped to steady falling prices, making it possible for potential home owners to finance when private mortgage insurers pulled out of oil producing states. The greatest effects of the Federal Housing Administration can be seen within minority populations and in cities. Nearly half of FHA's metropolitan area business is located in central cities, a percentage that is much higher than that of conventional loans. The FHA also lends to a higher percentage of African Americans and Hispanic Americans, as well as younger, credit constrained borrowers. Because some feel that these groups include riskier borrowers, it is believed that this is part of the reason for FHA's contribution to the home ownership increase.

As the capital markets in the United States mature, FHA has had less and less of an impact on the US housing market. In 2006, FHA made up less than 3 percent of all the loans originated in the United States. This had some members of Congress wondering why the government was still in the mortgage insurance business. A vocal minority of congressional leaders were calling for the end of the FHA. While many members supported reforming FHA in order to make it more competitive to the for-profit industry, several analysts questioned whether the taxpayers should be on the hook for a government-run "for-profit" business. See the Housing and Economic Recovery Act of 2008 (HERA) for recent revisions to FHA.

DEPARTMENT OF HOUSING AND URBAN DEVELOPMENT (HUD)

http://www.hud.gov

HUD's mission is to increase home ownership, support community development, and increase access to affordable housing free from discrimination. To fulfill this mission, HUD will embrace high standards of ethics, management, and accountability and forge new partnerships—particularly with faith-based and community organizations—that leverage resources and improve HUD's ability to be effective on the community level.

Complaints filed with HUD are investigated by the office of Fair Housing and Equal Opportunity (FHEO).

FEDERAL NATIONAL MORTGAGE ASSOCIATION (FNMA OR FANNIE MAE)

http://www.fanniemae.com

The Federal National Mortgage Association (NYSE: FNMA), commonly known as Fannie Mae, is a government-sponsored enterprise (GSE) of the United States government. As a GSE, it is a privately owned corporation authorized to make loans and loan guarantees. It is not backed or funded by the US government, nor do the securities it issues benefit from any explicit government guarantee or protection.

This secondary mortgage market helps to replenish the supply of lendable money for mortgages and ensures that money continues to be available for new home purchases. The name "Fannie Mae" is a creative acronym-portmanteau of the company's full name that has been adopted officially for ease of identification. Fannie Mae was originally founded as a government agency in 1938 as part of Franklin Delano Roosevelt's New Deal to provide liquidity to the mortgage market. For the next thirty years, Fannie Mae held a virtual monopoly on the secondary mortgage market in the United States. In 1968, to help balance the federal budget, Fannie Mae was converted into a private corporation. Fannie Mae ceased to be the guarantor of government-issued mortgages, and that responsibility was transferred to the new Government National Mortgage Association (Ginnie Mae).

Until recently, FNMA's primary method for making money was by charging a guarantee fee on loans that they have securitized into mortgage-backed security bonds. Investors, or purchasers of Fannie Mae MBSs, are willing to let Fannie Mae keep this fee in exchange for assuming the credit risk, that is, Fannie Mae's guarantee that the principal and interest on the underlying loan would be paid regardless of whether the borrower actually repaid. Alan Greenspan and Ben Bernanke have spoken publicly in favor of greater regulation of the GSEs, due to the size of their holdings and the public belief in a government guarantee that does not exist.

Fannie Mae (along with Freddie Mac) annually sets the limit of the size of a conforming loan based on the October-to-October changes in mean home price, above which a mortgage is considered a nonconforming jumbo loan. The GSEs only buy loans that are conforming, to repackage into the secondary market, making the demand for nonconforming loans lower. By virtue of the laws of supply and demand, then, it is harder for lenders to sell the loans, thus it would cost more to the consumers (typically 1/4 to 1/2 of a percent.) The conforming loan limit is 50 percent higher in Alaska, Hawaii, Guam, and the US Virgin Islands.

Until recently, Fannie Mae received no direct government funding or backing. Fannie Mae securities carried no government guarantee of being repaid. This was explicitly stated in the law that authorized GSEs, on the securities themselves, and in many public communications issued by Fannie Mae. Despite this, there was a wide perception that these notes carry an implied government guarantee, and the vast majority of investors believed that the government would prevent them from defaulting on their debt. Neither the certificates nor payments of principal and interest on the certificates were guaranteed by the United States government. The certificates did not constitute a debt or obligation of the United States or any of its agencies or instrumentalities other than Fannie Mae. There was a wide perception that FNMA securities were backed by some sort of implied federal guarantee, and a majority of investors believed that the government would prevent a disastrous default. Vernon L. Smith, 2002 Nobel Laureate in economics, has called FHLMC and FNMA "implicitly taxpayer-backed agencies." The *Economist* had referred to "[t]he implicit government guarantee" of FHLMC and FNMA.

Fannie Mae had looser restrictions placed on its activities than normal financial institutions: e.g., it was allowed to sell mortgage-backed securities with half as much capital backing them up as would be required of other financial institutions.

FNMA is a financial corporation that uses derivatives to "hedge" its cash flow. Derivative products it uses include interest rate swaps and options to enter interest rate swaps ("pay-fixed swaps," "receive-fixed swaps," "basis swaps," "interest rate caps and swaptions," "forward starting swaps").

In late 2004, Fannie Mae was under investigation for its accounting practices. The Office of Federal Housing Enterprise Oversight released a report on September 20, 2004, alleging widespread accounting errors, including shifting of losses allegedly so senior executives could earn bonuses. Fannie Mae was expected to spend more than $1 billion in 2006 alone to complete its internal audit and bring it closer to compliance. The anticipated restatement was estimated at $10.8 billion, however, after review resulted in $6.3 billion in restated earnings as listed in *Fannie Mae's Annual* Report on Form 10-K. Concerns with business and accounting practices at Fannie Mae predate the scandal itself. On June 15, 2000, the House Banking Subcommittee on Capital Markets, Securities and Government-Sponsored Enterprises held hearings on Fannie Mae. On December 18, 2006, US regulators filed 101 civil charges against chief executive Franklin Raines; chief financial officer J. Timothy Howard; and the former controller Leanne G. Spencer. The three are accused of allegedly manipulating Fannie Mae earnings to maximize their bonuses. The lawsuit sought to recoup more than $115 million in bonus payments, collectively accrued by the trio from 1998 to 2004, and about $100 million in penalties for their involvement in the accounting scandal.

GOVERNMENT NATIONAL MORTGAGE ASSOCIATION (GNMA OR GINNIE MAE)

http://www.ginniemae.gov/

The Government National Mortgage Association (GNMA) is a US government-owned corporation within the Department of Housing and Urban Development (HUD). Ginnie Mae, as it is called, provides guarantees on mortgage-backed securities (MBS) backed by federally insured or guaranteed loans, mainly loans issued by the Federal Housing Administration (FHA), Department of Veterans Affairs (VA), Rural Housing Service, and

Office of Public and Indian Housing. Ginnie Mae securities are the only MBS that are historically guaranteed by the United States government.

The GNMA was created by the United States federal government through a 1968 partition of the Federal National Mortgage Association (FNMA). As with other government-sponsored enterprises, Ginnie Mae uses a creative acronym-portmanteau of the company's full name, adopted officially for ease of identification. GNMA securities provided a connection between the capital markets and mortgage borrowers; investors purchased mortgage-backed securities (MBS also called RMBS), and borrowers gain access to investor funds. Capital market funding though MBS was thought to be more efficient and provide a much larger funding base than traditional deposit-funding (e.g., Savings and Loan model circa pre-1989 savings and loan crisis).

GNMA primarily does two things. First, it provides a computer platform that efficiently pools mortgages into bonds from pre-approved lenders. Second, GNMA provides, for six basis points of the outstanding principal balance of a bond, a guarantee of timely payment of principal and interest; this is essentially a guarantee that the US government would continue to pay investors even if the underlying collateral (government-insured mortgages) defaulted. GNMA securities thus have the same credit rating as the government of the United States and for capital purposes have risk-weighting of zero.

GNMA guaranties two "flavors" of MBS and also provides a CMO/REMIC program: (1) GNMA I securities. A GNMA I (Ginnie Mae one) represents a pool of mortgages all issued by one issuer, all with the same interest rate, and all issued within a three-month period. This is a basic pass-through security. (2) GNMA II securities. A GNMA II (Ginnie Mae two) is also a pass-through security, except that the collateral can have a range of interest rates and can include mortgages issued by more than one issuer. In this case, the service fees (see below) vary, so that the new interest rate being paid to the investor from each mortgage is the same. (3) GNMA "REMIC" securities. A REMIC (Real Estate Mortgage Investment Conduit), also known, as a CMO is an additional level of securitization. The collateral pool for a REMIC consists not of mortgages, but of mortgage-backed securities (such as GNMA I, GNMA II, or previously issued REMICs).

Pools are created by lenders. For example, a mortgage lender may sign up 100 home mortgages in which each buyer agrees to pay a fixed interest rate of 6% for a thirty-year term. The lender (who must be an approved issuer of GNMA certificates) obtains a guarantee from the GNMA and then sells the entire pool of mortgages to a bond dealer in the form of a "GNMA certificate." The bond dealer then sells GNMA mortgage-backed securities, paying 5.5% in this case, and backed by these mortgages, to investors. The original lender continues to collect payments from the home buyers, and forwards the money to a paying agent who pays the holders of the bonds. As these payments come in, the paying agent pays the principal that the home owners pay (or the amount that they are scheduled to pay, if some home owners fail to make the scheduled payment), and the 5.5% bond coupon payments to the investors. The difference between the 6% interest rate paid by the home owner and the 5.5% interest rate received by the investors consists of two components. Part of it is a guarantee fee (which GNMA gets) and part is a "servicing" fee, meaning a fee for collecting the monthly payments and dealing with the home owner. If a home buyer defaults on payments, GNMA pays the bond coupon, as well as the scheduled principal payment each month, until the property is foreclosed. If (as is often the case) there is a shortfall (meaning a loss) after a foreclosure, GNMA still makes a full payment to the investor. If a home buyer prematurely pays off all or part of his loan, that portion of the bond is retired, or "called," the investor is paid accordingly, and no longer earns interest on that proportion of his bond.

The GNMA said in its 2003 annual report that over its history, it had guaranteed securities on the mortgages for over 30 million homes totalling over $2 trillion. It guaranteed $215.8 billion in these securities for the purchase or refinance of 2.4 million homes in 2003.

According to the agencies' website: Ginnie Mae, helps make affordable housing a reality for millions of low- and moderate-income households across America by channeling global capital into the nation's housing markets. Specifically, the Ginnie Mae guarantee allows mortgage lenders to obtain a better price for their mortgage loans in the secondary market. The lenders can then use the proceeds to make new mortgage loans available. Ginnie Mae does not buy or sell loans or issue mortgage-backed securities (MBS). Therefore, Ginnie Mae's balance sheet doesn't use derivatives to hedge or carry long-term debt. What Ginnie Mae does is guarantee investors the timely payment of principal and interest on MBS backed by federally insured or guaranteed loans—mainly loans insured by the FHA or guaranteed by the Veterans Administration. Other guarantors or issuers of loans eligible as collateral for Ginnie Mae MBS include the Department of Agriculture's Rural Housing Service (RHS) and the Department of Housing and Urban Development's Office of Public and Indian Housing (PIH).

THE FEDERAL HOME LOAN MORTGAGE CORPORATION (FHLMC OR FREDDIE MAC)

http://www.freddiemac.com

Freddie Mac's mission is to provide liquidity, stability, and affordability to the housing market. Congress defined this mission in the 1970 charter, making America's mortgage markets liquid and stable and increasing opportunities for home ownership and affordable rental housing across the nation by creating:

- **Stability:** Freddie Mac's retained portfolio plays an important role in making sure there's a stable supply of money for lenders to make the home loans new homebuyers need and an available supply of workforce housing in our communities.
- **Affordability:** Financing housing for low- and moderate-income families. Freddie Mac's vision is that families must be able both to afford to purchase a home and to keep that home.
- **Liquidity:** Freddie Mac makes sure there's a stable supply of money for lenders to make the loans new homebuyers need.

OFFICE OF FEDERAL HOUSING ENTERPRISE OVERSIGHT (OFHEO)

http://www.ofheo.gov

OFHEO's mission is to promote housing and a strong national housing finance system by ensuring the safety and soundness of Fannie Mae and Freddie Mac. OFHEO works to ensure the capital adequacy and financial safety and soundness of these two housing government-sponsored enterprises. Fannie Mae and Freddie Mac are the nation's largest housing finance institutions.

OFHEO's oversight responsibilities include conducting broad-based examinations of Fannie Mae and Freddie Mac; developing a risk-based capital standard, using a "stress test" that simulates stressful interest rate and credit risk scenarios; making quarterly findings of capital adequacy based on minimum capital standards and a risk-based standard; prohibiting excessive executive compensation; issuing regulations concerning capital and enforcement standards; and taking necessary enforcement actions.

OFHEO is funded through assessments of Fannie Mae and Freddie Mac. OFHEO's operations represent no direct cost to the taxpayer. In its safety and soundness mission, OFHEO has regulatory authority similar to such other federal financial regulators as the Federal Deposit Insurance Corporation (FDIC), the Office of the Comptroller of the Currency (OCC), the Office of Thrift Supervision (OTS) and the Board of Governors of the Federal Reserve System.

The legislation that established OFHEO also requires Fannie Mae and Freddie Mac to meet certain affordable housing goals set annually by the secretary of housing and urban development. These goals specify the share of mortgages that the two GSEs are required to purchase annually from low-income, moderate-income and central-city homebuyers.

FAIR HOUSING AND EQUAL OPPORTUNITY OFFICE (FHEO)

http://www.hud.gov

FHEO's goal is to create equal housing opportunities for all persons living in America by administering laws that prohibit discrimination in housing on the basis of race, color, religion, sex, national origin, age, disability, and familial status.

The FHEO administers federal laws and establishes national policies that make sure all Americans have equal access to the housing of their choice. Particular activities it carries out include implementing and enforcing the Fair Housing Act and other civil rights laws, including Title VI of the Civil Rights Act of 1964, Section 109 of the Housing and Community Development Act of 1974, Section 504 of the Rehabilitation Act of 1973, Title II of the Americans with Disabilities Act of 1990, the Age Discrimination Act of 1975, Title IX of the Education Amendments Act of 1972, and the Architectural Barriers Act of 1968. In addition, FHEO is responsible to:

- Manage the Fair Housing Assistance Program, administer the award and management of Fair Housing Initiatives Program grants, and propose fair housing legislation;
- Work with other government agencies on fair housing issues;
- Review and comment on departmental clearances of proposed rules, handbooks, legislation, draft reports, and notices of funding availability for fair housing considerations;
- Interpret policy, process complaints, perform compliance reviews and offer technical assistance to local housing authorities and community development agencies regarding Section 3 of the Housing and Urban Development Act of 1968;
- Ensure the enforcement of federal laws relating to the elimination of all forms of discrimination in HUD's employment practices;
- Conduct oversight of the government-sponsored enterprises, Fannie Mae and Freddie Mac, to ensure consistency with the Fair Housing Act and the fair housing provisions of the Federal Housing Enterprises Financial Safety and Soundness Act; and
- Work with private industry and fair-housing and community advocates on the promotion of voluntary fair housing compliance.

UNITED STATES TREASURY FINANCIAL CRIMES ENFORCEMENT NETWORK (FinCEN)

http://www.fincen.gov

The Financial Crimes Enforcement Network is a bureau of the United States Department of the Treasury that collects and analyzes information about financial transactions in order to combat money laundering, terrorist financiers, and other financial crimes. As reflected in its name, FinCEN is a network, a means of bringing people and information together to fight the complex problem of money laundering. Since its creation in 1990, FinCEN has worked to maximize information sharing among law enforcement agencies and its other partners in the regulatory and financial communities. Working together is critical in succeeding against today's criminals. No organization, no agency, no financial institution can do it alone. Through cooperation and partnerships, FinCEN's network approach encourages cost-effective and efficient measures to combat money laundering domestically and internationally. The mission of FinCEN is to safeguard the financial system from the abuses of financial crime, including terrorist financing, money laundering, and other illicit activity. It was established by order of the secretary of the treasury on April 25, 1990. In May 1994, its mission was broadened to include regulatory responsibilities and the treasury department's Office of Financial Enforcement (OFE) was merged with FinCEN in October 1994. On September 26, 2002, after Title III of the USA PATRIOT Act was passed, Treasury Order 180-01 made it an official bureau in the Department of the Treasury.

The USA PATRIOT Act of 2001, §314(a) requires the secretary of the treasury to create a secure network for the transmission of information to enforce the relevant regulations. FinCEN's regulations under Section 314(a) enable federal law enforcement agencies, through FinCEN, to reach out to more than 45,000 points of contact at more than 27,000 financial institutions to locate accounts and transactions of persons who may be involved in terrorist financing and/or money laundering. This cooperative partnership between the financial community and law enforcement allows disparate bits of information to be identified, centralized, and rapidly evaluated.

Since its creation in 1990, FinCEN has worked to maximize information sharing among law enforcement agencies and its other partners in the regulatory and financial communities. The unique staffing of FinCEN both reflects and sustains its mission to safeguard the financial system from the abuses of financial crime, including terrorist financing, money laundering, and other illicit activity. The bureau consists of approximately 300 full-time employees, a third of whom are analysts, another third are administrative and managerial professionals, with the remaining third including regulatory specialists, technology experts, and federal agents. In addition, there are approximately forty long-term detailees from twenty different law enforcement and regulatory agencies.

FEDERAL TRADE COMMISSION (FTC)

http://www.ftc.gov

Handles complaints concerning most non-bank lenders, such as, mortgage and finance companies and state credit unions. Consumer Response Center, 600 Pennsylvania Avenue, NW, Washington, DC 20580, (877) 382-4357.

OFFICE OF THE COMPTROLLER OF THE CURRENCY (OCC)

http://www.occ.treas.gov

Handles complaints and regulates national banks. (These banks usually have "National" in their name or "N.A." after their names.) Compliance Management, 250 E Street SW, Mail Stop 3-9, Washington, DC 20219, (800) 613-6743.

OFFICE OF THRIFT SUPERVISION (OTS)

http://www.ots.treas.gov

Handles complaints and regulates federal savings and loans, and also federal savings banks. Consumer Affairs Division, 1700 G Street NW, Washington, DC 20552, (800) 842-6929.

NATIONAL CREDIT UNION ADMINISTRATION (NCUA)

http://www.ncua.gov

Handles complaints and regulates national credit unions. 1775 Duke Street, Alexandria, VA 22314-3428, (703) 518-6300.

DEPARTMENT OF AGRICULTURE

http://www.rurdev.usda.gov

Handles loans insured by Rural Development. Rural Development/Rural Housing Services, Mail Stop MC-0783, Washington, DC 20250, (202) 720-1474.

VETERANS ADMINISTRATION (VA)

http://www.va.gov

Handles complaints about loans guaranteed by Veterans Affairs. Consumer Affairs Service, 810 Vermont Avenue, NW, Washington, DC 20420, (202) 273-5770.

DEPARTMENT OF THE TREASURY

http://www.ustreas.gov

The treasury department is the executive agency responsible for promoting economic prosperity and ensuring the financial security of the United States. The department is responsible for a wide range of activities such as advising the president on economic and financial issues, encouraging sustainable economic growth, and fostering improved governance in financial institutions. The Department of the Treasury operates and maintains systems that are critical to the nation's financial infrastructure, such as the production of coin and currency, the disbursement of payments to the American public, revenue collection, and the borrowing of funds necessary to run the federal government. The department works with other federal agencies, foreign governments, and international financial institutions to encourage global economic growth, raise standards of living, and to the extent possible, predict and prevent economic and financial crises. The treasury department also performs a critical and far-reaching role in enhancing national security by implementing economic sanctions against foreign threats to the United States, identifying and targeting the financial support networks of national security threats, and improving the safeguards of our financial systems.

The Department of the Treasury is organized into two major components, the departmental offices and the operating bureaus. The departmental offices are primarily responsible for the formulation of policy and management of the department as a whole, while the operating bureaus carry out the specific operations assigned to the Department. The bureaus make up 98 percent of the treasury work force. The basic functions of the Department of the Treasury include:

- managing federal finances;
- collecting taxes, duties, and monies paid to and due to the United States and paying all bills of the federal government;
- currency and coinage;
- managing government accounts and the public debt;
- supervising national banks and thrift institutions;
- advising on domestic and international financial, monetary, economic, trade, and tax policy;
- enforcing federal finance and tax laws; and
- investigating and prosecuting tax evaders, counterfeiters, and forgery.

APPENDIX D
REGULATIONS

COMMUNITY REINVESTMENT ACT

http://www.ffiec.gov/cra

The Community Reinvestment Act (CRA), enacted by Congress in 1977 (12 U.S.C. 2901) and implemented by Regulations 12 CFR parts 25, 228, 345, and 563e, is intended to encourage depository institutions to help meet the credit needs of the communities in which they operate, including low- and moderate-income neighborhoods, consistent with safe and sound banking operations. In this section of the website, you can find out more about the regulation and its interpretation and information on CRA examinations.

The CRA requires that each insured depository institution's record in helping meet the credit needs of its entire community be evaluated periodically. That record is taken into account in considering an institution's application for deposit facilities, including mergers and acquisitions. CRA examinations are conducted by the federal agencies that are responsible for supervising depository institutions: the board of governors of the Federal Reserve System, the Federal Deposit Insurance Corporation, the Office of the Comptroller of the Currency, and the Office of Thrift Supervision.

EQUAL CREDIT OPPORTUNITY ACT (ECOA)

http://www.ftc.gov/bcp/conline/pubs/credit/ecoa.shtm

The Equal Credit Opportunity Act ensures that all consumers are given an equal chance to obtain credit. This doesn't mean all consumers who apply for credit get it: factors such as income, expenses, debt, and credit history are considerations for creditworthiness. The law protects you when you deal with any creditor who regularly extends credit, including banks, small loan and finance companies, retail and department stores, credit card companies, and credit unions. Anyone involved in granting credit, such as real estate brokers who arrange financing, is covered by the law. Businesses applying for credit also are protected by the law.

When you apply for credit, a creditor may not:

- Discourage you from applying because of your sex, marital status, age, race, national origin, or because you receive public assistance income.
- Ask you to reveal your sex, race, national origin, or religion. A creditor may ask you to voluntarily disclose this information (except for religion) if you're applying for a real estate loan. This information helps federal agencies enforce antidiscrimination laws. You may be asked about your residence or immigration status.
- Ask if you're widowed or divorced. When permitted to ask marital status, a creditor may only use the terms: married, unmarried, or separated.
- Ask about your marital status if you're applying for a separate, unsecured account. A creditor may ask you to provide this information if you live in "community property" states: Arizona, California, Idaho, Louisiana, Nevada, New Mexico, Texas, and Washington. A creditor in any state may ask for this information if you apply for a joint account or one secured by property.
- Request information about your spouse, except when your spouse is applying with you; your spouse will be allowed to use the account; you are relying on your spouse's income or on alimony or child support income from a former spouse; or if you reside in a community property state.
- Inquire about your plans for having or raising children.
- Ask if you receive alimony, child support, or separate maintenance payments, unless you're first told that you don't have to provide this information if you won't rely on these payments to get credit. A creditor may ask if you have to pay alimony, child support, or separate maintenance payments.

When deciding to give you credit, a creditor may not:

- Consider your sex, marital status, race, national origin, or religion.
- Consider whether you have a telephone listing in your name. A creditor may consider whether you have a phone.
- Consider the race of people in the neighborhood where you want to buy, refinance, or improve a house with borrowed money.
- Consider your age, unless:
  - you're too young to sign contracts, generally younger than eighteen years of age;
  - you're sixty-two or older, and the creditor will favor you because of your age;
  - it's used to determine the meaning of other factors important to creditworthiness. For example, a creditor could use your age to determine if your income might drop because you're about to retire;
  - it's used in a valid scoring system that favors applicants age sixty-two and older. A credit-scoring system assigns points to answers you provide to credit application questions. For example, your length of employment might be scored differently depending on your age.

When evaluating your income, a creditor may not:

- Refuse to consider public assistance income the same way as other income.
- Discount income because of your sex or marital status. For example, a creditor cannot count a man's salary at 100 percent and a woman's at 75 percent. A creditor may not assume a woman of childbearing age will stop working to raise children.
- Discount or refuse to consider income because it comes from part-time employment or pension, annuity, or retirement benefits programs.
- Refuse to consider regular alimony, child support, or separate maintenance payments. A creditor may ask you to prove you have received this income consistently.

You also have the right to:

- Have credit in your birth name (Mary Smith), your first and your spouse's last name (Mary Jones), or your first name and a combined last name (Mary Smith-Jones).

- Get credit without a cosigner, if you meet the creditor's standards.
- Have a cosigner other than your husband or wife, if one is necessary.
- Keep your own accounts after you change your name, marital status, reach a certain age, or retire, unless the creditor has evidence that you're not willing or able to pay.
- Know whether your application was accepted or rejected within thirty days of filing a complete application.
- Know why your application was rejected. The creditor must give you a notice that tells you either the specific reasons for your rejection or your right to learn the reasons if you ask within sixty days.
- Acceptable reasons include: "Your income was low," or "You haven't been employed long enough." Unacceptable reasons are: "You didn't meet our minimum standards," or "You didn't receive enough points on our credit-scoring system." Indefinite and vague reasons are illegal, so ask the creditor to be specific.
- Find out why you were offered less favorable terms than you applied for—unless you accept the terms. Ask for details. Examples of less favorable terms include higher finance charges or less money than you requested.
- Find out why your account was closed or why the terms of the account were made less favorable unless the account was inactive or delinquent.

For women in particular, a good credit history—a record of how you paid past bills—often is necessary to get credit. Unfortunately, this hurts many married, separated, divorced, and widowed women. There are two common reasons women don't have credit histories in their own names: they lost their credit histories when they married and changed their names; or creditors reported accounts shared by married couples in the husband's name only. If you're married, divorced, separated, or widowed, contact your local credit bureau(s) to make sure all relevant information is in a file under your own name.

If you suspect discrimination:

- Complain to the creditor. Make it known you're aware of the law. The creditor may find an error or reverse the decision.
- Check with your state attorney general to see if the creditor violated state equal credit opportunity laws. Your state may decide to prosecute the creditor.

- Bring a case in federal district court. If you win, you can recover damages, including punitive damages. You also can obtain compensation for attorney's fees and court costs. An attorney can advise you on how to proceed.
- Join with others and file a class action suit. You may recover punitive damages for the group of up to $500,000 or one percent of the creditor's net worth, whichever is less.
- Report violations to the appropriate government agency. If you're denied credit, the creditor must give you the name and address of the agency to contact. While some of these agencies don't resolve individual complaints, the information you provide helps them decide which companies to investigate. A list of agencies follows.

If a retail store, department store, small loan and finance company, mortgage company, oil company, public utility, state credit union, government lending program, or travel and expense credit card company is involved, contact Consumer Response Center, Federal Trade Commission, Washington, DC 20580. The FTC cannot intervene in individual disputes, but the information you provide may indicate a pattern of possible law violations that requires action by the commission. If your complaint concerns a nationally chartered bank ("National" or "N.A." will be part of the name), write to Comptroller of the Currency Compliance Management, Mail Stop 7-5, Washington, DC 20219. If your complaint concerns a state-chartered bank that is insured by the Federal Deposit Insurance Corporation but is not a member of the Federal Reserve System, write to Federal Deposit Insurance Corporation, Consumer Affairs Division Washington, DC 20429. If your complaint concerns a federally chartered or federally insured savings and loan association, write to Office of Thrift Supervision, Consumer Affairs Program, Washington, DC 20552. If your complaint concerns a federally chartered credit union, write to National Credit Union Administration, Consumer Affairs Division, Washington, DC 20456. Complaints against all kinds of creditors can be referred to Department of Justice, Civil Rights Division, Washington, DC 20530. The FTC works for the consumer to prevent fraudulent, deceptive, and unfair business practices in the marketplace and to provide information to help consumers spot, stop, and avoid them. To file a complaint or to get free information on consumer issues, visit ftc.gov or call toll-free, 1-877-FTC-HELP (1-877-382-4357); TTY: 1-866-653-4261.

EQUAL CREDIT OPPORTUNITY ACT—TITLE VII

§ 701. Prohibited discrimination; reasons for adverse action

(a) It shall be unlawful for any creditor to discriminate against any applicant, with respect to any aspect of a credit transaction—

(1) on the basis of race, color, religion, national origin, sex or marital status, or age (provided the applicant has the capacity to contract);

(2) because all or part of the applicant's income derives from any public assistance program; or

(3) because the applicant has in good faith exercised any right under the Consumer Credit Protection Act.

(b) It shall not constitute discrimination for purposes of this title for a creditor—

(1) to make an inquiry of marital status if such inquiry is for the purpose of ascertaining the creditor's rights and remedies applicable to the particular extension of credit and not to discriminate in a determination of credit-worthiness;

(2) to make an inquiry of the applicant's age or of whether the applicant's income derives from any public assistance program if such inquiry is for the purpose of determining the amount and probable continuance of income levels, credit history, or other pertinent element of credit-worthiness as provided in regulations of the board;

(3) to use any empirically derived credit system which considers age if such system is demonstrably and statistically sound in accordance with regulations of the board, except that in the operation of such system the age of an elderly applicant may not be assigned a negative factor or value; or

(4) to make an inquiry or to consider the age of an elderly applicant when the age of such applicant is to be used by the creditor in the extension of credit in favor of such applicant.

(c) It is not a violation of this section for a creditor to refuse to extend credit offered pursuant to—

(1) any credit assistance program expressly authorized by law for an economically disadvantaged class of persons;

(2) any credit assistance program administered by a nonprofit organization for its members or an economically disadvantaged class of persons; or

(3) any special purpose credit program offered by a profit-making organization to meet special social needs which meets standards prescribed in regulations by the board; if such refusal is required by or made pursuant to such program.

(d)(1) Within thirty days (or such longer reasonable time as specified in regulations of the board for any class of credit transaction) after receipt of a completed application for credit, a creditor shall notify the applicant of its action on the application.

(2) Each applicant against whom adverse action is taken shall be entitled to a statement of reasons for such action from the creditor. A creditor satisfies this obligation by—

(A) providing statements of reasons in writing as a matter of course to applicants against whom adverse action is taken; or

(B) giving written notification of adverse action which discloses (i) the applicant's right to a statement of reasons within thirty days after receipt by the creditor of a request made within sixty days after such notification, and (ii) the identity of the persons or office from which such statement may be obtained. Such statement may be given orally if the written notification advises the applicant of his right to have the statement of reasons confirmed in writing on written request.

(3) A statement of reasons meets the requirements of this section only if it contains the specific reasons for the adverse action taken.

(4) Where a creditor has been requested by a third party to make a specific extension of credit directly or indirectly to an applicant, the notification and statement of reasons required by this subsection may be made directly by such creditor, or indirectly through the third party, provided in either case that the identity of the creditor is disclosed.

(5) The requirements of paragraph (2), (3), or (4) may be satisfied by verbal statements or notifications in the case of any creditor who did not act

on more than one hundred and fifty applications during the calendar year preceding the calendar year in which the adverse action is taken, as determined under regulations of the board.

(6) For purposes of this subsection, the term "adverse action" means a denial or revocation of credit, a change in the terms of an existing credit arrangement, or a refusal to grant credit in substantially the amount or on substantially the terms requested. Such term does not include a refusal to extend additional credit under an existing credit arrangement where the applicant is delinquent or otherwise in default, or where such additional credit would exceed a previously established credit limit.

(e) Each creditor shall promptly furnish an applicant, upon written request by the applicant made within a reasonable period of time of the application, a copy of the appraisal report used in connection with the applicant's application for a loan that is or would have been secured by a lien on residential real property. The creditor may require the applicant to reimburse the creditor for the cost of the appraisal.

§ 702. Definitions

(a) The definitions and rules of construction set forth in this section are applicable for the purposes of this title. (b) The term "applicant" means any person who applies to a creditor directly for an extension, renewal, or continuation of credit, or applies to a creditor indirectly by use of an existing credit plan for an amount exceeding a previously established credit limit. (c) The term "Board" refers to the Board of Governors of the Federal Reserve System. (d) The term "credit" means the right granted by a creditor to a debtor to defer payment of debt or to incur debts and defer its payment or to purchase property or services and defer payment therefore. (e) The term "creditor" means any person who regularly extends, renews, or continues credit; any person who regularly arranges for the extension, renewal, or continuation of credit; or any assignee of an original creditor who participates in the decision to extend, renew, or continue credit. (f) The term "person" means a natural person, a corporation, government or governmental subdivision or agency, trust, estate, partnership, cooperative, or association. (g) Any reference to any requirement imposed under this title or any provision thereof includes reference to the regulations of the board under this title or the provision thereof in question.

§ 703. Regulations

(a)(1) The board shall prescribe regulations to carry out the purposes of this title. These regulations may contain but are not limited to such classifications, differentiation, or other provision, and may provide for such adjustments and exceptions for any class of transactions, as in the judgment of the board are necessary or proper to effectuate the purposes of this title, to prevent circumvention or evasion thereof, or to facilitate or substantiate compliance therewith.

(2) Such regulations may exempt from the provisions of this title any class of transactions that are not primarily for personal, family, or household purposes, or business or commercial loans made available by a financial institution, except that a particular type within a class of such transactions may be exempted if the board determines, after making an express finding that the application of this title or of any provision of this title of such transaction would not contribute substantially to effecting the purposes of this title.

(3) An exemption granted pursuant to paragraph (2) shall be for no longer than five years and shall be extended only if the board makes a subsequent determination, in the manner described by such paragraph, that such exemption remains appropriate.

(4) Pursuant to board regulations, entities making business or commercial loans shall maintain such records or other data relating to such loans as may be necessary to evidence compliance with this subsection or enforce any action pursuant to the authority of this act. In no event shall such records or data be maintained for a period of less than one year. The board shall promulgate regulations to implement this paragraph in the manner prescribed by chapter 5 of title 5, United States Code.

(5) The board shall provide in regulations that an applicant for a business or commercial loan shall be provided a written notice of such applicant's right to receive a written statement of the reasons for the denial of such loan.

(b) Consumer Advisory Council. The board shall establish a Consumer Advisory Council to advise and consult with it in the exercise of its functions under this chapter and to advise and consult with it concerning other consumer related matters it may place before the council. In appointing the members of the council, the board shall seek to achieve a fair representation of the interests of creditors and consumers. The council shall meet from time to time at the call of the board. Members of the council who are not regular full-time employees of the United States shall, while attending meetings of such council, be entitled to receive compensation at a rate fixed by the board, but not exceeding $100 per day, including travel time. Such members may be allowed travel expenses, including transportation and subsistence, while away from their homes or regular place of business.

§ 704. Administrative enforcement

(a) Compliance with the requirements imposed under this title shall be enforced under:

(1) section 8 of the Federal Deposit Insurance Act, in the case of—

(A) national banks, and federal branches and federal agencies of foreign banks, by the Office of the Comptroller of the Currency;

(B) member banks of the Federal Reserve System (other than national banks), branches and agencies of foreign banks (other than federal branches, federal agencies, and insured state branches of foreign banks), commercial lending companies owned or controlled by foreign banks, and organizations operating under section 25 or 25(a) of the Federal Reserve Act, by the Board of Governors of the Federal Reserve System; and

(C) banks insured by the Federal Deposit Insurance Corporation (other than members of the Federal Reserve System) and insured state branches of foreign banks, by the Board of Directors of the Federal Deposit Insurance Corporation;

(2) Section 8 of the Federal Deposit Insurance Act, by the director of the Office of Thrift Supervision, in the case of a savings association the deposits of which are insured by the Federal Deposit Insurance Corporation.

(3) The Federal Credit Union Act, by the administrator of the National Credit Union Administration with respect to any Federal Credit Union.

(4) The acts to regulate commerce, by the secretary of transportation, with respect to all carriers subject to the jurisdiction of the Surface Transportation Board.

(5) The Federal Aviation Act of 1958, by the Civil Aeronautics Board with respect to any carrier or foreign air carrier subject to that act.

(6) The Packers and Stockyards Act, 1921 (except as provided in section 406 of that Act), by the secretary of agriculture with respect to any activities subject to that Act.

(7) The Farm Credit Act of 1971, by the Farm Credit Administration with respect to any federal land bank, federal land bank association, federal intermediate credit bank, and production credit association;

(8) The Securities Exchange Act of 1934, by the Securities and Exchange Commission with respect to brokers and dealers; and

(9) The Small Business Investment Act of 1958, by the Small Business Administration, with respect to small business investment companies.

The terms used in paragraph (1) that are not defined in this title or otherwise defined in section 3(s) of the Federal Deposit Insurance Act (12

U.S.C. 1813(s)) shall have the meaning given to them in section 1(b) of the International Banking Act of 1978 (12 U.S.C. 3101).

(b) For the purpose of the exercise by any agency referred to in subsection (a) of its powers under any act referred to in that subsection, a violation of any requirement imposed under this title shall be deemed to be a violation of a requirement imposed under that act. In addition to its powers under any provision of law specifically referred to in subsection (a), each of the agencies referred to in that subsection may exercise for the purpose of enforcing compliance with any requirement imposed under this title, any other authority conferred on it by law. The exercise of the authorities of any of the agencies referred to in subsection (a) for the purpose of enforcing compliance with any requirement imposed under this title shall in no way preclude the exercise of such authorities for the purpose of enforcing compliance with any other provision of law not relating to the prohibition of discrimination on the basis of sex or marital status with respect to any aspect of a credit transaction.

(c) Except to the extent that enforcement of the requirements imposed under this title is specifically committed to some other Government agency under subsection (a), the Federal Trade Commission shall enforce such requirements. For the purpose of the exercise by the Federal Trade Commission of its functions and powers under the Federal Trade Commission Act, a violation of any requirement imposed under this title shall be deemed a violation of a requirement imposed under that Act. All of the functions and powers of the Federal Trade Commission under the Federal Trade Commission Act are available to the Commission to enforce compliance by any person with the requirements imposed under this title, irrespective of whether that person is engaged in commerce or meets any other jurisdictional tests in the Federal Trade Commission Act, including the power to enforce any Federal Reserve Board regulation promulgated under this title in the same manner as if the violation had been a violation of a Federal Trade Commission trade regulation rule.

(d) The authority of the Board to issue regulations under this title does not impair the authority of any other agency designated in this section to make rules respecting its own procedures in enforcing compliance with requirements imposed under this title.

704A. Incentives for self-testing and self-correction.

(a) PRIVILEGED INFORMATION.—

(1) CONDITIONS FOR PRIVILEGE.—A report or result of a self-test

(as that term is defined by regulations of the Board) shall be considered to be privileged under paragraph (2) if a creditor—

(A) conducts, or authorizes an independent third party to conduct, a self-test of any aspect of a credit transaction by a creditor, in order to determine the level or effectiveness of compliance with this title by the creditor; and

(B) has identified any possible violation of this title by the creditor and has taken, or is taking, appropriate corrective action to address any such possible violation.

(2) PRIVILEGED SELF-TEST.—If a creditor meets the conditions specified in subparagraphs (A) and (B) of paragraph (1) with respect to a self-test described in that paragraph, any report or results of that self-test

(A) shall be privileged; and

(B) may not be obtained or used by any applicant, department, or agency in any—

(i) proceeding or civil action in which one or more violations of this title are alleged; or

(ii) examination or investigation relating to compliance with this title.

(b) RESULTS OF SELF-TESTING.—

(1) IN GENERAL.—No provision of this section may be construed to prevent an applicant, department, or agency from obtaining or using a report or results of any self-test in any proceeding or civil action in which a violation of this title is alleged, or in any examination or investigation of compliance with this title if—

(A) the creditor or any person with lawful access to the report or results—

(i) voluntarily releases or discloses all, or any part of, the report or results to the applicant, department, or agency, or to the general public; or

(ii) refers to or describes the report or results as a defense to charges of violations of this title against the creditor to whom the self-test relates; or

(B) the report or results are sought in conjunction with an adjudication or admission of a violation of this title for the sole purpose of determining an appropriate penalty or remedy.

(2) Disclosure for determination of penalty or remedy.—Any report or results of a self-test that are disclosed for the purpose specified in paragraph (1)(B)—

(A) shall be used only for the particular proceeding in which the adjudication or admission referred to in paragraph (1)(B) is made; and

(B) may not be used in any other action or proceeding.

(c) ADJUDICATION.—An applicant, department, or agency that challenges a privilege asserted under this section may seek a determination of the existence and application of that privilege in—

(1) a court of competent jurisdiction; or

(2) an administrative law proceeding with appropriate jurisdiction.

§ 705. Relation to state laws

(a) A request for the signature of both parties to a marriage for the purpose of creating a valid lien, passing clear title, waiving inchoate rights to property, or assigning earnings, shall not constitute discrimination under this title: Provided, however, That this provision shall not be construed to permit a creditor to take sex or marital status into account in connection with the evaluation of creditworthiness of any applicant.

(b) Consideration or application of State property laws directly or indirectly affecting creditworthiness shall not constitute discrimination for purposes of this title.

(c) Any provision of State law which prohibits the separate extension of consumer credit to each party to a marriage shall not apply in any case where each party to a marriage voluntarily applies for separate credit from the same creditor: Provided, That in any case where such a State law is so preempted, each party to the marriage shall be solely responsible for the debt so contracted.

(d) When each party to a marriage separately and voluntarily applies for and obtains separate credit accounts with the same creditor, those accounts shall not be aggregated or otherwise combined for purposes of determining permissible finance charges or permissible loan ceilings under the laws of any State or of the United States.

(e) Where the same act or omission constitutes a violation of this title and of applicable State law, a person aggrieved by such conduct may bring a legal action to recover monetary damages either under this title or under such State law, but not both. This election of remedies shall not apply to court actions in which the relief sought does not include monetary damages or to administrative actions.

(f) This title does not annul, alter, or affect, or exempt any peron subject to the provisions of this title from complying with, the laws of any State with respect to credit discrimination, except to the extent that those laws are inconsistent with any provision of this title, and then only to the extent of the inconsistency. The Board is authorized to determine whether such inconsistencies exist. The Board may not determine that any State law is inconsistent with any provision of this title if the Board determines that such law gives greater protection to the applicant.

(g) The Board shall by regulation exempt from the requirements of sections 701 and 702 of this title any class of credit transactions within any State if it determines that under the law of that State that class of transactions is subject to requirements substantially similar to those imposed under this title or that such law gives greater protection to the applicant, and that there is adequate provision for enforcement. Failure to comply with any requirement of such State law in any transaction so exempted shall constitute a violation of this title for the purposes of section 706.

§ 706. Civil liability

(a) Any creditor who fails to comply with any requirement imposed under this title shall be liable to the aggrieved applicant for any actual damages sustained by such applicant acting either in an individual capacity or as a member of a class.

(b) Any creditor, other than a government or governmental subdivision or agency, who fails to comply with any requirement imposed under this title shall be liable to the aggrieved applicant for punitive damages in an amount not greater than $10,000, in addition to any actual damages provided in subsection (a), except that in the case of a class action the total recovery under this subsection shall not exceed the lesser of $500,000 or 1 per centum of the net worth of the creditor. In determining the amount of such damages in any action, the court shall consider, among other relevant factors, the amount of any actual damages awarded, the frequency and persistence of failures of compliance by the creditor, the resources of the creditor, the number of persons adversely affected, and the extent to which the creditor's failure of compliance was intentional.

(c) Upon application by an aggrieved applicant, the appropriate United States district court or any other court of competent jurisdiction may grant such equitable and declaratory relief as is necessary to enforce the requirements imposed under this title.

(d) In the case of any successful action under subsection (a), (b), or (c), the costs of the action, together with a reasonable attorney's fee as determined by the court, shall be added to any damages awarded by the court under such subsection.

(e) No provision of this title imposing liability shall apply to any act done or omitted in good faith in conformity with any official rule, regulation, or interpretation thereof by the Board or in conformity with any interpretation or approval by an official or employee of the Federal Reserve System duly authorized by the Board to issue such interpretations or approvals under such procedures as the Board may prescribe therefore, notwithstanding that after such act or omission has occurred, such rule, regulation, interpretation, or approval is amended, rescinded, or determined by judicial or other authority to be invalid for any reason.

(f) Any action under this section may be brought in the appropriate United States district court without regard to the amount in controversy, or in any other court of competent jurisdiction. No such action shall be brought later than two years from the date of the occurrence of the violation, except that—

(1) whenever any agency having responsibility for administrative enforcement under section 704 commences an enforcement proceeding within two years from the date of the occurrence of the violation,

(2) whenever the Attorney General commences a civil action under this section within two years from the date of the occurrence of the violation, then any applicant who has been a victim of the discrimination which is the subject of such proceeding or civil action may bring an action under this section not later than one year after the commencement of that proceeding or action.

(g) The agencies having responsibility for administrative enforcement under section 704, if unable to obtain compliance with section 701, are authorized to refer the matter to the Attorney General with a recommendation that an appropriate civil action be instituted. Each agency referred to in paragraphs (1), (2), and (3) of section 704(a) shall refer the matter to the Attorney General whenever the agency has reason to believe that 1 or more creditors has engaged in a pattern or practice of discouraging or denying applications for credit in violation of section 701(a). Each such agency may refer the matter to the Attorney General whenever the agency has reason to believe that 1 or more creditors has violated section 701(a).

(h) When a matter is referred to the Attorney General pursuant to subsection (g), or whenever he has reason to believe that one or more creditors are engaged in a pattern or practice in violation of this title, the Attorney General may bring a civil action in any appropriate United States district court for such relief as may be appropriate, including actual and punitive damages and injunctive relief.

(i) No person aggrieved by a violation of this title and by a violation of section 805 of the Civil Rights Act of 1968 shall recover under this title and section 812 of the Civil Rights Act of 1968, if such violation is based on the same transaction.

(j) Nothing in this title shall be construed to prohibit the discovery of a creditor's credit granting standards under appropriate discovery procedures in the court or agency in which an action or proceeding is brought.

(k) NOTICE TO HUD OF VIOLATIONS.—Whenever an agency referred to in paragraph (1), (2), or (3) of section 704(a)—

(1) has reason to believe, as a result of receiving a consumer complaint, conducting a consumer compliance examination, or otherwise, that a violation of this title has occurred;

(2) has reason to believe that the alleged violation would be a violation of the Fair Housing Act; and

(3) does not refer the matter to the Attorney General pursuant to subsection (g), the agency shall notify the Secretary of Housing and Urban Development of the violation, and shall notify the applicant that the Secretary of Housing and Urban Development has been notified of the alleged violation and that remedies for the violation may be available under the Fair Housing Act.

§ 707. Annual reports to Congress

Each year, the Board and the Attorney General shall, respectively, make reports to the Congress concerning the administration of their functions under this title, including such recommendations as the Board and the Attorney General, respectively, deem necessary or appropriate. In addition, each report of the Board shall include its assessment of the extent to which compliance with the requirements of this title is being achieved, and a summary of the enforcement actions taken by each of the agencies assigned administrative enforcement responsibilities under section 704.

§ 708. Effective date

This title takes effect upon the expiration of one year after the date of its enactment. The amendments made by the Equal Credit Opportunity Act Amendments of 1976 shall take effect on the date of enactment thereof and shall apply to any violation occurring on or after such date, except that the amendments made to section 701 of the Equal Credit Opportunity Act shall take effect 12 months after the date of enactment.

§ 709. Short title

This title may be cited as the "Equal Credit Opportunity Act."

FAIR DEBT COLLECTION PRACTICES ACT

http://www.ftc.gov/bcp/conline/pubs/credit/fdc

The Fair Debt Collection Practices Act (FDCPA), *15 U.S.C. § 1692* et seq., is a United States statute added in 1978 as Title VIII of the Consumer Credit Protection Act. Its purposes are to eliminate abusive practices in the collection of consumer debts, to promote fair debt collection, and to provide consumers with an avenue for disputing and obtaining validation of debt information in order to ensure the information's accuracy. The act creates guidelines under which debt collectors may conduct business, defines the rights of consumers involved with debt collectors, and prescribes penalties and remedies for violations of the act. It is sometimes used in conjunction with the Fair Credit Reporting Act.

The FDCPA broadly defines a debt collector as "any person who uses any instrumentality of interstate commerce or the mails in any business the principal purpose of which is the collection of any debts, or who regularly collects or attempts to collect, directly or indirectly, debts owed or due or asserted to be owed or due another." While the FDCPA generally only applies to third-party debt collectors—not internal collectors for an "original creditor"—some states, such as California, have similar state consumer protection laws which mirror the FDCPA, and regulate original creditors. In addition, courts have generally found debt buyers to be covered by the FDCPA even though they are collecting their own debts. The definitions and coverage have changed over time. The FDCPA itself contains numerous exceptions to the definition of a "debt collector," particularly after the October 13, 2006, passage of the Financial Services Regulatory Relief Act of 2006. Attorneys, originally explicitly excepted from the definition of a debt collector, have been included (to the extent that they otherwise meet the definition) since 1986.

The FDCPA's definitions of "consumers" and "debt" specifically restricts the coverage of the act to personal, family, or household transactions. Thus, debts owed by businesses (or by individuals for business purposes) are not subject to the FDCPA. The act prohibits certain types of "abusive and deceptive" conduct when attempting to collect debts, including the following:

- Hours for phone contact: contacting consumers by telephone outside of the hours of 8:00 a.m. to 9:00 p.m. local time

- Contact after being asked to stop: contacting consumers in any way (other than litigation) after receiving written notice that said consumer wishes no further contact or refuses to pay the alleged debt, with certain exceptions, including advising that collection efforts are being terminated or that the collector intends to file a lawsuit or pursue other remedies where permitted
- Contacting consumers at their place of employment after having been told verbally or in writing that this is not acceptable
- Contacting consumer known to be represented by an attorney
- Contacting consumer after request for validation: contacting the consumer or the pursuing of collection efforts by the debt collector after receipt of a consumer's written request for verification of a debt (or for the name and address of the original creditor on a debt) and before the debt collector mails the consumer the requested verification or original creditor's name and address
- Misrepresentation or deceit: misrepresenting the debt or using deception to collect the debt, including a debt collector's misrepresentation that he or she is an attorney or law enforcement officer
- Publishing the consumer's name or address on a "bad debt" list
- Seeking unjustified amounts, which would include demanding any amounts not permitted under an applicable contract or as provided under applicable law
- Threatening arrest or legal action that is either not permitted or not actually contemplated
- Abusive or *profane* language used in the course of communication related to the debt
- Contact with third parties: revealing or discussing the nature of debts with third parties (other than the consumer's spouse or attorney) or threatening such action
- Contact by embarrassing media, such as communicating with a consumer regarding a debt by post card, or using any language or symbol, other than the debt collector's address, on any envelope when communicating with a consumer by use of the mails or by telegram, except that a debt collector may use his business name if such name does not indicate that he is in the debt collection business
- Reporting false information on a consumer's credit report or threatening to do so in the process of collection.

Further, the FDCPA requires debt collectors to:

- Identify themselves and notify the consumer, in every communication, that the communication is from a debt collector, and that information received will be used to effect collection of the debt
- Give the name and address of the original creditor (company to which the debt was originally payable) upon the consumer's written request made within 30 days of receipt of the §1692g validation notice
- Notify the consumer of their right to dispute the debt, in part or in full, with the debt collector. This so-called 30-day §1692g validation notice is required to be sent by debt collectors within five days of the initial communication with the consumer, though in 2006 the definition of "initial communication" was amended to exclude "a formal pleading in a civil action" for purposes of triggering the §1692g validation notice, complicating the matter where the debt collector is an attorney or law firm. The consumer's receipt of this notice starts the clock running on the 30-day right to demand validation of the debt from the debt collector.
- Provide verification of the debt: If a consumer sends a written dispute or request for verification within 30 days of receiving the §1692g validation notice, then the debt collector must either mail the consumer the requested validation information or cease collection efforts altogether. Such asserted disputes must also be reported by the creditor to any credit bureau that reports the debt. Consumers may still dispute a debt verbally or after the thirty-day period has elapsed, but doing so waives the right to compel the debt collector to produce verification of the debt. Verification should include at a minimum the amount owed and the name and address of the original creditor.
- File a lawsuit in a proper venue: a debt collector may file a lawsuit, if at all, only in a place where the consumer lives or signed the contract.

This should not be understood to be an exhaustive list either of prohibited or required conduct. The Federal Trade Commission has the authority to administratively enforce the FDCPA using its powers under the Federal Trade Commission Act. Aggrieved consumers may also file a private lawsuit in a state or federal court to collect damages (actual, statutory, attorney's fee and court costs) from third-party debt collectors. The FDCPA is a strict liability law, which means that a consumer need not prove actual damages in order to claim statutory damages of up to $1,000 plus reasonable attorney fees if a debt collector is proven to have violated the FDCPA. The collector may, however, escape penalty if it shows that the violation (or violations) was the result of a "bona fide error." Alternately, if the consumer loses the lawsuit and the court determines that the consumer filed the case in bad faith and for the purposes of harassment, the court may then award attorney's fees to the debt collector.

Some consumer groups argue that the FDCPA does not go far enough, and does not provide sufficient deterrence against unscrupulous collection agencies. Consumer groups have complained that the maximum statutory damages contained in the original 1977 version of the law has not kept up with inflation. According to the inflation calculator at the Bureau of Labor Statistics' website, that same penalty would be the equivalent of $3,105.83 by 2006 standards. The Washington, DC–based National Association of Consumer Advocates is the largest consumer advocacy organization in the United States. Its member attorneys bring thousands of such FDCPA suits each year in virtually all fifty states. Many debt collectors, and the consumer rights attorneys who sue them for violations of the FDCPA rely heavily on the definitive legal treatise on the FDCPA produced by the National Consumer Law Center.

Conversely, many in the credit industry and some courts have taken the stance that the FDCPA has often been used to file frivolous lawsuits and seek damages for minor technical violations and has, at times, seriously impeded their ability to collect valid debts. Given the strict liability nature of the FDCPA, the collections industry and the insurance companies who provide liability coverage for them have repeatedly lobbied Congress to relax provisions of the law to reduce their civil exposure for these "hyper-technical" violations.

For its part, the Federal Trade Commission (FTC) produces an annual report to Congress of its findings with respect to its FDCPA enforcement activities. This report details consumer complaints to the FTC about alleged debt collector violations of the FDCPA. There were more than 69,000 consumer complaints made to the FTC about debt collectors in 2006, which is more complaints than the FTC receives about any other specific industry. This was an overall increase of 3.8 percent over 2005.

If you use credit cards, owe money on a personal loan, or are paying on a home mortgage, you are a "debtor." If you fall behind in repaying your creditors, or an error is made on your accounts, you may be contacted by a "debt collector." You should know that in either situation, the Fair Debt Collection Practices Act requires that debt collectors treat you fairly and prohibits certain methods of debt collection. Of course, the law does not erase any legitimate debt you owe. Debts covered are personal, family, and household debts are covered under the act. This includes money owed for the purchase of an automobile, for medical care, or for charge accounts. A debt collector is any person who regularly collects debts owed to others. This includes attorneys who collect debts on a regular basis. A collector may contact you in person, by mail, telephone, telegram, or fax. However, a debt collector may not contact you at inconvenient times or places, such as before 8 a.m. or after 9 p.m., unless you agree. A debt collector also may not contact you at work if the collector knows that your employer disapproves of such contacts. You can stop a debt collector from contacting you by writing a letter to the collector telling them to stop. Once the collector receives your letter, they may not contact you again except to say there will be no further contact or to notify you that the debt collector or the creditor intends to take some specific action. Please note, however, that sending such a letter to a collector does not make the debt go away if you actually owe it. You could still be sued by the debt collector or your original creditor. If you have an attorney, the debt collector must contact the attorney, rather than you. If you do not have an attorney, a collector may contact other people, but only to find out where you live, what your phone number is, and where you work. Collectors usually are prohibited from contacting such third parties more than once. In most cases, the collector may not tell anyone other than you and your attorney that you owe money. Within five days after you are first contacted, the collector must send you a written notice telling you the amount of money you owe; the name of the creditor to whom you owe the money; and what action to take if you believe you do not owe the money. A collector may not contact you if, within 30 days after you receive the written notice, you send the collection agency a letter stating you do not owe money. However, a collector can renew collection activities if you are sent proof of the debt, such as a copy of a bill for the amount owed. Harassment is prohibited. Debt collectors may not harass, oppress, or abuse you or any third parties they contact. For example, debt collectors may not:

- use threats of violence or harm;
- publish a list of consumers who refuse to pay their debts (except to a credit bureau);
- use obscene or profane language; or repeatedly use the telephone to annoy someone.

False statements. Debt collectors may not use any false or misleading statements when collecting a debt. For example, debt collectors may not:

- falsely imply that they are attorneys or government representatives;
- falsely imply that you have committed a crime;
- falsely represent that they operate or work for a credit bureau;
- misrepresent the amount of your debt;
- indicate that papers being sent to you are legal forms when they are not; or
- indicate that papers being sent to you are not legal forms when they are.

Debt collectors also may not state that:

- you will be arrested if you do not pay your debt;
- they will seize, garnish, attach, or sell your property or wages, unless the collection agency or creditor intends to do so, and it is legal to do so; or
- actions, such as a lawsuit, will be taken against you, when such action legally may not be taken, or when they do not intend to take such action.

Debt collectors may not:

- give false credit information about you to anyone, including a credit bureau;
- send you anything that looks like an official document from a court or government agency when it is not; or
- use a false name.

Unfair practices. Debt collectors may not engage in unfair practices when they try to collect a debt. For example, collectors may not:

- collect any amount greater than your debt, unless your state law permits such a charge;
- deposit a post-dated check prematurely;
- use deception to make you accept collect calls or pay for telegrams;
- take or threaten to take your property unless this can be done legally; or
- contact you by postcard.

If you owe more than one debt, any payment you make must be applied to the debt you indicate. A debt collector may not apply a payment to any debt you believe you do not owe. If you believe the law's been violated, you have the right to sue a collector in a state or federal court within one year from the date the law was violated. If you win, you may recover money for the damages you suffered plus an additional amount up to $1,000. Court costs and attorney' s fees also can be recovered. A group of people also may sue a debt collector and recover money for damages up to $500,000, or one percent of the collector' s net worth, whichever is less. Report any problems you have with a debt collector to your state Attorney General' s office and the Federal Trade Commission. Many states have their own debt collection laws, and your Attorney General' s office can help you determine your rights. The FTC works for the consumer to prevent fraudulent, deceptive and unfair business practices in the marketplace and to provide information to help consumers spot, stop, and avoid them. To file a complaint or to get free information on consumer issues, visit ftc.gov or call toll-free, 1-877-FTC-HELP (1-877-382-4357); TTY: 1-866-653-4261. The FTC enters Internet, telemarketing, identity theft, and other fraud-related complaints into Consumer Sentinel, a secure online database available to hundreds of civil and criminal law enforcement agencies in the United States and abroad.

FAIR HOUSING ACT

www.hud.gov/offices/fheo/FHLaws

Title VIII of the Civil Rights Act of 1968 (Fair Housing Act), as amended, prohibits discrimination in the sale, rental, and financing of dwellings, and in other housing-related transactions, based on race, color, national origin, religion, sex, familial status (including children under the age of eighteen living with parents of legal custodians, pregnant women, and people securing custody of children under the age of eighteen), and handicap (disability). HUD has played a lead role in administering the Fair Housing Act since its adoption in 1968. The 1988 amendments, however, have greatly increased the department's enforcement role. First, the newly protected classes have proven significant sources of new complaints. Second, HUD's expanded enforcement role took the department beyond investigation and conciliation into the area of mandatory enforcement.

Complaints filed with HUD are investigated by the Office of Fair Housing and Equal Opportunity (FHEO). If the complaint is not successfully conciliated, FHEO determines whether reasonable cause exists to believe that a discriminatory housing practice has occurred. Where reasonable cause is found, the parties to the complaint are notified by HUD's issuance of a Determination, as well as a Charge of Discrimination, and a hearing is scheduled before a HUD administrative law judge (ALJ). Either party—complainant or respondent—may cause the HUD-scheduled administrative proceeding to be terminated by electing instead to have the matter litigated in federal court. Whenever a party has so elected, the Department of Justice takes over HUD's role as counsel seeking resolution of the charge on behalf of aggrieved persons, and the matter proceeds as a civil action. Either form of action—the ALJ proceeding or the civil action in federal court—is subject to review in the US Court of Appeals. Significant recent changes include the Housing for Older Persons Act of 1995 (HOPA), making several changes to the fifty-five-and-older exemption. Since the 1988 amendments, the Fair Housing Act has exempted from its familial status provisions properties that satisfy the act's fifty-five-and-older housing condition. First, it eliminates the requirement that fifty-five-and-older housing have "significant facilities and services" designed for the elderly. Second, HOPA establishes a "good faith reliance" immunity from damages for persons who in good faith believe that the fifty-five-and-older exemption applies to a particular property, if they do not actually know that the property is not eligible for the exemption and if the party has formally stated in writing that the property qualifies for the exemption. HOPA retains the requirement that senior housing must have one person who is fifty-five years of age or older living in at least 80 percent of its occupied units. It also still requires that senior housing publish and follow policies and procedures that demonstrate an intent to be housing for persons fifty-five and older. An exempt property will not violate the Fair Housing Act if it includes families with children, but it does not have to do so. Of course, the property must meet the act's requirements that at least 80 percent of its occupied units have at least one occupant who is fifty-five or older, and that it publish and follow policies and procedures that demonstrate an intent to be fifty-five-and-older housing. A Department of Housing and Urban Development rule published in the April 2, 1999, *Federal Register* implements the Housing for Older Persons Act of 1995 and explains in detail those provisions of the Fair Housing Act that pertain to senior housing. Changes were made to enhance law enforcement, including making amendments to criminal penalties in section 901 of the Civil Rights Act of 1968 for violating the Fair Housing Act. Changes were made to provide incentives for self-testing by lenders for discrimination under the Fair Housing Act and the Equal Credit Opportunity Act.

The Fair Housing Act covers most housing. In some circumstances, the act exempts owner-occupied buildings with no more than four units, single-family housing sold or rented without the use of a broker, and housing operated by organizations and private clubs that limit occupancy to members.

In the sale and rental of housing: no one may take any of the following actions based on race, color, national origin, religion, sex, familial status, or handicap:

- Refuse to rent or sell housing
- Refuse to negotiate for housing
- Make housing unavailable
- Deny a dwelling
- Set different terms, conditions, or privileges for sale or rental of a dwelling
- Provide different housing services or facilities
- Falsely deny that housing is available for inspection, sale, or rental
- For profit, persuade owners to sell or rent (blockbusting) or
- Deny anyone access to or membership in a facility or service (such as a multiple-listing service) related to the sale or rental of housing.

In mortgage lending: no one may take any of the following actions based on race, color, national origin, religion, sex, familial status, or handicap (disability):

- Refuse to make a mortgage loan
- Refuse to provide information regarding loans
- Impose different terms or conditions on a loan, such as different interest rates, points, or fees
- Discriminate in appraising property
- Refuse to purchase a loan or
- Set different terms or conditions for purchasing a loan.

In addition: it is illegal for anyone to:

- Threaten, coerce, intimidate or interfere with anyone exercising a fair housing right or assisting others who exercise that right
- Advertise or make any statement that indicates a limitation or preference based on race, color, national origin, religion, sex, familial status, or handicap. This prohibition against discriminatory advertising applies to single-family and owner-occupied housing that is otherwise exempt from the Fair Housing Act.

If you or someone associated with you:

- Have a physical or mental disability (including hearing, mobility, and visual impairments, chronic alcoholism, chronic mental illness, AIDS, AIDS Related Complex, and mental retardation) that substantially limits one or more major life activities
- Have a record of such a disability or
- Are regarded as having such a disability

your landlord may not:

- Refuse to let you make reasonable modifications to your dwelling or common use areas, at your expense, if necessary for the disabled person to use the housing. (Where reasonable, the landlord may permit changes only if you agree to restore the property to its original condition when you move.)
- Refuse to make reasonable accommodations in rules, policies, practices or services if necessary for the disabled person to use the housing.

In buildings that are ready for first occupancy after March 13, 1991, and have an elevator and four or more units:

- Public and common areas must be accessible to persons with disabilities
- Doors and hallways must be wide enough for wheelchairs
- All units must have:
    - An accessible route into and through the unit
    - Accessible light switches, electrical outlets, thermostats, and other environmental controls
    - Reinforced bathroom walls to allow later installation of grab bars and
    - Kitchens and bathrooms that can be used by people in wheelchairs.

If a building with four or more units has no elevator and will be ready for first occupancy after March 13, 1991, these standards apply to ground-floor units. These requirements for new buildings do not replace any more stringent standards in state or local law. Unless a building or community qualifies as housing for older persons, it may not discriminate based on familial status. That is, it may not discriminate against families in which one or more children under eighteen live with:

- A parent
- A person who has legal custody of the child or children or
- The designee of the parent or legal custodian, with the parent or custodian's written permission.

Familial status protection also applies to pregnant women and anyone securing legal custody of a child under eighteen. Exemption: Housing for older persons is exempt from the prohibition against familial status discrimination if:

- The HUD secretary has determined that it is specifically designed for and occupied by elderly persons under a federal, state, or local government program or
- It is occupied solely by persons who are sixty-two or older or

- It houses at least one person who is fifty-five or older in at least 80 percent of the occupied units, and adheres to a policy that demonstrates an intent to house persons who are fifty-five or older.

A transition period permits residents on or before September 13, 1988, to continue living in the housing, regardless of their age, without interfering with the exemption.

You have one year after an alleged violation to file a complaint with HUD, but you should file it as soon as possible. What to tell HUD:

- Your name and address
- The name and address of the person your complaint is against (the respondent)
- The address or other identification to the housing involved
- A short description of the alleged violation (the event that caused you to believe your rights were violated)
- The date(s) to the alleged violation.

HUD will notify you when it receives your complaint. Normally, HUD also will:

- Notify the alleged violator of your complaint and permit that person to submit an answer
- Investigate your complaint and determine whether there is reasonable cause to believe the Fair Housing Act has been violated
- Notify you if it cannot complete an investigation within 100 days of receiving your complaint.

HUD will try to reach an agreement with the person your complaint is against (the respondent). A conciliation agreement must protect both you and the public interest. If an agreement is signed, HUD will take no further action on your complaint. However, if HUD has reasonable cause to believe that a conciliation agreement is breached, HUD will recommend that the attorney general file suit. If HUD has determined that your state or local agency has the same fair housing powers as HUD, it will refer your complaint to that agency for investigation and notify you of the referral. That agency must begin work on your complaint within 30 days or HUD may take it back. If you need immediate help to stop a serious problem that is being caused by a Fair Housing Act violation, HUD may be able to assist you as soon as you file a complaint. HUD may authorize the attorney general to go to court to seek temporary or preliminary relief, pending the outcome of your complaint, if:

- Irreparable harm is likely to occur without HUD's intervention
- There is substantial evidence that a violation of the Fair Housing Act occurred.

If, after investigating your complaint, HUD finds reasonable cause to believe that discrimination occurred, it will inform you. Your case will be heard in an administrative hearing within 120 days, unless you or the respondent want the case to be heard in federal district court. Either way, there is no cost to you. If your case goes to an administrative hearing HUD attorneys will litigate the case on your behalf. You may intervene in the case and be represented by your own attorney if you wish. An administrative law ludge (ALJ) will consider evidence from you and the respondent. If the ALJ decides that discrimination occurred, the respondent can be ordered:

- To compensate you for actual damages, including humiliation, pain and suffering
- To provide injunctive or other equitable relief, for example, to make the housing available to you
- To pay the federal government a civil penalty to vindicate the public interest (the maximum penalties are $10,000 for a first violation and $50,000 for a third violation within seven years)
- To pay reasonable attorney's fees and costs.

If you or the respondent choose to have your case decided in federal district court, the attorney general will file a suit and litigate it on your behalf. Like the ALJ, the district court can order relief, and award actual damages, attorney's fees and costs. In addition, the court can award punitive damages. You may file suit, at your expense, in federal district court or state court within two years of an alleged violation. If you cannot afford an attorney, the court may appoint one for you. You may bring suit even after filing a complaint, if you have not signed a conciliation agreement and an ALJ has not started a hearing. A court may award actual and punitive damages and attorney's fees and costs. If there is noncompliance with the order of an ALJ, HUD may seek temporary relief, enforcement of the order or a restraining order in a United States court of appeals. The attorney general may file a suit in a federal district court if there is reasonable cause to believe a pattern or practice of housing discrimination is occurring.

FEDERAL DEPOSIT INSURANCE CORPORATION IMPROVEMENT ACT

In 1991, Congress, via the Federal Deposit Insurance Corporation Improvement Act, authorized the Federal Reserve Board, in consultation with the Department of Housing and Urban Development, to develop a new exemption standard for nondepository mortgage lenders that is comparable to the exemption for depository institutions. In 1992, the board adopted a standard that further expanded coverage of independent mortgage lenders. Under the adopted standard, a nondepository mortgage lender with an office in a metropolitan statistical area is covered if it meets either an asset-size test or a lending activity test.

FEDERAL RESERVE ACT

To provide for the establishment of Federal Reserve banks, to furnish an elastic currency, to afford means of rediscounting commercial paper, to establish a more effective supervision of banking in the United States, and for other purposes.

HOME MORTGAGE DISCLOSURE ACT

http://www.ffiec.gov/hmda

The Home Mortgage Disclosure Act (HMDA), enacted by Congress in 1975 and implemented by the Federal Reserve Board's Regulation C, requires lending institutions to report public loan data. This regulation provides the public loan data that can be used to assist in determining whether financial institutions are serving the housing needs of their communities, by public officials in distributing public-sector investments so as to attract private investment to areas where it is needed and in identifying possible discriminatory lending patterns. Using the loan data submitted by these financial institutions, the Federal Financial Institutions Examination Council (FFIEC) creates aggregate tables for each metropolitan statistical area (MSA) or metropolitan division (MD) and individual institution disclosure reports. Many amendments followed including in 1994, when Regulation C was amended by the Federal Reserve Board to make HMDA data available to the public earlier, to improve the accuracy of the HMDA data, and to clarify and simplify the reporting requirements.

HOME OWNERSHIP AND EQUITY PROTECTION ACT (HOEPA)

http://www.inmanwiki.com/RealEstate/Home_Ownership_and_Equity_Protection_Act

The Home Ownership and Equity Protection Act of 1994 was intended to protect consumers refinancing their mortgages or applying for home equity loans from deceptive and unfair practices. HOEPA is an amendment to the Truth in Lending Act (TILA), and establishes rules for certain loans that carry high rates or fees. Loans subject to HOEPA are sometimes called "Section 32 Mortgages" after the section of the regulation that implements TILA. Consumer groups including the Center for Responsible Lending have called for lawmakers to strengthen HOEPA by lowering the thresholds that trigger its requirements, and increasing penalties for violations. The mortgage lending industry has opposed such action, in part because an expansion of HOEPA could make it more difficult to bundle packages of loans for securitization and sale on Wall Street. HOEPA applies to:

- First-lien loans with an annual percentage rate (APR) that exceeds by more than 8 percent the rate on treasury securities of comparable maturity, and second-lien loans with APRs more than 10 percent higher.
- Loans in which total fees and points payable at or before closing exceed $547 or 8 percent of the total loan amount, whichever is larger.

The $547 figure was set by the Federal Reserve Board and applies to 2007. The board adjusts the amount annually. Credit insurance premiums are counted as fees.

- Loans subject to HOEPA subject lenders to additional requirements and allow borrowers some additional rights, including:
- Written notice at least three days before a HOEPA loan is finalized, informing prospective borrowers of their right to change their minds. After signing a loan application and receiving the required disclosures, consumers have three business days to decide whether to sign a loan agreement.
- The lender must disclose the APR, regular payment amount (including any balloon payment), and the loan amount (including credit insurance premiums). For variable rate loans, the lender must disclose that the rate and monthly payment may increase and state the amount of the maximum monthly payment.

Lenders are barred from:

- Making loans based on the collateral value of a property without regard to the borrower's ability to repay the loan. Proceeds for home improvement loans must be directly disbursed to the borrower, to the borrower and the home improvement contractor or, in some instances, an escrow agent.
- Refinancing a HOEPA loan into another HOEPA loan within the first 12 months of origination, unless the new loan is in the borrower's best interest. The prohibition also applies to assignees holding or servicing the loan.
- Documenting a closed-end, high-cost loan as an open-end loan. A high-cost mortgage may not be structured as a home equity line of credit, for instance, if there is no reasonable expectation that repeat transactions will occur.
- HOEPA bans the following features from high rate, high fee loans subject to its requirements:
    - Balloon payments on loans with less than five-year terms if a lump sum payment of more than twice the amount of the regular payments is required. Balloon payments are allowed for bridge loans of less than one year that are used buy or build a home.

- Negative amortization, or monthly payments so small they do not repay all the interest due and cause the loan principal to increase.
- Default interest rates higher than pre-default rates.
- Rebates of interest upon default calculated by any method less favorable than the actuarial method.
- A repayment schedule that consolidates more than two periodic payments that are to be paid in advance from the proceeds of the loan.
- Most prepayment penalties, including refunds of unearned interest calculated by any method less favorable than the actuarial method.
- Due-on-demand clauses, unless there is fraud or material misrepresentation by the consumer in connection with the loan or the consumer fails to meet the repayment terms.

HOEPA gives borrowers the right to sue lenders for violations of its requirements, and recover statutory and actual damages, court costs and attorney's fees. Borrowers have up to three years to cancel a loan that violates the requirements for high-rate, high-fee loans under HOEPA. The Federal Trade Commission handles HOEPA complaints and distributes free information. For more information or to file a complaint, visit www.ftc.gov or call toll-free, 1-877-FTC-HELP (1-877-382-4357); TTY: 1-866-653-4261

HOUSING AND COMMUNITY DEVELOPMENT ACT OF 1992

www.hud.gov/progdesc/sec-109.cfm

President Bush's Statement on Signing the Housing and Community Development Act of 1992

October 28th, 1992

Today I am signing into law H.R. 5334, the "Housing and Community Development Act of 1992." This bill establishes a sound regulatory structure for government-sponsored enterprises, combats money laundering, provides essential regulatory relief to financial institutions, authorizes several key administration housing initiatives, and reduces the risk of lead-based paint poisoning.

This legislation addresses the problems created by the rapid expansion of certain GSEs in the last decade. It establishes a means to protect taxpayers from the possible risks posed by GSEs in housing finance. The bill creates a regulator within the Department of Housing and Urban Development (HUD) to ensure that the housing GSEs are adequately capitalized and operated safely.

H.R. 5334 includes many of my administration's regulatory relief proposals for depository institutions. The regulatory burden that the Congress has placed on our banking system has reached a staggering level that prevents banks from providing the credit that is necessary to assure economic growth. By reducing the regulatory burden, this bill will assist banks, borrowers, and the economy as a whole.

. . . My administration worked diligently to craft a compromise housing bill that would target assistance where it is needed most, expand home ownership opportunities, ensure fiscal integrity, and empower recipients of Federal housing assistance.

I also note that two provisions of the bill must be narrowly construed to avoid constitutional difficulties. Section 1313 would authorize the director of the newly established Office of Federal Housing Enterprise Oversight within HUD to submit "reports, recommendations, testimony, or comments" to the Congress without prior approval or review by "any officer or agency of the United States." The bill also provides the director authority, exclusive of the secretary of housing and urban development, to promulgate safety and soundness regulations and to formulate an annual budget. When a member of the executive branch acts in an official capacity, the Constitution requires that I have the ultimate authority to supervise that officer in the exercise of his or her duties. In order to avoid constitutional difficulties, and without recognizing the Congress' authority to prevent the secretary from supervising on my behalf an agency within HUD, I will interpret this provision to permit me to supervise the director through other means, such as through the Office of Management and Budget.

Section 911 of the bill requires the secretary of housing and urban development to establish guidelines for housing credit agencies to "implement" section 102(d) of the Department of Housing and Urban Development Reform Act of 1989 (42 U.S.C. 3545(d)). That provision requires the secretary to certify that HUD assistance to housing projects is not more than necessary to provide affordable housing, after taking other federal and state assistance into account, and to adjust the amount of HUD assistance to compensate for changes in assistance amounts from other sources. To avoid the constitutional difficulties that would arise if section 911 were understood to vest in housing credit agencies the exercise of significant authority under federal law, I interpret section 911 to permit the secretary to formulate guidelines under which he will retain the ultimate authority to make the determinations required by section 102(d).

President George Bush

NATIONAL HOUSING ACT OF 1934

http://www.hud.gov/offices/adm/about/admguide

The National Housing Act of 1934 was passed during the Great Depression in order to make housing and home mortgages more affordable. It created the Federal Housing Administration (FHA) and the Federal Savings and Loan Insurance Corporation. It was designed to stop the tide of bank foreclosures on family homes. Both the FHA and the Federal Savings and Loan Insurance Corporation worked to create the backbone of the mortgage and homebuilding industries. Some unintended consequences were that it did little to improve inner-city housing, it intensified segregation of races, and further promoted the single-family detached dwelling as the prevailing mode of housing, which furthered the phenomenon of suburban sprawl. It lead to a litany of federal housing initiatives including those we see today.

The 1930s

In the midst of the Depression, widespread unemployment, and financial collapse, Congress passed the Emergency Relief and Construction Act of 1932, creating the Reconstruction Finance Corporation (RFC). This was the government's first major involvement in the housing field. The RFC was authorized to make loans to private corporations providing housing for low-income families. Also in 1932, the Federal Home Loan Bank Board was established to make advances on the security of home mortgages and establish a Home Loan Bank System.

However, these efforts did little to assist individual homebuyers. The average home loan at that time required very short-term credit, with terms generally ranging from three to five years. Large down payments, second mortgages, and high interest rates were commonplace. As the depression ended, and the prospect of improved financial status for individual families increased, the National Housing Act of 1934 was passed to relieve unemployment and stimulate the release of private credit in the hands of banks and lending institutions for home repairs and construction. To accomplish this, the act of 1934 created the Federal Housing Administration (FHA). The FHA continues to this day, under the assistant secretary for housing, Federal Housing Commission, as the main federal agency handling mortgage insurance. Title II of the act of 1934 established two basic mortgage insurance programs: Section 203 mortgage insurance for one-to-four family homes; and Section 207 multifamily project mortgages. The FHA's assumption of risk, through its insurance programs, made possible the amortization of mortgage loans with regular monthly payments to reduce the size of the loan. The act of 1934 also authorized the FHA to create a national mortgage association to provide a secondary market where home mortgages could be sold. This allowed more money to be available for home loans. In 1937, the Federal National Mortgage Association, or Fannie Mae, was chartered by the FHA as a subsidiary of the RFC.

While these early measures were a major government effort to stimulate housing construction, they did not help those lower-income families most in need of housing. Because of the needs of this group, the United States Housing Act of 1937 established the public housing program. The act, administered by the United States Public Housing Authority, authorized loans to local public housing agencies for lower-rent public housing construction expenses. The programs created by these acts guided the direction of federal housing policy for the next ten years, leading to the creation of the urban renewal program. Over the years, all of these original programs have undergone some changes and additions. However, they continue to reflect the federal government's aim to marshal both public and private resources to improve housing conditions for low-and moderate-income families. The same year that the public housing program was approved by Congress, the Bankhead-Jones Farm Tenant Act was passed to allow the secretary of agriculture to make rural housing loans. The separate administration of rural loans continues to the present with the Farmers Home Administration (FmHA), which offers direct loans for rural housing that may be used in conjunction with other housing assistance such as Section 8 housing assistance.

While another major housing act would not be passed until 1949, government housing agencies underwent several reorganizations between 1937 and 1949. In 1939, the United States Public Housing Authority was transferred to the newly created Federal Works Agency; and the Federal Loan Agency was created to assume responsibility for the FHA, the RFC, Fannie Mae, the Federal Home Loan Bank Board, and the Home Owners Loan Corporation. Three years later, the National Housing Agency (NHA) was established to handle all nonfarm housing programs. The Federal Home Loan Bank Administration, the FHA, and the Federal Public Housing Administration became constituent agencies of NHA. In 1943, the Housing and Home Finance Agency (HHFA), HUD's immediate predecessor, replaced the NHA.

The 1940s

World War II caused a temporary moratorium on domestic housing construction except for defense purposes. Legislation during this period, however, had a major impact on housing. The 1944 authorization of the Veterans Administration (VA) home loan program has guaranteed millions of single-family and mobile home loans since its inception. The market increase in housing construction following World War II, which led to the growth of suburban areas, is in part attributable to this financing program. This exodus to the suburbs in turn led to the need for new housing programs to deal with declining urban areas. Congress responded to this urban decline with the Housing Act of 1949. Title I of the 1949 act authorized funds to localities to assist in slum clearance and urban redevelopment. This program, as had earlier programs, once again emphasized new construction. In addition, it provided funding for activities not directly related to housing construction. Open space land, neighborhood facilities and basic water and sewer facilities were all made eligible for federal assistance.

The 1950s

The Housing Act of 1954 amended the 1949 act to provide funding, not only for new construction and demolition, but for the rehabilitation and conservation of deteriorating areas. These amendments represented a substantive change in the evaluation of housing problems. The gradually shift from new construction to conservation has had a major impact on today's housing policies where rehabilitation rather than demolition is encouraged. Two years later the Housing Act of 1956 added special provisions under Sections 203 and 207 and the public housing programs to give preference to the elderly, and amended the 1949 act to authorize relocation payments to persons displaced by urban renewal. Federal involvement in housing was rapidly expanding to include not only the financing of new construction but measures to preserve existing housing resources and develop better communities. This trend continued throughout the 1960s and into the 1970s.

The 1960s

Legislation in the 1960s expressed the social concerns of providing decent and sanitary housing and ensuring that such housing is made available to all. In that spirit, Executive Order 11063, Equal Opportunity in Housing, was issued in 1962 and represented the first major effort by the federal government to combine civil rights with housing. Title VI of the Civil Rights Act of 1964 assured nondiscrimination on federally assisted programs. Equality in housing opportunity was legislated by Title VII of the Civil Rights Act of 1968, the Fair Housing Act, which prohibited discrimination in the sale, financing, or leading of housing. The full protection of the law was expanded by the Fair Housing Amendments of 1988, further prohibiting discrimination based on familial status or handicap. In 1965, the Housing and Urban Development Act created HUD to succeed the HHFA as a cabinet-level agency. The 1960s brought a new method of developing low-income housing. The Housing and Urban Development Act of 1965 initiated a new leased housing program to make privately owned housing available to low-income families. The Housing and Community Development Act of 1974 replaced Section 23 with the Section 8 Leased Housing Assistance Payment Program. Title I of the 1974 act created a new community development block grant (CDBG) program.

The 1970s

In the late 1960s to the mid-1970s, laws were enacted to define and protect the rights of consumers in the areas of interstate land sales and real estate settlement procedures (RESPA). The Home Mortgage Disclosure Act of 1976 and the Community Reinvestment Act of 1978 attempted to have lending institutions reveal where they were making their housing loans in an effort to discourage geographical discrimination in the mortgage lending industry.

The 1980s

The 1980s represented an era of retrenchment in new housing construction programs funded by HUD. Project based Section 8 assistance, which proliferated during the 1970s, obligated the government to long-term housing assistance payments. Budgetary constraints during the 1980s led to the elimination of the Section 8 new construction program in order to limit the scope of its assistance to existing housing.

The 1990s

The 1990s presented a different set of crises for the department, much of which related to the cost of expiring Section 8 contracts and deteriorating properties. Several new programs were established to ensure the survival of affordable units and the viability of subsidized housing programs. The Low-Income Housing Preservation and Resident Homeownership Act of 1990 attempted to maintain the supply of affordable housing by offering project incentives not to prepay mortgages and to continue the low-income rental use of their properties. In addition, HUD was facing the high cost of renewing expiring Section 8 contracts. At the crux of the problem, was the high cost of FHA-insured mortgages, which necessitated higher than market-rate rents, thereby making HUD Section 8 subsidies extremely expensive. The Multifamily Assisted Housing Reform and Affordability Act of 1997 created a mechanism to restructure the mortgages in order to maintain affordable Section 8 subsidies.

HUD was also beset by budgetary pressures and was forced to look to management reform and personnel cutbacks. Significant organizational reconfiguration was necessary, based on the long-range HUD 2020 Management Reform Plan (2020 Plan), which was announced in 1997 as an attempt to streamline the department through significant staff cuts and reorganizing operations by function. The intent of the plan was to eliminate "stovepipe" bureaucratic processes in which offices operate independently, with duplication of operations. Under the 2020 Plan, programs were consolidated and some functions were to be privatized, with the number of HUD programs to be reduced from 300 to 70. Although significant staff reductions were achieved, program consolidation had only limited success.

The Present

The mission of HUD, to "promote adequate and affordable housing, economic opportunity, and a suitable living environment free from discrimination" continues to focus the department's initiatives. Over the past two years, the national home ownership rate for all Americans has reached a record of 68 percent, but minority home ownership rates lag far behind. The department is committed to former president Bush's goal of creating 5.5 million new minority home owners by the end of the decade. Together with the housing industry, HUD programs play a key role in helping to reach this goal, including FHA mortgage insurance, an important source of financing, especially for minority and lower-income homebuyers; home ownership vouchers; the HOME program; CDBG; housing counseling; and other focused efforts.

During fiscal year 2002, HUD launched a major consumer advocacy initiative: reforming outdated and needlessly complex regulatory requirements under RESPA.

To assist citizens who decide against or who may not be prepared for home ownership, HUD also maintains a commitment to increasing quality affordable rental housing. Working with public agencies, nonprofit, faith-based, and community organizations as well as private partners, the department has helped expand the availability of affordable housing and improve structural and living conditions at HUD-insured and assisted rental housing projects. Moreover, a variety of HUD program offices offer specially targeted programs to provide housing and other essential support to populations with special needs, including the elderly, persons with disabilities, individuals with HIV/AIDS, and the homeless.

REAL ESTATE SETTLEMENT PROCEDURE ACT (RESPA)

http://www.hud.gov/offices/hsg/sfh/res/respa

RESPA is about closing costs and settlement procedures. RESPA requires that consumers receive disclosures at various times in the transaction and outlaws kickbacks that increase the cost of settlement services. RESPA is a HUD consumer protection statute designed to help home buyers be better shoppers in the home buying process, and is enforced by HUD. RESPA is a consumer protection statute, first passed in 1974. Some disclosures spell out the costs associated with the settlement, outline lender servicing and escrow account practices and describe business relationships between settlement service providers. RESPA also prohibits certain practices that increase the cost of settlement services. Section 8 of RESPA prohibits a person from giving or accepting any thing of value for referrals of settlement service business related to a federally related mortgage loan. It also prohibits a person from giving or accepting any part of a charge for services that are not performed. Section 9 of RESPA prohibits home sellers from requiring home buyers to purchase title insurance from a particular company. RESPA covers loans secured with a mortgage placed on a one-to-four family residential property. These include most purchase loans, assumptions, refinances, property improvement loans, and equity lines of credit. HUD's Office of RESPA and Interstate Land Sales is responsible for enforcing RESPA.

When borrowers apply for a mortgage loan, mortgage brokers and/or lenders must give the borrowers:

- A Special Information Booklet, which contains consumer information regarding various real estate settlement services. (Required for purchase transactions only.)
- A Good Faith Estimate (GFE) of settlement costs, which lists the charges the buyer is likely to pay at settlement. This is only an estimate and the actual charges may differ. If a lender requires the borrower to use a particular settlement provider, then the lender must disclose this requirement on the GFE.
- A Mortgage Servicing Disclosure Statement, which discloses to the borrower whether the lender intends to service the loan or transfer it to another lender. It also provides information about complaint resolution.

If the borrowers don't get these documents at the time of application, the lender must mail them within three business days of receiving the loan application. If the lender turns down the loan within three days, however, then RESPA does not require the lender to provide these documents. The RESPA statute does not provide an explicit penalty for the failure to provide the Special Information Booklet, Good Faith Estimate or Mortgage Servicing Statement. However, bank regulators may choose to impose penalties on lenders who fail to comply with federal law. Please read the section on RESPA enforcement for more information. At the time of closing, borrowers must be given an Affiliated Business Arrangement (AfBA) Disclosure is required whenever a settlement service provider involved in a RESPA covered transaction refers the consumer to a provider with whom the referring party has an ownership or other beneficial interest. The referring party must also give the AfBA disclosure to the consumer at or prior to the time of referral. The disclosure must describe the business arrangement that exists between the two providers and give the borrower an estimate of the second provider's charges. Except in cases where a lender refers a borrower to an attorney, credit reporting agency, or real estate appraiser to represent the lender's interest in the transaction, the referring party may not require the consumer to use the particular provider being referred. The HUD-1 Settlement Statement is a standard form that clearly shows all charges imposed on borrowers and sellers in connection with the settlement. RESPA allows the borrower to request to see the HUD-1 Settlement Statement one day before the actual settlement. The settlement agent must then provide the borrowers with a completed HUD-1 Settlement Statement based on information known to the agent at that time.

The HUD-1 Settlement Statement shows the actual settlement costs of the loan transaction. Separate forms may be prepared for the borrower and the seller. Where it is not the practice that the borrower and the seller both attend the settlement, the HUD-1 should be mailed or delivered as soon as practicable after settlement.

The Initial Escrow Statement itemizes the estimated taxes, insurance premiums, and other charges anticipated to be paid from the Escrow Account during the first twelve months of the loan. It lists the escrow payment amount and any required cushion. Although the statement is usually given at settlement, the lender has 45 days from settlement to deliver it. Loan servicers must deliver to borrowers an Annual Escrow Statement once a year. The annual escrow account statement summarizes all escrow account deposits and payments during the servicer's twelve month computation year. It also notifies the borrower of any shortages or surpluses in the account and advises the borrower about the course of action being taken.

A Servicing Transfer Statement is required if the loan servicer sells or assigns the servicing rights to a borrower's loan to another loan servicer. Generally, the loan servicer must notify the borrower 15 days before the effective date of the loan transfer. As long the borrower makes a timely payment to the old servicer within 60 days of the loan transfer, the borrower cannot be penalized. The notice must include the name and address of the new servicer, toll-free telephone numbers, and the date the new servicer will begin accepting payments.

Section 8 of RESPA prohibits anyone from giving or accepting a fee, kickback or any thing of value in exchange for referrals of settlement service business involving a federally related mortgage loan. In addition, RESPA prohibits fee splitting and receiving unearned fees for services not actually performed. Violations of Section 8's anti-kickback, referral fees and unearned fees provisions of RESPA are subject to criminal and civil penalties. In a criminal case a person who violates Section 8 may be fined up to $10,000 and imprisoned up to one year. In a private law suit a person who violates Section 8 may be liable to the person charged for the settlement service an amount equal to three times the amount of the charge paid for the service.

Section 9 of RESPA prohibits a seller from requiring the home buyer to use a particular title insurance company, either directly or indirectly, as a condition of sale. Buyers may sue a seller who violates this provision for an amount equal to three times all charges made for the title insurance.

Section 10 of RESPA sets limits on the amounts that a lender may require a borrower to put into an escrow account for purposes of paying taxes, hazard insurance and other charges related to the property. RESPA does not require lenders to impose an escrow account on borrowers; however, certain government loan programs or lenders may require escrow accounts as a condition of the loan. During the course of the loan, RESPA prohibits a lender from charging excessive amounts for the escrow account. Each month the lender may require a borrower to pay into the escrow account no more than 1/12 of the total of all disbursements payable during the year, plus an amount necessary to pay for any shortage in the account. In addition, the lender may require a cushion, not to exceed an amount equal to 1/6 of the total disbursements for the year. The lender must perform an escrow account analysis once during the year and notify borrowers of any shortage. Any excess of $50 or more must be returned to the borrower.

Individuals have one (1) year to bring a private lawsuit to enforce violations of Section 8 or 9. A person may bring an action for violations of Section 6 within three years. Lawsuits for violations of Section 6, 8, or 9 may be brought in any federal district court in the district in which the property is located or where the violation is alleged to have occurred. HUD, a state attorney general or state insurance commissioner may bring an injunctive action to enforce violations of Section 6, 8 or 9 of RESPA within three (3) years. Section 6 provides borrowers with important consumer protections relating to the servicing of their loans. Under Section 6 of RESPA, borrowers who have a problem with the servicing of their loan (including escrow account questions), should contact their loan servicer in writing, outlining the nature of their complaint. The servicer must acknowledge the complaint in writing within 20 business days of receipt of the complaint. Within 60 business days the servicer must resolve the complaint by correcting the account or giving a statement of the reasons for its position. Until the complaint is resolved, borrowers should continue to make the servicer's required payment. A borrower may bring a private lawsuit, or a group of borrowers may bring a class action suit, within three years, against a servicer who fails to comply with Section 6's provisions. Borrowers may obtain actual damages, as well as additional damages if there is a pattern of noncompliance. Under Section 10, HUD has authority to impose a civil penalty on loan servicers who do not submit initial or annual escrow account statements to borrowers. Borrowers should contact HUD's Office of RESPA and Interstate Land Sales to report servicers who fail to provide the required escrow account statements. Persons who believe a settlement service provider has violated RESPA in an area in which the department has enforcement authority (primarily sections 6, 8 and 9), may wish to file a complaint. The complaint should outline the violation and identify the violators by name, address and phone number. Complainants should also provide their own name and phone number for follow up questions from HUD. Requests for confidentiality will be honored. Complaints should be sent to: Director, Office of RESPA and Interstate Land Sales US Department of Housing and Urban Development, Room 9154, 451 7th Street, SW, Washington, DC 20410

Your home mortgage may be the largest and most important loan you get during your lifetime. You should be aware of certain rights before you enter into any loan agreement:

- You have the RIGHT to shop for the best loan for you and compare the charges of different mortgage brokers and lenders.
- You have the RIGHT to be informed about the total cost of your loan including the interest rate, points and other fees.

- You have the RIGHT to ask for a Good Faith Estimate of all loan and settlement charges before you agree to the loan and pay any fees.
- You have the RIGHT to know what fees are not refundable if you decide to cancel the loan agreement.
- You have the RIGHT to ask your mortgage broker to explain exactly what the mortgage broker will do for you.
- You have the RIGHT to know how much the mortgage broker is getting paid by you and the lender for your loan.
- You have the RIGHT to ask questions about charges and loan terms that you do not understand.
- You have the RIGHT to a credit decision that is not based on your race, color, religion, national origin, sex, marital status, age, or whether any income is from public assistance.
- You have the RIGHT to know the reason if your loan was turned down.
- You have the RIGHT to ask for the HUD settlement costs booklet "Buying Your Home."

RESPA was created in part because various companies associated with the buying and selling of real estate, such as lenders, realtors, and title insurance companies were often engaging in providing undisclosed kickbacks to each other, inflating the costs of real estate transactions and obscuring price competition by facilitating bait and switch tactics. For example, a lender advertising a home loan might have advertised the loan with a 5 percent interest rate, but then when one applies for the loan one is told that one must use the lender's affiliated title insurance company and pay $5,000 for the service (whereas the normal rate is $1,000). The title company would then have paid $4,000 to the lender. This was made illegal. The act prohibits kickbacks between lenders and third-party settlement service agents in the real estate settlement process (Section 8 of RESPA), requires lenders to provide a good faith estimate for all the approximate costs of a particular loan and finally a HUD-1 (for purchase real estate loans) or a HUD-1A (for refinances of real estate loans) at the closing of the real estate loan. The final HUD-1 or HUD-1A allows the borrower to know specifically the costs of the loan and to whom the fees are being allotted.

If the borrower believes there is an error in the mortgage account, he or she can make a "qualified written request" to the loan servicer. The request must be in writing, identify the borrower by name and account, and include a statement of reasons why the borrower believes the account is in error. The request should include the words "qualified written request." It cannot be written on the payment coupon, but must be on a separate piece of paper. The Department of Housing and Urbana Development provides a sample letter. The servicer must acknowledge receipt of the request within 20 days. The servicer then has 60 days (from the request) to take action on the request. The servicer has to either provide a written notification that the error has been corrected, or provide a written explanation as to why the servicer believes the account is correct. Either way, the servicer has to provide the name and telephone number of a person with whom the borrower can discuss the matter. The servicer cannot provide information to any credit agency regarding any overdue payment during the 60-day period. If the servicer fails to comply with the "qualified written request," the borrower is entitled to actual damages, up to $1000 of additional damages if there is a pattern of noncompliance, costs and attorneys fees.

Critics say however that kickbacks still occur. For example, lenders often provide captive insurance to the title insurance companies they work with, which critics say is essentially a kickback mechanism. Others counter that, economically, the transaction is a zero sum game, where if the kickback were forbidden, a lender would simply charge higher prices. One of the core elements of the debate is the fact that customers overwhelmingly go with the default service providers associated with a lender or a realtor, even though they sign documents explicitly stating that they can choose to use any service provider. Some say that if the profits of the service providers were truly excessive or if the price of the services were excessively inflated because of illegal or quasi-legal kickbacks, then at some point nonaffiliated service providers would attempt to target consumers directly with lower prices to entice them to choose the unaffiliated provider.

There have been various proposals to modify the Real Estate Settlement Procedures Act. One proposal is to change the "open architecture" system currently in place, where a customer can choose to use any service provider for each service, to one where the services are bundled, but where the realtor or lender must pay directly for all other costs. Under this system, lenders, who have more buying power, would more aggressively seek the lowest price for real estate settlement services.

THE TRUTH IN LENDING ACT (TILA) OF 1968

http://www.fdic.gov/regulations/laws/rules/6500-1400.html

A United States federal law designed to protect consumers in credit transactions by requiring clear disclosure of key terms of the lending arrangement and all costs. The statute is contained in title I of the Consumer Credit Protection Act, as amended (15 *USC* 1601 et seq.). The regulations implementing the statute, which are known as "Regulation Z," are codified at 12 CFR Part 226. Most of the specific requirements imposed by TILA are found in Regulation Z, so a reference to the requirements of TILA usually refers to the requirements contained in Regulation Z as well as the statute itself. The purpose of TILA is to promote the informed use of consumer credit by requiring disclosures about its terms, cost to standardize the manner in which costs associated with borrowing are calculated and disclosed. TILA also gives consumers the right to cancel certain credit transactions that involve a lien on a consumer's principal dwelling, regulates certain credit card practices, and provides a means for fair and timely resolution of credit billing disputes. With the exception of certain high-cost mortgage loans, TILA does not regulate the charges that may be imposed for consumer credit. Rather, it requires uniform or standardized disclosure of costs and charges so that consumers can shop. It also imposes limitations on home equity plans that are subject to the requirements of Sec. 226.5b and certain higher-cost mortgages that are subject to the requirements of Sec. 226.32. The regulation prohibits certain acts or practices in connection with credit secured by a consumer's principal dwelling.

The statute is divided into subparts and appendices as follows:

- Subpart A contains general information. It sets forth: (i) The authority, purpose, coverage, and organization of the regulation; (ii) the definitions of basic terms; (iii) the transactions that are exempt from coverage (which would be any business purpose loan); and (iv) the method of determining the finance charge.
- Subpart B contains the rules for open-end credit. It requires that initial disclosures and periodic statements be provided, as well as additional disclosures for credit and charge card applications and solicitations and for home equity plans subject to the requirements of Sec. 226.5a

and Sec. 226.5b, respectively. The Subpart also covers the right of rescission requirements and the advertising restrictions for open-end credit. For example, a home equity line of credit advertisement cannot mention any tax benefits without verbiage suggesting that the consumer consult a tax adviser.

- Subpart C relates to closed-end credit. It contains rules on disclosures, treatment of credit balances, annual percentage rate calculations, right of rescission requirements, and advertising.
- Subpart D contains rules on oral disclosures, Spanish language disclosure in Puerto Rico, record retention, effect on state laws, state exemptions (which only apply to states that had Truth in Lending-type laws prior to the Federal Act, and rate limitations.
- Subpart E contains special rules for mortgage transactions. Section 226.32 requires certain disclosures and provides limitations for loans that have rates and fees above specified amounts. Section 226.33 requires disclosures, including the total annual loan cost rate, for reverse mortgage transactions. Section 226.34 prohibits specific acts and practices in connection with mortgage transactions.

Several appendices contain information such as the procedures for determinations about state laws, state exemptions and issuance of staff interpretations, special rules for certain kinds of credit plans, a list of enforcement agencies, model disclosures which if used properly will ensure compliance with the Act, and the rules for computing annual percentage rates in closed-end credit transactions and total annual loan cost rates for *reverse mortgage* transactions.

The lender must disclose to the borrower the *annual percentage rate* (APR). The APR reflects the cost of the credit to the consumer. It contains things other than interest such as origination fees and discount points. The Truth-in-Lending Act defines "finance charge" as all fees paid either directly or indirectly by the person to whom the credit is extended, incident to the extension of the credit. There are exceptions to this rule found at 12 CFR 226.4. Generally fees paid to the lender are considered finance charges regardless of any costs they are designed to cover.

OTHER HOUSING RELATED REGULATIONS IN CHRONOLOGICAL ORDER

- **National Housing Act** (48 Stat. 1246). Creates the Federal Housing Administration. June 27, 1934.
- **United States Housing Act of 1937** (50 Stat. 888). Creates the United States Housing Authority for low-rent housing and slum clearance projects. September 1, 1937.
- **Reorganization Plan Number 3** (61 Stat. 954). Establishes the Housing and Home Finance Agency. July 27, 1947.
- **Housing Act of 1949** (63 Stat. 413). Establishes the national housing objective to provide federal aid to assist slum-clearance, community development, and redevelopment programs. July 15, 1949.
- **Housing Act of 1954** (68 Stat. 590). Section 701 comprehensive planning assistance. August 2, 1954.
- **Housing Act of 1959** (73 Stat. 654). Direct loans for senior citizen housing. September 23, 1959.
- **Housing Act of 1964** (78 Stat. 769). Section 312 rehabilitation loans. September 2, 1964.
- **The Department of Housing and Urban Development Act** (79 Stat. 667). Establishes a Department of Housing and Urban Development. September 9, 1965.
- **Civil Rights Act of 1968** (82 Stat. 73). Title VIII of this act provides for fair housing. April 11, 1968.
- **Housing and Urban Development Act of 1968** (82 Stat. 476). Adds sections 235, 236, 237, and 238 to the National Housing Act. Enacts the New Communities Act of 1968, National Flood Insurance Act of 1968, Urban Property Protection and Reinsurance Act of 1968, and Interstate Land Sales Full Disclosure Act. Creates Government National Mortgage Association (Ginnie Mae). August 1, 1968.
- **Housing and Urban Development Act of 1970** (84 Stat. 1770). Provides for the establishment of a national growth policy, encourages and supports the proper growth and development of the states, metropolitan areas, cities, counties, and towns with emphasis upon new community and inner-city development, and extends and amends laws relating to housing and urban development. December 31, 1970.
- **Reorganization Plan Number 1 of 1973** (87 Stat. 1089). Transfers the Office of Emergency Preparedness to HUD. July 1, 1973.

- **Housing and Community Development Act of 1974** (88 Stat. 633). Establishes Community Development Block Grants. Adds National Mobile Home Construction and Safety Standards Act of 1974, the Consumer Home Mortgage Assistance Act of 1974, and provides for Urban Homesteading. August 22, 1974.
- **Solar Heating and Cooling Demonstration Act of 1974** (88 Stat. 1069). Provides for the early development and commercial demonstrations of the technology of solar heating and cooling systems. September 3, 1974.
- **Emergency Home Purchase Assistance Act of 1974** (88 Stat. 1364). Gives Government National Mortgage Association tandem authority to increase on an emergency basis the availability of reasonably priced mortgage credit. October 18, 1974.
- **Emergency Housing Act of 1975** (89 Stat. 249). Includes Emergency Homeowners' Relief Act and authorizes temporary assistance to unemployed or underemployed for purpose of defraying mortgage payments. July 2, 1975.
- **Housing Authorization Act of 1976** (90 Stat. 1067). Amends and extends housing and community development laws with key changes to flood insurance and home ownership counseling. August 3, 1976.
- **Supplemental Housing Authorization Act of 1977** (91 Stat. 55). Title II establishes the National Commission on Neighborhoods. April 30, 1977.
- **Housing and Community Development Act of 1977** (91 Stat. 1111). Substantial changes to the Community Development Block Grant Program; establishes Urban Development Action Grants and Small Cities Development Study; allows graduated payment mortgages; extends elderly and handicapped provisions; directs submission of an annual report on National Urban Policy; extends flood insurance provisions; establishes the Community Reinvestment Act of 1977. October 12, 1977.
- **Reorganization Plan Number 3 of 1978** (92 Stat. 3788). Transfers the Federal Insurance Administration and the Federal Disaster Assistance Administration to the Federal Emergency Management Agency. July 19, 1978.
- **Housing and Community Development Amendments of 1978** (92 Stat. 2080). Substantial changes to the Community Development Block Grant Program; establishes assistance payments to owners of multi-family projects; extends elderly and handicapped provisions;

establishes the Neighborhood Self-Help Development Act of 1978. October 31, 1978.

- **National Energy Conservation Policy Act** (92 Stat. 3206). Authorizes financing for energy conservation improvements and solar energy research, demonstration, and implementation. November 9, 1978.
- **Housing and Community Development Amendments of 1979** (93 Stat. 1101). Variety of amendments to the Community Development Block Grant, Action Grant, Neighborhood Self-Help Development, and Urban Homesteading programs; changes in rent supplement program; establishes higher mortgage limits for FHA homes; and transfers the position of Federal Insurance Administrator (Urban Property Protection and Reinsurance Act of 1968) to the Federal Emergency Management Agency. December 21, 1979.
- **Veterans' Disability Compensation and Housing Benefits Amendments of 1980** (94 Stat. 1528). Amends title 38, United States Code to provide for limited grants for special home adaptations for certain severely disabled veterans, to provide for Veterans' Administration guaranties for loans to refinance certain existing veterans' home loans, and to increase the maximum loan guaranties for home loans made to veterans. October 7, 1980.
- **Housing and Community Development Act of 1980** (94 Stat. 1614). Amends and extends certain Federal laws relating to housing, community and neighborhood development and preservation, and related programs. October 8, 1980.
- **Housing and Community Development Amendments of 1981** (95 Stat. 384). Amends the Housing and Community Development Act of 1974. August 13, 1981.
- **Veterans' Disability Compensation, Housing, and Memorial Benefits Amendments of 1981** (95 Stat. 1026). Amends Title 38, United States Code to authorize the administrator of Veterans' Affairs to guarantee home loans with provisions for graduated-payment plans. October 17, 1981.
- **Housing and Urban-Rural Recovery Act of 1983** (97 Stat. 1153). An act making supplemental appropriations for the fiscal year ending September 30, 1984. Creates housing voucher program as an alternative to Section 8 rent certificates. Creates Rental Rehabilitation Program. November 30, 1983.

- **Housing and Community Development Technical Amendments Act of 1984** (98 Stat. 2218). Makes technical and conforming amendments to the Housing and Urban-Rural Recovery Act of 1983, the Housing and Community Development Act of 1974, and the National Housing Act. October 17, 1984.
- **Housing and Community Development Reconciliation Amendments of 1985** (100 Stat. 101). Amends various provisions of the Housing and Community Development Act of 1974 and extends FHA mortgage insurance programs and rural housing authorities. April 7, 1986.
- **Stewart B. McKinney Homeless Assistance Act** (101 Stat. 482). Provides assistance to the homeless, with special emphasis on elderly persons, persons with disabilities, and families with children. July 22, 1987.
- **Housing and Community Development Act of 1987** (101 Stat. 1815). Makes housing vouchers a permanent program. Allows sales of public housing to resident management corporations. Authorizes enterprise zones. February 5, 1988.
- **Indian Housing Act** (102 Stat. 676). Amends the United States Housing Act of 1937 to establish a separate program to address housing assistance for Indian and Alaskan natives. June 28, 1988.
- **Fair Housing Amendments Act of 1988** (102 Stat. 1619). Amends Title VIII of the Civil Rights Act of 1968, to expand the scope of fair housing provisions. Gives HUD enforcement responsibility. September 13, 1988.
- **Stewart B. McKinney Homeless Assistance Amendments Act of 1988** (102 Stat. 3224). Amends the Stewart B. McKinney Homeless Assistance Act to extend programs providing assistance for the homeless. November 7, 1988.
- **Housing and Urban Development Reform Act** (103 Stat. 1987). Establishes over fifty legislative, regulatory, and administrative reforms to help insure ethical, financial, and management integrity. December 15, 1989.
- **Cranston-Gonzalez National Affordable Housing Act** (104 Stat. 4079). Creates the HOME Investment Partnerships program, a National Homeownership Trust program, HOPE program, and provides funding for homeless programs. November 28, 1990.
- **VA-HUD Independent Agencies Appropriations Act** (105 Stat. 743). Provides funding and authorization for a Capital Grants program

to construct or substantially rehabilitate housing for the elderly and disabled, replacing the Section 202 direct loan program. Creates the Office of Lead-Based Paint Abatement and Poisoning Prevention. (105 Stat. 753, 42 U.S.C. 3532 note). October 28, 1991.

- **Housing and Community Development Act of 1992** (106 Stat. 3672). Creates the Office of Federal Housing Enterprise Oversight to supervise Fannie Mae and Freddie Mac. Enacts the Residential Lead-Based Paint Hazard Reduction Act of 1992, to develop a national strategy to eliminate lead-based paint hazard in all housing, and the Removal of Regulatory Barriers to Affordable Housing Act of 1992, to identify and remove governmental barriers that increase housing costs and limit the supply of affordable housing. October 28, 1992.
- **Omnibus Budget Reconciliation Act of 1993** (107 Stat. 312). Authorizes the establishment of enterprise zones to stimulate economic development within designated distressed areas through a combination of tax incentives and direct funding. Nine empowerment zones and ninety-five enterprise communities, which receive a lower level of support, are authorized. The designated areas must be nominated by state and local governments and meet criteria for economic distress. The six empowerment zones and sixty-five enterprise communities in urban areas were designated by HUD in December 1994. The Department of Agriculture designated rural areas on August 10, 1993.
- **Multifamily Housing Property Disposition Reform Act of 1994** (108 Stat. 342). Gives HUD greater flexibility in disposing of apartment buildings that have fallen into government possession through foreclosure. Contains HOME and public housing technical changes, expansion of Section 108 loan guarantees, and changes to multifamily financing risk-sharing demonstrations enacted in the 1992 Housing Act. April 11, 1994.
- **Housing Opportunity Program Extension Act of 1996** (110 Stat. 834). Gives owners of multifamily properties in the low-income housing preservation program the right to prepay their mortgages and includes new drug and alcohol abuse provisions designed to help Public Housing Authorities screen applicants and evict individuals with criminal records, or those whose behavior is found to endanger other residents. March 28, 1996.
- **Quality Housing and Work Responsibility Act of 1998.** Provides

additional public housing units for moderate-income working families, raises the limit on FHA loans, creates a home ownership voucher program and authorizes a home rehabilitation program.

APPENDIX E

CONSUMER ADVOCACY AND RESEARCH GROUPS

AMERICANS FOR FAIRNESS IN LENDING (AFFIL)

http://www.affil.org

AFFIL focuses on abusive credit and lending practices and calls for re-regulation of the industry. This organization is the collaborative effort of numerous partner and ally organizations, each contributing their expertise to AFFIL and the public through AFFIL activities. In 2004, a group of consumer advocates, economists, and policy makers began discussing how to reverse certain economic trends. They determined that what was needed was a public awareness campaign that could move forward the advocacy, educational, legal, and policy work already being done to protect consumers. The National Consumer Law Center organized a conference, assisted by ACORN, the Center for Responsible Lending, and the Consumer Federation of America. The conference, Changing Attitudes, Reforming Policy in the Credit Marketplace, took place in Cleveland, Ohio, at Cleveland State University, on October, 7–8, 2004. Over 100 prominent advocates, experts, and community organizers attended, ranging from the Rainbow Push Coalition and LA Chinatown Service Center to the American Association of Retired Persons (AARP). The conference allowed participants to exchange information, watch presentations by two ad firms, and discuss the most effective strategies for moving forward. As an essential first step, AFFIL representatives met with key nonprofit organizations to develop the vision for the message campaign. Many of these organizations formally become AFFIL partners. AFFIL also maintained contact with locally focused groups from the formative Cleveland conference, many of whom became the first AFFIL allies. In the summer and fall of 2006, AFFIL began to solidify as its own organization. AFFIL was incorporated in the state of Massachusetts on August 31, 2006, and filed for 501(c)(3) tax status soon thereafter. During the fall of 2006, the partners met three times in Washington, DC, twice at AARP and once at the National Council of La Raza. At these meetings, they jointly wrote AFFIL's *Six Principles of Fairness in Lending.*

ASSOCIATION OF COMMUNITY ORGANIZATIONS FOR REFORM NOW (ACORN)

http://www.acorn.org

The Association of Community Organizations for Reform Now, is the nation's largest community organization of low- and moderate-income families, with over 175,000 member families organized into 850 neighborhood chapters in 80 cities across the country. Since 1970, ACORN has taken action and won victories on issues of concern to its members. Its priorities include: better housing for first-time home buyers and tenants, living wages for low-wage workers, more investment in our communities from banks and governments, and better public schools. It achieves these goals by building community organizations that have the power to win changes—through direct action, negotiation, legislation, and voter participation.

The sixties were an important time in the history of American politics. The decade witnessed struggles for freedom for low-income people and minorities across the nation as well as a war that deeply divided all Americans. Amid the confusion and conflict, some important lessons were learned by those who cared deeply about America and her people—lessons that would endure and make a lasting impact on the nation. One of the groups that took risks, explored new ideas and developed a unique formula for a politics of justice in America was the National Welfare Rights Organization (NWRO), led by George Wiley. Wiley developed and led the National Welfare Rights Organization in the mid-sixties to become a national force for the needs and rights of low-income people. By 1966, the NWRO had 170 groups in sixty cities across the nation. Despite the very real needs of its members, the NWRO was destined to remain a small minority with limited power in American politics unless it could build a network of friends and allies. When Rathke arrived in Little Rock in 1970, he began a campaign to help welfare recipients attain their basic needs—clothing and furniture. This drive, inspired by a clause in the Arkansas welfare laws, began the effort to create and sustain a social justice movement that would grow to become the Arkansas Community Organizations for Reform Now—ACORN. The goal was to unite welfare recipients with working people in need around issues of free school lunches for schoolchildren, unemployed workers' concerns, Vietnam Veterans' rights, and hospital emergency room care. The inclusion of many groups in a single coalition came with costs. In particular, many welfare rights members wanted a strictly welfare rights group and withdrew from the organization, fearing that they would lose control. After the split, the organization diversified further with the addition of the Vietnam Veterans Organizing Committee (VVOC) and the Unemployed Workers Organizing Committee (UWOC). The following year, ACORN leaders organized a "Save the City" campaign in Little Rock. The campaign addressed blue-collar home owners' concerns that their neighborhoods were being destroyed by traffic problems in the Centennial section, and by unscrupulous real estate agencies who engaged in blockbusting in the Oak Forest section. ACORN began growing geographically, establishing six regional offices in the state. Campaigns were developed around issues of concern to small town and rural Arkansans and the foundations were laid for statewide campaigns. In 1972, ACORN made its first entry into electoral politics. In 1975, ACORN became a multistate organization with new branches in Texas and South Dakota. Each year thereafter saw three or more states join ACORN with a total in 1980 of twenty states. The great expansion of the organization led to multistate campaigns beginning with a mass meeting of 1,000 members in Memphis in 1978. ACORN national conventions and actions in 1978, 1979, and 1980 led to an entry into national politics. In December 1978, ACORN held its first national convention in Memphis, Tennessee, to discuss and initiate a national platform for low- and moderate-income people. The following summer, July 1, 1979, ACORN's second National Convention and Platform Conference was held in St. Louis. The ACORN Commission was a proposal for changes in the Democratic Party that would mandate more low- to moderate-income delegates in their national convention and in important positions on committees. ACORN members reasoned that if the best route to power for low- and moderate-income people is through organization, it would be wise to create organizational means for power within the Democratic Party. ACORN members ran as delegates to the Democratic National Convention in New York in caucuses and primaries. The result was a contingent of forty-two delegates and alternates representing ACORN in the convention. On the floor of the convention, ACORN passed a resolution by voice vote establishing the ACORN Commission. Meanwhile, ACORN members got Republican attention by testifying at the Republican Platform Committee. The campaign won some valuable victories for ACORN and its members. First, it made ACORN a truly national organization of some 30,000 ACORN families in every section of the country and helped to unify an organization that had grown from three states to twenty in only five years. Most importantly, it brought together different groups of people from a far-flung constituency of Westerners, rural Southerners, big-city Northerners and so on, into a unified group with a shared set of goals. The eighties proved to be a time when the political elite in America was less concerned with the needs of low- and moderate-income people than ever. The immediate impact of Reagan's presidency was a severe recession with increased unemployment, a rapid increase in the cost of necessities and serious economic hardship for the lower end of the income scale. Reagan also set about changing the shape of American politics by taking important responsibilities away from national control and placing them at state and local levels. Tax cuts, vastly increased defense spending, and dramatic cuts in social spending saddled state and local governments with severe social problems. Meanwhile the federal government piled up unheard-of budget deficits. ACORN launched a campaign to obtain affordable housing. Long before it became fashionable to be concerned about the homeless, ACORN was fighting for homes for low- and moderate-income people. Noting that economic upheaval had forced many people to default on mortgages, ACORN sought to place needy people in the resulting vacant homes. This required the forceful and illegal (though logical and moral) seizing of the properties—squatting. The squatting campaigns involved personal, community, and political dimensions. The personal needs of people without homes attracted many to advertisements ACORN placed in papers asking "Do you need a home?" The squatting campaign required a personal commitment to move into a vacant, usually poorly kept house and refit it for comfortable living. It also involved the risk of arrest if local authorities refused them the legal occupation of the home. Nevertheless, the response was great. Through these campaigns ACORN gained national exposure on housing issues and cemented its reputation as the leading authority on low-income community development. Tent cities symbolizing the homelessness Reagan's policies created sprang up in city after city, including Washington, DC. Internally, ACORN developed and strengthened its ACORN Political Action Committees (APACs). ACORN also established a legislative office to coordinate national ACORN goals and translate them into legislation at the national level. Working out of Washington, the office informed national leaders and media of ACORN's agenda and sought allies for the organization. This period also marked a diversification of ACORN organizing. The United Labor Unions (ULU) became an effective labor organizing arm of ACORN. The years 1980 to 1985 were a trying time for ACORN organizing. As the needs of low- and moderate-income people increased, the means of serving those needs declined. This period witnessed the maturity of ACORN in preparation for the nineties. The people and the organization they comprise, 70,000-plus in twenty-eight states, grew in size, numbers, and maturity. The original vision of the movement to win the power to control important decisions in American life for the majority continued to guide ACORN members and allies across the country. The five years between 1990 and 1995 follow the building and consolidation of the previous five years. Working at all levels of politics and in every corner of the country, ACORN has parlayed its building efforts into major victories. While some of ACORN's most exciting efforts were in the area of housing, its victories also included health, public safety, education, representation, work and workers' rights and communications concerns. The housing issue continued to heat up in 1991, when ACORN fought back against bank lobbyist efforts to gut the CRA. At the ACORN convention in New York in 1992, the "ACORN-Bank Summit" was organized to hammer out deals with giant banks like Continental, First Fidelity, Mellon, PriMerit, and Chemical. Representatives signed agreements to establish programs for low- and moderate-income people to qualify for mortgages in their communities. It made major strides in the area of education, too. ACORN expanded and won major victories in the late 1990s and early 2000s. On the political front, ACORN pursued new directions in the 1990s. Through an initiative process, ACORN put strong campaign finance reform measures on the ballot and won overwhelming voter support. ACORN members also spearheaded creation of locally based independent parties that have put dozens of progressive candidates in office. ACORN took the lead in organizing broad-based community and labor coalitions in support of a living wage. By the close of the 1990s, forty-one cities had passed living-wage laws requiring employers that receive government contracts or subsidies to pay their employees at least enough to lift a family of four above the poverty level. With the advent of welfare "reform," ACORN organized workfare workers to demand the same rights other workers enjoy as well as the child care, transportation, and job training necessary to make the transition from welfare to work. ACORN launched a new fight for fair lending, this time targeting the subprime loan industry that preys on low-income and minority neighborhoods. At the close of the 1990s, ACORN was 125,000 members strong. In 2000, ACORN escalated the fight against predatory lending. Actions and negotiations have won reforms from some of the largest subprime lenders. The campaign persists in pressuring lenders directly and pushing for stronger laws and regulations governing the industry. Affordable housing, fair lending, jobs at living wages, and better schools remain at the top of ACORN's agenda. At the same time, ACORN groups respond to members' concerns, as they always have, addressing a wide range of issues and building power for low- and moderate-income Americans.

CENTER FOR HOUSING POLICY, NATIONAL HOUSING CENTER (NHC)

http://www.nhc.org/housing/chp-about

The Center for Housing Policy is the NHC's research affiliate. In partnership with the NHC and its members, the center works to broaden understanding of the nation's housing challenges and to examine the impact of policies and programs developed to address these needs. Combining research and practical, real-world expertise, the center helps to develop effective policy solutions at the national, state and local levels that increase the availability of affordable homes. The center works by:

Expanding Awareness of the Nation's Housing Challenges: By working closely with some of the nation's leading housing researchers, as well as conducting its own analyses, the center seeks to raise awareness of the housing challenges facing American households, with a particular emphasis on the housing needs of working families with low to moderate incomes.

Strengthening Housing Policies for Working Families: The center goes beyond documenting housing problems to identify proven solutions and bring them to the attention of community leaders. Through research, it collects and analyzes information on programs and policies from around the country that have been shown to expand housing opportunities for working families. The center shares this information in an easy-to-follow format that provides a roadmap for developing effective state and local housing strategies.

Documenting and Strengthening the Connections between Affordable Housing and Key Social Objectives: The center works to identify the important connections between stable, affordable housing and other social objectives, such as improved health, stronger educational outcomes, reduced crime, and community and economic development. Through this work, the center seeks to expand the base of support for affordable housing and to develop housing policies that more effectively achieve key social objectives.

CENTER FOR RESPONSIBLE LENDING (CRL)

http://www.responsiblelending.org/about/index.html

The Center for Responsible Lending (CRL) is a nonprofit, nonpartisan research and policy organization dedicated to protecting home ownership and family wealth by working to eliminate abusive financial practices. The CRL is affiliated with Self-Help, one of the nation's largest community development financial institutions. In the late 1990s, home owners began coming to Self-Help Credit Union, a subsidiary of CRL, seeking help to avoid foreclosure. Unfortunately, it was too late for many of these families. Unscrupulous lenders already had stolen their home equity—their greatest source of wealth and future financial security. The targets for this theft are often among our most vulnerable citizens, including the elderly and working families in minority communities. In 1999, Self-Help worked with a state coalition to help pass the North Carolina Predatory Lending Law, the first such law in the country. In 2002, Self-Help established the Center for Responsible Lending to build on initial successes and expand its focus to include practices outside of mortgage lending, such as payday lending. Since then, CRL has conducted or commissioned landmark studies on predatory lending practices and the impact of state laws that protect borrowers. The CRL has also supported state efforts to combat predatory lending and worked for regulatory changes to require responsible practices among lenders nationwide. The CRL's staff includes attorneys, researchers, and policy analysts in North Carolina; Washington, DC; and California who study and report on predatory lending matters and monitor legislative and regulatory activity in state capitols and in the US Congress. CRL's work has five main components:

Policy and Technical Assistance: sharing market and legal knowledge with advocates and policymakers across the country interested in reforming lending practices.

Research: producing research on predatory lending to inform policymakers, regulators, and others on its extent and impact.

Coalition Building: supporting national and state organizations concerned about predatory lending.

Litigation: partnering with other advocates to advance predatory lending litigation and submitting legal briefs on key legal issues.

Communications: promoting public awareness and providing a web-based archive of information for local legislators and advocates.

CONSUMER CREDIT COUNSELING SERVICES (CCCS)

Consumer Credit Counseling Services (CCCA) are regional nonprofit 501(c)(3) community-service agencies dedicated to helping families achieve financial stability. CCCS members provide confidential budget counseling, money management education, debt management programs, bankruptcy counseling and education, and comprehensive housing counseling. Families turn to Consumer Credit Counseling Service for help with money problems. CCCS work with local business communities to educate consumers about money management, promote the wise use of credit as a tool for financial planning and assist people in overcoming financial difficulties. CCCS serves clients across the entire socioeconomic spectrum. The average client in debt management programs is age 42 with income of $35,753 and $25,000 of unsecured debt owed to 8.4 creditors: 59% are home owners; 62% are female; 12% are divorced. The average household has three members and 59% are Caucasian, 34% African American, 3% are Hispanic. Services include professional, certified counselors offering individual advice for developing and balancing budgets; managing money; using credit wisely; and building a savings plan. Some area CCCS members provide as many as 50,000 free, confidential budget and debt counseling sessions annually. CCCS develop reduced payment programs with creditors for consumers who are overextended. In many cases, debt repayment plans provide sound alternatives to bankruptcy. CCCSs provide money-management education in classroom settings and through interactive online courses. Seminars are conducted by certified education specialists and trained CCCS representatives for employed and employable adults in the workplace and through churches, civic organizations, educational institutions and professional associations. Programs cover many topics including Home-buyer Workshops, Conquering Credit Challenges, Road to Financial Health, Coping with Change, Money in Motion, and Identify Theft and Senior Scams. Presentations are offered in English or Spanish and can be customized for a specific audience. CCCS is certified by the US Department of Housing and Urban Development as a group of comprehensive housing counseling agencies. The agencies help consumers with prepurchase counseling, mortgage default, rent delinquency, post-occupancy counseling, and loan declinations. CCCS also serves home buyers through community organizations and governmental agencies. CCCS provide budget and credit counseling for bankruptcy filers nationwide in English and Spanish, 24 hours a day, 365 days a year. All consumers who plan to file for bankruptcy must complete a credit counseling session from an approved provider and receive a Certificate of Counseling before filing. All bankruptcy filers must complete a personal financial management course and receive a Certificate of Debtor Education before their case can be discharged. CCCS provide free or low-cost services to consumers. Support for CCCS comes from corporations, foundations, contributions from individuals, and clients on debt management plans, grants contracts, and donated services from a variety of partners. CCCS counselors are certified by the National Foundation for Credit Counseling and the agency is accredited by the Council on Accreditation. CCCS partners with United Way and members of Better Business Bureaus and Chambers of Commerce throughout its service areas.

CONSUMER FEDERATION OF AMERICA (CFA)

http://www.consumerfed.org

Since 1968, the Consumer Federation of America (CFA) has provided consumers a well-reasoned and articulate voice in decisions that affect their lives. Day in and day out, CFA's professional staff gathers facts, analyzes issues, and disseminates information to the public, policymakers, and rest of the consumer movement. The size and diversity of its membership — some 300 nonprofit organizations from throughout the nation with a combined membership exceeding fifty million people — enables CFA to speak for virtually all consumers. In particular, CFA looks out for those who have the greatest needs, especially the least affluent. CFA is an advocacy, research, education, and service organization. As an advocacy group, it works to advance pro-consumer policy on a variety of issues before Congress, the White House, federal and state regulatory agencies, state legislatures, and the courts. Its staff works with public officials to promote beneficial policies, to oppose harmful policies, and to ensure a balanced debate on important issues in which consumers have a stake. As a research organization, CFA investigates consumer issues, behavior, and attitudes using surveys, polling, focus groups, and literature reviews. The findings of such projects are published in reports that assist consumer advocates and policymakers as well as individual consumers. This research also provides the basis for new consumer initiatives, public service advertising, and consumer information and education efforts. As an education organization, CFA disseminates information on consumer issues to the public and the media, as well as to policymakers and other public-interest advocates. Conferences, reports, books, brochures, news releases, a newsletter, and a website all contribute to CFA's education program. Finally, as a service organization, CFA provides support to national, state, and local organizations committed to the goals of consumer advocacy, research, and education. Some of these organizations are consumer advocacy, education, or cooperative organizations that belong to the federation.

CONSUMERS UNION (CU)

http://www.consumerreports.org

Consumers Union (CU) is an expert, independent, nonprofit organization, whose mission is to work for a fair, just, and safe marketplace for all consumers. CU publishes *Consumer Reports* and *ConsumerReports.org* in addition to two newsletters, *Consumer Reports on Health* and *Consumer Reports Money Adviser* with combined subscriptions of more than seven million. Consumers Union also has more than 500,000 online activists who help work to change legislation and the marketplace in favor of the consumer interest and several public education Web sites. Since its founding in 1936, Consumers Union has never taken any advertising or freebies of any kind. The organization generates more than $160 million in revenue and a staff of more than five hundred work at either CU's fifty state-of-the-art labs in Yonkers, NY; its 327-acre auto test facility in East Haddam, CT; or its three advocacy offices (Washington, DC; Austin, TX; and San Francisco, CA).

HARVARD JOINT CENTER FOR HOUSING STUDIES

http://www.jchs.harvard.edu/

The Joint Center for Housing Studies is Harvard University's center for information and research on housing in the United States. The joint center analyzes the dynamic relationships between housing markets and economic, demographic, and social trends, providing leaders in government, business, and the nonprofit sector with the knowledge needed to develop effective policies and strategies.

Established in 1959, the joint center is a collaborative unit affiliated with the Harvard Design School and the Kennedy School of Government. Through its rich array of research, education, and public outreach programs, the joint center serves as a convener for informed discussion on a broad range of issues in the housing sector of the nation's economy. In doing so, it educates business leaders, government officials, policy makers, and the public on critical and emerging factors affecting housing and our communities.

The joint center investigates, evaluates and reports on emerging housing issues and community development policies. The annual report, The State of the Nation's Housing, identifies and analyzes demographic, economic and social trends to inform industry leaders and public officials and helps them to prepare for the future. The center generates new information on housing and mortgage markets by analyzing large-scale databases, designing housing market indicators, and applying innovative analytical approaches to housing problems.

HOMEOWNERSHIP PRESERVATION FOUNDATION (HPF)

www.hpfonline.org

The Homeownership Preservation Foundation (HPF) develops innovative solutions for preserving and expanding home ownership by partnering with consumers, policy makers, and the mortgage-lending industry.

The counselors for the 888-995-HOPE hotline are provided by six HUD-approved nonprofit allies: Auriton Solutions, Consumer Credit Counseling Services of Atlanta, Consumer Credit Counseling Services of San Francisco, Novadebt, Springboard Nonprofit Consumer Credit Management, and Money Management International (MMI).

INDIAN COMMUNITY DEVELOPMENT BLOCK GRANT (ICDBG)

http://www.hud.gov/offices/pih/ih/grants/icdbg.cfm

The ICDBG program provides eligible grantees with direct grants for use in developing viable American Indian and Alaska Native Communities, including decent housing, a suitable living environment, and economic opportunities, primarily for low and moderate income persons. Eligible applicants for assistance include any Indian tribe, band, group, or nation (including Alaska Indians, Aleutes, and Eskimos), or Alaska Native village that has established a relationship to the federal government as defined in the program regulations. In certain instances, tribal organizations may be eligible to apply. The ICDBG program can provide funding for recipients in the following categories:

Housing: Housing rehabilitation, land acquisition to support new housing construction, and under limited circumstances, new housing construction.

Community Facilities: Infrastructure construction (e.g., roads, water and sewer facilities) and single or multipurpose community buildings.

Economic Development: Wide variety of commercial, industrial, and agricultural projects that may be recipient owned and operated or that may be owned and/or operated by a third party.

The program is administered by the six area Office(s) of Native American Projects (ONAP) with policy development and oversight provided by the Denver National Program Office of ONAP. Each area ONAP is responsible for a geographic jurisdiction that includes from 26 to over 200 eligible applicants. The program regulations provide for two categories of grants, Imminent Threat and Single Purpose. Single-purpose grants are awarded on a competitive basis pursuant to the terms published in an annual Notice of Funding Availability (NOFA). The secretary of HUD may set aside 5 percent of each year's allocation for the noncompetitive, first come–first served, funding of grants to eliminate or lessen problems that pose an imminent threat to public health or safety.

NATIONAL AMERICAN INDIAN HOUSING COUNCIL (NAIHC)

http://www.naihc.net

Founded in 1974, the National American Indian Housing Council (NAIHC), a 501(c)(3) corporation, is the only national organization representing housing interests of tribes and housing entities across the United States. The NAIHC is guided by a ten-member board of directors representing tribal housing agencies in nine geographical regions throughout the United States. The NAIHC currently has 267 voting members, representing 458 Indian tribes and Alaska Native villages. The NAIHC also has 29 associate and individual members, organizations and individuals who support our mission. It promotes, supports, and upholds tribes and tribal housing agencies in their efforts to provide culturally relevant, decent, safe, sanitary and quality affordable housing for Native people in American Indian communities and Alaska Native villages. Toward this end it provides training, technical assistance, research, communications, and advocacy.

NAIHC services to its members and the general public include:

- Advocacy for housing opportunities and increased funding for Native American housing and community development programs,

- Training in many areas of Indian housing management,
- On-site technical assistance to Indian housing professionals,
- Research and information services on Indian housing issues and programs.

The NAIHC is supported by member dues and fees as well as government, foundation, association, and private grants.

NATIONAL ASSOCIATION FOR THE ADVANCEMENT OF COLORED PEOPLE (NAACP)

http://www.naacp.org

The mission of the National Association for the Advancement of Colored People (NAACP) is to ensure the political, educational, social, and economic equality of rights of all persons and to eliminate racial hatred and racial discrimination. The vision of the NAACP is to ensure a society in which all individuals have equal rights and there is no racial hatred or racial discrimination. The NAACP's objectives are as follows:

to ensure the political, educational, social, and economic equality of all citizens;

to achieve equality of rights and eliminate race prejudice among the citizens of the United States;

to remove all barriers of racial discrimination through democratic processes;

to seek enactment and enforcement of federal, state, and local laws securing civil rights;

to inform the public of the adverse effects of racial discrimination and to seek its elimination;

to educate persons as to their constitutional rights and to take all lawful action to secure the exercise thereof, and to take any other lawful action in furtherance of these objectives, consistent with the NAACP's Articles of Incorporation and this Constitution.

NATIONAL ASSOCIATION OF CONSUMER ADVOCATES (NACA)

http://www.naca.net

The National Association of Consumer Advocates (NACA) is a nationwide organization of more than one thousand attorneys who represent and have represented hundreds of thousands of consumers victimized by fraudulent as well as abusive and predatory business practices. As an organization fully committed to promoting justice for consumers, NACA's members and their clients are actively engaged in promoting a fair and open marketplace that forcefully protects the rights of consumers, particularly those of modest means.

NATIONAL ASSOCIATION OF HOME BUILDERS (NAHB)

http://www.nahb.org

The NAHB produces in-depth economic analyses of the home building industry based on private and government data. It's economics group surveys builders, home buyers, and renters to gain insight into the issues and trends driving the industry. The NAHB also hosts the Construction Forecast Conference, held twice a year to help keep on top of housing and the economy.

NATIONAL COMMUNITY REINVESTMENT COALITION (NCRC)

http://www.ncrc.org

The National Community Reinvestment Coalition (NCRC) is an association of more than 600 community-based organizations that promote access to basic banking services, including credit and savings, to create and sustain affordable housing, job development, and vibrant communities for America's working families. Members include community reinvestment organizations, community development corporations; local and state government agencies; faith-based institutions; community organizing and civil rights groups; minority and women-owned business associations as well as local and social service providers from across the nation.

The NCRC pursues its work through a variety of partnerships and programs. It's National Homeownership Sustainability Fund makes use of the expertise of a national network of mortgage finance advisors, working with servicers and lenders, on behalf of home owners, to keep working families from losing their homes to foreclosure. The NCRC's National Training Academy provides training and technical assistance on topics such as understanding how to use the Community Reinvestment Act, fair lending laws, the Home Mortgage Disclosure Act, the Truth in Lending Act, the Real Estate Settlement Procedures Act, and the Homeownership and Equity Protection Act, fair housing and foreclosure prevention. It's Economic Justice Campaign sites pilot innovative community partnerships to enhance the delivery of financial, technical, and social services to individual consumers, home owners, and small businesses.

The NCRC's work is enhanced by two financial service advisory councils consisting of the nation's largest banks and mortgage finance companies. Quarterly roundtables examine issues involving responsible financial service-related policies; regulations and legislation; as well as innovative products, services, and best practices. The NCRC represents its members before Congress, federal regulatory agencies, and the press. It routinely testifies before the US Congress and meets with the leadership of banking and lending regulatory agencies. The NCRC frequently provides expert commentary on national television, and its research and policy papers have been cited in hundreds of newspapers in the United States.

NATIONAL CONSORTIUM OF HOUSING RESEARCH CENTERS

http://www.housingresearch.net

The National Consortium of Housing Research Centers has many accomplishments since its establishment in 1988.

Through attendance at the International Builders' Show and other national meetings, universities throughout the country have gained a better perspective of the home-building industry. Conversely, the industry has gained a better perspective of the universities' roles in housing research and education.

More housing courses are being taught at US universities, and these are providing an educated workforce for industry, government, and academia.

There has been immediate recognition of a study area, consequently, there are more, higher-quality theses and dissertation projects being produced, and these studies are contributing to the knowledge base about housing issues, to the advancement of housing science, and to the development of a better educated work force.

Through both scientific and applied research universities have contributed to technology transfer in the home-building industry through a variety of venues, including the following:

- technical reports
- workshops
- regional, national, and international conferences
- publications
- a national newsletter
- a peer-reviewed journal

An interdisciplinary research infrastructure is in place with bylaws, operating policies, and procedures that help to govern, coordinate, and focus activities of the consortium.

Stronger links to home builders associations around America have been made through the participation of industry advisory councils to housing research centers.

Consortia research proposals and housing research partnerships have been facilitated. Joint ventures between universities, consultants, and industry laboratories have produced a number of winning proposals for funding of housing research.

During the first ten years of the consortium's existence, member universities have collectively invested over two hundred and fifty thousand dollars in hard cash in development of the consortium (this does not include faculty and staff salaries, telecommunications, and other costs that would probably double this figure).

Student interns have been supported in the housing industry, at the NAHB Research Center, with home builders and in other organizations, and this, too, is supporting an educated work force.

Because the consortium members are scattered geographically across the United States, each having its unique interests and capabilities, regional, national, and international foci in housing research topics and activities have been facilitated. These are affecting policies at many levels worldwide.

Students have been attracted to the home-building industry through activities at local housing research centers such as with NAHB student chapters, faculty advising, and the like.

Communication within the consortium has helped to avoid wasteful redundancy in research by facilitated replication of results and by advancing the knowledge base of housing research in technology, policy, and delivery systems.

Consortium members have developed associations with research organizations such as the Energy Efficient Buildings Association (EEBA), the National Institute of Building Sciences (NIBS), the Architectural Research Centers Consortium (ARCC), the American Institute of Architects (AIA), the American Society of Civil Engineers (ASCE), and others, and these associations have helped to advance the science of housing and construction research.

Regional consortia for housing research center have been started in Florida, Pennsylvania, Nevada, and California. These help to bring the research needs of the housing industry into focus locally.

There has been immediate recognition of a study area on housing that could have been focused on other aspects of construction.

Housing research gives individuals at member schools of the consortium a context in which to conduct housing research within the framework of a larger organization.

The consortium has helped to define the national agenda for housing research.

NATIONAL CONSUMER LAW CENTER (NCLC)

http://www.consumerlaw.org

The National Consumer Law Center (NCLC) is the nation's consumer law expert, helping consumers, their advocates, and public policy makers use powerful and complex consumer laws on behalf of low-income and vulnerable Americans seeking economic justice.

To most effectively address the unique challenges faced by different segments of the low-income population, NCLC conducts targeted consumer rights initiatives. In addition to disadvantaged consumers everywhere, it devotes special attention to the problems of immigrants, vulnerable elders, home owners, former welfare recipients, victims of domestic violence, military personnel, and others. NCLC uses the courts to promote marketplace justice by providing expert issue identification, case assistance, and legal research, as well as advocacy workshops for legal services and private attorneys, lay advocates, and community-based organizations representing low-income clients.

NCLC's sixteen-volume legal practice series provides expert analysis in all major aspects of consumer and energy law and has been recognized by the American Bar Association as "A monumental undertaking [which] should become a standard reference set. . . . These manuals make consumer law accessible to office practitioners and litigators." Issues on which NCLC has had a significant impact include the Equal Credit Opportunity Act, the federal Truth in Lending law, Low-Income Home Energy Assistance Program, the Home Ownership Equity Protection Act of 1994, development of state unfair and deceptive acts and practices legislation, consumer protections in the foreclosure process, and numerous federal and state statutes, including the Fair Debt Collection Practices Act, Home Mortgage Abuse Act, and Uniform Commercial Code. A top priority for NCLC is providing support on issues involving consumer fraud, debt collection, consumer finance, energy assistance programs, predatory lending, and sustainable home ownership programs. Boston Headquarters: 77 Summer Street, 10th Floor, Boston, MA 02110-1006; Phone: 617/542-8010; Fax 617/542-8028. Washington Office: 1001 Connecticut Avenue, NW, Suite 510, Washington, DC, 20036; Phone: 202/452-6252; Fax 202/463-9462, E-mail: consumerlaw @nclc.org.

NATIONAL COUNCIL OF LA RAZA (NCLR)

http://www.nclr.org

The National Council of La Raza (NCLR) is the largest national Hispanic civil rights and advocacy organization in the United States. The NCLR works to improve opportunities for Hispanic Americans. Through its network of nearly 300 affiliated community-based organizations (CBOs), the NCLR reaches millions of Hispanics each year in 41 states, Puerto Rico, and the District of Columbia. To achieve its mission, the NCLR conducts applied research, policy analysis, and advocacy, providing a Latino perspective in five key areas: assets/investments, civil rights/immigration, education, employment and economic status, and health. In addition, it provides capacity-building assistance to its affiliates who work at the state and local level to advance opportunities for individuals and families. Founded in 1968, the NCLR is a private, nonprofit, nonpartisan, tax-exempt organization headquartered in Washington, DC. The NCLR serves all Hispanic subgroups in all regions of the country and has operations in Atlanta, Chicago, Los Angeles, New York, Phoenix, Sacramento, San Antonio, and San Juan, Puerto Rico. The NCLR traces its origins to the civil rights movement of the 1960s, as well as to previous efforts that preceded World War II, such as those related to early school and housing desegregation. Although Hispanics, especially Mexican Americans and Puerto Ricans, participated in both movements, they did not gain widespread media coverage or national visibility for their efforts. Without such recognition, legislation such as the Civil Rights Act of 1964 and the Economic Opportunity Act of 1964, while creating enormous change in other areas of the country, had relatively little impact on the Hispanic community. In large part, the invisibility that plagued the Mexican American civil rights movement was a result of the movement's geographic isolation, which caused it to be overshadowed by the more highly visible national movements. Additionally, Mexican Americans lacked the kinds of institutions that were critical to the success of the Black civil rights movement, and around which they could rally, unify, and organize.

NATIONAL FOUNDATION FOR CREDIT COUNSELING (NFCC)

http://www.nfcc.org

With over 100 member agencies and more than 900 local offices throughout the country, the NFCC is the national voice for its members, which are nonprofit, mission-driven, community-based agencies. Many NFCC members are known as Consumer Credit Counseling Services ® (CCCS). An increasing number of agencies operate under other names, but all members can be identified by the NFCC member seal. This seal represents accredited agencies with high standards, ethical practices, certified counselors, and policies and practices that help consumers achieve financial stability.

Each year, more than one million people receive counseling and educational services from NFCC member agencies. More than one-third of all consumers who come to an NFCC agency for counseling are able to manage their debt on their own after receiving financial education and counseling.

NFCC member agencies provide a variety of services, including:

budget counseling and education
debt management plans
counseling referral services
financial literacy courses
housing counseling

Every client of NFCC member agencies receives comprehensive money management services based on their individual needs. Members provide free and/or affordable services, which are offered in-person or by phone. Many agencies also offer Web-based services. Housing counseling is also provided by many members for consumers who want to purchase homes and those who have fallen behind on their mortgage payments.

Each NFCC member is individually accredited by the Council on Accreditation (COA), an independent, third-party, not-for-profit, accrediting organization that has reviewed more than 1,500 social service programs to ensure compliance with best-practices standards. All NFCC member agencies must be re-accredited by COA every four years. The NFCC is highly recognized within the industry and by creditors for its trademarked Counselor Certification Program. All NFCC member counselors must complete the NFCC's comprehensive, quality training program to guarantee their ability to provide quality education and assistance to consumers. National Foundation for Credit Counseling, 801 Roeder Road, Suite 900, Silver Spring, MD 20910, 301-589-5600, www.nfcc.org

NATIVE AMERICAN HOUSING ASSISTANCE (NAHA)

http://www.hud.gov/progdesc/ihbg1208.cfm

The Native American Housing Assistance and Self-Determination Act of 1996 reorganized the system of federal housing assistance to Native Americans by eliminating several separate programs and replacing them with a single block grant program that recognizes the right of Indian self-determination and tribal self-governance. It provides for tribal governing bodies to name a tribally designated housing entity (TDHE)—which may be the former Indian Housing Authority—to prepare an Indian Housing Plan (IHP). The act aims to simplify the process of federal housing assistance for Indian tribes and to make such assistance better fit the circumstances of Native Americans. It became effective October 1, 1997. It replaces assistance previously authorized under the Housing Act of 1937, the Indian Housing Child Development Program, the Public Housing Youth Sports Program, and the HOME Investment Partnership Program under the Cranston-Gonzalez National Affordable Housing Act, and the Innovative Homeless Demonstration Program. Some existing contracts will remain in force until they expire or are renegotiated. Assistance is in the form of a block grant made available on an annual basis using an allocation formula for Indian tribes with approved IHPs.

Eligible Indian tribes and Alaska Native villages designate who will receive the block grant. The block grant serves the housing needs of low-income American Indians and Alaska Natives. Eligible affordable housing activities must develop or support rental or ownership housing or provide housing services to benefit low-income Indian families on Indian reservations and other Indian areas. Affordable housing must cost no more than 30 percent of the family's adjusted income. Eligible activities include modernization or operating assistance for housing previously developed using HUD resources; acquisition, new construction, or rehabilitation of additional units; housing-related services such as housing counseling, self-sufficiency services, energy auditing, and establishment of resident organizations; housing management services; crime prevention and safety activities; rental assistance; model activities; and administrative expenses. Every tribe that submits an IHP (which is approved) is awarded a block grant. The IHP has two parts: a five-year plan and a one-year plan. The five-year plan must contain a mission statement, goals, objectives, and an activities plan. The one-year plan must contain goals, objectives, a statement of needs, an operating budget, a statement of the affordable housing resources currently available, and certifications of compliance. In fiscal year 1998, $600 million was appropriated to the IHBG. The Native American Housing Assistance Act authorized the Indian Housing Block Grant (IHBG) program, which replaces the Indian housing programs under the Housing Act of 1937. Section 106 of the 1996 act establishes the procedure for developing the regulations for the program. The act is administered by the Office of Native American Programs (ONAP).

NEIGHBORWORKS AMERICA

http://www.nw.org

NeighborWorks® America, local NeighborWorks organizations, and Neighborhood Housing Services of America make up the system, which has successfully built healthy communities since 1978. The roots of the NeighborWorks system go back to a resident-led, 1968 campaign for better housing in Pittsburgh, Pennsylvania's central north side neighborhood. Dorothy Mae Richardson, a homemaker and community activist, enlisted city bankers and government officials to join with her block club to improve her neighborhood. Together, they persuaded sixteen financial institutions to make conventional loans in the community; a local foundation capitalized a revolving loan fund. They rented a trailer, hired staff, and named the effort Neighborhood Housing Services (NHS). In 1970, the Federal Home Loan Bank (FHLB), under the direction of Preston Martin, concluded that savings-and-loan officers needed special training in lending in older, urban markets. These trainings were led by Bill Whiteside, who soon discovered that the accomplishments of NHS of Pittsburgh could serve as a model for the rest of the country. The FHLB trainings continued around the country, but, more and more, they turned into workshops for starting other Neighborhood Housing Services organizations, now referred to as NeighborWorks organizations. In 1973, President Nixon prepared to announce a moratorium on federal housing programs. To help soften the announcement, the Department of Housing and Urban Development (HUD) entered into a handshake agreement with the FHLB on a five-year initiative to expand NeighborWorks organizations across the country. The initiative would be coordinated by a specially created Urban Reinvestment Task Force, for which HUD would provide the funding and the FHLB would provide the staff. The HUD-FHLB partnership was expanded the next year to include the Federal Reserve, the Comptroller of the Currency, and the Federal Deposit Insurance Corporation. Limited access to funding for the NeighborWorks organizations' revolving loan funds threatened the network's effectiveness and further expansion. At the time, private foundations were practically the only resource. Then Congress enacted the Community Development Block Grant (CDBG) program, and provided that CDBG grants could capitalize NeighborWorks loan funds. In 1974, NHS partners in Oakland conceived of a national loan-purchase resource that would buy loans from local NHSs, thus replenishing their local loan funds. They named it Neighborhood Housing Services of America (NHSA). Its initial funding came from the Urban Reinvestment Task Force. The Federal Home Loan Bank established the Office of Neighborhood Reinvestment in 1975 with Bill Whiteside serving as its first director. A year later, the office expanded to fourteen staff members working with NHSs in 45 cities. The new entity established regional offices in Boston, New York, Atlanta, Kansas City, Cincinnati, and San Francisco to support the growing NHS network. In 1978, Congress institutionalized the NHS network by establishing the Neighborhood Reinvestment Corporation to carry on the work of the Urban Reinvestment Task Force. [In April 2005, the corporation began doing business as NeighborWorks America.] The congressional act (Public Law 95-557) charged Neighborhood Reinvestment with promoting reinvestment in older neighborhoods by local financial institutions in cooperation with the community, residents and local governments. Bill Whiteside was named executive director. The act defined Neighborhood Reinvestment's mission as "revitalizing older urban neighborhoods by mobilizing public, private, and community resources at the neighborhood level." In their first decade, local organizations concentrated on perfecting their core services for owner-occupied housing in their initially targeted neighborhoods. Pittsburgh's NHS staff, for example, helped central north side residents with referrals to reputable contractors, follow-up inspections to assure work quality, counseling and assistance in securing work-related financing, referrals to participating financial institutions for credit-worthy clients, and custom-tailored loans from the NHS's loan fund for others. But blight and decay infected whole swaths of territory, including apartment buildings, shopping areas, and rural communities. So local organizations adjusted their strategies by expanding into additional neighborhoods and adding new programs. Neighborhood Reinvestment staff helped devise new programs, such as revitalizing distressed apartment buildings and shopping areas, promoting home ownership, and training jobless youth in home construction. In the meantime other communities formed new NeighborWorks organizations, and rural communities experimented with adapting the model to their areas. Soon, almost half the local organizations had expanded their core services beyond rehabbing owner-occupied housing. In the early 1980s, network organizations were beginning to see themselves as lasting institutions, assuming long-term responsibility for neighborhoods in need. Then double-digit inflation and sharp drops in state and federal resources combined to pose a formidable threat. Fewer residents were bankable; soaring demand drained NeighborWorks loan funds; and even raising operating funds became a challenge.

Selected insurance companies that Neighborhood Reinvestment had been gradually bringing into the NeighborWorks partnership provided key support. Insurance executives, for example, had been experimenting in Chicago NeighborWorks neighborhoods, testing out new insurance products and marketing strategies. Nearly $30 million in below-market insurance company commitments were secured to expand NeighborWorks lending throughout the network.

Major financial institutions and corporations provided other crucial support. Together, the commitments enabled local NeighborWorks organizations to continue and even accelerate their neighborhood revitalization work. Local organizations, searching for broader public support, learned the media value of selected projects, such as major in-fill housing, owner-built homes, and massed-volunteer neighborhood painting projects. Local organizations in 1984 gained further visibility as part of a national network in the first Congressionally proclaimed NeighborWorks Week (then called Neighborhood Housing Services Week). President Ronald Reagan signed a proclamation calling for a national observance of the week in a special Oval Office ceremony.

Even as some local organizations were struggling to survive, others were experimenting with adapting the European concept of mutual housing to American neighborhoods. Mutual housing, a variation on the cooperative-housing model, was seen as a strategy for providing reliable affordability for a community's ongoing renters. Alameda Place in Baltimore became the site of the network's first mutual housing association demonstration.

For the country's burgeoning homeless population, NeighborWorks organizations also pursued single-room occupancy and transitional-housing projects.

The Ad Council worked with Neighborhood Reinvestment to create a new identity for the NHS network and "NeighborWorks" was born.

As the complexities of revitalizing neighborhoods continued to grow, network executive directors, board members, and key staff could keep pace through training institutes, which Neighborhood Reinvestment launched in 1987. The institutes further professionalized available network training opportunities

Network organizations moved toward still greater professionalism in the early 1990s with Neighborhood Reinvestment's move to charter qualified local efforts. Chartering, among other things, confirmed an organization's financial stability and its partnership with residents, government officials, and business. Rutland West NHS of rural West Rutland, Vermont, became the first NeighborWorks organization to receive a Neighborhood Reinvestment charter in 1993. As the 1990s unfolded, Neighborhood Reinvestment increasingly was able to attract investments from national financial partners. To harness the investments, it developed a series of new programmatic strategies in home ownership, asset management, community organizing, resident leadership, and access to affordable financing and insurance products. In the first effort in 1991, Neighborhood Reinvestment facilitated the launch of RNA Community Builders Inc. This alliance of rural NeighborWorks organizations banded together to find creative ways of addressing rural housing concerns and increasing the focus on organizational resources for rural development. In 1992, twenty NeighborWorks organizations came together and launched the NeighborWorks Campaign for Home Ownership. The initial, 1993–97 campaign grew to involve more than one hundred organizations, assist 15,880 families into home ownership, and attract more than $1.1 billion in total investments. A second, five-year campaign was launched in 1998. Out of the campaigns emerged two nationally recognized strategies. One was Full-Cycle Lending, an innovative, comprehensive system of pre- and postpurchase home buyer education and flexible financing products. The other, NeighborWorks HomeOwnership Centers, offers in a convenient, retail location, all the services and training that customers need to locate, purchase, rehabilitate, insure, and maintain a home. In 1994, the National Insurance Task Force was organized to help the insurance industry and community-based organizations better understand each other. Community residents were able to explore the difficulties they faced in obtaining affordable property insurance, and the industry was able to refine its marketing approaches. To enhance the role of residents in revitalization, in 1996 Neighborhood Reinvestment began developing a series of initiatives that focused on community organizing, strengthening neighborhood associations, developing resident leaders, and building capacity in communities. The series, in time, evolved into the Resident Leadership Initiatives. The last year of the millennium was a banner one for Neighborhood Reinvestment and the network. The NeighborWorks Multifamily Initiative was created to increase organizations' capacity to take on new housing development by attracting additional public and private investment, strengthen their asset-management systems, and help them develop resident leaders. NHSA celebrated its twenty-fifth anniversary and achieved from Standard and Poor's AA rating for its $75 million collateralized mortgage bond that was fully subscribed at issue. And, for the first time, Neighborhood Reinvestment hit the $1 billion mark for annual direct investment in distressed communities. The late 1990s also saw the organization move into the digital age, as a new Neighborhood Reinvestment/NeighborWorks Web site began to capture the successes of the NeighborWorks network, promote training institutes, and made available for download many Neighborhood Reinvestment publications, including *NeighborWorks Bright Ideas Magazine*. The second five-year NeighborWorks Campaign for Home Ownership exceeded its goals when it came to a close at the end of 2002, with 47,648 new home owners, $4.5 billion in total investments, and 272,976 home buyer counseling participants. Of the new home owners, 94 percent purchased their home for the first time. A new five-year NeighborWorks Campaign for Home Ownership began in 2003 with a goal of creating 50,000 new home owners, including 30,000 minority homebuyers. In April 2005, Neighborhood Reinvestment began doing business as NeighborWorks America. Neighborhood Reinvestment Corporation remains the legal, incorporated name, as provided in the 1978 statute. Approved by the board of directors in September 2004, the NeighborWorks America trade name (or DBA) clearly aligns the corporation with NeighborWorks organizations and all of the other components in the overall NeighborWorks system. The transition to NeighborWorks America demonstrates the corporation's belief in the value of the NeighborWorks network of community development organizations, while helping to raise the network's visibility in order to attract increased resources to NeighborWorks and the communities served.

NEIGHBORHOOD ASSISTANCE CORPORATION (NCAC)

https://www.naca.com

The Neighborhood Assistance Corporation of America (NACA) is a nonprofit, community advocacy and home ownership organization. NACA's primary goal is to build strong, healthy neighborhoods in urban and rural areas nationwide through affordable home ownership. NACA has made the dream of home ownership a reality for thousands of working people by counseling them honestly and effectively, enabling even those with poor credit to purchase a home or refinance a predatory loan with far better terms than those provided even in the prime market. The NACA home ownership program is NCAC's answer to the huge subprime and predatory lending industry. Started in 1988, NACA has a tremendous track record of successful advocacy against predatory and discriminatory lenders. NACA is the largest housing services organization in the country and is rapidly expanding by growing its more than thirty existing offices, headquartered in Boston, Massachusetts, opening many new offices nationwide, and expanding the services it offers its membership. NACA's confrontational community organizing and unprecedented mortgage program have set the national standard for assisting low- and moderate-income people to achieve the dream of home ownership.

NACA began in 1988 in Boston as the Union Neighborhood Assistance Corporation (UNAC). Its roots are with the Hotel Workers Union-Local 26, an activist union that won and established the country's first housing trust fund for union members. NACA employed the union's activist tactics to confront lenders that were redlining communities by denying credit to minority neighborhoods and exploiting low- and moderate-income home owners.

THE RESEARCH INSTITUTE FOR HOUSING AMERICA of the MORTGAGE BANKERS ASSOCIATION (MBA)

http://www.housingamerica.org

The Research Institute for Housing America of the Mortgage Bankers Association is a 501(c)(3) trust fund. Its chief purpose is to encourage and aid—through grants and sponsored research to distinguished scholars, educational institutions, research facilities, and government organizations—the pursuit of knowledge of mortgage markets and real estate finance. Its mission emphasizes rigorous analysis furthering understanding of how to expand rental opportunities and home ownership among the underserved, and how to encourage equal access to mortgage credit for all qualified borrowers.

APPENDIX F

AN EXAMPLE OF A MORTGAGE MODIFICATION SOLICITATION

YOUR ESTIMATED EQUITY MAY BE AS MUCH AS $264,379[1] — AVAILABLE TO YOU RIGHT NOW

Limited Time Offer!

Call Toll Free:

(Press Option 2)

Available Cash:
Up to $264,379

Preferred Customer #:
M83124-0037107

000164

HOME LOANS

IMPORTANT INFORMATION REGARDING YOUR REFINANCE OPPORTUNITY

Dear

We've set aside time for you to contact for a complimentary loan consultation to see if refinancing your mortgage may help meet your family's changing financial needs.[2] **And get your Exclusive Customer Discount when you call this Saturday,**

Now May Be The Time To Plan For Your Future.
Please Contact Right Away!

With a wide variety of refinance mortgage programs, you may discover one that could allow you to:

- If you have available home equity, you may be able to access it to pay off bills or take care of unexpected expenses.[3]
- Consolidate multiple, higher-interest debts into one, simple monthly mortgage payment with a lower interest rate.[4]
- If you are currently in the first years of a 30-year mortgage, potentially save thousands of dollars in interest payments with a 10-, 15-, or 20-year mortgage.[5]

Plus, you may be eligible for our Fastrack Loan Program,[6] allowing you to receive your closing documents in as little as 3 days. That means you could close your loan and access your cash even faster!

It's easy to get started. A simple phone consultation may be the key to gaining the financial flexibility that you need! Take advantage of our dedicated, toll-free hotline and call us this **Saturday,**
(Press Option 2)!

Sincerely,

Executive Vice President

P.S. PLEASE CALL A home loan expert will explain all the Fastrack options now available to you. **Se Habla Español**

APPENDIX G

TYPICAL PROMISSORY NOTE DEFAULT PROVISIONS

1.1 *Events of Default.* Each of the following constitute an event of default under this note ("default"): (a) failure of borrower to pay any amount of indebtedness when due, whether interest, principal or otherwise and whether as an installment, on the maturity date or otherwise; (b) any other default or event of default under any of the loan documents that continue for a period exceeding the cure [pay off] period provided in the loan documents; (c) borrower's failure to pay, when due, any amount payable under any other obligation of the borrower, or any related entity (as hereinafter defined) of the borrower, to the lender, however created, arising or evidenced, whether direct or indirect, absolute or contingent, now or hereafter existing, or due or to become due, subject to applicable cure periods, if any; (d) an indictment or other charge is filed against the borrower, or any related entity (as defined below) of the borrower, in any jurisdiction, under any federal or state law, for which forfeiture of any collateral securing the loan, as described in the loan documents, or of any other funds, property or other assets of the borrower is a potential penalty unless such charge is dismissed within thirty (30) days after filing; or (e) the death or legal incapacity of any borrower being a natural person. For purposes of this note, a "Related Entity" shall be defined as the borrower or any corporation, partnership, limited liability company or other entity owned or controlled by the borrower.

1.2 *Acceleration of Maturity.* At any time after the occurrence of any default and at the option of the lender, the entire principal balance under this note, together with interest accrued thereon and all other indebtedness (including all sums expended by the lender in connection with such default), shall without further notice become immediately due and payable. The mortgage and the other loan documents restrict changes in the ownership of the real estate (as defined in the mortgage) and other changes relating to such ownership, and provide for acceleration, under certain circumstances; of the indebtedness upon the breach of such restrictions.

1.3 *Default Interest Rate*. While any default exists, interest on the unpaid principal balance of the loan from time to time shall accrue at a rate per annum ("default interest rate") equal to eighteen percent (18%), and the borrower shall pay such interest upon demand, or if no such demand is made, then at the times installments of interest and/or principal are due as provided herein. All unpaid interest that has accrued under this note, whether prior (at the interest rate) or subsequent (at the default interest rate) to the occurrence of the default, shall be paid at the time of, and as a condition precedent to, the curing of the default.

1.4 *Attorneys' Fees*. If any counsel (whether an employee of the lender or otherwise) is employed, retained or engaged to: (a) collect the indebtedness or any part thereof, whether or not legal proceedings are instituted by the lender; (b) represent the lender in any bankruptcy, reorganization, receivership, or other proceedings affecting creditors' rights and involving a claim under this note; (c) protect the liens or security interests created by any of the loan documents; or (d) represent the lender in any other proceedings in connection with the loan documents or the property described therein, then the borrower shall pay to the lender all related reasonable attorneys' fees, time charges and expenses as a part of the indebtedness.

1.5 *Lender's Remedies*. Upon the occurrence of a default, the lender, at its option, may proceed to foreclose the mortgage, to exercise any other rights and remedies available to the lender under the mortgage or the other loan documents and to exercise any other rights and remedies against the borrower or with respect to this note which the lender may have at law, at equity or otherwise.

The lender's remedies under this note, the mortgage, and all other loan documents shall be cumulative and concurrent and may be pursued singly, successively, or together against any or all of the borrower and any other obligors (as defined below), the real estate described in the mortgage, and any other security described in the loan documents or any portion or combination of such real estate and other security. The lender may resort to every other right or remedy available at law or in equity without first exhausting the rights and remedies contained herein, all in the lender's sole discretion. Failure of the lender, for any period of time or on more than one occasion, to exercise its option to accelerate the maturity date shall not constitute a waiver of that right at any time during the default or in the event of any subsequent default. The lender shall not by any other omission or act be deemed to waive any of its rights or remedies unless such waiver is written and signed by an officer of the lender, and then only to the extent specifically set forth. A waiver in connection with one event shall not be construed as continuing or as a bar to or waiver of any right or remedy in connection with a subsequent event.

1.6 *Late Charges.* If any installment of interest or the unpaid principal balance due under this note or any required escrow fund payment for taxes or insurance becomes overdue for a period in excess of fifteen (15) days, the borrower shall pay to the lender upon demand a late charge of five cents ($.05) for each dollar so overdue in order to defray part of the increased cost of collection resulting from such late payments. Payment of such late charges does not excuse or cure a late payment.

DEFAULT PROVISIONS

1. *Events of Default.* Each of the following shall constitute an event of default ("event of default") under this mortgage:

a. Mortgagor's failure to pay any amount due herein or secured hereby, or any installment of principal or interest when due and payable whether at maturity or by acceleration or otherwise under the note, this mortgage, or any other loan document;

b. Mortgagor's failure to pay any and all annual or quarterly real estate taxes or any other taxes for the property;

c. Mortgagor's failure to perform or observe any other covenant, agreement, representation, warranty or other provision contained in the note, this mortgage (other than an event of default described elsewhere in this paragraph) or any other document or instrument evidencing, guarantying or securing the secured indebtedness, and such failure continues for more than thirty (30) days after the earlier of the mortgagor's becoming aware of such failure or notice thereof given by the lender to the mortgagor; provided, however, that such thirty (30)-day cure period shall not apply to the other subparagraphs of this paragraph;

d. The occurrence of any breach of any representation or warranty contained in this mortgage or any other loan document and such breach continues for more than thirty (30) days after the earlier of the mortgagor's becoming aware of the breach or written notice from the lender;

e. A prohibited transfer occurs;

f. A court having jurisdiction shall enter a decree or order for relief in respect of the mortgagor in any involuntary case brought under any bankruptcy, insolvency, debtor relief, or similar law; or if the mortgagor, or any beneficiary of or person in control of the mortgagor, shall: (i) file a voluntary petition in bankruptcy, insolvency, debtor relief or for arrangement, reorganization or other relief under the Federal Bankruptcy Act or any similar state or federal law; (ii) consent to or suffer the appointment of or taking possession by a receiver, liquidator, or trustee (or similar official) of the mortgagor or for any part of the property or any substantial part of the mortgagor's other property; (iii) make any assignment for the benefit of the mortgagor's creditors; (iv) fail generally to pay the mortgagor's debts as they become due;

g. All or a substantial part of the mortgagor's assets are attached, seized, subjected to a writ or distress warrant, or are levied upon;

h. If the mortgagor is other than a natural person or persons: (i) the dissolution or termination of existence of the mortgagor, voluntarily or involuntarily; (ii) the amendment or modification in any respect of the mortgagor's operating agreement or its articles of organization that would affect the mortgagor's performance of its obligations under the note, this mortgage or the other loan documents;

i. This mortgage shall not constitute a valid lien on and security interest in the property (subject only to the permitted encumbrances), or if such lien and security interest shall not be perfected;

j. The property is abandoned;

k. An indictment or other charge is filed against the mortgagor in any jurisdiction, under any federal or state law, for which forfeiture of the property or of other collateral securing the secured indebtedness or of any other funds, property or other assets of the mortgagor or the lender, is a potential penalty (unless such charge is dismissed within thirty (30) days after filing);

l. Mortgagor's, or any related entity's, failure to pay, when due, any amount payable under any other obligation of the mortgagor, or any related entity of the mortgagor, to the lender, however created, arising or evidenced, whether direct or indirect, absolute or contingent, now or hereafter existing, or due or to become due, subject to applicable cure periods, if any. For purposes of this mortgage, the loan and the loan documents, (i) a "related entity," shall be defined as the mortgagor, any member of the mortgagor or any corporation, partnership, limited liability company or other entity owned or controlled by the mortgagor, (ii) a "mortgagor affiliate" shall be defined as any member, general partner, venturer or controlling shareholder of the mortgagor or a guarantor of all or any part of the secured indebtedness; or

m. The death or legal incapacity of any Mortgagor being a natural person.

n. Borrower specifically agrees that a default under the note, the loan agreement, this mortgage or any other loan document is and shall constitute a default under this mortgage and visa versa and shall entitle the lender to any and all remedies as provided under this mortgage and in any and all of the loan documents. In the event that such a default occurs, the entire principal and accrued interest secured by the loan documents and all other sums or indebtedness and accrued interest, shall become due and payable at once, without notice. Failure by the lender to enforce this remedy with respect to any default shall not constitute a waiver of the lender's right to exercise the remedy in the event of a subsequent default.

2. *Acceleration; Remedies*. At any time after an event of default, the lender, at lender's option, may declare all sums secured by this mortgage and the other loan documents to be immediately due and payable without further demand and may foreclose this mortgage by judicial proceeding. The lender shall be entitled to collect in such proceeding all expenses of foreclosure, including, but not limited to, reasonable attorneys' fees and costs including abstracts and title reports, all of which shall become a part of the secured indebtedness and immediately due and payable, with interest at the default rate. the proceeds of any foreclosure sale of the property shall be applied as follows: first, to all costs, expenses and fees incident to the foreclosure proceedings; second, as set forth in this mortgage; and third, any balance to mortgagor.

APPENDIX H

JUDICIAL V. TRUSTEE OR NONJUDICIAL STATES

The foreclosure process varies from state to state, and depends primarily on whether the state uses mortgages or deeds of trust for the financing of real property. Generally, states that use mortgages conduct judicial foreclosures, using the court system to execute the foreclosure; states that use deeds of trust conduct nonjudicial foreclosures, using an out-of-court procedure defined by state law. Some states utilize both or a hybrid combination of judicial and trustee foreclosure theory. In general, foreclosures are quicker in nonjudicial states than in judicial states.

To foreclose in accordance with the judicial procedure, a mortgagee (lender) must prove in court that the mortgagor (the borrower) is in default. Once the mortgagee has exhausted its attempts to resolve the default with the mortgagor, the mortgagee's attorney pursues court action. The attorney contacts the mortgagor to try to resolve the default. If the mortgagor is unable to pay off the default or reach another type of work-out agreement, the attorney files a lawsuit against the mortgagor to establish the default amount and the right to have the loan collateral (home) sold and the sale proceeds applied toward the outstanding loan. The purpose of the action is to provide evidence of a default and get the court's approval to initiate foreclosure. In connection with the lawsuit, a lis pendens (lawsuit pending notice) is filed with the county clerk or other public property records repository. The lis pendens gives notice to the public that a pending action has been filed against the mortgagor in default to collect the defaulted debt, including having the collateral sold. Judicial foreclosures are processed through the courts, beginning with the lender filing a complaint and recording a notice of lis pendens. The complaint will state what the debt is, and why the default should allow the lender to foreclose and take the property given as security. The home owner will be served notice of the complaint, either by mail, direct service, or publication of the notice, and will have the opportunity to be heard before the court. If the court finds the debt valid, and in default, it will issue a judgment for the total amount owed, including the costs of the foreclosure process. After the judgment has been entered, a writ will be issued by the court authorizing a sheriff's sale. The sheriff's sale is an auction, open to anyone, and is held in a public place, which can range from in front of the courthouse steps, to in front of the property being auctioned. Sheriff's sales will require either cash to be paid at the time of sale, or a substantial deposit, with the balance paid from later that same day up to 30 days after the sale. At the end of the auction, the highest bidder will be the owner of the property, subject to the court's confirmation of the sale. After the court has confirmed the sale, a sheriff's deed (also known by other names cuh as clerk's certificate of title) will be prepared and delivered to the highest bidder, when that deed is recorded, the highest bidder is the owner of the property.

Nonjudicial foreclosures are based on deeds of trust that contain a power-of-sale clause. The clause enables the trustee to initiate a foreclosure sale of the collateral, without having to file a lawsuit or go to court. The trustee is typically required to issue a notice of default and notify the trustor (borrower) accordingly about the defaulted loan status. If the trustor does not respond, the trustee then initiates the steps for conducting the foreclosure sale of the collateral. Nonjudicial foreclosures are processed without court intervention, with the requirements for the foreclosure established by state statutes. When a loan default occurs, the home owner will be mailed a default letter, and in many states, a notice of default will be recorded at approximately the same time. If the home owner does not cure (remedy) the default, a notice of sale will be mailed to the home owner, posted in public places, recorded at the county recorder's office, and published in area legal publications. After the legally required time period has expired, a public auction will be held, with the highest bidder becoming the owner of the property, subject to their receipt and recordation of the deed. Auctions of nonjudicial foreclosures will generally require cash, or cash equivalent either at the sale, or very shortly thereafter. Each nonjudicial foreclosure state has different procedures. Some do not require a notice of default, but start with a notice of sale. Others require only the publication of the notice of sale to announce the sale, with no direct owner notification required.

A redemption period enables a mortgagor to pay off the loan and reclaim the collateral (home) for a period after the foreclosure sale. In some states an owner of an underlying junior lien also has this right. The time allowed to redeem foreclosed collateral varies from state to state from zero days all the way up to almost a year. This time period has a big impact on how long a borrower can stay in his home and the risk and costs involved in foreclosures for mortgagees, but also for foreclosure investors.

SAMPLE NONJUDICIAL FORECLOSURE TIMELINE:

CALENDAR	DESCRIPTION
After approx. 90 days without borrower making a mortgage payment	Request to initiate foreclosure received. Default documents prepared and sent for signature/recording (substitution/notice of default). Search ordered from title company.
Start (day 1)	Notice of default recorded with county recorder.
Within 10 business days	Notice of default and important notice are mailed to trustor/new owner on the deed of trust at the property address, address on deed of trust and any other addresses known to lender/trustee. Notice is also sent to any parties with a recorded request for notice as required under Statute.
Within 1 month	Title search is received and reviewed. Notice of default mailed to all entitled parties with an interest in the property (i.e., new owners/ junior lien holders) as required under Statute.
3 months after recordation of notice of default	Notice of trustee's sale is prepared and sent for publication.

25 days prior to sale date	Send notice of sale to IRS (if applicable).
20 days prior to sale date	Begin publishing notice of sale in an adjudicated newspaper (must run once a week for 3 consecutive weeks).
20 days prior to sale date	Post the notice of sale on the property itself. Most posting services will photograph the posting location for your records.
20 days prior to sale date	Mail notice of sale to the trustor and all other parties to which the notice of default was mailed as required under Statute.
14 days prior to sale date	The notice of trustee's sale is recorded in the county recorder's office.
5 days prior to sale date	The borrower's right to reinstate expires.
On sale date	The property sale is postponed to a new sale date or the property is sold to highest bidder, or the property reverts to the foreclosing beneficiary.

JUDICIAL V. TRUSTEE OR NONJUDICIAL BY STATE

State	Security Instrument	Foreclosure Type	Initial Step	# of Months	Redemption	Deficiency
Alabama	Mortgage	Nonjudicial	Publication	1	12 MM	Allowed
Alaska	Trust Deed	Nonjudicial	Notice of Default	3	None	Allowed
Arizona	Trust Deed	Nonjudicial	Notice of Sale	3	None	Allowed
Arkansas	Mortgage	Judicial	Complaint	4	None	Allowed
California	Trust Deed	Nonjudicial	Notice of Default	4	None	Prohibited
Colorado	Trust Deed	Nonjudicial	Notice of Default	2	75 DD	Allowed
Connecticut	Mortgage	Strict	Complaint	5	None	Allowed
Delaware	Mortgage	Judicial	Complaint	3	None	Allowed
Dist. of Col.	Trust Deed	Nonjudicial	Notice of Default	2	None	Allowed
Florida	Mortgage	Judicial	Complaint	5	None	Allowed
Georgia	Security Deed	Nonjudicial	Publication	2	None	Allowed

State	Security Instrument	Foreclosure Type	Initial Step	# of Months	Redemption	Deficiency
Hawaii	Mortgage	Nonjudicial	Publication	3	None	Allowed
Idaho	Trust Deed	Nonjudicial	Notice of Default	5	None	Allowed
Illinois	Mortgage	Judicial	Complaint	7	None	Allowed
Indiana	Mortgage	Judicial	Complaint	5	3 MM	Allowed
Iowa	Mortgage	Judicial	Petition	5	6 MM	Allowed
Kansas	Mortgage	Judicial	Complaint	4	6-12 MM	Allowed
Kentucky	Mortgage	Judicial	Complaint	6	None	Allowed
Louisiana	Mortgage	Exec.Process	Petition	2	None	Allowed
Maine	Mortgage	Judicial	Complaint	6	None	Allowed
Maryland	Trust Deed	Nonjudicial	Notice	2	None	Allowed
Massachusetts	Mortgage	Judicial	Complaint	3	None	Allowed
Michigan	Mortgage	Nonjudicial	Publication	2	6 MM	Allowed
Minnesota	Mortgage	Nonjudicial	Publication	2	6 MM	Prohibited
Mississippi	Trust Deed	Nonjudicial	Publication	2	None	Prohibited
Missouri	Trust Deed	Nonjudicial	Publication	2	None	Allowed
Montana	Trust Deed	Nonjudicial	Notice	5	None	Prohibited
Nebraska	Mortgage	Judicial	Petition	5	None	Allowed
Nevada	Trust Deed	Nonjudicial	Notice of Default	4	None	Allowed
New Hampshire	Mortgage	Nonjudicial	Notice of Sale	2	None	Allowed
	Trust Deed	Nonjudicial	Notice Hearing	2	None	Allowed
New Jersey	Mortgage	Judicial	Complaint	3	10 DD	Allowed
New Mexico	Mortgage	Judicial	Complaint	4	None	Allowed
New York	Mortgage	Judicial	Complaint	4	None	Allowed
North Carolina						
North Dakota	Mortgage	Judicial	Complaint	3	60 DD	Prohibited
Ohio	Mortgage	Judicial	Complaint	5	None	Allowed
Oklahoma	Mortgage	Judicial	Complaint	4	None	Allowed
Oregon	Trust Deed	Both	Publication	6	365	Allowed
Pennsylvania	Mortgage	Judicial	Complaint	3	None	Allowed
Rhode Island	Mortgage	Nonjudicial	Publication	2	None	Allowed
South Carolina	Mortgage	Judicial	Complaint	6	None	Allowed
South Dakota	Mortgage	Judicial	Complaint	3	180 DD	Allowed
Tennessee	Trust Deed	Nonjudicial	Publication	2	None	Allowed
Texas	Trust Deed	Nonjudicial	Publication	2	None	Allowed
Utah	Trust Deed	Nonjudicial	Notice of Default	4	None	Allowed
Vermont	Mortgage	Judicial	Complaint	7	None	Allowed
Virginia	Trust Deed	Nonjudicial	Publication	2	None	Allowed
Washington	Trust Deed	Nonjudicial	Notice of Default	4	None	Allowed
West Virginia	Trust Deed	Nonjudicial	Publication	2	None	Prohibited
Wisconsin	Mortgage	Judicial	Complaint	Varies	None	Allowed
Wyoming	Mortgage	Nonjudicial	Publication	2	3 MM	Allowed

APPENDIX I

SAMPLE FORECLOSURE COMPLAINT

IN THE CIRCUIT COURT OF THE JUDICIAL CIRCUIT
IN AND FOR COUNTY, FLORIDA.

CASE NO.

	)	
Plaintiff(s),	)	
vs.	)	COMPLAINT FOR FORECLOSURE
	)	OF MORTGAGE
if the above Defendants are	)	
alive and if one or more of	)	
said Defendants are dead,	)	
their unknown spouses, heirs,	)	
devisees, grantees, personal	)	
representatives, creditors	)	
and all other parties claiming	)	
by, through or against them;	)	
and all parties having or	)	
claiming to have any right,	)	
title or interest in the	)	
property described in the	)	
complaint,	)	
	)	
Defendant(s).	)	

______________________________/

Plaintiff sues the Defendants and alleges:

1. This is an action to foreclose a mortgage on real property in the County where it lies.

2. The Notice Required by the Fair Debt Collection Practices Act, (The Act), 15 U.S.C. Section 1601 as Amended, is attached hereto as Exhibit "A."

3. On [date], Defendant(s), [state Defendants' name(s)], executed and delivered a promissory note and a mortgage securing payment of the note to Plaintiff, a copy is attached hereto and incorporated herein. The mortgage was recorded on [state date], in Official Records Book [book number], at Page [page number], of the Public Records of [county name], Florida, and mortgaged the property described in the mortgage then owned by and in possession of the mortgagor(s).

4. The mortgage of the Plaintiff is a lien superior in dignity to any prior or subsequent right, title, claim, lien or interest arising out of mortgagor or the mortgagor's predecessors in interest.

5. Plaintiff owns the note and mortgage and holds same.

6. Defendant(s) has defaulted under the covenants, terms, and agreements of the note and mortgage in that the payment due [state date], and all subsequent payments have not been paid.

7. Plaintiff declares the full amount payable under the note and mortgage to be due.

8. Defendant(s) owe Plaintiff what is due and owing on principal, plus interest from and after [state date], and title search expenses for ascertaining necessary parties to this action.

9. In order to protect its security, the Plaintiff may have advanced and paid Ad Valorem Taxes, premiums on insurance required by the mortgage and other necessary costs, or may be required to make such advances during the pendency of this action. Any such sum so paid will be due and owing Plaintiff.

10. The record legal title to said mortgaged property is now vested in Defendant(s), [state names], and upon information and belief Defendant(s) hold possession.

11. All conditions precedent to the acceleration of this mortgage note and to foreclosure of the mortgage have been fulfilled and have occurred.

12. For purposes of collection and foreclosure, the Plaintiff has retained the undersigned attorney and is obligated to pay said attorney a reasonable fee for his/her services.

13. This mortgage is insured under the provisions of the National Housing Act, as amended and regulations thereunder, if applicable.

14. Plaintiff alleges that the claims of the remaining Defendants are secondary, junior, inferior, and subject to the prior claim of Plaintiff, and more particularly the remaining Defendants claim some right, title, and interest in and to the mortgaged premises in the following manner:

a) The Defendant, [state name(s)], may claim some right, title, or interest in the property herein sought to be foreclosed by virtue of [state defendant's reasons]; however, said interest, if any, is subordinate, junior, and inferior to the lien of Plaintiff's mortgage.

(b) The Defendant, an unknown tenant or tenants, may claim some right, title or interest in the property herein sought to be foreclosed by virtue of possession or some other unknown interest, the exact nature of which is unknown to Plaintiff and not a matter of public record; however, said interest, if any, is subordinate, junior, and inferior to the lien of Plaintiff's mortgage.

WHEREFORE, Plaintiff prays the Court as follows:

1. Plaintiff demands an accounting of the sums due under the terms of the mortgage note and mortgage, and if the sum is not paid within the time set by the Court, that the property be sold to satisfy Plaintiff's claim.

2. That the estate of the Defendants and all persons claiming under or against Defendants since the filing of the Lis Pendens be foreclosed.

3. That the Court reserve jurisdiction to enter a deficiency judgment for any portion of a deficiency, should one exist, all in accordance with Chapter 702, Florida Statutes Annotated, unless any Defendant personally liable shall have been discharged from liability under the subject note pursuant to the provisions of the Bankruptcy Code 11 U.S.C. Section 101, et.seq.

Name
Address
Telephone
of Plaintiff's attorney

By:
Plaintiff's attorney
name and registration #
at the Bar

(Our File No.)

NOTICE REQUIRED BY THE FAIR DEBT COLLECTION PRACTICES ACT, (THE ACT) 15 U.S.C. SECTION 1601 AS AMENDED

1. The amount of the debt is stated in Paragraph 8 of the complaint attached hereto.

2. The Plaintiff as named in the attached summons and complaint is the creditor to whom the debt is owed and/or is the servicing agent for the creditor to whom the debt is owed.

3. The debt described in the complaint attached hereto and evidenced by the copy of the mortgage note attached hereto will be assumed to be valid by the creditor's law firm, unless the debtor, within thirty (30) days after the receipt of this notice, disputes, in writing, the validity of the debt or some portion thereof.

4. If the debtor notifies the creditor's law firm in writing within thirty (30) days of the receipt of this notice that the debt or any portion thereof is disputed, the creditor's law firm will obtain verification of the debt and a copy of the verification will be mailed to the debtor by the creditor's law firm.

5. The name of the original creditor is set forth in the mortgage and mortgage note attached hereto. If the creditor named as Plaintiff in the attached summons and complaint is not the original creditor and if the debtor makes a written request to the creditor's law firm within thirty (30) days from receipt of this notice, the name and address of the original creditor will be mailed to the debtor by the creditor's law firm.

6. Written requests should be addressed to the Fair Debt Collection Clerk, Law Office of [name and address of Plaintiff's law firm].

THIS IS AN ATTEMPT TO COLLECT A DEBT AND ANY INFORMATION OBTAINED WILL BE USED FOR THAT PURPOSE.

THE THIRTY (30) DAY TIME PERIOD FOR REQUESTING VERIFICATION OF THE DEBT OWED TO THE PLAINTIFF IS <u>NOT</u> AFFECTED BY THE TWENTY (20) DAY TIME PERIOD SET FORTH IN THE SUMMONS YOU HAVE RECEIVED WITH THIS COMPLAINT. ALTHOUGH YOU MUST RESPOND TO THE COMPLAINT WITHIN TWENTY (20) DAYS, YOU STILL HAVE THE

FULL THIRTY (30) DAYS TO REQUEST IN WRITING, VERIFICATION OF THE MORTGAGE DEBT AND OTHERWISE DEMAND COMPLIANCE WITH THE FAIR DEBT AND COLLECTION PRACTICES ACT.

APPENDIX J

SAMPLE LIS PENDENS

IN THE CIRCUIT COURT OF THE JUDICIAL CIRCUIT
IN AND FOR COUNTY, FLORIDA

CASE NO.

	)	
Plaintiff(s), [name(s) here]	)	
vs.	)	NOTICE OF LIS PENDENS
	)	
if the above Defendants are	)	
alive and if one or more of	)	
said Defendants are dead,	)	
their unknown spouses, heirs,	)	
devisees, grantees, personal	)	
representatives, creditors	)	
and all other parties claiming	)	
by, through or against them;	)	
and all parties having or	)	
claiming to have any right,	)	
title or interest in the	)	
property described in the	)	
complaint,	)	
	)	
Defendant(s). [name(s) here]	)	

_______________________________/

TO: THE DEFENDANTS NAMED ABOVE AND ALL OTHERS TO WHOM IT MAY CONCERN:

NOTICE IS HEREBY GIVEN that a suit has been instituted in the above Court by the above named Plaintiff(s) and against you seeking to foreclose a mortgage on the following real property in the County indicated in the description:

Dated this _____ day of __________, 20___.

[Name, address, and Bar # for Plaintiff's attorney]

By:
[Name of Plaintiff's attorney]
(Our File No.)

APPENDIX K

SAMPLE DEFENDANT ANSWER

IN THE CIRCUIT COURT OF THE
NTH JUDICIAL CIRCUIT IN
AND FOR Ye Old COUNTY, Any State.

ANYMORTGAGE, INC.) CASE NO. 00-00000 DA 00
)
Plaintiff,)
vs.)
)
SUBPRIME BORROWER; ET AL.,)
)
Defendant(s),)
[name(s) here])

ANSWER AND AFFIRMATIVE DEFENSE OF ONE GUY AND ANOTHER

COMES NOW, ONE GUY AND ANOTHER, by and through undersigned counsel and files this answer and affirmative defense to Plaintiff's complaint and states:

Answer

1. That the allegations set forth in Paragraphs 1 and 2 showing these answering Defendants interest in the real property by virtue of that certain mortgage recorded in Official Records Book 00000, Page 0, of the Public Records of Ye Old County, Any State, are admitted.

2. The remaining allegations contained in Plaintiff's complaint are denied and Defendant demands strict proof thereof.

Affirmative Defense

3. Should the Plaintiff's mortgage be found superior to that of these answering Defendants, and a sale ensue then ONE GUY AND ANOTHER prays for an award of any surplus or overage at the time of sale.

THEIR ATTORNEY, P.A.
Attorney for ONE GUY AND ANOTHER
AND DEFENDANT'S NAME
THIS Avenue
YE OLD CITY, ANY STATE 00000
(000)000-0000
ANY STATE Bar# 0000000000

By:
ONE GUY ATTORNEY, ESQ.

CERTIFICATE OF SERVICE

I HEREBY CERTIFY that a true and correct copy of the foregoing ANSWER and AFFIRMATIVE DEFENSE, was faxed and mailed this _____ day of ____________, 2009, to the following:

BANK'S ATTORNEY, ESQ., LAW FIRM, ATTORNEY FOR PLAINTIFF, ADDRESS

____
ONE GUY ATTORNEY, ESQ.

APPENDIX L

SAMPLE FORECLOSURE BIDDING RULES

OFFICE OF THE CLERK ADMINISTRATIVE ORDER

SUBJECT: JUDICIAL SALES PROCEDURES

Where not otherwise provided by an Order or Final Judgment, the Clerk may set up any reasonable criteria and procedures in conducting judicial sales that he may deem advisable, which would have the purpose of selling the property for cash at public sale to the highest and best bidder for the highest and best bid.

Therefore, the following criteria and procedures are hereby established:

All bidders shall fill out a Registration Form for each sale, prior to bidding.

At 11:00 a.m. on the day of a sale, the Auctioneer will read the terms of the sale that are contained in the Registration Form.

If time allows, canceled sales will be posted. However, in any event, they will be announced before the start of all sales, or when received during or after the sales.

The Auctioneer will announce each sale by case number, Plaintiff's name, Defendant's name, and legal description of the property. The Auctioneer will request that the Plaintiff or his representative make an opening bid. If the Plaintiff or his representative makes an opening bid, the bidding shall continue until there is a successful high bidder.

If the Plaintiff or his representative states that an opening bid will not be forthcoming, the Auctioneer repeats that the Plaintiff is not making a bid at this time and asks any interested parties if there are any opening bids. A deputy clerk documents on the bid sheet that the Plaintiff offers no bid at this time. If no bids are received from anyone, a Certificate of No Sale is filed by the Clerk. If bids are received, the bidding continues until there is a successful high bidder.

When the Plaintiff or his representative is not present, a deputy clerk will read the Final Judgment to see if there is a clause that states that the sale cannot be held unless there is a representative of the Plaintiff present at the sale. The deputy clerk will also check the case in the computer to see if there is anything else that will stop the sale. If there is no reason to stop the sale, the Auctioneer will proceed to sell the property to the highest bidder.

When the property is sold, a deputy clerk documents on the bid sheet that the Plaintiff or his representative was not present.

All those bidding on a particular piece of property, with the exception of the Plaintiff, will be told that they must stand in the area immediately in front of and visible to the Auctioneer but behind the stanchion poles. The Plaintiff may stand at the designated podium. Sale attendees not bidding on the property must remain in the rear or on the sides of the room and may not approach the other bidders during the sale. Bidders or observers who do not comply with this policy will be disqualified from bidding or attending the sales for the remainder of that day as well as the sales conducted on the next auction date.

All Registration Forms for a particular sale must be submitted to the Clerk at the Auctioneer's table prior to the commencement of bidding. Prior to the Plaintiff submitting the opening bid, the Auctioneer will ask if there are any Registration Forms to be submitted for this sale. After pausing for forms to be submitted, the Auctioneer will announce that no more Registration Forms will be submitted. Registration Forms not submitted at this time will not be honored. If the Auctioneer determines that there were no Registration Forms submitted for a particular sale, the Plaintiff will submit their opening bid. At that time, the Auctioneer will announce, "Since there were no Registration Forms submitted, the Plaintiff is the successful bidder for the amount of ____________."

With the exception of the aforementioned cases that are sold to the Plaintiff, all final bids are repeated three times. When the last bid appears to have been made, the Auctioneer will make an announcement using language substantially the same as the following. The Auctioneer will call "Going once to (name of successful bidder) for (the amount of last offer)," call "Going twice to (name of successful bidder) for (the amount of last offer)," pause, call

"Your attention please, I am about to make the third and final call. Are there any other bids?" and call "Going three times to (name of successful bidder) for (the amount of the last offer)." If no other bids are placed, the Auctioneer will announce "Sold to (name of successful bidder) for (the amount of the winning bid).

The Auctioneer will only accept bids that are at least in increments of $100.00 more than the previous bid. All bid increments must be made in multiples of $100.00. All bids announced by a bidder and repeated by the Auctioneer are written on a bid sheet by a deputy clerk. The Auctioneer will acknowledge an invalid bid and state why the bid is invalid by making an announcement using language substantially the same as the following example: "That is not a valid bid. A valid bid must be a minimum of $100.00 above the previous bid." A bidder who consistently bids in increments less that $100.00 will be disqualified from bidding as well as the corporation, partnership, business, or nonprofit organization under whose name they bid for the remainder of that date's sales as well as the sales conducted on the next auction date.

During the bidding process, all bidders and observers are expected to treat each other and Clerk's Office employees with respect. Any disruptive behavior (e.g., engaging in conversation or using a cellular phone while a sale is being conducted, arguing with a clerk or another bidder, etc.) will result in disqualification from bidding or attending the sales for the remainder of that day as well as the sales conducted on the next auction date.

All bidding must be done in good faith. If any bidder fails to immediately make the required deposit, rescinds a bid after a property has been declared sold, or engages in disruptive behavior, the individual bidding as well as the corporation, partnership, business, or nonprofit organization under whose name they bid will be disqualified from bidding for the remainder of that date's sales as well as the sales conducted on the next auction date. If a bidder is disqualified from bidding due to bad faith bidding and/or disruptive behavior on three occasions in any thirty-day period or on six occasions in one year, the individual bidder as well as the corporation, partnership, business, or nonprofit organization under whose name they bid may be disqualified from bidding for one year from the date of the last disruption. Any involvement in a physical altercation will result in an immediate disqualification for up to six months.

A deposit, as required by law or court order, is immediately requested from the successful bidder. This deposit shall be payable in cash or cashier's check only, in US funds made payable to the Clerk of the Courts.

If the successful bidder does not post the deposit as set forth above at the time of the sale, the bidder will be disqualified for that day as well as the sales conducted on the next auction day, the bid will be considered invalid, and the bidding will continue from the last highest bid.

All sales are final and will not be reopened.

All successful bidders shall pay the balance of their bid and the costs of the sale (Clerk's fee, registry fee, publication cost, stamps) in cash or cashier's check only, in US funds payable to the Clerk of the Court by 3:00 p.m. the day of the sale. Only the costs of the sale may be paid by attorney's trust account check. If final payment is not made by 3:00 p.m., the Clerk shall re-advertise the sale and pay all costs of the sale from the deposit. Any remaining funds shall be applied toward the judgment.

The Mortgage Foreclosure Unit will remain and make available for viewing, upon request, copies of the Clerk's Administrative Order.

APPENDIX M

EXAMPLE OF FORECLOSURE SALE INFORMATION AVAILABLE FOR PURCHASE

26 Years Reporting Foreclosures

With the F. I. S. Premium Report, you get even more information.

www.FisReports.com · 305-552-8994 · Miami, FL

Foreclosure Information Systems, Inc. (305) 552-8994
P.O. Box 650490, Miami, Fl 33265-0490 - Fax (305) 227-9599
FISReports.com Internet foreclosure research service

Date of Sale 11/20/2008 Thursday Page: 9
Book Date Range: 11/20/2008 To: 11/20/2008
Copyright 2008 FIS Inc ANY REPRODUCTION is strictly PROHIBITED
FIS Inc does its best to obtain and report all details correctly, but assumes NO responsibilty for errors or omissions

(1) 07-45463-CA-01 (2) Sale: 11/20/2008 (3) Doc: MORTGAGE,Pos/Unk 07/03/2007 25751-4634 (4) L-P: 12/26/2007 26126-4697 (10) Judgment for the Plaintiff: 428,999
(5) Pltf: CHASE HOME FIN (LLC) (6) Atty: BARBARA LEON 813/251-4766
(7) Defts: ROBERTO J PUBLIC
(11) Adj Active Mls $ 473,621
(12) Adj Pending Mls $ 268,968
(8) D02 BOARD OF COUNTY FJUDG 20879-3592 | D04 CLEARING THE WAY FJUDG 25967-2328 | D06 SEARS ROEBUCK & CO FJUDG 19056-2908
(13) Adj 3 Months Closed Mls $ 362,858
D03 CITIBANK (F S B) MOR-UN 24961-1338 | D05 PREMIUM ASSET FJUDG 22328-4131 | D07 STATE OF FL DEPT OF FJUDG 20879-3592
(14) Adj 6 Months Closed Mls $ 362,858
(9) Dockets: 09/17/08 TEXT CANCEL 09/17/08 RESET 11/20/08 . <>09/17/08 SALE: 11-20-2008 <>09/18/08 SALE: 09-17-2008 <>08/17/08 JUDGMENT $ 428999.07 BK:26448 PG:0570 <>06/04/08 DEFAULT D02 <>01/05/08 ANS

(15) 3125 SW 71 AVE (16) Lot Size: 9,045 SQ FT (17) Folio: 30-4014-006-1600 (34) Bldg Size.: 1,985 (40) Tax Assmt: 08 $405,548
(18) Owner: ROBERTO J PUBLIC 3125 SW 71 AVE MIAMI FL 33155-385 (28) Built 47 (35) Mls Type Mls Adj (41) Taxes Due: 11-19 $7,989
(19) Legal.: CENTRAL MIAMI PART 4 PB 25-43 LOTS 19 & 20 & S17FT OF LOT 21 BLK 65 LOT SIZE (29) Floors 1
(20) Use....: RESIDENTIAL - SINGLE FAMILY (25) Zoning: SINGLE FAMILY - GENERAL (30) Units 1 (36) (5) Active $ 473,621 (42) MLS Status: Closed Sale
(21) Last Sale 06/07 $490,000 25751 - 4632 GOOD SALE (26) Homestead : YES (31) Beds 3 (37) (2) Pending $ 268,968 (43) Status Date: 06/20/2007
(22) Location: INTERIOR - WITH NO VIEW (27) Extras: POOL (32) Baths 2 (38) 5) 3 Mo Closed $ 341,420 (44) MLS List $... $ 495,000
(23) Code Citations: B014462 7/18/2007 $10,510.00 == B014461 7/18/2007 $7,860.00 == B053715 (33) 1/2 Baths 1 (39) 5) 6 Mo Closed $ 341,420 (45) Days Market: 14
(24) Escrow: CHASE HOME FIN LLC - SUPRIME (46) Lowest Adj MLS with same # Beds: $ 307,675 (47) Lowest Mls: $ 269,960 (48)

1. Court Case Number
2. Auction Sale Date
3. Foreclosing Document Type
4. Lis Pendens
5. Plaintiff (Lender)
6. Plaintiff's Attorney
7. First Defendant
8. List of Inferior Liens
9. Docket Case History
10. Judgment Amount (in favor of...)
11. Total Adjusted Active MLS Value
12. Total Adjusted Pending MLS Value
13. Total Adjusted 3 Month Closed Sales MLS Value
14. Total Adjusted 6 Month Closed Sales MLS Value
15. Property Address
16. Property Lot Size
17. Property Tax Folio Number
18. Owner of Record with Address
19. Property Legal Description
20. Property Use
21. Last Recorded Sale Details
22. Property Location Description
23. Property Code Violations
24. Escrow Agent: Lender that collects real estate taxes
25. Property Zoning
26. Homestead Exemption
27. Property Extras
28. Year Built
29. Number of Floors
30. Number of Living Units
31. Number of Bedrooms
32. Number of Baths
33. Number of Half Baths
34. Property Building Size
35. Assorted Adjusted MLS Values
36. Average of Current Active MLS Values Adjusted to Property
37. Average of Current Pending MLS Values Adjusted to Property
38. Average of Current 3 Month Closed MLS Values Adjusted to Property
39. Average of Current 6 Month Closed MLS Values Adjusted to Property
40. Property Tax Market Assessment
41. Total of Current and Delinquent Real Estate Taxes
42. Property Current MLS Status
43. Property Current MLS Status Date
44. MLS Listing Price at Status Date
45. Property's Days on Market at Status Date
46. Property's Adjusted Value Using Active Listing with Same Number of Bedrooms and Lowest Listed Square Foot Value
47. Property's Adjusted Value Using Active Listing with Lowest Listed Square Foot Value
48. MLS Photo (when available) Prints in Black and white

Adjusted MLS values are calculated by taking the average square foot value of the properties listed in each group and adjusting the value to the subject property by multiplying that average against the square footage of the property.

Delivered Nationally

APPENDIX N

SAMPLE BROKER PRICE OPINION

View BPO - Order Number: Printer-friendly version) (Client) Page 1

Residential RealEstate Review, Inc.
10401 Deerwood Park Blvd.
Jacksonville, FL 32256

904-722-7012
www.rrreview.com
info@rrreview.com

Exterior Broker Price Opinion (BPO) #:

Client:
Order #:
Inspection Type: Exterior
Mortgagor:
Property Address:

Date Completed: 12/7/2007
Loan #:
Inspection Date: 12/5/2007
City, State, ZIP:

Subject Property

Type/Style: Single Family - 1 Story

Occupancy: Occupied - Occupant Unknown

Location	Condition	Sq. Ft. Living	No Units	Rooms	Bed-rooms	Full Baths	Half Baths	Base-ment	Garages	Lot Size (Sq. ft.)	Lot Size (Acres)	Age (Yrs)
Suburban	Average	1,482	1	7	3	2	0	None	1 Attached	7,700	0.177	25

Purchase Price: $215,000

Purchase Date: 7/14/2005

Currently Listed: No

Comments: It is unknown if property is vacant or occupied. Property is in average condition, showing inferior curb appeal and pride of ownership. Roof shows several patches throughought. No landscaping at all. Property features older windows and no recent updates, but no obvious signs of neglect observed. Owner acquired this property thru a conventional mortgage recorded by Long Beach Mortgage on 8/19/2005 for a combined amount of $215,000 (80/20 loan). An additional Private Party Lender loan for $15,000 was recorded on 10/31/2005. Property has a mortgage Lis Pendens filed by

Comparable Sales

Address	City	Zip	Sq. Ft. Living	No. Units	Rooms	Bed-rooms	Full Baths	Half Baths	Base-ment	Garages	Lot Size (Sq. Ft.)	Lot Size (Acres)	Age (Yrs)	DOM	Prox. to Subject	See Map
			1,395	1	7	3	2	0	None	1 Attached	4,500	0.103	15	89	0.36 Miles	1
			1,846	1	8	4	2	0	None	1 Attached	8,000	0.184	22	79	0.28 Miles	2
			1,782	1	8	4	2	0	None	None	7,500	0.172	25	112	0.08 Miles	3

	Condition	Style	List Price	Sale Price	Sale Date	Location	PUD?	Concessions/Comments
1	Good	1 Story	$275,000	$275,000	8/9/2007	Same as subject	No	Although this property is younger than subject property, it's lot sqft is considerably smaller.
2	Good	1 Story	$278,400	$278,400	9/27/2007	Same as subject	No	Superior to subject: larger room count, lot and LA sqft and better curb appeal and pride of ownership.
3	Average	1 Story	$335,500	$294,500	7/5/2007	Same as subject	No	This property is most comparable to subject in exterior condition, curb appeal and pride of ownership, subject price adjustment to be made to reflect pool.

Competitive Properties

Address	City	Zip	Sq. Ft. Living	No. Units	Rooms	Bed-rooms	Full Baths	Half Baths	Base-ment	Garages	Lot Size (Sq. Ft.)	Lot Size (Acres)	Age (Yrs)	DOM	Prox. to Subject	See Map
			1,531	1	7	3	2	0	None	1 Attached	7,600	0.174	24	55	0.13 Miles	4
			1,713	1	7	3	2	0	None	1 Attached	7,500	0.172	24	15	0.07 Miles	5
			1,846	1	7	3	2	0	None	2 Attached	7,500	0.172	22	104	0.26 Miles	6

	Condition	Style	Original List Price	Current List Price	Location	PUD?	Concessions/Comments
1	Average	1 Story	$260,000	$260,000	Same as subject	No	Most comparable to subject: similar LA and lot sqft, same room count, and similar exterior condition and curb appeal.
2	Average	1 Story	$264,000	$264,000	Same as subject	No	Similar to subject in room count, lot and LA sqft. This property shows average pride of ownership and curb appeal.
							Younger property, larger LA sqft, but inferior curb appeal and exterior condition.

View BPO - Order Number: (Printer-friendly version) (Client) Page 2

3	Fair	1 Story	$274,000	$274,000	Same as subject	No	Short sale, cosmetic repairs required. Property is overpriced given current market trend.

Valuation Information

Marketing Time:	Quick Sale 30 Days	90 -120 Days	Est. Days to Sell: 120 Days
As Is Value:	$221,000	$260,000	$260,000
Repaired Value:	$222,500	$261,500	$261,500

Estimate repair costs on:	Amount (in dollars)		
Painting:	$1,200.00		
Structural:	$0.00		
Landscaping:	$300.00		
Roof:	$0.00		
Windows:	$0.00		
Other($):	$0.00		
Other Notes:	N/A		
Est. Cost of Repairs:	$1,500.00	Est. Days to Repair: 14	Land Value: $122,200

Marketability of Subject

Do neighborhood environmental issues affect that value of the subject property? no

Explain environmental issues:

Are repairs recommend? yes

Property should be listed: As Repaired

Explain any functional or economic obsolescence factors: Exterior needs to be painted, existing paint is fading and peeling. Front yard needs landscaping in order to show curb appeal and pride of ownership. No functional or economic obsolescence observed at time of drive-by.

Estimated Days to Sell under Current Market Conditions: 120

Will this property be a problem for resale? No

Neighborhood Trend: Stable

Pride of Ownership: Average

Number of Listings in Immediate Area: 11

Neighborhood Low Price: $214,500

Neighborhood High Price: $289,000

Describe any negative neighborhood factors that detract from subject's value: No negative factors detracting from subject's resale value observed at time of drive-by.

Quality Control Review

QC comments: The subject is an older SFR in an established suburban neighborhood. The value of the subject is below the values of the closed comparable sales. The closed sales bracket the subject's GLA and age. The sales are timely and proximate. The agent's estimate of value appears reasonable and reflects the current active listings.

APPENDIX O

SAMPLE MORTGAGE MODIFICATION PACKAGE AND AGREEMENT

This instrument prepared by/RETURN TO:
ATTORNEY, P.A.
ADDRESS

MORTGAGE MODIFICATION AGREEMENT

THIS AGREEMENT, made and executed this _____ day of ___________, 2009, by BORROWERS, A SINGLE MAN, hereinafter called the Mortgagors, whose post office address is ADDRESS shall include the heirs, legal and personal representatives, successors, and assigns of said Mortgagors wherever the context so requires or admits, to LENDER, INC., hereinafter called the Mortgagee, whose post office address is ADDRESS, which term shall include the heirs, legal and personal representatives, successors, and assigns of said Mortgagee wherever the context so requires or admits,

WITNESSETH: That for divers good and valuable consideration, including the Lender's agreement to forebear from exercising its legal right to accelerate the mortgage loan and foreclose, the parties hereby agree to amend and supplement the Mortgage dated WHENEVER and recorded ALSO WHENEVER in Official Records Book 000000, Page 0000 in the Public Records of YE OLD, ANY STATE, more particularly described as follows:

THIS IS MY CONDO LEGAL DESCRIPTION

BORROWER FURTHER COVENANT AND AGREE:

1. That as of A DAY WE PICKED, the principal balance due on the loan is MORE MONEY THAN THE BORROWER HAS ($0000000). In addition

to said principal balance, additional charges have accrued on the loan, including but not limited to default interest, late charges, attorneys fees and costs, and corporate advances to protect the lender's interest.

2. That as of THE DAY THE MONEY WAS DUE, the subject mortgage loan is in default for the payment due on THE DAY THE MONEY WAS DUE and subsequent months.

3. The parties have agreed that the delinquent interest in the amount of A LOT MORE MONEY ($00000), late charges, and attorneys fees and costs shall be waived by Lender provided there is no default under the terms of this Modification Agreement. The monthly payments shall be due in the amount of A PAYMENT THE BORROWER CAN AFFORD WE HOPE ($0000). The final maturity date shall be A DATE WE ALL AGREED ON.

4. To pay all and singular the principal and interest and other sums of money payable by virtue of the promissory note and mortgage, or either, promptly on the days, respectively, the same severally become due. The first payment to commence on SOON DATE. The first payment of $0000 together with fees and costs of $000.00 shall be remitted to THE BANK'S LAWYER, Trust account. All subsequent payments due hereunder and commencing on THE NEXT PAYMENT DATE, shall be paid directly to BANK at BANK ADDRESS. In the event that additional documentary stamps are required by the Department of Revenue, borrowers shall pay same immediately upon demand.

3. To abide by all the terms, covenants and conditions set forth in the mortgage dated DATE OF MORTGAGE and described above.

NO ADDITIONAL FUNDS HAVE BEEN ADVANCED OR LOANED TO BORROWER BY LENDER. ALL DOCUMENTARY STAMPS HAVE PREVIOUSLY BEEN PAID IN CONNECTION WITH THE ORIGINAL MORTGAGE AND NOTE.

IN WITNESS WHEREOF, the said Lender has executed this mortgage under seal on this day and year herein first above written.

Signed, sealed and delivered in the presence of:

Print name: _______________ BORROWER _______________

STATE OF ANY)

SS:

COUNTY OF YE OLD)

THE FOREGOING INSTRUMENT WAS ACKNOWLEDGED BEFORE ME THIS _____ DAY OF_________, 2008, BY BORROWER PERSONALLY KNOWN TO ME OR HAS PRODUCED ____________ AS IDENTIFICATION AND DID (DID NOT) TAKE AN OATH.

Notary Public

My Commission Expires:

APPENDIX P

SHORT SALE TIPS FOR BUYERS AND SELLERS

IF YOU ARE A BUYER

- **Do Your Homework:** Research the property you are interested in before making an offer by reviewing the county public records. Many counties are fully automated now so this research can be done on the Internet. For those counties that are not online you will need to go to the Office of County Records to do this research. An alternative is to order a title search report from a reputable title insurance underwriter such as First American Title Insurance Company. These cost about $150, but if you are not comfortable doing your own research and fairly certain that you will be able to negotiate a purchase, they are well worth the cost (which may be shared with the seller if you can negotiate that). This research will tell you who owns the property (for example, the person who is holding herself out as thc owner may have a deceased person who is still on the title or a parent who cosigned for the loan and is still on title. Anyone who is on the title to the property should sign the contract as seller since each of these folks will need to sign over the deed to you at closing. If you want to avoid a last-minute surprise at the closing table, like finding out there's another owner who refuses to sell to you at the short-sale price, it is important to identify each of these people up front and make sure they each sign the purchase contract (which usually obligates them to sell you the property and indicates their acceptance of the terms of your offer).
- **Find an Experienced Realtor:** If the listing realtor does not have short-sale experience, make sure to find your own realtor who does. On the other hand, if the listing agent is experienced in short sales and you are comfortable moving forward with your own realtor, you want to do so since bringing one more realtor into the mix means one more

person to negotiate fees with and in short sales there's only so much money to go around. Make sure you are clear with the realtor about who will be paying his commission. Most lenders will only agree to pay discounted realtor commissions and some will not pay any at all. Other times the amount of commission the lender will pay depends on the purchase price. If the realtor is expecting to make up the difference, you want to be aware of that added cost and factor it into your offer calculations.

- **Find Out What Your Lender's Short-Sale Procedures Are:** Some lenders submit short-sale offers to a committee that meets on a set schedule. If that's the case, you will want to submit your offer in time for the next meeting. In all cases, it is imperative that you work with the right contact person at the bank branch in order to avoid delays. It is currently taking most lenders at least 2 or 3 weeks to respond to short-sale offers and up to several months to close. For this reason, a concurrent closing with the house you are selling* may not be possible. Be aware that most lenders will want to do their own comparative market analysis of area sales or at least get a broker price opinion (BPO) before accepting your offer since, as we've discussed, they have investors they need to answer to. And remember, most lenders will insist that you buy the property as is and may not be willing to pay traditional seller paid closing costs. Be sure to calculate possible added costs (such as repairs and past due association fees) due to this condition when you are deciding what to offer. Often times, a lender will try to reserve the right to renegotiate the contract terms (and in particular, the purchase price) if the market improves before closing. Unfortunately, they will not agree to allow you to do this if the market worsens. Some lenders will also not agree to an inspection or a financing contingency in the contract. It is fairly risky for a buyer to waive either unless these items can be fully vested (i.e., finalized) before signing the contract.
- **Make Sure the Seller Knows What to Expect:** Lenders will only agree to short sales when the seller has no equity in the home and no money to pay the lender the difference between the price you agree to pay and the loans that need to be paid off. The seller will need to pro-

---

*Those buyers who may need to sell their home before buying another home (often termed a contingency sale).

vide a financial hardship letter to his lender. The seller may also have to pay income taxes on the amount of the mortgage loan that is forgiven. Congress passed and later extended a law waiving this income tax in certain cases, but those cases may not apply to your seller, and your purchase may occur after the law expires.

- **Submit Proper Documentation and Purchase Offer to Lender:** Once you have reached an agreement on the purchase terms with the seller, send the signed contract together with the seller's hardship letter and financial information to the lender for approval.
- **Set Deadlines:** Be sure to establish a clear deadline by which the lender must accept your offer. This does not mean that the lender will respond by that date but it gives you the legal right to cancel your offer and look for another property if they do not. The timeframes in your contract offer, for example, the amount of time you have to inspect the property and get a mortgage loan, should all begin when the lender approves your offer. This way you will not have to lay out money for these items until you know you have a deal.
- **Remember Psychology:** Remember the seller's psychology is different in a short sale than a conventional sale. When a seller is not getting any money and is in the midst of financial duress, he may not be as motivated or cooperative as one would wish.

IF YOU ARE A SELLER

- **Make Sure You Understand Your Lender's Short Sale Procedures and Requirements:** This may require multiple telephone calls to find the right contact person and get answers. Ideally, you can speak directly with the decision maker. If you are working with a Realtor, he can do this legwork for you, but your lender may require him to provide them with an authorization letter from you. The letter should contain: (1) the property address, (2) your loan reference number, (3) your name, and (4) your Realtor's name and contact information.
- **Find an Experienced Realtor:** If you're going to work with a Realtor, you will want to work with a Realtor who has plenty of experience with short sales. If you can find a Realtor who has done short sales with your lender, all the better. Each lender has its own unique proce-

dures. If your Realtor already knows your lender's procedures and contact people, it can save you a lot of time and hassles. Your Realtor should be able to obtain a payoff letter from your lender that will give you an idea of the full amount due to your lender including late fees, penalties, default interest, and costs, if any. Start by asking your Realtor for a preliminary net sheet. This is an estimated closing statement showing the sales price you can expect to receive, the costs you will incur, including real estate commissions, if any. Eventually, your lender will also want a hardship letter from you. The letter should describe how you got into the financial bind and make a plea to the lender to accept less than full payment to satisfy your mortgage loan. Your lender will also want proof of income and assets. Be truthful and honest. Include savings accounts, money market accounts, stocks or bonds, cash or other real estate, or anything of value. Remember, lenders have investors to whom they need to justify short sale decisions. Bank deposits that reflect large deposits or withdrawals should be explained.

- **Make Proper Disclosures:** If you are working with a Realtor experienced in short sales, he will know the proper way to disclose that the transaction will be a short sale in the multiple listing service, in any advertising, and in the purchase contract. If you do not plan on working with an experienced Realtor, you should consider investing a few dollars in a short-sale book or a few hours educating yourself about short sales online to avoid potentially costly mistakes and liability.
- **Know the Laws, Taxes, and Impacts:** Above all else, be sure you understand how your lender will reflect the short sale on your credit report and release you from liability for the amount they discount the mortgage payoff. If the lender intends to pursue you for his deficiency amount, it is not a true short sale and you're better off knowing that up front.

APPENDIX Q

SAMPLE DEED-IN-LIEU OF FORECLOSURE

This instrument prepared by:

LAW FIRM, P.A.
ADDRESS

Record and Return to:

WARRANTY DEED

THIS INDENTURE, made this _____ day of __________, __________, between ______________, whose post office address is ______________, herein after called the Grantor(s), to ______________, a ______________ corporation, whose post office address is ____________________, hereinafter called the Grantees. (Wherever used herein the terms "grantor" and "grantee" include all the parties to this instrument and the heirs, legal representatives and assigns of individuals, and the successors and assigns.)

WITNESSETH: That the Grantor, for and in consideration of the sum of Ten Dollars ($10.00) and other good and valuable consideration, the receipt whereof is hereby acknowledged, hereby grant, bargain, sell, alien, remise, release, convey and confirm unto the Grantee, and the Grantee's heirs, and assigns forever, all that certain land situate in YE OLD County, ANY STATE, to wit:

Subject to:

a. Taxes for the year of closing and subsequent years.

b. Easements, restrictions, conditions, limitations and covenants of record and zoning ordinances common to the neighborhood.

This deed is an absolute conveyance, the Grantor having sold said land to Grantee for a fair and adequate consideration, such consideration, in addition to the above-recited, being the Grantee's covenant not to sue the Grantor in regard to his/her personal obligation secured by the mortgage from _______, dated __________, recorded , in Official Records Book 0000, Page 0000, of the Public Records of YE OLD County, ANY STATE, and in consideration of the Grantee waiving all rights to seek any deficiency judgment against the Grantor in regard to any foreclosure of said mortgage. Both Grantor and the Grantee specifically intend that this conveyance shall not result in a merger of the equitable and legal titles in regard to the above-described property and that the mortgage lien created in the mortgage recorded in Official Records Book 00000, Page 000, shall not be cancelled or satisfied by delivery of this Warranty Deed.

Grantor declares that this conveyance is free and fairly made and that there are no agreements, oral or written, other than this deed between Grantor and Grantee with respect to said land, and said Grantor does hereby fully warrant the title to said land, and will defend the same against the lawful claims of all person whomsoever.

IN WITNESS WHEREOF, the said Grantor has hereunto set Grantor's hand and seal the day and year first above written.

Signed, sealed and delivered
in our presence:

Witness #1 ____

Print Name: ____

Witness #2 ____

Print Name: ____

STATE OF ________________)

SS:

COUNTY OF ______________)

THE FOREGOING INSTRUMENT was acknowledged before me this _____ day of ______________________, ________________, by , who is (or are) personally known to me or who has/have produced _________________ as identification and who did (did not) take an oath.

Notary Public

My Commission Expires:

APPENDIX R

EXAMPLES OF LAWS GOVERNING COLLECTIONS

THE FAIR DEBT COLLECTION PRACTICES ACT

There are many rules and regulations lenders must follow when foreclosing. The Fair Debt Collection Practices Act contains rules that must be followed when collecting any debt, including a mortgage. Each time a debt collector contacts you, he must give you what is known as a "Mini-Miranda Warning" This warning received that name because it is reminiscent of the warnings that police should give you if you are arrested, however, "Mini-Miranda Warnings" have nothing to do with criminal law. The warning must contain the following words (or words imparting this meaning):

> Hello, I am ______(name of collector). I am (or this office is) a debt collector representing __________(creditor). Information obtained during the course of this call will be used for the purpose of collecting the debt.

If the creditor has not been advising you as above, you may have a right to sue.

Letters you receive in the mail from collectors also must contain similar warnings such as:

> This is an attempt to collect a debt. Any information obtained will be used for that purpose. Unless within 30 days of your receipt of this notice, you notify us that you dispute the validity of this debt, it will be assumed to be correct. If you notify this office within thirty days that you dispute the validity of the debt, we will obtain verification of the debt or a copy of the judgment. If you request it within 30 days, we will provide you with the name and address of the original creditor (if different from the current creditor).

If the letter does not state the above, or words similar or close to the above, you may also have a right of action. Furthermore, did you know that no bill collector or creditor has the right to contact any third person about your debt, except to get information solely to locate you? This means that if a bill collector or a creditor tells anyone except you that you owe them money, they, too, can be sued.

In addition to federal rules and regulations, each state has it's own statutes lenders must follow when foreclosing. Below, by way of example, is the foreclosure Statute for the State of Florida:

SAMPLE STATE FORECLOSURE STATUTES

702.01 Equity.—All mortgages shall be foreclosed in equity. In a mortgage foreclosure action, the court shall sever for separate trial all counterclaims against the foreclosing mortgagee. The foreclosure claim shall, if tried, be tried to the court without a jury.

702.035 Legal notice concerning foreclosure proceedings.—Whenever a legal advertisement, publication, or notice relating to a foreclosure proceeding is required to be placed in a newspaper, it is the responsibility of the petitioner or petitioner's attorney to place such advertisement, publication, or notice. For counties with more than 1 million total population as reflected in the 2000 Official Decennial Census of the United States Census Bureau as shown on the official web site of the United States Census Bureau, any notice of publication required by this section shall be deemed to have been published in accordance with the law if the notice is published in a newspaper that has been entered as a periodical matter at a post office in the county in which the newspaper is published, is published a minimum of 5 days a week, exclusive of legal holidays, and has been in existence and published a minimum of 5 days a week, exclusive of legal holidays, for 1 year or is a direct successor to a newspaper that has been in existence for 1 year that has been published a minimum of 5 days a week, exclusive of legal holidays. The advertisement, publication, or notice shall be placed directly by the attorney for the petitioner, by the petitioner if acting pro se, or by the clerk of the court. Only the actual costs charged by the newspaper for the advertisement, publication, or notice may be charged as costs in the action.

702.04 Mortgaged lands in different counties.—When a mortgage includes lands, railroad track, right-of-way, or terminal facilities and station grounds, lying in two or more counties, it may be foreclosed in any one of said counties, and all proceedings shall be had in that county as if all the mortgaged land, railroad track, right-of-way, or terminal facilities and station grounds lay therein, except that notice of the sale must be published in every county wherein any of the lands, railroad track, right-of-way, or terminal facilities and station grounds to be sold lie. After final disposition of the suit, the clerk of the circuit court shall prepare and forward a certified copy of the decree of foreclosure and sale and of the decree of confirmation of sale to the clerk of the circuit court of every county wherein any of the mortgaged lands, railroad tracks, right-of-way, or terminal facilities and station grounds lie, to be recorded in the foreign judgment book of each such county, and the costs of such copies and of the record thereof shall be taxed as costs in the cause.

702.05 Mortgaged lands sold for taxes.—Any person who has a lien by mortgage or otherwise upon lands sold for taxes may, within the time allowed by law for redemption, redeem such lands, and the receipt of the officer authorized to receive the amount paid for redemption money shall entitle the lienholder to collect the said amount, with interest at the rate of 10 percent per annum, as a part of and in the same manner as the amount secured by her or his original lien.

702.06 Deficiency decree; common-law suit to recover deficiency.—In all suits for the foreclosure of mortgages heretofore or hereafter executed the entry of a deficiency decree for any portion of a deficiency, should one exist, shall be within the sound judicial discretion of the court, but the complainant shall also have the right to sue at common law to recover such deficiency, provided no suit at law to recover such deficiency shall be maintained against the original mortgagor in cases where the mortgage is for the purchase price of the property involved and where the original mortgagee becomes the purchaser thereof at foreclosure sale and also is granted a deficiency decree against the original mortgagor.

History.—s. 1, ch. 11993, 1927; CGL 5751; s. 1, ch. 13625, 1929.

702.065 Final judgment in uncontested proceedings where deficiency judgment waived; attorney's fees when default judgment entered.—

(1) In uncontested mortgage foreclosure proceedings in which the mortgagee waives the right to recoup any deficiency judgment, the court shall enter final judgment within 90 days from the date of the close of pleadings. For the purposes of this subsection, a mortgage foreclosure proceeding is

uncontested if an answer not contesting the foreclosure has been filed or a default judgment has been entered by the court.

(2) In a mortgage foreclosure proceeding, when a default judgment has been entered against the mortgagor and the note or mortgage provides for the award of reasonable attorney's fees, it is not necessary for the court to hold a hearing or adjudge the requested attorney's fees to be reasonable if the fees do not exceed 3 percent of the principal amount owed at the time of filing the complaint, even if the note or mortgage does not specify the percentage of the original amount that would be paid as liquidated damages. Such fees constitute liquidated damages in any proceeding to enforce the note or mortgage. This section does not preclude a challenge to the reasonableness of the attorney's fees.

History.—s. 2, ch. 2001-215.

702.07 Power of courts and judges to set aside foreclosure decrees at any time before sale.—The circuit courts of this state, and the judges thereof at chambers, shall have jurisdiction, power, and authority to rescind, vacate, and set aside a decree of foreclosure of a mortgage of property at any time before the sale thereof has been actually made pursuant to the terms of such decree, and to dismiss the foreclosure proceeding upon the payment of all court costs.

History.—s. 1, ch. 11881, 1927; CGL 5752.

702.08 Effect of setting aside foreclosure decree.—Whenever a decree of foreclosure has been so rescinded, vacated, and set aside and the foreclosure proceedings dismissed as provided in s. 702.07, the mortgage, together with its lien and the debt thereby secured, shall be, both in law and equity, completely relieved of all effects of any kind whatsoever resulting from or on account of the foreclosure proceedings and the decree of foreclosure and fully restored in all respects to the original status of the same as it existed prior to the foreclosure proceedings and the decree of foreclosure, and thereafter the same shall be for all purposes whatsoever legally of force and effect just as if foreclosure proceeding had never been instituted and a decree of foreclosure had never been made.

History.—s. 2, ch. 11881, 1927; CGL 5753.

702.09 Definitions.—For the purposes of ss. 702.07 and 702.08 the words "decree of foreclosure" shall include a judgment or order rendered or passed in the foreclosure proceedings in which the decree of foreclosure shall be rescinded, vacated, and set aside; the word "mortgage" shall mean any written instrument securing the payment of money or advances and includes liens to secure payment of assessments arising under chapters 718 and 719 and liens created pursuant to the recorded covenants of a home owners' association as defined in s. 712.01; the word "debt" shall include promissory notes, bonds, and all other written obligations given for the payment of money; the words "foreclosure proceedings" shall embrace every action in the circuit or county courts of this state wherein it is sought to foreclose a mortgage and sell the property covered by the same; and the word "property" shall mean and include both real and personal property.

History.—s. 3, ch. 11881, 1927; CGL 5754; s. 4, ch. 2002-27; s. 13, ch. 2003-14.

702.10 Order to show cause; entry of final judgment of foreclosure; payment during foreclosure.—

(1) After a complaint in a foreclosure proceeding has been filed, the mortgagee may request an order to show cause for the entry of final judgment and the court shall immediately review the complaint. If, upon examination of the complaint, the court finds that the complaint is verified and alleges a cause of action to foreclose on real property, the court shall promptly issue an order directed to the defendant to show cause why a final judgment of foreclosure should not be entered.

(a) The order shall:

1. Set the date and time for hearing on the order to show cause. However, the date for the hearing may not be set sooner than 20 days after the service of the order. When service is obtained by publication, the date for the hearing may not be set sooner than 30 days after the first publication. The hearing must be held within 60 days after the date of service. Failure to hold the hearing within such time does not affect the validity of the order to show cause or the jurisdiction of the court to issue subsequent orders.

2. Direct the time within which service of the order to show cause and the complaint must be made upon the defendant.

3. State that the filing of defenses by a motion or by a verified or sworn answer at or before the hearing to show cause constitutes cause for the court not to enter the attached final judgment.

4. State that the defendant has the right to file affidavits or other papers at the time of the hearing and may appear personally or by way of an attorney at the hearing.

5. State that, if the defendant files defenses by a motion, the hearing time may be used to hear the defendant's motion.

6. State that, if the defendant fails to appear at the hearing to show cause or fails to file defenses by a motion or by a verified or sworn answer or files an answer not contesting the foreclosure, the defendant may be considered to have waived the right to a hearing and in such case the court may enter a final judgment of foreclosure ordering the clerk of the court to conduct a foreclosure sale.

7. State that if the mortgage provides for reasonable attorney's fees and the requested attorney's fees do not exceed 3 percent of the principal amount owed at the time of filing the complaint, it is unnecessary for the court to hold a hearing or adjudge the requested attorney's fees to be reasonable.

8. Attach the final judgment of foreclosure the court will enter, if the defendant waives the right to be heard at the hearing on the order to show cause.

9. Require the mortgagee to serve a copy of the order to show cause on the mortgagor in the following manner:

a. If the mortgagor has been served with the complaint and original process, service of the order may be made in the manner provided in the Florida Rules of Civil Procedure.

b. If the mortgagor has not been served with the complaint and original process, the order to show cause, together with the summons and a copy of the complaint, shall be served on the mortgagor in the same manner as provided by law for original process.

Any final judgment of foreclosure entered under this subsection is for in rem relief only. Nothing in this subsection shall preclude the entry of a deficiency judgment where otherwise allowed by law.

(b) The right to be heard at the hearing to show cause is waived if the defendant, after being served as provided by law with an order to show cause, engages in conduct that clearly shows that the defendant has relinquished the right to be heard on that order. The defendant's failure to file defenses by a motion or by a sworn or verified answer or to appear at the hearing duly scheduled on the order to show cause presumptively constitutes conduct that clearly shows that the defendant has relinquished the right to be heard. If a defendant files defenses by a motion or by a verified or sworn answer at or before the hearing, such action constitutes cause and precludes the entry of a final judgment at the hearing to show cause.

(c) In a mortgage foreclosure proceeding, when a default judgment has been entered against the mortgagor and the note or mortgage provides for the award of reasonable attorney's fees, it is unnecessary for the court to hold a hearing or adjudge the requested attorney's fees to be reasonable if the fees do not exceed 3 percent of the principal amount owed on the note or mortgage at the time of filing, even if the note or mortgage does not specify the percentage of the original amount that would be paid as liquidated damages.

(d) If the court finds that the defendant has waived the right to be heard as provided in paragraph (b), the court shall promptly enter a final judgment of foreclosure. If the court finds that the defendant has not waived the right to be heard on the order to show cause, the court shall then determine whether there is cause not to enter a final judgment of foreclosure. If the court finds that the defendant has not shown cause, the court shall promptly enter a judgment of foreclosure.

(2) In an action for foreclosure, other than residential real estate, the mortgagee may request that the court enter an order directing the mortgagor defendant to show cause why an order to make payments during the pendency of the foreclosure proceedings or an order to vacate the premises should not be entered.

(a) The order shall:

1. Set the date and time for hearing on the order to show cause. However, the date for the hearing shall not be set sooner than 20 days after the service of the order. Where service is obtained by publication, the date for the hearing shall not be set sooner than 30 days after the first publication.

2. Direct the time within which service of the order to show cause and the complaint shall be made upon the defendant.

3. State that the defendant has the right to file affidavits or other papers at the time of the hearing and may appear personally or by way of an attorney at the hearing.

4. State that, if the defendant fails to appear at the hearing to show cause and fails to file defenses by a motion or by a verified or sworn answer, the defendant may be deemed to have waived the right to a hearing and in such case the court may enter an order to make payment or vacate the premises.

5. Require the mortgagee to serve a copy of the order to show cause on the mortgagor in the following manner:

a. If the mortgagor has been served with the complaint and original process, service of the order may be made in the manner provided in the Florida Rules of Civil Procedure.

b. If the mortgagor has not been served with the complaint and original process, the order to show cause, together with the summons and a copy of the complaint, shall be served on the mortgagor in the same manner as provided by law for original process.

(b) The right to be heard at the hearing to show cause is waived if the defendant, after being served as provided by law with an order to show cause, engages in conduct that clearly shows that the defendant has relinquished the right to be heard on that order. The defendant's failure to file defenses by a motion or by a sworn or verified answer or to appear at the hearing duly scheduled on the order to show cause presumptively constitutes conduct that clearly shows that the defendant has relinquished the right to be heard.

(c) If the court finds that the defendant has waived the right to be heard as provided in paragraph (b), the court may promptly enter an order requiring payment in the amount provided in paragraph (f) or an order to vacate.

(d) If the court finds that the mortgagor has not waived the right to be heard on the order to show cause, the court shall, at the hearing on the order to show cause, consider the affidavits and other showings made by the parties appearing and make a determination of the probable validity of the underlying claim alleged against the mortgagor and the mortgagor's defenses. If the court determines that the mortgagee is likely to prevail in the foreclosure action, the court shall enter an order requiring the mortgagor to make the payment described in paragraph (e) to the mortgagee and provide for a remedy as described in paragraph (f). However, the order shall be stayed pending final adjudication of the claims of the parties if the mortgagor files with the court a written undertaking executed by a surety approved by the court in an amount equal to the unpaid balance of the mortgage on the property, including all principal, interest, unpaid taxes, and insurance premiums paid by the mortgagee.

(e) In the event the court enters an order requiring the mortgagor to make payments to the mortgagee, payments shall be payable at such intervals and in such amounts provided for in the mortgage instrument before acceleration or maturity. The obligation to make payments pursuant to any order entered under this subsection shall commence from the date of the motion filed hereunder. The order shall be served upon the mortgagor no later than 20 days before the date specified for the first payment. The order may permit, but shall not require the mortgagee to take all appropriate steps to secure the premises during the pendency of the foreclosure action.

(f) In the event the court enters an order requiring payments the order shall also provide that the mortgagee shall be entitled to possession of the premises upon the failure of the mortgagor to make the payment required in the order unless at the hearing on the order to show cause the court finds good cause to order some other method of enforcement of its order.

(g) All amounts paid pursuant to this section shall be credited against the mortgage obligation in accordance with the terms of the loan documents, provided, however, that any payments made under this section shall not constitute a cure of any default or a waiver or any other defense to the mortgage foreclosure action.

(h) Upon the filing of an affidavit with the clerk that the premises have not been vacated pursuant to the court order, the clerk shall issue to the sheriff a writ for possession which shall be governed by the provisions of s. 83.62.

Additionally, default servicers and the attorney's they retain to conduct the foreclosures must follow rules and regulations laid out by the FHA, GSE's, banks, investor and other entities that have purchased, insured or otherwise have an interest in the loan being foreclosed. These will typically require the attorney's accomplish certain foreclosure-related tasks within certain time periods.

The point here is that default servicers and attorney's handling foreclosures are typically under a great deal of pressure to comply with rules, regulations and expectations at many different levels. Oftentimes these measure intended to protect consumers put default servicers and attorneys under so much pressure that they may actually harm consumers instead. The increase of foreclosure volume to current levels lends itself to serious systemic strains.

APPENDIX S

DISTRESSED BORROWER LOSS MITIGATION WORKSHEET

QUESTIONNAIRE

Date: ______________________

Name: ______________________

Phone Number: ______________________

Address: ______________________

1. Why are you seeking advice? ______________________________
____

2. What is the address of the property you are seeking advice about? ____
____
____

3. Has a foreclosure case been filed in court? If so, please provide the case number and the county in which the case was filed. ______________
____

4. Are you behind in your mortgage payments? Yes _____ No _____

5. Do you know the amount that you owe to the mortgage company?
Yes _____ No _____ If yes, how much $ ______________________

6. Do you have more than one mortgage on the property?
Yes _____ No _____
If yes, how much do you owe on your second mortgage line of credit?
$ ____

7. Do you live on the property as your primary residence?
   Yes _____ No _____
   If not, what is your home address? ______________________________
   If not, do you have any tenants living on the property?
   Yes _____ No _____

8. Do you want to save the property or give it back to the bank?
   __________ Save it
   __________ Give it to bank

9. Have you talked to anyone at the bank regarding your current situation?
   Yes _____ No _____ If yes, please provide the name and phone number of the person with whom you spoke ______________________

10. Have you ever sent any letters, e-mails, or faxes to the bank?
    Yes _____ No _____

11. Do you know the value of your property? Yes _____ No _____
    If yes, please write in the approximate value $____________________

12. How many properties do you own? ______________________________

13. If you have more than one property and are behind on mortgage payments, how many other properties are at risk? ____________________

14. Are you interested in selling this property? Yes _____ No _____
    If yes, for how much? $ _______________________________________

15. Do you already have a buyer interested in buying your property?
    Yes _____ No _____ If yes, do you already have a signed contract?
    Yes _____ No _____

16. Have you tried to refinance in the past two years? Yes _____ No _____

17. Have you been denied for a loan in the past two years?
    Yes _____ No _____

18. Are you currently working? Yes _____ No _____

19. What caused you to fall behind in your mortgage? _______________
____

20. Have you discussed your current situation with an attorney?
Yes_____ No _____ If yes, what advice was given to you? _________
____

21. Have you ever filed bankruptcy? Yes _____ No _____
If yes, where? _______________ When? _____ What Chapter? _____

22. Do you agree with the bank that you are behind on your mortgage payments? Yes _____ No _____

23. Does anyone else own the property with you? Yes _____No _____
If yes, does that person know about the current situation?
Yes_____ No _____

24. Are the real estate taxes current? Yes _____ No _____
Is insurance in effect? Yes _____ No _____

FORECLOSURE PRESCRIPTION

Homeowner Name: ______________________
Date: __________________________________

Based upon the information provided to us, we recommend the following:

_____ Contact the Bank/Lender to try to give them a deed-in-lieu of foreclosure in exchange for a release from any potential deficiency.

_____ Contact the Bank/Lender to try to negotiate a payment plan, a/k/a a forbearance agreement.

_____ Contact the Bank/Lender to try to negotiate a loan modification.

_____ Contact the Bank/Lender to try to negotiate a short sale.

_____ Contact a loan officer or mortgage broker to try to refinance the loan.

_____ Contact a Realtor to list the property for sale.

_____ Contact an attorney to discuss other available legal options.